CAMBRIDGE GREEK AN

HERODOTUS

HISTORIES

BOOK VIII

EDITED BY

A. M. BOWIE

University Lecturer in Classical Languages and Literature and Fellow of The Queen's College, Oxford

CAMBRIDGE
UNIVERSITY PRESS

CAMBRIDGE
UNIVERSITY PRESS

University Printing House, Cambridge CB2 8BS, United Kingdom

Cambridge University Press is part of the University of Cambridge.

It furthers the University's mission by disseminating knowledge in the pursuit of education, learning and research at the highest international levels of excellence.

www.cambridge.org
Information on this title: www.cambridge.org/9780521575713

First published 2007
Reprinted 2009

A catalogue record for this publication is available from the British Library

ISBN 978-0-521-57328-3 Hardback
ISBN 978-0-521-57571-3 Paperback

IN MEMORIAM
BOB COLEMAN
PRAECEPTORIS AMICI

CONTENTS

MAPS

PREFACE

In this edition I have had two intentions especially in mind: to try to bring to life for the reader the Achaemenid empire, and to offer a good deal of help with the grammatical aspects of the text. The first intention responds to a growing interest in Greece's relationships with the Ancient Near East, and will I hope prevent the commentary and its readers from taking too Hellenocentric a view of Herodotus' account. That Herodotus makes a strong distinction between 'Greeks' and 'Persians' is an idea that is slowly being revised, as the complexity of his presentation is more and more explored. The second intention responds to my experience at the JACT Greek Summer School, held annually now at Bryanston School, in Dorset. I am very grateful to my various students there not only for making it clearer to me what is required in a modern commentary on a classical text, but also for permitting me to try out on them earlier drafts of the commentary.

Although a new text of Herodotus, based on fresh study of the MSS and a consideration of the linguistic problems involved in constituting such a text, is much to be desired, the text offered here is not the result of a new inspection of the MSS, but aims to be an accessible and readable text. I have been conservative in the matter of emendation and deletion, but I have introduced a good deal more punctuation than is usual, in order to offer the reader more guidance in the structuring of Herodotus' sentences. Accessibility has also been increased by the introduction of subtitles in English into the Greek text. This is an innovation for the series, but I hope it will make using the text more manageable. This and the emphasis on grammatical questions make this edition rather like nineteenth-century editions, but this may be no bad thing. Numbers in bold refer to chapters in book 8.

As must be the case in an undertaking such as this, I have a number of debts of gratitude in addition to that mentioned above. James Morwood brought his acute skills to a reading of the grammatical portions of the commentary, thus saving me from various errors, unclarities and infelicities. John Penney read the section of the Introduction on the language of Herodotus. Stephanie West contributed the sections on the transmission and reception of the text and on Herodotus' biography. Finally, anyone who has been involved in the 'Green and Yellows' will know how much authors owe to the Editors of the series. Their assiduity and advice have brought innumerable improvements both in style and substance.

ABBREVIATIONS

I. ANCIENT AUTHORS AND WORKS

Abbreviations of ancient authors and inscriptional collections are largely those of LSJ, of journals those of *L'Année philologique*.

II. TEXTS AND EDITIONS OF BOOK 8

Asheri	Asheri, D., *Erodoto: le Storie, libro* VIII, *la vittoria di Themistocle*, Milan 2003 (now translated and updated in Asheri, D., Lloyd, A. and Corcella, A., *A Commentary on Herodotus Books I–II* (eds. O. Murray and A. Moreno), Oxford 2007).
Hude	Hude, C., *Herodoti Historiae*, 3rd edn, II, Oxford 1927.
Legrand	Legrand, P. E., *Hérodote: Histoires livre 8 Uranie*, Paris 1953.
Macan	Macan, R. W., *Herodotus: the seventh, eighth and ninth books*, 2 vols. in 3, London 1908.
Masaracchia	Masaracchia, A., *Erodoto: le Storie, libro* VIII, *la battaglia di Salamina*, Milan 1977.
Powell	Powell, J. E., *Herodotus: book 8*, Cambridge 1939.
Rosén	Rosén, H. B.: *Herodoti Historiae*, Leipzig 1987–97.
Shuckburgh	Shuckburgh, E. S., *Herodotus* VIII *Urania*, Cambridge 1893.
Stein	Stein, H., *Herodotus*, 6th edn, Berlin 1901.

III. MODERN WORKS

ANET	Pritchard, J. B., *Ancient Near Eastern texts relating to the Old Testament*, 3rd edn with supplement, Princeton 1969.
BM	British Museum
Brosius	Brosius, M., *The Persian empire from Cyrus II to Artaxerxes I* (*LACTOR* 16), London 2000.
BHAch I	*Topoi*, Supplément I: Lyons 1997.
BHAch 2	*Bulletin d'histoire achéménide* II, ed. P. Briant, Paris 2001.
CAH	*Cambridge Ancient History*
CANE	Sasson, J. (ed.), *Civilizations of the ancient Near East*, I–IV, New York 1995.
Chantraine	Chantraine, P., *Dictionnaire étymologique de la langue Grecque: histoire des mots*, 2nd edn, Paris 1999.

F&M	Flower, M. A. and Marincola, J., *Herodotus: Histories book 9*, Cambridge 2002.
FdD	*Fouilles de Delphes*, Paris 1902–.
FGH	Jacoby, F., *Fragmente der griechischen Historiker*, Berlin and Leiden 1923–58.
Fornara	Fornara, C. W., *Archaic times to the end of the Peloponnesian War*, 2nd edn, Cambridge 1983.
Fort.	Unpublished Persepolis fortification tablet.
GP	Denniston, J. D., *The Greek particles*, 2nd edn, Oxford 1954.
H–N	Hansen M. H. and Nielsen, T. H., *An inventory of archaic and classical* poleis, Oxford 2004.
Humbert	Humbert, J., *Syntaxe grecque*, 3rd edn., Paris 1960.
IEG	West, M. L. (ed.), *Iambi et elegi graeci*, 2 vols., 2nd edn, Oxford 1989–92.
K–G	Kühner, R. and Gerth, B., *Ausführliche Grammatik der griechischen Sprache*, I–II, 3rd edn, Hanover 1890–1904.
Lex.	Powell, J. E., *A Lexicon to Herodotus*, 2nd edn, Hildesheim 1977.
LGPN	Fraser, P. M. and Matthews, E. (eds.), *Lexicon of Greek Personal Names*, Oxford 1987–.
LIMC	*Lexicon iconographicum mythologiae graecae*, Zurich 1966–97.
M&T	Goodwin, W. W., *Syntax of the moods and tenses of the Greek verb*, London 1889.
ML	Meiggs, R. and Lewis, D. M., *A selection of Greek historical inscriptions to the end of the fifth century*, Oxford 1988.
PF, PFa	*Persepolis Fortification Tablets* (see Hallock 1969, 1978).
PTT	Cameron, G. G., *Persepolis Treasury Tablets*, Chicago 1948.
PFS	Persepolis Fortification Seals.
RdA	*Reallexikon der Assyriologie und vorderasiatischen Archäologie*, Berlin, Leipzig and New York 1928–.
RE	Pauly, A., Wissowa, G. and Kroll, W. (eds.), *Real-encyclopädie der classischen Altertumswissenschaft*, Stuttgart 1893–1979.
Schmidt	Schmidt, E. F., *Persepolis* I–III, Chicago 1953–70.
Smyth	Smyth, H. W., *Greek Grammar* (rev. by G. M. Messing), Harvard 1956.
VS	*Vorderasiatische Schriftdenkmäler der königlichen Museen zu Berlin*, Leipzig, 1907–.

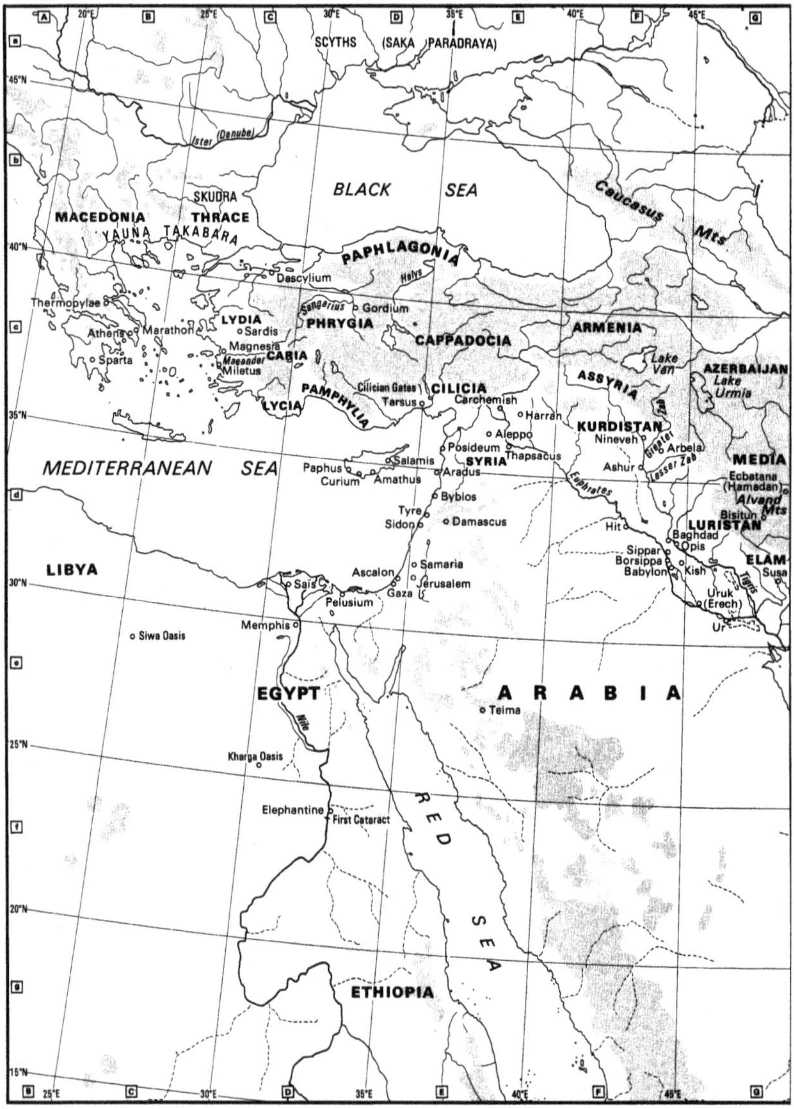

Map 1. The Achaemenid empire.

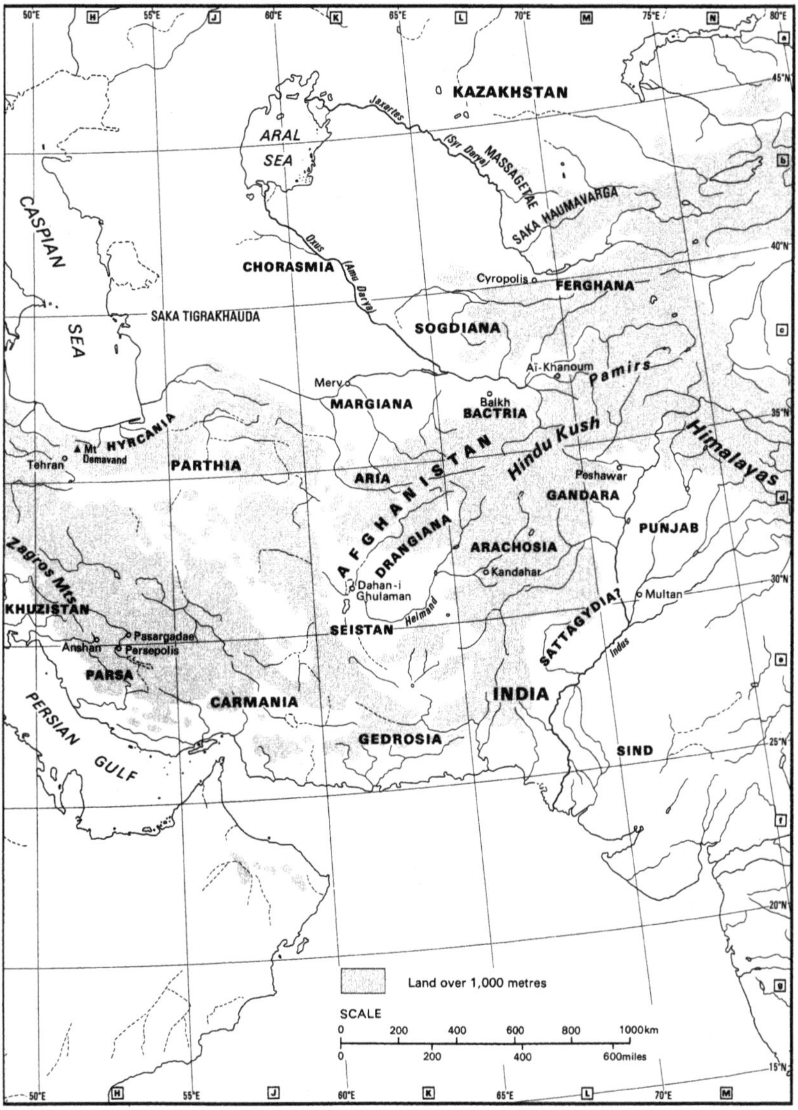

KAZAKHSTAN
ARAL SEA
CASPIAN SEA
Jaxartes (Syr Darya)
MASSAGETAE
SAKA HAUMAVARGA
Oxus (Amu Darya)
CHORASMIA
Cyropolis
FERGHANA
SAKA TIGRAKHAUDA
SOGDIANA
Aï-Khanoum
Pamirs
Merv
MARGIANA
Balkh
BACTRIA
HYRCANIA
Mt Demavand
Tehran
PARTHIA
AFGHANISTAN
Hindu Kush
Himalayas
ARIA
Peshawar
GANDARA
PUNJAB
DRANGIANA
ARACHOSIA
Kandahar
Zagros Mts
Dahan-i Ghulaman
Multan
KHUZISTAN
Helmand
SATTAGYDIA?
SEISTAN
Pasargadae
Anshan
Persepolis
Indus
PARSA
INDIA
CARMANIA
PERSIAN GULF
GEDROSIA
SIND
Land over 1,000 metres
SCALE
0 200 400 600 800 1000km
0 200 400 600miles

Map 1. *(cont.)*

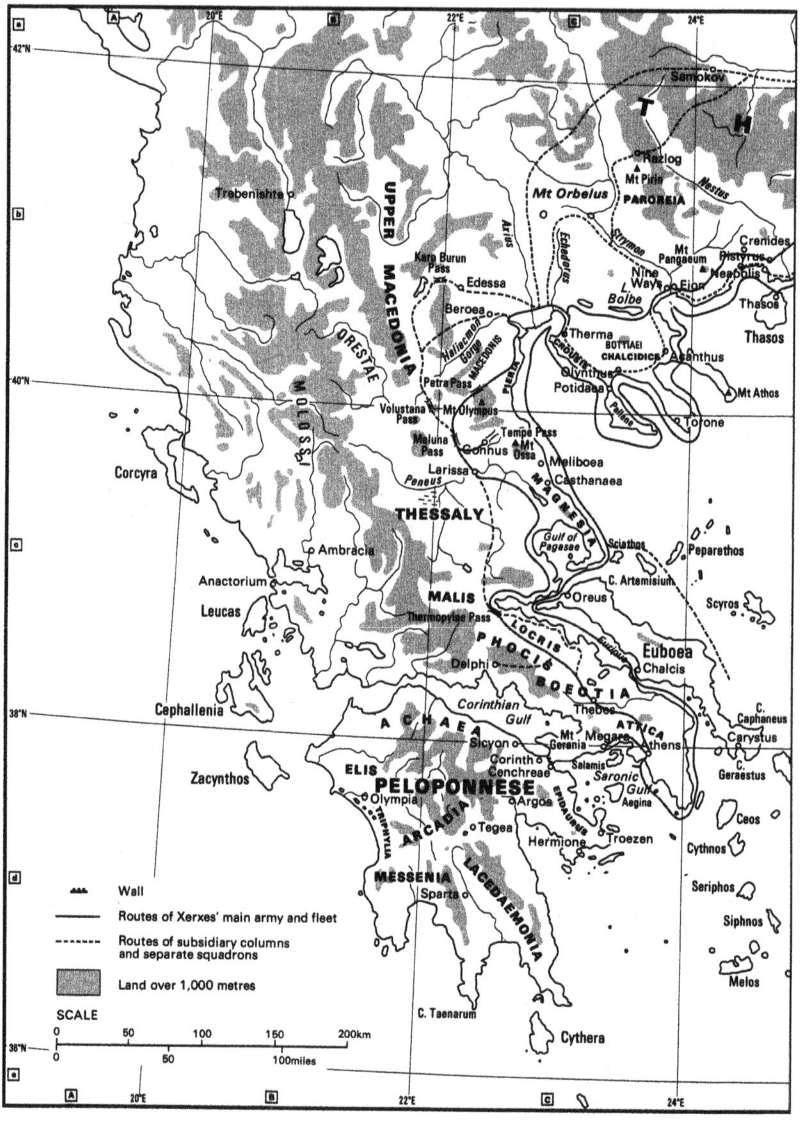

Map 2. Xerxes' routes in Greece.

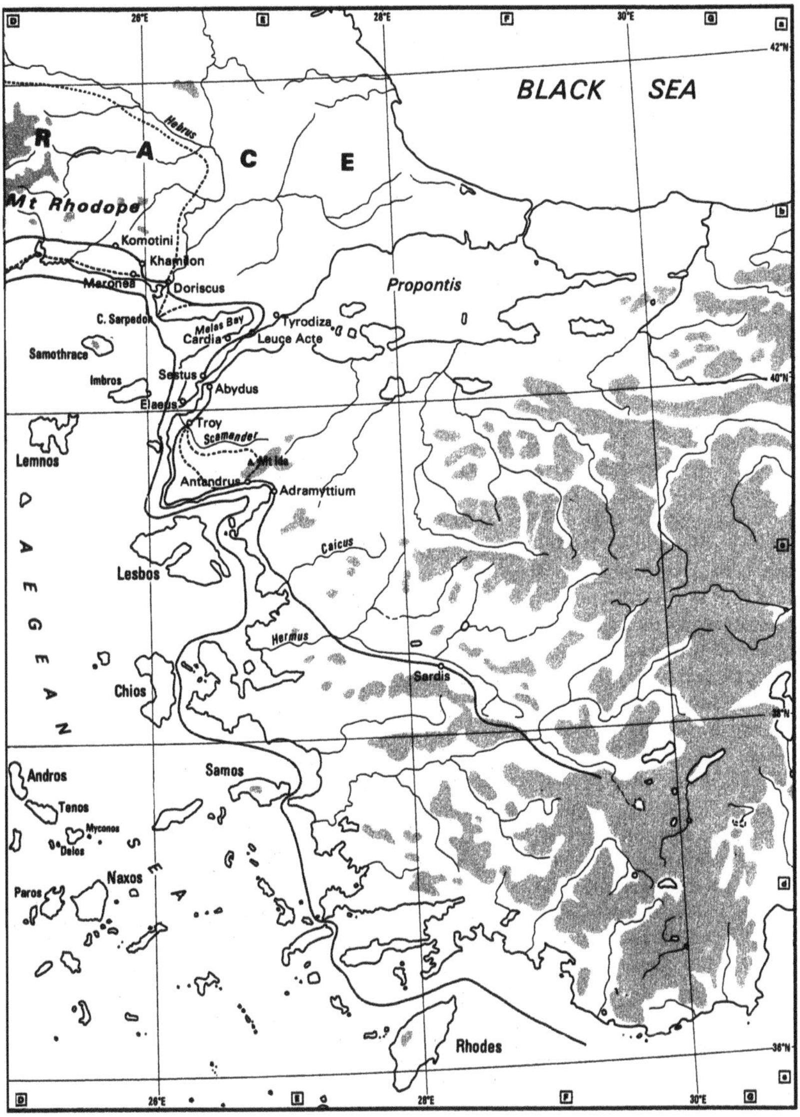

BLACK SEA
Mt Rhodope
Hebrus
Komotini
Khamilon
Maronea
Doriscus
C. Serpedon
Melas Bay
Cardia
Tyrodiza
Leuce Acte
Propontis
Samothrace
Imbros
Sestus
Abydus
Elaeus
Troy
Scamander
Mt Ida
Antandrus
Adramyttium
Lemnos
Caicus
Lesbos
Hermus
Sardis
Chios
Samos
Andros
Tenos
Myconos
Delos
Naxos
Paros
Rhodes
A E G E A N
S E A

Map 2. *(cont.)*

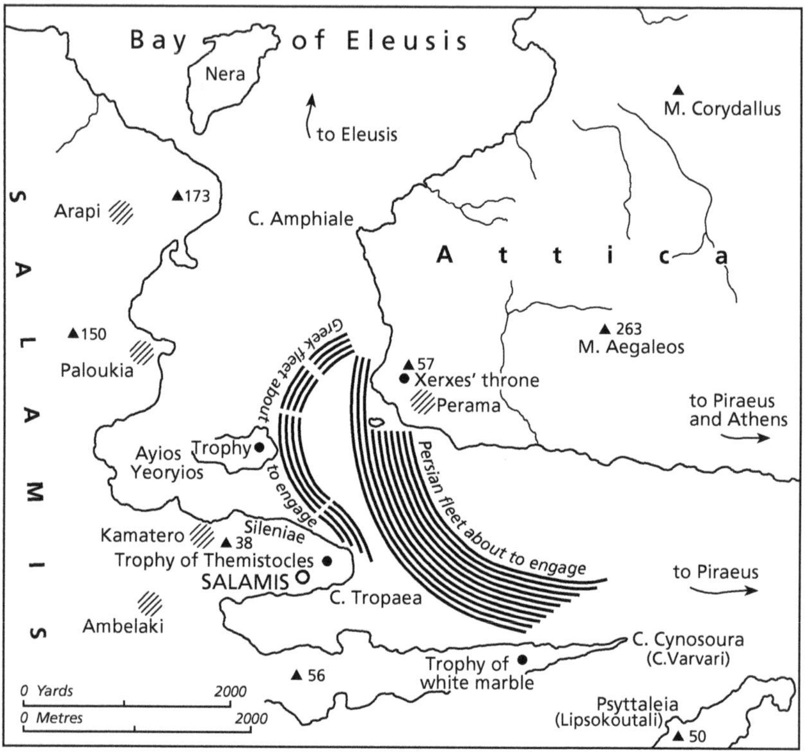

Map 3. The battle of Salamis.

INTRODUCTION

I MEDES AND PERSIANS

'Darius the king says: this is the kingdom which I hold: from the Scythians who are beyond Sogdiana to Ethiopia, from Sind to Sardis'.[1] Xerxes inherited from his father an empire that stretched from the Asia Minor coast to India and from the Caucasus to the Persian Gulf, and included Egypt.[2] It far surpassed anything the Near East had seen before, and would not be surpassed in size until the Roman empire.[3]

One unusual feature of this empire is that, despite the fact that it was the successor to the Elamite, Babylonian and Assyrian empires, which made much use of at least nominally 'historical' texts recording the deeds of their kings, the Persian empire has left us very little of the kind.[4] There is only one document that can be described as a historical account of specific events, Darius' great inscription at Bisitun (DB = Brosius no. 44), which recounts his crushing of the revolts that greeted his accession to power. Other royal inscriptions list the peoples of the empire, describe the building of great palaces and outline royal ideology, but they do not concern themselves with specific events. Again, apart from the carving that accompanies DB, Achaemenid art does not use representations of individual events. Records were kept of battles, acts of benevolence towards the King etc., but these would have been on perishable material and have not survived (cf. **85**.3 and n.). Two archives written in Elamite on clay are of prime importance for economic history, the Persepolis Fortification Tablets, which record the issue of provisions and livestock to workers, travellers and others for the period 509–494 BC, and the Persepolis Treasury Tablets, which record payment to workers for 492–458.[5] We have a certain amount of material from Babylonian and Egyptian sources, and the Old Testament books of Ezra, Nehemiah and Esther are also important. However, the absence of historical accounts from the Persian point of view means we have to rely heavily on those written by their victorious opponents,

[1] DPh (=Brosius no. 134) §2; cf. DB (=Brosius no. 44) I §6, DSe (=Brosius no. 46) §3, DNa (=Brosius no. 48) §3, DPe (=Brosius no. 133) §2 for more detailed lists of up to 29 countries. Xerxes lists 31 in XPh (=Brosius no. 191) §3.

[2] The degree of actual control exercised over different parts of the empire did, of course, vary over time and space.

[3] For magisterial surveys of the Persian Empire, see Briant 2002 (note especially the 'research notes' after the main text) and Kuhrt 2007. For bibliography after 1995, cf. Briant 1997: 1–127, 2001; and for a massive analytical bibliography, cf. Weber-Wiesehöfer 1996. For new Achaemenid research, cf. http://www.achemenet.com (it includes the ongoing *Encyclopaedia Iranica*); cf. also http://www.museum-achemenet.college-de-france.fr/ and http://oi.uchicago.edu/OI/default.html for texts, images, electronic resources etc. Also useful for an overview are Cook 1983; Young, *CAH*² IV 1–111; Dandamayev and Lukonin 1989; Briant 1990; Brentjes, *CANE* II 1001–21; Sancisi-Weerdenburg, *CANE* II 1035–50; Kuhrt 1995: 647–701; Wiesehöfer 1996; Cawkwell 2005; Curtis and Tallis 2005; Flower 2006. For Greece's place in a Near Eastern–Aegean cultural community, cf. Burkert 2005.

[4] Brosius is a very useful collection of texts in translation.

[5] Cf. Hallock 1985.

the Greeks.[6] One should not operate a rigorous scepticism about anything found in a Greek source,[7] but caution is always wise when using documents written by one people about another, especially when the writers come from one race that has unexpectedly vanquished the other, and also made great use of that victory in the construction of their self-image.[8] Of course, uncritical acceptance of Persian sources would be equally unwise.

The Medes and Persians were amongst the peoples who appeared in the Zagros Mountains, between the Caspian Sea and the Persian Gulf, around the start of the first millennium BC. They came either from central Asia to the east or (less likely) from southern Russia to the north.[9] The Medes and Persians were speakers of languages from the Iranian branch of Indo-European.[10] The first reference to them comes in an inscription of Shalmaneser III (858–824), king of Assyria: 'I received tribute from twenty-seven kings of the land Parsua. Moving on from the land Parsua I went down to the lands of . . . Media (*Amadaiia*).'[11] The name *Parsua* is connected with the region which the Persians called *Pārsa* and the Greeks *Persis*, and which is now Fars in south-west Iran.[12] In the ninth to seventh centuries we hear sketchily of the periodic defeats of Medes and Persians by the Assyrians, as they became participants in the shifting power politics and wars between the Assyrians, Babylonians, Elamites and Urartians.[13]

The picture becomes clearer from the middle of the seventh century. In 646, the Assyrians crushed Elam, the very ancient kingdom centred on Susa and Anshan, and King Ashurbanipal records that, 'Kurash [Cyrus I], the king of the country of Parsumash, . . . sent Arukku, his eldest son, with his tribute to Nineveh, my capital city, in order to declare his obedience.'[14] The Assyrian empire, however, was soon to fall,

[6] Cf. the list of Greek sources in Brosius xx–xxi; Dandamayev and Lukonin 1989: 368–99 for a discussion of written sources; Cawkwell 2005: 1–29. Apart from Herodotus, the principal early sources on Persian history are Aeschylus' *Persae*; Timotheus' *Persae* (cf. Hordern 2002); the valuable but somewhat sensationalist *Persica* of Ctesias of Cnidus (*FGH* 688), a doctor at the court of Artaxerxes II from 405 to 388, which are preserved largely in paraphrase (cf. Gilmore 1885); Xenophon's *Anabasis*, a first-hand account of the failed revolt of Cyrus the Younger against his brother Artaxerxes II in 401 and of the subsequent Greek retreat, *Cyropedia*, a treatise on good government composed through a fictionalised life of Cyrus the Great, and *Oeconomicus* gives an account of the administration of the Persian empire in §4. Also important are the *Histories* of Diodorus Siculus (books 9–11), preserving material from the earlier writers Hecataeus, Ctesias, Ephorus and Hieronymus of Cardia; Strabo's *Geographia*, especially books 12–15 on Asia Minor and Persia and 16–17 on Egypt and Mesopotamia; Plutarch's *Lives*, especially those of Themistocles, Aristeides and Artaxerxes I (many remarks on Persian matters are scattered through his works); and Arrian's *Anabasis of Alexander*. Cf. in general, Drews 1973; Stevenson 1997.

[7] On Herodotus' knowledge of Persia, cf. Miller 1997: 105–8.

[8] Cf. §2 below. [9] Young 1980.

[10] For Old Persian (and Median) language and texts, cf. Kent 1953; Brandenstein-Mayrhofer 1964; Lecoq 1997; for the languages of the empire, cf. Stolper 2005.

[11] Cf. Grayson 1996: 68.

[12] The country was 'Persia' until 1934, when its government requested the use of 'Iran', derived ultimately from OP *ariya*, 'Aryan' and cognate with Skt. *arya-* 'noble' (cf. *Eire* 'Ireland'); cf. Wiesehöfer 1996: xi–xii.

[13] Luckenbill 1926–7: Index, *s.v.* 'Parsua', 'Parsuai', 'Parsuash', 'Matai'.

[14] Weidner 1931/2: 4–5.

as the Medes under Cyaxares (Median *Uvaxshtra*;[15] ruled *ca.* 625–585), having in ways we do not know increased their power, captured first Ashur, the former capital and major religious centre of the Assyrian empire in 614, and then helped the Babylonians utterly destroy the capital Nineveh in 612: 'the city [they turned] into ruin-hills and heaps (of debris)'.[16] According to the traditional account, Cyaxares also took control of Persia *ca.* 625.[17] He was succeeded by his son Astyages.

Persian domination then began with Cyrus II, the Great (OP *Kūrush*). He had become king of Anshan in 559, and revolted against and eventually conquered the Medes in 549,[18] thus inaugurating what became the great 'Achaemenid' dynasty. Around 546 he conquered Lydia and its fabulously wealthy king Croesus, who by now ruled the Greek cities of the coast and much of western Anatolia (H. 1.46–94). He then campaigned successfully in eastern Iran, central Asia and Afghanistan, taking control of land as far as north-western India and the Hindu Kush. In 539/8, he conquered Babylon.[19] Cyrus had therefore conquered three of the four major Near Eastern kingdoms, and was in effective control of the whole Near East apart from Egypt. Building on the complex bureaucracies of Babylon and Elam, he saw to the organisation of his enormous empire. He inaugurated the Achaemenid habit of showing considerable tolerance to local religions, customs and laws, and also the distinctively Persian, eclectic style of art and architecture, which blended features of the crafts of the peoples in his kingdom.[20] He probably instituted the system of 'satraps' (OP *xshaçapāvā*, 'protector of the kingdom'). He was killed in 530, fighting in the east,[21] and his tomb still stands at Pasargadae, the most ancient Achaemenid capital. The splendour of his achievements led Greek writers to chart a spiral of decline through the reigns of his successors.

Cyrus was succeeded by his son Cambyses (OP *Kambūjiya*; 530–522), who added Egypt to the empire (H. 3.1–29). The hostile account of his rule in Herodotus probably depends on traditions created by Egyptian priests angered by Cambyses' changes to the organisation of temple finances, which were intended to reduce the power of the priesthood;[22] Egyptian sources give a more complimentary picture.[23] Cambyses died of a gangrenous wound in Syria, as he was returning to Persia on learning that his brother Bardiya (Gk. *Smerdis*) had seized the throne in Persia.

[15] *x* is pronounced rather like *ch* in 'loch'.

[16] Babylonian Chronicle in *ANET* 304–5; cf. Xen. *Anab.* 3.4.6–12.

[17] For the problems, cf. Brown 1988; Sancisi-Weerdenburg 1994.

[18] Cf. 'Nabonidus Chronicle' 7.2.1–2; *ANET* 305; Brosius no. 11.

[19] Cf. H. 1.178–91; and the different version in the 'Nabonidus Chronicle' (cf. Grayson 1975: 109–110; *ANET*, 306–7; Brosius no. 11).

[20] Lecoq 1997: 42–50 argues that 'Old Persian' is also a mixture, of Persian and Median (and possibly other languages), again created to express the unity of Medes and Persians, which is expressed in art too.

[21] There are different versions in H. 1.201–14 and Ctesias, *FGrH* 688 F 9.

[22] Cf. Brosius no. 24.

[23] Contrast Brosius nos. 19–22, 24 with fig. 3 with H. 3.25–30, 37; cf. Fried 2004: 68–73.

The events surrounding the succession of Darius (OP *Dārayavaush*, 'He who holds firm the good') are very murky. According to both Darius (DB (= Brosius no. 44) I §§29–32) and Herodotus (3.30.3), Cambyses had secretly killed his brother Bardiya, but Gaumata, a Median Magus, took Bardiya's identity and seized the throne; he was then overthrown by Darius and his fellow conspirators. What really happened cannot be divined, since the main source is from the winning side. Revolts in at least nine different parts of the empire, including Babylon, Persia, Media, Elam and Assyria, suggest general turmoil in the empire, which Darius may have exploited. By June 521, he had crushed them all: 'this is what I have done by the favour of Ahura Mazda in one and the same year, after I became king' (DB (= Brosius no. 44) IV §52).

Darius was not of Cyrus' family and so not in line to succeed. When on the throne, he was keen to assert his legitimacy. He invented an ancestor Achaemenes (*Haxāmanish*) as father both of Teispes (OP *Cishpish*), great-grandfather of Cyrus, and of his own ancestor Ariaramnes, thus making his family part of the same 'Achaemenid' line as Cyrus (DB (= Brosius no. 44) I §§1–2). Cyrus is described as 'an Achaemenid' at Pasargadae, on inscriptions which are attributed to him but may have been made by Darius (CMa-c).[24] Darius also married two daughters of Cyrus, Atossa and Artystone (Elam. *Irtashduna*), and a granddaughter, Parmys. It was Darius who consolidated the empire by campaigns in countries at the edges of it, such as India and Scythia (H. 4.1–143). He also gave the empire the accoutrements expressive of its greatness. He began immense palaces at Persepolis and Susa, which were built and decorated by the many peoples of the empire, the mixture of styles symbolising the heterogeneity yet unity of the empire (DSf (= Brosius no. 45) §4). The spectacular decorations on the Audience Hall (*Apadāna*) at Persepolis and those on Darius' tomb at Naqsh-i Rustam convey a timeless sense of harmony between King and peoples.[25] Darius ordered major engineering works, such as the building of the Bosporus bridge, involving 200 ships carrying a road across a strait with powerful current and winds (4.85), and the restoration of the Nile canal (2.158.1–2). He may have developed the Old Persian cuneiform to give his empire its own script, which his inscriptions carry alongside the old Babylonian and Elamite cuneiforms, implying an equivalence of prestige. In religious matters, he seems to have made Zoroastrianism and its main god Ahura Mazda a central feature of Persian religion, perhaps as a focus of loyalty to his regime (cf. **115**.4n.).

In Darius' time the Persians begin to take control of the Greek islands and areas of the mainland. In 499/8 the Ionians revolted against their Persian masters, and this 'Ionian revolt' lasted till 493.[26] Athens and Eretria sent ships to help the Ionians. The Greeks succeeded in burning the lower town of Sardis, but the revolt, never notable for its unity of purpose or loyalty to the cause, collapsed when the Persians

[24] An idea opposed by Lecoq 1997: 81–2.

[25] Cf. Root 1979: esp. 131–61. It is noteworthy that the Achaemenids did not refer to their 'empire' but rather to *dahyāva*, 'peoples'.

[26] Cf. Tozzi 1978; Murray, *CAH*² IV 461–90; Georges 2000; Cawkwell 2005: 61–86.

captured Miletus and the Greek fleet was defeated at Lade nearby. Severe reprisals followed, but inter-Ionian hostilities were curbed, taxation revised and a measure of self-rule instituted (6.42–3). Darius sought to punish Athens and Eretria, and in 490 sent Datis (Elam. *Datiya*) and Artaphernes (Elam. *Irdapirna*) to attack mainland Greece. They were repulsed at Marathon, but Darius planned a further attempt, which was interrupted by his death in 486.

His successor was his son by Atossa, Xerxes (OP *Xshayārshā* 'ruling over heroes'; Elam. *Iksherishsha*; OT Ahasuerus). Though not the eldest of Darius' sons, he was the eldest of those born to a wife who was a daughter of Cyrus; choosing Xerxes thus meant the kingship remained in the Achaemenid family.[27] His attack on Greece has resulted in Xerxes generally being given a very poor reputation in subsequent western accounts and conceptions of the East, but this does not accurately reflect his reign.[28] He preserved the empire as he had inherited it, and completed the palaces at Susa and Persepolis. His engineering projects were monumental. For his invasion of Greece, he caused to be dug through the Athos peninsula a canal which was 2200 m long and 20 m wide, so that triremes could row past each other. He also made a bridge over the Hellespont, which involved 674 warships anchored under hemp and papyrus cables, a feat that has never been repeated to this day. The four-year planning of the expedition, the marshalling of his vast army from Cappadocia to Athens and the co-ordination with the huge fleet were also extraordinary feats of military organisation.

The defeat, for which Mardonius must take a large share of the blame, appears not to have affected Xerxes' rule:[29] it is too easy to exaggerate the interest the Persians had in Greece, a very small country on the edge of their vast empire. Indeed, there is some evidence that it may have been presented as something of a triumph. Booty was set up in various capitals: for instance, the statues of the tyrannicides Harmodius and Aristogeiton, taken from Athens, were displayed in Babylon, whence they were returned by Alexander.[30] Xerxes could after all point to his defeat and killing of one Spartan king at Thermopylae and to the destruction of Athens, which was one of his prime objectives (7.8β.3). The failure of the expedition could be also compared to those of Cyrus against the Massagetae, Cambyses in Egypt and Darius in Scythia: Xerxes was in distinguished company. He continued as King until August 465, when he was the first Achaemenid king (unless we count Bardiya/Smerdis) to be assassinated, in a palace coup. His son Arses succeeded as Artaxerxes I (OP *Artaxshaça*),[31] and the Achaemenid

[27] Cf. Sancisi-Weerdenburg 1993. Xerxes' comment was 'other sons of Darius there were, (but) it was the desire of Ahura Mazda that my father Darius made me the greatest after himself' (XPF §4 (= Brosius no. 107)); cf. H. 7.3.

[28] Current scholarship is convincingly revaluing his reign: cf. Wiesehöfer 1996: 42–55; Briant 2002: 515–68.

[29] Cf. Young 1980 and Briant 2002: 535–42 for attempts to look at this outcome from the Persian perspective; cf. **97**n. on a possible reason for Xerxes' flight from Greece after Salamis.

[30] Arrian, *Anab.* 7.19.2; cf. 3.16.7–8; Paus. 1.8.5, and cf. 16.3, 8.46.3 for the bronze Apollo of Branchidae.

[31] For Achaemenid throne-names, cf. Ctesias, *FGH* 688 F 15 §50–1, 55; Plut. *Art.* 1.2; Schmitt 1982.

empire continued until Alexander's final defeat of Darius III at Gaugamela (Syria) in 331.

2 GREEKS AND PERSIANS

In her account of Aeschylus' presentation of the Persians in the *Persae*, Edith Hall identifies three main psychological flaws attributed to them, hierarchicalism, immoderate luxuriousness and unrestrained emotionalism;[32] matters are different in Herodotus.[33]

It is true that these features may be found in his Persians, but they are not the defining features. There is indeed a very strong hierarchical element in the Persians' view of the world:

> After themselves, they hold their immediate neighbours in the highest regard, then those who live the next furthest away, and so on in order of proximity; so they have the least respect for those who live furthest away from their own land. The reason for this is that they regard themselves as by far the best people in the world in all respects, and others as gradually decreasing in goodness, so that those who live the furthest away from them are the worst people in the world.
> (1.134.2; tr. Waterfield)

This is also reflected in their social relations: meetings between equals are accompanied by a kiss on the lips, between those slightly distinguished in rank by a kiss on the cheek and between those of divergent standing by *proskynesis* by the lower ranker (1.134.1).[34] It is plain too that the King stands at the head of the hierarchy. On the other hand, though courtiers are respectful to the King, they do not in Herodotus fawn upon him in quite the way characters do in Aeschylus' play, and some speak their minds with complete openness, as in Achaemenes' rude dismissal of Demaratus' advice to Xerxes to occupy the island of Cythera (7.236), or Artemisia's forthright opposition to a strategy at Salamis supported by Xerxes himself (**68**). Even Mardonius' immensely courtly speech at **100** is steeped in self-interest. The King is often found consulting his closest associates, and even accepting their advice, despite a sense that a minority opinion may be wiser (**69**.2).

Eastern luxuriousness as opposed to Greek poverty and austerity is a cliché of Greek thinking which has echoes as early as epic representations of Troy and the Trojans, and such luxuriousness can indeed be found in Herodotus. Cyrus establishes his empire by offering the Persians the choice between the life of the banquet and that of slavish toil (1.126), and certain Persians when lavishly entertained by Amyntas, king of Macedonia, molest the Macedonians' wives, claiming this to be the Persian custom

[32] Hall 1989: 80.

[33] On Herodotus' depiction of Greeks and Persians, cf. Momigliano 1979; Hartog 1988; Hall 1989; Cartledge 1990; Pelling 1997a (especially for the deconstruction of this opposition); Harrison 2002b.

[34] On *proskynesis*, cf. **118**.4.

(5.18). Most famously, after Plataea, the Spartan king Pausanias, on discovering the fabulously caparisoned tent of Xerxes, has Persian and Greek cooks each produce a typical meal, to 'display the folly of the leader of the Medes, who, though he enjoyed such a lifestyle as this, came to take away the pitiful one that is ours' (9.82.3). On the other hand, this aspect of the Persians is not over-emphasised by Herodotus. Xerxes' expeditionary force is described in all its finery (7.40–1, 59–100) but, though its grandeur will have had a hybristic aspect in Greek eyes, Herodotus does not make any explicit comment. Many of the formal occasions on which Xerxes appears before his army will have been spectacular events, but Herodotus does not emphasise this (cf. **67**.2n). The work ends with Cyrus' warning that, if the Persians abandon their poor land for more fertile pastures, they will end up slaves (9.122).

Nor is unrestrained emotionalism a regular feature of Persian behaviour. Xerxes bursts into tears at his review when he realises that all his great force will be dead in a hundred years (7.44–6), but he is not given to tears elsewhere, more to laughter (**114**.2n.). He can react violently, as when he has Pythius' eldest son cut in half because of an inappropriate request (7.38–9), but this is not a feature restricted to Persians (cf. 9.5 and 9.120.4 for similar Greek savagery). Outpourings of lamentation and mourning are an especial trait of Aeschylus' Persians; there are two occasions when Herodotus' Persians also give themselves over to similar emotion, when news of the defeat at Salamis is brought (**99**.2) and when Masistius is killed (9.24), but the description is brief, and the grief understandable in the circumstances.

Recent work has begun to stress how Herodotus breaks down any simple opposition between Greeks and Persians. The ideology of Persian and Greek is sometimes explicitly contrasted, notably in Demaratus' discussion with Xerxes in 7.101–5. Demaratus speaks of Greek freedom and respect for *nomos*: 'they are free, but not wholly so, since there is a master over them, Law, which they fear much more than your men do you' (104.4). Xerxes praises tyranny: the Persians 'under the rule of one man, as is our way, might through fear of him show unnatural courage, and compelled by whips might confront greater numbers in battle' (103.4).[35] However, this opposition is not as clear-cut as it may appear. Demaratus is not speaking about all Greeks, but only the Spartans (102.1–2), and even they at times show reluctance to fight (**72**.1n., 9.6–11, 46–9). Though the Persians do sometimes fight under the whip (7.223.3), the improved Persian performance under Xerxes' gaze at Salamis (**86**) supports his argument, and immediately after this debate, Herodotus gives two examples of entirely voluntary and unshakable loyalty to the King in Mascames and Boges (106–7). Nor are the Persians notably deficient in courage: they are no less tentative than the Greeks at Artemisium, and after Salamis both sides are shown to be frightened of entering unfamiliar territory (**132**.3). At Salamis, it is their disorder which causes their defeat (**86**), and at Plataea, they again advanced 'in no sort of order or array' (9.59.2), but 'were not inferior in courage or strength, but they wore no armour and were also

[35] Cf. 5.78, where the Athenians are said to have become the best fighters once they had thrown off tyranny.

less experienced and could not match the skill (*sophia*) of their opponents' (9.62.3); at Mycale too, they held out for a long time, before all but the ethnic Persians fled (9.102.3).

In Persian debates, there is sometimes the suggestion that speaking openly and frankly to the King is dangerous (**65**.5n.), and this is implicitly contrasted with Greek *isegorie* ('the equal right to speak' enjoyed by all men; cf. 5.78). But in the debate in **59–64**, Themistocles is explicitly said to be unable to speak openly (**60** *init.*), and an attempt is even made to forbid him to speak at all (**59**). We noted above Xerxes' command that the view of the majority on Salamis should be followed (**69**.2), and it is Themistocles the Greek who acts in an autocratic manner. It is notable too that it is the Persians Artaphernes and Mardonius who forced the Ionians to use law rather than violence to settle their disputes, and introduced 'democracies' (7.42–3).

In **144**.2, the Athenians nobly state that one reason for their refusal to come to terms with Xerxes is 'Greekness (*to Hellenikon*), which shares one blood and one language, the shrines of the gods and sacrifices we have in common, and the similarity of our customs', but this is somewhat tarnished when, finding the Spartans have not sent help, they threaten to go over to Persia (9.6–11). Indeed, throughout books 5–9, the fissiparous nature of the Greeks is constantly emphasised, not least in the Ionian Revolt, and in book 6 in particular the Greeks treat each other abominably: note especially the shameful treatment of the people of Zancle by the Samians to whom they had offered a home, and the contrast between such actions and the behaviour of Datis there and elsewhere in the book (6.22–4). Herodotus puts down the troubles that befell the Greeks in the century between Darius and Artaxerxes I (522–424) 'in part to the Persians, but in part to the wars fought by the leading nations for supremacy' (6.98.2). There is therefore no simple opposition between admirable Greeks and deficient Persians.

3 XERXES IN HERODOTUS

Greek accounts of the expedition were to give Xerxes[36] a reputation for arrogance, excess and intolerance from which scholarship has only recently begun to free him.[37] In Aeschylus, he is the inadequate son of the great Darius, who destroys his empire by his miscalculations and returns to his mother in ragged shame.[38] Herodotus' account of Persian history has been interpreted as structured on a series of eastern potentates, all with an overreaching ambition, but with Xerxes as the epitome of the flawed king.[39] His expedition has been depicted as the final example of the tendency of Persian kings

36 References in this section are to book 7 unless it is otherwise stated.
37 Cf. Wiesehöfer 1996: 43–55; Sancisi-Weerdenburg 2002.
38 For a comparison of Aeschylus' and Herodotus' portrayal of Xerxes, cf. Saïd 2002: 137–45.
39 Cf. Immerwahr 1966: 176–83.

to overstep one too many boundaries,[40] and his comprehensive defeat has been seen as surpassing all of the earlier defeats, in a final demonstration of the unwisdom of imperial expansionism. These views need some qualification.

Book 7 provides the background to Xerxes in book 8, and presents Xerxes undertaking his expedition in response to a number of pressures, internal and external, divine and human, which leave him little room for manoeuvre.[41] It is true that Xerxes does act at times like a wilful tyrant, but for each action that supports that idea, there is often another that negates it. If he insults Artabanus for opposing his wish to invade Greece (11.1), he sends him home with honour from the Hellespont (52.2). He may act inconsistently in first rewarding royally a benefactor, Pythius the Lydian, and then, in anger at Pythius' request for one son to be spared the expedition, cutting his eldest son in half (27–9, 38–9), and he may abuse Leonidas' corpse savagely (238); but he also declines to punish Spartan heralds who fail to show him reverence, thereby refusing to imitate the Spartans' killing of Persian heralds and acting, as Herodotus says, 'with greatness of heart' (ὑπὸ μεγαλοφροσύνης, 136.2, cf. 134–7). He also saves captured Spartan spies from execution by his own generals (145–7). If he flogs, fetters and abuses the Hellespont (35), he makes sumptuous offerings to it as he crosses (53–4). If he makes dangerously arrogant claims, such as 'we will make the land of Persia border on Zeus's aether' (8γ.1), he can also weep at the shortness of human life and at the thought that all on his great and impressive expedition will be dead in a hundred years (45–46.2).

The question of whether the expedition should be undertaken is examined in a detailed and sophisticated manner by Herodotus.[42] Initially reluctant to concern himself with Greece (5.1), Xerxes comes under a variety of pressures, internal and external. Exiled Greeks encourage him, seeking the restoration of their rule (6), as does the powerful Persian Mardonius, who sees Greece as potentially his personal fiefdom (5). Furthermore, as Xerxes says himself, being a new king, he must establish himself as worthy of his highly successful predecessors: put another way, he must satisfy the Persian nobility who look to him for their own continued wealth and power, and he must cement his own position by increasing the Persian dominions and their tribute. There is also the unfinished business of his father's planned vengeance on the Greeks (8α.2).

His uncle Artabanus, as a 'warner',[43] counsels caution (10). In this, he has been seen as the wise counsellor who knows the truth, with Xerxes' refusal to follow it as a sign of his flawed nature. But there is an artificiality about Artabanus' words, in that his predictions are *too* accurate and so obviously the product of hindsight (cf. esp. 8β.2, 10ε, 10θ, 49). This perception of their artificiality puts them into perspective: they are

40 Cf. Boedeker 1988.

41 On motivation in Herodotus generally, cf. Baragwanath 2005; for Xerxes, cf. 219–61.

42 Cf. de Jong 2001 for a narratological analysis of this debate and how Herodotus uses prolepses and analepses to comment on Xerxes' decision.

43 Cf. Bischoff 1932; Lattimore 1939; cf. **54**n.

not necessarily what any sensible man would have thought. In response, Xerxes looks for justification to the past. The Persians have succeeded because, 'ever since we took our kingdom from the Medes, we have never stayed still' (8α.1), and

> it is better to be courageous in everything and to suffer half of what one fears, than to be fearful of everything and never to suffer anything . . . How can one who is mortal know what is sure? I do not think he can. However, the prizes tend generally to go to those who are willing to act, but not to those who consider everything and hesitate . . . Great achievements are usually attained through great dangers. (50.1–3)

These sentiments would not be out of place in the mouth of a Homeric hero.

Furthermore, four dreams add their own considerable pressures for invasion. Xerxes ignores the first's warnings (12–13), but a second makes it plain that if he does not invade, 'just as you became mighty and powerful in a short time, so you will be as quickly reduced to insignificance' (14). To test Artabanus' claim that dreams can simply be the reflection of matters uppermost in a man's mind (16β.2), Artabanus is dressed up as Xerxes; the dream-figure gives a similar warning, and reinforces the message by trying to burn out his eyes (17). This figure also accuses Artabanus of obstructing 'what must be' (τὸ χρεὸν γενέσθαι), an ominous indication that Xerxes has no choice in the matter of invasion, and that disaster will follow. All this does not suggest an unthinking act of aggrandisement by a greedy and hybristic tyrant.

Once on campaign, the Spartan Demaratus takes the place of Artabanus as Xerxes' adviser. Xerxes rejects his arguments with laughter (**114**.2n.), but always with reasons for doing so. At the end of the book, Demaratus advises Xerxes to use part of his fleet to attack the Peloponnese from the island of Cythera, but Xerxes prefers the advice of Achaemenes, who argues against giving up their numerical superiority by dividing the fleet (234–7). Again, with hindsight Demaratus' idea might have been a good one, but there is no glaring tactical error here, since the Persians did rely on force of numbers in battle.

The episodes featuring Xerxes in book 8 are dealt with in the commentary. He makes a final major appearance in the erotic intrigues of 9.108–13.[44] Failing to seduce his brother Masistes' wife, Xerxes marries his son to Masistes' daughter and seduces her. He promises her any gift and, 'because she and all her house were doomed to an evil end' (109.2), she insists on the robe Xerxes' wife Amestris had woven him, and wears it openly. Amestris presumes Masistes' wife is to blame, and at Xerxes' birthday feast, when custom compelled him grant any request, demands Masistes' wife, whom she mutilates horribly. Xerxes advises an unaware Masistes to repudiate his wife and marry one of Xerxes' daughters; he refuses and, suspecting danger, takes his sons and

[44] For a historical interpretation of this story as reflecting a usurpation attempt by Xerxes' eldest brother Ariamenes, cf. Wiesehöfer 1996: 52–3 summarising arguments from Sancisi-Weerdenburg 1980. The motif of wearing the King's robe is repeated from the start of the narrative of Xerxes' reign. Cf. also F&M on 9.108–13.

men to foment revolt from Bactria. He is intercepted and all are killed.[45] The elements of earlier episodes reappear: divine compulsion and the demands of the Persian court constrain the King, who operates under a mixture of licence and compulsion.

One must beware therefore of accepting uncritically the prevalent Greek view of Xerxes as a man of hybris and unwisdom, unwilling to listen to good advice and marked down by fate for a bad end. Herodotus' narrative helped to create, but also offers the means to qualify, traditional western conceptions both of Xerxes and of the East.

4 ACHAEMENID CAMPAIGNS

Though Xerxes' invasion of Greece was a military campaign, it would be a mistake to think only fighting men were involved. The King periodically progressed round the royal capitals, partly for reasons of climate, but also to display himself, his court and his power to subject countries, to renew loyalties and a sense of belonging to the empire, to receive gifts, reward benefactors, hear petitions and so on.[46] The distinction between royal progress and military expedition was thus blurred: the business of the empire had to go on.[47]

Luxury in particular was not foregone. Eunuchs, cooks, pastry-chefs, specialists in dairy products, pot-boys, servants of table and bedchamber, wine-filterers, perfumers, garland-makers, musicians, dancers, etc. all feature in the sources. After Mycale, the Greeks found 'tents decorated with gold and silver, gilded and silver-plated couches, gold *craters*, cups and other drinking-vessels; they discovered sacks on wagons, in which could be seen gold and silver cooking vessels; from the dead that lay there they stripped armbands and torques and golden daggers; they did not bother with the embroidered clothing' (9.80.1–2). There was a huge tent, 'decked out in gold and silver and decorated tapestries . . . Pausanias was amazed when he saw the gold and silver couches richly covered, the gold and silver tables, and the whole magnificent dinner service' (9.821–1).[48] In such tents the King lived, with the same elaborate rituals as in his palaces: he drank a wine exclusive to himself from a special egg-shaped cup (Athen. 145C, 503F), and water only from the Choaspes at Susa, boiled, stored in silver vessels and transported in numerous wagons (H. 1.188). Suitably gargantuan quantities of food and drink were taken along to fuel this lifestyle,[49] or were requisitioned on the way (7.118–20). As Xenophon puts it, 'Most of the peoples of Asia go on campaign with

45 Xerxes' actual last appearance is 9.116, again in a context of royal gift-giving, where he is duped by Artaÿctes into giving him the shrine of Protesilaus and all its treasures.

46 Cf. Briant 2002: 183–95; Wiesehöfer 1996: 38–41.

47 Book 1 of Xenophon's *Anabasis* gives an idea of aristocratic life on the road, in describing Cyrus' the Younger's movements; note especially the account of the trial of Orontas in 1.6.

48 On the King's tent, cf. Xen. *Cyr.* 8.5.1–14 for a fictionalised account no doubt based on reality; Xen. *Anab.* 4.4.21 for the tent of Tiribazus, a commander; cf. also Theopompus, *FGH* 115 F 263; Miller 1997: 34–7. For pictures of Assyrian kings' pavilions, cf. Reade 1988: figs. 40 (BM WA 124548) and 74 (BM WA 124913–15).

49 Cf. Polyaen. 4.3.32; Briant 2002: 290 for the evidence of the Persepolis tablets.

their households . . . They say that they would fight better if what they hold dearest were there . . . This may be true, but perhaps also they do this for sensual gratification' (*Cyr.* 4.2.2, 3.2). Households certainly accompanied the Persians. Xerxes travelled to Greece with some of his sons by lesser wives (**103**). Whether he was accompanied by any principal wives we do not know, but Cambyses took his sister-wife to Egypt (3.31.1), and Darius III had his half-sister wife, sons and daughters with him when defeated by Alexander at Issus (Arr. *Anab.* 2.11.9). Concubines accompanied their masters,[50] whether high-born consorts, like the concubine of Pharandates, daughter of Hegetorides of Cos (9.76), or dancers, musicians etc. (Xen. *Cyr.* 4.3.1).

In the light of the nature of such expeditions, one should not judge the outcome purely in military terms. Xerxes was able to display his power to a large number of races, and indeed, albeit briefly, extended his empire to the Isthmus of Corinth and the islands of Andros and the Cyclades. He recorded for reward those who deserved well of him (**85**.3, **90**.4), and passed judgement on those who did not (**90**). He was able to reward cities for their efforts on his behalf (**120**), and established relationships with many Greeks, not least Themistocles, which could have been useful in any later campaign (**75**n.). In other words, in Greece the normal business of the empire continued, with the King at its margins rather than more centrally placed.

5 THE BATTLES OF BOOK 8

It is natural to wish to reconstruct ancient battles from Herodotus' accounts, but the amount of patterning, by means of repeated motifs, narrative structures and even names, in and between them suggests that he is interested in more than simply what happened.[51]

Herodotus associates Artemisium (**1–26**) and Thermopylae (7.210–225) by noting that they were fought on the same three days and that the defence of the pass at Thermopylae was equivalent to the fleet's defence of the Euripus channel (**15**); but the parallelisms go further. There is a similar pattern of two inconclusive battles followed by a conclusive one; in each episode, the Peloponnesians wish to retreat (7.207 and **4**.1; the language is similar); the Persians carry out a 'flanking manoeuvre', at Thermopylae successfully taking the Greeks by surprise, but at Artemisium unsuccessfully sending a squadron round Euboea in an attempt to encircle them (**7**.1); the exiled Spartan king, Demaratus, features in an episode before each battle (7.209 and 239).

Salamis is also linked to Artemisium. The motif of secretive actions by Themistocles in the context of debates is prominent. Artemisium begins and ends with councils, and Themistocles treats secretly with Eurybiades, Adeimantus and the Euboeans (**4–5**, **18–19**). At Salamis, there is Mnesiphilus' secret meeting with Themistocles (**57**), Themistocles' sending of Sicinnus on a secret mission to Xerxes (**75**; cf. also **110**), and Themistocles' private meeting with Aristeides outside the assembly

[50] For the distinction between wives and concubines, cf. **103**n.

[51] On the battles in these later books, cf. Pohlenz 1937: 120–63; Immerwahr 1966: 238–305.

(**78–82**); Eurybiades and Adeimantus also feature again (**56–64**). There are again more detailed links. The very name of the Carian queen who plays a major role in events before, during and after Salamis (**68–9**, **87–8**, **101–3**), Artemisia, evokes the earlier battle, and Salamis is also prefigured at Artemisium by the capture of the brother of the king of Cypriot Salamis (**11**.2), and a gift of land on the island of Salamis to a deserter from the Persians (**11**.3).[52] Reading the Salamis narrative in the light of Artemisium and Thermopylae now offers an implicit commentary on Greek decision-making after Artemisium.[53] At Thermopylae, the Greeks put their trust in a wall, which fails them (7.223.2); at Artemisium, they are comparatively successful at sea. The motif of the wall is crucial. Delphi tells Athens to trust a 'wooden wall' (7.141–3): some interpret this as meaning a wall on the Acropolis, and they are killed (**51**.2); Themistocles interprets it as meaning the fleet and wins at Salamis. The Peloponnesians build a wall across the Isthmus of Corinth (**71**.2–**73**), preferring to trust this rather than fight at Salamis, but Herodotus has already given his opinion on this, when attributing the major role in Xerxes' defeat to the Athenians:

> If no one had opposed Xerxes by sea, this is what would have happened on land: even if the Spartans had built lots of walls across the Isthmus, they would have been betrayed by their allies, not willingly but by necessity, as their cities were individually captured by the barbarian fleet; they would have been isolated and, undertaking great exploits, would have died nobly.[54] (7.139.3)

Implicit in Herodotus' narrative therefore is an ongoing justification for Themistocles' strategy of a sea-battle at Salamis: narration becomes analysis.

These three battles also have links with the final two battles, at Plataea and Mycale. This latter pair were similarly fought on the same day, again with one involving the army, the other naval forces (though fought on the shore). Herodotus draws attention to the similarities between the two: at Mycale, a herald's staff found on the shore is associated with a rumour of the victory at Plataea, and each conflict takes place by a temple of Demeter (9.100–1). There are other similarities, such as the reference to temples of Hera (52, 61.3, 69.1), the capture of a wall as (again) the crucial event (70, 102), desertions (66, 103–4), and the importance of seers and their histories (33–6, 93–5). The earlier battles are also explicitly recalled: the only Spartan survivor of Thermopylae, Aristodemus, who was shunned in Sparta because he had not died with the others (7.229–31), purges his disgrace by becoming the bravest fighter at Plataea (9.71.2). Leotychidas' appeal to the Ionians at Mycale 'had the same purpose as Themistocles' at Artemisium' (98.4). Salamis is recalled by the temples of Demeter, of which the one at Mycale was called 'Eleusinia' (97), recalling the Eleusinian portent in **65**; Alexander's night-time embassy to the Greek lines at Plataea (44–5) is reminiscent of Sicinnus' to the Persians (**75**).[55]

[52] Salamis is also linked to Marathon: **60**α n. [53] Cf. further Bowie 2004.
[54] The same point is made about the uselessness of the wall by Chileus in 9.9.2.
[55] Cf. also Lachenaud 1978: 323–404 on the religious aspects.

Finally, Plataea and Mycale close a ring that goes right back to the Ionian Revolt, where yet again two battles are fought on the same day, at Cypriot Salamis, one on land, lost like Thermopylae through treachery, and one at sea, like Artemisium won by the Greeks (5.108–15). As at Salamis, the Greeks subsequently entrust their fortunes to a sea-battle: at Lade, the Ionians are finally defeated, as a result of treachery (6.7, 11–16), while at Salamis Themistocles' cunning secures a Greek victory. At Lade, the battle is lost when the Samians, followed by most of the Ionians, desert the Greek lines (6.14.2); at Mycale, the Samians, followed by the Milesians, this time reverse their treachery and desert the Persians (9.103–4). Herodotus' comment on this latter desertion is: 'thus Ionia revolted from the Persians a second time' (104), cementing the parallelism between the two sets of battles.

Two points can be made. First, the insistent parallelisms between the battles can be seen as part of Herodotus' portrayal of these events as not random, but subject to some divine or cosmic ordering. Sometimes this is made explicit, as when he comments on the storm that destroyed the Persian ships rounding Euboea, saying that 'everything was done by the god to make the Persian fleet the same size as the Greek and not much greater' (**13**), or when he notes the divine aspects at Plataea and Mycale. Second, there is an implicit contrast between the Revolt and Xerxes' invasion. The reader is encouraged to compare the two and ponder exactly why the Greeks, in each case divided against themselves, were once defeated and once victorious. The intelligence and tactical brilliance of Themistocles may, for instance, be contrasted with the numerous miscalculations by the Ionians.

Not that matters stop with Mycale. Herodotus subsequently recounts Greek discussions about the future of the Ionians, held 'because they thought it would be impossible for them to guard the Ionians continually, but if they did not guard them they could not hope that the Persians would let them off scot-free' (9.106.2). The problems remain, and the Ionians will be central to the problems between Athens and Sparta, which the narrative looks forward to. The splitting up of the Greek fleet (114.2), as the Athenians go their own way, separately from the Spartans, is symbolic of what the rest of the century holds.

6 STRUCTURE AND NARRATIVE MODES

Recent work on Herodotus' narrative technique has tended to move away from the ideas either that there is a main theme, from which, for various reasons, Herodotus 'digresses', or that Herodotus is a simple story-teller with little concern or capacity for organising his material. The complexity of the work, and the varying ways in which it can be analysed are being progressively revealed, but much remains to be done.[56] Here will be considered some of the major structuring principles of the work, which,

[56] On the structure of Herodotus' work, cf. e.g. Immerwahr 1966; Wood 1972; Lateiner 1989; Lang 1984; F&M 4–9; and on the Persian wars, Harrison 2002a. For a useful brief survey of narratological approaches to Herodotus, cf. de Jong 2002: 245–54. Cf. also Luraghi 2006.

as far as we know, had no parallel in range and scope in early Greek literature except Homer: to call Herodotus the 'prose Homer' is not unjust in this area, at any rate.

1 Individuals

Herodotus will sometimes organise his narrative around an important individual,[57] weaving into his narration a whole range of congruent material on other peoples, places and institutions. For instance, the first section of the work tells of the downfall of the Lydian king Croesus, but weaves in a spell-binding variety of topics. Basically, it is ordered through rough concentration first on Lydia, then on Delphi, Athens and Sparta, then on Media and the Scythians, and finally on Lydia again.

It starts with a history of Lydia (1.6–45). This begins with a first mention of Croesus, before regressing to the usurpation of the throne of Candaules by Croesus' ancestor Gyges (Assyrian *Guggu* of *Ludu*), and the Delphic prophecy that Gyges and his successors would rule for only five generations (6–15). Then Herodotus fills in Lydian history through brief accounts of the three intervening kings, Ardys, Sadyattes and Alyattes (16–25), before returning to Croesus and his fabulous wealth and power and his pride in it (26–8). This is counterpointed by two stories, Solon's visit and warning about the mutability of human happiness (29–33), and the tragic death of Croesus' son, Atys (34–45).

Cyrus' rise in Persia provokes Croesus' desire to crush this threat and prompts his first contacts with mainland Greeks. After Delphi has successfully answered the question which Croesus posed to various oracles, Croesus gives it lavish gifts (46–55; cf. 53.3), which will at the end of the story be seen to be crucial to all that has happened. He seeks out for alliance the most important peoples among the Greeks, the Athenians and Spartans, which enables Herodotus to give a partial history of the two cities, by means of a disquisition on the Pelasgian and Hellenic races, to which they respectively belonged (56–70).

Similarly, a fuller account of Croesus' reasons for attacking Cyrus then allows Herodotus to recount some of the history of the Medes, the chief power to the east. Astyages, the king of Media deposed by Cyrus, is revealed as Croesus' brother-in-law, having married his sister to settle a war which was started by a dispute over some Scythians. The activities of these Scythians in Media and their ultimate quarrel with Cyaxares, Astyages' father, are then described (71–5).

The account of Croesus' attack on Cyrus, his defeat and rescue from the pyre on which Cyrus intended to immolate him all bring us back in a circle to Solon's visit and Delphi and its role in Croesus' life. Croesus calls out Solon's name on the pyre, which catches Cyrus' interest and leads to the reprieve. When Croesus complains to Apollo about his lack of gratitude for Croesus' gifts, Delphi's role in his downfall is

57 This is perhaps not surprising, given that Near Eastern and Egyptian kings constructed narratives around themselves and their exploits, and Greek tyrants also sought accounts of themselves in the same way.

explained (72–92). The account of Lydia is completed by a description of its geography, remarkable buildings and customs, many of the latter invented during a famine which led some of the Lydians to go to Italy and become the Etruscans (93–4).

These ninety-four chapters thus contain: aspects of the history of the major peoples and cities of the time, Lydians, Medes, Scythians, Etruscans, Delphi, Athens, Sparta, and preparation for the rise of the Persians; geographical accounts of Cappadocia and Lydia; ethnographic accounts of the Lydians, Scythians, Pelasgians, Hellenes, Spartans, Argives and Athenians; notable oral traditions, such as Arion's ride on the Dolphin, Solon's visit to Croesus and the discovery of Orestes' bones at Tegea; description of remarkable buildings and artworks; and the introduction of ethical ideas which will inform the work as a whole, all skilfully contained within an account of the rise and fall of Croesus. More on Media and then an account of Persia will follow.

2 *Military campaigns*

A good deal of Herodotus' work is structured around campaigns of the Persian Kings, but what is noticeable is how, except in books 7–9, there is often a dearth of precise information about the military campaigning: this is true of Cambyses' conquest of Egypt, but most strikingly so of Darius' conquest of lands in India, which is not described at all. What we tend to get instead of military history is ethnography.

Thus, in book 4, the narrative of Darius' expedition against the Scythians contains substantial accounts of the geography, history and customs of those races, and the actual campaigning takes up relatively little space (1–144; campaigning 83–5, 87–92, 118–44). These accounts are not there purely for interest, but provide the explanation for the failure of Darius to conquer Scythia: their nomadic lifestyle is ideal for outwitting the heavily armed Persian troops, who are lucky to escape the trackless wastes that Herodotus describes. Again, in the subsequent account of the Persian invasion of Libya, there are substantial narratives of the histories of Cyrene (145–64) and of the Libyans (168–99); the actual campaigning once more takes second place.

In book 5, Aristagoras' journey to Sparta for help with the Ionian Revolt allows description of relationships within the Spartan royal families, an account of the races who live between Ionian and Susa, and a description of the Royal Road from Sardis to Susa (39–54). When Aristagoras goes to Athens, this enables Herodotus to continue the history of Athens begun in book 1, with the death of Peisistratus' son Hipparchus and an account of the activities of the newly democratic state (55–97).[58] Again, during the expedition of Xerxes, Herodotus describes the nations he passes through (e.g. the Thracian tribes, 7.110–12; Thessaly, 7.128–30; conflict of Phocians and Thessalians, **27–31**), and Salamis is marked by a summary account of the histories and origins of the Greek peoples who fought and were victorious there (**43–8**).

[58] Cf. the narratological analysis of this passage in de Jong 2002: 263–6.

Book 2 may be included here, since its account of Egypt's geography (5–34), ethology and ethnology, flora, fauna (35–98) and history (99–182), though in fact in part a travelogue involving Herodotus himself, is placed between the announcement of Cambyses' intention to invade (2.1) and the account of that invasion in book 3. Similar too in technique is 3.88–116, where Darius' accession is the excuse for a descriptive survey of his empire and the tribute the various nations paid him, followed by an account of Indian customs and of the ends of the world. These sections, apart from their intrinsic interest, emphasise Persia's power and control of its empire.

3 Episodes

The economy of Herodotus' writing can be appreciated also in shorter episodes, such as the Spartan and Corinthian attack on Polycrates of Samos, instigated by the Samians who founded Cydonia in Crete (3.39–60). As in the narratives of Darius' campaigns, little of the episode (less than 10 per cent) concerns the actual invasion (39.1, 54–6). The rest is taken up with three episodes providing the background and outcome of the invasion: one involves Polycrates and the Samians (39–47), another Periander and the Corinthians and Corcyreans (48–53), and the last the foundation of Cydonia and engineering marvels on Samos (57–60).

Polycrates' conflict with Sparta is announced, but the description is immediately postponed, as Polycrates' rise to immense prosperity and power (39.2–40) is contrasted with the prophetic story that, advised by pharaoh Amasis to counter this prosperity by deliberate loss of his most prized possession, Polycrates threw a signet ring into the sea only to have it returned to him in a fish (41–3). Returning to the conflict, the reasons for the Samians' request to Sparta are given, along with an analeptic (i.e. 'retrospective') discussion of their ultimate fate (44–6). When the Spartans agree to help, the narrative appears most interested in describing the remarkable linen breastplate, sent to Sparta by Amasis but stolen by Samians, which is the reason the Spartans give for helping (47); even in a complex narrative, Herodotus maintains his interest in marvels.

The involvement of the Corinthians with the attack on Samos is then explained by another story of theft. The Samians had stolen from their Corinthian escort three hundred noble Corcyrean youths sent by the Corinthian tyrant Periander for castration at Sardis, through a desire to avenge himself on the Corcyreans for killing his own younger son (49). The story of this killing constitutes then the longest section of this whole episode (50–3), and is told in a leisurely manner, with lengthy speeches, so that it becomes the most striking part of the episode. After this lengthy build-up, the failure of the Spartan expedition comes almost as something of an anti-climax (54–6), the main part of the narrative concerning the exploits of the ancestor of a man whom Herodotus had actually met (55). The episode closes with the foundation of Cydone by these Samians and their enslavement by the Argives, in revenge for earlier attacks by the Samians (57–9). Herodotus then justifies spending so much time on the

Samians, on the grounds that they have created the three greatest engineering works in Greece (60).

This fruitless Spartan attack therefore is the framework on which to hang a complex series of interlocking events involving the major powers of the time, Egypt, Samos, Corinth and Corcyra, and accounts of the major rulers, Amasis, Polycrates and Periander, as well as descriptions of artefacts and engineering works, an *aition* for a festival, folk-tale-like episodes, personal reminiscence and a long tale of a family feud. The chronology of the events is considerably varied in the telling, so that Herodotus solves the problems of how to tell of several interlocked and roughly contemporaneous events, without being enslaved to chronology. These shifts of chronology and unexpected distributions of emphasis enable him to give due weight to all the events. What is announced as the subject of the episode turns out to be less important than what that episode allows Herodotus to recount around it.

4 *Narrative modes*

We have so far looked at how Herodotus handles space and time; we now turn to the formal presentation of the narrative. For the greater part of his narrative, Herodotus is the 'primary narrator' and, though he records many traditions, he does not often pass the narration of events directly to 'secondary' narrators in the story, as for instance Homer does with Odysseus in *Odyssey* 9–12. The main exception to this is Socles' opposition to the restoration of Hippias as tyrant in Athens, using a long, retrospective account of the horrors of Cypselus' tyranny in Corinth (5.92). Though Socles' speech is given in his own words, the speech still resembles Herodotus' own style of narrative: it addresses questions of tyranny and freedom, and nests a tale within a tale, when Cypselus' messenger visits Thrasybulus, tyrant of Miletus, whose destruction of his finest stalks of corn symbolises how a tyrant must behave. This episode relates thematically to an earlier one in the work (but later in time), where Cypselus' son Periander helped Thrasybulus avoid destruction by Alyattes (1.19–23), the two episodes sharing the motif of the piling of items in the central agora. The centrality of oracles also reflects Herodotus' own analysis of historical process. Socles takes up the story, therefore, but his speech is woven into the fabric of Herodotus' narrative.[59]

Herodotus seldom gives the names of his individual sources (**65**n.), as opposed to collective ones such as 'the Greeks', and only twice are they made to give information at any length. In **65**, Dicaeus is the source, in indirect speech (enlivened by direct quotations), of the description of the mystical Eleusinian procession before Salamis; and in 9.16, Thersander of Thebes, again in indirect speech, tells of a Persian's prophetic lament about the outcome of the battle of Plataea. Rarely, nations collectively may become the narrators, as in the tales from their mythical past told by the Tegeans and

59 Another example of a lengthy warning narrative, this time unsuccessful, is found in Leotychides' tale of Glaucus (6.86).

Athenians in support of their claims to occupy the left wing at Plataea (9.26–7). Elsewhere, Herodotus will give long accounts of stories told him, but they are in indirect speech, as in the case of the cunning thief who plundered pharaoh Rhampsinitus' treasury (2.121).

Herodotus does, however, use his characters in other ways as vehicles for the presentation of his subject matter, and not just as 'focalisers', i.e. the eyes or ears through which the story is perceived.[60] There is a striking example of this technique at Doriscus, when Xerxes reviews his forces and Herodotus gives an account of the dress and backgrounds of the peoples in Xerxes' army: as Xerxes conducts the review, so Herodotus makes them pass before the reader's eye in all their colour and variety (7.59–100). Sometimes, Herodotus will help out a character who has been carrying the narrative. When Aristagoras expounds his map of Asia Minor to the Spartans, he describes the effeteness and riches of the easterners, and lists the races who live between Ionia and Susa, with emphasis on the wealth of their fields, flocks, tribute and treasure houses (5.49–51). He is, however, thrown out of Sparta before he can describe the Royal Road from Sardis to Susa, so Herodotus does this for him in his own voice (52–4). Characters can also be used to convey factual information in an integrated way: as Xerxes' messenger travels to Susa after Salamis, the messenger-system he is using is described in some detail (**98**).

Herodotus will often give political analysis in his own voice, as when he gives his 'unpopular' opinion that the Athenians were central to the Greek victory over Xerxes (7.139); the remark is not gratuitous, since it marks the move from the narrative of Xerxes' advance to the Greeks' opposition to it. At other times, he will convey such analysis through other mouths, as when the seven conspirators discuss whether they should institute a democracy, oligarchy or monarchy when they have overthrown Smerdies (3.80–2),[61] or when Demaratus and Xerxes debate the merits of Greek and Persian politics and warfare (7.101–4, 209, 234–8). Strategic matters can be similarly treated: the merits to the Greeks and demerits to the Persians of fighting at Salamis are set out in the speeches of Artemisia and Themistocles, and the question of whether Xerxes should invade Greece is examined at length in Persian councils (7.5–18), as is that of whether to retreat after Salamis (**100–2**).

Herodotus is the primary moral commentator on events, but by no means the dominant one. At times, the judgements will be his own: he opines on the 'wisest' and the 'most shameful' Babylonian customs (1.196–9), and elsewhere his judgement may be tacitly corroborated by a character: Panionius 'made his living from the most godless actions' towards the boys he bought and sold (**105**.1), and one of his victims then addresses Panionius as 'you who among all men make your living from the most godless actions' (**106**.3). The moral import of episodes is regularly given by characters in the narrative, as when Solon warns the fabulously successful Croesus of divine jealousy and the need to judge a man's happiness at the end of his life and not during

[60] For focalisation and history-writing, cf. Rood 1998.
[61] On this debate, cf. Pelling 2002.

it (1.29–33). The same idea occurs more complexly when Xerxes proudly reviews his remarkable expeditionary force before breaking down in tears at the thought that all will be dead in a hundred years. Artabanus reminds him that all men will at one time or another wish for the release from trouble that death brings (7.44–6), and the fact that many of the men in the review will achieve that release before the year is out prevents this from being mere clichéd moralising.

Comment on events can also be conveyed by the juxtaposition of episodes, as when Tritantaechmes' praise of Greek virtue, as shown by their willingness to compete at Olympia without the incentive of riches (**26**), is immediately followed by the Thessalians' cruel treatment of their fellow Greeks, the Phocians, which involves the demand for a massive sum to be paid to buy the Thessalians off (**27–30**). Before Salamis, the two sides receive portents, but only the Greeks take steps to act on them.[62] Juxtaposition is also used with prolepses (i.e. narratives that look forward to the future) to events outside the narrative: as Pelling has noted, 'these are never casual, nor casually placed: it is no coincidence . . . that the most important flash-forward to the Peloponnesian War comes just before Herodotus' praise of Athens for not fragmenting Greece during the Persian War (7.139).'[63]

When the historical truth about particular events is unknowable, Herodotus will give competing versions, sometimes offering an opinion as to which is more likely, sometimes not. Thus the opening chapters of the work present the causes of the conflict between East and West in Greek and Persian variants. Readers may be offered guidance in judging the variants, but must ultimately make up their own mind. Not infrequently, stories from some sources are told only to be dismissed, but even these stories contribute to the account. Of the three versions of how Cambyses came to invade Egypt (3.1–3), two are rejected, but in rejecting one Herodotus is able to convey, not only the lineage of Cambyses, but also the ethnographic facts that the Egyptians are the best informed people about Persian customs, and that no bastard could be King of Persia if legitimate sons were alive: significant information is woven into the text at a convenient moment. Similarly, in **94**, he tells at some length an Athenian tale, which is rejected by all Greeks besides the Athenians, but looks forward to the conflict between Athens and Corinth later in the century (see note *ad loc.*).

Some of Herodotus' stories look very much like what we would call 'folk-tales', and he has in the past been criticised for apparently accepting them uncritically. How far his acceptance was uncritical is of course impossible to tell, since we have no access to the tales as he heard them, but that he should have used such 'tales' is inevitable when he was collecting material on oral or predominantly oral cultures. Members of an oral culture cannot possibly preserve the mass of historical events they live through in the way a literate culture can, and there is a tendency therefore to give events meaning by casting them into pre-existing, significant story-patterns.[64] To

[62] Cf. **64–5**n.; Griffiths 2001. [63] Cf. Pelling 1997a.

[64] This is a massive topic that can only be touched on here. A classic discussion can be found in Eliade 1965: 3–48; cf. also Vansina 1973. For Herodotus, cf. e.g. Murray 1987; Gould 1989: 27–41.

take a well-known example, the extraordinary achievements of Cyrus led to his early years being narrated according to the pattern of the great leader who has humble and yet also divinely influenced beginnings, a pattern that is widespread across many cultures. In a manner that has similarities with the stories of, for instance, Moses, the Babylonian king Sargon, Oedipus, Romulus and Remus and others, he begins in rural poverty, having been saved by good fortune, before rising to great heights (H. 1.95–122). Fitting Cyrus into this pattern thus establishes him as a great man: this pattern conveys much more about Cyrus than the 'truth' about his background would have. In retailing these stories, Herodotus may not be stating what actually happened, but he is stating what people believed happened, which is as much a historical fact as a precise account of the events would have been. For the purposes of this section, what is notable is the way in which Herodotus takes these traditional stories and works them so that they contribute to his greater purposes. This story of Cyrus' youth in the countryside and rise to power in a mighty empire can be seen to be part of, and a frame for, a series of narratives of kings' reigns and descriptions of cities, which reflect upon kingship, the values inherent in cities and countryside, on freedom and the need for political control and so on. It is thus very much more than simply the repetition of a story-pattern.[65]

Furthermore, such stories can contain important information. In reality, Darius is unlikely to have become master of the Achaemenid empire simply because his horse was first to whinny at dawn and thunder rang out (3.84–7). However, the elements of the story seem to reflect the ideology of Achaemenid kingship: dawn is a time associated with royal activities;[66] kings were believed to be able to control thunder and lightning, which often accompany royal acts;[67] and horses figure regularly in regal iconography. In the case of the story of the eunuch Hermotimus and the slave-dealer Panionius, we seem to have a story, cast in the form of a moral tale of wickedness appropriately punished, which is allegorical of relations between Persians and Ionians.[68]

Finally, Herodotus will also play with different levels of knowledge between character and reader. Xerxes' expedition against Greece is constantly attended by signs of divine displeasure, which are either misinterpreted by the Persians, or not seen as significant by them, because they do not have the reader's perspective.[69] The Magi wrongly see the eclipse which takes place as the army leaves Sardis as portending the eclipse of the Greek cities (7.37), and Xerxes ignores two prodigies involving mares (7.57), one of which comes immediately after the offerings to the Hellespont and his crossing. Equally ill-omened is the reference to Xerxes as Zeus, made at the same time in 'inspired speech'[70] by a local man. Xerxes is apparently unaware of this, as he is of the fact that the Greeks have been specifically told to call on the help of the

[65] Cf. Bowie 2006: 122–9. [66] Cf. e.g. 7.54; Polyaen. 7.11.12.

[67] Cf. Ctesias *FGH* 688 F 45b (9), *Indica* 4. [68] Cf. Hornblower 2003; **104–6**n.

[69] Contrast the way that good fortune smiles repeatedly on Darius and his fellow conspirators as they overthrow the Magi (3.67–79).

[70] A *kledon*: cf. **114**.2n.

winds (**12–14**n.): as a result, he does not see the frequent disastrous storms and other omens as significant. The reader's and Xerxes' perspectives on matters here diverge in a kind of dramatic irony.

There is, therefore, enormous variety in Herodotus' narrative, and the reader has to be alert to the many things that are going on. Into the broadly chronological framework are woven studies in a remarkable number of areas of human research.

7 THE LANGUAGE OF HERODOTUS[71]

Our MSS are descended from an 'archetype' written probably in the first century AD.[72] These MSS and the few surviving papyri do not suggest there is a wide divergence between our text and Herodotus' original in terms of expression, word order, order of incidents, etc. However, in matters of dialect, morphology, spelling, etc., considerable confusion reigns.[73] In the representation of particular forms, the MSS disagree with each other, are inconsistent with themselves, and contain some very peculiar spellings. It is clear that Herodotus' text has been heavily corrupted by the introduction of Attic and false Ionic forms by scribes and scholars who were more used to Attic or had their own theories about how his Ionic dialect should look. Furthermore, we have too little contemporary Ionic from inscriptions against which to check the MSS' readings, and the texts of other Ionic writers close in time to Herodotus, such as the early historians and Hippocrates, are themselves heavily Atticised (and in the former case, very fragmentary).

Faced with the plethora of competing variants in the MSS, editors have hard choices to make: when the MSS write ποιέει and ποιέειν more often than ποιεῖ and ποιεῖν, but by contrast prefer νοεῖ and νοεῖν to the corresponding uncontracted forms, do editors go with the majority verdict in the case of each individual verb or form, do they standardise either the contracted or uncontracted form, or do they have a mixture of the two, and if so, how do they decide what the mixture will be? When standardisation and consistency of spelling is a relatively late feature of English, how much should we demand of fifth-century BC Ionia?

Again, it is difficult when we come across unusual forms to know how they should be accounted for. There are a number of possibilities. (1) They might be 'false' Ionicisms, that is, forms created as a result of insufficient knowledge of how that dialect works. A good instance of this problem concerns the genitive plural of the pronoun αὐτός, in which Ionic distinguishes between the feminine in -εων (< -ηων < -ᾱων) and the masculine/neuter in -ων (< *-*ōm*). However, in the MSS we find the feminine αὐτέων used as a masculine or neuter. This might have been introduced by a scribe who saw -εων frequently in his text and extended its use falsely, but we have ἑκαστέων (neut.) on a Milesian inscription. The document itself dates from the mid-fifth century, which

[71] There is appended to this section a brief guide to the language of Herodotus, for those who wish speedily to see the differences from Attic.

[72] See further §8 below.

[73] Most useful on Herodotus' dialect are Smyth 1894; Untersteiner 1949; Legrand 1955: 179–223; Rosén 1962; for later literary Ionic, Lightfoot 2003: 97–142.

is promising, but the actual version we have was carved only *ca.* 100: is ἑκαστέων an original form or a later one, based on what the writer thought it should be in Ionic?[74] (2) They might be Atticisms, wrongly substituted for Ionic forms: πόλει (beside usual πόλι) is also found in Homer, but is likely to be an Attic form both there and in Herodotus. However, not all Atticisms need be copyists' errors: Herodotus seems to have spent time in Athens, and his lexicon (especially in later books) shows words that seem to have been specifically Attic (e.g. καραδοκέω, δωροδοκέω, ἐπ' αὐτοφώρωι): why not Attic spellings as well? (3) They might be poeticisms borrowed by Herodotus perhaps from epic and used as part of an attempt to create a language suitably elevated for his great subject. (4) It has been argued that such doublets as μοῦνος / μόνος found in the MSS might be variant spellings of the same sound,[75] introduced by copyists if not Herodotus himself. (5) They might simply be mistakes. In the list that follows, therefore, there are many uncertainties.

Because Attic is the dialect that most people learn first, Herodotus' dialect will be discussed below largely in terms of the differences between Attic and his Ionic. Herodotus came from Halicarnassus (modern-day Bodrum) in Caria. This was a Dorian colony, but inscriptions from that area are in a form of 'East Ionic', a dialect spoken in the Ionic areas of the Asia Minor coast and some of the adjacent islands, as well as in their colonies around the Hellespont and Black Sea. Historically, Attic and Ionic are two branches of an earlier 'Attic-Ionic' dialect, one of the five main groupings into which the historical Greek dialects are divided.[76] This Attic-Ionic group separated from other dialects after the Mycenean period, and subsequently divided into its two branches during the migrations that marked that period. This is important for understanding the material that follows. '*x* for *y*' below is merely a short-hand way of saying 'where in Attic we find form *y*, in Ionic we find form *x*'. It does *not* mean that 'Ionic replaced Attic *y* with its own *x*'. The differences between the two dialects are sometimes the result of *Attic* introducing innovations after it split from 'Attic-Ionic' (e.g. the contraction of ε + ο > ου: Ion. γένεος, Att. γένους < *γένε(σ)ος), sometimes the result of Ionic and Attic independently treating an inherited form in different ways after the split (e.g. Ion. μοῦνος, Att. μόνος < *μόνϝος).

Here is a general account of the differences between Herodotus' language and Attic, with some historical explanations. It is followed by a much briefer survey for those who wish to see quickly what the differences are.

General. (a) ***Psilosis***, the loss of the 'rough breathing', was a feature of East Ionic, but modern texts keep the initial aspirate as 'a venerable absurdity' (Powell):[77] e.g. Ἕλληνες should strictly be printed Ἔλληνες. In some compounds, which were no longer felt as compounds, the aspirate was preserved (e.g. καθεύδουσι), as it was

74 Κροισέω etc. found in some MSS, with the first declension genitive ending transferred to the second declension, is a better candidate for falsehood.

75 ο is written in many forms for which the usual later spelling is ου.

76 The others are Doric, North-West Greek, Aeolic and Arcado-Cyprian. For a clear account of the Greek dialects, cf. Chadwick 1956.

77 Papyri of Herodotus display *psilosis* more often than not.

in some non-Ionic names (Ἀφεταί (< ἀπό + ἵημι), ἔφορος (< ἐπί + ὁράω).[78] **(b)** ***Etacism*** involved the wholesale replacement in Ionic of original ᾱ by η, where Attic keeps ᾱ after ρ, ε, ι (πρῆγμα, Πυθέης, προθυμίη). Forms like πᾶσα (< *πάνσα < *πάντ-yα), which developed a secondary long α, were created after the shift ᾱ > η had ceased to operate.[79] **(c)** ***Hiatus*** (conjunction of two vowels, often caused by loss of intervocalic *-j-*, *-s-*, *-w-*) is regularly found, especially between *e* and another vowel: Attic employs contraction more. Many examples of hiatus (e.g. νόος, πλήρεες, κυνέη, the many verbal forms in -έει, -έεις, -έειν etc.) are also alien to spoken Ionic but are found in Homer: it is not absolutely certain whether they were written by Herodotus, but most editors keep them. Others we know to be Ionic (e.g. genitives Ξέρξεω, μοιρέων, γένεος, ἔσεαι 'you will be', δοκέοι opt.).

Vowels. These are the most important differences in the treatment of vowels (note that in many cases here we are talking about a small number of particular words, not general rules).

α for ε	τάμνω, μέγαθος (Att. μέγεθος innovates by assimilation of α to the earlier ε).
α for η	μεσαμβρίη.
ε for α	τέσσερες, ἔρσην ('male').
ε for ει	κρέσσων (<κρέτ-yων: Att. κρείττων on analogy with χείρων etc.), μέζων; ἡμίσεαι (fem. pl. of adj. in -υς); ἀποδέξω etc. (but uncompounded δείξω); ἔργω 'restrain' < root *ϝεργ-; Att. εἵργω < *ἐ-(ϝ)εργω with a prothetic vowel); τέλεος (adj., Att. -ειος).
ει for ε	κεινός ('empty'), ξεῖνος, εἵνεκα/-εν (< κενϝός etc.; East Ionic is unusual in lengthening the vowel thus); εἰρωτῶ, εἰρόμην, εἰρύω, ἠνείχθην.
ε for η	ἑσσοῦμαι (but ἥσσων).
ε for ο	πεντηκόντερος.
ευ for ου	regularly in ποιεῖν (ποιεῦσι, ποιεῦντες), and when -εο, -εου is preceded by a vowel (θηεύμενος): the original sequence is εο, which contracts to ου in Attic, and either remains εο in Ionic or becomes ευ. These sounds were very close, so the variants are probably orthographic, i.e. two ways of representing basically the same sound.
η for ε	μαχήσομαι, ἠώς 'dawn'.
ηι for ει	nouns in -ήιον, -ηίη (ἀριστήιον); adjs. in -ήιος (οἰκήιος).
ι for ε	ἱστίη 'hearth' (by assimilation from ἑστία (cf. μέγαθος above); Att. is unusual in keeping the original form; cf. also Ἱστιαιεύς).
ι for ει	ἴκελος (but εἰκ- in compounds, which is a secondary form).
ι for ευ	ἰθύς, ἰθέως (Att. εὐθύς is unclear).
ο for ω	χρεόν (< χρεὼ ὄν 'it being necessary').

[78] Such non-Ionic words and names often keep their own dialectal forms.

[79] I.e. the change from short vowel + -νσ- to long vowel + -σ- started after the ᾱ > η shift stopped.

ου for ο οὖρος, μοῦνος, νοῦσος (but νοσέω etc.) from *ὄρϝος, *μόνϝος etc. (cf. κεινός above); οὔνομα is a borrowing of a metrically lengthened form from Homer (contrast ὀνομάζω).
ω for αυ θῶμα, τρῶμα.
ω for ευ ἔπλωσα (from πλώω 'sail' rather than πλέω).
ω for ου ὦν (= οὖν; unexplained), τοιγαρῶν etc.

Consonants. (**a**) **κῶς, κως, ὁκότε, κότερος** etc., i.e. interrogative and indefinite pronouns and enclitics derived from the root *k^w*o*- have forms with -κ-, where Attic and other dialects have -π-.[80] (**b**) **δέκομαι** in Herodotus, literary Ionic and other dialects: Attic δέχομαι, with -χ- from δέχαται. (**c**) **οὐκί** (< οὐ + k^w*i*) for οὐχί. (**d**) **γίνομαι, γινώσκω** for γίγνομαι, γιγνώσκω, probably with a weakening of the articulation of the second γ, by dissimilation (perhaps helped by forms in γεν- in the case of γίνομαι). (**e**) **ἐνθαῦτα, ἐνθεῦτεν** were turned by Attic through metathesis into ἐνταῦθα, ἐντεῦθεν.

Nouns and adjectives. (**a**) ***a-stems***. (i) Gen. sg. masc. -εω (Ξέρξεω < -ηο < -ᾱο). (ii) Gen. pl. -έων (μοιρέων, ἐουσέων < -ηων < -ᾱων). (iii) Dat. pl. -ησι, which is descended from the locative in *-āsu/i*, and developed the iota on analogy with -οισι, locative of the *o*-stems: when Greek dispensed with the locative, some dialects used it to represent the dative; Attic -αις was created on analogy with -οις, an old instrumental. (**b**) ***o-stems***. Dat. pl. -οισι, another locative; Attic again uses the instrumental *-ōis*. Note however τοῖσδε, also found in Homer. (**c**) ***Consonant stems***. (i) Nouns and adjectives in -ος and -ης are uncontracted: γένος, γένεος, γένεϊ, γένεα, γενέων, γένεσι; Ἀστυάγης, Ἀστάγεα etc.; ἀληθής, ἀληθέα, ἀληθέος etc. (ii) So nouns in -εύς: βασιλέα, βασιλέος etc. (iii) πόλις, ὕβρις, φύσις etc. retain the stem in -ι- throughout the paradigm (πόλιος, πόλι, πόλιες, πόλῑς, πολίων, πόλισι).

Pronouns. (**a**) **ἐμέο, σέο, τέο** for ἐμοῦ, σοῦ, and also with more closed pronunciation ἐμεῦ etc. (**b**) **ὅστις** gives ὅτευ, ὅτεωι, ὅτεων, ὁτέοισι. (**c**) **ὅς, ἥ, τό**, τόν, τήν, τό etc. is the relative; note also Herodotus' rare use of καὶ ὅς 'and he'; cf. ἦ δὲ ὅς 'he said'. They tend to be used where there is no preposition or a preposition that cannot be elided. Herodotus also uses ὅς, ἥ, ὅ; ὅν, ἥν, ὅ etc., especially in phrases such as ἐν ὧι = 'while', ἐς ὅ = 'until'. (**d**) **σφεας**, σφεων, σφι and σφισι are used like αὐτούς etc., not just to refer to the subject of the main clause as in Attic. (**e**) **ἑωυτόν** stands for ἑαυτόν (ἑω- generalised from crasis of ἓο αὐτοῦ). (**f**) Note also accusative sg. **μιν** = αὐτόν, αὐτήν.

Verbs. (**a**) ***Syllabic augment*** is omitted in pluperfects (παρατετάχατο) and iteratives in -σκον (ἔχεσκον). (**b**) ***Temporal augment*** is sometimes absent, especially in verbs beginning with the diphthongs αι, αυ, ει, ευ, οι (e.g. αἴνεσα); in some cases, imitation of Homer may be involved. ***(c) Uncontracted terminations***: 2nd p. sg. mid. -εαι for Att. -ει or -ηι (ἔσεαι 'you will be'); -εο for -ου (πείθεο pres. mid. imper.); -εε for -η (ἐγεγόνεε (ppf.), ἐτίθεε (impf.)). (**d**) **δείκνυμι** etc. have forms from the -ω

[80] A problematic feature: the inscriptions usually give forms in π, but these are inscriptions where Koine influence is notable, so the π-forms may not be original. Forms in κ appear very rarely in the Ionic of the Asia Minor cities and their colonies. Cf. Lillo 1991, Stüber 1996.

conjugation in 2nd and 3rd p. sg. and 3rd p. pl. pres. indic. and 3rd p. sg. impf.: προσαπολλύεις (for -υς), προδεικνύει (for -υσι), δεικνύουσι (for -ύασι), ἐδείκνυε (for -υ). **(e) -αται, -ατο** appear in the 3rd p. pl. of optatives, perfects and pluperfects (ἀνελοίατο, ἀπίκαται, διεφθάρατο), and in the present and imperfects of some verbs in -μι: regularly in δύναμαι, ἐπίσταμαι, ἵσταμαι (δυνέαται, ἠπιστέατο); less certainly also τιθέαται, ἐτιθέατο.[81] **-αται** etc. arose as a treatment of -νται after a consonant, and was then extended to other contexts. **(f)** ***Contract verbs***. (i) Verbs in -έω are usually uncontracted, but note δεῖ, ἔδει. (ii) -ε- sometimes replaces -α- in -αω verbs: τολμέω, ὁρέων (part,), ὁρέωσι (subj.), beside expected 2nd and 3rd p. sg. ὁρᾶις and ὁρᾶι (contracted forms are also frequent: ὁρῶ etc.). **(g) -μι** ***verbs***, in the 2nd and 3rd p. sg. and 3rd p. pl. of the present, have forms which show the influence of contract verbs: thus τίθημι, but τιθεῖς (Att. τίθης), τιθεῖ (Att. τίθησι), τιθεῖσι (as -εω verbs); δίδωμι, διδοῖς, διδοῖ, διδοῦσι (as -οω verbs); ἵστημι, ἱστᾶις, ἱστᾶι, ἱστᾶσι (as -αω verbs). **(h)** ***Other forms***. (i) οἴδαμεν and οἴδασι beside ἴδμεν, ἴσασι. (ii) εἶπα, εἴπας (part.) beside εἶπον, εἰπών. (iii) λάμψομαι, ἐλάμφθην etc. from λαμβάνω. (iv) εἶς, εἰμέν are used for εἶ, ἐσμέν (cf. εἰμί < *ἐσμί); ἔωσι, ἐών, ἐοῦσα for ὦσι etc.; opt. εἴησαν is used beside εἶεν. (v) The frequentative suffix -σκον with the present or aorist stem: ἄγεσκον, λάβεσκον.

Brief guide to the language of Herodotus

(In this brief guide, Attic equivalents are given in brackets.)

Vowels and consonants

η for ᾱ: προθυμίη (προθυμία).

Uncontracted forms: νόος (νοῦς), γένεος (γένους), γένεϊ (γένει), πλήρεες (πλήρεις), προσπλέειν (προσπλεῖν), ἐπεβοήθεον (ἐπεβοήθουν), ἐτίθεε (ἐτίθει).

ει for ε: κεινός (κενός, 'empty'), ξεῖνος (ξένος), εἵνεκα/-εν (ἕνεκα).

ευ for ου: ποιεῦσι (ποιοῦσι), ποιεῦντες (ποιοῦντες).

ου for ο: οὖρος (ὅρος), μοῦνος (μόνος), νοῦσος (νόσος), οὔνομα (ὄνομα).

κ for π: κῶς (πῶς), ὁκότε (ὁπότε), κότερος (πότερος).

γίνομαι (γίγνομαι), γινώσκω (γιγνώσκω).

Nouns, adjectives and pronouns

Gen. sg. masc. -εω (ου): Ξέρξεω (Ξέρξου).

Gen. pl. -εων (-ων): μοιρέων (μοιρῶν).

Dat. pl. -ηισι (-αις), -οισι (-οις): ἡμέρηισι (ἡμέραις), λόγοισι (λόγοις).

Words like πόλις keep their iota: πόλιος (πόλεως), πόλι (πόλει).

ἐμέο (ἐμοῦ), σέο (σοῦ).

[81] Where the verb stem has a long vowel, that is shortened: ὁρμέ-αται 'they have set out' (cf. ὥρμη-σα etc.).

ὅστις: ὅτευ (οὗτινος, ὅτου), ὅτεῳ (ᾧτινι, ὅτῳ), ὅτεων (ὧντινων ὅτων), ὁτέοισι (οἷστισι, ὅτοις).

Verbs

Augments are sometimes missing: ἀμειβόμην (ἠμειβόμην), αἴνεσα (ᾔνεσα).

-μι verbs sometimes conjugate like contract verbs: τίθημι but τιθεῖς (τίθης), τιθεῖ (τίθησι), τιθεῖσι (τιθέασι); δίδωμι but διδοῖς (δίδως), διδοῖ (δίδωσι), διδοῦσι (διδόασι).

In εἰμί an initial epsilon is often preserved: ἔωσι (ὦσι), ἐών (ὤν), ἐοῦσα (οὖσα). Note also εἷς (εἶ), εἰμέν (ἐσμέν).

-αται, -ατο for -νται -ντο: ἀπίκαται (ἀφίκονται), ἀνελοίατο (ἀνέλοιντο).

Various

ὦν (οὖν); ἴθεως (εὐθύς); ἐνθαῦτα (ἐνταῦθα); ἑωυτόν (ἑαυτόν); μιν = αὐτόν, αὐτήν; σφεας often = αὐτούς; δέκομαι (δέχομαι); οἴδαμεν (ἴδμεν), οἴδασι (ἴσασι); εἶπα (εἶπον), εἴπας (εἰπών).

8 LIFE OF HERODOTUS (BY S. R. WEST)[82]

Herodotus tells us, in his opening sentence, that he came from Halicarnassus, modern Bodrum on the Aegean coast of Turkey, but he gives no further explicit information about himself, notwithstanding the pervasive sense of authorial presence conveyed by references to his own opinions and observations. Extensive travels are indicated by his claims to have visited Elephantine in Upper Egypt (2.29.1), the North Pontic region (4.81.2), Metapontum in South Italy (4.15), Tyre (2.44) and Palestine (2.106.1); perhaps we should extend his range even further east, since he writes of Babylon in a manner strongly suggesting that he had been there (1.183.3; 193.4). He presents himself as one who, like Odysseus, has seen the cities of many men and come to know their minds, though we must remember that he could have talked to (e.g.) Colchians and Cyrenians without going to Colchis or Cyrene and that his references to local traditions need not imply that he had visited the places concerned. His appeals to his own observation are intended to validate what he reports, and cannot be treated as reference points for reconstructing his biography and intellectual development. Thus, while he mentions visits to Thasos (2.44), Dodona (2.55), Zacynthus (4.195), Thebes (5.59) and Thessaly (7.129), he simply leaves us to infer that he must have spent time in such important sources of his material as Delphi, Samos, and, above all, Athens. But, while there is room for debate as to whether he owed to first-hand observation and enquiry quite as much as he would have us believe (particularly since he appears to have spoken no language other than Greek),[83] his self-presentation has been enormously influential

[82] Any discussion of Herodotus' life must owe a very substantial debt to Jacoby's magisterial treatment, 1913: 205–80. Among more recent accounts I have profited particularly from that of Asheri 1988: ix–xvii.

[83] For the sceptics' case see Armayor 1978 and 1980; Fehling 1989; against this trend see Kendrick Pritchett 1993. These discussions represent the extremes; but it should be emphasised

in establishing the importance of travel for an understanding of the world, because it enables an enquirer not merely to collect information, but also to escape from the cultural narrowness which results from knowing only one's own people.

Though he never actually says that he had lived at Athens, his work certainly suggests a period of extended residence there. He cites the Athenians as informants more often than any other Greek people (they are surpassed only by the Egyptians), and from time to time he uses comparisons familiar to those who know Attica (e.g. 1.98.5, 192.3; 2.7; 4.99.4), a reflection of Athens' outstanding political and intellectual importance rather than an indication that he wrote with an Athenian public in mind.

The latest event to which he refers (7.137.1–3) can be dated from Thucydides (2.67) to summer 430. Unfulfilled promises (1.106.2; 184; 7.213.3) suggest that he had not formally finished his work, but the last chapter (9.122) has a marked closural effect, and we certainly should not suppose that he planned to continue beyond 479.

What we can infer from his work may be cautiously supplemented by information from later sources, of which the most important is the brief biography given in the Byzantine historical encyclopedia known as the *Suda* (*Fortress*):

> Herodotus: son of Lyxes and Dryo, of Halicarnassus, from a prominent family, brother of Theodorus. He moved to Samos on account of Lygdamis, the third tyrant of Halicarnassus, grandson of Artemisia . . . In Samos he became fluent in the Ionic dialect and wrote a history in nine books, starting from Cyrus the Persian and Candaules the Lydian. After returning to Halicarnassus and driving out the tyranny, he later saw that he was unpopular with his fellow citizens, and went voluntarily to Thurii, which was being settled by the Athenians. He died there and was buried in the market place; but some say that he died at Pella.

From the *Suda* we also learn (*s.v.* 'Panyassis') that Herodotus was the nephew (or cousin) of the poet and diviner Panyassis, author of an epic about Heracles and executed by Lygdamis, and (*s.v.* 'Thucydides') that he reassured Olorus, father of Thucydides, when the boy burst into tears during a public reading of the *Histories*.[84]

Not knowing the source(s) of this information, we must treat it with some reserve, but it cannot be disregarded. The Carian names of Herodotus' father and uncle exemplify the mixed character of the population of Halicarnassus (well attested in its inscriptions); though we may assume that Herodotus' family was thoroughly hellenized, an upbringing among people of partly non-Greek stock would be likely to result in a more open-minded attitude towards foreigners than could be expected from a contemporary Athenian (or indeed from most Greeks).[85] Herodotus' opposition to tyranny in general is clear from his work, as is his familiarity with Samos. Not only

that the sceptics are more concerned with analysing Herodotus' aims and literary technique than with impugning his honesty. The problem is most acute in his account of Egypt.

[84] *S.v.* 'Hellanicus', we are told that he and Herodotus stayed at the Macedonian court at Pella, but this detail fails to inspire confidence: see Jacoby, *RE* 8 *s.v.* 'Hellanikos' (7), 106; FGH I p. 431.

[85] See further Hall 1989.

is he well informed about the island's remarkable sights, above all the great temple of Hera (1.70; 2.182; 3.123.1; 4.88, 152.4), but he devotes to Samian internal politics what he evidently realised some would judge disproportionate space (3.60.1), the bias of his account indicating that his informants were aristocrats of the party which was opposed alike to tyranny and friendship with Persia, and which gained power after the Persian Wars.[86] The *Suda*'s explanation of Herodotus' Samian period raises no obvious cause for scepticism. However, though Halicarnassus was originally a Dorian foundation (cf. 1.144.3; 2.178.2; 7.99.3), already in Lygdamis' time its inscriptions were in Ionic,[87] and Herodotus did not need to go to Samos to achieve fluency in the conventional dialect of early prose-writing. That the composition of the *Histories* belongs to this period has generally been regarded as incredible; it is also disturbing that the *Suda* says nothing of Herodotus' travels.[88] We note too the lack of any mention of a sojourn at Athens. Herodotus' participation in Pericles' panhellenic foundation at Thurii (444/3), on the site of Sybaris, is attested by the ancient variant in his opening sentence, Θουρίου[89] instead of Ἁλικαρνησσέος; as a new colony it offered citizenship and a land grant.

Apart from the *Suda*'s anecdote about the youthful Thucydides' reaction to Herodotus' work (cf. *Vita Marcellini* 54), we have two further scraps of evidence for his reception at Athens.[90] According to Eusebius (*Chron.* Ol. 83.4), in 445/4 Herodotus 'was honoured by the Athenian Council after reading his books to them'.[91] More specifically, the Athenian historian Diyllus (*FGH* 73 F 3, quoted by Plut. *MH* 26) recorded that 'on the proposal of Anytus[92] he received from the Athenians a gift of ten talents'. As a reward for purely literary achievement the figure is incredible (compare the Athenian gift of one and two-thirds talents (= 10,000 drachmae) to Pindar (Isocr. 15.166)); it is diverting to speculate about Herodotus' potential for protecting or furthering Athenian interests by the judicious deployment of suitable sums.[93]

Despite his enthusiasm for Athens, he never names any individual Athenian informant; perhaps he had to protect his sources. It seems, however, that Sophocles became his friend. Plutarch, *Mor.* 785B quotes the opening of an epigram evidently intended to accompany a song which the tragedian had composed: ᾠιδὴν Ἡροδότωι τεῦξεν Σοφοκλῆς ἐτέων ὤν | πέντ' ἐπὶ πεντήκοντα ('Sophocles at the age of 55 composed a song for Herodotus'; Page *Epigrammata Graeca* 466f., Sophocles, *IEG* F 5). It

86 See further Mitchell 1975. 87 See ML 32.

88 Should we see in these oddities reflections of a theory that Samos' extensive trading connections had supplied Herodotus with informants sufficiently familiar with foreign parts to provide him with his material about the wider world without his needing to travel further?

89 Vigorously championed by Jacoby 1913: 205–9, 224–6, though few have been convinced.

90 See further Ostwald 1991.

91 The ancient dating of his birth 'a little before the Persian Wars' (D. H. *Th.* 5), in 484 according to Gellius (15.23), surely rests on the assumption that he must have been about forty at the time.

92 Not to be identified with Socrates' accuser.

93 For some possibilities see Jacoby 1913: 228f.

is not quite certain that the dedicatee was the historian; but at all events the name was not favoured by Athenians. Of course, literary influence need not be connected with personal contact; this is not the place to consider reminiscences of Herodotus in Sophocles' work.[94]

For much of his life Herodotus was effectively stateless, his ties with his homeland broken. He must have been short of military experience compared with the average able-bodied Greek male and, notwithstanding the youthful resistance to tyranny which led to his period in Samos, he would have lacked the opportunities to participate in political debate and decision-making which were enjoyed by his Athenian contemporaries and by other Greeks living in democracies or moderate oligarchies. On the other hand, a life so spent must have stimulated scepticism, detachment, and immunity to chauvinism. We do not know how he supported himself, though we might guess that like the sophists he made money by peripatetic lecturing. His liability to error in calculation rather tells against the once popular idea that his travels were undertaken partly (or primarily) with a commercial purpose.

We cannot tell whether he stayed permanently in the West after his departure for Thurii, but presumably it was then that he shaped what had been the material for successful lectures into a continuous narrative. It is pointless to try to determine a date of publication; this was a period when the dissemination of ideas was mediated by the spoken rather than the written word, and no doubt Herodotus continued to tinker with his text until he died.

Though the place and date of his death are uncertain, he lived to see the beginning of the Peloponnesian War, and his presentation of earlier events must have been coloured by contemporary developments. His lifetime coincided with the period when the Delian League, a grand alliance of freedom-loving Greek cities against Persia, changed into the Athenian empire, while Persia was more powerful than it had ever been, and its financial support an object of keen competition between Athens and Sparta. 479 was a good stopping point.

9 THE TEXT

1 Transmission and ancient reception (by S. R. West)

(a) Transmission[95]

Our texts of Herodotus are based on medieval MSS, of which the oldest (**A**) may be dated *ca.* 900. Their testimony is occasionally supplemented by fragments of ancient copies, dating mainly from the first to the third centuries AD, collectively designated as

94 On this, see Dewald and Kitzinger 2006.

95 On the medieval tradition see further Pasquali 1952: 306–18; Hemmerdinger 1981; McNeal 1983; the *Praefatio* to Rosén's edition, vol. 1. I am indebted to Nigel Wilson for advice on the dating of **A** and **D**. On papyri, see further Paap 1948; Chambers *et al.* 1981: 22–9; Alberti 1983; Saerens 1990; Mertens and Strauss 1992; Bandiera 1997.

papyri even though a few are in fact written on parchment, and by ancient citations, generally rather brief.

The medieval MSS are conventionally divided into two groups designated Florentine (a) and Roman (b), from the cities whose libraries hold the principal, and oldest, representatives. The MSS used in this edition are denoted by the following sigla:

A: *Laurentianus* 70.3, *ca.* 900
B: *Romanus Angelicus gr.* 83, late eleventh or early twelfth century
C: *Laurentianus Conv. Suppr. gr.* 207, eleventh century
D: *Vaticanus gr.* 2369, probably *ca.* 950–*ca.* 975
P: *Parisinus gr.* 1633, fourteenth century
R: *Vaticanus gr.* 123, fourteenth century
S: *Cantabrigiensis Sancroftianus coll. Emmanuelis gr.* 30, fifteenth century
V: *Vindobonensis gr.* 85, fourteenth century

To the Florentine 'family' belong **A** and **B**, to the Roman **D**, **R**, **S**, **V**. Some other MSS waver between the two traditions, presumably reflecting collation against a second exemplar; of these **C** and **P** are the most important.

The division into two 'families' is not observable in the papyri; already in 1919 it was a reasonable inference that this division was not earlier than the fourth century AD,[96] and subsequently published papyri have confirmed this conclusion. At present *ca.* 40 Herodotus papyri have been published. All come from Egypt, apart from one piece from Dura-Europus; somewhat surprisingly, none is Ptolemaic. About half come from book 1; books 4, 6 and 9 are poorly attested. Whether all our papyri represent continuous copies of the books to which they belong might be questioned; the striking predominance of book 1, peculiarly rich in *novelle*, might partly reflect selection of memorable episodes, 'Tales from Herodotus'. In view of the uneven attestation of the several books, the change of format from rolls holding no more than a single book to codices may be regarded as a watershed, and the division of the tradition into two 'families' might well belong to this phase.

To date, four papyri of book 8 have been published:

P.Oxy. 48.3382, late second or early third century AD: 1.1–2
P.Oxy. 48. 3383, late second or early third century: 2.3–3.1; 4.2–5.1
P.Oxy. 17.2099, first half of second century: 22.2–23
P.Harris 40, early third century: 126.3–127; 129.2

There are also four unpublished papyri:[97]

P.Oxy. ined. A early second century (from the same roll as P.Oxy. 2099): 24.1–2
P.Oxy. ined. B: 109–112
P.Oxy. ined. C, early first century: 129.1, 130.1–2
P.Oxy. ined. D, third century: 130.2–131.2.

[96] See Grenfell and Hunt 1919 on P.Oxy. 1619.
[97] I am very grateful to Dirk Obbink for permission to refer to these new papyri.

The papyri show that already in the early Imperial period Herodotus' text was infected with epicisms, hyperionicisms, and Atticisms; it suffered from tendencies both to import *Koine* forms and to restore supposed Ionic. Viewed more positively, these scanty remains of ancient copies indicate that the medieval tradition gives us a good idea of the range of variants current in post-Ptolemaic times.

The most exciting contribution from papyri hitherto has been the evidence for Aristarchus' commentary (*hypomnema*) on book 1, the earliest known commentary on a prose author, provided by the colophon of P.Amherst 12 (third century): Ἀριστάρχου Ἡροδότου α΄ ὑπόμνημα. Notes are preserved on 194.3 and 215.1; the latter records Aristarchus' reading ἄμιπποι, not attested in any of the medieval MSS. The lack of any notes on the intervening chapters suggests that this copy must represent extracts from Aristarchus' work, if it is not actually defective. We are not entitled on the strength of this tantalizing fragment to credit Aristarchus with an edition of book 1, much less of the whole of Herodotus.[98]

Whether the division of the work into books is due to Alexandrian scholarship or developed earlier is not clear; but it is not likely to go back to Herodotus himself. The ninefold division (first attested by Diodorus Siculus (11.37.6) produces some lengthy books which might conveniently have been divided between two rolls (1, 4, 7). We do not know when the practice of naming each book after a Muse was introduced (cf. Lucian, *Hist. conscr.* 42, *Herod.* 1), though this fancy is unlikely to have dictated the ninefold division.

Neither the age of a MS (whether ancient or medieval) nor its relationship to other MSS relieves the editor of the duty of weighing every variant on its merits. Decisions are made harder by the fact that, as inscriptions show, orthography is for Herodotus' time an anachronistic conception, and oscillation between alternative forms may go back to the author. His dialect must be judged to some extent artificial and individual, a literary language appropriate to his view of his subject matter.[99]

Our picture of the transmission is further complicated by uncertainties about the manner of publication. Did Herodotus himself regard his work as finished? May we suppose that at some time in the 420s he oversaw the production of a fair copy of the whole? Or did he authorize piecemeal copying of extracts and the circulation of individual *logoi*[100] on request, with minor updating? We must be wary of assumptions derived from the book trade as it developed after the invention of printing; ancient authors were free to continue to alter their texts for as long as suited them, while readers must often have had cause to wonder whether the copy before them represented the latest version which the author had allowed to be circulated. The ancient variant in Herodotus' ethnic, Θουρίου for Ἁλικαρνασσέος (Arist. *Rhet.* 1409a34, cf. Plut. *Mor.* 604F) highlights our ignorance and should discourage any complacency arising from the basic uniformity of the direct tradition observable from the first century AD onwards.

98 See further Pfeiffer 1968: 224–5. 99 Cf. §7 above. 100 Cf. Cagnazzi 1975.

(b) Reception in antiquity[101]

The transmission of Herodotus' work cannot be discussed without regard to its reception. What follows is merely a sketch-map of an area that calls for much further exploration.

The immediate impact of Herodotus' work can be seen in Sophocles (e.g. *Ant.* 904–20, cf. Hdt. 3.119; *OC* 337–45, cf. 2.35),[102] perhaps also in Aristophanes (e.g. *Ach.* 523–9, cf.1.1–5; *Birds* 551f., cf. 1.178f.).[103] It is significant that Thucydides, though he seems to seek critical confrontation with Herodotus in his chapters on methodology (1.20f.), takes his narrative back to the point where Herodotus left off (1.89–118). The work of local historians like Antiochus of Syracuse (*FGH* 555) was undoubtedly stimulated by the *Histories*, and the polemic of Ctesias (*FGH* 688) is clearly inspired by the desire to trump Herodotus as the recognized authority on Persian matters. We have a tribute of a rather different kind in the epitomisation of the *Histories* in two books by Theopompus of Chios (*FGH* 115 F 1–4), apparently the first significant literary work to undergo this treatment. Aristotle made extensive use of Herodotean material (geographical, ethnographical, zoological); though he refers to Herodotus as *mythologos*, a story-teller (*GA* 756b6), in the *Poetics* (1451b2) he cites him to exemplify the historian contrasted with the poet. His immense range made him a crucial influence on Hellenistic writers responding to the expansion of the known world as a result of Alexander's conquests. His work was a treasure house for poets and paradoxographers; in particular, the learned poets of Ptolemaic Alexandria, Callimachus, Apollonius Rhodius and Lycophron, owed Herodotus an incalculable debt.[104]

The ethnographic element in his work was more influential than the strictly historical. The narrative of the Persian Wars, as an indispensable element in encomia of Athens, developed a life of its own, independent of Herodotus, and the imputation of unreliability and insufficient regard for truth (already observable in the fifth century) could not be satisfactorily refuted. But rhetoric early concerned itself with Herodotus, and his literary achievement ensured that his work became familiar at an early stage in education. [Longinus'] characterization of Herodotus (*de subl.* 13.3) as most Homeric, Ὁμηρικώτατος (along with Stesichorus, Archilochus, and Plato), is nicely paralleled by a recently published inscription of the second century BC celebrating Halicarnassus' distinguished citizens in elegiac verse, among them Ἡρόδοτον τὸν πεζὸν ἐν ἱστορίαισιν Ὅμηρον, 'Herodotus, in history the prose Homer'.[105] There is indeed abundant evidence that he was honoured in his birthplace; in particular, he was depicted on its coinage.

Quintilian's characterization (10.1.73; cf. 101), in terms of a comparison which certainly now seems a cliché, shows that he had a place in the rhetorical schools of the Latin West: *Historiam multi scripsere praeclare, sed nemo dubitat longe duos ceteris praeferendos,*

[101] For further orientation see Riemann 1967; Ehrhardt 1988: 850–61; Pernot 1995; Bichler and Rollinger 2000: 114–21; Gibson 2004.

[102] See further West 1999. [103] See further Sansone 1985.

[104] See further Pearson 1960 passim; Murray 1972.

[105] Isager 1998; see also Lloyd-Jones 1999; Merkelbach and Stauber 1998: 39–45.

quorum diversa virtus laudem paene est parem consecuta. Densus et brevis et semper instans sibi Thucydides, dulcis et candidus et fusus Herodotus: ille concitatis, hic remissis adfectibus melior, ille contionibus, hic sermonibus, ille vi, hic voluptate. ('History has been written by many with distinction, but no one questions that there are two far superior to the rest, whose very different excellences have won them almost equal praise. Thucydides is close-textured, concise, always pressing himself hard: Herodotus is pleasing, transparent, expansive. Thucydides is better at the tenser emotions, Herodotus at the more relaxed; Thucydides at set speeches, Herodotus at dialogue; Thucydides excels in force, Herodotus in giving pleasure' (tr. D. A. Russell).) Quintilian appears quite uninterested in content. Not so Plutarch who, in his essay *de malignitate Herodoti*, while paying tribute to Herodotus' literary artistry, offers a sustained assault on his proclivity to malicious misrepresentation. Protests regarding Herodotus' lack of concern for truth were nothing new, but Plutarch goes much further in his determination to discredit Herodotus as a historian. But his oddly adversarial analysis of Herodotus' presentational skills and ingenious use of innuendo is also a tribute to the fascination of the narrative technique, and we are left in no doubt that Plutarch knew the *Histories* extremely well.[106]

So too did Lucian, whose treatise *On the Syrian goddess* is a virtuoso display of nuanced and thoughtful Herodotean imitation. Though its inspiration is primarily the combination of ethnography and periegesis offered by Herodotus' account of Egypt, it provides invaluable insight into the way in which the work as a whole was read in the second century AD.[107]

In view of Herodotus' well-established place in the school curriculum it is not surprising that his work was familiar to very many writers of the Imperial age. But not all references are evidence of first-hand familiarity with his work as a whole. Episodes like Solon's conversation with Croesus and the latter's dealings with the Delphic oracle were common currency; not surprisingly, allusions to book 1 predominate. But it is reassuring to note that in the ninth century Photius thought it necessary to devote to the *Histories* only one short chapter in his *Bibliotheca* (60), apparently confident that it was not worth making extracts as the work was generally known.

Cicero (*de leg.* 1.5) memorably expresses the Janus-like image of Herodotus current in antiquity: *apud Herodotum patrem historiae . . . sunt innumerabiles fabulae* ('there are innumerable tales in Herodotus, the father of history'). His distinctive literary achievement could not be questioned; his concern for truth was deemed of secondary importance.

2 *The text of this edition*

The following is a list of the major differences between the text of this edition, Hude's Oxford Classical Text and Rosén's Teubner edition. Minor differences and most orthographic differences are not listed. I have also paragraphed and punctuated the text in ways different from theirs, and added the sub-headings. The small *apparatus* contains variants and emendations that I have not thought strong enough to put in

[106] See further Russell 1973: 60–1; Bowen 1992.

[107] Cf. in general Lightfoot 2003.

the text, but which merit not being lost sight of; they also draw attention to places where the text is not absolutely certain.

Hude	Rosén	Bowie
3.2 διωσάμενοι	δὴ ὠσάμενοι	δὴ ὠσάμενοι
15.1 παρασκευασάμενοι	παρασκευασάμενοι	παρακελευσάμενοι
15.2 παρήσουσι . . . κρατήσουσι	παρήσωσι . . . κρατήσωσι	παρήσουσι . . . κρατήσουσι
38.1 φύσιν ἐόντας	φύσιν ἔχοντας	φύσιν ἐόντας
46.1 ἄλλαι	ἄλλαι <δυώδεκα>	ἄλλαι
48 γένος ἐόντες	γεγονότες	γένος ἐόντες
57.2 οὔ τοι ἄρα	οὔτοι ἄρα	οὔ τοι ἄρα
57.2 οὐδὲ περὶ μιῆς	περὶ οὐδεμιῆς	περὶ οὐδεμιῆς
60a [ἐς] τὸ ἥκιστα	ἐς ὃ ἥκιστα	[ἐς] τὸ ἥκιστα
62.1 εἰ μενέεις	εἰ μενέεις	εἰ <μὲν> μενέεις
70.1 παρήγγελλε	παρήγγελλον	παρήγγελλον
74.1 <τὸν> περὶ τοῦ παντὸς ἤδη δρόμον	περὶ τοῦ παντὸς ἤδη δρόμου	περὶ τοῦ παντὸς ἤδη [δρόμον]
76.2 μηδὲ φυγεῖν	μηδὲ φυγεῖν	μὴ διαφυγεῖν
77 χρησμοῖσι . . . ἐνδέκομαι	χρησμοῖσι . . . ἐνδέκομαι	[χρησμοῖσι . . . ἐνδέκομαι]
86 καὶ ἐγένοντο	καὶ ἐγένοντο	[καὶ ἐγένοντο]
96.2 τὸν χρησμὸν . . . ἐξενειχθέντα	τὸν χρησμὸν . . . ἐξενειχθέντα	[τὸν χρησμὸν . . . ἐξενειχθέντα]
96.2 φρύξουσι	φρίξουσι	φρύξουσι
98.2 κατ’ ἄλλον <καὶ ἄλλον>	κατ’ ἄλλον	κατ’ ἄλλον <καὶ ἄλλον>
100.1 γενόμενον	γενόμενον	γινόμενα
104–5 [οἱ δέ . . . ῾Ερμότιμος ἦν]	(οἱ δέ . . . ἐγένετο.) ἐκ τούτων . . . ῾Ερμότιμος ἦν	[οἱ δέ . . . ῾Ερμότιμος ἦν]
107.2 τῆς ἠπείρου ταύτηι	τῆς ἠπείρου ταύτης	τῆς ἠπείρου ταύτης
108.2 ἐργασαίατο	ἐργάσαιτο	ἐργασαίατο
111.3 οὐδέκοτε γὰρ <ἄν>	οὐδέκοτε γάρ	οὐδέκοτε γάρ <ἄν>
123.2 διένεμον	διένεμον	ἔφερον
126.2 κατεπείγων αὐτός	κατεπείγοντος	κατεπείγοντος
129.3 [καὶ τῆς πλημυρίδος]	καὶ τῆς πλημμυρίδος	καὶ τῆς πλημυρίδος
140a.2 ἀναγκαίως ἔχει μοι . . . ἢν μή	ἀναγκαίως <εἰ> ἔχει μοι . . . ἢ μή	ἀναγκαίως ἔχει μοι . . . ἢν μή
140a.2 ἀντίον	αἴτιον	αἴτιον
142.2 ἀρχῆθεν	ἀρχῆς	ἀρχῆς
144.5 ὑμέας	ἡμέας	ἡμέας

ΗΡΟΔΟΤΟΥ ΙΣΤΟΡΙΩΝ Θ ΟΥΡΑΝΙΑ

ΗΡΟΔΟΤΟΥ ΙΣΤΟΡΙΩΝ Θ ΟΥΡΑΝΙΑ

1–26 Battles at Artemisium and the aftermath

1–5 The Greeks

Οἱ δὲ Ἑλλήνων ἐς τὸν ναυτικὸν στρατὸν ταχθέντες ἦσαν οἵδε, **1**
Ἀθηναῖοι μὲν νέας παρεχόμενοι ἑκατὸν καὶ εἴκοσι καὶ ἑπτά· ὑπὸ δὲ
ἀρετῆς τε καὶ προθυμίης Πλαταιέες, ἄπειροι τῆς ναυτικῆς ἐόντες,
συνεπλήρουν τοῖσι Ἀθηναίοισι τὰς νέας. Κορίνθιοι δὲ τεσσεράκοντα
νέας παρείχοντο, Μεγαρέες δὲ εἴκοσι. καὶ Χαλκιδέες ἐπλήρουν εἴκοσι, 2
Ἀθηναίων σφι παρεχόντων τὰς νέας, Αἰγινῆται δὲ ὀκτωκαίδεκα,
Σικυώνιοι δὲ δυοκαίδεκα, Λακεδαιμόνιοι δὲ δέκα, Ἐπιδαύριοι δὲ
ὀκτώ, Ἐρετριέες δὲ ἑπτά, Τροιζήνιοι δὲ πέντε, Στυρέες δὲ δύο,
καὶ Κήιοι δύο τε νέας καὶ πεντηκοντέρους δύο· Λοκροὶ δέ σφι οἱ
Ὀπούντιοι ἐπεβοήθεον πεντηκοντέρους ἔχοντες ἑπτά. Ἦσαν μὲν **2**
ὦν οὗτοι οἱ στρατευόμενοι ἐπ᾽ Ἀρτεμίσιον, εἴρηται δέ μοι καὶ ὡς
τὸ πλῆθος ἕκαστοι τῶν νεῶν παρείχοντο. ἀριθμὸς δὲ τῶν συλ-
λεχθεισέων νεῶν ἐπ᾽ Ἀρτεμίσιον ἦν, πάρεξ τῶν πεντηκοντέρων,
διηκόσιαι καὶ ἑβδομήκοντα καὶ μία.

Τὸν δὲ στρατηγὸν τὸν τὸ μέγιστον κράτος ἔχοντα παρεί- 2
χοντο Σπαρτιῆται, Εὐρυβιάδην Εὐρυκλείδεω· οἱ γὰρ σύμμαχοι οὐκ
ἔφασαν, ἢν μὴ ὁ Λάκων ἡγεμονεύῃ, Ἀθηναίοισι ἕψεσθαι ἡγεομένοισι,
ἀλλὰ λύσειν τὸ μέλλον ἔσεσθαι στράτευμα. Ἐγένετο γὰρ κατ᾽ἀρχὰς **3**
λόγος, πρὶν ἢ καὶ ἐς Σικελίην πέμπειν ἐπὶ συμμαχίην, ὡς τὸ ναυ-
τικὸν Ἀθηναίοισι χρεὸν εἴη ἐπιτρέπειν. ἀντιβάντων δὲ τῶν συμ-
μάχων, εἶκον οἱ Ἀθηναῖοι, μέγα πεποιημένοι περιεῖναι τὴν Ἑλλάδα,
καὶ γνόντες, εἰ στασιάσουσι περὶ τῆς ἡγεμονίης, ὡς ἀπολέεται ἡ
Ἑλλάς, ὀρθὰ νοεῦντες· στάσις γὰρ ἔμφυλος πολέμου ὁμοφρονέοντος
τοσούτωι κάκιόν ἐστι, ὅσωι πόλεμος εἰρήνης. ἐπιστάμενοι ὦν αὐτὸ 2
τοῦτο, οὐκ ἀντέτεινον ἀλλ᾽εἶκον, μέχρι ὅσου κάρτα ἐδέοντο αὐτῶν,
ὡς διέδεξαν· ὡς γὰρ δὴ ὠσάμενοι τὸν Πέρσην περὶ τῆς ἐκείνου ἤδη
τὸν ἀγῶνα ἐποιεῦντο, πρόφασιν τὴν Παυσανίεω ὕβριν προϊσχό-
μενοι, ἀπείλοντο τὴν ἡγεμονίην τοὺς Λακεδαιμονίους. ἀλλὰ ταῦτα
μὲν ὕστερον ἐγένετο.

Τότε δὲ οὗτοι οἱ καὶ ἐπ᾽ Ἀρτεμίσιον Ἑλλήνων ἀπικόμενοι, ὡς **4**
εἶδον νέας τε πολλὰς καταχθείσας ἐς τὰς Ἀφέτας, καὶ στρατιῆς

1.1 ταῦτα μὲν δὴ οὕτω γενέσθαι· οἱ δὲ Ἑλλήνων codd. (ex 7.239.4) 3.1 μέγα τε ποιεύμενοι Stein

ἅπαντα πλέα, ἐπεὶ αὐτοῖσι παρὰ δόξαν τὰ πρήγματα τῶν βαρβάρων ἀπέβαινε ἢ ὡς αὐτοὶ κατεδόκεον, καταρρωδήσαντες
2 δρησμὸν ἐβούλευον ἀπὸ τοῦ Ἀρτεμισίου ἔσω ἐς τὴν Ἑλλάδα. γνόντες δέ σφεας οἱ Εὐβοέες ταῦτα βουλευομένους, ἐδέοντο Εὐρυβιάδεω προσμεῖναι χρόνον ὀλίγον, ἔστ᾽ ἂν αὐτοὶ τέκνα τε καὶ τοὺς οἰκέτας ὑπεκθέωνται. ὡς δ᾽ οὐκ ἔπειθον, μεταβάντες τὸν Ἀθηναίων στρατηγὸν πείθουσι Θεμιστοκλέα ἐπὶ μισθῶι τριήκοντα ταλάντοισι, ἐπ᾽ ὧι τε καταμείναντες πρὸ τῆς Εὐβοίης ποιήσονται τὴν ναυμαχίην.

5 Ὁ δὲ Θεμιστοκλέης τοὺς Ἕλληνας ἐπισχεῖν ὧδε ποιέει· Εὐρυβιάδηι τούτων τῶν χρημάτων μεταδιδοῖ πέντε τάλαντα, ὡς παρ᾽ ἑωυτοῦ δῆθεν διδούς. ὡς δέ οἱ οὗτος ἀνεπέπειστο (Ἀδείμαντος γὰρ ὁ Ὠκύτου ὁ Κορίνθιος στρατηγὸς τῶν λοιπῶν ἤσπαιρε μοῦνος, φάμενος ἀποπλεύσεσθαί τε ἀπὸ τοῦ Ἀρτεμισίου καὶ οὐ παραμενέειν),
2 πρὸς δὴ τοῦτον εἶπε ὁ Θεμιστοκλέης ἐπομόσας· "οὐ σύ γε ἡμέας ἀπολείψεις, ἐπεί τοι ἐγὼ μέζω δῶρα δώσω ἢ βασιλεὺς ἄν τοι ὁ Μήδων πέμψειε ἀπολιπόντι τοὺς συμμάχους." ταῦτά τε ἅμα ἠγόρευε καὶ πέμπει ἐπὶ τὴν νέα τὴν Ἀδειμάντου τάλαντα ἀργυρίου
3 τρία. οὗτοί τε δὴ πληγέντες δώροισι ἀναπεπεισμένοι ἦσαν, καὶ τοῖσι Εὐβοεῦσι ἐκεχάριστο, αὐτός τε ὁ Θεμιστοκλέης ἐκέρδηνε, ἐλάνθανε δὲ τὰ λοιπὰ ἔχων· ἀλλ᾽ ἠπιστέατο οἱ μεταλαβόντες τούτων τῶν χρημάτων ἐκ τῶν Ἀθηνέων ἐλθεῖν ἐπὶ τῶι λόγωι τούτωι.

6–8 The Persians

6 Οὕτω δὴ κατέμεινάν τε ἐν τῆι Εὐβοίηι καὶ ἐναυμάχησαν· ἐγένετο δὲ ὧδε. ἐπείτε δὴ ἐς τὰς Ἀφέτας περὶ δείλην πρωίην γινομένην ἀπίκατο οἱ βάρβαροι, πυθόμενοι μὲν ἔτι καὶ πρότερον περὶ τὸ Ἀρτεμίσιον ναυλοχέειν νέας Ἑλληνίδας ὀλίγας, τότε δὲ αὐτοὶ ἰδόντες, πρόθυμοι
2 ἦσαν ἐπιχειρέειν, εἴ κως ἕλοιεν αὐτάς. ἐκ μὲν δὴ τῆς ἀντίης προσπλέειν οὔ κώ σφι ἐδόκεε τῶνδε εἵνεκα, μή κως ἰδόντες οἱ Ἕλληνες προσπλέοντας ἐς φυγὴν ὁρμήσειαν, φεύγοντάς τε εὐφρόνη καταλαμβάνηι· καὶ ἔμελλον δῆθεν ἐκφεύξεσθαι, ἔδει δὲ μηδὲ πυρφόρον τῶι ἐκείνων λόγωι ἐκφυγόντα περιγενέσθαι.

7 Πρὸς ταῦτα ὦν τάδε ἐμηχανέοντο· τῶν νεῶν ἁπασέων ἀποκρίναντες διηκοσίας, περιέπεμπον ἔξωθεν Σκιάθου, ὡς ἂν μὴ ὀφθείησαν ὑπὸ τῶν πολεμίων περιπλέουσαι Εὔβοιαν κατά τε Καφηρέα καὶ περὶ Γεραιστὸν ἐς τὸν Εὔριπον, ἵνα δὴ περιλάβοιεν, οἱ μὲν ταύτηι

5.1 Τῶν λοιπῶν om. PDRSV 7.1 ὀφθέωσι DPRSV

ἀπικόμενοι καὶ φράξαντες αὐτῶν τὴν ὀπίσω φέρουσαν ὁδόν, σφεῖς
δὲ ἐπισπόμενοι ἐξ ἐναντίης. ταῦτα βουλευσάμενοι ἀπέπεμπον τῶν 2
νεῶν τὰς ταχθείσας, αὐτοὶ οὐκ ἐν νόωι ἔχοντες ταύτης τῆς ἡμέρης
τοῖσι Ἕλλησι ἐπιθήσεσθαι, οὐδὲ πρότερον ἢ τὸ σύνθημά σφι ἔμελλε
φανήσεσθαι παρὰ τῶν περιπλεόντων, ὡς ἡκόντων. ταύτας μὲν δὴ
περιέπεμπον, τῶν δὲ λοιπέων νεῶν ἐν τῆισι Ἀφέτηισι ἐποιεῦντο
ἀριθμόν.

Ἐν δὲ τούτωι τῶι χρόνωι, ἐν ὧι οὗτοι ἀριθμὸν ἐποιεῦντο τῶν **8**
νεῶν, ἦν γὰρ ἐν τῶι στρατοπέδωι τούτωι Σκυλλίης Σκιωναῖος, δύτης
τῶν τότε ἀνθρώπων ἄριστος, ὃς καὶ ἐν τῆι ναυηγίηι τῆι κατὰ Πήλιον
γενομένηι πολλὰ μὲν ἔσωσε τῶν χρημάτων τοῖσι Πέρσηισι, πολλὰ
δὲ καὶ αὐτὸς περιεβάλετο, οὗτος ὁ Σκυλλίης ἐν νόωι μὲν εἶχε ἄρα καὶ
πρότερον αὐτομολήσειν ἐς τοὺς Ἕλληνας, ἀλλ' οὐ γάρ οἱ παρέσχε ἐς
τότε. ὅτεωι μὲν δὴ τρόπωι τὸ ἐνθεῦτεν ἔτι ἀπίκετο ἐς τοὺς Ἕλληνας, 2
οὐκ ἔχω εἰπεῖν ἀτρεκέως, θωμάζω δὲ εἰ τὰ λεγόμενά ἐστι ἀληθέα.
λέγεται γὰρ ὡς ἐξ Ἀφετέων δὺς ἐς τὴν θάλασσαν οὐ πρότερον ἀνέσχε,
πρὶν ἢ ἀπίκετο ἐπὶ τὸ Ἀρτεμίσιον, σταδίους μάλιστά κηι τούτους ἐς
ὀγδώκοντα διὰ τῆς θαλάσσης διεξελθών. λέγεται μέν νυν καὶ ἄλλα 3
ψευδέσι ἴκελα περὶ τοῦ ἀνδρὸς τούτου, τὰ δὲ μετεξέτερα ἀληθέα·
περὶ μέντοι τούτου γνώμη μοι ἀποδεδέχθω πλοίωι μιν ἀπικέσθαι
ἐπὶ τὸ Ἀρτεμίσιον. ὡς δὲ ἀπίκετο, αὐτίκα ἐσήμηνε τοῖσι στρατηγοῖσι
τήν τε ναυηγίην ὡς γένοιτο, καὶ τὰς περιπεμφθείσας τῶν νεῶν περὶ
Εὔβοιαν.

9–14 The first battle and a violent storm

Τοῦτο δὲ ἀκούσαντες οἱ Ἕλληνες, λόγον σφίσι αὐτοῖσι ἐδίδοσαν. **9**
πολλῶν δὲ λεχθέντων, ἐνίκα τὴν ἡμέρην ἐκείνην αὐτοῦ μείναντάς τε
καὶ αὐλισθέντας, μετέπειτα νύκτα μέσην παρέντας, πορεύεσθαι καὶ
ἀπαντᾶν τῆισι περιπλεούσηισι τῶν νεῶν. μετὰ δὲ τοῦτο, ὡς οὐδείς
σφι ἐπέπλεε, δείλην ὀψίην γινομένην τῆς ἡμέρης φυλάξαντες, αὐτοὶ
ἐπανέπλεον ἐπὶ τοὺς βαρβάρους, ἀπόπειραν αὐτῶν ποιήσασθαι
βουλόμενοι τῆς τε μάχης καὶ τοῦ διεκπλόου. Ὁρῶντες δέ σφεας οἵ τε **10**
ἄλλοι στρατιῶται οἱ Ξέρξεω καὶ οἱ στρατηγοὶ ἐπιπλέοντας νηυσὶ
ὀλίγηισι, πάγχυ σφι μανίην ἐπενείκαντες, ἀνῆγον καὶ αὐτοὶ τὰς
νέας, ἐλπίσαντές σφεας εὐπετέως αἱρήσειν, οἰκότα κάρτα ἐλπίσαν-
τες, τὰς μέν γε τῶν Ἑλλήνων ὁρῶντες ὀλίγας νέας, τὰς δὲ ἑωυτῶν
πλήθεΐ τε πολλαπλησίας καὶ ἄμεινον πλεούσας. καταφρονήσαν-
τες ταῦτα, ἐκυκλοῦντο αὐτοὺς ἐς μέσον. ὅσοι μέν νυν τῶν Ἰώνων 2

8.1 ἐς τότε Pingel: ὡς τότε codd.

ἦσαν εὔνοοι τοῖσι Ἕλλησι ἀέκοντές τε ἐστρατεύοντο, συμφορήν [τε]
ἐποιεῦντο μεγάλην, ὁρῶντες περιεχομένους αὐτοὺς καὶ ἐπιστάμενοι
ὡς οὐδεὶς αὐτῶν ἀπονοστήσει· οὕτω ἀσθενέα σφι ἐφαίνετο εἶναι τὰ
3 τῶν Ἑλλήνων πρήγματα. ὅσοισι δὲ καὶ ἡδομένοισι ἦν τὸ γινόμενον,
ἅμιλλαν ἐποιεῦντο, ὅκως αὐτὸς ἕκαστος πρῶτος νέα Ἀττικὴν ἑλὼν,
παρὰ βασιλέος δῶρα λάμψεται· Ἀθηναίων γὰρ αὐτοῖσι λόγος ἦν
πλεῖστος ἀνὰ τὰ στρατόπεδα.

11 Τοῖσι δὲ Ἕλλησι ὡς ἐσήμηνε, πρῶτα μὲν ἀντίπρωιροι τοῖσι βαρ-
βάροισι γενόμενοι ἐς τὸ μέσον τὰς πρύμνας συνήγαγον· δεύτερα δὲ
σημήναντος, ἔργου εἴχοντο, ἐν ὀλίγωι περ ἀπολαμφθέντες καὶ κατὰ
2 στόμα. ἐνθαῦτα τριήκοντα νέας αἱρέουσι τῶν βαρβάρων καὶ τὸν
Γόργου τοῦ Σαλαμινίων βασιλέος ἀδελφεὸν, Φιλάονα τὸν Χέρσιος,
λόγιμον ἐόντα ἐν τῶι στρατοπέδωι ἄνδρα. πρῶτος δὲ Ἑλλήνων
νέα τῶν πολεμίων εἷλε ἀνὴρ Ἀθηναῖος, Λυκομήδης Αἰσχραίου, καὶ
3 τὸ ἀριστήιον ἔλαβε οὗτος. τοὺς δ' ἐν τῆι ναυμαχίηι ταύτηι ἑτερ-
αλκέως ἀγωνιζομένους νὺξ ἐπελθοῦσα διέλυσε. οἱ μὲν δὴ Ἕλληνες
ἐπὶ τὸ Ἀρτεμίσιον ἀπέπλεον, οἱ δὲ βάρβαροι ἐς τὰς Ἀφέτας, πολ-
λὸν παρὰ δόξαν ἀγωνισάμενοι. ἐν ταύτηι τῆι ναυμαχίηι Ἀντίδωρος
Λήμνιος μοῦνος τῶν σὺν βασιλέϊ Ἑλλήνων ἐόντων αὐτομολέει ἐς
τοὺς Ἕλληνας, καὶ οἱ Ἀθηναῖοι διὰ τοῦτο τὸ ἔργον ἔδοσαν αὐτῶι
χῶρον ἐν Σαλαμῖνι.

12 Ὡς δὲ εὐφρόνη ἐγεγόνεε, ἦν μὲν τῆς ὥρης μέσον θέρος, ἐγίνετο
δὲ ὕδωρ τε ἄπλετον διὰ πάσης τῆς νυκτὸς καὶ σκληραὶ βρονταὶ
ἀπὸ τοῦ Πηλίου. οἱ δὲ νεκροὶ καὶ τὰ ναυήγια ἐξεφορέοντο ἐς τὰς
Ἀφέτας, καὶ περί τε τὰς πρώιρας τῶν νεῶν εἱλέοντο, καὶ ἐτάρασσον
2 τοὺς ταρσοὺς τῶν κωπέων. οἱ δὲ στρατιῶται οἱ ταύτηι ἀκούοντες
ταῦτα ἐς φόβον κατιστέατο, ἐλπίζοντες πάγχυ ἀπολέεσθαι, ἐς οἷα
κακὰ ἧκον. πρὶν γὰρ ἢ καὶ ἀναπνεῦσαί σφεας ἔκ τε τῆς ναυηγίης
καὶ τοῦ χειμῶνος τοῦ γενομένου κατὰ Πήλιον, ὑπέλαβε ναυμαχίη
καρτερή, ἐκ δὲ τῆς ναυμαχίης ὄμβρος τε λάβρος καὶ ῥεύματα ἰσχυρὰ
ἐς θάλασσαν ὁρμημένα βρονταί τε σκληραί.

13 Καὶ τούτοισι μὲν τοιαύτη ἡ νὺξ ἐγίνετο, τοῖσι δὲ ταχθεῖσι αὐτῶν περιπλέειν Εὔβοιαν ἡ αὐτή περ ἐοῦσα νὺξ πολλὸν ἦν ἔτι ἀγριωτέρη, τοσούτωι ὅσωι ἐν πελάγεϊ φερομένοισι ἐπέπιπτε, καὶ τὸ τέλος σφι ἐγένετο ἄχαρι. ὡς γὰρ δὴ πλέουσι αὐτοῖσι χειμών τε καὶ τὸ ὕδωρ ἐπεγίνετο ἐοῦσι κατὰ τὰ Κοῖλα τῆς Εὐβοίης, φερόμενοι τῶι πνεύματι καὶ οὐκ εἰδότες τῆι ἐφέροντο, ἐξέπιπτον πρὸς τὰς πέτρας· ἐποιέετό τε πᾶν ὑπὸ τοῦ θεοῦ, ὅκως ἂν ἐξισωθείη τῶι Ἑλληνικῶι τὸ Περσικόν, μηδὲ πολλῶι πλέον εἴη.

12.1 ἐτάρασσον codd.: ἀπάρασσον Emper

Οὗτοι μέν νυν περὶ τὰ Κοῖλα τῆς Εὐβοίης διεφθείροντο· οἱ δ' ἐν 14 Ἀφέτῃσι βάρβαροι, ὥς σφι ἀσμένοισι ἡμέρη ἐπέλαμψε, ἀτρέμας τε εἶχον τὰς νέας, καί σφι ἀπεχρᾶτο κακῶς πρήσσουσι ἡσυχίην ἄγειν ἐν τῶι παρεόντι. τοῖσι δὲ Ἕλλησι ἐπεβοήθεον νέες τρεῖς καὶ πεντήκοντα Ἀττικαί. αὗταί τε δή σφεας ἐπέρρωσαν ἀπικόμεναι, καὶ ἅμα ἀγγελίη 2 ἐλθοῦσα, ὡς τῶν βαρβάρων οἱ περιπλέοντες τὴν Εὔβοιαν πάντες εἴησαν διεφθαρμένοι ὑπὸ τοῦ γενομένου χειμῶνος. φυλάξαντες δὴ τὴν αὐτὴν ὥρην, πλέοντες ἐπέπεσον νηυσὶ Κιλίσσῃσι· ταύτας δὲ διαφθείραντες, ὡς εὐφρόνη ἐγίνετο, ἀπέπλεον ὀπίσω ἐπὶ τὸ Ἀρτεμίσιον.

15–18 The second battle

Τρίτηι δὲ ἡμέρηι, δεινόν τι ποιησάμενοι οἱ στρατηγοὶ τῶν βαρ- 15 βάρων νέας οὕτω σφι ὀλίγας λυμαίνεσθαι, καὶ τὸ ἀπὸ Ξέρξεω δειμαίνοντες, οὐκ ἀνέμειναν ἔτι τοὺς Ἕλληνας μάχης ἄρξαι, ἀλλὰ παρακελευσάμενοι κατὰ μέσον ἡμέρης ἀνῆγον τὰς νέας. συνέπιπτε δὲ ὥστε τὰς αὐτὰς ταύτας ἡμέρας τάς τε ναυμαχίας γίνεσθαι ταύτας καὶ τὰς πεζομαχίας τὰς ἐν Θερμοπύλῃσι. ἦν δὲ πᾶς ὁ ἀγὼν τοῖσι 2 κατὰ θάλασσαν περὶ τοῦ Εὐρίπου, ὥσπερ τοῖσι ἀμφὶ Λεωνίδην τὴν ἐσβολὴν φυλάσσειν. οἱ μὲν δὴ παρεκελεύοντο, ὅκως μὴ παρήσουσι ἐς τὴν Ἑλλάδα τοὺς βαρβάρους, οἱ δ' ὅκως τὸ Ἑλληνικὸν στράτευμα διαφθείραντες τοῦ πόρου κρατήσουσι. Ὡς δὲ ταξάμενοι οἱ 16 Ξέρξεω ἐπέπλεον, οἱ Ἕλληνες ἀτρέμας εἶχον πρὸς τῶι Ἀρτεμισίωι. οἱ δὲ βάρβαροι μηνοειδὲς ποιήσαντες τῶν νεῶν ἐκυκλεῦντο, ὡς περιλάβοιεν αὐτούς. ἐνθεῦτεν οἱ Ἕλληνες ἐπανέπλεόν τε καὶ συνέμισγον. ἐν ταύτηι τῆι ναυμαχίηι παραπλήσιοι ἀλλήλοισι ἐγίνοντο. ὁ γὰρ Ξέρξεω στρατὸς ὑπὸ μεγάθεός τε καὶ πλήθεος αὐτὸς ὑπ' 2 ἑωυτοῦ ἔπιπτε, ταρασσομένων τε τῶν νεῶν καὶ περιπιπτουσέων περὶ ἀλλήλας. ὅμως μέντοι ἀντεῖχε καὶ οὐκ εἶκε· δεινὸν γὰρ χρῆμα ἐποιεῦντο ὑπὸ νεῶν ὀλιγέων ἐς φυγὴν τράπεσθαι. πολλαὶ μὲν δὴ 3 τῶν Ἑλλήνων νέες διεφθείροντο, πολλοὶ δὲ ἄνδρες, πολλῶι δ' ἔτι πλεῦνες νέες τε τῶν βαρβάρων καὶ ἄνδρες. οὕτω δὲ ἀγωνιζόμενοι, διέστησαν χωρὶς ἑκάτεροι.

Ἐν ταύτηι τῆι ναυμαχίηι Αἰγύπτιοι μὲν τῶν Ξέρξεω στρατι- 17 ωτέων ἠρίστευσαν, οἳ ἄλλα τε μεγάλα ἔργα ἀπεδέξαντο, καὶ νέας αὐτοῖσι ἀνδράσι εἷλον Ἑλληνίδας πέντε. τῶν δὲ Ἑλλήνων κατὰ ταύτην τὴν ἡμέρην ἠρίστευσαν Ἀθηναῖοι, καὶ Ἀθηναίων Κλεινίης ὁ Ἀλκιβιάδεω, ὃς δαπάνην οἰκηίην παρεχόμενος ἐστρατεύετο ἀνδράσι

15.1 παρασκευασάμενοι DRSV

18 τε διηκοσίοισι καὶ οἰκηίηι νηί. Ὡς δὲ διέστησαν, ἄσμενοι ἑκάτεροι
ἐς ὅρμον ἠπείγοντο. οἱ δὲ Ἕλληνες, ὡς διακριθέντες ἐκ τῆς ναυ-
μαχίης ἀπηλλάχθησαν, τῶν μὲν νεκρῶν καὶ τῶν ναυηγίων ἐπεκρά-
τεον· τρηχέως δὲ περιεφθέντες, καὶ οὐκ ἥκιστα Ἀθηναῖοι, τῶν αἱ
ἡμίσεαι τῶν νεῶν τετρωμέναι ἦσαν, δρησμὸν δὴ ἐβούλευον ἔσω ἐς
τὴν Ἑλλάδα.

19–22 Greek tactics

19 Νόωι δὲ λαβὼν ὁ Θεμιστοκλέης, ὡς εἰ ἀπορραγείη ἀπὸ τοῦ βαρ-
βάρου τό τε Ἰωνικὸν φῦλον καὶ τὸ Καρικόν, οἷοί τε εἴησαν τῶν
λοιπῶν κατύπερθε γενέσθαι, ἐλαυνόντων τῶν Εὐβοέων πρόβατα
ἐπὶ τὴν θάλασσαν, ταύτηι συλλέξας τοὺς στρατηγούς, ἔλεγέ σφι
ὡς δοκέοι ἔχειν τινὰ παλάμην, τῆι ἐλπίζοι τῶν βασιλέος συμμάχων
2 ἀποστήσειν τοὺς ἀρίστους. ταῦτα μέν νυν ἐς τοσοῦτο παρεγύμ-
νου, ἐπὶ δὲ τοῖσι κατήκουσι πρήγμασι τάδε ποιητέα σφι εἶναι
ἔλεγε, τῶν τε προβάτων τῶν Εὐβοϊκῶν καταθύειν ὅσα τις ἐθέλοι,
κρέσσον γὰρ εἶναι τὴν στρατιὴν ἔχειν ἢ τοὺς πολεμίους· παραίνεέ
τε προειπεῖν τοῖσι ἑωυτῶν ἑκάστους πυρὰ ἀνακαίειν. κομιδῆς δὲ
πέρι τὴν ὥρην αὐτῶι μελήσειν, ὥστε ἀσινέας ἀπικέσθαι ἐς τὴν
Ἑλλάδα. ταῦτα ἤρεσέ σφι ποιέειν, καὶ αὐτίκα πυρὰ ἀνακαυσάμενοι
20 ἐτρέποντο πρὸς τὰ πρόβατα. Οἱ γὰρ Εὐβοέες, παραχρησάμενοι τὸν
Βάκιδος χρησμὸν ὡς οὐδὲν λέγοντα, οὔτε τι ἐξεκομίσαντο οὐδὲν
οὔτε προεσάξαντο, ὡς παρεσομένου σφι πολέμου, περιπετέα τε
2 ἐποιήσαντο σφίσι αὐτοῖσι τὰ πρήγματα. Βάκιδι γὰρ ὧδε ἔχει περὶ
τούτων ὁ χρησμός·

φράζεο, βαρβαρόφωνος ὅταν ζυγὸν εἰς ἅλα βάλληι
βύβλινον, Εὐβοίης ἀπέχειν πολυμηκάδας αἶγας.

τούτοισι οὐδὲν τοῖσι ἔπεσι χρησαμένοισι ἐν τοῖσι τότε παρεοῦσί τε
καὶ προσδοκίμοισι κακοῖσι παρῆν σφι συμφορῆι χρᾶσθαι πρὸς τὰ
μέγιστα.

21 Οἱ μὲν δὴ ταῦτα ἔπρησσον, παρῆν δὲ ὁ ἐκ Τρηχῖνος κατάσκοπος.
ἦν μὲν γὰρ ἐπ᾽ Ἀρτεμισίωι κατάσκοπος Πολύας, γένος Ἀντικυρεύς,
τῶι προσετέτακτο (καὶ εἶχε πλοῖον κατῆρες ἕτοιμον), εἰ παλή-
σειε ὁ ναυτικὸς στρατός, σημαίνειν τοῖσι ἐν Θερμοπύληισι
ἐοῦσι· ὣς δ᾽ αὔτως ἦν Ἀβρώνιχος ὁ Λυσικλέος Ἀθηναῖος καὶ
παρὰ Λεωνίδηι ἕτοιμος τοῖσι ἐπ᾽ Ἀρτεμισίωι ἐοῦσι ἀγγέλλειν

19.2 πυρά Cobet: πυράς S: πῦρ rell. 20 del. Powell

τριηκοντέρωι, ἤν τι καταλαμβάνηι νεώτερον τὸν πεζόν. οὗτος ὦν ὁ 2
Ἀβρώνιχος ἀπικόμενός σφι ἐσήμηνε τὰ γεγονότα περὶ Λεωνίδην καὶ
τὸν στρατὸν αὐτοῦ. οἱ δὲ ὡς ἐπύθοντο ταῦτα, οὐκέτι ἐς ἀναβολὰς
ἐποιεῦντο τὴν ἀποχώρησιν, ἐκομίζοντο δὲ ὡς ἕκαστοι ἐτάχθησαν,
Κορίνθιοι πρῶτοι, ὕστατοι δὲ Ἀθηναῖοι.

Ἀθηναίων δὲ νέας τὰς ἄριστα πλεούσας ἐπιλεξάμενος, Θεμιστοκ- **22**
λέης ἐπορεύετο περὶ τὰ πότιμα ὕδατα, ἐντάμνων ἐν τοῖσι λίθοισι
γράμματα, τὰ Ἴωνες ἐπελθόντες τῆι ὑστεραίηι ἡμέρηι ἐπὶ τὸ Ἀρτεμί-
σιον ἐπελέξαντο. τὰ δὲ γράμματα τάδε ἔλεγε· "ἄνδρες Ἴωνες, οὐ
ποιέετε δίκαια ἐπὶ τοὺς πατέρας στρατευόμενοι, καὶ τὴν Ἑλλάδα
καταδουλούμενοι. ἀλλὰ μάλιστα μὲν πρὸς ἡμέων γίνεσθε· εἰ δὲ ὑμῖν 2
ἐστι τοῦτο μὴ δυνατὸν ποιῆσαι, ὑμεῖς δὲ ἔτι καὶ νῦν ἐκ τοῦ μέσου
ἡμῖν ἕζεσθε, καὶ αὐτοὶ καὶ τῶν Καρῶν δέεσθε τὰ αὐτὰ ὑμῖν ποιέειν. εἰ
δὲ μηδέτερον τούτων οἷόν τε γίνεσθαι, ἀλλ᾽ ὑπ᾽ ἀναγκαίης μέζονος
κατέζευχθε ἢ ὥστε ἀπίστασθαι, ὑμεῖς δὲ ἐν τῶι ἔργωι, ἐπεὰν συμ-
μίσγωμεν, ἐθελοκακέετε, μεμνημένοι ὅτι ἀπ᾽ ἡμέων γεγόνατε, καὶ
ὅτι ἀρχῆθεν ἡ ἔχθρη πρὸς τὸν βάρβαρον ἀπ᾽ ὑμέων ἡμῖν γέγονε."
Θεμιστοκλέης δὲ ταῦτα ἔγραφε, δοκέειν ἐμοί, ἐπ᾽ ἀμφότερα νοέων, 3
ἵνα ἢ λαθόντα τὰ γράμματα βασιλέα Ἴωνας ποιήσηι μεταβαλεῖν
καὶ γενέσθαι πρὸς ἑωυτῶν, ἢ ἐπείτε ἀνενειχθῆι καὶ διαβληθῆι πρὸς
Ξέρξην, ἀπίστους ποιήσηι τοὺς Ἴωνας καὶ τῶν ναυμαχιέων αὐτοὺς
ἀπόσχηι.

23–6 On the Persian side

Θεμιστοκλέης μὲν ταῦτα ἐνέγραψε· τοῖσι δὲ βαρβάροισι αὐτίκα μετὰ **23**
ταῦτα πλοίωι ἦλθε ἀνὴρ Ἱστιαιεύς, ἀγγέλλων τὸν δρησμὸν τὸν ἀπ᾽
Ἀρτεμισίου τῶν Ἑλλήνων. οἱ δ᾽ ὑπ᾽ ἀπιστίης τὸν μὲν ἀγγέλλοντα
εἶχον ἐν φυλακῆι, νέας δὲ ταχέας ἀπέστειλαν προκατοψομένας.
ἀπαγγειλάντων δὲ τούτων τὰ ἦν, οὕτω δὴ ἅμα ἡλίωι σκιδναμένωι
πᾶσα ἡ στρατιὴ ἐπέπλεε ἁλὴς ἐπὶ τὸ Ἀρτεμίσιον. ἐπισχόντες δὲ 2
ἐν τούτωι τῶι χώρωι μέχρι μέσου ἡμέρης, τὸ ἀπὸ τούτου ἔπλεον
ἐς Ἱστιαίην. ἀπικόμενοι δέ, τὴν πόλιν ἔσχον τῶν Ἱστιαιέων, καὶ
τῆς Ἐλλοπίης μοίρης, γῆς δὲ τῆς Ἱστιαιώτιδος, τὰς παραθαλασσίας
κώμας πάσας ἐπέδραμον.

Ἐνθαῦτα δὲ τούτων ἐόντων, Ξέρξης, ἑτοιμασάμενος τὰ περὶ τοὺς **24**
νεκρούς, ἔπεμπε ἐς τὸν ναυτικὸν στρατὸν κήρυκα· προετοιμάσατο
δὲ τάδε. ὅσοι τοῦ στρατοῦ τοῦ ἑωυτοῦ ἦσαν νεκροὶ ἐν Θερ-
μοπύληισι (ἦσαν δὲ καὶ δύο μυριάδες), ὑπολιπόμενος τούτων ὡς
χιλίους, τοὺς λοιποὺς τάφρους ὀρυξάμενος ἔθαψε, φυλλάδα τε

ἐπιβαλὼν καὶ γῆν ἐπαμησάμενος, ἵνα μὴ ὀφθείησαν ὑπὸ τοῦ ναυ-
2 τικοῦ στρατοῦ. ὡς δὲ διέβη ἐς τὴν Ἱστιαίην ὁ κῆρυξ, σύλλο-
γον ποιησάμενος παντὸς τοῦ στρατοπέδου, ἔλεγε τάδε· "ἄνδρες
σύμμαχοι, βασιλεὺς Ξέρξης τῶι βουλομένωι ὑμέων παραδίδωσι,
ἐκλιπόντα τὴν τάξιν, ἐλθόντα θεήσασθαι ὅκως μάχεται πρὸς τοὺς
ἀνοήτους τῶν ἀνθρώπων, οἳ ἤλπισαν τὴν βασιλέος δύναμιν ὑπερ-
25 βαλέεσθαι." Ταῦτα ἐπαγγειλαμένου, μετὰ ταῦτα οὐδὲν ἐγίνετο
πλοίων σπανιώτερον, οὕτω πολλοὶ ἤθελον θεήσασθαι. διαπεραι-
ωθέντες δέ, ἐθηεῦντο διεξιόντες τοὺς νεκρούς· πάντες δὲ ἠπιστέατο
τοὺς κειμένους εἶναι πάντας Λακεδαιμονίους καὶ Θεσπιέας, ὁρῶντες
2 καὶ τοὺς εἵλωτας. οὐ μὲν οὐδ' ἐλάνθανε τοὺς διαβεβηκότας Ξέρξης,
ταῦτα πρήξας περὶ τοὺς νεκροὺς τοὺς ἑωυτοῦ. καὶ γὰρ δὴ καὶ
γελοῖον ἦν· τῶν μὲν χίλιοι ἐφαίνοντο νεκροὶ κείμενοι, οἱ δὲ πάντες
ἐκέατο ἁλέες συγκεκομισμένοι ἐς τὠυτὸ χωρίον, τέσσερες χιλιάδες.
3 ταύτην μὲν τὴν ἡμέρην πρὸς θέην ἐτράποντο, τῆι δ' ὑστεραίηι οἱ
μὲν ἀπέπλεον ἐς Ἱστιαίην ἐπὶ τὰς νέας, οἱ δὲ ἀμφὶ Ξέρξην ἐς ὁδὸν
ὁρμέατο.

26 Ἧκον δέ σφι αὐτόμολοι ἄνδρες ἀπ' Ἀρκαδίης ὀλίγοι τινές, βίου τε
δεόμενοι καὶ ἐνεργοὶ βουλόμενοι εἶναι. ἄγοντες δὲ τούτους ἐς ὄψιν τὴν
βασιλέος, ἐπυνθάνοντο οἱ Πέρσαι περὶ τῶν Ἑλλήνων τί ποιέοιεν· εἷς
2 δέ τις πρὸ πάντων ἦν ὁ εἰρωτῶν αὐτοὺς ταῦτα. οἱ δέ σφι ἔλεγον,
ὡς Ὀλύμπια ἄγουσι καὶ θεωρέοιεν ἀγῶνα γυμνικὸν καὶ ἱππικόν.
ὁ δὲ ἐπείρετο ὅ τι τὸ ἄεθλον εἴη σφι κείμενον, περὶ ὅτευ ἀγωνίζον-
ται· οἱ δ' εἶπον τῆς ἐλαίης τὸν διδόμενον στέφανον. ἐνθαῦτα εἴπας
γνώμην γενναιοτάτην Τριτανταίχμης ὁ Ἀρταβάνου δειλίην ὦφλε
3 πρὸς βασιλέος. πυθόμενος γὰρ τὸ ἄεθλον ἐὸν στέφανον ἀλλ' οὐ
χρήματα, οὔτε ἠνέσχετο σιγῶν, εἶπέ τε ἐς πάντας τάδε· "παπαῖ,
Μαρδόνιε, κοίους ἐπ' ἄνδρας ἤγαγες μαχησομένους ἡμέας, οἳ οὐ περὶ
χρημάτων τὸν ἀγῶνα ποιεῦνται ἀλλὰ περὶ ἀρετῆς." τούτωι μὲν δὴ
ταῦτα εἴρητο.

27–33 Hostility between Thessaly and Phocis

27 Ἐν δὲ τῶι διὰ μέσου χρόνωι, ἐπείτε τὸ ἐν Θερμοπύληισι τρῶμα
ἐγεγόνεε, αὐτίκα Θεσσαλοὶ πέμπουσι κήρυκα ἐς Φωκέας, ἅτε σφι
ἐνέχοντες αἰεὶ χόλον, ἀπὸ δὲ τοῦ ὑστάτου τρώματος καὶ τὸ κάρτα.
2 ἐσβαλόντες γὰρ πανστρατιῆι αὐτοί τε οἱ Θεσσαλοὶ καὶ οἱ σύμμα-
χοι αὐτῶν ἐς τοὺς Φωκέας, οὐ πολλοῖσι ἔτεσι πρότερον ταύτης

26.2 Τιγράνης ABC

τῆς βασιλέος στρατηλασίης, ἑσσώθησαν ὑπὸ τῶν Φωκέων καὶ περι-
έφθησαν τρηχέως. ἐπείτε γὰρ κατειλήθησαν ἐς τὸν Παρνησσὸν οἱ 3
Φωκέες, ἔχοντες μάντιν Τελλίην τὸν Ἠλεῖον, ἐνθαῦτα ὁ Τελλίης
οὗτος σοφίζεται αὐτοῖσι τοιόνδε· γυψώσας ἄνδρας ἑξακοσίους τῶν
Φωκέων τοὺς ἀρίστους, αὐτούς τε τούτους καὶ τὰ ὅπλα αὐτῶν,
νυκτὸς ἐπεθήκατο τοῖσι Θεσσαλοῖσι, προείπας αὐτοῖσι, τὸν ἂν μὴ
λευκανθίζοντα ἴδωνται, τοῦτον κτείνειν. τούτους ὦν αἵ τε φυλακαὶ 4
τῶν Θεσσαλῶν πρῶται ἰδοῦσαι ἐφοβήθησαν, δόξασαι ἄλλο τι
εἶναι τέρας, καὶ μετὰ τὰς φυλακὰς αὐτὴ ἡ στρατιὴ οὕτω, ὥστε
τετρακισχιλίων κρατῆσαι νεκρῶν καὶ ἀσπίδων Φωκέας, τῶν τὰς μὲν
ἡμισέας ἐς Ἄβας ἀνέθεσαν, τὰς δὲ ἐς Δελφούς. ἡ δὲ δεκάτη ἐγένετο τῶν 5
χρημάτων ἐκ ταύτης τῆς μάχης οἱ μεγάλοι ἀνδριάντες, οἱ περὶ τὸν
τρίποδα συνεστεῶτες ἔμπροσθε τοῦ νηοῦ τοῦ ἐν Δελφοῖσι, καὶ ἕτεροι
τοιοῦτοι ἐν Ἄβηισι ἀνακέαται. Ταῦτα μέν νυν τὸν πεζὸν ἐργάσαντο **28**
τῶν Θεσσαλῶν οἱ Φωκέες πολιορκέοντας ἑωυτούς· ἐσβαλοῦσαν δὲ
ἐς τὴν χώρην τὴν ἵππον αὐτῶν ἐλυμήναντο ἀνηκέστως. ἐν γὰρ
τῆι ἐσβολῆι ἥ ἐστι κατὰ Ὑάμπολιν, ἐν ταύτηι τάφρον μεγάλην
ὀρύξαντες, ἀμφορέας κεινοὺς ἐς αὐτὴν κατέθηκαν, χοῦν δὲ ἐπι-
φορήσαντες καὶ ὁμοιώσαντες τῶι ἄλλωι χώρωι, ἐδέκοντο τοὺς
Θεσσαλοὺς ἐσβάλλοντας. οἱ δέ, ὡς ἀναρπασόμενοι τοὺς Φωκέας,
φερόμενοι ἐσέπεσον ἐς τοὺς ἀμφορέας· ἐνθαῦτα οἱ ἵπποι τὰ σκέλεα
διεφθάρησαν.

Τούτων δή σφι ἀμφοτέρων ἔχοντες ἔγκοτον οἱ Θεσσαλοί, **29**
πέμψαντες κήρυκα ἠγόρευον τάδε· "ὦ Φωκέες, ἤδη τι μᾶλλον γνωσι-
μαχέετε μὴ εἶναι ὅμοιοι ἡμῖν. πρόσθε τε γὰρ ἐν τοῖσι Ἕλλησι, ὅσον 2
χρόνον ἐκεῖνα ἡμῖν ἥνδανε, πλέον αἰεί κοτε ὑμέων ἐφερόμεθα, νῦν
τε παρὰ τῶι βαρβάρωι τοσοῦτον δυνάμεθα, ὥστε ἐπ' ἡμῖν ἐστι
τῆς γῆς ἐστερῆσθαι, καὶ πρὸς ἠνδραποδίσθαι ὑμέας. ἡμεῖς μέντοι
τὸ πᾶν ἔχοντες οὐ μνησικακέομεν, ἀλλ' ἡμῖν γενέσθω ἀντ' αὐτῶν
πεντήκοντα τάλαντα ἀργυρίου, καὶ ὑμῖν ὑποδεκόμεθα τὰ ἐπιόντα
ἐπὶ τὴν χώρην ἀποτρέψειν." Ταῦτά σφι ἐπαγγέλλοντο οἱ Θεσσα- **30**
λοί. οἱ γὰρ Φωκέες μοῦνοι τῶν ταύτηι ἀνθρώπων οὐκ ἐμήδιζον,
κατ' ἄλλο μὲν οὐδέν, ὡς ἐγὼ συμβαλλόμενος εὑρίσκω, κατὰ δὲ τὸ
ἔχθος τὸ Θεσσαλῶν· εἰ δὲ Θεσσαλοὶ τὰ Ἑλλήνων ηὖξον, ὡς ἐμοὶ 2
δοκέειν, ἐμήδιζον ἂν οἱ Φωκέες. οἳ ταῦτα ἐπαγγελλομένων Θεσ-
σαλῶν οὔτε δώσειν ἔφασαν χρήματα, παρέχειν τέ σφι Θεσσαλοῖσι
ὁμοίως μηδίζειν, εἰ ἄλλως βουλοίατο· ἀλλ' οὐκ ἔσεσθαι ἑκόντες εἶναι
προδόται τῆς Ἑλλάδος.

Ἐπειδὴ δὲ ἀνηνείχθησαν οὗτοι οἱ λόγοι, οὕτω δὴ οἱ Θεσσαλοὶ **31**
κεχολωμένοι τοῖσι Φωκεῦσι, ἐγένοντο ἡγεμόνες τῶι βαρβάρωι τῆς

ὁδοῦ. ἐκ μὲν δὴ τῆς Τρηχινίης ἐς τὴν Δωρίδα ἐσέβαλον· τῆς γὰρ Δωρίδος χώρης ποδεὼν στεινὸς ταύτηι κατατείνει, ὡς τριήκοντα σταδίων μάλιστά κηι εὖρος, κείμενος μεταξὺ τῆς τε Μηλίδος καὶ Φωκίδος χώρης, ἥ περ ἦν τὸ παλαιὸν Δρυοπίς· ἡ δὲ χώρη αὕτη ἐστὶ μητρόπολις Δωριέων τῶν ἐν Πελοποννήσωι. ταύτην ὦν τὴν Δωρίδα γῆν οὐκ ἐσίναντο ἐσβαλόντες οἱ βάρβαροι· ἐμήδιζόν τε γὰρ καὶ οὐκ ἐδόκεε Θεσσαλοῖσι.

32 Ὡς δὲ ἐκ τῆς Δωρίδος ἐς τὴν Φωκίδα ἐσέβαλον, αὐτοὺς μὲν τοὺς Φωκέας οὐκ αἱρέουσι. οἱ μὲν γὰρ τῶν Φωκέων ἐς τὰ ἄκρα τοῦ Παρνησσοῦ ἀνέβησαν· ἔστι δὲ καὶ ἐπιτηδέη δέξασθαι ὅμιλον τοῦ Παρνησσοῦ ἡ κορυφή <ἡ> κατὰ Νέωνα πόλιν, κειμένη ἐπ᾽ ἑωυτῆς (Τιθορέα οὔνομα αὐτῆι)· ἐς τὴν δὴ ἀνηνείκαντο καὶ αὐτοὶ ἀνέβησαν.
2 οἱ δὲ πλεῦνες αὐτῶν ἐς τοὺς Ὀζόλας Λοκροὺς ἐξεκομίσαντο, ἐς Ἄμφισσαν πόλιν τὴν ὑπὲρ τοῦ Κρισαίου πεδίου οἰκεομένην. οἱ δὲ βάρβαροι τὴν χώρην πᾶσαν ἐπέδραμον τὴν Φωκίδα· Θεσσαλοὶ γὰρ οὕτω ἦγον τὸν στρατόν· ὁκόσα δὲ ἐπέσχον, πάντα ἐπέφλεγον καὶ ἔκειρον,
33 καὶ ἐς τὰς πόλις ἐνιέντες πῦρ καὶ ἐς τὰ ἱρά. Πορευόμενοι γὰρ ταύτηι παρὰ τὸν Κηφισὸν ποταμὸν ἐδηίουν πάντα, καὶ κατὰ μὲν ἔκαυσαν Δρυμὸν πόλιν, κατὰ δὲ Χαράδραν καὶ Ἔρωχον καὶ Τεθρώνιον καὶ Ἀμφίκαιαν καὶ Νέωνα καὶ Πεδιέας καὶ Τριτέας καὶ Ἐλάτειαν καὶ Ὑάμπολιν καὶ Παραποταμίους καὶ Ἄβας, ἔνθα ἦν ἱρὸν Ἀπόλλωνος πλούσιον, θησαυροῖσί τε καὶ ἀναθήμασι πολλοῖσι κατεσκευασμένον· ἦν δὲ καὶ τότε καὶ νῦν ἔστι χρηστήριον αὐτόθι, καὶ τοῦτο τὸ ἱρὸν συλήσαντες ἐνέπρησαν. καί τινας διώκοντες εἷλον τῶν Φωκέων πρὸς τοῖσι ὄρεσι, καὶ γυναῖκάς τινας διέφθειραν μισγόμενοι ὑπὸ πλήθεος.

34–9 The Persian attack on Delphi

34 Παραποταμίους δὲ παραμειβόμενοι οἱ βάρβαροι, ἀπίκοντο ἐς Πανοπέας. ἐνθεῦτεν δὲ ἤδη διακρινομένη ἡ στρατιὴ αὐτῶν ἐσχίζετο. τὸ μὲν πλεῖστον καὶ δυνατώτατον τοῦ στρατοῦ ἅμα αὐτῶι Ξέρξηι πορευόμενον, ἐπ᾽ Ἀθήνας ἐσέβαλε ἐς Βοιωτούς, ἐς γῆν τὴν Ὀρχομενίων. Βοιωτῶν δὲ πᾶν τὸ πλῆθος ἐμήδιζε, τὰς δὲ πόλις αὐτῶν ἄνδρες Μακεδόνες διατεταγμένοι ἔσωιζον, ὑπὸ Ἀλεξάνδρου ἀποπεμφθέντες· ἔσωιζον δὲ τῆιδε, δῆλον βουλόμενοι ποιέειν Ξέρξηι ὅτι τὰ Μήδων Βοιωτοὶ φρονέοιεν.

35 Οὗτοι μὲν δὴ τῶν βαρβάρων ταύτηι ἐτράποντο· ἄλλοι δὲ αὐτῶν ἡγεμόνας ἔχοντες ὁρμέατο ἐπὶ τὸ ἱρὸν τὸ ἐν Δελφοῖσι, ἐν δεξιῆι τὴν Παρνησσὸν ἀπέργοντες. ὅσα δὲ καὶ οὗτοι ἐπέσχον τῆς

Φωκίδος, πάντα ἐσιναμώρεον· καὶ γὰρ τῶν Πανοπέων τὴν πόλιν
ἐνέπρησαν καὶ Δαυλίων καὶ Αἰολιδέων. ἐπορεύοντο δὲ ταύτηι, 2
ἀποσχισθέντες τῆς ἄλλης στρατιῆς τῶνδε εἵνεκα, ὅκως συλήσαν-
τες τὸ ἱρὸν τὸ ἐν Δελφοῖσι βασιλέϊ Ξέρξηι ἀποδέξαιεν τὰ χρήματα.
πάντα δ᾽ ἠπίστατο τὰ ἐν τῶι ἱρῶι ὅσα λόγου ἦν ἄξια Ξέρξης, ὡς
ἐγὼ πυνθάνομαι, ἄμεινον ἢ τὰ ἐν τοῖσι οἰκίοισι ἔλιπε, πολλῶν αἰεὶ
λεγόντων, καὶ μάλιστα τὰ Κροίσου τοῦ Ἀλυάττεω ἀναθήματα.

Οἱ δὲ Δελφοὶ πυνθανόμενοι ταῦτα ἐς πᾶσαν ἀρρωδίην ἀπίκα- **36**
το· ἐν δείματι δὲ μεγάλωι κατεστεῶτες, ἐμαντεύοντο περὶ τῶν ἱρῶν
χρημάτων, εἴτε σφέα κατὰ γῆς κατορύξωσι εἴτε ἐκκομίσωσι ἐς ἄλλην
χώρην. ὁ δὲ θεός σφεας οὐκ ἔα κινέειν, φὰς αὐτὸς ἱκανὸς εἶναι τῶν ἑωυ-
τοῦ προκατῆσθαι· Δελφοὶ δὲ ταῦτα ἀκούσαντες, σφέων αὐτῶν πέρι 2
ἐφρόντιζον. τέκνα μέν νυν καὶ γυναῖκας πέρην ἐς τὴν Ἀχαιίην διέπεμ-
ψαν· αὐτῶν δέ, οἱ μὲν πλεῖστοι ἀνέβησαν ἐς τοῦ Παρνησσοῦ τὰς
κορυφὰς καὶ ἐς τὸ Κωρύκιον ἄντρον ἀνηνείκαντο, οἱ δὲ ἐς Ἄμφισσαν
τὴν Λοκρίδα ὑπεξῆλθον. πάντες δὲ ὦν οἱ Δελφοὶ ἐξέλιπον τὴν πόλιν,
πλὴν ἑξήκοντα ἀνδρῶν καὶ τοῦ προφήτεω.

Ἐπεὶ δὲ ἀγχοῦ τε ἦσαν οἱ βάρβαροι ἐπιόντες καὶ ἀπώρων τὸ ἱρόν, **37**
ἐν τούτωι ὁ προφήτης, τῶι οὔνομα ἦν Ἀκήρατος, ὁρᾶι πρὸ τοῦ
νηοῦ ὅπλα προκείμενα ἔσωθεν ἐκ τοῦ μεγάρου ἐξενηνειγμένα ἱρά,
τῶν οὐκ ὅσιον ἦν ἅπτεσθαι ἀνθρώπων οὐδενί. ὁ μὲν δὴ ἤιε Δελφῶν 2
τοῖσι παρεοῦσι σημανέων τὸ τέρας. οἱ δὲ βάρβαροι, ἐπειδὴ ἐγίνοντο
ἐπειγόμενοι κατὰ τὸ ἱρὸν τῆς Προνηίης Ἀθηναίης, ἐπιγίνεταί σφι
τέρεα ἔτι μέζονα τοῦ πρὶν γενομένου τέρεος. θῶμα μὲν γὰρ καὶ
τοῦτο κάρτα ἐστί, ὅπλα ἀρήια αὐτόματα φανῆναι ἔξω προκείμενα
τοῦ νηοῦ· τὰ δὲ δὴ ἐπὶ τούτωι δεύτερα ἐπιγενόμενα καὶ διὰ πάντων
φασμάτων ἄξια θωμάσαι μάλιστα. ἐπεὶ γὰρ δὴ ἦσαν ἐπιόντες οἱ 3
βάρβαροι κατὰ τὸ ἱρὸν τῆς Προνηίης Ἀθηναίης, ἐν τούτωι ἐκ μὲν
τοῦ οὐρανοῦ κεραυνοὶ αὐτοῖσι ἐνέπιπτον, ἀπὸ δὲ τοῦ Παρνησσοῦ
ἀπορραγεῖσαι δύο κορυφαὶ ἐφέροντο πολλῶι πατάγωι ἐς αὐτούς,
καὶ κατέλαβον συχνούς σφεων, ἐκ δὲ τοῦ ἱροῦ τῆς Προνηίης βοή τε
καὶ ἀλαλαγμὸς ἐγίνετο. Συμμιγέντων δὲ τούτων πάντων, φόβος **38**
τοῖσι βαρβάροισι ἐνεπεπτώκεε. μαθόντες δὲ οἱ Δελφοὶ φεύγοντάς
σφεας, ἐπικαταβάντες ἀπέκτειναν πλῆθός τι αὐτῶν· οἱ δὲ περιεόντες
ἰθὺ Βοιωτῶν ἔφευγον. ἔλεγον δὲ οἱ ἀπονοστήσαντες οὗτοι τῶν βαρ-
βάρων, ὡς ἐγὼ πυνθάνομαι, ὡς πρὸς τούτοισι καὶ ἄλλα ὥρων θεῖα·
δύο γὰρ ὁπλίτας μέζονας ἢ κατ᾽ ἀνθρώπων φύσιν ἐόντας ἕπεσθαί
σφι κτείνοντας καὶ διώκοντας. Τούτους δὲ τοὺς δύο Δελφοὶ λέγουσι **39**

36.1 θεός σφεα Stein   37.3 κατέβαλον Reiske   38 ἐόντας Koen: ἔχοντας codd.

εἶναι ἐπιχωρίους ἥρωας, Φύλακόν τε καὶ Αὐτόνοον, τῶν τὰ τεμένεά
ἐστι περὶ τὸ ἱρόν, Φυλάκου μὲν παρ᾽ αὐτὴν τὴν ὁδὸν κατύπερθε
τοῦ ἱροῦ τῆς Προνηίης, Αὐτονόου δὲ πέλας τῆς Κασταλίης ὑπὸ τῆι
2 Ὑαμπείηι κορυφῆι. οἱ δὲ πεσόντες ἀπὸ τοῦ Παρνησσοῦ λίθοι ἔτι καὶ
ἐς ἡμέας ἦσαν σόοι, ἐν τῶι τεμένεϊ τῆς Προνηίης Ἀθηναίης κείμενοι,
ἐς τὸ ἐνέσκηψαν διὰ τῶν βαρβάρων φερόμενοι. τούτων μέν νυν τῶν
ἀνδρῶν αὕτη ἀπὸ τοῦ ἱροῦ ἀπαλλαγὴ γίνεται.

40–82 The prelude to Salamis

40–50.1 The abandoning of Athens; the Greek forces

40 Ὁ δὲ Ἑλλήνων ναυτικὸς στρατὸς ἀπὸ τοῦ Ἀρτεμισίου, Ἀθηναίων
δεηθέντων, ἐς Σαλαμῖνα κατίσχει τὰς νέας. τῶνδε δὲ εἵνεκα
προσεδεήθησαν αὐτῶν σχεῖν πρὸς Σαλαμῖνα Ἀθηναῖοι, ἵνα αὐτοὶ
παῖδάς τε καὶ γυναῖκας ὑπεξαγάγωνται ἐκ τῆς Ἀττικῆς, πρὸς δὲ
καὶ βουλεύσωνται τὸ ποιητέον αὐτοῖσι ἔσται. ἐπὶ γὰρ τοῖσι κατή-
κουσι πρήγμασι βουλὴν ἔμελλον ποιήσεσθαι, ὡς ἐψευσμένοι
2 γνώμης. δοκέοντες γὰρ εὑρήσειν Πελοποννησίους πανδημεὶ ἐν τῆι
Βοιωτίηι ὑποκατημένους τὸν βάρβαρον, τῶν μὲν εὗρον οὐδὲν
ἐόν, οἱ δὲ ἐπυνθάνοντο τὸν Ἰσθμὸν αὐτοὺς τειχέοντας, ὡς τὴν
Πελοπόννησον περὶ πλείστου τε ποιευμένους περιεῖναι καὶ ταύτην
ἔχοντας ἐν φυλακῆι, τὰ ἄλλα δὲ ἀπιέναι. ταῦτα πυνθανόμενοι οὕτω
δὴ προσεδεήθησάν σφεων σχεῖν πρὸς τὴν Σαλαμῖνα.

41 Οἱ μὲν δὴ ἄλλοι κατέσχον ἐς τὴν Σαλαμῖνα, Ἀθηναῖοι δὲ ἐς τὴν
ἑωυτῶν. μετὰ δὲ τὴν ἄπιξιν κήρυγμα ἐποιήσαντο, Ἀθηναίων τῆι τις
δύναται σώιζειν τέκνα τε καὶ τοὺς οἰκέτας· ἐνθαῦτα οἱ μὲν πλεῖστοι ἐς
2 Τροιζῆνα ἀπέστειλαν, οἱ δὲ ἐς Αἴγιναν, οἱ δὲ ἐς Σαλαμῖνα. ἔσπευσαν
δὲ ταῦτα ὑπεκθέσθαι, τῶι χρηστηρίωι τε βουλόμενοι ὑπηρετέειν
καὶ δὴ καὶ τοῦδε εἵνεκα οὐκ ἥκιστα· λέγουσι Ἀθηναῖοι ὄφιν μέγαν
φύλακα τῆς ἀκροπόλιος ἐνδιαιτᾶσθαι ἐν τῶι ἱρῶι· λέγουσί τε ταῦτα
καὶ δὴ καὶ ὡς ἐόντι ἐπιμήνια ἐπιτελέουσι προτιθέντες· τὰ δ᾽ ἐπιμήνια
3 μελιτόεσσά ἐστι. αὕτη δὴ ἡ μελιτόεσσα, ἐν τῶι πρόσθε αἰεὶ χρόνωι
ἀναισιμουμένη, τότε ἦν ἄψαυστος. σημηνάσης δὲ ταῦτα τῆς ἱρείης,
μᾶλλόν τι οἱ Ἀθηναῖοι καὶ προθυμότερον ἐξέλιπον τὴν πόλιν, ὡς καὶ
τῆς θεοῦ ἀπολελοιπυίης τὴν ἀκρόπολιν. ὡς δέ σφι πάντα ὑπεξέκειτο,
ἔπλεον ἐς τὸ στρατόπεδον.

42 Ἐπεὶ δὲ οἱ ἀπ᾽ Ἀρτεμισίου ἐς Σαλαμῖνα κατέσχον τὰς νέας,
συνέρρεε καὶ ὁ λοιπὸς πυνθανόμενος ὁ τῶν Ἑλλήνων ναυτικὸς

40.1 αὐτοῖσί ἐστι Powell   40.2 ὡς τὴν Stein: ε(ἰ)ς τὴν ABCP Ald.: τὴν Schaefer

στρατὸς ἐκ Τροιζῆνος· ἐς γὰρ Πώγωνα τὸν Τροιζηνίων λιμένα
προείρητο συλλέγεσθαι. συνελέχθησάν τε δὴ πολλῶι πλεῦνες νέες
ἢ ἐπ᾽ Ἀρτεμισίωι ἐναυμάχεον, καὶ ἀπὸ πολίων πλεύνων. ναύαρχος 2
μέν νυν ἐπῆν ὡυτὸς ὅς περ ἐπ᾽ Ἀρτεμισίωι, Εὐρυβιάδης ὁ Εὐρυ-
κλείδεω ἀνὴρ Σπαρτιήτης, οὐ μέντοι γένεός γε τοῦ βασιληίου
ἐών· νέας δὲ πολλῶι πλείστας τε καὶ ἄριστα πλεούσας παρείχοντο
Ἀθηναῖοι.

Ἐστρατεύοντο δὲ οἵδε· ἐκ μὲν Πελοποννήσου, Λακεδαιμόνιοι **43**
ἑκκαίδεκα νέας παρεχόμενοι, Κορίνθιοι δὲ τὸ αὐτὸ πλήρωμα παρεχό-
μενοι τὸ καὶ ἐπ᾽ Ἀρτεμισίωι· Σικυώνιοι δὲ πεντεκαίδεκα παρείχοντο
νέας, Ἐπιδαύριοι δὲ δέκα, Τροιζήνιοι δὲ πέντε, Ἑρμιονέες δὲ τρεῖς,
ἐόντες οὗτοι πλὴν Ἑρμιονέων Δωρικόν τε καὶ Μακεδνὸν ἔθνος, ἐξ
Ἐρινεοῦ τε καὶ Πίνδου καὶ τῆς Δρυοπίδος ὕστατα ὁρμηθέντες. οἱ δὲ
Ἑρμιονέες εἰσὶ Δρύοπες, ὑπὸ Ἡρακλέος τε καὶ Μηλιέων ἐκ τῆς νῦν
Δωρίδος καλεομένης χώρης ἐξαναστάντες.

Οὗτοι μέν νυν Πελοποννησίων ἐστρατεύοντο· οἵδε <δὲ> ἐκ τῆς **44**
ἔξω ἠπείρου, Ἀθηναῖοι μὲν πρὸς πάντας τοὺς ἄλλους παρεχόμενοι
νέας ὀγδώκοντα καὶ ἑκατόν, μοῦνοι. ἐν Σαλαμῖνι γὰρ οὐ συνε-
ναυμάχησαν Πλαταιέες Ἀθηναίοισι διὰ τοιόνδε τι πρῆγμα· ἀπαλ-
λασσομένων τῶν Ἑλλήνων ἀπὸ τοῦ Ἀρτεμισίου, ὡς ἐγίνοντο κατὰ
Χαλκίδα, οἱ Πλαταιέες, ἀποβάντες ἐς τὴν περαίην τῆς Βοιωτίης
χώρης, πρὸς ἐκκομιδὴν ἐτράποντο τῶν οἰκετέων. οὗτοι μέν νυν τού-
τους σώιζοντες ἐλείφθησαν. Ἀθηναῖοι δέ, ἐπὶ μὲν Πελασγῶν ἐχόντων 2
τὴν νῦν Ἑλλάδα καλεομένην ἦσαν Πελασγοί, ὀνομαζόμενοι Κραναοί·
ἐπὶ δὲ Κέκροπος βασιλέος ἐπεκλήθησαν Κεκροπίδαι· ἐκδεξα-
μένου δὲ Ἐρεχθέος τὴν ἀρχήν, Ἀθηναῖοι μετωνομάσθησαν· Ἴωνος
δὲ τοῦ Ξούθου στρατάρχεω γενομένου Ἀθηναίοισι, ἐκλήθησαν ἀπὸ
τούτου Ἴωνες. Μεγαρέες δὲ τὠυτὸ πλήρωμα παρείχοντο τὸ καὶ **45**
ἐπ᾽ Ἀρτεμισίωι, Ἀμπρακιῶται δὲ ἑπτὰ νέας ἔχοντες ἐπεβοήθησαν,
Λευκάδιοι δὲ τρεῖς, ἔθνος ἐόντες οὗτοι Δωρικὸν ἀπὸ Κορίνθου.

Νησιωτέων δέ, Αἰγινῆται τριήκοντα παρείχοντο· ἦσαν μέν νύν **46**
σφι καὶ ἄλλαι πεπληρωμέναι νέες, ἀλλὰ τῆισι μὲν τὴν ἑωυτῶν
ἐφύλασσον, τριήκοντα δὲ τῆισι ἄριστα πλεούσηισι ἐν Σαλαμῖνι
ἐναυμάχησαν. Αἰγινῆται δέ εἰσι Δωριέες ἀπὸ Ἐπιδαύρου· τῆι δὲ 2
νήσωι πρότερον οὔνομα ἦν Οἰνώνη. μετὰ δὲ Αἰγινήτας, Χαλκιδέες
τὰς ἐπ᾽ Ἀρτεμισίωι εἴκοσι παρεχόμενοι, καὶ Ἐρετριέες τὰς ἑπτά· οὗτοι
δὲ Ἴωνές εἰσι. μετὰ δὲ Κήιοι τὰς αὐτὰς παρεχόμενοι, ἔθνος ἐὸν Ἰωνικὸν
ἀπὸ Ἀθηνέων. Νάξιοι δὲ παρείχοντο τέσσερας, ἀποπεμφθέντες μὲν 3

46.1 <δυώδεκα> post ἄλλαι add. van Herwerden, post νέες Stein

ἐς τοὺς Μήδους ὑπὸ τῶν πολιητέων, κατά περ ὦλλοι νησιῶται,
ἀλογήσαντες δὲ τῶν ἐντολέων, ἀπίκατο ἐς τοὺς Ἕλληνας, Δημοκρί-
του σπεύσαντος, ἀνδρὸς τῶν ἀστῶν δοκίμου καὶ τότε τριηραρχέον-
4 τος. Νάξιοι δέ εἰσι Ἴωνες ἀπὸ Ἀθηνέων γεγονότες. Στυρέες δὲ τὰς
αὐτὰς παρείχοντο νέας τὰς καὶ ἐπ᾽ Ἀρτεμισίωι· Κύθνιοι δὲ μίαν καὶ
πεντηκόντερον, ἐόντες συναμφότεροι οὗτοι Δρύοπες. καὶ Σερίφιοί τε
καὶ Σίφνιοι καὶ Μήλιοι ἐστρατεύοντο· οὗτοι γὰρ οὐκ ἔδοσαν μοῦνοι
νησιωτέων τῶι βαρβάρωι γῆν τε καὶ ὕδωρ.

47 Οὗτοι μὲν ἅπαντες, ἐντὸς οἰκημένοι Θεσπρωτῶν καὶ Ἀχέροντος
ποταμοῦ, ἐστρατεύοντο· Θεσπρωτοὶ γάρ εἰσι ὁμουρέοντες Ἀμπρα-
κιώτηισι καὶ Λευκαδίοισι, οἳ ἐξ ἐσχατέων χωρέων ἐστρατεύοντο.
τῶν δὲ ἐκτὸς τούτων οἰκημένων, Κροτωνιῆται μοῦνοι ἦσαν οἳ
ἐβοήθησαν τῆι Ἑλλάδι κινδυνευούσηι, μιῆι νηὶ τῆς ἦρχε ἀνὴρ
48 τρὶς πυθιονίκης Φάυλλος· Κροτωνιῆται δὲ γένος εἰσὶ Ἀχαιοί. Οἱ
μέν νυν ἄλλοι τριήρεας παρεχόμενοι ἐστρατεύοντο, Μήλιοι δὲ καὶ
Σίφνιοι καὶ Σερίφιοι πεντηκοντέρους· Μήλιοι μέν, γένος ἐόντες ἀπὸ
Λακεδαίμονος, δύο παρείχοντο· Σίφνιοι δὲ καὶ Σερίφιοι, Ἴωνες ἐόν-
τες ἀπ᾽ Ἀθηνέων, μίαν ἑκάτεροι. ἀριθμὸς δὲ ἐγένετο ὁ πᾶς τῶν
νεῶν, πάρεξ τῶν πεντηκοντέρων, τριηκόσιαι καὶ ἑβδομήκοντα καὶ
ὀκτώ.

49 Ὡς δὲ ἐς τὴν Σαλαμῖνα συνῆλθον οἱ στρατηγοὶ ἀπὸ τῶν εἰρημένων
πολίων, ἐβουλεύοντο, προθέντος Εὐρυβιάδεω γνώμην ἀποφαί-
νεσθαι τὸν βουλόμενον, ὅκου δοκέοι ἐπιτηδεότατον εἶναι ναυμαχίην
ποιέεσθαι, τῶν αὐτοὶ χωρέων ἐγκρατέες εἰσί· ἡ γὰρ Ἀττικὴ ἀπεῖτο
2 ἤδη, τῶν δὲ λοιπέων πέρι προετίθεε. αἱ γνῶμαι δὲ τῶν λεγόν-
των αἱ πλεῖσται συνεξέπιπτον πρὸς τὸν Ἰσθμὸν πλώσαντας ναυ-
μαχέειν πρὸ τῆς Πελοποννήσου, ἐπιλέγοντες τὸν λόγον τόνδε, ὡς
εἰ νικηθέωσι τῆι ναυμαχίηι, ἐν Σαλαμῖνι μὲν ἐόντες πολιορκήσον-
ται ἐν νήσωι, ἵνα σφι τιμωρίη οὐδεμία ἐπιφανήσεται, πρὸς δὲ τῶι
50 Ἰσθμῶι ἐς τοὺς ἑωυτῶν ἐξοίσονται. Ταῦτα τῶν ἀπὸ Πελοποννήσου
στρατηγῶν ἐπιλεγομένων, ἐληλύθεε ἀνὴρ Ἀθηναῖος ἀγγέλλων ἥκειν
τὸν βάρβαρον ἐς τὴν Ἀττικὴν καὶ πᾶσαν αὐτὴν πυρπολέεσθαι.

50.2–55 The capture and burning of Athens

2 ὁ γὰρ διὰ Βοιωτῶν τραπόμενος στρατὸς ἅμα Ξέρξηι, ἐμπρήσας
Θεσπιέων τὴν πόλιν, αὐτῶν ἐκλελοιπότων ἐς Πελοπόννησον, καὶ
τὴν Πλαταιέων ὡσαύτως, ἧκέ τε ἐς τὰς Ἀθήνας καὶ πάντα ἐκεῖνα
ἐδήιου. ἐνέπρησε δὲ Θέσπειάν τε καὶ Πλάταιαν, πυθόμενος Θηβαίων
51 ὅτι οὐκ ἐμήδιζον. Ἀπὸ δὲ τῆς διαβάσιος τοῦ Ἑλλησπόντου, ἔνθεν

πορεύεσθαι ἤρξαντο οἱ βάρβαροι, ἕνα αὐτοῦ διατρίψαντες μῆνα, ἐν τῶι διέβαινον ἐς τὴν Εὐρώπην, ἐν τρισὶ ἑτέροισι μησὶ ἐγένοντο ἐν τῆι Ἀττικῆι, Καλλιάδεω ἄρχοντος Ἀθηναίοισι. καὶ αἱρέουσι ἔρημον τὸ 2
ἄστυ, καί τινας ὀλίγους εὑρίσκουσι τῶν Ἀθηναίων ἐν τῶι ἱρῶι ἐόντας, ταμίας τε τοῦ ἱροῦ καὶ πένητας ἀνθρώπους, οἳ φραξάμενοι τὴν ἀκρόπολιν θύρηισί τε καὶ ξύλοισι ἠμύνοντο τοὺς ἐπιόντας, ἅμα μὲν ὑπ᾽ ἀσθενείης βίου οὐκ ἐκχωρήσαντες ἐς Σαλαμῖνα, πρὸς δὲ καὶ αὐτοὶ δοκέοντες ἐξευρηκέναι τὸ μαντήιον, τὸ ἡ Πυθίη σφι ἔχρησε, τὸ ξύλινον τεῖχος ἀνάλωτον ἔσεσθαι· αὐτὸ δὴ τοῦτο εἶναι τὸ κρησφύγετον κατὰ τὸ μαντήιον καὶ οὐ τὰς νέας.

Οἱ δὲ Πέρσαι, ἱζόμενοι ἐπὶ τὸν καταντίον τῆς ἀκροπόλιος ὄχθον, 52
τὸν Ἀθηναῖοι καλέουσι Ἀρήιον πάγον, ἐπολιόρκεον τρόπον τοιόνδε· ὅκως στυππεῖον περὶ τοὺς ὀϊστοὺς περιθέντες ἅψειαν, ἐτόξευον ἐς τὸ φράγμα. ἐνθαῦτα Ἀθηναίων οἱ πολιορκεόμενοι ὅμως ἠμύνοντο, καίπερ ἐς τὸ ἔσχατον κακοῦ ἀπιγμένοι, καὶ τοῦ φράγματος προδεδωκότος. οὐδὲ λόγους τῶν Πεισιστρατιδέων προσφερόντων περὶ 2
ὁμολογίης ἐνεδέκοντο, ἀμυνόμενοι δέ, ἄλλα τε ἀντεμηχανῶντο καὶ δὴ καί, προσιόντων τῶν βαρβάρων πρὸς τὰς πύλας, ὀλοιτρόχους ἀπίεσαν, ὥστε Ξέρξην ἐπὶ χρόνον συχνὸν ἀπορίηισι ἐνέχεσθαι, οὐ δυνάμενόν σφεας ἑλεῖν. Χρόνωι δ᾽ ἐκ τῶν ἀπόρων ἐφάνη δή τις 53
ἔξοδος τοῖσι βαρβάροισι· ἔδεε γὰρ κατὰ τὸ θεοπρόπιον πᾶσαν τὴν Ἀττικὴν τὴν ἐν τῆι ἠπείρωι γενέσθαι ὑπὸ Πέρσηισι. ἔμπροσθε ὦν τῆς ἀκροπόλιος, ὄπισθε δὲ τῶν πυλέων καὶ τῆς ἀνόδου, τῆι δὴ οὔτε τις ἐφύλασσε, οὔτ᾽ ἂν ἤλπισε μή κοτέ τις κατὰ ταῦτα ἀναβαίη ἀνθρώπων, ταύτηι ἀνέβησάν τινες κατὰ τὸ ἱρὸν τῆς Κέκροπος θυγατρὸς Ἀγλαύρου, καίπερ ἀποκρήμνου ἐόντος τοῦ χώρου. ὡς δὲ 2
εἶδον αὐτοὺς ἀναβεβηκότας οἱ Ἀθηναῖοι ἐπὶ τὴν ἀκρόπολιν, οἱ μὲν ἐρρίπτεον ἑωυτοὺς κατὰ τοῦ τείχεος κάτω καὶ διεφθείροντο, οἱ δὲ ἐς τὸ μέγαρον κατέφευγον. τῶν δὲ Περσέων οἱ ἀναβεβηκότες, πρῶτον μὲν ἐτράποντο πρὸς τὰς πύλας· ταύτας δὲ ἀνοίξαντες, τοὺς ἱκέτας ἐφόνευον. ἐπεὶ δέ σφι πάντες κατέστρωντο, τὸ ἱρὸν συλήσαντες, ἐνέπρησαν πᾶσαν τὴν ἀκρόπολιν.

Σχὼν δὲ παντελέως τὰς Ἀθήνας, Ξέρξης ἀπέπεμψε ἐς Σοῦσα 54
ἄγγελον ἱππέα, Ἀρταβάνωι ἀγγελέοντα τὴν παρεοῦσάν σφι εὐπρηξίην. ἀπὸ δὲ τῆς πέμψιος τοῦ κήρυκος δευτέρηι ἡμέρηι, συγκαλέσας Ἀθηναίων τοὺς φυγάδας, ἑωυτῶι δὲ ἑπομένους, ἐκέλευε τρόπωι τῶι σφετέρωι θῦσαι τὰ ἱρά, ἀναβάντας ἐς τὴν ἀκρόπολιν, εἴτε δὴ ὦν ὄψιν τινὰ ἰδὼν ἐνυπνίου ἐνετέλλετο ταῦτα, εἴτε καὶ ἐνθύμιόν οἱ ἐγένετο ἐμπρήσαντι τὸ ἱρόν. οἱ δὲ φυγάδες τῶν Ἀθηναίων ἐποίησαν τὰ ἐντεταλμένα. Τοῦ δὲ εἵνεκεν τούτων ἐπεμνήσθην, 55

φράσω. ἔστι ἐν τῆι ἀκροπόλι ταύτηι Ἐρεχθέος τοῦ γηγενέος λεγομένου εἶναι νηός, ἐν τῶι ἐλαίη τε καὶ θάλασσα ἔνι, τὰ λόγος παρὰ Ἀθηναίων Ποσειδέωνά τε καὶ Ἀθηναίην, ἐρίσαντας περὶ τῆς χώρης, μαρτύρια θέσθαι. ταύτην ὦν τὴν ἐλαίην ἅμα τῶι ἄλλωι ἱρῶι κατέλαβε ἐμπρησθῆναι ὑπὸ τῶν βαρβάρων· δευτέρηι δὲ ἡμέρηι ἀπὸ τῆς ἐμπρήσιος, Ἀθηναίων οἱ θύειν ὑπὸ βασιλέος κελευόμενοι, ὡς ἀνέβησαν ἐς τὸ ἱρόν, ὥρων βλαστὸν ἐκ τοῦ στελέχεος ὅσον τε πηχυαῖον ἀναδεδραμηκότα. οὗτοι μέν νυν ταῦτα ἔφρασαν.

56–63 Greek despondency and deliberations

56 Οἱ δὲ ἐν Σαλαμῖνι Ἕλληνες, ὥς σφι ἐξηγγέλθη ὡς ἔσχε τὰ περὶ τὴν Ἀθηναίων ἀκρόπολιν, ἐς τοσοῦτον θόρυβον ἀπίκοντο, ὥστε ἔνιοι τῶν στρατηγῶν οὐδὲ κυρωθῆναι ἔμενον τὸ προκείμενον πρῆγμα, ἀλλ᾽ἔς τε τὰς νέας ἐσέπιπτον καὶ ἱστία ἀείροντο ὡς ἀποθευσόμενοι· τοῖσί τε ὑπολειπομένοισι αὐτῶν ἐκυρώθη πρὸ τοῦ Ἰσθμοῦ ναυμαχέειν. νύξ τε ἐγίνετο, καὶ οἳ διαλυθέντες ἐκ τοῦ συνεδρίου ἐσέβαινον ἐς τὰς νέας.

57 Ἐνθαῦτα δὴ Θεμιστοκλέα ἀπικόμενον ἐπὶ τὴν νέα εἴρετο
Μνησίφιλος, ἀνὴρ Ἀθηναῖος, ὅ τι σφι εἴη βεβουλευμένον. πυθόμενος
δὲ πρὸς αὐτοῦ, ὡς εἴη δεδογμένον ἀνάγειν τὰς νέας πρὸς τὸν Ἰσθμὸν
2 καὶ πρὸ τῆς Πελοποννήσου ναυμαχέειν, εἶπε· "οὔ τοι ἄρα, ἢν ἀπάρωσι [τὰς νέας] ἀπὸ Σαλαμῖνος, περὶ οὐδεμιῆς ἔτι πατρίδος ναυμαχήσεις· κατὰ γὰρ πόλις ἕκαστοι τρέψονται, καὶ οὔτε σφέας Εὐρυβιάδης κατέχειν δυνήσεται οὔτε τις ἀνθρώπων ἄλλος, ὥστε μὴ οὐ διασκεδασθῆναι τὴν στρατιήν· ἀπολέεταί τε ἡ Ἑλλὰς ἀβουλίηισι. ἀλλ᾽εἴ τις ἔστι μηχανή, ἴθι καὶ πειρῶ διαχέαι τὰ βεβουλευμένα, ἤν κως δύνηι ἀναγνῶσαι Εὐρυβιάδην μεταβουλεύσασθαι, ὥστε αὐτοῦ μένειν."

58 Κάρτα τε τῶι Θεμιστοκλέι ἤρεσε ἡ ὑποθήκη, καὶ οὐδὲν πρὸς
ταῦτα ἀμειψάμενος ἤιε ἐπὶ τὴν νέα τὴν Εὐρυβιάδεω. ἀπικόμενος
δέ, ἔφη ἐθέλειν οἱ κοινόν τι πρῆγμα συμμεῖξαι· ὁ δ᾽αὐτὸν ἐς τὴν νέα
2 ἐκέλευε ἐσβάντα λέγειν, εἴ τι θέλοι. ἐνθαῦτα ὁ Θεμιστοκλέης παριζόμενός οἱ καταλέγει ἐκεῖνά τε πάντα, τὰ ἤκουσε Μνησιφίλου, ἑωυτοῦ ποιεύμενος, καὶ ἄλλα πολλὰ προστιθείς, ἐς ὃ ἀνέγνωσε, χρηίζων ἔκ τε τῆς νεὸς ἐκβῆναι, συλλέξαι τε τοὺς στρατηγοὺς ἐς τὸ συνέδριον.

59 Ὡς δὲ ἄρα συνελέχθησαν, πρὶν ἢ τὸν Εὐρυβιάδην προθεῖναι τὸν λόγον τῶν εἵνεκα συνήγαγε τοὺς στρατηγούς, πολλὸς ἦν ὁ

57.2 τὰς νέας del. Stein 57.2 περὶ οὐδὲ μιῆς codd. (περὶ δὲ οὐδὲ μιῆς R): οὐδὲ περὶ μιῆς Plut. 59 τὸν λόγον del. Powell

Θεμιστοκλέης ἐν τοῖσι λόγοισι, οἷα κάρτα δεόμενος. λέγοντος δὲ
αὐτοῦ, ὁ Κορίνθιος στρατηγὸς Ἀδείμαντος ὁ Ὠκύτου εἶπε· "ὦ
Θεμιστόκλεες, ἐν τοῖσι ἀγῶσι οἱ προεξανιστάμενοι ῥαπίζονται." ὁ
δὲ ἀπολυόμενος ἔφη· "οἱ δέ γε ἐγκαταλειπόμενοι οὐ στεφανοῦνται."
Τότε μὲν ἠπίως [πρὸς] τὸν Κορίνθιον ἀμείψατο, πρὸς δὲ τὸν Εὐρυ- **60**
βιάδην ἔλεγε ἐκείνων μὲν οὐκέτι οὐδὲν τῶν πρότερον λεχθέντων,
ὡς ἐπεὰν ἀπάρωσι ἀπὸ Σαλαμῖνος διαδρήσονται· παρεόντων γὰρ
τῶν συμμάχων, οὐκ ἔφερέ οἱ κόσμον οὐδένα κατηγορέειν· ὁ δὲ ἄλλου
λόγου εἴχετο, λέγων τάδε·

"Ἐν σοὶ νῦν ἐστι σῶσαι τὴν Ἑλλάδα, ἢν ἐμοὶ πείθηι ναυμαχίην α
αὐτοῦ μένων ποιέεσθαι, μηδὲ πειθόμενος τούτων τοῖσι λόγοισι
ἀναζεύξηις πρὸς τὸν Ἰσθμὸν τὰς νέας. ἀντίθες γὰρ ἑκάτερον ἀκούσας.
πρὸς μὲν τῶι Ἰσθμῶι συμβάλλων, ἐν πελάγεϊ ἀναπεπταμένωι ναυ-
μαχήσεις, [ἐς] τὸ ἥκιστα ἡμῖν σύμφορόν ἐστι νέας ἔχουσι βαρυτέρας
καὶ ἀριθμὸν ἐλάσσονας· τοῦτο δὲ ἀπολέεις Σαλαμῖνά τε καὶ Μέγαρα
καὶ Αἴγιναν, ἤν περ καὶ τὰ ἄλλα εὐτυχήσωμεν. ἅμα δὲ τῶι ναυτικῶι
αὐτῶν ἕψεται καὶ ὁ πεζὸς στρατός, καὶ οὕτω σφέας αὐτὸς ἄξεις ἐπὶ
τὴν Πελοπόννησον, κινδυνεύσεις τε ἁπάσηι τῆι Ἑλλάδι.

Ἢν δὲ τὰ ἐγὼ λέγω ποιήσηις, τοσάδε ἐν αὐτοῖσι χρηστὰ εὑρή- β
σεις· πρῶτα μὲν ἐν στεινῶι συμβάλλοντες νηυσὶ ὀλίγηισι πρὸς πολ-
λάς, ἢν τὰ οἰκότα ἐκ τοῦ πολέμου ἐκβαίνηι, πολλὸν κρατήσομεν· τὸ
γὰρ ἐν στεινῶι ναυμαχέειν πρὸς ἡμέων ἐστί, ἐν εὐρυχωρίηι δὲ πρὸς
ἐκείνων. αὖτις δὲ Σαλαμὶς περιγίνεται, ἐς τὴν ἡμῖν ὑπέκκειται τέκνα τε
καὶ γυναῖκες. καὶ μὲν καὶ τόδε ἐν αὐτοῖσι ἔνεστι, τοῦ καὶ περιέχεσθε
μάλιστα· ὁμοίως αὐτοῦ τε μένων προναυμαχήσεις Πελοποννήσου
καὶ πρὸς τῶι Ἰσθμῶι, οὐδέ σφεας, εἴ περ εὖ φρονέεις, ἄξεις ἐπὶ τὴν
Πελοπόννησον.

Ἢν δέ γε τὰ ἐγὼ ἐλπίζω γένηται, καὶ νικήσωμεν τῆισι νηυσί, γ
οὔτε ὑμῖν ἐς τὸν Ἰσθμὸν παρέσονται οἱ βάρβαροι, οὔτε προβήσον-
ται ἑκαστέρω τῆς Ἀττικῆς, ἀπίασί τε οὐδενὶ κόσμωι, Μεγάροισί
τε κερδανέομεν περιεοῦσι καὶ Αἰγίνηι καὶ Σαλαμῖνι, ἐν τῆι ἡμῖν
καὶ λόγιόν ἐστι τῶν ἐχθρῶν κατύπερθε γενέσθαι. οἰκότα μέν νυν
βουλευομένοισι ἀνθρώποισι ὡς τὸ ἐπίπαν ἐθέλει γίνεσθαι· μὴ δὲ
οἰκότα βουλευομένοισι οὐκ ἐθέλει οὐδὲ ὁ θεὸς προσχωρέειν πρὸς τὰς
ἀνθρωπηίας γνώμας."

Ταῦτα λέγοντος Θεμιστοκλέος, αὖτις ὁ Κορίνθιος Ἀδείμαντος **61**
ἐπεφέρετο, σιγᾶν τε κελεύων τῶι μὴ ἔστι πατρίς, καὶ Εὐρυβιάδην οὐκ

60.1 πρός del. Krueger 60α λόγοισι Krueger, Blakesley: λέγουσι (ν) codd.
60α ἐς del. Krueger

ἐῶν ἐπιψηφίζειν ἀπόλι ἀνδρί· πόλιν γὰρ τὸν Θεμιστοκλέα παρεχό-
μενον οὕτω ἐκέλευε γνώμας συμβάλλεσθαι. ταῦτα δέ οἱ προέφερε,
2 ὅτι ἡλώκεσάν τε καὶ κατείχοντο αἱ Ἀθῆναι. τότε δὴ ὁ Θεμιστοκλέης
κεῖνόν τε καὶ τοὺς Κορινθίους πολλά τε καὶ κακὰ ἔλεγε, ἑωυτοῖσι τε
ἐδήλου λόγωι ὡς εἴη καὶ πόλις καὶ γῆ μέζων ἤ περ ἐκείνοισι, ἔστ᾽
ἂν διηκόσιαι νέες σφι ἔωσι πεπληρωμέναι· οὐδαμοὺς γὰρ Ἑλλήνων
αὐτοὺς ἐπιόντας ἀποκρούσεσθαι.

62 Σημαίνων δὲ ταῦτα, τῶι λόγωι διέβαινε ἐς Εὐρυβιάδην, λέγων
μᾶλλον ἐπεστραμμένα· "σὺ εἰ <μὲν> μενέεις αὐτοῦ καὶ μένων ἔσεαι
ἀνὴρ ἀγαθός· εἰ δὲ μή, ἀνατρέψεις τὴν Ἑλλάδα· τὸ πᾶν γὰρ ἡμῖν
2 τοῦ πολέμου φέρουσι αἱ νέες. ἀλλ᾽ ἐμοὶ πείθεο. εἰ δὲ ταῦτα μὴ
ποιήσηις, ἡμεῖς μέν, ὡς ἔχομεν, ἀναλαβόντες τοὺς οἰκέτας κομιεύμεθα
ἐς Σῖριν τὴν ἐν Ἰταλίηι, ἥ περ ἡμετέρη τέ ἐστι ἐκ παλαιοῦ ἔτι,
καὶ τὰ λόγια λέγει ὑπ᾽ ἡμέων αὐτὴν δεῖν κτισθῆναι· ὑμεῖς δὲ συμ-
63 μάχων τοιῶνδε μουνωθέντες, μεμνήσεσθε τῶν ἐμῶν λόγων." Ταῦτα
δὲ Θεμιστοκλέος λέγοντος, ἀνεδιδάσκετο Εὐρυβιάδης. δοκέειν δέ
μοι, ἀρρωδήσας μάλιστα τοὺς Ἀθηναίους ἀνεδιδάσκετο, μή σφεας
ἀπολίπωσι, ἢν πρὸς τὸν Ἰσθμὸν ἀγάγηι τὰς νέας· ἀπολιπόντων
γὰρ Ἀθηναίων, οὐκέτι ἐγίνοντο ἀξιόμαχοι οἱ λοιποί. ταύτην δὲ
αἱρέεται τὴν γνώμην, αὐτοῦ μένοντας διαναυμαχέειν.

64–5 Divine manifestations

64 Οὕτω μὲν οἱ περὶ Σαλαμῖνα ἔπεσι ἀκροβολισάμενοι, ἐπείτε Εὐρυ-
βιάδηι ἔδοξε, αὐτοῦ παρεσκευάζοντο ὡς ναυμαχήσοντες. ἡμέρη τε
ἐγίνετο, καὶ ἅμα τῶι ἡλίωι ἀνιόντι σεισμὸς ἐγένετο ἔν τε τῆι γῆι καὶ
2 τῆι θαλάσσηι. ἔδοξε δέ σφι εὔξασθαι τοῖσι θεοῖσι καὶ ἐπικαλέσασθαι
τοὺς Αἰακίδας συμμάχους. ὡς δέ σφι ἔδοξε, καὶ ἐποίευν ταῦτα· εὐξά-
μενοι γὰρ πᾶσι τοῖσι θεοῖσι, αὐτόθεν μὲν ἐκ Σαλαμῖνος Αἴαντά τε καὶ
Τελαμῶνα ἐπεκαλέοντο, ἐπὶ δὲ Αἰακὸν καὶ τοὺς ἄλλους Αἰακίδας νέα
ἀπέστελλον ἐς Αἴγιναν.

65 Ἔφη δὲ Δίκαιος ὁ Θεοκύδεος, ἀνὴρ Ἀθηναῖος, φυγάς τε καὶ παρὰ
Μήδοισι λόγιμος γενόμενος, τοῦτον τὸν χρόνον ἐπείτε ἐκείρετο ἡ
Ἀττικὴ χώρη ὑπὸ τοῦ πεζοῦ στρατοῦ τοῦ Ξέρξεω, ἐοῦσα ἔρημος
Ἀθηναίων, τυχεῖν τότε ἐὼν ἅμα Δημαρήτωι τῶι Λακεδαιμονίωι ἐν
τῶι Θριασίωι πεδίωι. ἰδεῖν δὲ κονιορτὸν χωρέοντα ἀπ᾽ Ἐλευσῖνος
ὡς ἀνδρῶν μάλιστά κηι τρισμυρίων· ἀποθωμάζειν τέ σφεας τὸν

61.2 ἀποκρούσεσθαι BRSV: ἀποκρούεσθαι rell.: (fort. <ἂν>) ἀποκρούσασθαι Powell
62.1 <μέν> add. Werfer

κονιορτόν, ὅτεων κοτὲ εἴη ἀνθρώπων, καὶ πρόκατε φωνῆς ἀκούειν, καί οἱ φαίνεσθαι τὴν φωνὴν εἶναι τὸν μυστικὸν ἴακχον. εἶναι δ᾽ 2
ἀδαήμονα τῶν ἱρῶν τῶν ἐν Ἐλευσῖνι γινομένων τὸν Δημάρητον, εἰρέσθαι τε αὐτὸν, ὅ τι τὸ φθεγγόμενον εἴη τοῦτο. αὐτὸς δὲ εἰπεῖν· "Δημάρητε, οὐκ ἔστι ὅκως οὐ μέγα τι σίνος ἔσται τῆι βασιλέος στρατιῆι. τάδε γὰρ ἀρίδηλα, ἐρήμου ἐούσης τῆς Ἀττικῆς, ὅτι θεῖον τὸ φθεγγόμενον, ἀπ᾽ Ἐλευσῖνος ἰὸν ἐς τιμωρίην Ἀθηναίοισί τε καὶ τοῖσι συμμάχοισι. καὶ ἢν μέν γε κατασκήψηι ἐς τὴν Πελοπόννησον, 3
κίνδυνος αὐτῶι τε βασιλέϊ καὶ τῆι στρατιῆι τῆι ἐν τῆι ἠπείρωι ἔσται· ἢν δὲ ἐπὶ τὰς νέας τράπηται τὰς ἐν Σαλαμῖνι, τὸν ναυτικὸν στρατὸν κινδυνεύσει βασιλεὺς ἀποβαλεῖν. τὴν δὲ ὁρτὴν ταύτην 4
ἄγουσι Ἀθηναῖοι ἀνὰ πάντα ἔτεα τῆι Μητρὶ καὶ τῆι Κούρηι, καὶ αὐτῶν τε ὁ βουλόμενος καὶ τῶν ἄλλων Ἑλλήνων μυεῖται· καὶ τὴν φωνὴν τῆς ἀκούεις ἐν ταύτηι τῆι ὁρτῆι ἰακχάζουσι." πρὸς ταῦτα εἰπεῖν Δημάρητον· "σίγα τε καὶ μηδενὶ ἄλλωι τὸν λόγον τοῦτον εἴπηις. ἢν γάρ τοι ἐς βασιλέα ἀνενειχθῆι τὰ ἔπεα ταῦτα, 5
ἀποβαλέεις τὴν κεφαλήν, καί σε οὔτε ἐγὼ δυνήσομαι ῥύσασθαι οὔτ᾽ ἄλλος ἀνθρώπων οὐδὲ εἷς. ἀλλ᾽ ἔχ᾽ ἥσυχος, περὶ δὲ στρατιῆς τῆσδε θεοῖσι μελήσει." τὸν μὲν δὴ ταῦτα παραινέειν, ἐκ δὲ τοῦ κονιορ- 6
τοῦ καὶ τῆς φωνῆς γενέσθαι νέφος καὶ μεταρσιωθὲν φέρεσθαι ἐπὶ Σαλαμῖνος ἐς τὸ στρατόπεδον τὸ τῶν Ἑλλήνων. οὕτω δὴ αὐτοὺς μαθεῖν ὅτι τὸ ναυτικὸν τὸ Ξέρξεω ἀπολέεσθαι μέλλοι. ταῦτα μὲν Δίκαιος ὁ Θεοκύδεος ἔλεγε, Δημαρήτου τε καὶ ἄλλων μαρτύρων καταπτόμενος.

66–70 Persian deliberations

Οἱ δὲ ἐς τὸν Ξέρξεω ναυτικὸν στρατὸν ταχθέντες, ἐπειδὴ ἐκ Τρηχῖνος **66**
θεησάμενοι τὸ τρῶμα τὸ Λακωνικὸν διέβησαν ἐς τὴν Ἱστιαίην, ἐπισχόντες ἡμέρας τρεῖς, ἔπλεον δι᾽ Εὐρίπου, καὶ ἐν ἑτέρηισι τρισὶ ἡμέρηισι ἐγένοντο ἐν Φαλήρωι. ὡς μὲν ἐμοὶ δοκέειν, οὐκ ἐλάσσονες ἐόντες ἀριθμὸν ἐσέβαλον ἐς τὰς Ἀθήνας, κατά τε ἤπειρον καὶ τῆισι νηυσὶ ἀπικόμενοι, ἢ ἐπί τε Σηπιάδα ἀπίκοντο καὶ ἐς Θερμοπύλας. ἀντιθήσω γὰρ τοῖσί τε ὑπὸ τοῦ χειμῶνος αὐτῶν 2
ἀπολομένοισι καὶ τοῖσι ἐν Θερμοπύληισι καὶ τῆισι ἐπ᾽ Ἀρτεμισίωι ναυμαχίηισι τούσδε τοὺς τότε οὔκω ἑπομένους βασιλέϊ, Μηλιέας καὶ Δωριέας καὶ Λοκροὺς καὶ Βοιωτούς, πανστρατιῆι ἑπομένους πλὴν Θεσπιέων καὶ Πλαταιέων, καὶ μάλα Καρυστίους τε καὶ Ἀνδρίους καὶ Τηνίους τε καὶ τοὺς λοιποὺς νησιώτας πάντας, πλὴν τῶν πέντε πολίων τῶν ἐπεμνήσθην πρότερον τὰ οὐνόματα. ὅσωι γὰρ δὴ

προέβαινε ἐσωτέρω τῆς Ἑλλάδος ὁ Πέρσης, τοσούτωι πλέω ἔθνεά οἱ εἵπετο.

67 Ἐπεὶ ὦν ἀπίκατο ἐς τὰς Ἀθήνας πάντες οὗτοι πλὴν Παρίων (Πάριοι δὲ ὑπολειφθέντες ἐν Κύθνωι ἐκαραδόκεον τὸν πόλεμον, κῆι ἀποβήσεται), οἱ δὲ λοιποὶ ὡς ἀπίκοντο ἐς τὸ Φάληρον, ἐνθαῦτα κατέβη αὐτὸς Ξέρξης ἐπὶ τὰς νέας, ἐθέλων σφι συμμεῖξαί
2 τε καὶ πυθέσθαι τῶν ἐπιπλεόντων τὰς γνώμας. ἐπεὶ δὲ ἀπικόμενος προΐζετο, παρῆσαν μετάπεμπτοι οἱ τῶν ἐθνέων τῶν σφετέρων τύραννοι καὶ ταξίαρχοι ἀπὸ τῶν νεῶν, καὶ ἵζοντο ὥς σφι βασιλεὺς ἑκάστωι τιμὴν ἐδεδώκεε, πρῶτος μὲν ὁ Σιδώνιος βασιλεύς, μετὰ δὲ ὁ Τύριος, ἐπὶ δὲ ὦλλοι. ὡς δὲ κόσμωι ἐπεξῆς ἵζοντο, πέμψας Ξέρξης Μαρδόνιον, εἰρώτα ἀποπειρώμενος ἑκάστου εἰ ναυμαχίην ποιέοιτο.

68 Ἐπεὶ δὲ περιιὼν εἰρώτα ὁ Μαρδόνιος, ἀρξάμενος ἀπὸ τοῦ Σιδωνίου, οἱ μὲν ἄλλοι κατὰ τὠυτὸ γνώμην ἐξεφέροντο, κελεύοντες ναυμαχίην ποιέεσθαι. Ἀρτεμισίη δὲ τάδε ἔφη·

α "Εἰπεῖν μοι πρὸς βασιλέα, Μαρδόνιε, ὡς ἐγὼ τάδε λέγω, οὔτε κακίστη γενομένη ἐν τῆισι ναυμαχίηισι τῆισι πρὸς Εὐβοίηι, οὔτε ἐλάχιστα ἀποδεξαμένη. 'δέσποτα, τὴν δὲ ἐοῦσαν γνώμην με δίκαιόν ἐστι ἀποδείκνυσθαι, τὰ τυγχάνω φρονέουσα ἄριστα ἐς πρήγματα τὰ σά. καί τοι τάδε λέγω, φείδεο τῶν νεῶν μηδὲ ναυμαχίην ποιέο· οἱ γὰρ ἄνδρες τῶν σῶν ἀνδρῶν κρέσσονες τοσοῦτόν εἰσι κατὰ
2 θάλασσαν, ὅσον ἄνδρες γυναικῶν. τί δὲ πάντως δεῖ σε ναυμαχίηισι ἀνακινδυνεύειν; οὐκ ἔχεις μὲν τὰς Ἀθήνας, τῶν περ εἵνεκα ὁρμήθης στρατεύεσθαι, ἔχεις δὲ τὴν ἄλλην Ἑλλάδα; ἐμποδὼν δέ τοι ἵσταται οὐδείς· οἳ δέ τοι ἀντέστησαν, ἀπήλλαξαν οὕτω ὡς κείνους ἔπρεπε.

β Τῆι δὲ ἐγὼ δοκέω ἀποβήσεσθαι τὰ τῶν ἀντιπολέμων πρήγματα, τοῦτο φράσω. ἢν μὲν μὴ ἐπειχθῆις ναυμαχίην ποιεύμενος, ἀλλὰ τὰς νέας αὐτοῦ ἔχηις πρὸς γῆι μένων, ἢ καὶ προβαίνων ἐς τὴν Πελοπόννησον, εὐπετέως τοι, δέσποτα, χωρήσει τὰ νοέων
2 ἐλήλυθας. οὐ γὰρ οἷοί τε πολλὸν χρόνον εἰσί τοι ἀντέχειν οἱ Ἕλληνες, ἀλλά σφεας διασκεδᾶις, κατὰ πόλις δὲ ἕκαστοι φεύξονται. οὔτε γὰρ σῖτος πάρα σφι ἐν τῆι νήσωι ταύτηι, ὡς ἐγὼ πυνθάνομαι, οὔτε αὐτοὺς οἰκός, ἢν σὺ ἐπὶ τὴν Πελοπόννησον ἐλαύνηις τὸν πεζὸν στρατόν, ἀτρεμιεῖν τοὺς ἐκεῖθεν αὐτῶν ἥκοντας, οὐδέ σφι μελήσει πρὸ τῶν Ἀθηνέων ναυμαχέειν.

γ Ἢν δὲ αὐτίκα ἐπειχθῆις ναυμαχῆσαι, δειμαίνω μὴ ὁ ναυτικὸς στρατὸς κακωθεὶς τὸν πεζὸν προσδηλήσηται. πρὸς δέ, ὦ βασιλεῦ, καὶ τόδε ἐς θυμὸν βάλευ, ὡς τοῖσι μὲν χρηστοῖσι τῶν ἀνθρώπων κακοὶ δοῦλοι φιλέουσι γίνεσθαι, τοῖσι δὲ κακοῖσι χρηστοί. σοὶ δὲ

67.2 ποιέοιτο DPRSV: ποιέοιντο C: ποιοῖντο rell.

ἐόντι ἀρίστωι ἀνδρῶν πάντων κακοὶ δοῦλοι εἰσί, οἳ ἐν συμμάχων
λόγωι λέγονται εἶναι, ἐόντες Αἰγύπτιοί τε καὶ Κύπριοι καὶ Κίλικες
καὶ Πάμφυλοι, τῶν ὄφελός ἐστι οὐδέν.'"

Ταῦτα λεγούσης πρὸς Μαρδόνιον, ὅσοι μὲν ἦσαν εὔνοοι τῆι 69
Ἀρτεμισίηι, συμφορὴν ἐποιεῦντο τοὺς λόγους ὡς κακόν τι πει-
σομένης πρὸς βασιλέος, ὅτι οὐκ ἔα ναυμαχίην ποιέεσθαι· οἱ δὲ ἀγεό-
μενοί τε καὶ φθονέοντες αὐτῆι, ἅτε ἐν πρώτοισι τετιμημένης διὰ πάν-
των τῶν συμμάχων, ἐτέρποντο τῆι κρίσι, ὡς ἀπολεομένης αὐτῆς.
ἐπεὶ δὲ ἀνηνείχθησαν αἱ γνῶμαι ἐς Ξέρξην, κάρτα τε ἥσθη τῆι γνώμηι 2
τῆι Ἀρτεμισίης, καὶ νομίζων ἔτι πρότερον σπουδαίην εἶναι, τότε
πολλῶι μᾶλλον αἴνεε. ὅμως δὲ τοῖσι πλέοσι πείθεσθαι ἐκέλευε, τάδε
καταδόξας, πρὸς μὲν Εὐβοίηι σφέας ἐθελοκακέειν ὡς οὐ παρεόντος
αὐτοῦ, τότε δὲ αὐτὸς παρεσκεύαστο θεήσασθαι ναυμαχέοντας.

Ἐπεὶ δὲ παρήγγελλον ἀναπλέειν, ἀνῆγον τὰς νέας ἐπὶ τὴν 70
Σαλαμῖνα, καὶ παρεκρίθησαν διαταχθέντες κατ' ἡσυχίην. τότε
μέν νυν οὐκ ἐξέχρησέ σφι ἡ ἡμέρη ναυμαχίην ποιήσασθαι, νὺξ
γὰρ ἐπεγένετο, οἱ δὲ παρεσκευάζοντο ἐς τὴν ὑστεραίην. τοὺς 2
δὲ Ἕλληνας εἶχε δέος τε καὶ ἀρρωδίη, οὐκ ἥκιστα δὲ τοὺς ἀπὸ
Πελοποννήσου· ἀρρώδεον δέ, ὅτι αὐτοὶ μὲν ἐν Σαλαμῖνι κατή-
μενοι ὑπὲρ γῆς τῆς Ἀθηναίων ναυμαχέειν μέλλοιεν, νικηθέντες τε
ἐν νήσωι, ἀπολαμφθέντες πολιορκήσονται, ἀπέντες τὴν ἑωυτῶν
ἀφύλακτον.

71–7 Greek disagreements and Themistocles' message to Xerxes

Τῶν δὲ βαρβάρων ὁ πεζὸς ὑπὸ τὴν παρεοῦσαν νύκτα ἐπορεύετο 71
ἐπὶ τὴν Πελοπόννησον. καίτοι τὰ δυνατὰ πάντα ἐμεμηχάνητο,
ὅκως κατ' ἤπειρον μὴ ἐσβάλοιεν οἱ βάρβαροι. ὡς γὰρ ἐπύθοντο
τάχιστα Πελοποννήσιοι τοὺς ἀμφὶ Λεωνίδην ἐν Θερμοπύληισι
τετελευτηκέναι, συνδραμόντες ἐκ τῶν πολίων ἐς τὸν Ἰσθμὸν ἵζοντο,
καί σφι ἐπῆν στρατηγὸς Κλεόμβροτος ὁ Ἀναξανδρίδεω, Λεωνίδεω
δὲ ἀδελφεός. ἱζόμενοι δὲ ἐν τῶι Ἰσθμῶι καὶ συγχώσαντες τὴν Σκιρ- 2
ωνίδα ὁδόν, μετὰ τοῦτο ὥς σφι ἔδοξε βουλευομένοισι, οἰκοδόμεον
διὰ τοῦ Ἰσθμοῦ τεῖχος. ἅτε δὲ ἐουσέων μυριάδων πολλέων καὶ
παντὸς ἀνδρὸς ἐργαζομένου, ἤνετο τὸ ἔργον· καὶ γὰρ λίθοι καὶ
πλίνθοι καὶ ξύλα καὶ φορμοὶ ψάμμου πλήρεες ἐσεφορέοντο, καὶ
ἐλίνυον οὐδένα χρόνον οἱ βοηθήσαντες ἐργαζόμενοι, οὔτε νυκτὸς
οὔτε ἡμέρης. Οἱ δὲ βοηθήσαντες ἐς τὸν Ἰσθμὸν πανδημεὶ οἵδε ἦσαν 72

69.1 κρίσει DRSV: ἀνακρίσι P: ἀνακρίσει ABC Valckenaer 70.1 παρήγγελλον ABD: παρήγγελλε

Ἑλλήνων· Λακεδαιμόνιοί τε καὶ Ἀρκάδες πάντες καὶ Ἠλεῖοι καὶ Κορίν-
θιοι καὶ Σικυώνιοι καὶ Ἐπιδαύριοι καὶ Φλιάσιοι καὶ Τροιζήνιοι καὶ
Ἑρμιονέες. οὗτοι μὲν ἦσαν οἱ βοηθήσαντες καὶ ὑπεραρρωδέοντες
τῆι Ἑλλάδι κινδυνευούσηι. τοῖσι δὲ ἄλλοισι Πελοποννησίοισι ἔμελε
οὐδέν· Ὀλύμπια δὲ καὶ Κάρνεια παροιχώκεε ἤδη.

73 Οἰκέει δὲ τὴν Πελοπόννησον ἔθνεα ἑπτά. τούτων δέ, τὰ μὲν δύο
αὐτόχθονα ἐόντα κατὰ χώρην ἵδρυται νῦν τῆι καὶ τὸ πάλαι οἴκεον,
Ἀρκάδες τε καὶ Κυνούριοι. ἓν δὲ ἔθνος τὸ Ἀχαιϊκὸν ἐκ μὲν Πελοποννή-
σου οὐκ ἐξεχώρησε, ἐκ μέντοι τῆς ἑωυτῶν, οἰκέει δὲ γὴν ἀλλοτρίην.
2 τὰ δὲ λοιπὰ ἔθνεα τῶν ἑπτὰ τέσσερα ἐπήλυδά ἐστι, Δωριέες τε καὶ
Αἰτωλοὶ καὶ Δρύοπες καὶ Λήμνιοι. Δωριέων μὲν πολλαί τε καὶ δόκιμοι
πόλιες, Αἰτωλῶν δὲ Ἦλις μούνη, Δρυόπων δὲ Ἑρμιών τε καὶ Ἀσίνη
ἡ πρὸς Καρδαμύληι τῆι Λακωνικῆι, Λημνίων δὲ Παρωρεῆται πάν-
3 τες. οἱ δὲ Κυνούριοι, αὐτόχθονες ἐόντες, δοκέουσι μοῦνοι εἶναι Ἴωνες,
ἐκδεδωρίευνται δὲ ὑπό τε Ἀργείων ἀρχόμενοι καὶ τοῦ χρόνου, ἐόντες
Ὀρνεῆται καὶ [οἱ] περίοικοι. τούτων ὦν τῶν ἑπτὰ ἐθνέων αἱ λοιπαὶ
πόλιες, πάρεξ τῶν κατέλεξα, ἐκ τοῦ μέσου κατέατο· εἰ δὲ ἐλευθέρως
ἔξεστι εἰπεῖν, ἐκ τοῦ μέσου κατήμενοι, ἐμήδιζον.

74 Οἱ μὲν δὴ ἐν τῶι Ἰσθμῶι τοιούτωι πόνωι συνέστασαν, ἅτε περὶ
τοῦ παντὸς ἤδη [δρόμου] θέοντες καὶ τῆισι νηυσὶ οὐκ ἐλπίζοντες
ἐλλάμψεσθαι· οἱ δὲ ἐν Σαλαμῖνι ὅμως ταῦτα πυνθανόμενοι ἀρρώδεον,
οὐκ οὕτω περὶ σφίσι αὐτοῖσι δειμαίνοντες, ὡς περὶ τῆι Πελοπον-
2 νήσωι. ἕως μὲν δὴ αὐτῶν ἀνὴρ ἀνδρὶ παραστὰς σιγῆι λόγον
ἐποιέετο, θῶμα ποιεύμενοι τὴν Εὐρυβιάδεω ἀβουλίην· τέλος δὲ ἐξερ-
ράγη ἐς τὸ μέσον. σύλλογός τε δὴ ἐγίνετο, καὶ πολλὰ ἐλέγετο περὶ
τῶν αὐτῶν, οἱ μὲν ὡς ἐς τὴν Πελοπόννησον χρεὸν εἴη ἀποπλέειν
καὶ περὶ ἐκείνης κινδυνεύειν, μηδὲ πρὸ χώρης δοριαλώτου μένοντας
μάχεσθαι, Ἀθηναῖοι δὲ καὶ Αἰγινῆται καὶ Μεγαρέες αὐτοῦ μένοντας
ἀμύνεσθαι.

75 Ἐνθαῦτα Θεμιστοκλέης, ὡς ἑσσοῦτο τῆι γνώμηι ὑπὸ τῶν
Πελοποννησίων, λαθὼν ἐξέρχεται ἐκ τοῦ συνεδρίου, ἐξελθὼν δὲ
πέμπει ἐς τὸ στρατόπεδον τὸ Μήδων ἄνδρα πλοίωι, ἐντειλάμενος
τὰ λέγειν χρεόν, τῶι οὔνομα μὲν ἦν Σίκιννος, οἰκέτης δὲ καὶ παιδα-
γωγὸς ἦν τῶν Θεμιστοκλέος παίδων· τὸν δὴ ὕστερον τούτων
τῶν πρηγμάτων Θεμιστοκλέης Θεσπιέα τε ἐποίησε, ὡς ἐπεδέκοντο
2 οἱ Θεσπιέες πολιήτας, καὶ χρήμασι ὄλβιον. ὃς τότε πλοίωι
ἀπικόμενος, ἔλεγε πρὸς τοὺς στρατηγοὺς τῶν βαρβάρων τάδε·

73.1 τῆι Stein: τε codd. 73.1 γῆν Pingel, Krueger: τήν codd. 73.3 οἱ om. DRSV: καὶ οἱ περίοικοι del. Stein

"ἔπεμψέ με στρατηγὸς ὁ Ἀθηναίων λάθρηι τῶν ἄλλων Ἑλλήνων
(τυγχάνει γὰρ φρονέων τὰ βασιλέος, καὶ βουλόμενος μᾶλλον τὰ
ὑμέτερα κατύπερθε γίνεσθαι ἢ τὰ τῶν Ἑλλήνων πρήγματα), φρά-
σοντα ὅτι οἱ Ἕλληνες δρησμὸν βουλεύονται καταρρωδηκότες, καὶ
νῦν παρέχει κάλλιστον ὑμέας ἔργον ἁπάντων ἐξεργάσασθαι, ἢν μὴ
περιίδητε διαδράντας αὐτούς. οὔτε γὰρ ἀλλήλοισι ὁμοφρονέουσι, 3
οὔτ᾽ ἔτι ἀντιστήσονται ὑμῖν, πρὸς ἑωυτούς τε σφέας ὄψεσθε ναυ-
μαχέοντας, τοὺς τὰ ὑμέτερα φρονέοντας καὶ τοὺς μή."

Ὁ μὲν ταῦτά σφι σημήνας, ἐκποδὼν ἀπαλλάσσετο. τοῖσι δὲ ὡς **76**
πιστὰ ἐγίνετο τὰ ἀγγελθέντα, τοῦτο μὲν ἐς τὴν νησῖδα τὴν Ψυτ-
τάλειαν, μεταξὺ Σαλαμῖνός τε κειμένην καὶ τῆς ἠπείρου, πολλοὺς
τῶν Περσέων ἀπεβιβάσαν· τοῦτο δέ, ἐπειδὴ ἐγίνοντο μέσαι νύκτες,
ἀνῆγον μὲν τὸ ἀπ᾽ ἑσπέρης κέρας, κυκλούμενοι πρὸς τὴν Σαλαμῖνα,
ἀνῆγον δὲ οἱ ἀμφὶ τὴν Κέον τε καὶ τὴν Κυνόσουραν τεταγμένοι,
κατεῖχόν τε μέχρι Μουνυχίης πάντα τὸν πορθμὸν τῆισι νηυσί. τῶνδε 2
δὲ εἵνεκα ἀνῆγον τὰς νέας, ἵνα δὴ τοῖσι Ἕλλησι μὴ διαφυγεῖν ἐξῆι,
ἀλλ᾽ ἀπολαμφθέντες ἐν τῆι Σαλαμῖνι, δοῖεν τίσιν τῶν ἐπ᾽ Ἀρτεμισίωι
ἀγωνισμάτων. ἐς δὲ τὴν νησῖδα τὴν Ψυττάλειαν καλεομένην ἀπε-
βίβαζον τῶν Περσέων τῶνδε εἵνεκα, ὡς ἐπεὰν γένηται ναυμαχίη,
ἐνθαῦτα μάλιστα ἐξοισομένων τῶν τε ἀνδρῶν καὶ τῶν ναυηγίων
(ἐν γὰρ δὴ πόρωι τῆς ναυμαχίης τῆς μελλούσης ἔσεσθαι ἔκειτο ἡ
νῆσος), ἵνα τοὺς μὲν περιποιῶσι, τοὺς δὲ διαφθείρωσι. ἐποίευν δὲ 3
σιγῆι ταῦτα, ὡς μὴ πυνθανοίατο οἱ ἐναντίοι. οἱ μὲν δὴ ταῦτα τῆς
νυκτὸς οὐδὲν ἀποκοιμηθέντες παραρτέοντο.

[Χρησμοῖσι δὲ οὐκ ἔχω ἀντιλέγειν ὡς οὐκ εἰσὶ ἀληθέες, οὐ βουλό- **77**
μενος ἐναργέως λέγοντας πειρᾶσθαι καταβάλλειν, ἐς τοιάδε πρήγ-
ματα ἐσβλέψας.

> ἀλλ᾽ ὅταν Ἀρτέμιδος χρυσαόρου ἱερὸν ἀκτήν
> νηυσὶ γεφυρώσωσι καὶ εἰναλίην Κυνόσουραν,
> ἐλπίδι μαινομένηι, λιπαρὰς πέρσαντες Ἀθήνας,
> δῖα Δίκη σβέσσει κρατερὸν Κόρον, Ὕβριος υἱόν,
> δεινὸν μαιμώοντα, δοκεῦντ᾽ ἀνὰ πάντα πιθέσθαι.
> χαλκὸς γὰρ χαλκῶι συμμίξεται, αἵματι δ᾽ Ἄρης 2
> πόντον φοινίξει. τότ᾽ ἐλεύθερον Ἑλλάδος ἦμαρ
> εὐρύοπα Κρονίδης ἐπάγει καὶ πότνια Νίκη.

ἐς τοιαῦτα μὲν καὶ οὕτω ἐναργέως λέγοντι Βάκιδι ἀντιλογίας
χρησμῶν πέρι οὔτε αὐτὸς λέγειν τολμέω οὔτε παρ᾽ ἄλλων
ἐνδέκομαι.]

76.2 μὴ διαφυγεῖν Stein: μὴ φυγέειν DRSV: μὴ δὲ φυγέειν Ald. 77 del. Krueger

78–82 Aristeides and Themistocles

78 Τῶν δὲ ἐν Σαλαμῖνι στρατηγῶν ἐγίνετο ὠθισμὸς λόγων πολλός.
ἤιδεσαν δὲ οὔκω ὅτι σφέας περιεκυκλεῦντο τῆισι νηυσὶ οἱ βάρβαροι,
ἀλλ᾽ ὥσπερ τῆς ἡμέρης ὥρων αὐτοὺς τεταγμένους, ἐδόκεον κατὰ
79 χώρην εἶναι. Συνεστηκότων δὲ τῶν στρατηγῶν, ἐξ Αἰγίνης διέβη
Ἀριστείδης ὁ Λυσιμάχου, ἀνὴρ Ἀθηναῖος μέν, ἐξωστρακισμένος δὲ
ὑπὸ τοῦ δήμου, τὸν ἐγὼ νενόμικα, πυνθανόμενος αὐτοῦ τὸν τρόπον,
2 ἄριστον ἄνδρα γενέσθαι ἐν Ἀθήνηισι καὶ δικαιότατον. οὗτος ὡνὴρ
στὰς ἐπὶ τὸ συνέδριον ἐξεκαλέετο Θεμιστοκλέα, ἐόντα μὲν ἑωυτῶι
οὐ φίλον, ἐχθρὸν δὲ τὰ μάλιστα· ὑπὸ δὲ μεγάθεος τῶν παρεόντων
κακῶν λήθην ἐκείνων ποιεύμενος ἐξεκαλέετο, θέλων αὐτῶι συμμεῖξαι.
προακηκόεε δὲ ὅτι σπεύδοιεν οἱ ἀπὸ Πελοποννήσου ἀνάγειν τὰς νέας
3 πρὸς τὸν Ἰσθμόν. ὡς δὲ ἐξῆλθέ οἱ Θεμιστοκλέης, ἔλεγε Ἀριστείδης
τάδε· "ἡμέας στασιάζειν χρεόν ἐστι ἔν τε τῶι ἄλλωι καιρῶι καὶ δὴ
καὶ ἐν τῶιδε, περὶ τοῦ ὁκότερος ἡμέων πλέω ἀγαθὰ τὴν πατρίδα
4 ἐργάσεται. λέγω δέ τοι ὅτι ἴσον ἐστὶ πολλά τε καὶ ὀλίγα λέγειν
περὶ ἀποπλόου τοῦ ἐνθεῦτεν Πελοποννησίοισι. ἐγὼ γὰρ αὐτόπτης
τοι λέγω γενόμενος, ὅτι νῦν οὐδ᾽ ἢν θέλωσι Κορίνθιοί τε καὶ αὐτὸς
Εὐρυβιάδης οἷοί τε ἔσονται ἐκπλῶσαι· περιεχόμεθα γὰρ ὑπὸ τῶν
πολεμίων κύκλωι. ἀλλ᾽ ἐσελθών σφι ταῦτα σήμηνον."
80 Ὁ δ᾽ ἀμείβετο τοισίδε· "κάρτα τε χρηστὰ διακελεύεαι καὶ εὖ
ἤγγειλας· τὰ γὰρ ἐγὼ ἐδεόμην γενέσθαι, αὐτὸς αὐτόπτης γενό-
μενος ἥκεις. ἴσθι γὰρ ἐξ ἐμέο τὰ ποιεύμενα ὑπὸ Μήδων· ἔδεε γάρ,
ὅτε οὐκ ἑκόντες ἤθελον ἐς μάχην κατίστασθαι οἱ Ἕλληνες, ἀέκοντας
παραστήσασθαι. σὺ δὲ ἐπεί περ ἥκεις χρηστὰ ἀπαγγέλλων, αὐτός
2 σφι ἄγγειλον. ἢν γὰρ ἐγὼ αὐτὰ λέγω, δόξω πλάσας λέγειν καὶ οὐ
πείσω, ὡς οὐ ποιεύντων τῶν βαρβάρων ταῦτα. ἀλλά σφι σήμη-
νον αὐτὸς παρελθὼν ὡς ἔχει. ἐπεὰν δὲ σημήνηις, ἢν μὲν πείθωνται,
ταῦτα δὴ τὰ κάλλιστα· ἢν δὲ αὐτοῖσι μὴ πιστὰ γένηται, ὅμοιον ἡμῖν
ἔσται· οὐ γὰρ ἔτι διαδρήσονται, εἴ περ περιεχόμεθα πανταχόθεν, ὡς
σὺ λέγεις."
81 Ταῦτα ἔλεγε παρελθὼν ὁ Ἀριστείδης, φάμενος ἐξ Αἰγίνης τε ἥκειν
καὶ μόγις ἐκπλῶσαι λαθὼν τοὺς ἐπορμέοντας· περιέχεσθαι γὰρ
πᾶν τὸ στρατόπεδον τὸ Ἑλληνικὸν ὑπὸ τῶν νεῶν τῶν Ξέρξεω·
παραρτέεσθαί τε συνεβούλευε ὡς ἀλεξησομένους. καὶ ὁ μὲν ταῦτα
εἴπας μετεστήκεε, τῶν δὲ αὖτις ἐγίνετο λόγων ἀμφισβασίη· οἱ γὰρ
82 πλεῦνες τῶν στρατηγῶν οὐκ ἐπείθοντο τὰ ἐσαγγελθέντα. Ἀπισ-
τεόντων δὲ τούτων, ἧκε τριήρης ἀνδρῶν Τηνίων αὐτομολέουσα,

79.3 εἰ ἔν τεωι ἄλλωι Stein: ἐν τεωι Gomperz 80.1 τὰ ποιεύμενα codd.: τάδε π Krueger

τῆς ἦρχε ἀνὴρ Παναίτιος ὁ Σωσιμένεος, ἥ περ δὴ ἔφερε τὴν ἀληθείην
πᾶσαν. διὰ δὲ τοῦτο τὸ ἔργον ἐνεγράφησαν Τήνιοι ἐν Δελφοῖσι ἐς
τὸν τρίποδα ἐν τοῖσι τὸν βάρβαρον κατελοῦσι. σὺν δὲ ὦν ταύτηι τῆι 2
νηὶ τῆι αὐτομολησάσηι ἐς Σαλαμῖνα καὶ τῆι πρότερον ἐπ' Ἀρτεμί-
σιον τῆι Λημνίηι, ἐξεπληροῦτο τὸ ναυτικὸν τοῖσι Ἕλλησι ἐς τὰς
ὀγδώκοντα καὶ τριηκοσίας νέας· δύο γὰρ δὴ νεῶν τότε κατέδεε ἐς
τὸν ἀριθμόν.

83–96 The battle of Salamis

83–90 The battle begins; the Persian perspective

Τοῖσι δὲ Ἕλλησι ὡς πιστὰ δὴ τὰ λεγόμενα ἦν τῶν Τηνίων ῥήματα, **83**
παρεσκευάζοντο ὡς ναυμαχήσοντες. ἠώς τε διέφαινε, καὶ οἳ σύλλο-
γον τῶν ἐπιβατέων ποιησάμενοι, προηγόρευε εὖ ἔχοντα μὲν ἐκ πάν-
των Θεμιστοκλέης· τὰ δὲ ἔπεα ἦν πάντα <τὰ> κρέσσω τοῖσι ἥσσοσι
ἀντιτιθέμενα, ὅσα δὴ ἐν ἀνθρώπου φύσι καὶ καταστάσι ἐγγίνεται.
παραινέσας δὲ τούτων τὰ κρέσσω αἱρέεσθαι, καὶ καταπλέξας τὴν 2
ῥῆσιν, ἐσβαίνειν ἐκέλευε ἐς τὰς νέας. καὶ οὗτοι μὲν δὴ ἐσέβαινον,
καὶ ἧκε ἡ ἀπ' Αἰγίνης τριήρης, ἣ κατὰ τοὺς Αἰακίδας ἀπεδήμησε.
ἐνθαῦτα ἀνῆγον τὰς νέας ἁπάσας <οἱ> Ἕλληνες, ἀναγομένοισι δέ
σφι αὐτίκα ἐπεκέατο οἱ βάρβαροι.

Οἱ μὲν δὴ ἄλλοι Ἕλληνες [ἐπὶ] πρύμνην ἀνεκρούοντο καὶ ὤκελ- **84**
λον τὰς νέας, Ἀμεινίης δὲ Παλληνεύς, ἀνὴρ Ἀθηναῖος, ἐξαναχθεὶς νηὶ
ἐμβάλλει· συμπλεκείσης δὲ τῆς νεὸς καὶ οὐ δυναμένων ἀπαλλαγῆ-
ναι, οὕτω δὴ οἱ ἄλλοι Ἀμεινίηι βοηθέοντες συνέμισγον. Ἀθηναῖοι 2
μὲν οὕτω λέγουσι τῆς ναυμαχίης γενέσθαι τὴν ἀρχήν, Αἰγινῆται
δὲ τὴν κατὰ τοὺς Αἰακίδας ἀποδημήσασαν ἐς Αἴγιναν, ταύτην
εἶναι τὴν ἄρξασαν. λέγεται δὲ καὶ τάδε, ὡς φάσμα σφι γυναικὸς
ἐφάνη, φανεῖσαν δὲ διακελεύσασθαι, ὥστε καὶ ἅπαν ἀκοῦσαι τὸ τῶν
Ἑλλήνων στρατόπεδον, ὀνειδίσασαν πρότερον τάδε· "ὦ δαιμόνιοι,
μέχρι κόσου ἔτι πρύμνην ἀνακρούεσθε;"

Κατὰ μὲν δὴ Ἀθηναίους ἐτετάχατο Φοίνικες, οὗτοι γὰρ εἶχον τὸ **85**
πρὸς Ἐλευσῖνός τε καὶ ἑσπέρης κέρας· κατὰ δὲ Λακεδαιμονίους Ἴωνες,
οὗτοι δ' εἶχον τὸ πρὸς τὴν ἠῶ τε καὶ τὸν Πειραιέα. ἐθελοκάκεον
μέντοι αὐτῶν κατὰ τὰς Θεμιστοκλέος ἐντολὰς ὀλίγοι, οἱ δὲ
πλεῦνες οὔ. ἔχω μέν νυν συχνῶν οὐνόματα τριηράρχων καταλέξαι 2
τῶν νέας Ἑλληνίδας ἑλόντων, χρήσομαι δὲ αὐτοῖσι οὐδὲν πλὴν

83.1 τά post ἦν transp. Powell: ῥήματα secl. Stein 83.1 τά post πάντα add. Dobree
84.1 ἐπί del. Bekker 85.1 Ἐλευσῖνός codd.: Σαλαμῖνός Loeschke

Θεομήστορός τε τοῦ Ἀνδροδάμαντος καὶ Φυλάκου τοῦ Ἱστιαίου,
3 Σαμίων ἀμφοτέρων. τοῦδε <δὲ> εἵνεκα μέμνημαι τούτων μούνων,
ὅτι Θεομήστωρ μὲν διὰ τοῦτο τὸ ἔργον Σάμου ἐτυράννευσε,
καταστησάντων τῶν Περσέων, Φύλακος δὲ εὐεργέτης βασιλέος ἀνε-
γράφη καὶ χώρηι ἐδωρήθη πολλῆι. οἱ δ' εὐεργέται βασιλέος ὀροσάγ-
γαι καλέονται Περσιστί.

86 Περὶ μέν νυν τούτους οὕτω εἶχε. τὸ δὲ πλῆθος τῶν νεῶν ἐν τῆι
Σαλαμῖνι ἐκεραΐζετο, αἱ μὲν ὑπ' Ἀθηναίων διαφθειρόμεναι, αἱ δὲ ὑπ'
Αἰγινητέων. ἅτε γὰρ τῶν μὲν Ἑλλήνων σὺν κόσμωι ναυμαχεόντων
<καὶ> κατὰ τάξιν, τῶν δὲ βαρβάρων οὔτε τεταγμένων ἔτι οὔτε σὺν
νόωι ποιεόντων οὐδέν, ἔμελλε τοιοῦτό σφι συνοίσεσθαι, οἷόν περ
ἀπέβη. καίτοι ἦσάν γε [καὶ ἐγένοντο] ταύτην τὴν ἡμέρην μακρῶι
ἀμείνονες αὐτοὶ ἑωυτῶν ἢ πρὸς Εὐβοίηι, πᾶς τις προθυμεόμενος καὶ
δειμαίνων Ξέρξην, ἐδόκεέ τε ἕκαστος ἑωυτὸν θεήσασθαι βασιλέα.

87 Κατὰ μὲν δὴ τοὺς ἄλλους οὐκ ἔχω [μετεξετέρους] εἰπεῖν ἀτρεκέως,
ὡς ἕκαστοι τῶν βαρβάρων ἢ τῶν Ἑλλήνων ἠγωνίζοντο· κατὰ
δὲ Ἀρτεμισίην τάδε ἐγένετο, ἀπ' ὧν εὐδοκίμησε μᾶλλον ἔτι παρὰ
2 βασιλέϊ. ἐπειδὴ γὰρ ἐς θόρυβον πολλὸν ἀπίκετο τὰ βασιλέος πρήγ-
ματα, ἐν τούτωι τῶι καιρῶι ἡ νηῦς ἡ Ἀρτεμισίης ἐδιώκετο ὑπὸ
νεὸς Ἀττικῆς· καὶ ἣ οὐκ ἔχουσα διαφυγεῖν (ἔμπροσθε γὰρ αὐτῆς
ἦσαν ἄλλαι νέες φίλιαι, ἡ δὲ αὐτῆς πρὸς τῶν πολεμίων μάλιστα
ἐτύγχανε ἐοῦσα), ἔδοξέ οἱ τόδε ποιῆσαι, τὸ καὶ συνήνεικε ποιη-
σάσηι. διωκομένη γὰρ ὑπὸ τῆς Ἀττικῆς, φέρουσα ἐνέβαλε νηὶ
φιλίηι, ἀνδρῶν τε Καλυνδέων καὶ αὐτοῦ ἐπιπλέοντος τοῦ Καλυνδέων
3 βασιλέος Δαμασιθύμου. εἰ μὲν καί τι νεῖκος πρὸς αὐτὸν ἐγεγόνεε
ἔτι περὶ Ἑλλήσποντον ἐόντων, οὐ μέντοι ἔχω γε εἰπεῖν, οὔτε εἰ ἐκ
προνοίης αὐτὰ ἐποίησε, οὔτε εἰ συνεκύρησε ἡ τῶν Καλυνδέων κατὰ
4 τύχην παραπεσοῦσα νηῦς. ὡς δὲ ἐνέβαλέ τε καὶ κατέδυσε, εὐτυχίηι
χρησαμένη διπλᾶ ἑωυτὴν ἀγαθὰ ἐργάσατο· ὅ τε γὰρ τῆς Ἀττικῆς
νεὸς τριήραρχος, ὡς εἶδέ μιν ἐμβάλλουσαν νηὶ ἀνδρῶν βαρβάρων,
νομίσας τὴν νέα τὴν Ἀρτεμισίης ἢ Ἑλληνίδα εἶναι ἢ αὐτομολέειν
ἐκ τῶν βαρβάρων καὶ αὐτοῖσι ἀμύνειν, ἀποστρέψας πρὸς ἄλλας
ἐτράπετο.

88 Τοῦτο μὲν τοιοῦτο αὐτῆι συνήνεικε γενέσθαι διαφυγεῖν τε καὶ
μὴ ἀπολέσθαι· τοῦτο δὲ συνέβη, ὥστε κακὸν ἐργασαμένη, ἀπὸ
2 τούτων αὐτὴν μάλιστα εὐδοκιμῆσαι παρὰ Ξέρξηι. λέγεται γὰρ

85.3 δέ add.Reiske 86 <καί> add. Stein 86 καὶ ἐγένοντο del. Blakesley
86 θεήσασθαι CPS: θηήσεσθαι B: θηήσασθαι ADRV 87.1 μετεξετέρους del. Stein
88.1 <ὥστε> γενέσθαι Stein

βασιλέα θηεύμενον μαθεῖν τὴν νέα ἐμβαλοῦσαν, καὶ δή τινα εἰπεῖν
τῶν παρεόντων· "δέσποτα, ὁρᾶις Ἀρτεμισίην ὡς εὖ ἀγωνίζεται καὶ
νέα τῶν πολεμίων κατέδυσε;" καὶ τὸν ἐπειρέσθαι, εἰ ἀληθέως ἐστὶ
Ἀρτεμισίης τὸ ἔργον, καὶ τοὺς φάναι, σαφέως τὸ ἐπίσημον τῆς νεὸς
ἐπισταμένους· τὴν δὲ διαφθαρεῖσαν ἠπιστέατο εἶναι πολεμίην. τά 3
τε γὰρ ἄλλα, ὡς εἴρηται, αὐτῆι συνήνεικε ἐς εὐτυχίην γενόμενα,
καὶ τὸ τῶν ἐκ τῆς Καλυνδικῆς νεὸς μηδένα ἀποσωθέντα κατήγορον
γενέσθαι. Ξέρξην δὲ εἰπεῖν λέγεται πρὸς τὰ φραζόμενα· "οἱ μὲν ἄνδρες
γεγόνασί μοι γυναῖκες, αἱ δὲ γυναῖκες ἄνδρες." ταῦτα μὲν Ξέρξην
φασὶ εἰπεῖν.

Ἐν δὲ τῶι πόνωι τούτωι, ἀπὸ μὲν ἔθανε ὁ στρατηγὸς Ἀριαβίγνης **89**
ὁ Δαρείου, Ξέρξεω ἐὼν ἀδελφεός, ἀπὸ δὲ ἄλλοι πολλοί τε καὶ ὀνομασ-
τοὶ Περσέων καὶ Μήδων καὶ τῶν ἄλλων συμμάχων· ὀλίγοι δέ τινες
καὶ Ἑλλήνων· ἅτε γὰρ νέειν ἐπιστάμενοι, τοῖσι αἱ νέες διεφθείροντο,
οἱ μὴ ἐν χειρῶν νόμωι ἀπολλύμενοι ἐς τὴν Σαλαμῖνα διένεον. τῶν 2
δὲ βαρβάρων οἱ πολλοὶ ἐν τῆι θαλάσσηι διεφθάρησαν, νέειν οὐκ
ἐπιστάμενοι. ἐπεὶ δὲ αἱ πρῶται ἐς φυγὴν ἐτράποντο, ἐνθαῦτα αἱ
πλεῖσται διεφθείροντο· οἱ γὰρ ὄπισθε τεταγμένοι, ἐς τὸ πρόσθε τῆισι
νηυσὶ παριέναι πειρώμενοι, ὡς ἀποδεξόμενοί τι καὶ αὐτοὶ ἔργον
βασιλέϊ, τῆισι σφετέρηισι νηυσὶ φευγούσηισι περιέπιπτον.

Ἐγένετο δὲ καὶ τόδε ἐν τῶι θορύβωι τούτωι. τῶν τινες Φοινίκων, **90**
τῶν αἱ νέες διεφθάρατο, ἐλθόντες παρὰ βασιλέα διέβαλλον τοὺς
Ἴωνας, ὡς δι᾽ ἐκείνους ἀπολοίατο αἱ νέες, ὡς προδόντων. συνήνεικε
ὦν οὕτω, ὥστε Ἰώνων τε τοὺς στρατηγοὺς μὴ ἀπολέσθαι, Φοινίκων
τε τοὺς διαβάλλοντας λαβεῖν τοιόνδε μισθόν. ἔτι τούτων ταῦτα 2
λεγόντων, ἐνέβαλε νηὶ Ἀττικῆι Σαμοθρηικίη νηῦς. ἥ τε δὴ Ἀττικὴ
κατεδύετο, καὶ ἐπιφερομένη Αἰγιναίη νηῦς κατέδυσε τῶν Σαμο-
θρήικων τὴν νέα. ἅτε δὲ ἐόντες ἀκοντισταὶ οἱ Σαμοθρήικες, τοὺς
ἐπιβάτας ἀπὸ τῆς καταδυσάσης νεὸς βάλλοντες ἀπήραξαν, καὶ
ἐπέβησάν τε καὶ ἔσχον αὐτήν. ταῦτα γενόμενα τοὺς Ἴωνας 3
ἐρρύσατο· ὡς γὰρ εἶδέ σφεας Ξέρξης ἔργον μέγα ἐργασαμένους,
ἐτράπετο πρὸς τοὺς Φοίνικας, οἷα ὑπερλυπεόμενός τε καὶ πάν-
τας αἰτιώμενος, καί σφεων ἐκέλευσε τὰς κεφαλὰς ἀποταμεῖν, ἵνα
μὴ αὐτοὶ κακοὶ γενόμενοι τοὺς ἀμείνονας διαβάλλωσι. ὅκως γάρ 4
τινα ἴδοι Ξέρξης τῶν ἑωυτοῦ ἔργον τι ἀποδεικνύμενον ἐν τῆι ναυ-
μαχίηι, κατήμενος ὑπὸ τῶι ὄρεϊ τῶι ἀντίον Σαλαμῖνος, τὸ καλέε-
ται Αἰγάλεως, ἀνεπυνθάνετο τὸν ποιήσαντα, καὶ οἱ γραμματισταὶ
ἀνέγραφον πατρόθεν τὸν τριήραρχον καὶ τὴν πόλιν. πρός δέ τι

89.1 οἱ μὴ Krueger: καὶ μὴ codd. 90.4 πρὸς δέ τι Schaefer: πρὸς δ(ὲ) ἔτι codd.

καὶ προσεβάλετο φίλος ἐὼν <Ἰώνων> Ἀριαράμνης, ἀνὴρ Πέρσης, παρεὼν τούτου τοῦ Φοινικηίου πάθεος.

91–6 The battle from the Greek side

91 Οἱ μὲν δὴ πρὸς τοὺς Φοίνικας ἐτράποντο. τῶν δὲ βαρβάρων ἐς φυγὴν τραπομένων καὶ ἐκπλεόντων πρὸς τὸ Φάληρον, Αἰγινῆται ὑποστάντες ἐν τῶι πορθμῶι ἔργα ἀπεδέξαντο λόγου ἄξια. οἱ μὲν γὰρ Ἀθηναῖοι ἐν τῶι θορύβωι ἐκεράϊζον τάς τε ἀντισταμένας καὶ τὰς φευγούσας τῶν νεῶν, οἱ δὲ Αἰγινῆται τὰς ἐκπλεούσας· ὅκως δέ τινες τοὺς Ἀθηναίους διαφύγοιεν, φερόμενοι ἐσέπιπτον ἐς τοὺς Αἰγινήτας.

92 Ἐνθαῦτα συνεκύρεον νέες, ἥ τε Θεμιστοκλέος διώκουσα νέα, καὶ ἡ Πολυκρίτου τοῦ Κριοῦ, ἀνδρὸς Αἰγινήτεω, νηὶ ἐμβαλοῦσα Σιδωνίηι, ἥ περ εἷλε τὴν προφυλάσσουσαν ἐπὶ Σκιάθωι τὴν Αἰγιναίην, ἐπ᾽ ἧς ἔπλεε Πυθέης ὁ Ἰσχενόου, τὸν οἱ Πέρσαι κατακοπέντα ἀρετῆς εἵνεκα εἶχον ἐν τῆι νηὶ ἐκπαγλεόμενοι. τὸν δὴ περιάγουσα ἅμα τοῖσι Πέρσηισι ἥλω νηῦς ἡ Σιδωνίη, ὥστε Πυθέην οὕτω σωθῆναι ἐς Αἴγιναν.
2 ὡς δὲ ἐσεῖδε τὴν νέα τὴν Ἀττικὴν ὁ Πολύκριτος, ἔγνω τὸ σημήιον ἰδὼν τῆς στρατηγίδος, καὶ βώσας τὸν Θεμιστοκλέα ἐπεκερτόμησε ἐς τῶν Αἰγινητέων τὸν μηδισμὸν ὀνειδίζων. ταῦτα μέν νυν νηὶ ἐμβαλὼν ὁ Πολύκριτος ἀπέρριψε ἐς Θεμιστοκλέα. οἱ δὲ βάρβαροι, τῶν αἱ νέες περιεγένοντο, φεύγοντες ἀπίκοντο ἐς Φάληρον ὑπὸ τὸν πεζὸν στρατόν.

93 Ἐν δὲ τῆι ναυμαχίηι ταύτηι ἤκουσαν Ἑλλήνων ἄριστα Αἰγινῆται, ἐπὶ δὲ Ἀθηναῖοι, ἀνδρῶν δὲ Πολύκριτός τε ὁ Αἰγινήτης καὶ Ἀθηναῖοι Εὐμένης τε ὁ Ἀναγυράσιος καὶ Ἀμεινίης <ὁ> Παλληνεύς, ὃς καὶ Ἀρτεμισίην ἐπεδίωξε. εἰ μέν νυν ἔμαθε ὅτι ἐν ταύτηι πλέοι Ἀρτεμισίη,
2 οὐκ ἂν ἐπαύσατο πρότερον ἢ εἷλέ μιν ἢ καὶ αὐτὸς ἥλω. τοῖσι γὰρ Ἀθηναίων τριηράρχοισι παρεκεκέλευστο, πρὸς δὲ καὶ ἄεθλον ἔκειτο μύριαι δραχμαί, ὃς ἄν μιν ζωὴν ἕληι· δεινὸν γάρ τι ἐποιεῦντο γυναῖκα ἐπὶ τὰς Ἀθήνας στρατεύεσθαι. αὕτη μὲν δή, ὡς πρότερον εἴρηται, διέφυγε· ἦσαν δὲ καὶ οἱ ἄλλοι, τῶν αἱ νέες περιεγεγόνεσαν, ἐν τῶι Φαλήρωι.

94 Ἀδείμαντον δὲ τὸν Κορίνθιον στρατηγὸν λέγουσι Ἀθηναῖοι αὐτίκα κατ᾽ ἀρχάς, ὡς συνέμισγον αἱ νέες, ἐκπλαγέντα τε καὶ ὑπερδείσαντα, τὰ ἱστία ἀειράμενον οἴχεσθαι φεύγοντα· ἰδόντας δὲ τοὺς Κορινθίους τὴν στρατηγίδα φεύγουσαν, ὡσαύτως οἴχεσθαι.
2 ὡς δὲ ἄρα φεύγοντας γίνεσθαι τῆς Σαλαμινίης κατὰ ἱρὸν Ἀθηναίης Σκιράδος, περιπίπτειν σφι κέλητα θείηι πομπῆι, τὸν οὔτε πέμψαντα

90.4 προσελάβετο Reiske 90.4 Ἰώνων add. Abresch

φανῆναι οὐδένα, οὔτε τι τῶν ἀπὸ τῆς στρατιῆς εἰδόσι προσφέρεσθαι
τοῖσι Κορινθίοισι. τῆιδε δὲ συμβάλλονται εἶναι θεῖον τὸ πρῆγμα·
ὡς γὰρ ἀγχοῦ γενέσθαι τῶν νεῶν, τοὺς ἀπὸ τοῦ κέλητος λέγειν
τάδε· "Ἀδείμαντε, σὺ μὲν ἀποστρέψας τὰς νέας ἐς φυγὴν ὅρμη- 3
σαι, καταπροδοὺς τοὺς Ἕλληνας· οἱ δὲ καὶ δὴ νικῶσι, ὅσον αὐτοὶ
ἠρῶντο ἐπικρατῆσαι τῶν ἐχθρῶν." ταῦτα λεγόντων, ἀπιστέειν γὰρ
τὸν Ἀδείμαντον, αὖτις τάδε λέγειν, ὡς αὐτοὶ οἷοί τε εἶεν ἀγόμενοι
ὅμηροι ἀποθνήισκειν, ἢν μὴ νικῶντες φαίνωνται οἱ Ἕλληνες. οὕτω 4
δὴ ἀποστρέψαντα τὴν νέα, αὐτόν τε καὶ τοὺς ἄλλους ἐπ᾽ ἐξεργασ-
μένοισι ἐλθεῖν ἐς τὸ στρατόπεδον. τούτους μὲν τοιαύτη φάτις ἔχει
ὑπὸ Ἀθηναίων· οὐ μέντοι αὐτοί γε Κορίνθιοι ὁμολογέουσι, ἀλλ᾽ ἐν
πρώτοισι σφέας αὐτοὺς τῆς ναυμαχίης νομίζουσι γενέσθαι· μαρ-
τυρέει δέ σφι καὶ ἡ ἄλλη Ἑλλάς.

Ἀριστείδης δὲ ὁ Λυσιμάχου, ἀνὴρ Ἀθηναῖος, τοῦ καὶ ὀλίγωι τι **95**
πρότερον τούτων ἐπεμνήσθην ὡς ἀνδρὸς ἀρίστου, οὗτος ἐν τῶι θορύβωι τούτωι τῶι περὶ Σαλαμῖνα γενομένωι τάδε ἐποίεε· παραλαβὼν πολλοὺς τῶν ὁπλιτέων, οἳ παρατετάχατο παρὰ τὴν ἀκτὴν τῆς Σαλαμινίης χώρης, γένος ἐόντες Ἀθηναῖοι, ἐς τὴν Ψυττάλειαν νῆσον ἀπέβησε ἄγων, οἳ τοὺς Πέρσας τοὺς ἐν τῆι νησῖδι ταύτηι κατεφόνευσαν πάντας.

Ὡς δὲ ἡ ναυμαχίη διελέλυτο, κατειρύσαντες ἐς τὴν Σαλαμῖνα οἱ **96**
Ἕλληνες τῶν ναυηγίων ὅσα ταύτηι ἐτύγχανε ἔτι ἐόντα, ἕτοιμοι
ἦσαν ἐς ἄλλην ναυμαχίην, ἐλπίζοντες τῆισι περιεούσηισι νηυσὶ ἔτι
χρήσεσθαι βασιλέα. τῶν δὲ ναυηγίων πολλὰ ὑπολαβὼν ἄνεμος 2
ζέφυρος, ἔφερε τῆς Ἀττικῆς ἐπὶ τὴν ἠιόνα τὴν καλεομένην Κωλιάδα,
ὥστε ἀποπλῆσαι [τὸν χρησμὸν τόν τε ἄλλον πάντα τὸν περὶ
τῆς ναυμαχίης ταύτης εἰρημένον Βάκιδι καὶ Μουσαίωι, καὶ δὴ καὶ
κατὰ τὰ ναυήγια τὰ ταύτηι ἐξενειχθέντα] τὸ εἰρημένον πολλοῖσι
ἔτεσι πρότερον τούτων ἐν χρησμῶι Λυσιστράτωι, Ἀθηναίωι ἀνδρὶ
χρησμολόγωι, τὸ ἐλελήθεε πάντας τοὺς Ἕλληνας·

> Κωλιάδες δὲ γυναῖκες ἐρετμοῖσι φρύξουσι.

τοῦτο δὲ ἔμελλε ἀπελάσαντος βασιλέος ἔσεσθαι.

97–129 The aftermath

97–103 Persian reactions to the defeat

Ξέρξης δέ, ὡς ἔμαθε τὸ γεγονὸς πάθος, δείσας μή τις τῶν Ἰώνων ὑπο- **97**
θῆται τοῖσι Ἕλλησι, ἢ αὐτοὶ νοήσωσι, πλέειν ἐς τὸν Ἑλλήσποντον

96.2 ἀποπλῆσαι codd.: *ut impletum sit* Valla: ἀποπλῆσθαι Buttmann: ἀποπεπλῆσθαι Abicht
96.2 τὸν χρησμόν . . . ἐξενειχθέντα del. Powell 96.2 φρύξουσι I. Kuhn: φρίξουσι codd.

λύσοντες τὰς γεφύρας, καὶ ἀπολαμφθεὶς ἐν τῆι Εὐρώπηι κινδυνεύσηι
ἀπολέσθαι, δρησμὸν ἐβούλευε. θέλων δὲ μὴ ἐπίδηλος εἶναι μήτε τοῖσι
Ἕλλησι μήτε τοῖσι ἑωυτοῦ, ἐς τὴν Σαλαμῖνα χῶμα ἐπειρᾶτο διαχοῦν,
γαύλους τε Φοινικηίους συνέδεε, ἵνα ἀντί τε σχεδίης ἔωσι καὶ τείχεος,
2 ἀρτέετό τε ἐς πόλεμον ὡς ναυμαχίην ἄλλην ποιησόμενος. ὁρῶντες δέ
μιν πάντες οἱ ἄλλοι ταῦτα πρήσσοντα, εὖ ἠπιστέατο ὡς ἐκ παντὸς
νόου παρεσκεύασται μένων πολεμήσειν· Μαρδόνιον δ᾽οὐδὲν τούτων
ἐλάνθανε, ὡς μάλιστα ἔμπειρον ἐόντα τῆς ἐκείνου διανοίης.
98 Ταῦτά τε ἅμα Ξέρξης ἐποίεε καὶ ἔπεμπε ἐς Πέρσας ἀγγελέοντα τὴν
παρεοῦσάν σφι συμφορήν. τούτων δὲ τῶν ἀγγέλων ἔστι οὐδὲν ὅ τι
θᾶσσον παραγίνεται, θνητὸν ἐόν· οὕτω τοῖσι Πέρσηισι ἐξεύρηται
τοῦτο. λέγουσι γὰρ ὡς, ὁσέων ἂν ἡμερέων <ἦι> ἡ πᾶσα ὁδός,
τοσοῦτοι ἵπποι τε καὶ ἄνδρες διεστᾶσι, κατὰ ἡμερησίην ὁδὸν
ἑκάστην ἵππος τε καὶ ἀνὴρ τεταγμένος· τοὺς οὔτε νιφετός, οὐκ
ὄμβρος, οὐ καῦμα, οὐ νὺξ ἔργει, μὴ οὐ κατανύσαι τὸν προκείμενον
2 αὐτῶι δρόμον τὴν ταχίστην. ὁ μὲν δὴ πρῶτος δραμὼν παραδιδοῖ τὰ
ἐντεταλμένα τῶι δευτέρωι, ὁ δὲ δεύτερος τῶι τρίτωι· τὸ δὲ ἐνθεῦτεν
ἤδη κατ᾽ἄλλον <καὶ ἄλλον> διεξέρχεται παραδιδόμενα, κατά περ
ἐν Ἕλλησι ἡ λαμπαδηφορίη, τὴν τῶι Ἡφαίστωι ἐπιτελέουσι. τοῦτο
τὸ δράμημα τῶν ἵππων καλέουσι Πέρσαι ἀγγαρήιον.
99 Ἡ μὲν δὴ πρώτη ἐς Σοῦσα ἀγγελίη ἀπικομένη, ὡς ἔχοι Ἀθήνας
Ξέρξης, ἔτερψε οὕτω δή τι Περσέων τοὺς ὑπολειφθέντας, ὡς τάς τε
ὁδοὺς μυρσίνηι πάσας ἐστόρεσαν καὶ ἐθυμίων θυμιήματα, καὶ αὐτοὶ
2 ἦσαν ἐν θυσίηισί τε καὶ εὐπαθείηισι. ἡ δὲ δευτέρη σφι ἀγγελίη ἐπ-
εσελθοῦσα συνέχεε οὕτω ὥστε τοὺς κιθῶνας κατερρήξαντο πάντες,
βοῆι τε καὶ οἰμωγῆι ἐχρέωντο ἀπλέτωι, Μαρδόνιον ἐν αἰτίηι τιθέν-
τες. οὐκ οὕτω δὲ περὶ τῶν νεῶν ἀχθόμενοι ταῦτα οἱ Πέρσαι ἐποίευν,
ὡς περὶ αὐτῶι Ξέρξηι δειμαίνοντες.
100 Καὶ περὶ Πέρσας μὲν ἦν ταῦτα τὸν πάντα μεταξὺ χρόνον γινό-
μενα, μέχρι οὗ Ξέρξης αὐτός σφεας ἀπικόμενος ἔπαυσε. Μαρδόνιος δέ,
ὁρῶν μὲν Ξέρξην συμφορὴν μεγάλην ἐκ τῆς ναυμαχίης ποιεύμενον,
ὑποπτεύων δὲ αὐτὸν δρησμὸν βουλεύειν ἐκ τῶν Ἀθηνέων, φροντίσας
πρὸς ἑωυτόν, ὡς δώσει δίκην ἀναγνώσας βασιλέα στρατεύεσθαι ἐπὶ
τὴν Ἑλλάδα, καί οἱ κρέσσον εἴη ἀνακινδυνεῦσαι ἢ κατεργάσασθαι
τὴν Ἑλλάδα ἢ αὐτὸν καλῶς τελευτῆσαι τὸν βίον ὑπὲρ μεγάλων
αἰωρηθέντα· πλέον μέντοι ἔφερέ οἱ ἡ γνώμη κατεργάσασθαι

98.1 ἦι add. Schaefer 98.2 καὶ ἄλλον add. Stein; cf. *alium atque alium* Valla 98.2 κατά περ . . . ἐπιτελέουσι del. Powell 99.2 ἐπεσελθοῦσα Reiske: ἐπεξελθοῦσα codd. 100.1 γινόμενα Stein: γενόμενον codd. 100.1 ἀνακινδυνεύσαντα van Herwerden

τὴν Ἑλλάδα. λογισάμενος ὦν ταῦτα, προσέφερε τὸν λόγον τόν-
δε· "δέσποτα, μήτε λυπέο μήτε συμφορὴν μηδεμίαν μεγάλην ποιεῦ 2
τοῦδε τοῦ γεγονότος εἵνεκα πρήγματος. οὐ γὰρ ξύλων ἀγὼν ὁ τὸ
πᾶν φέρων ἐστὶ ἡμῖν, ἀλλ' ἀνδρῶν τε καὶ ἵππων. σοὶ δὲ οὔτε τις
τούτων τῶν τὸ πᾶν σφίσι ἤδη δοκεόντων κατεργάσθαι, ἀποβὰς
ἀπὸ τῶν νεῶν, πειρήσεται ἀντιωθῆναι, οὔτ' ἐκ τῆς ἠπείρου τῆσ-
δε· οἵ τε ἡμῖν ἠντιώθησαν, ἔδοσαν δίκας. εἰ μέν νυν δοκέει, αὐτίκα 3
πειρώμεθα τῆς Πελοποννήσου· εἰ δὲ καὶ δοκέει ἐπισχεῖν, παρέχει
ποιέειν ταῦτα. μὴ δὲ δυσθύμεε· οὐ γὰρ ἔστι Ἕλλησι οὐδεμία ἔκδυ-
σις μὴ οὐ, δόντας λόγον τῶν ἐποίησαν νῦν τε καὶ πρότερον, εἶναι
σοὺς δούλους. μάλιστα μέν νυν ταῦτα ποίεε· εἰ δ' ἄρα τοι βεβούλευ-
ται αὐτὸν ἀπελαύνοντα ἀπάγειν τὴν στρατιήν, ἄλλην ἔχω καὶ ἐκ
τῶνδε βουλήν. σὺ Πέρσας, βασιλεῦ, μὴ ποιήσῃς καταγελάστους 4
γενέσθαι Ἕλλησι· οὐδὲν γὰρ ἐν Πέρσῃσί τοι δεδήληται τῶν πρηγ-
μάτων, οὐδὲ ἐρέεις ὅκου ἐγενόμεθα ἄνδρες κακοί. εἰ δὲ Φοίνικές τε καὶ
Αἰγύπτιοι καὶ Κύπριοί τε καὶ Κίλικες κακοὶ ἐγένοντο, οὐδὲν πρὸς
Πέρσας τοῦτο προσήκει τὸ πάθος. ἤδη ὦν, ἐπειδὴ οὐ Πέρσαι τοι 5
αἴτιοί εἰσι, ἐμοὶ πείθεο· εἴ τοι δέδοκται μὴ παραμένειν, σὺ μὲν ἐς ἤθεα
τὰ σεωυτοῦ ἀπέλαυνε, τῆς στρατιῆς ἀπάγων τὸ πολλόν, ἐμὲ δὲ σοὶ
χρὴ τὴν Ἑλλάδα παρασχεῖν δεδουλωμένην, τριήκοντα μυριάδας
τοῦ στρατοῦ ἀπολεξάμενον."

Ταῦτα ἀκούσας Ξέρξης, ὡς ἐκ κακῶν ἐχάρη τε καὶ ἥσθη, πρὸς **101**
Μαρδόνιόν τε βουλευσάμενος ἔφη ἀποκρινέεσθαι ὁκότερον ποιήσει
τούτων. ὡς δὲ ἐβουλεύετο ἅμα Περσέων τοῖσι ἐπικλήτοισι, ἔδοξέ
οἱ καὶ Ἀρτεμισίην ἐς συμβουλίην μεταπέμψασθαι, ὅτι πρότερον
ἐφαίνετο μούνη νοέουσα τὰ ποιητέα ἦν. ὡς δὲ ἀπίκετο ἡ Ἀρτεμισίη, 2
μεταστησάμενος τοὺς ἄλλους, τούς τε συμβούλους Περσέων καὶ
τοὺς δορυφόρους, ἔλεξε Ξέρξης τάδε· "κελεύει με Μαρδόνιος μένοντα
αὐτοῦ πειρᾶσθαι τῆς Πελοποννήσου, λέγων ὥς μοι Πέρσαι τε καὶ
ὁ πεζὸς στρατὸς οὐδενὸς μεταίτιοι πάθεός εἰσι, ἀλλὰ βουλομένοισί
σφι γένοιτ' ἂν ἀπόδεξις. ἐμὲ ὦν ἢ ταῦτα κελεύει ποιέειν, ἢ αὐτὸς 3
ἐθέλει, τριήκοντα μυριάδας ἀπολεξάμενος τοῦ στρατοῦ, παρασχεῖν
μοι τὴν Ἑλλάδα δεδουλωμένην, αὐτὸν δέ με κελεύει ἀπελαύνειν σὺν
τῶι λοιπῶι στρατῶι ἐς ἤθεα τὰ ἐμά. σὺ ὦν ἐμοί, καὶ γὰρ περὶ τῆς 4
ναυμαχίης εὖ συνεβούλευσας τῆς γενομένης, οὐκ ἐῶσα ποιέεσθαι,
νῦν τε συμβούλευσον ὁκότερα ποιέων ἐπιτύχω εὖ βουλευσάμενος."

Ὁ μὲν ταῦτα συνεβουλεύετο, ἡ δὲ λέγει τάδε· "βασιλεῦ, χαλεπὸν **102**
μέν ἐστι συμβουλευομένωι τυχεῖν τὰ ἄριστα εἴπασαν, ἐπὶ μέντοι

100.4 Πέρσῃσί τοι Stein: Πέρσῃσι τοῖσι ABCP

τοῖσι κατήκουσι πρήγμασι δοκέει μοι αὐτὸν μέν σε ἀπελαύνειν ὀπίσω, Μαρδόνιον δέ, εἰ ἐθέλει τε καὶ ὑποδέκεται ταῦτα ποιήσειν,
2 αὐτοῦ καταλιπεῖν σὺν τοῖσι ἐθέλει. τοῦτο μὲν γάρ, ἢν καταστρέψηται τά φησι θέλειν καί οἱ προχωρήσηι τὰ νοέων λέγει, σὸν τὸ ἔργον, ὦ δέσποτα, γίνεται· οἱ γὰρ σοὶ δοῦλοι κατεργάσαντο· τοῦτο δέ, ἢν τὰ ἐναντία τῆς Μαρδονίου γνώμης γένηται, οὐδεμία συμφορὴ μεγάλη ἔσται, σέο τε περιεόντος καὶ ἐκείνων τῶν πρηγμάτων περὶ
3 οἶκον τὸν σόν. ἢν γὰρ σύ τε περιῆις καὶ οἶκος ὁ σός, πολλοὺς πολλάκις ἀγῶνας δραμέονται περὶ σφέων αὐτῶν οἱ Ἕλληνες. Μαρδονίου δέ, ἤν τι πάθηι, λόγος οὐδεὶς γίνεται· οὐδέ τι νικῶντες οἱ Ἕλληνες νικῶσι, δοῦλον σὸν ἀπολέσαντες· σὺ δέ, τῶν εἵνεκα τὸν στόλον ἐποιήσαο, πυρώσας τὰς Ἀθήνας, ἀπελᾶις."

103 Ἥσθη τε δὴ τῆι συμβουλίηι Ξέρξης· λέγουσα γὰρ ἐπετύγχανε τά περ αὐτὸς ἐνόεε. οὐδὲ γὰρ εἰ πάντες καὶ πᾶσαι συνεβούλευον αὐτῶι μένειν, ἔμενε ἄν, δοκέειν ἐμοί· οὕτω καταρρωδήκεε. ἐπαινέσας δὲ τὴν Ἀρτεμισίην, ταύτην μὲν ἀποστέλλει ἄγουσαν αὐτοῦ τοὺς παῖδας ἐς Ἔφεσον· νόθοι γάρ τινες παῖδές οἱ συνείποντο.

104–7 The revenge of the eunuch Hermotimus

104 Συνέπεμπε δὲ τοῖσι παισὶ φύλακον Ἑρμότιμον, γένος μὲν ἐόντα Πηδασέα, φερόμενον δὲ οὐ τὰ δεύτερα τῶν εὐνούχων παρὰ βασιλέϊ, [οἱ δὲ Πηδασέες οἰκέουσι ὑπὲρ Ἁλικαρνησσοῦ· ἐν δὲ τοῖσι Πηδάσοισι τούτοισι τοιόνδε συμφέρεται πρῆγμα γίνεσθαι· ἐπεὰν τοῖσι ἀμφικτυόσι πᾶσι τοῖσι ἀμφὶ ταύτης οἰκέουσι τῆς πόλιος μέλληι τι ἐντὸς χρόνου ἔσεσθαι χαλεπόν, τότε ἡ ἱρείη αὐτόθι τῆς Ἀθηναίης
105 φύει πώγωνα μέγαν. τοῦτο δέ σφι δὶς ἤδη ἐγένετο. Ἐκ τούτων δὴ τῶν Πηδασέων ὁ Ἑρμότιμος ἦν] τῶι μεγίστη τίσις ἤδη ἀδικηθέντι ἐγένετο πάντων τῶν ἡμεῖς ἴδμεν. ἁλόντα γὰρ αὐτὸν ὑπὸ πολεμίων καὶ πωλεόμενον ὠνέεται Πανιώνιος ἀνὴρ Χῖος, ὃς τὴν ζόην κατεστήσατο ἀπ' ἔργων ἀνοσιωτάτων· ὅκως γὰρ κτήσαιτο παῖδας εἴδεος ἐπαμμένους, ἐκτάμνων ἐπώλεε ἀγινέων ἐς Σάρδις τε καὶ Ἔφεσον
2 χρημάτων μεγάλων. παρὰ γὰρ τοῖσι βαρβάροισι τιμιώτεροί εἰσι οἱ εὐνοῦχοι πίστιος εἵνεκα τῆς πάσης τῶν ἐνορχέων. ἄλλους τε δὴ ὁ Πανιώνιος ἐξέταμε πολλούς, ἅτε ποιεύμενος ἐκ τούτου τὴν ζόην, καὶ δὴ καὶ τοῦτον. καὶ οὐ γὰρ τὰ πάντα ἐδυστύχεε ὁ Ἑρμότιμος, ἀπικνέεται ἐκ τῶν Σαρδίων παρὰ βασιλέα μετ' ἄλλων δώρων, χρόνου δὲ προϊόντος, πάντων τῶν εὐνούχων ἐτιμήθη μάλιστα παρὰ Ξέρξηι.

104 οἱ δέ . . . Ἑρμότιμος ἦν del. Valckenaer: om. Const.

Ὡς δὲ τὸ στράτευμα τὸ Περσικὸν ὅρμα βασιλεὺς ἐπὶ τὰς Ἀθήνας **106**
ἐὼν ἐν Σάρδισι, ἐνθαῦτα καταβὰς κατὰ δή τι πρῆγμα ὁ Ἑρμότιμος
ἐς γῆν τῆς Μυσίης, τὴν Χῖοι μὲν νέμονται, Ἀταρνεὺς δὲ καλέεται,
εὑρίσκει τὸν Πανιώνιον ἐνθαῦτα. ἐπιγνοὺς δέ, ἔλεγε πρὸς αὐτὸν 2
πολλοὺς καὶ φιλίους λόγους, πρῶτα μέν οἱ καταλέγων ὅσα αὐτὸς
δι᾽ ἐκεῖνον ἔχοι ἀγαθά, δεύτερα δέ οἱ ὑπισχνεύμενος ἀντὶ τούτων
ὅσα μιν ἀγαθὰ ποιήσει, ἢν κομίσας τοὺς οἰκέτας οἰκέηι ἐκείνηι·
ὥστε ὑποδεξάμενον ἄσμενον τοὺς λόγους τὸν Πανιώνιον, κομί-
σαι τὰ τέκνα καὶ τὴν γυναῖκα. ὡς δὲ ἄρα πανοικίηι μιν περι- 3
έλαβε, ἔλεγε ὁ Ἑρμότιμος τάδε· "ὦ πάντων ἀνδρῶν ἤδη μάλιστα
ἀπ᾽ ἔργων ἀνοσιωτάτων τὸν βίον κτησάμενε, τί σε ἐγὼ κακὸν
ἢ αὐτὸς ἢ τῶν ἐμῶν τις ἐργάσατο, ἢ σὲ ἢ τῶν σῶν τινα, ὅτι
με ἀντ᾽ ἀνδρὸς ἐποίησας τὸ μηδὲν εἶναι; ἐδόκεές τε θεοὺς λήσειν
οἷα ἐμηχανῶ τότε, οἵ σε ποιήσαντα ἀνόσια, νόμωι δικαίωι χρεώ-
μενοι, ὑπήγαγον ἐς χεῖρας τὰς ἐμάς, ὥστε σε μὴ μέμψασθαι τὴν
ἀπ᾽ ἐμέο τοι ἐσομένην δίκην." ὡς δέ οἱ ταῦτα ὠνείδισε, ἀχθέν- 4
των τῶν παίδων ἐς ὄψιν, ἠναγκάζετο ὁ Πανιώνιος τῶν ἑωυτοῦ
παίδων, τεσσέρων ἐόντων, τὰ αἰδοῖα ἀποτάμνειν, ἀναγκαζόμενος
δὲ ἐποίεε ταῦτα· αὐτοῦ τε, ὡς ταῦτα ἐργάσατο, οἱ παῖδες ἀναγκαζό-
μενοι ἀπέταμνον. Πανιώνιον μέν νυν οὕτω περιῆλθε ἥ τε τίσις καὶ
Ἑρμότιμος.

Ξέρξης δέ, ὡς τοὺς παῖδας ἐπέτρεψε Ἀρτεμισίηι ἀπάγειν ἐς **107**
Ἔφεσον, καλέσας Μαρδόνιον ἐκέλευέ μιν τῆς στρατιῆς διαλέγειν τοὺς
βούλεται, καὶ ποιέειν τοῖσι λόγοισι τὰ ἔργα πειρώμενον ὅμοια.
ταύτην μὲν τὴν ἡμέρην ἐς τοσοῦτον ἐγίνετο, τῆς δὲ νυκτός, κελεύσαν-
τος βασιλέος, τὰς νέας οἱ στρατηγοὶ ἐκ τοῦ Φαλήρου ἀπῆγον ὀπίσω
ἐς τὸν Ἑλλήσποντον, ὡς τάχεος εἶχε ἕκαστος, διαφυλαξούσας τὰς
σχεδίας πορευθῆναι βασιλέϊ. ἐπεὶ δὲ ἀγχοῦ ἦσαν Ζωστῆρος πλέον- 2
τες οἱ βάρβαροι, ἀνατείνουσι γὰρ ἄκραι λεπταὶ τῆς ἠπείρου ταύτης,
ἔδοξάν τε νέας εἶναι καὶ ἔφευγον ἐπὶ πολλόν. χρόνωι δὲ μαθόντες ὅτι
οὐ νέες εἶεν ἀλλ᾽ ἄκραι, συλλεχθέντες ἐκομίζοντο.

108–12 Greek military activity

Ὡς δὲ ἡμέρη ἐγίνετο, ὁρῶντες οἱ Ἕλληνες κατὰ χώρην μένοντα **108**
τὸν στρατὸν τὸν πεζόν, ἤλπιζον καὶ τὰς νέας εἶναι περὶ
Φάληρον, ἐδόκεόν τε ναυμαχήσειν σφέας, παραρτέοντό τε ὡς

106.1 τῆς Μυσίης Pingel: τὴν Μυσίην codd. 106.3 μέμψεσθαι Madvig, Cobet: μέμψασθαι codd.

ἀλεξησόμενοι. ἐπεὶ δὲ ἐπύθοντο τὰς νέας οἰχωκυίας, αὐτίκα μετὰ
ταῦτα ἐδόκεε ἐπιδιώκειν. τὸν μέν νυν ναυτικὸν τὸν Ξέρξεω στρατὸν
οὐκ ἐπεῖδον διώξαντες μέχρι Ἄνδρου, ἐς δὲ τὴν Ἄνδρον ἀπικό-
2 μενοι ἐβουλεύοντο. Θεμιστοκλέης μέν νυν γνώμην ἀπεδείκνυτο, διὰ
νήσων τραπομένους καὶ ἐπιδιώξαντας τὰς νέας, πλέειν ἰθέως ἐπὶ τὸν
Ἑλλήσποντον, λύσοντας τὰς γεφύρας. Εὐρυβιάδης δὲ τὴν ἐναντίην
ταύτηι γνώμην ἐτίθετο, λέγων ὡς εἰ λύσουσι τὰς σχεδίας, τοῦτ᾽
3 ἂν μέγιστον πάντων σφεῖς κακῶν τὴν Ἑλλάδα ἐργασαίατο. εἰ γὰρ
ἀναγκασθείη ἀπολαμφθεὶς ὁ Πέρσης μένειν ἐν τῆι Εὐρώπηι, πειρῶιτο
ἂν ἡσυχίην μὴ ἄγειν, ὡς ἄγοντι μέν οἱ ἡσυχίην οὔτε τι προχωρέειν
οἷόν τε ἔσται τῶν πρηγμάτων, οὔτε τις κομιδὴ τὸ ὀπίσω φανήσεται,
λιμῶι τέ οἱ ἡ στρατιὴ διαφθερέεται· ἐπιχειρέοντι δὲ αὐτῶι καὶ ἔργου
ἐχομένωι πάντα τὰ κατὰ τὴν Εὐρώπην οἷά τε ἔσται προσχωρῆ-
σαι, κατὰ πόλις τε καὶ κατὰ ἔθνεα, ἤτοι ἁλισκομένων γε ἢ πρὸ
τούτου ὁμολογεόντων, τροφήν τε ἕξειν σφέας τὸν ἐπέτειον αἰεὶ τὸν
4 τῶν Ἑλλήνων καρπόν. ἀλλὰ δοκέειν γὰρ νικηθέντα τῆι ναυμαχίηι
οὐ μενέειν ἐν τῆι Εὐρώπηι τὸν Πέρσην· ἐατέον ὦν εἶναι φεύγειν,
ἐς ὃ ἔλθηι φεύγων ἐς τὴν ἑωυτοῦ· τὸ ἐνθεῦτεν δὲ περὶ τῆς ἐκείνου
ποιέεσθαι ἤδη τὸν ἀγῶνα ἐκέλευε. ταύτης δὲ εἴχοντο τῆς γνώμης
καὶ Πελοποννησίων τῶν ἄλλων οἱ στρατηγοί.
109 Ὡς δὲ ἔμαθε ὅτι οὐ πείσει τούς γε πολλοὺς πλέειν ἐς τὸν
Ἑλλήσποντον ὁ Θεμιστοκλέης, μεταβαλὼν πρὸς τοὺς Ἀθηναίους
(οὗτοι γὰρ μάλιστα ἐκπεφευγότων περιημέκτεον, ὁρμέατό τε ἐς
τὸν Ἑλλήσποντον πλέειν καὶ ἐπὶ σφέων αὐτῶν βαλόμενοι, εἰ
2 ὦλλοι μὴ βουλοίατο), ἔλεγέ σφι τάδε· "καὶ αὐτὸς ἤδη πολλοῖσι
παρεγενόμην καὶ πολλῶι πλέω ἀκήκοα τοιάδε γενέσθαι, ἄνδρας ἐς
ἀναγκαίην ἀπειληθέντας νενικημένους ἀναμάχεσθαί τε καὶ ἀναλαμ-
βάνειν τὴν προτέρην κακότητα. ἡμεῖς δέ, εὕρημα γὰρ εὑρήκαμεν
ἡμέας τε αὐτοὺς καὶ τὴν Ἑλλάδα, νέφος τοσοῦτον ἀνθρώπων
3 ἀνωσάμενοι, μὴ διώκωμεν ἄνδρας φεύγοντας. τάδε γὰρ οὐκ ἡμεῖς
κατεργασάμεθα, ἀλλὰ θεοί τε καὶ ἥρωες, οἳ ἐφθόνησαν ἄνδρα ἕνα
τῆς τε Ἀσίης καὶ τῆς Εὐρώπης βασιλεῦσαι, ἐόντα ἀνόσιόν τε καὶ
ἀτάσθαλον· ὃς τά τε ἱρὰ καὶ τὰ ἴδια ἐν ὁμοίωι ἐποιέετο, ἐμπιπράς
τε καὶ καταβάλλων τῶν θεῶν τὰ ἀγάλματα· ὃς καὶ τὴν θάλασσαν
4 ἀπεμαστίγωσε πέδας τε κατῆκε. ἀλλ᾽ εὖ γὰρ ἔχει ἐς τὸ παρεὸν ἡμῖν,
νῦν μὲν ἐν τῆι Ἑλλάδι καταμείναντας, ἡμέων τε αὐτῶν ἐπιμεληθῆναι
καὶ τῶν οἰκετέων, καί τις οἰκίην τε ἀναπλασάσθω καὶ σπόρου
ἀνακῶς ἐχέτω, παντελέως ἀπελάσας τὸν βάρβαρον· ἅμα δὲ τῶι ἔαρι

108.2 ἐργασαίατο Dindorf: ἐργάσαιτο ABCDPV

καταπλέωμεν ἐπὶ Ἑλλησπόντου καὶ Ἰωνίης." ταῦτα ἔλεγε ἀποθήκην
μέλλων ποιήσεσθαι ἐς τὸν Πέρσην, ἵνα ἢν ἄρα τί μιν καταλαμβάνηι
πρὸς Ἀθηναίων πάθος ἔχηι ἀποστροφήν· τά περ ὦν καὶ ἐγένετο.

Θεμιστοκλέης μὲν ταῦτα λέγων διέβαλλε, Ἀθηναῖοι δὲ ἐπείθοντο· **110**
ἐπειδὴ γὰρ καὶ πρότερον δεδογμένος εἶναι σοφός, ἐφάνη ἐὼν ἀληθέως
σοφός τε καὶ εὔβουλος, πάντως ἕτοιμοι ἦσαν λέγοντι πείθεσθαι. ὡς 2
δὲ οὗτοί οἱ ἀνεγνωσμένοι ἦσαν, αὐτίκα μετὰ ταῦτα ὁ Θεμιστοκλέης
ἄνδρας ἀπέπεμπε ἔχοντας πλοῖον, τοῖσι ἐπίστευε σιγᾶν ἐς πᾶσαν
βάσανον ἀπικνεομένοισι τὰ αὐτὸς ἐνετείλατο βασιλέϊ φράσαι· τῶν
καὶ Σίκιννος ὁ οἰκέτης αὖτις ἐγένετο. οἳ ἐπείτε ἀπίκοντο πρὸς τὴν
Ἀττικήν, οἱ μὲν κατέμενον ἐπὶ τῶι πλοίωι, Σίκιννος δὲ ἀναβὰς παρὰ
Ξέρξην ἔλεγε τάδε· "ἔπεμψέ με Θεμιστοκλέης ὁ Νεοκλέος, στρατηγὸς 3
μὲν Ἀθηναίων, ἀνὴρ δὲ τῶν συμμάχων πάντων ἄριστος καὶ σοφώ-
τατος, φράσοντά τοι ὅτι Θεμιστοκλέης ὁ Ἀθηναῖος, σοὶ βουλόμενος
ὑπουργέειν, ἔσχε τοὺς Ἕλληνας τὰς νέας βουλομένους διώκειν καὶ
τὰς ἐν Ἑλλησπόντωι γεφύρας λύειν. καὶ νῦν κατ' ἡσυχίην πολλὴν
κομίζεο."

Οἱ μὲν ταῦτα σημήναντες ἀπέπλεον ὀπίσω. οἱ δὲ Ἕλληνες, ἐπείτε **111**
σφι ἀπέδοξε μήτ' ἐπιδιώκειν ἔτι προσωτέρω τῶν βαρβάρων τὰς
νέας, μήτε πλέειν ἐς τὸν Ἑλλήσποντον λύσοντας τὸν πόρον, τὴν
Ἄνδρον περικατέατο ἐξελεῖν ἐθέλοντες. πρῶτοι γὰρ Ἄνδριοι νησι- 2
ωτέων, αἰτηθέντες πρὸς Θεμιστοκλέος, χρήματα οὐκ ἔδοσαν, ἀλλὰ
προϊσχομένου Θεμιστοκλέος λόγον τόνδε, ὡς ἥκοιεν Ἀθηναῖοι περὶ
ἑωυτοὺς ἔχοντες δύο θεοὺς μεγάλους, Πειθώ τε καὶ Ἀναγκαίην,
οὕτω τέ σφι κάρτα δοτέα εἶναι χρήματα, ὑπεκρίναντο πρὸς ταῦτα
λέγοντες ὡς κατὰ λόγον ἦσαν ἄρα αἱ Ἀθῆναι μεγάλαι τε καὶ εὐδαί-
μονες, <αἳ> καὶ θεῶν χρηστῶν ἥκοιεν εὖ· ἐπεὶ Ἀνδρίους γε εἶναι 3
γεωπείνας ἐς τὰ μέγιστα ἀνήκοντας, καὶ θεοὺς δύο ἀχρήστους οὐκ
ἐκλείπειν σφέων τὴν νῆσον ἀλλ' αἰεὶ φιλοχωρέειν, Πενίην τε καὶ
Ἀμηχανίην, καὶ τούτων τῶν θεῶν ἐπηβόλους ἐόντας Ἀνδρίους οὐ
δώσειν χρήματα· οὐδέκοτε γὰρ <ἂν> τῆς ἑωυτῶν ἀδυναμίης τὴν
Ἀθηναίων δύναμιν εἶναι κρέσσω. οὗτοι μὲν δὴ ταῦτα ὑποκρινάμενοι
καὶ οὐ δόντες τὰ χρήματα ἐπολιορκέοντο.

Θεμιστοκλέης δέ, οὐ γὰρ ἐπαύετο πλεονεκτέων, ἐσπέμπων ἐς **112**
τὰς ἄλλας νήσους ἀπειλητηρίους λόγους, αἴτεε χρήματα διὰ τῶν
αὐτῶν ἀγγέλων χρεώμενος, τοῖσι καὶ πρὸς βασιλέα ἐχρήσατο,
λέγων ὡς εἰ μὴ δώσουσι τὸ αἰτεόμενον, ἐπάξει τὴν στρατιὴν

111.2 αἳ add. Dobree 111.3 ἂν add. Dobree 112.1 χρεώμενος τοῖσι codd.: χρεώμενος del. Cobet, Madvig:]cτοιc[P.Oxy. ined. B

2 τῶν Ἑλλήνων καὶ πολιορκέων ἐξαιρήσει. λέγων ταῦτα συνέλεγε
χρήματα μεγάλα παρὰ Καρυστίων τε καὶ Παρίων, οἳ πυνθανόμενοι
τήν τε Ἄνδρον ὡς πολιορκέοιτο διότι ἐμήδισε, καὶ Θεμιστοκλέα ὡς εἴη
ἐν αἴνηι μεγίστηι τῶν στρατηγῶν, δείσαντες ταῦτα ἔπεμπον χρή-
ματα. εἰ δὲ δή τινες καὶ ἄλλοι ἔδοσαν νησιωτέων, οὐκ ἔχω εἰπεῖν·
3 δοκέω δέ τινας καὶ ἄλλους δοῦναι καὶ οὐ τούτους μούνους. καίτοι
Καρυστίοισί γε οὐδὲν τούτου εἵνεκα τοῦ κακοῦ ὑπερβολὴ ἐγένετο·
Πάριοι δὲ Θεμιστοκλέα χρήμασι ἱλασάμενοι διέφυγον τὸ στράτευμα.
Θεμιστοκλέης μέν νυν ἐξ Ἄνδρου ὁρμώμενος, χρήματα παρὰ νησι-
ωτέων ἐκτᾶτο λάθρηι τῶν ἄλλων στρατηγῶν.

113–20 Mardonius selects his army and Xerxes returns to Persia

113 Οἱ δ᾽ ἀμφὶ Ξέρξην, ἐπισχόντες ὀλίγας ἡμέρας μετὰ τὴν ναυμαχίην,
ἐξήλαυνον ἐς Βοιωτοὺς τὴν αὐτὴν ὁδόν. ἔδοξε γὰρ Μαρδονίωι, ἅμα
μὲν προπέμψαι βασιλέα, ἅμα δὲ ἀνωρίη εἶναι τοῦ ἔτεος πολεμέειν,
χειμερίσαι τε ἄμεινον εἶναι ἐν Θεσσαλίηι, καὶ ἔπειτα ἅμα τῶι ἔαρι
2 πειρᾶσθαι τῆς Πελοποννήσου. ὡς δὲ ἀπίκατο ἐς τὴν Θεσσαλίην,
ἐνθαῦτα Μαρδόνιος ἐξελέγετο πρώτους μὲν τοὺς Πέρσας πάντας
τοὺς ἀθανάτους καλεομένους, πλὴν Ὑδάρνεος τοῦ στρατηγοῦ,
οὗτος γὰρ οὐκ ἔφη λείψεσθαι βασιλέος, μετὰ δὲ τῶν ἄλλων Περ-
σέων τοὺς θωρηκοφόρους καὶ τὴν ἵππον τὴν χιλίην, καὶ Μήδους τε
καὶ Σάκας καὶ Βακτρίους τε καὶ Ἰνδούς, καὶ τὸν πεζὸν καὶ τὴν ἵππον.
3 ταῦτα μὲν ἔθνεα ὅλα εἵλετο, ἐκ δὲ τῶν ἄλλων συμμάχων ἐξελέγετο
κατ᾽ ὀλίγους, τοῖσι εἶδεά τε ὑπῆρχε διαλέγων καὶ εἰ τέοισί τι χρηστὸν
συνήιδεε πεποιημένον· ἓν δὲ πλεῖστον ἔθνος Πέρσας αἱρέετο, ἄνδρας
στρεπτοφόρους τε καὶ ψελιοφόρους, ἐπὶ δὲ Μήδους· οὗτοι δὲ τὸ
πλῆθος μὲν οὐκ ἐλάσσονες ἦσαν τῶν Περσέων, ῥώμηι δὲ ἥσσονες.
ὥστε σύμπαντας τριήκοντα μυριάδας γενέσθαι σὺν ἱππεῦσι.
114 Ἐν δὲ τούτωι τῶι χρόνωι, ἐν τῶι Μαρδόνιός τε τὴν στρατιὴν
διέκρινε καὶ Ξέρξης ἦν περὶ Θεσσαλίην, χρηστήριον ἐληλύθεε ἐκ
Δελφῶν Λακεδαιμονίοισι, Ξέρξην αἰτέειν δίκας τοῦ Λεωνίδεω φόνου,
καὶ τὸ διδόμενον ἐξ ἐκείνου δέκεσθαι. πέμπουσι δὴ κήρυκα τὴν
ταχίστην Σπαρτιῆται, ὃς ἐπειδὴ κατέλαβε ἐοῦσαν ἔτι πᾶσαν τὴν
στρατιὴν ἐν Θεσσαλίηι, ἐλθὼν ἐς ὄψιν τὴν Ξέρξεω ἔλεγε τάδε·
2 "ὦ βασιλεῦ Μήδων, Λακεδαιμόνιοί τέ σε καὶ Ἡρακλεῖδαι οἱ ἀπὸ
Σπάρτης αἰτέουσι φόνου δίκας, ὅτι σφέων τὸν βασιλέα ἀπέκτεινας
ῥυόμενον τὴν Ἑλλάδα." ὁ δὲ γελάσας τε καὶ κατασχὼν πολλὸν

113.1: ἀνωρίη ABC: ἀνωρίην PRSV ἀωρίη Cobet

χρόνον, ὥς οἱ ἐτύγχανε παρεστεὼς Μαρδόνιος, δεικνὺς ἐς τοῦτον
εἶπε· "τοιγάρ σφι Μαρδόνιος ὅδε δίκας δώσει τοιαύτας οἵας ἐκείνοισι
πρέπει."

Ὁ μὲν δὴ δεξάμενος τὸ ῥηθὲν ἀπαλλάσσετο. Ξέρξης δέ, Μαρδόνιον 115
ἐν Θεσσαλίηι καταλιπών, αὐτὸς ἐπορεύετο κατὰ τάχος ἐς τὸν
Ἑλλήσποντον, καὶ ἀπικνέεται ἐς τὸν πόρον τῆς διαβάσιος ἐν πέντε
καὶ τεσσεράκοντα ἡμέρηισι, ἀπάγων τῆς στρατιῆς οὐδὲν μέρος, ὡς
εἰπεῖν. ὅκου δὲ πορευόμενοι γινοίατο καὶ κατ᾽ οὕστινας ἀνθρώπους, 2
τὸν τούτων καρπὸν ἁρπάζοντες ἐσιτέοντο· εἰ δὲ καρπὸν μηδένα
εὕροιεν, οἱ δὲ τὴν ποίην τὴν ἐκ τῆς γῆς ἀναφυομένην καὶ τῶν
δενδρέων τὸν φλοιὸν περιλέποντες, καὶ τὰ φύλλα καταδρέποντες,
κατήσθιον, ὁμοίως τῶν τε ἡμέρων καὶ τῶν ἀγρίων, καὶ ἔλειπον
οὐδέν· ταῦτα δ᾽ ἐποίεον ὑπὸ λιμοῦ. ἐπιλαβὼν δὲ λοιμός τε τὸν 3
στρατὸν καὶ δυσεντερίη, κατ᾽ ὁδὸν ἔφθειρε. τοὺς δὲ καὶ νοσέοντας
αὐτῶν κατέλειπε, ἐπιτάσσων τῆισι πόλισι, ἵνα ἑκάστοτε γίνοιτο
ἐλαύνων, μελεδαίνειν τε καὶ τρέφειν, ἐν Θεσσαλίηι τέ τινας καὶ ἐν Σίρι
τῆς Παιονίης καὶ ἐν Μακεδονίηι. ἔνθα καὶ τὸ ἱρὸν ἅρμα καταλιπὼν 4
τοῦ Διός, ὅτε ἐπὶ τὴν Ἑλλάδα ἤλαυνε, ἀπιὼν οὐκ ἀπέλαβε, ἀλλὰ
δόντες οἱ Παίονες τοῖσι Θρήιξι, ἀπαιτέοντος Ξέρξεω ἔφασαν νεμομέ-
νας ἁρπασθῆναι ὑπὸ τῶν ἄνω Θρηίκων τῶν περὶ τὰς πηγὰς τοῦ
Στρυμόνος οἰκημένων.

Ἔνθα καὶ ὁ τῶν Βισαλτέων βασιλεὺς γῆς τε τῆς Κρηστωνικῆς 116
Θρῆιξ ἔργον ὑπερφυὲς ἐργάσατο· ὃς οὔτε αὐτὸς ἔφη τῶι Ξέρξηι
ἑκὼν εἶναι δουλεύσειν, ἀλλ᾽ οἴχετο ἄνω ἐς τὸ ὄρος τὴν Ῥοδόπην·
τοῖσί τε παισὶ ἀπηγόρευε μὴ στρατεύεσθαι ἐπὶ τὴν Ἑλλάδα. οἱ δὲ 2
ἀλογήσαντες, ἢ ἄλλως σφι θυμὸς ἐγένετο θεήσασθαι τὸν πόλεμον,
ἐστρατεύοντο ἅμα τῶι Πέρσηι. ἐπεὶ δὲ ἀνεχώρησαν ἀσινέες πάντες
ἓξ ἐόντες, ἐξώρυξε αὐτῶν ὁ πατὴρ τοὺς ὀφθαλμοὺς διὰ τὴν αἰτίην
ταύτην.

Καὶ οὗτοι μὲν τοῦτον τὸν μισθὸν ἔλαβον. οἱ δὲ Πέρσαι ὡς ἐκ 117
τῆς Θρηίκης πορευόμενοι ἀπίκοντο ἐπὶ τὸν πόρον, ἐπειγόμενοι τὸν
Ἑλλήσποντον τῆισι νηυσὶ διέβησαν ἐς Ἄβυδον· τὰς γὰρ σχεδίας
οὐκ εὗρον ἔτι ἐντεταμένας, ἀλλ᾽ ὑπὸ χειμῶνος διαλελυμένας. ἐνθαῦτα 2
δὲ κατεχόμενοι σιτία [τε] πλέω ἢ κατ᾽ ὁδὸν ἐλάγχανον, οὐδένα τε
κόσμον ἐμπιπλάμενοι καὶ ὕδατα μεταβάλλοντες, ἀπέθνηισκον τοῦ
στρατοῦ τοῦ περιεόντος πολλοί. οἱ δὲ λοιποὶ ἅμα Ξέρξηι ἀπικνέον-
ται ἐς Σάρδις.

Ἔστι δὲ καὶ ἄλλος ὅδε λόγος λεγόμενος, ὡς ἐπειδὴ Ξέρξης 118
ἀπελαύνων ἐξ Ἀθηνέων ἀπίκετο ἐπ᾽ Ἠιόνα τὴν ἐπὶ Στρυμόνι,
ἐνθεῦτεν οὐκέτι ὁδοιπορίηισι διεχρᾶτο, ἀλλὰ τὴν μὲν στρατιὴν

Ὑδάρνεϊ ἐπιτρέπει ἀπάγειν ἐς τὸν Ἑλλήσποντον, αὐτὸς δ᾽ ἐπὶ νεὸς
2 Φοινίσσης ἐπιβὰς ἐκομίζετο ἐς τὴν Ἀσίην. πλέοντα δέ μιν ἄνεμον
Στρυμονίην ὑπολαβεῖν μέγαν καὶ κυματίην. καὶ δὴ μᾶλλον γάρ
τι χειμαίνεσθαι, γεμούσης τῆς νεὸς ὥστε ἐπὶ τοῦ καταστρώματος
ἐπεόντων συχνῶν Περσέων τῶν σὺν Ξέρξηι κομιζομένων, ἐνθαῦτα
ἐς δεῖμα πεσόντα τὸν βασιλέα, εἰρέσθαι βώσαντα τὸν κυβερνήτην, εἴ
3 τις ἐστί σφι σωτηρίη. καὶ τὸν εἶπαι· "δέσποτα, οὐκ ἔστι οὐδεμία, εἰ μὴ
τούτων ἀπαλλαγή τις γένηται τῶν πολλῶν ἐπιβατέων." καὶ Ξέρξην
λέγεται ἀκούσαντα ταῦτα εἰπεῖν· "ἄνδρες Πέρσαι, νῦν τις διαδεξάτω
ὑμέων βασιλέος κηδόμενος· ἐν ὑμῖν γὰρ οἶκε εἶναι ἐμοὶ ἡ σωτηρίη."
4 τὸν μὲν ταῦτα λέγειν, τοὺς δὲ προσκυνέοντας ἐκπηδᾶν ἐς τὴν θάλασ-
σαν, καὶ τὴν νέα ἐπικουφισθεῖσαν οὕτω δὴ ἀποσωθῆναι ἐς τὴν
Ἀσίην. ὡς δὲ ἐκβῆναι τάχιστα ἐς γῆν τὸν Ξέρξην ποιῆσαι τοιόνδε·
ὅτι μὲν ἔσωσε βασιλέος τὴν ψυχήν, δωρήσασθαι χρυσέωι στεφάνωι
τὸν κυβερνήτην, ὅτι δὲ Περσέων πολλοὺς ἀπώλεσε, ἀποταμεῖν τὴν
κεφαλὴν αὐτοῦ.

119 Οὗτος δὲ ἄλλος λέγεται λόγος περὶ τοῦ Ξέρξεω νόστου, οὐδαμῶς ἔμοιγε πιστός, οὔτε ἄλλως οὔτε τὸ Περσέων τοῦτο πάθος. εἰ γὰρ δὴ ταῦτα οὕτω εἰρέθη ἐκ τοῦ κυβερνήτεω πρὸς Ξέρξην, ἐν μυρίηισι γνώμηισι μίαν οὐκ ἔχω ἀντίξοον, μὴ οὐκ ἂν ποιῆσαι βασιλέα τοιόνδε· τοὺς μὲν ἐπὶ τοῦ καταστρώματος καταβιβάσαι ἐς κοίλην νέα, ἐόντας Πέρσας καὶ Περσέων τοὺς πρώτους, τῶν δ᾽ ἐρετέων, ἐόντων Φοινίκων, ὅκως οὐκ ἂν ἴσον πλῆθος τοῖσι Πέρσηισι ἐξέβαλε ἐς τὴν θάλασσαν. ἀλλ᾽ ὁ μέν, ὡς καὶ πρότερόν μοι εἴρηται, ὁδῶι χρεώμενος ἅμα τῶι ἄλλωι στρατῶι ἀπενόστησε ἐς τὴν Ἀσίην.

120 Μέγα δὲ καὶ τόδε μαρτύριον· φαίνεται γὰρ Ξέρξης ἐν τῆι ὀπίσω κομιδῆι ἀπικόμενος ἐς Ἄβδηρα, καὶ ξεινίην τέ σφι συνθέμενος, καὶ δωρησάμενος αὐτοὺς ἀκινάκηι τε χρυσέωι καὶ τιήρηι χρυσοπάστωι. καὶ ὡς αὐτοὶ λέγουσι Ἀβδηρῖται, λέγοντες ἔμοιγε οὐδαμῶς πιστά, πρῶτον ἐλύσατο τὴν ζώνην φεύγων ἐξ Ἀθηνέων ὀπίσω, ὡς ἐν ἀδείηι ἐών. τὰ δὲ Ἄβδηρα ἵδρυται πρὸς τοῦ Ἑλλησπόντου μᾶλλον τοῦ Στρυμόνος καὶ τῆς Ἠιόνος, ὅθεν δή μίν φασι ἐπιβῆναι ἐπὶ τὴν νέα.

121–5 Greek honours to gods and men

121 Οἱ δὲ Ἕλληνες, ἐπείτε οὐκ οἷοί τε ἐγίνοντο ἐξελεῖν τὴν Ἄνδρον, τραπόμενοι ἐς Κάρυστον καὶ δηιώσαντες αὐτῶν τὴν χώρην, ἀπαλλάσσοντο ἐς Σαλαμῖνα. πρῶτα μέν νυν τοῖσι θεοῖσι ἐξεῖλον ἀκροθίνια

119–20 del. Blakesley 119 <κατά> τό Περσέων Powell

ἄλλα τε καὶ τριήρεας τρεῖς Φοινίσσας, τὴν μὲν ἐς Ἰσθμὸν ἀναθεῖ-
ναι, ἥ περ ἔτι καὶ ἐς ἐμὲ ἦν, τὴν δὲ ἐπὶ Σούνιον, τὴν δὲ τῶι Αἴαντι
αὐτοῦ ἐς Σαλαμῖνα. μετὰ δὲ τοῦτο διεδάσαντο τὴν ληίην καὶ τὰ 2
ἀκροθίνια ἀπέπεμψαν ἐς Δελφούς, ἐκ τῶν ἐγένετο ἀνδριὰς ἔχων ἐν
τῆι χειρὶ ἀκρωτήριον νεός, ἐὼν μέγαθος δυώδεκα πηχέων· ἕστηκε
δὲ οὗτος τῆι περ ὁ Μακεδὼν Ἀλέξανδρος ὁ χρύσεος. Πέμψαντες 122
δὲ ἀκροθίνια οἱ Ἕλληνες ἐς Δελφούς, ἐπειρώτων τὸν θεὸν κοινῆι,
εἰ λελάβηκε πλήρεα καὶ ἀρεστὰ τὰ ἀκροθίνια. ὁ δὲ παρ' Ἑλλήνων
μὲν τῶν ἄλλων ἔφησε ἔχειν, παρὰ Αἰγινητέων δὲ οὔ, ἀλλὰ ἀπαίτεε
αὐτοὺς τὰ ἀριστήια τῆς ἐν Σαλαμῖνι ναυμαχίης. Αἰγινῆται δὲ πυθό-
μενοι ἀνέθεσαν ἀστέρας χρυσέους, οἳ ἐπὶ ἱστοῦ χαλκέου ἑστᾶσι τρεῖς
ἐπὶ τῆς γωνίης, ἀγχοτάτω τοῦ Κροίσου κρητῆρος.

Μετὰ δὲ τὴν διαίρεσιν τῆς ληίης, ἔπλεον οἱ Ἕλληνες ἐς τὸν 123
Ἰσθμόν, ἀριστήια δώσοντες τῶι ἀξιωτάτωι γενομένωι Ἑλλήνων
ἀνὰ τὸν πόλεμον τοῦτον. ὡς δὲ ἀπικόμενοι οἱ στρατηγοὶ ἔφερον 2
τὰς ψήφους ἐπὶ τοῦ Ποσειδέωνος τῶι βωμῶι, τὸν πρῶτον καὶ
τὸν δεύτερον κρίνοντες ἐκ πάντων, ἐνθαῦτα πᾶς τις αὐτῶν ἑωυτῶι
ἐτίθετο τὴν ψῆφον, αὐτὸς ἕκαστος δοκέων ἄριστος γενέσθαι· δεύτερα
δὲ οἱ πολλοὶ συνεξέπιπτον Θεμιστοκλέα κρίνοντες. οἱ μὲν δὴ
ἐμουνοῦντο, Θεμιστοκλέης δὲ δευτερείοισι ὑπερεβάλλετο πολλόν.

Οὐ βουλομένων δὲ ταῦτα κρίνειν τῶν Ἑλλήνων φθόνωι, ἀλλ' 124
ἀποπλεόντων ἑκάστων ἐς τὴν ἑωυτῶν ἀκρίτων, ὅμως Θεμιστοκ-
λέης ἐβώσθη τε καὶ ἐδοξώθη εἶναι ἀνὴρ πολλὸν Ἑλλήνων σοφώ-
τατος ἀνὰ πᾶσαν τὴν Ἑλλάδα. ὅτι δὲ νικῶν οὐκ ἐτιμήθη πρὸς 2
τῶν ἐν Σαλαμῖνι ναυμαχησάντων, αὐτίκα μετὰ ταῦτα ἐς Λακεδαί-
μονα ἀπίκετο, θέλων τιμηθῆναι· καί μιν Λακεδαιμόνιοι καλῶς μὲν
ὑπεδέξαντο, μεγάλως δὲ ἐτίμησαν. ἀριστήια μέν νυν ἔδοσαν Εὐρυ-
βιάδηι ἐλαίης στέφανον, σοφίης δὲ καὶ δεξιότητος Θεμιστοκλέϊ, καὶ
τούτωι στέφανον ἐλαίης· ἐδωρήσαντό τέ μιν ὄχωι τῶι ἐν Σπάρτηι
καλλιστεύοντι. αἰνέσαντες δὲ πολλά, προέπεμψαν ἀπιόντα τριηκό- 3
σιοι Σπαρτιητέων λογάδες (οὗτοι οἵ περ ἱππέες καλέονται) μέχρι
οὔρων τῶν Τεγεητικῶν. μοῦνον δὴ τοῦτον πάντων ἀνθρώπων τῶν
ἡμεῖς ἴδμεν Σπαρτιῆται προέπεμψαν.

Ὡς δὲ ἐκ τῆς Λακεδαίμονος ἀπίκετο ἐς τὰς Ἀθήνας, ἐνθαῦτα 125
Τιμόδημος Ἀφιδναῖος, τῶν ἐχθρῶν μὲν τῶν Θεμιστοκλέος ἐών,
ἄλλως δὲ οὐ τῶν ἐπιφανέων ἀνδρῶν, φθόνωι καταμαργέων ἐνείκεε
τὸν Θεμιστοκλέα, τὴν ἐς Λακεδαίμονα ἄπιξιν προφέρων, ὡς διὰ τὰς

123.2 ἔφερον DRSV: διένεμον ABC: διέφερον van Herwerden 123.2 ἀπὸ . . . τοῦ βωμοῦ Powell 124.2 ἔδοσαν <ἀνδρηίης μέν> Cobet; cf. *primas partes rei bene gestae* Valla

Ἀθήνας ἔχοι τὰ γέρεα τὰ παρὰ Λακεδαιμονίων, ἀλλ᾽ οὐ δι᾽ ἑωυτόν.
2 ὁ δέ, ἐπείτε οὐκ ἐπαύετο λέγων ταῦτα ὁ Τιμόδημος, εἶπε· "οὕτω ἔχει
τοι· οὔτ᾽ ἂν ἐγὼ ἐὼν Βελβινίτης ἐτιμήθην οὕτω πρὸς Σπαρτιητέων,
οὔτ᾽ ἂν σύ, ὤνθρωπε, ἐὼν Ἀθηναῖος."

126–9 Artabazus attacks Olynthus and Potidaea

126 Ταῦτα μέν νυν ἐς τοσοῦτο ἐγένετο. Ἀρτάβαζος δὲ ὁ Φαρνάκεος,
ἀνὴρ ἐν Πέρσῃσι λόγιμος καὶ πρόσθε ἐών, ἐκ δὲ τῶν Πλαται-
ικῶν καὶ μᾶλλον ἔτι γενόμενος, ἔχων ἓξ μυριάδας στρατοῦ τοῦ
2 Μαρδόνιος ἐξελέξατο, προέπεμπε βασιλέα μέχρι τοῦ πόρου. ὡς δὲ
ὁ μὲν ἦν ἐν τῆι Ἀσίηι, ὁ δὲ ὀπίσω πορευόμενος κατὰ τὴν Παλλήνην
ἐγίνετο, ἅτε Μαρδονίου τε χειμερίζοντος περὶ Θεσσαλίην τε καὶ
Μακεδονίην, καὶ οὐδέν κω κατεπείγοντος ἥκειν ἐς τὸ ἄλλο στρατόπε-
δον, οὐκ ἐδικαίου, ἐντυχὼν ἀπεστεῶσι Ποτειδαιήτῃσι, μὴ οὐκ ἐξαν-
3 δραποδίσασθαί σφεας. οἱ γὰρ Ποτειδαιῆται, ὡς βασιλεὺς παρεξελη-
λάκεε καὶ ὁ ναυτικὸς τοῖσι Πέρσῃσι οἰχώκεε φεύγων ἐκ Σαλαμῖνος,
ἐκ τοῦ φανεροῦ ἀπέστασαν ἀπὸ τῶν βαρβάρων· ὣς δὲ καὶ ὧλλοι
127 οἱ τὴν Παλλήνην ἔχοντες. Ἐνθαῦτα δὴ Ἀρτάβαζος ἐπολιόρκεε τὴν
Ποτείδαιαν. ὑποπτεύσας δὲ καὶ τοὺς Ὀλυνθίους ἀπίστασθαι ἀπὸ
βασιλέος, καὶ ταύτην ἐπολιόρκεε· εἶχον δὲ αὐτὴν Βοττιαῖοι ἐκ τοῦ
Θερμαίου κόλπου, ἐξαναστάντες ὑπὸ Μακεδόνων. ἐπεὶ δέ σφεας εἷλε
πολιορκέων, κατέσφαξε ἐξαγαγὼν ἐς λίμνην, τὴν δὲ πόλιν παραδι-
δοῖ Κριτοβούλωι Τορωναίωι ἐπιτροπεύειν καὶ τῶι Χαλκιδικῶι γένεϊ·
καὶ οὕτω Ὄλυνθον Χαλκιδέες ἔσχον.
128 Ἐξελὼν δὲ ταύτην ὁ Ἀρτάβαζος, τῆι Ποτειδαίηι ἐντεταμένως
προσεῖχε. προσέχοντι δέ οἱ προθύμως συντίθεται προδοσίην Τιμό-
ξεινος ὁ τῶν Σκιωναίων στρατηγός, ὅντινα μὲν τρόπον ἀρχὴν ἔγωγε
οὐκ ἔχω εἰπεῖν, οὐ γὰρ ὦν λέγεται, τέλος μέντοι τοιάδε ἐγίνετο. ὅκως
βυβλίον γράψειε ἢ Τιμόξεινος ἐθέλων παρὰ Ἀρτάβαζον πέμψαι,
ἢ Ἀρτάβαζος παρὰ Τιμόξεινον, τοξεύματος παρὰ τὰς γλυφίδας
περιειλίξαντες καὶ πτερώσαντες, τὸ βυβλίον ἐτόξευον ἐς συγκεί-
2 μενον χωρίον. ἐπάϊστος δὲ ἐγένετο ὁ Τιμόξεινος προδιδοὺς τὴν
Ποτείδαιαν· τοξεύων γὰρ ὁ Ἀρτάβαζος ἐς τὸ συγκείμενον, ἁμαρτὼν
τοῦ χωρίου τούτου βάλλει ἀνδρὸς Ποτειδαιήτεω τὸν ὦμον· τὸν
δὲ βληθέντα περιέδραμε ὅμιλος, οἷα φιλέει γίνεσθαι ἐν πολέμωι, οἳ
αὐτίκα τὸ τόξευμα λαβόντες, ὡς ἔμαθον τὸ βυβλίον, ἔφερον ἐπὶ
τοὺς στρατηγούς· παρῆν δὲ καὶ τῶν ἄλλων Παλληναίων συμμαχίη.

126.2 κατεπείγων αὐτός Pingel

τοῖσι δὲ στρατηγοῖσι ἐπιλεξαμένοισι τὸ βυβλίον, καὶ μαθοῦσι τὸν 3
αἴτιον τῆς προδοσίης, ἔδοξε μὴ καταπλέξαι Τιμόξεινον προδοσίηι
τῆς Σκιωναίων πόλιος εἵνεκα, μὴ νομιζοίατο εἶναι Σκιωναῖοι ἐς τὸν
μετέπειτα χρόνον αἰεὶ προδόται.

Ὁ μὲν δὴ τοιούτωι τρόπωι ἐπάϊστος ἐγεγόνεε. Ἀρταβάζωι δὲ 129
ἐπειδὴ πολιορκέοντι ἐγεγόνεσαν τρεῖς μῆνες, γίνεται ἄμπωτις τῆς
θαλάσσης μεγάλη καὶ χρόνον ἐπὶ πολλόν. ἰδόντες δὲ οἱ βάρβαροι
τέναγος γενόμενον, παρήισαν ἐς τὴν Παλλήνην. ὡς δὲ τὰς δύο μὲν 2
μοίρας διοδοιπορήκεσαν, ἔτι δὲ τρεῖς ὑπόλοιποι ἦσαν, τὰς διελθόν-
τας χρῆν εἶναι ἔσω ἐν τῆι Παλλήνηι, ἐπῆλθε πλημυρὶς τῆς θαλάσσης
μεγάλη, ὅση οὐδαμά κω, ὡς οἱ ἐπιχώριοι λέγουσι, πολλάκις
γινομένη. οἱ μὲν δὴ νέειν αὐτῶν οὐκ ἐπιστάμενοι διεφθείροντο, τοὺς
δὲ ἐπισταμένους οἱ Ποτειδαιῆται ἐπιπλώσαντες πλοίοισι ἀπώλε-
σαν. αἴτιον δὲ λέγουσι Ποτειδαιῆται τῆς τε ῥηχίης καὶ τῆς πλημυρί- 3
δος καὶ τοῦ Περσικοῦ πάθεος γενέσθαι τόδε, ὅτι τοῦ Ποσειδέωνος
ἐς τὸν νηὸν καὶ τὸ ἄγαλμα τὸ ἐν τῶι προαστίωι ἠσέβησαν οὗτοι
τῶν Περσέων, οἵ περ καὶ διεφθάρησαν ὑπὸ τῆς θαλάσσης· αἴτιον
δὲ τοῦτο λέγοντες, εὖ λέγειν ἔμοιγε δοκέουσι. τοὺς δὲ περιγενομέ-
νους ἀπῆγε Ἀρτάβαζος ἐς Θεσσαλίην παρὰ Μαρδόνιον. οὗτοι μὲν
οἱ προπέμψαντες βασιλέα οὕτω ἔπρηξαν.

130–44 The following spring

130–2 Mutual fear keeps the two sides apart

Ὁ δὲ ναυτικὸς ὁ Ξέρξεω <ὁ> περιγενόμενος, ὡς προσέμειξε τῆι 130
Ἀσίηι φεύγων ἐκ Σαλαμῖνος, καὶ βασιλέα τε καὶ τὴν στρατιὴν ἐκ
Χερσονήσου διεπόρθμευσε ἐς Ἄβυδον, ἐχειμέριζε ἐν Κύμηι. ἔαρος δὲ
ἐπιλάμψαντος, πρώιος συνελέγετο ἐς Σάμον· αἱ δὲ τῶν νεῶν καὶ
ἐχειμέρισαν αὐτοῦ· Περσέων δὲ καὶ Μήδων οἱ πλεῦνες ἐπεβάτευον.
στρατηγοὶ δέ σφι ἐπῆλθον Μαρδόντης τε ὁ Βαγαίου καὶ Ἀρταΰντης 2
ὁ Ἀρταχαίεω· συνῆρχε δὲ τούτοισι καὶ ἀδελφιδέος αὐτοῦ Ἀρταΰντεω
προσελομένου Ἰθαμίτρης. ἅτε δὲ μεγάλως πληγέντες, οὐ προήισαν
ἀνωτέρω τὸ πρὸς ἑσπέρης, οὐδ᾽ ἐπηνάγκαζε οὐδείς, ἀλλ᾽ ἐν τῆι
Σάμωι κατήμενοι, ἐφύλασσον τὴν Ἰωνίην μὴ ἀποστῆι, νέας ἔχοντες

129.3 καὶ τῆς πλημυρίδος del. Valckenaer sed]λη|[P.Oxy. ined. C   130.2 βαρδοντ̣η̣[P.Oxy. ined. C   130.2 αδ̣ε̣λ̣φεο̣[P.Oxy. ined. C: ἀδελφιδέος ABCPRVD[c]   130.2 Ἀρταχαίεω Stein: αρτ̣αχα̣ί̣ου P.Oxy. ined. C, codd.   130.2 Ἀρταΰντεω DPRSV: αρ] | [τ]α̣υντεο̣[P.Oxy. ined. C: Ἀρταΰντεω αὐτοῦ Krueger   130.2 Ἰθαμίτρης Wesseling ex 9.102.4: οαμ[P.Oxy. ined. C: ὀαμίτηρ R: ὁ ἀμίτρης rell.   130.2 τό P.Oxy. ined. C(post corr.) D, ABC: τά DPRSV

3 σὺν τῆισι Ἰάσι τριηκοσίας. οὐ μὲν οὐδὲ προσεδέκοντο τοὺς Ἕλληνας
ἐλεύσεσθαι ἐς τὴν Ἰωνίην, ἀλλ᾽ ἀποχρήσειν σφι τὴν ἑωυτῶν φυλάσ-
σειν, σταθμεύμενοι ὅτι σφέας οὐκ ἐπεδίωξαν φεύγοντας ἐκ Σαλαμῖνος,
ἀλλ᾽ ἄσμενοι ἀπαλλάσσοντο. κατὰ μέν νυν τὴν θάλασσαν ἑσσωμένοι
ἦσαν τῶι θυμῶι, πεζῆι δὲ ἐδόκεον πολλῶι κρατήσειν τὸν Μαρδόνιον.
4 ἐόντες δὲ ἐν Σάμωι, ἅμα μὲν ἐβουλεύοντο εἴ τι δυναίατο κακὸν τοὺς
πολεμίους ποιέειν, ἅμα δὲ καὶ ὠτακούστεον ὅκηι πεσέεται τὰ Μαρ-
δονίου πρήγματα.

131 Τοὺς δὲ Ἕλληνας τό τε ἔαρ γινόμενον ἤγειρε καὶ Μαρδόνιος ἐν Θεσ-
σαλίηι ἐών. ὁ μὲν δὴ πεζὸς οὔκω συνελέγετο, ὁ δὲ ναυτικὸς ἀπίκετο
2 ἐς Αἴγιναν, νέες ἀριθμὸν δέκα καὶ ἑκατόν. στρατηγὸς δὲ καὶ ναύαρ-
χος ἦν Λευτυχίδης ὁ Μενάρεος τοῦ Ἡγησίλεω τοῦ Ἱπποκρατίδεω
τοῦ Λευτυχίδεω τοῦ Ἀναξίλεω τοῦ Ἀρχιδήμου τοῦ Ἀναξαν-
δρίδεω τοῦ Θεοπόμπου τοῦ Νικάνδρου τοῦ Χαρίλεω τοῦ Εὐνόμου
τοῦ Πολυδέκτεω τοῦ Πρυτάνιος τοῦ Εὐρυφῶντος τοῦ Προκλέος τοῦ
Ἀριστοδήμου τοῦ Ἀριστομάχου τοῦ Κλεοδαίου τοῦ Ὕλλου τοῦ
3 Ἡρακλέος, ἐὼν τῆς ἑτέρης οἰκίης τῶν βασιλέων. οὗτοι πάντες, πλὴν
τῶν δυῶν τῶν μετὰ Λευτυχίδεα πρώτων καταλεχθέντων, οἱ ἄλλοι
βασιλέες ἐγένοντο Σπάρτης. Ἀθηναίων δὲ ἐστρατήγεε Ξάνθιππος ὁ
Ἀρίφρονος.

132 Ὡς δὲ παρεγένοντο ἐς τὴν Αἴγιναν πᾶσαι αἱ νέες, ἀπίκοντο
Ἰώνων ἄγγελοι ἐς τὸ στρατόπεδον τῶν Ἑλλήνων, οἳ καὶ ἐς
Σπάρτην ὀλίγωι πρότερον τούτων ἀπικόμενοι ἐδέοντο Λακεδαι-
2 μονίων ἐλευθεροῦν τὴν Ἰωνίην· τῶν καὶ Ἡρόδοτος ὁ Βασι-
ληίδεω ἦν. οἳ στασιῶται σφίσι γενόμενοι, ἐπεβούλευον θάνατον
Στράττι τῶι Χίου τυράννωι, ἐόντες ἀρχὴν ἑπτά. ἐπιβουλεύοντες
δέ ὡς φανεροὶ ἐγένοντο, ἐξενείκαντος τὴν ἐπιχείρησιν ἑνὸς τῶν
μετεχόντων, οὕτω δὴ οἱ λοιποὶ ἓξ ἐόντες ὑπεξέσχον ἐκ τῆς Χίου,
καὶ ἐς Σπάρτην τε ἀπίκοντο καὶ δὴ καὶ τότε ἐς τὴν Αἴγιναν,
τῶν Ἑλλήνων δεόμενοι καταπλῶσαι ἐς τὴν Ἰωνίην· οἳ προήγαγον
3 αὐτοὺς μόγις μέχρι Δήλου. τὸ γὰρ προσωτέρω πᾶν δεινὸν ἦν τοῖσι
Ἕλλησι, οὔτε τῶν χώρων ἐοῦσι ἐμπείροισι, στρατιῆς τε πάντα
πλέα ἐδόκεε εἶναι· τὴν δὲ Σάμον ἐπιστέατο δόξηι καὶ Ἡρακλέας
στήλας ἴσον ἀπέχειν. συνέπιπτε δὲ τοιοῦτον, ὥστε τοὺς μὲν βαρ-
βάρους τὸ πρὸς ἑσπέρης ἀνωτέρω Σάμου μὴ τολμᾶν [κατα]πλῶσαι
καταρρωδηκότας, τοὺς δὲ Ἕλληνας, χρηιζόντων τῶν Χίων, τὸ

130.2 αποστηι P.Oxy. ined. D, codd.: ?αποστη]ναι P.Oxy. ined. C 130.4 καί om. P.Oxy. ined. D, DRSV 131.3 τῶν ἑπτά Paulmier
132.3 [κατα]πλῶσαι van Herwerden; ἀναπλῶσαι Stein

πρὸς τὴν ἠῶ κατωτέρω Δήλου. οὕτω δέος τὸ μέσον ἐφύλασσέ σφεων.

133–9 Two ambassadors of Mardonius: Mys and Alexander; the origin of the Macedonian monarchy

Οἱ μὲν δὴ Ἕλληνες ἔπλεον ἐς τὴν Δῆλον, Μαρδόνιος δὲ περὶ τὴν Θεσσαλίην ἐχείμαζε. ἐνθεῦτεν δὲ ὁρμώμενος, ἔπεμπε κατὰ τὰ χρηστήρια ἄνδρα Εὐρωπέα γένος, τῶι οὔνομα ἦν Μῦς, ἐντειλάμενος πανταχῆι μιν χρησόμενον ἐλθεῖν, τῶν οἷά τε ἦν σφι ἀποπειρήσασθαι. ὅ τι μὲν βουλόμενος ἐκμαθεῖν πρὸς τῶν χρηστηρίων ταῦτα ἐνετέλλετο, οὐκ ἔχω φράσαι, οὐ γὰρ ὦν λέγεται· δοκέω δ᾽ ἔγωγε περὶ τῶν παρεόντων πρηγμάτων καὶ οὐκ ἄλλων πέρι πέμψαι. Οὗτος ὁ Μῦς ἔς τε **134** Λεβάδειαν φαίνεται ἀπικόμενος καὶ μισθῶι πείσας τῶν ἐπιχωρίων ἄνδρα καταβῆναι παρὰ Τροφώνιον, καὶ ἐς Ἄβας τὰς Φωκέων ἀπικόμενος ἐπὶ τὸ χρηστήριον· καὶ δὴ καὶ ἐς Θήβας πρῶτα ὡς ἀπίκετο, τοῦτο μὲν τῶι Ἰσμηνίωι Ἀπόλλωνι ἐχρήσατο (ἔστι δὲ κατά περ ἐν Ὀλυμπίηι ἱροῖσι αὐτόθι χρηστηριάζεσθαι), τοῦτο δὲ ξεῖνόν τινα καὶ οὐ Θηβαῖον χρήμασι πείσας, κατεκοίμησε ἐς Ἀμφιάρεω. Θηβαίων 2 δὲ οὐδενὶ ἔξεστι μαντεύεσθαι αὐτόθι διὰ τόδε· ἐκέλευσέ σφεας ὁ Ἀμφιάρεως, διὰ χρηστηρίων ποιεύμενος, ὁκότερα βούλονται ἑλέσθαι τούτων, ἑωυτῶι ἢ ἅτε μάντι χρᾶσθαι ἢ ἅτε συμμάχωι, τοῦ ἑτέρου ἀπεχομένους· οἱ δὲ σύμμαχόν μιν εἵλοντο εἶναι. διὰ τοῦτο μὲν οὐκ ἔξεστι Θηβαίων οὐδενὶ αὐτόθι ἐγκατακοιμηθῆναι. **133**

135 Τότε δὲ θῶμά μοι μέγιστον γενέσθαι λέγεται ὑπὸ Θηβαίων. ἐλθεῖν ἄρα τὸν Εὐρωπέα Μῦν, περιστρωφώμενον πάντα τὰ χρηστήρια, καὶ ἐς τοῦ Πτώιου Ἀπόλλωνος τὸ τέμενος. τοῦτο δὲ τὸ ἱρὸν καλέεται μὲν Πτῶιον, ἔστι δὲ Θηβαίων, κεῖται δὲ ὑπὲρ τῆς Κωπαΐδος λίμνης πρὸς ὄρεϊ ἀγχοτάτω Ἀκραιφίης πόλιος. ἐς τοῦτο 2 τὸ ἱρὸν ἐπείτε παρελθεῖν τὸν καλεόμενον τοῦτον Μῦν, ἕπεσθαι δέ οἱ τῶν ἀστῶν αἱρετοὺς ἄνδρας τρεῖς ἀπὸ τοῦ κοινοῦ, ὡς ἀπογραψομένους τὰ θεσπιεῖν ἔμελλε· καὶ πρόκατε τὸν πρόμαντιν βαρβάρωι γλώσσηι χρᾶν. καὶ τοὺς μὲν ἑπομένους τῶν Θηβαίων 3 ἐν θώματι ἔχεσθαι, ἀκούοντας βαρβάρου γλώσσης ἀντὶ Ἑλλάδος, οὐδὲ ἔχειν ὅ τι χρήσωνται τῶι παρεόντι πρήγματι. τὸν δὲ Εὐρωπέα Μῦν, ἐξαρπάσαντα παρ᾽ αὐτῶν τὴν ἐφέροντο δέλτον, τὰ λεγόμενα ὑπὸ τοῦ προφήτεω γράφειν ἐς αὐτήν, φάναι δὲ Καρίηι μιν γλώσσηι χρᾶν· συγγραψάμενον δέ, οἴχεσθαι ἀπιόντα ἐς Θεσσαλίην.

136 Μαρδόνιος δὲ ἐπιλεξάμενος ὅ τι δὴ λέγοντα ἦν τὰ χρηστήρια,
μετὰ ταῦτα ἔπεμψε ἄγγελον ἐς Ἀθήνας Ἀλέξανδρον τὸν Ἀμύν-
τεω, ἄνδρα Μακεδόνα, ἅμα μὲν ὅτι οἱ προσκηδέες οἱ Πέρσαι
ἦσαν, Ἀλεξάνδρου γὰρ ἀδελφεὴν Γυγαίην, Ἀμύντεω δὲ θυγατέρα,
Βουβάρης ἀνὴρ Πέρσης ἔσχε, ἐκ τῆς οἱ ἐγεγόνεε Ἀμύντης ὁ ἐν τῆι
Ἀσίηι, ἔχων τὸ οὔνομα τοῦ μητροπάτορος, τῶι δὴ ἐκ βασιλέος
τῆς Φρυγίης ἐδόθη Ἀλάβανδα πόλις μεγάλη νέμεσθαι· ἅμα δὲ ὁ
Μαρδόνιος, πυθόμενος ὅτι πρόξεινός τε εἴη καὶ εὐεργέτης ὁ Ἀλέξαν-
2 δρος, ἔπεμπε. τοὺς γὰρ Ἀθηναίους οὕτω ἐδόκεε μάλιστα προσ-
κτήσεσθαι, λεών τε πολλὸν ἄρα ἀκούων εἶναι καὶ ἄλκιμον, τά
τε κατὰ τὴν θάλασσαν συντυχόντα σφι παθήματα κατεργασαμέ-
3 νους μάλιστα Ἀθηναίους ἐπίστατο. τούτων δὲ προσγενομένων,
κατήλπιζε εὐπετέως τῆς θαλάσσης κρατήσειν, τά περ ἂν καὶ ἦν,
πεζῆι τε ἐδόκεε πολλῶι εἶναι κρέσσων· οὕτω τε ἐλογίζετο κατύπερθέ
οἱ τὰ πρήγματα ἔσεσθαι τῶν Ἑλληνικῶν. τάχα δ' ἂν καὶ τὰ
χρηστήρια ταῦτά οἱ προλέγοι, συμβουλεύοντα σύμμαχον τὸν
Ἀθηναῖον ποιέεσθαι. τοῖσι δὴ πειθόμενος ἔπεμπε.

137 Τοῦ δὲ Ἀλεξάνδρου τούτου ἕβδομος γενέτωρ Περδίκκης ἐστί, ὁ
κτησάμενος τῶν Μακεδόνων τὴν τυραννίδα τρόπωι τοιῶιδε. ἐξ
Ἄργεος ἔφυγον ἐς Ἰλλυριοὺς τῶν Τημένου ἀπογόνων τρεῖς ἀδελφεοί,
Γαυάνης τε καὶ Ἀέροπος καὶ Περδίκκης· ἐκ δὲ Ἰλλυριῶν ὑπερβαλόντες
2 ἐς τὴν ἄνω Μακεδονίην, ἀπίκοντο ἐς Λεβαίην πόλιν. ἐνθαῦτα δὲ ἐθή-
τευον ἐπὶ μισθῶι παρὰ τῶι βασιλέϊ, ὁ μὲν ἵππους νέμων, ὁ δὲ βοῦς, ὁ
δὲ νεώτατος αὐτῶν Περδίκκης τὰ λεπτὰ τῶν προβάτων. ἦσαν δὲ τὸ
πάλαι καὶ αἱ τυραννίδες τῶν ἀνθρώπων ἀσθενέες χρήμασι, οὐ μοῦνον
3 ὁ δῆμος· ἡ δὲ γυνὴ τοῦ βασιλέος αὐτὴ τὰ σιτία σφι ἔπεσσε. ὅκως δὲ
ὀπτώιη ὁ ἄρτος τοῦ παιδὸς τοῦ θητός, τοῦ Περδίκκεω, διπλήσιος
ἐγίνετο αὐτὸς ἑωυτοῦ. ἐπεὶ δὲ αἰεὶ τὠυτὸ τοῦτο ἐγίνετο, εἶπε πρὸς
τὸν ἄνδρα τὸν ἑωυτῆς· τὸν δὲ ἀκούσαντα ἐσῆλθε αὐτίκα, ὡς εἴη
τέρας καὶ φέροι ἐς μέγα τι. καλέσας δὲ τοὺς θῆτας, προηγόρευέ σφι
4 ἀπαλλάσσεσθαι ἐκ γῆς τῆς ἑωυτοῦ. οἱ δὲ τὸν μισθὸν ἔφασαν δίκαιοι
εἶναι ἀπολαβόντες οὕτω ἐξιέναι. ἐνθαῦτα ὁ βασιλεὺς τοῦ μισθοῦ πέρι
ἀκούσας, ἦν γὰρ κατὰ τὴν καπνοδόκην ἐς τὸν οἶκον ἐσέχων ὁ ἥλιος,
εἶπε θεοβλαβὴς γενόμενος, "μισθὸν δὲ ὑμῖν ἐγὼ ὑμέων ἄξιον τόνδε
5 ἀποδίδωμι," δέξας τὸν ἥλιον. ὁ μὲν δὴ Γαυάνης τε καὶ ὁ Ἀέροπος οἱ
πρεσβύτεροι ἕστασαν ἐκπεπληγμένοι, ὡς ἤκουσαν ταῦτα· ὁ δὲ παῖς,
ἐτύγχανε γὰρ ἔχων μάχαιραν, εἴπας τάδε, "δεκόμεθα, ὦ βασιλεῦ, τὰ
διδοῖς", περιγράφει τῆι μαχαίρηι ἐς τὸ ἔδαφος τοῦ οἴκου τὸν ἥλιον,

137.2 ἦσαν . . . δῆμος del. van Herwerden; post ἔπεσσε transp. Stein

περιγράψας δέ, ἐς τὸν κόλπον τρὶς ἀρυσάμενος τοῦ ἡλίου, ἀπαλ-
λάσσετο αὐτός τε καὶ οἱ μετ᾽ ἐκείνου.
Οἱ μὲν δὴ ἀπήισαν, τῶι δὲ βασιλέϊ σημαίνει τις τῶν παρέδρων **138**
οἷόν τι χρῆμα ποιήσειε ὁ παῖς, καὶ ὡς σὺν νόωι κείνων ὁ νεώτα-
τος λάβοι τὰ διδόμενα. ὁ δὲ ταῦτα ἀκούσας καὶ ὀξυνθείς, πέμπει ἐπ᾽
αὐτοὺς ἱππέας ἀπολέοντας. ποταμὸς δέ ἐστι ἐν τῆι χώρηι ταύτηι,
τῶι θύουσι οἱ τούτων τῶν ἀνδρῶν ἀπ᾽ Ἄργεος ἀπόγονοι σωτῆρι.
οὗτος, ἐπείτε διέβησαν οἱ Τημενίδαι, μέγας οὕτω ἐρρύη, ὥστε τοὺς 2
ἱππέας μὴ οἵους τε γενέσθαι διαβῆναι. οἱ δὲ ἀπικόμενοι ἐς ἄλλην γῆν
τῆς Μακεδονίης, οἴκησαν πέλας τῶν κήπων τῶν λεγομένων εἶναι
Μίδεω τοῦ Γορδίεω, ἐν τοῖσι φύεται αὐτόματα ῥόδα, ἓν ἕκαστον ἔχον
ἑξήκοντα φύλλα, ὀδμῆι τε ὑπερφέροντα τῶν ἄλλων. ἐν τούτοισι καὶ ὁ 3
Σιληνὸς τοῖσι κήποισι ἥλω, ὡς λέγεται ὑπὸ Μακεδόνων. ὑπὲρ δὲ τῶν
κήπων ὄρος κεῖται, Βέρμιον οὔνομα, ἄβατον ὑπὸ χειμῶνος. ἐνθεῦτεν
δὲ ὁρμώμενοι, ὡς ταύτην ἔσχον, κατεστρέφοντο καὶ τὴν ἄλλην
Μακεδονίην. Ἀπὸ τούτου δὴ τοῦ Περδίκκεω Ἀλέξανδρος ὧδε ἐγένε- **139**
το· Ἀμύντεω παῖς ἦν Ἀλέξανδρος, Ἀμύντης δὲ Ἀλκέτεω, Ἀλκέτεω δὲ
πατὴρ ἦν Ἀέροπος, τοῦ δὲ Φίλιππος, Φιλίππου δὲ Ἀργαῖος, τοῦ δὲ
Περδίκκης ὁ κτησάμενος τὴν ἀρχήν.

140–4 Debate at Athens

Ἐγεγόνεε μὲν δὴ ὧδε ὁ Ἀλέξανδρος ὁ Ἀμύντεω. ὡς δὲ ἀπίκετο **140α**
ἐς τὰς Ἀθήνας, ἀποπεμφθεὶς ὑπὸ Μαρδονίου, ἔλεγε τάδε· "ἄνδρες
Ἀθηναῖοι, Μαρδόνιος τάδε λέγει· ἐμοὶ ἀγγελίη ἥκει παρὰ βασιλέος
λέγουσα οὕτως· Ἀθηναίοισι τὰς ἁμαρτάδας τὰς ἐς ἐμὲ ἐξ ἐκείνων
γενομένας πάσας μετίημι. νῦν τε ὧδε, Μαρδόνιε, ποίεε· τοῦτο μὲν 2
τὴν γῆν σφι ἀπόδος, τοῦτο δὲ ἄλλην πρὸς ταύτηι ἑλέσθων αὐτοί,
ἥντινα ἂν ἐθέλωσι, ἐόντες αὐτόνομοι. ἱρά τε πάντα σφι, ἢν δὴ βού-
λωνταί γε ἐμοὶ ὁμολογέειν, ἀνόρθωσον, ὅσα ἐγὼ ἐνέπρησα. τούτων
δὲ ἀπιγμένων, ἀναγκαίως ἔχει μοι ποιέειν ταῦτα, ἢν μὴ τὸ ὑμέτερον
αἴτιον γένηται. λέγω δὲ ὑμῖν τάδε. νῦν τί μαίνεσθε πόλεμον βασιλέϊ 3
ἀνταειρόμενοι; οὔτε γὰρ ἂν ὑπερβάλοισθε, οὔτε οἷοί τέ ἐστε ἀντ-
έχειν τὸν πάντα χρόνον. εἴδετε μὲν γὰρ τῆς Ξέρξεω στρατηλασίης
τὸ πλῆθος καὶ τὰ ἔργα, πυνθάνεσθε δὲ καὶ τὴν νῦν παρ᾽ ἐμοὶ ἐοῦσαν
δύναμιν· ὥστε καὶ ἢν ἡμέας ὑπερβάλησθε καὶ νικήσητε, τοῦ περ ὑμῖν
οὐδεμία ἐλπίς, εἴ περ εὖ φρονέετε, ἄλλη παρέσται πολλαπλησίη.
μὴ ὢν βούλεσθε, παρισούμενοι βασιλέϊ, στέρεσθαι μὲν τῆς χώρης, 4

138.1 ὁ παῖς del. Stein 138.1 ὡς add. Pingel 140α.2 ἀντίον Valckenaer

θέειν δὲ αἰεὶ περὶ ὑμέων αὐτῶν· ἀλλὰ καταλύσασθε. παρέχει δὲ
ὑμῖν κάλλιστα καταλύσασθαι, βασιλέος ταύτηι ὁρμημένου. ἔστε
ἐλεύθεροι, ἡμῖν ὁμαιχμίην συνθέμενοι ἄνευ τε δόλου καὶ ἀπάτης.
140β "Μαρδόνιος μὲν ταῦτα, ὦ Ἀθηναῖοι, ἐνετείλατό μοι εἰπεῖν πρὸς
ὑμέας. ἐγὼ δὲ περὶ μὲν εὐνοίης τῆς πρὸς ὑμέας ἐούσης ἐξ ἐμεῦ οὐδὲν
λέξω, οὐ γὰρ ἂν νῦν πρῶτον ἐκμάθοιτε, προσχρηίζω δὲ ὑμέων
2 πείθεσθαι Μαρδονίωι. ἐνορῶ γὰρ ὑμῖν οὐκ οἵοισί τε ἐσομένοισι τὸν
πάντα χρόνον πολεμέειν Ξέρξηι. εἰ γὰρ ἐνώρων τοῦτο ἐν ὑμῖν, οὐκ
ἄν κοτε ἐς ὑμέας ἦλθον ἔχων λόγους τούσδε· καὶ γὰρ δύναμις ὑπὲρ
3 ἄνθρωπον ἡ βασιλέος ἐστὶ καὶ χεὶρ ὑπερμήκης. ἢν ὦν μὴ αὐτίκα
ὁμολογήσητε, μεγάλα προτεινόντων ἐπ' οἷσι ὁμολογέειν ἐθέλουσι,
δειμαίνω ὑπὲρ ὑμέων, ἐν τρίβωι τε μάλιστα οἰκημένων τῶν συμ-
μάχων πάντων, αἰεί τε φθειρομένων μούνων, ἐξαίρετον μεταίχμιόν τε
4 τὴν γῆν ἐκτημένων. ἀλλὰ πείθεσθε· πολλοῦ γὰρ ὑμῖν ἄξια ταῦτα, εἰ
βασιλεύς γε ὁ μέγας, μούνοισι ὑμῖν Ἑλλήνων τὰς ἁμαρτάδας ἀπιείς,
ἐθέλει φίλος γενέσθαι."
141 Ἀλέξανδρος μὲν ταῦτα ἔλεξε. Λακεδαιμόνιοι δέ, πυθόμενοι
ἥκειν Ἀλέξανδρον ἐς Ἀθήνας ἐς ὁμολογίην ἄξοντα τῶι βαρβάρωι
Ἀθηναίους, ἀναμνησθέντες τῶν λογίων ὥς σφεας χρεόν ἐστι ἅμα
τοῖσι ἄλλοισι Δωριεῦσι ἐκπίπτειν ἐκ Πελοποννήσου ὑπὸ Μήδων
τε καὶ Ἀθηναίων, κάρτα τε ἔδεισαν μὴ ὁμολογήσωσι τῶι Πέρσηι
2 Ἀθηναῖοι· αὐτίκα τέ σφι ἔδοξε πέμπειν ἀγγέλους. καὶ δὴ συνέπιπτε,
ὥστε ὁμοῦ σφεων γίνεσθαι τὴν κατάστασιν· ἐπανέμειναν γὰρ οἱ
Ἀθηναῖοι διατρίβοντες, εὖ ἐπιστάμενοι ὅτι ἔμελλον Λακεδαιμόνιοι
πεύσεσθαι ἥκοντα παρὰ τοῦ βαρβάρου ἄγγελον ἐπ' ὁμολογίηι,
πυθόμενοί τε πέμψειν κατὰ τάχος ἀγγέλους. ἐπίτηδες ὦν ἐποίευν,
ἐνδεικνύμενοι τοῖσι Λακεδαιμονίοισι τὴν ἑωυτῶν γνώμην.
142 Ὡς δὲ ἐπαύσατο λέγων Ἀλέξανδρος, διαδεξάμενοι ἔλεγον οἱ ἀπὸ
Σπάρτης ἄγγελοι· "ἡμέας δὲ ἔπεμψαν Λακεδαιμόνιοι δεησομένους
ὑμέων μήτε νεώτερον ποιέειν μηδὲν κατὰ τὴν Ἑλλάδα, μήτε λόγους
2 ἐνδέκεσθαι παρὰ τοῦ βαρβάρου. οὔτε γὰρ δίκαιον οὐδαμῶς, οὔτε
κόσμον φέρον οὔτι γε ἄλλοισι Ἑλλήνων οὐδαμοῖσι, ὑμῖν δὲ δὴ
καὶ διὰ πάντων ἥκιστα πολλῶν εἵνεκα. ἠγείρατε γὰρ τόνδε τὸν
πόλεμον ὑμεῖς, οὐδὲν ἡμέων βουλομένων, καὶ περὶ τῆς ὑμετέρης
ἀρχῆς ὁ ἀγὼν ἐγένετο· νῦν δὲ φέρει καὶ ἐς πᾶσαν τὴν Ἑλλάδα.
3 ἄλλως τε τούτων ἁπάντων αἰτίους γενέσθαι <καὶ> δουλοσύνης
τοῖσι Ἕλλησι Ἀθηναίους οὐδαμῶς ἀνασχετόν, οἵτινες αἰεὶ καὶ τὸ

142.2 οὔτι Werfer: οὔτε codd. 142.2 ἀρχήν Schaefer: ἀρχῆθεν Wesseling
142.3 γενέσθαι <καί> A.M. Bowie: alii alia

πάλαι φαίνεσθε πολλοὺς ἐλευθερώσαντες ἀνθρώπων. πιεζευμένοισι
μέντοι ὑμῖν συναχθόμεθα, καὶ ὅτι καρπῶν ἐστερήθητε διξῶν ἤδη,
καὶ ὅτι οἰκοφθόρησθε χρόνον ἤδη πολλόν. ἀντὶ τούτων δὲ ὑμῖν 4
Λακεδαιμόνιοί τε καὶ οἱ σύμμαχοι ἐπαγγέλλονται γυναῖκάς τε καὶ
τὰ ἐς πόλεμον ἄχρηστα οἰκετέων ἐχόμενα πάντα ἐπιθρέψειν, ἔστ᾽
ἂν ὁ πόλεμος ὅδε συνεστήκηι. μηδὲ ὑμέας Ἀλέξανδρος ὁ Μακεδὼν
ἀναγνώσηι, λεήνας τὸν Μαρδονίου λόγον. τούτωι μὲν γὰρ ταῦτα 5
ποιητέα ἐστί· τύραννος γὰρ ἐών, τυράννωι συγκατεργάζεται· ὑμῖν
δέ γε οὐ ποιητέα, εἴ περ εὖ τυγχάνετε φρονέοντες, ἐπισταμένοισι ὡς
βαρβάροισί ἐστι οὔτε πιστὸν οὔτε ἀληθὲς οὐδέν." ταῦτα ἔλεξαν οἱ
ἄγγελοι.

Ἀθηναῖοι δὲ πρὸς μὲν Ἀλέξανδρον ὑπεκρίναντο τάδε· "καὶ αὐτοὶ **143**
τοῦτό γε ἐπιστάμεθα, ὅτι πολλαπλησίη ἐστὶ τῶι Μήδωι δύναμις ἤ
περ ἡμῖν, ὥστε οὐδὲν δεῖ τοῦτό γε ὀνειδίζειν. ἀλλ᾽ ὅμως, ἐλευθερίης
γλιχόμενοι, ἀμυνεύμεθα οὕτω ὅκως ἂν καὶ δυνώμεθα. ὁμολογῆ-
σαι δὲ τῶι βαρβάρωι μήτε σὺ ἡμέας πειρῶ ἀναπείθειν, οὔτε ἡμεῖς
πεισόμεθα. νῦν τε ἀπάγγελλε Μαρδονίωι ὡς Ἀθηναῖοι λέγουσι, ἔστ᾽ 2
ἂν ὁ ἥλιος τὴν αὐτὴν ὁδὸν ἴηι τῆι περ καὶ νῦν ἔρχεται, μήκοτε
ὁμολογήσειν ἡμέας Ξέρξηι· ἀλλὰ θεοῖσί τε συμμάχοισι πίσυνοί
μιν ἐπέξιμεν ἀμυνόμενοι καὶ τοῖσι ἥρωσι, τῶν ἐκεῖνος, οὐδεμίαν
ὄπιν ἔχων, ἐνέπρησε τούς τε οἴκους καὶ τὰ ἀγάλματα. σύ τε τοῦ 3
λοιποῦ λόγους ἔχων τοιούσδε μὴ ἐπιφαίνεο Ἀθηναίοισι, μηδὲ δοκέων
χρηστὰ ὑπουργέειν, ἀθέμιστα ἔρδειν παραίνεε. οὐ γάρ σε βουλόμεθα
οὐδὲν ἄχαρι πρὸς Ἀθηναίων παθεῖν, ἐόντα πρόξεινόν τε καὶ φίλον."

Πρὸς μὲν Ἀλέξανδρον ταῦτα ὑπεκρίναντο, πρὸς δὲ τοὺς ἀπὸ **144**
Σπάρτης ἀγγέλους τάδε· "τὸ μὲν δεῖσαι Λακεδαιμονίους μὴ
ὁμολογήσωμεν τῶι βαρβάρωι κάρτα ἀνθρωπήιον ἦν. ἀτὰρ
αἰσχρῶς γε οἴκατε ἐξεπιστάμενοι τὸ Ἀθηναίων φρόνημα ἀρρωδῆ-
σαι, ὅτι οὔτε χρυσός ἐστι γῆς οὐδαμόθι τοσοῦτος, οὔτε χώρη κάλλεϊ
καὶ ἀρετῆι μέγα ὑπερφέρουσα, τὰ ἡμεῖς δεξάμενοι ἐθέλοιμεν ἂν
μηδίσαντες καταδουλῶσαι τὴν Ἑλλάδα. πολλά τε γὰρ καὶ μεγάλα 2
ἐστὶ τὰ διακωλύοντα ταῦτα μὴ ποιέειν, μηδ᾽ ἢν ἐθέλωμεν· πρῶτα μὲν
καὶ μέγιστα τῶν θεῶν τὰ ἀγάλματα καὶ τὰ οἰκήματα ἐμπεπρησμένα
τε καὶ συγκεχωσμένα, τοῖσι ἡμέας ἀναγκαίως ἔχει τιμωρέειν ἐς τὰ
μέγιστα, μᾶλλον ἤ περ ὁμολογέειν τῶι ταῦτα ἐργασαμένωι· αὖτις δὲ
τὸ Ἑλληνικόν, ἐὸν ὅμαιμόν τε καὶ ὁμόγλωσσον, καὶ θεῶν ἱδρύματά
τε κοινὰ καὶ θυσίαι ἤθεά τε ὁμότροπα, τῶν προδότας γενέσθαι
Ἀθηναίους οὐκ ἂν εὖ ἔχοι. ἐπίστασθέ τε οὕτω, εἰ μὴ καὶ πρότερον 3

143.2 τήν περ Cobet

ἐτυγχάνετε ἐπιστάμενοι, ἔστ᾽ ἂν καὶ εἷς περιῇ Ἀθηναίων, μηδαμὰ
ὁμολογήσοντας ἡμέας Ξέρξῃ. ὑμέων μέντοι ἀγάμεθα τὴν προνοίην
τὴν ἐς ἡμέας ἔχουσαν, ὅτι προείδετε ἡμέων οἰκοφθορημένων οὕτω
4 ὥστε ἐπιθρέψαι ἐθέλειν ἡμέων τοὺς οἰκέτας. καὶ ὑμῖν μὲν ἡ χάρις ἐκπε-
πλήρωται, ἡμεῖς μέντοι λιπαρήσομεν οὕτω ὅκως ἂν ἔχωμεν, οὐδὲν
λυπέοντες ὑμέας. νῦν δέ, ὡς οὕτω ἐχόντων, στρατιὴν ὡς τάχιστα
5 ἐκπέμπετε. ὡς γὰρ ἡμεῖς εἰκάζομεν, οὐκ ἑκὰς χρόνου παρέσται ὁ
βάρβαρος ἐσβαλὼν ἐς τὴν ἡμετέρην, ἀλλ᾽ ἐπειδὰν τάχιστα πύθηται
τὴν ἀγγελίην, ὅτι οὐδὲν ποιήσομεν τῶν ἐκεῖνος ἡμέων προσεδέετο.
πρὶν ὦν παρεῖναι ἐκεῖνον ἐς τὴν Ἀττικήν, ἡμέας καιρός ἐστι προβο-
ηθῆσαι ἐς τὴν Βοιωτίην." οἱ μέν, ταῦτα ὑποκριναμένων Ἀθηναίων,
ἀπαλλάσσοντο ἐς Σπάρτην.

144.5 ὑμέας Wesseling

COMMENTARY

The story so far. After the defeat of his generals Datis and Artaphernes at Marathon in 490, Darius intended to invade Greece again, but was distracted by a revolt in Egypt in 486, during which year he died. His son by Atossa, Xerxes, succeeded him and crushed the revolt in 485. Xerxes spent four years preparing his expedition against Greece, the first act being the digging of a canal through the Athos peninsula in 483 (7.22). Late in 481, envoys were sent to demand 'earth and water' from the northern Greek states down to Boeotia (**46**.4n.). The army mustered in Cappadocia, and marched to Sardis, whence in spring 480 it began the expedition; the fleet collected at Abydos (7.20–40). H. gives a total of 5,283,220 men (7.186.2), a fantastic exaggeration no doubt, but indicative of the vast scale of the force. On the way, roads and bridges were constructed, and the Hellespont spanned by pontoons at Abydos (7.33–7). Progress was measured, partly because of the sheer numbers involved, and partly because Xerxes wanted to be able to use the crops in northern Greece to help feed his troops (7.50.4). Army and fleet advanced in contact with each other so as to coordinate their actions (7.236.2), but at the head of the Thermaic gulf in Macedonia, the land route diverged from the coast and they separated, reuniting at Aphetae on the Gulf of Pagasae, where the fleet is waiting at the start of book 8. H. does not tell us enough to be certain which route or (more likely) routes the army took. See map for possible solutions.

Once most of the northern states had sided with the Persians, the Greeks began to organise resistance in earnest. At the Hellenium in Laconia, they called themselves the 'Hellenes' and swore a pact of mutual aid and conferred the leadership on Sparta (Paus. 3.12.6). Steps were taken to persuade those who had submitted to the King to change their allegiance. Unsuccessful attempts were made to enlist the help of the Argives and Gelon of Syracuse (H. 7.145–71). The Thessalians asked for help and, after an abortive occupation of the Vale of Tempe, the Greeks decided to make a stand, with the army at the pass of Thermopylae and with the fleet at Artemisium (7.172–7). These were the only places before the Isthmus of Corinth that they could have hoped to hold with the forces at their disposal.

After the Persian land victory at Thermopylae, the way to central Greece was open to the Persians, and the Greek fleet had to retreat south, but the question remained of where they should make their next stand, at the Isthmus or further north. The Isthmus was an obvious place to make a stand with the land army, unlike Attica with its long northern frontier vulnerable at a number of points and absence of a suitable naval base to protect the north-east coast; but fighting at the Isthmus would mean abandoning the whole of central Greece and Euboea to the invaders, which the Athenians were not happy with, and their wishes could not easily be ignored.

We are now in late September 480, but the only certain date is the solar eclipse in 9.10.3, datable to 2 October. For the problems of Herodotean chronology, cf. **11**.3n.;

for a proposed summary chronology of the campaign, cf. Hammond, *CAH*² IV 591; more generally, cf. Rhodes 2003.

For narratives of events after Marathon, cf. Burn 1984: 313–77; Hammond, *CAH*² IV 518–63; Green 1996: 41–105; Cawkwell 2005: 87–125.

ΟΥΡΑΝΙΑ. The division of the *Histories* into books is first referred to in the Lindian temple chronicle (*FGH* 532 (29).1–4 Ἄμασις . . . περὶ οὗ μ[αρτ]υρεῖ Ἡρόδοτος . . . ἐν τᾶι β τᾶν ἱστοριᾶ[ν; 99 BC or before) and Diod. 11.37.6; the attachment of the names of the Muses to the books appears first in Lucian, *Hist. Conscr.* 42 ὁ δ' οὖν Θουκυδίδης . . . ὁρῶν μάλιστα θαυμαζόμενον τὸν Ἡρόδοτον, ἄχρι τοῦ καὶ Μούσας κληθῆναι αὐτοῦ τὰ βιβλία.

1–26 BATTLES AT ARTEMISIUM AND THE AFTERMATH

This episode consists of four sections, in which the narrative focuses first on one side in the conflict and then on the other, and an 'episode' closes each section, two 'athletic' ones enclosing two military:

A. **1–8:** Greek fleet and reactions (**1–5**); Persian plans (**6–7**); episode (**8:** Scyllies' defection and miraculous swim).
B. **9–11:** Greek plans (**9**); Persian reactions (**10**); episode (**11:** battle; and another defection).
C. **12–18:** Persian reverses (**12–13**); Greek successes (**14**); episode (**15–18:** battle).
D. **19–26:** Greek actions and retreat (**19–22**); Persian actions (**23–5**); episode (**26:** discussion of Olympic games).

1 The narrative is picked up from 7.175–96, where the Greeks decide to base themselves at Thermopylae and Artemisium, and the Persians arrive at Aphetae.

1–2.1 Catalogue of the Greek forces

In the later books, H. employs catalogues of forces to mark important battles, the catalogues being tailored to the event: 6.8, a short, bald list of the Ionian fleet before Lade, a prelude to their undistinguished performance which ended the Ionian Revolt; 7.59–100, a spectacular and detailed description of the many races in Xerxes' army at Doriscus, which inaugurates its time in Greece, but whose grandeur also has a hubristic aspect to it; 7.202–203.1, detailed origins of the Greeks at Thermopylae; **43–8**, before their great victory, the national origins of the Greek fleet at Salamis are described in historical detail, giving them a prestige to match the grandeur of the Persians; this contrasts almost ironically with **73**, the catalogue of medisers, also with their histories; 9.28.2–32, the importance of Plataea indicated by lengthy catalogues of the Greek and Persian armies at Plataea, this the longest catalogue except the Doriscus review. Such catalogues have epic antecedents in Near Eastern literature and Homer's lists of the Greek and Trojan forces, given as the fighting is about to break out for the first time (2.484–785, 811–77; M. L. West 1997: 208). The list here is relatively bald, the order being determined by the number of triremes each state provides.

1.1 The MSS all repeat at the start of this book the last line of book 7 ταῦτα μὲν δὴ οὕτω λέγεται γενέσθαι. The book divisions are not authorial, but the work of Alexandrian editors. Since the sentence sums up the last events of book 7, it is better to attach it to that book.

οἱ . . . οἵδε: join οἱ with ταχθέντες.

Ἀθηναῖοι: the Athenians were able to build up a substantial navy after Themistocles persuaded them to use for that purpose the surplus income of some 50 talents from the new seams of silver discovered in Laurium (near Sunium) at sometime before 483 (7.144.1; Aes. *Pers.* 238). These ships were intended for the war against Aegina (Thuc. 1.14.3), which had the paradoxical result that 'this war saved Greece', when the ships were used against Persia (cf. 7.144; *Ath. Pol.* 22.7; Labarbe 1957; Wallinga 1993: 148–57). The difference made by this silver can be seen from the fact that in 489 they had seventy ships to give to Miltiades (6.132), but in 480 two hundred. The timber for the ships may have come from Alexander of Macedon, who was honoured as a benefactor before 480 (**136**.1 with n.).

νέας: triremes, which gradually replaced penteconters (**1**.2n.) as the main mediterranean battle-ship from the latter part of the sixth century. They are first mentioned by Hipponax of Ephesus (fr. 28W), and probably came into existence shortly before Cambyses' expedition against Egypt in 525, for which Polycrates of Samos provided 40 triremes (3.44.2). A Phoenician or Egyptian origin is likely, and Thuc. 1.13.2 makes Corinth the first city to build them in Greece. The remains of the ship sheds at the Attic harbour of Zea suggest that the trireme had a maximum length of about 121 feet (37 m) and width of about 19 feet (6 m), with partial decking. Its main battle-weapon was the bronze-sheathed ram, and it was capable of considerable speed: a modern version has exceeded 9 knots. When fully crewed in the later fifth century, 170 men rowed it in battle, sitting in three rows on each side, one above the other; there were also typically ten marines (*epibatai*), four archers and 16 sailors also on board (for the number of 200, cf. 7.185.1, **17**). There was a mast, which could be removed before battle (**94**.1n.). Triremes were expensive to build and run, and the crews required much training (cf. 6.11–12; Thuc. 1.142.6–9). Cf. Morrison, Coates and Rankov 2000; for technical details from the experience of sailing the reconstructed *Olympias*, cf. Coates, Platis and Shaw 1990.

παρεχόμενοι . . . συνεπλήρουν: note how these verbs alternate in this list. It is a feature of H.'s style to repeat words thus, sometimes together with cognate words and sometimes with a certain punning sense (Powell 1937): cf. in this book **2**.2 ἡγεμονεύηι . . . ἡγεομένοισι; **20**.1–2 παραχρησάμενοι . . . χρησμὸν . . . χρησαμένοισι . . . χρᾶσθαι; **22**.1 ἐπιλεξάμενος . . . ἐπελέξαντο . . . ἔλεγε, etc. At times, the pun emphasises an important aspect of the narrative: cf. **68**α.1, 9.53.3 (twice, F&M *ad loc.*)

ὑπὸ δὲ ἀρετῆς '(inspired) by their valour', an extension to active verbs of the use of ὑπό + genitive of the agent with passives; cf. **23**.1 ὑπ' ἀπιστίης 'through disbelief', 7.22.1 ὤρυσσον ὑπὸ μαστίγων 'they dug, urged on by whips'; the idea of causality is still felt. The courage of the Plataeans is emphasised by the fact that this is the only evaluative language in an otherwise plain passage. Plataean courage had been displayed at Marathon: having resisted Theban pressure to join their Boeotian Confederacy, they allied themselves with Athens, at whose behest they immediately sent all their 1,000 men; this loyalty was commemorated at Athenian festivals (6.108, 111.1–2). It is at Plataea that Mardonius' army is finally repulsed, and 600 Plataeans fought on the Greek side (9.28.6). The Plataeans pleaded these services against Persia in vain when Sparta and Thebes destroyed the city in 427 (Thuc. 3.54.3–4).

ἄπειροι τῆς ναυτικῆς ἐόντες 'although they had no experience of naval matters'. This contrasts with ὑπὸ ἀρετῆς, ἐόντες being concessive. The Plataeans were thus serving as marines.

συνεπλήρουν: συμπληρόω, normally 'to fill completely', is here used uniquely to mean 'man alongside with'; it governs τοῖσι Ἀθηναίοισι.

Κορίνθιοι: after the Athenians, they provided the largest fleet of the allies; they were the first Greeks to have a potent fleet, being involved in 'the oldest sea-battle that we know of' (Thuc. 1.13.4; *ca.* 610).

1.2 Χαλκιδέες: the reference to them as 'Ionians' in **46**.2 suggests these were actual Chalcidians, not Athenian cleruchs living there (for whom, cf. 5.77.2, 6.100.1).

Ἀθηναίων . . . παρεχόντων: the distinction between this active form and the middle παρεχόμενοι in §1 is that the former means 'supplied (for the use of the Chalcidians)', the latter 'supplied (for their own use)'. The Athenians had not enough men to crew all of the ships available to them.

Αἰγινῆται δὲ ὀκτωκαίδεκα: the low number for Aegina, a naval power second only to Athens, is a mystery. Other manned Aeginetan ships are being used to guard Aegina, and they supplied 30 at Salamis (**46**.1), but even that number is still small. Perhaps the relatively small numbers for the Peloponnesian states were due to the contemporaneous celebration of the Spartan Carneia and the Olympic games (Hammond, *CAH*^{2} IV 549). Athens and Aegina had been at war before the Persians came (**1**.1n).

Ἐρετριέες: they and the Athenians amongst the mainland Greeks had supported the Ionian revolt and taken part in the burning of Sardis (5.100–102.1). Darius thus sent first Mardonius and then Datis and Artaphernes to destroy these cities and bring the people to him as captives. The Eretrians were divided between flight and submission, but the city was finally betrayed by two leading citizens and burned in 490, shortly before Marathon. The people in the city were enslaved and brought to Darius, who settled them at Cissia by the Red Sea (5.99.1, 6.100–1, 119; cf. Grosso 1958). *A.P.* 7.256 and 259 are poignant epigrams attributed to Plato on their exile. In 480, the Eretrians were more united against the Persians; Gongylus alone supported medising and he was exiled as a result (Xen. *HG* 3.1.6).

πεντηκοντέρους: these were smaller than triremes (**1**.1n.), and were originally rowed by fifty men in two rows, one on each side; later, the oarsmen were placed in two rows on each side, one above the other. Unlike the trireme, they had considerable stowage space, and so could be used for other than purely military purposes: they were used for instance by the Phocaeans for their voyages of discovery and their flight *en masse* from the Persians (1.163.2, 164.3). Cf. Morrison, Coates and Rankov 2000: 28–30, 40–1.

Λοκροὶ . . . Ὀπούντιοι: they had, along with neighbouring peoples, 'given earth and water' to Xerxes as tokens of submission (7.132.1), but when summoned by the Greeks came with all their forces to fight at Thermopylae (7.203.1). Their refusal to retreat and abandon their lands, when the Persian army appeared at the gates of the pass, was a major reason why Leonidas decided to stay and fight (7.207). They are at Salamis (**66**.2), but, perhaps because they had no choice, they fight for Mardonius at Plataea (9.31.5).

Στυρέες: from Styra, in southern Euboea, opposite Marathon.

2.1 μὲν ὦν 'so, on the one hand'; ὦν is transitional and retrospective, μέν looks forward to the δέ-clause (*GP* 470–3).

Ἀρτεμίσιον: the coastline of northern Euboea, where there was a temple of Artemis Proseoea ('To the East'; cf. 7.176.1; Plut. *Them.* 8.2–3); it is now the bay of Pevki where Potoki stands. Stationing the fleet here meant the Greeks could not only maintain some contact with the army at Thermopylae (cf. 7.175.2, and **21** for how it was done), but also prevent the Persians landing troops in northern Euboea and moving easily south towards Chalcis, thus blocking any Greek retreat through the Euripus channel between Euboea and Boeotia. The Greeks could also escape from it out to sea, east of Euboea.

εἴρηται δέ μοι 'I have said' with perfects and pluperfects passive the dative is used to express the interest of a person in the action (cf. Smyth §1488). For this type of concluding formula, cf. 7.100.1 ἐς μὲν τοσόνδε ὁ ναυτικὸς στρατὸς εἴρηται, at the end of the catalogue of Persian ships. τῶν νέων depends on πλῆθος.

2.2–3.2 The question of leadership

This section introduces the themes of Athenian selflessness, which will include the sacrifice of their city and provide the climax to the book (**143–4**), and of the fragile nature of the Greek alliance. Problems of leadership and precedence beset the Greek alliance generally: cf. 7.145.2–52 (problems with Argives), 153–62 (Gelon's demands), 9.26–28.1 (Athenian refusal to cede one wing to the Tegeans); for disunity as a salient feature of the Greeks in H., cf. Immerwahr 1966: 189–237. This disunity, immediately revealed, contrasts with the unity implied by the catalogue. Plutarch, in *MH*, was especially critical of H.'s emphasis on the fractiousness of the Greeks (cf. esp. *MH* 35).

That the Spartans were the most powerful of the Greeks has been regularly acknowledged before in H.: cf. 1.56.1, 69.1, 152, 3.148, 5.49, 6.84, 108, 7.161.2.

2.2 Εὐρυβιάδην Εὐρυκλείδεω: Eurybiades (*LGPN* IIIA *s.v.*(2)) is first mentioned here; nothing is known of his father. Though he is the leader, Eurybiades is not a member of either of the Spartan royal families (cf. **42**.2n.).

ἡγεμονεύῃ . . . ἡγεομένοισι: the two verbs have very slightly different senses: the allies will serve under Athenian commanders, so long as Eurybiades is the over-all leader.

3.1 κατ' ἀρχάς: perhaps at the meeting of the allies at the Isthmus in autumn 481, when it was decided to send an embassy to ask help from Gelon in Sicily (7.145.2), or when the Athenians recognised Spartan supremacy on the embassy (7.161.2).

λόγος 'talk'.

πρὶν ἤ . . . πέμπειν: πρὶν ἤ + infinitive = 'before' is a developed form of simple πρίν + infinitive; the combination is found only twice in Homer, and rarely in Attic, but H. uses it regularly with indicative, subjunctive and infinitive (*M&T* §651; Smyth §2460).

μέγα πεποιημένοι 'considering it very important'. For this use of ποιεῖσθαι, cf. **15**.1 δεινόν τι ποιησάμενοι 'considered it a disgrace', **16**.2 δεινὸν χρῆμα ἐποιεῦντο. The perfect indicates that they had decided this in the past and still felt it.

ὀρθὰ νοεῦντες 'and they were right'. H. is not afraid to state his opinions forthrightly; cf. 7.139 where, in language echoed here, he says that the Athenians' resistance to the Persians was the crucial factor in Greece's victory, despite the fact that such a view is likely to be 'invidious' (ἐπίφθονον) to many. This poetically charged (see below) praise of Athens looks forward to their crucial role in the Salamis campaign.

H. here explicitly views the Athenian concession proleptically, in the light of events after the end of his history: for such explicit references, cf. also 6.90, 7.137.3, 233, 9.73; see the summary in Forsdyke 2006: 228–35. On H.'s portrayal of Athens, the classic positive view is Jacoby 1913; Strasburger 1955 modified this. Cf. more recently Immerwahr 1966: 206–25; Fornara 1971: 37–58 (balanced views); Carrière 1988 (strongly pro-Athenian); Stadter 1992 (critical of Athens); Moles 1996 (H. warning Athens); Fowler 2003 (richly complex). For a review of scholarship on this topic, cf. Blösel 2004: 21–30; this work offers (not always compelling) suggestions about possible references to later events (summary in Blösel 2001). The disagreements amongst scholars show how complex H.'s analysis of empire and realpolitik is. His work should not be seen as directed in a reductive way mainly at a contemporary or Athenian readership (cf. Gould 1989: 14–16), but it has many points of contact with the outbreak of and events during the Peloponnesian War. Cf. also Fornara 1971: 75–91; Raaflaub 1987.

στάσις . . . εἰρήνης: this gnomic remark is reminiscent in phraseology and sentiment of archaic poetry: cf. e.g. Solon, 4.19 (δουλοσύνη) ἣ στάσιν ἔμφυλον πόλεμόν θ' εὕδοντ' ἐπεγείρει; Theogn. 51 στάσιές τε καὶ ἔμφυλοι φόνοι ἀνδρῶν. It also contains the striking poeticism πολέμου ὁμοφρονέοντος. For another passage with notable poeticisms, cf. **65**.2n.

3.2 εἶκον, μέχρι ὅσου κάρτα ἐδέοντο κτλ. 'the Athenians yielded as long as they needed the allies badly, as they showed, when, having repulsed the Persians . . . they took the command from the Spartans.' There are grammatical and historical problems however (cf. Immerwahr 1966: 220 n. 87). It is most natural to keep the Athenians as subject, rather than making an abrupt change to 'the allies' after εἶκον, despite the fact that μέχρι ὅσου is found only here in H. and is generally rare = 'as long as' (e.g. Pl. *Mx.* 245A). Thuc. 1.95.1 says the allies not the Athenians took the initiative, but other sources support H.; the truth is probably a complex mixture of the two traditions: cf. Hornblower 1983: 142–3; Munson 2001: 214–17.

περὶ τῆς ἐκείνου: *sc.* γῆς. This refers to the naval campaign against Persian territories of 478, which led to the transfer of the leadership to Athens and the formation of the Delian League.

τὴν Παυσανίεω ὕβριν: Pausanias was son of King Cleombrotus (for whom, cf. **71**.1) and came to the throne on his death in 480. He commanded the Greek land forces at Plataea, claiming credit for the victory. His autocratic behaviour on an expedition to Cyprus and Byzantium alienated the other Greeks, and helped Athens build up her alliance. He was eventually starved to death in Athena's temple in Sparta, when he faced charges of improper dealings with the Persians and of complicity in a helot revolt: cf. Thuc. 1.94–7, 128.3–135.1.

4–5 Greek terror and Euboean bribery of Themistocles

Fear and desire for flight characterises the Greeks with remarkable regularity, until Salamis; cf. 7.173.3–4, 183.1, 207, 219; **18, 49**.2, **56, 74**.2, **75**.2. Afterwards, it is Xerxes' turn: **97**.1 δρησμὸν ἐβούλευε, **100**.1. The story of bribery is probably part of the anti-Themistoclean tradition that grew up after his defection to Persia, but as often H.'s text provides its own implicit commentary on it: Themistocles is not the only one who takes the money, and the fact that the Euboeans and their families are saved is perhaps more important than who is enriched. The pattern of these two chapters, (1) Greek desire to retreat, (2) Themistocles' reaction and (3) involvement of Euboeans, will be repeated in **19–20**. The motif of secret discussions involving Themistocles, conducted behind the backs of the rest of the Greeks, will recur regularly, in **57–8, 75, 79–80**, and **110**. The story also introduces the man who embodies the opposition to Themistocles, the Corinthian Adeimantus (cf. **59–61** and **94**). These two, with Eurybiades, are the principal debaters of Greek policy in H.'s account: he restricts the number of speakers in both the Greek and Persian camps.

4.1 καί emphasises ἐπὶ Ἀρτεμίσιον . . . ἀπικόμενοι: 'these Greeks who had finally arrived at Artemisium', as opposed, it seems, to the reserves at Pogon (**42**).

νέας τε πολλάς: cf. **66**.1n.

τὰς Ἀφέτας: probably Plataniá Bay on the southern coast of Magnesia, opposite Artemisium. It was so called because it was from there that the Argonauts had set out (ἀφιέναι); H. gives this etymology in 7.193.2, and cf. A.R. 1.589–91.

αὐτοῖσι παρὰ δόξαν 'unexpectedly (and otherwise) than they expected'. αὐτοῖσι is the Greeks, a dative of disadvantage; παρὰ δόξαν is pleonastically reinforced by the clause ἢ ὡς αὐτοὶ κατεδόκεον (cf. K–G II 586).

ἔσω ἐς τὴν Ἑλλάδα 'further into Greece' (cf. also **18**). Trachis, which is near Thermopylae, is similarly said to be the ἔσοδος ἐς τὴν Ἑλλάδα in 7.176.2; cf. also 6.33.2 οἴχοντο ἔσω ἐς τὸν Εὔξεινον πόντον. Ἑλλάς and Ἕλληνες seem originally to have referred to the area round Thermopylae, but here the phrase is being used rather imprecisely to mean 'further south'.

4.2 Θεμιστοκλέα: *ca.* 524–459; (*LGPN* II *s.v.*(39)); he is first introduced in 7.143.1. Son of Neocles and a mother who may not have been Athenian, he was from the Lycomid family, of the deme of Phrearrhii. He was eponymous archon in 493/2, when he set in train the development and fortification of the Piraeus as the main harbour of Athens, which replaced the more exposed landing place at Phaleron (Thuc. 1.93.3). He also developed Athens' fleet (**1**.2n.), to the advantage of the Athenians in their conflict against Aegina. Though more ostraca with his name on have been found than with anyone else's (more than 2,000 (Lang 1990: 102–32, 142–61; Brenne 2001: 297–300), he survived the frequent use of ostracism in the 480s (*Ath. Pol.* 22), but was exiled towards the end of the 470s. He eventually ended up in Persia as governor of Magnesia, having fled mainland Greece on being accused by the Spartans (who suspected his activities in the Peloponnese) of having dealings with Persia. H.'s account contains much that can be read as criticism of him (though cf. Fornara 1971: 66–74); Thucydides is much more complimentary (1.90–3, 135.2–38). On his life, cf. Podlecki 1975; Lenardon 1978; for H.'s characterisation of him, cf. Blösel 2004.

ἐπὶ μισθῶι τριήκοντα ταλάντοισι: ταλάντοισι shares the case of μισθῶι; a genitive would also be possible (K–G I 265). The actual sum is remarkably large: Adeimantus is happy with three talents (**5**.2), and the Thessalians will forget a bloody past for fifty (**29**.2). Such offers of money are a feature of diplomacy in H., and though moral stigma can be involved, this is not always so: cf. 5.51, 63.1, 6.72, 9.2, 41.3, 88. Interestingly, bribery is never a feature of Persian attempts to win people over (Lewis 1997: 372), and Mardonius, perhaps unwisely, refuses to use bribes to buy the support of Greeks cities when he is left to conquer Greece by Xerxes after Salamis (9.2.2–3.1). On the protean concept of political 'bribery' in Greece, cf. Harvey 1985.

ἐπ' ὧι τε . . . ποιήσονται: ἐπ' ὧι (τε) 'on condition that', normally constructed with the infinitive, is found with the future indicative in Herodotus (6× plus twice with the present) and Thucydides (always). The subject is the Greeks generally.

5.1 ὡς παρ' ἑωυτοῦ δῆθεν διδούς 'as if it were from his *own* resources that he was making a gift'. δῆθεν 'is commonly used of apparent or pretended truth, and mostly with an ironical tone' (Smyth §2849; cf. *GP* 265): H. indicates that though Eurybiades was fooled, he himself is not. Cf. the grisly story of how the Scythians cooked a Median boy and fed him to Cyaxares φέροντες ὡς ἄγρην δῆθεν, 'as if they were bringing him game [which of course they were not]' (1.73.5).

ὡς δέ οἱ οὗτος ἀνεπέπειστο 'when Eurybiades had been persuaded to his satisfaction by him'. οἱ is Themistocles, a dative of the agent, as often with perfects and pluperfects (**2**.1n.).

Ἀδείμαντος γάρ: 'anticipatory' γάρ, introducing an explanatory clause which precedes, or is inserted parenthetically into, the clause it explains (*GP* 68–73). Such sentences are not easy to translate literally, but here the sense is something like

'When Eurybiades had been persuaded – you see there was one Adeimantus who alone . . . – , so it was to him . . .' This apparently illogical putting of the explanation before what is to be explained has the rhetorical function of emphasising the importance of the γάρ-clause. In an oral presentation, it lends a colloquial and informal air to the narrative, as if the speaker had just realised that he needed to provide some information to make his narrative comprehensible. It is frequent in H.: cf. **8**.1, **94**.3. Gould 1989: 64–5 notes how H., with his interest in explanation in his histories, uses backward-looking connectives like 'for' three and a half times more often than forward-looking ones like 'and so'; cf. de Jong 1997. For Adeimantus, cf. *RE s.v.* (2); *LGPN* IIIA *s.v.* (6).

ἤσπαιρε 'strongly resisted'; in Homer usually of the dying, but cf. *Il.* 12.203 ζωὸν ἔτ' ἀσπαίροντα, of a snake that is seized by an eagle but frees itself.

πρὸς δὴ τοῦτον: 'so it was to *this* man . . .'; δή is emphatic after the preposition, as often in H. (*GP* 229). It is used resumptively with pronouns to 'pick up the thread of a train of thought that is beginning to wander' (ibid. 225): note therefore the mildly disjointed syntax of this sentence.

5.2 Μήδων: OP *Māda* > Ion. Μῆδος. Outside strictly ethnographic passages, H. usually refers to the Persians as 'Persians', but often uses 'Medes' in contexts which impute an element of actual 'medising' to a person or people; cf. **46**.3, **65**.1, **141**.1, **143**.1 (Tuplin 1994: 246–8; cf. 238–51 on Greek usage of 'Medes' and 'Persians' generally, and 245–9 on H.). On the Medes, see Introduction, §1.

ταῦτά τε ἅμα ἠγόρευε καὶ πέμπει 'the words were hardly out of his mouth before he sent . . .'; the historic present is often used alongside imperfects or aorists to mark the more significant action, as in Thuc. 7.29.3 ἅμα δὲ τῆι ἡμέραι τῆι πόλει προσέκειτο . . . καὶ αἱρεῖ (K–G I 132–4).

5.3 οὗτοί τε δὴ πληγέντες . . . τῶι λόγωι τούτωι 'these men then were fully won over by the gifts, a favour had been done for the Euboeans, and Themistocles benefited; he got away with keeping the rest of the money and those who shared the money mistakenly thought it had come from Athens for this purpose.' The use of tenses in this sentence is noteworthy. The pluperfects ἀναπεπεισμένοι ἦσαν and ἐκεχάριστο imply a state achieved in the past whose effects continue to be felt; the instantaneous aorist ἐκέρδηνε marks the fact of Themistocles' profiting, and the imperfects ἐλάνθανε and ἠπιστέατο describe the continuance of his deception.

τε δή: δή emphasises οὗτοι, and τε looks forward to καί . . . τε; τε . . . καί . . . τε is a rare combination in prose (Smyth §2977). H. is particularly fond of this combination: he uses it 60 times to Thucydides' three (*GP* 260).

πληγέντες: this metaphorical use of πλήσσω with bribes is hard to parallel, the nearest example being Plut. *Demosth.* 25.4 πληγεὶς ὑπὸ τῆς δωροδοκίας, which is possibly a reminiscence of this passage. It is found of being smitten emotionally in e.g. Aes. *Ag.* 544 ἱμέρωι πεπληγμένοι; Pl. *Symp.* 218A τὴν καρδίαν . . . πληγεὶς . . . ὑπὸ τῶν ἐν φιλοσοφίαι λόγων.

ἠπιστέατο: the verb is often used of mistaken ideas, as in **25**.1.

λόγωι 'purpose', as in 3.36.5 κατακρύπτουσι τὸν Κροῖσον ἐπὶ τῶιδε τῶι λόγωι ὥστε . . .

6–7 Persian reactions

The focus now turns on the Persians. The Greeks were surprised to see the number of Persians, but here the Persians have their expectations of small Greek numbers confirmed. Their confidence is high, because in both naval and military campaigns the Persians tended to rely on superior numbers for victory, and H. conveys their thoughts in a more vivid manner than those of the Greeks (see nn.). A squadron is sent round Euboea to prevent a Greek retreat south down the Euripus channel.

6.1 δείλην πρωίην 'early afternoon'; δείλη could be divided in 'early' and 'late' (ὀψίη, **9**; Thuc. 8.26.1).

πυθόμενοι μὲν ἔτι καὶ πρότερον: perhaps from the captured lookout ships of 7.179–82, though that is not specifically said there. There is a contradiction here with **4**.1, where the Greeks arrive after the Persians.

ἐπιχειρέειν, εἴ κως ἕλοιεν 'to see whether they might capture them', lit. 'to try if somehow they might . . .' The εἰ-clause does not in this construction depend on the apodosis, but on the idea of purpose or desire expressed in it, here by ἐπιχειρέειν; cf. *Il.* 5.279 νῦν αὖτ' ἐγχείηι πειράσομαι, αἴ κε τύχωμι 'now I will make trial with my spear (to see) whether I may hit you'. In Homer, the purpose or desire is often implicit, but in Herodotus and later Greek it is more common for verbs like θέλω and βούλομαι to be actually expressed: cf. 6.52.4 βουλομένην δὲ εἴ κως ἀμφότεροι γενοίατο βασιλέες, lit. 'wishing if perhaps both might become kings'. Cf. *M&T* §§486–90; Smyth §2354.

6.2 ἐκ . . . τῆς ἀντίης 'head-on'; for this type of adverbial feminine, cf. ἐξ ἐναντίης (**7**.1), ἐκ τῆς ἰθείης 'openly'.

μὲν δή 'is frequently used by the historians as a formula of transition' (*GP* 258). Since this sentence introduces a qualification to the Persian enthusiasm described in the previous one, one might see δή here emphasising μέν, which introduces a long sentence explaining the course of action rejected; πρὸς ταῦτα ὦν in **7**.1 then marks the contrasting account of what they actually did.

μή κως . . . ὁρμήσειαν . . . καταλαμβάνηι: when two or more purpose clauses follow each other, subjunctive and optative may be used interchangeably, typically with the subjunctive expressing the principal aim or concern and the optative other possible consequences (K–G II 387–8; Smyth §2199). Here, the actual escape of the Greeks is more to be avoided than simply an attempt at flight. This usage is perhaps connected with the use of the subjunctive after secondary tenses in purpose clauses to convey a certain vivid quality, because it represents the mood and tense of the speaker's original words or idea.

εὐφρόνη lit. 'the Kindly One', i.e. 'Night'. This is a 'kenning', an expression which, perhaps for superstitious reasons, describes but does not actually name a person or thing which is in some way feared: cf. Σεμναὶ Θεαί for the Furies, 'Euxine' ('kind to strangers') for the stormy Pontus etc. 'This kenning had some currency in Ionic speech, as appears from its use in Heraclitus, Herodotus (books 7–9), and Hippocratica' (M. L. West on Hes. *Op.* 560); it is otherwise mainly confined to poetry.

καὶ ἔμελλον δῆθεν κτλ. 'and it was likely indeed that they would get away'; δῆθεν expresses a certain outrage or indignation on the Persians' part that such a thing should happen (cf. *GP* 265–6; a different use in **5**.1n.).

μηδὲ πυρφόρον . . . περιγενέσθαι 'not even a fire-bearer (to use their expression) must escape and live'. The meaning is fairly clear, but the explanation is not so easy. There are two problems: the significance of '*even* a fire-bearer' and the meaning of τῶι ἐκείνων λόγωι. The point of killing the fire-bearer is clearly that killing such men equalled the complete annihilation of an army, but it has been uncertain since antiquity whether this is because the fire-bearer was very important, as the man in charge of the fires of sacrifice and so sacrosanct and to be spared in a massacre, or because he was the least important and so not usually bothered with in a slaughter. The first explanation is preferable, because fire was an important aspect of Persian royal ceremonial and cult practice (Briant 2002: 248–50), and fire-bearers had an important role. In Xenophon's description of Cyrus' great procession (*Cyr.* 8.3.11–12), the procession is led by bulls dedicated to Zeus, after which there are horses for the sun, three grand chariots 'and men came after them bearing fire on a great altar'; Cyrus himself was next. The prominent position of these men suggests the fire-bearer was of great importance. That the fire-bearer was important is the view of e.g. Zenob. 5.34 and schol. Eur. *Phoen.* 1377, but the other view is supported by Photius, *Lexicon s.v.* οὐδὲ πυρφόρος: 'when we want to say that many were killed, we say that "not even a fire-bearer was left", that is, not even the man who would bring fire into the city . . . or not even a camp-guard, or some such.' The Septuagint translators seem to have taken this view too. In what looks like a learned imitation of H., they wrote in Obadiah 18 καὶ οὐκ ἔσται πυροφόρος τῶι οἴκωι Ἡσαῦ, where the Hebrew does not refer to fire-bearers, but means simply 'there shall not be any remaining of the house of Esau' (King James Version; cf. the Latin Vulgate's *non erunt reliquiae domus Esau*).

As to τῶι ἐκείνων λόγωι, this is more likely to mean 'to use their expression', not 'for their express purpose' because, as is shown by δῆθεν (see above), this passage is focalised through the mind of the Persians, so using ἐκείνων of them would be odd: it looks more like an authorial intervention to explain the presence of the unusual expression about the fire-bearer.

7.1 ἔξωθεν Σκιάθου: this episode has been questioned because Skiathos is an island about ten miles north-east from Artemisium and in sight of it, so the Persians could not avoid being seen when they sailed out of Aphetae (cf. Hignett 1963: 386–92). But H. says specifically that they did not want to be seen sailing round Euboea: in other words, the Greeks could have seen them, but would not have known exactly what they were going to do. Watchers on the high ground in Euboea may have been able to see them, but the Persians need not have known this. Euboea is about 120 miles long, and the total distance to be covered just under 200 miles, so in optimal conditions, the Persians could have completed the journey in just over a day. On the other hand, this circumnavigation is a very elaborate means of blocking the strait, which could have been done much more easily in other ways, and some scholars reject it as a fiction.

ὡς ἂν μὴ ὀφθείησαν 'so that they might not be seen'. ὡς ἄν in purpose clauses is very rare in Attic prose except in Xenophon.

ἵνα δὴ περιλάβοιεν 'in order (as they thought) to surround them'. H. is especially fond of using δή after ἵνα to describe 'an ingenious stratagem or device: often, but not always, indignant or contemptuous in tone' (*GP* 232). The clause gives the thoughts of the Persians and, in the light of the failure of this stratagem, perhaps passes adverse retrospective judgement on them.

οἱ μὲν . . . σφεῖς: i.e. the men sent round Euboea . . . the rest at Aphetae, through whom the sentence is focalised.

7.2 ταῦτα βουλευσάμενοι: asyndeton between sentences, though a device more exploited in later writers, is frequent in earlier prose when a pronoun in the second sentence effectively creates a link with the preceding one (Denniston 1952: 109).

οὐδὲ πρότερον ἤ . . . ὡς ἡκόντων 'nor (did they intend to attack) until the signal should arrive (as they expected) from those who were sailing round (Euboea), (indicating) that they had indeed arrived'. πρότερον ἤ is sometimes used like πρὶν ἤ (*M&T* §653; cf. πρὶν ἤ **3**.1n.); πρότερον ἤ . . . ἔμελλε φανήσεσθαι is essentially the equivalent of πρὶν ἂν φαίνηται, but the use of ἔμελλε indicates that the focalisation is still that of the Persians. The participle after φαίνομαι usually states what is the case (**110**.1n.); ὡς adds a little emphasis, 'the Persians could be assured that they had arrived' (cf. *M&T* §916; Cooper 2002: 2554).

σύνθημα: there is a problem of how the signal was to be given, when the Euripus channel is fifty miles away from Aphetae.

ἀριθμόν: 'a muster'. Such counting of forces had important logistical purposes, as here for instance to see how many ships had been lost in the storm, but also psychological ones, to allow men to see their leading commanders, the size of their forces etc., and so to have their confidence boosted. The last muster of Xerxes' forces was carried out at Doriscus (7.59–100). The Persians since then had lost many ships, 3 hitting reefs (7.183.2), 400 in a storm (7.190), and 15 in a battle (7.194); they had also gained 120 (7.185.1).

8 Scyllies the diver

The arrival of an informant or messenger is a frequent narrative device in this book, here covering the shift from the Persian to the Greek camp: cf. **21, 23, 24**.2, **26**.1, **50**.1, **79, 82**.1.

Scyllies' unlikely aquatic exploit, performed to the detriment of the Persians, stands as an emblem of the coming remarkable Greek naval success at Salamis, and is one of a number of notable occurrences that accompany that triumph. The Greeks had 'a cultural pride in their prowess in the water, and a conviction that it was one of the many features which signified their superiority over non-Greek peoples and enabled them to beat them in sea-battles' (E. M. Hall 1994: 56). The distinction is not in fact absolute, since in e.g. 6.44.3, **89**, and **129**.2 it is only some of the barbarians who cannot swim, but the implied Greek superiority here would be mirrored in the last section of the Artemisium episode where the Greeks' moral superiority in not fighting for wealth is highlighted (**26**). Swimming was often done with the aid of stuffed or inflated skins or rafts of skin (e.g. DB (= Brosius no. 44) I §18, V §74; Arr. *Anab.* 3.29.4), but warriors are also shown swimming without, e.g. on Ashurnasirpal's palace at Nineveh (BM WA 124538).

The episode also illustrates a frequent aspect of H.'s narrative, whereby he will recount a story, sometimes one that pushes at the bounds of credibility, and then refute or reject it; the readers are given a hint as to H.'s view, but left to make up their own minds as to the likelihood of the story: cf. **87**.1–3, **94**, **112**.2, **118–21**, **128**.1; Cartledge and Greenwood 2002.

8.1 γάρ: 'anticipatory'; cf. **5**.1n.

Σκυλλίης: in contrast to H.'s story, Paus. 10.19.1–2 records a statue of him set up by the Amphictyons at Delphi to commemorate how he and his daughter Hydna had worked on the *Greeks'* behalf during the storm, by pulling away from below the anchors and moorings of the Persian ships. Scyllies and his daughter became legendary figures: the invention of submarine warfare is attributed to him (Apollonides, *A.P.* 9.296 (1st century AD)), and Hydna enters mythology as a lover of the sea-god Glaucus (Aeschrion of Samos, *ap.* Athen. 296E). Cf. Frost 1968.

ἐν τῆι ναυηγίηι: the storm and shipwreck off Mt Pelion in 7.188–92. H. keeps back the account of Scyllies' actions in that storm until the time of his most famous exploit.

περιεβάλετο: as elsewhere in H., simply 'obtained' (3.71.4 etc.).

ἐν νόωι μὲν εἶχε ἄρα . . . ἀλλ' οὐ γάρ οἱ παρέσχε ἐς τότε 'so he probably had in mind . . . but it was not possible until then'. ἄρα adds the sense 'as was subsequently suggested by his actions' (*GP* 36); what he actually intended remains uncertain. ἀλλ' οὐ γάρ then implies that the previous clause is rendered irrelevant by, or is of less importance than, what follows (*GP* 101): whatever Scyllies had in mind, he had no opportunity to do anything about it. παρέσχε is impersonal.

8.2 ἔτι reinforces τὸ ἐνθεῦτεν 'after that time'; cf. ἐκ παλαιοῦ ἔτι (**62**.2) and τὸ ἐνθεῦτεν ἤδη (**98**.2 etc.).

οὐκ ἔχω εἰπεῖν ἀτρεκέως: when H. uses this adverb of his own knowledge, it is almost always found in negative expressions; cf. **87**.1 and F&M on 9.18.2. For H.'s expressions of ignorance and uncertainty, cf. the list in Lateiner 1989: 69–72, and ibid. 76–90 on alternative versions of events.

θωμάζω δὲ εἰ: θωμάζω is used with εἰ rather than ὅτι when the object of amazement is not stated as a fact but as a possibility or as something that is questionable (*M&T* §494; Smyth §2247). Since the distance involved is about nine miles, some scepticism would be justified. For H.'s expressions of wonder, cf. Barth 1968.

σταδίους μάλιστά κηι τούτους ἐς ὀγδώκοντα: μάλιστά κηι and ἐς both mean 'approximately'; for the tautology, cf. ὡς . . . μάλιστά κηι in **31**.1.

8.3 μέν νυν 'and so' is often used in H. at the end or in the course of a narration. νυ(ν) is an enclitic form of νῦν, found mainly in Ionic prose and poetry (and seen in Lat. *nu-per*, *nu-dius*), which has a mildly consecutive rather than temporal force (K–G II 118).

ψεύδεσι ἴκελα: reminiscent of *Od.* 19.203 ἴσκε ψεύδεα πολλὰ λέγων ἐτύμοισιν ὁμοῖα; Hes. *Th.* 27; Theog. 713.

γνώμη μοι ἀποδεδέχθω 'let it be made clear that my opinion is'. The perfect imperative (here of δείκνυμι), most often in the passive, implies that an action about to be completed (or just completed) is decisive (*M&T* §105): there is to be no doubt about H.'s opinion. H. brings himself into his narrative no fewer than 1,086 times (Dewald 1987), but this is not self-importance: 'he has not tried . . . to use his own voice as author to confirm the authority of the third person narrative. He has rather presented the "I" of the authorial persona as an alternative voice, one that goes to some lengths to distinguish itself from the *logoi* it recounts' (ibid. 151). H. set a trend for later ancient historians: 'as opposed to the assured narrative of the contemporary historian, [the non-contemporary historian] . . . portrays himself within the narrative as an organiser and sifter, if not solver, of the tradition' (Marincola 1997: 262–3; cf. 95–127). The reader or audience is left with work to do: for H.'s relation to his audience, cf. Brock 2003. Thomas 2000: 235–48 sees the prevalent use of the first person as a feature of the style of live performance, used also by sophists and medical writers.

9–11 The first battle

This narrative falls into five roughly equal sections: (a) Greek deliberations and change of plan (as in the previous section); (b) Persian reaction; (c) reactions of the Ionians, (i) friendly to Greeks, (ii) hostile; (d) the fighting; (e) the retreat of both sides. An incident involving a man from Cypriot Salamis ends (d); a gift of land on the island of Salamis ends (e). Salamis, the site of the great battle in this book, is once again evoked by events at Artemisium (**8**n.).

The Greeks carry out skilled manoeuvres, despite the fact that they had never fought together thus as a navy and many would have had no experience of naval warfare at all, nor much training for it; their leaders were similarly inexperienced. The same was true of the Persians: the Ionian Revolt and Datis' and Artaphernes' expedition that ended at Marathon had given the Persians some experience of campaigning on this scale, but how many men from the latter were in Xerxes' expedition is not known. The Persians had crack naval forces like the Phoenicians (**85**.1n.), but other contingents need not have been so skilled. Furthermore, their commanders owed their positions largely to birth or royal favour, and not necessarily to military skill. Nonetheless, both navies carried out complex manoeuvres with considerable skill in the course of the campaign.

On the fighting at Artemisium, cf. Hignett 1963: 149–92; Hammond, *CAH*² IV 546–63; Lazenby 1993: 117–50; Morrison, Coates and Rankov 2000: 50–5; Bowen 1998.

9–10.1 Preparations for battle. Persian confidence, which will be their final downfall, is again evident, and again H. focalises the Persian reactions more vividly than the Greek (ὁρῶντες . . . ἐλπίσαντες . . . ὁρῶντες . . . καταφρονήσαντες . . . ὁρῶντες . . . ἐπιστάμενοι).

9 λόγον σφίσι αὐτοῖσι ἐδίδοσαν 'gave one another the opportunity to speak', i.e. 'debated' cf. **132**.2n.

ἐνίκα . . . πορεύεσθαι impersonal, 'the view prevailed that they should sail'; cf. 6.101.2; Thuc. 2.54.3.

αὐλισθέντας 'having camped on shore', as crews of triremes always had to at night, since bunks and cooking facilities did not exist on board (cf. e.g. [Dem.] 50.22). In this case it would also confirm to the enemy that they did not plan any naval activity that night.

ἀπαντᾶν τῇσι περιπλεούσῃσι τῶν νεῶν: presumably H. means that a proportion of the fleet would have sailed to meet the Persians, since only a few ships would have been needed to block the channel, and contact needed to be maintained with the men at Thermopylae (**2**.1n).

μετὰ δὲ τοῦτο: i.e. after the making of the decision, but on the same day. H. has made this a very busy day, with the arrival of the Persian fleet at Aphetae and the dispatch of the squadron round Euboea, Scyllies' arrival, the council of war, the first battle and the capture of the ships as mentioned in 7.194.

αὐτοὶ ἐπανέπλεον: it is a little strange that the Greeks, having decided to leave by night, then fight late in the day. Perhaps the Greeks were thus able both to convince the Persians that they did not have flight in mind, and to fight when there was not enough time left in the day for anything catastrophic to happen.

ἀπόπειραν . . . διεκπλόου: the *diekplous* essentially involved an attempt to break through the enemy line and attack from the rear, either by individual ships or by columns of ships (cf. Gomme on Thuc. 2.83.5; Lazenby 1987; Morrison 1991: 197–200; Cawkwell 2005: 221–32). It seems to have been a relatively new manoeuvre, and, as the Ionians found before Lade in 494, it required considerable skill and practice to get right (6.11–12); the Chians used it successfully in that battle (6.15.2). The Greek desire to see how the Persians went about it would be understandable therefore. The Persians in fact seem to employ the encircling movement, the *periplous:* ἐκυκλοῦντο (**10**.1; cf. Whitehead 1987). The *diekplous* was a ramming manoeuvre, favoured by the Greeks at Salamis; the Persians seem to have preferred bumping into ships and boarding them (**84**.1n.). For the development of the Persian navy, cf. Cawkwell 2005: 255–73.

10.1 Ξέρξεω: cf. Introduction, §3.

μανίην ἐπενείκαντες 'thinking them mad'. The Persians reacted in the same way to the Greek attack at the run at Marathon: μανίην . . . ἐπέφερον (6.112.2); this intertext bodes well for the Greeks here. Coupled with καταφρονήσαντες, this phrase suggests the hubristic arrogance of the Persians.

μέν γε: γε 'concentrate[s] attention momentarily on the μέν clause, with a deliberate temporary exclusion of the δέ clause' (*GP* 159); the μέν-clause thus gains slightly more importance than usual.

ἄμεινον πλεούσας: probably because they had better-trained and more experienced crews, rather than because of some aspect of their construction.

ἐκυκλοῦντο: i.e. they employed the *periplous* manoeuvre, where one tried to encircle the enemy fleet. It is not exactly clear exactly how the Greeks responded, but they seem to have employed what became the standard defence against the *periplous*, of forming their ships up with sterns together and bows pointing outwards, from which position they could attack the Persian ships side-on or at an angle, which posed a grave threat to the trireme.

10.2–3 The reactions of the Ionians here illustrate a problem for the Persians, that some of their forces, being Greeks fighting Greeks, were potentially ambivalent about their role; the Ionians, as related to the Athenians (**22**.1n.), would have felt this ambivalence especially. Before the expedition, Artabanus warned Xerxes of the likely problems of including the Ionians in his army during an expedition against the Greek mainland, but Xerxes countered with proof of their loyalty in the past (7.49–50). Themistocles will try to exploit their ambivalence in **22**, but in the end the majority of the Ionians did their duty by the Persians at Salamis (**85**.1). At Plataea, however, they fought more slackly (9.67), and at Mycale actually revolted and attacked the Persians (9.103.2).

10.2 Ἰώνων: in H., 'Ionians' tends to mean the Greeks of Asia Minor generally, whether actually 'racially' Ionian or not (cf. 1.142–8; **90**.2.n). 'Ionians' (Myc. *iawone*, Gk. Ἴωνες, *Ἰάϝονες, Akk. *Yawanaya*, Elam. *Yaunā-ip*, OP *Yaunā*, cf. Pseudartabas' address Ἰαοναῦ in Ar. *Ach.* 104, Genesis 10.2 *Javan*) appear in Assyrian and Babylonian sources from the eighth century on, though who exactly they are is a problem (cf. Brinkman 1989). They came under Persian control when Cyrus defeated and took over Croesus' Lydian empire *ca.* 546 (1.46–87). They revolted from Persia in 500, but after quelling the revolt in 493, the Persians took care to improve relationships between the Ionians and to permit them a measure of self-government (6.42–3). Ionians first appear as subjects in Achaemenid sources under Darius: cf. DB (= Brosius no. 44) I §6, *ca.* 520. DPe (= Brosius no. 133) §2 distinguishes two branches: 'those who are on the mainland and those who are by the sea [i.e. on the Asia Minor coast]'; and DSe (= Brosius no. 46) § 3 mentions the *Yaunā takabarā* '*petasos*-wearing Ionians', the *petasos* being a flat, broad-rimmed hat, which the Ionians wear on the royal tombs: Bearer 26, Schmidt III fig. 49. They are recorded as working on Darius' palace at Susa as wood-hauliers and stonemasons (DSf (= Brosius no. 45) § 4), on the columned hall at Persepolis (*PTT* 15.6, 483–482 BC; cf. also PF 2072.84, 86, 1224.8–9 = Fornara no. 45) and at Pasargadae. The appearance of an individual called 'Yauna' on PF 1807 (Brosius no. 143) shows they were also employed in important posts in the bureaucracy ('Yauna' is probably an ethnic name: Lewis 1997: 351–2; cf. Brinkman 1989: 61–3 on Akkadian references to Ionians in Achaemenid sources). At Persepolis, they are depicted bare-headed, in possibly woollen robes, with scarves over their shoulders (Schmidt I 88, with Pl. 38, III 153 with Pl. 104B; not certain). They provided 100 ships for Xerxes' expedition (7.94). On H.'s portrayal of the Ionians, cf. Immerwahr 1966: 229–33; Alty 1982: 11–14; Murray, *CAH*² IV 461–90.

10.3 **ὅσοισι δὲ καὶ . . . ἦν το γινόμενον** 'but those to whom the situation actually gave pleasure'. For this mode of expression, cf. **101**.2 βουλομένοισί σφι γένοιτ' ἂν ἀπόδεξις, 9.46.3 ἡδομένοισι ἡμῖν οἱ λόγοι γεγόνασι. The particles express disjunction (δέ) and emphasis (καί; *GP* 305).

λάμψεται: the future indicative in an object clause after the phrase ἅμιλλαν ἐποιεῦντο which expresses effort (*M&T* §339; Smyth §2211). For the custom of Persian rulers giving rewards in war, cf. **85**.3n.

αὐτὸς ἕκαστος πρῶτος: αὐτός emphasises ἕκαστος.

στρατόπεδα: used because fleets camped on shore at night (**9**n.); the plural indicates the separate contingents.

11.1 **ἐσήμηνε** 'when the signal was given'; either the verb is used impersonally, as in the following σημήναντος, or one should understand ὁ σαλπιγκτής; cf. Krentz 1991.

ἔργου εἴχοντο 'they set to work', a partitive genitive.

ἐν ὀλίγῳ περ ἀπολαμφθέντες 'though they were hemmed into a small area'. περ = καίπερ is poetic, found in prose elsewhere only in H. 3.131.1, **13** and Pl. *Epin.* 975C (*GP* 485), but it seems to have no particular force here.

κατὰ στόμα 'ranged prow to prow against the enemy'.

11.2 **Γόργου:** Gorgus (*LGPN* I *s.v.*(2)) had refused to join the unsuccessful revolt of Cyprus against Darius during the Ionian Revolt (5.104–16) and, when he was shut out of the city by his younger brother Onesilus and his faction, took refuge with the Persians. His loyalty will explain the fact that he was λόγιμος; cf. **85**.3n.

πρῶτος . . . εἷλε ἀνὴρ Ἀθηναῖος: reminiscent of the epic habit of indicating which warrior was first to strike an opponent and inaugurate a battle; cf. the first death in the *Iliad* πρῶτος δ' Ἀντίλοχος Τρώων ἕλεν ἄνδρα κορυστήν (4.457). Cf. **84** for the question of the initiator of the battle at Salamis. H.'s accounts of battles often give the exploits of significant fighters, presumably preserved by families and friends. By contrast, both the epigrams commemorating the final Greek victory and Aeschylus' tragedy laid stress on the actions of all Greece: cf. Simonides in ML 26 and *AP* 7.253 (= IX Page); Barron, *CAH*² IV 619–20. This represents an interesting difference between private oral traditions and official literature.

Λυκομήδης: Plut. *Them.* 15.2 attributes this action to him at Salamis; cf. *LGPN* II *s.v.*(11).

ἀριστήιον: for such awards and judgement passed on the best fighters, cf. **123**; Hamel 1998: 64–70. Greek aristocratic competitiveness extends even to warfare.

11.3 **ἑτεραλκέως:** here more probably 'with uncertain outcome, indecisively' rather than 'with victory going to the other (i.e. unexpected) side'. Diod. 11.12.6 says of this battle that 'they parted at nightfall, with neither side profiting from a complete victory', and indeed, though the Greeks seem to have had the best of the encounter, it was a brief affair and finished nothing. However, ἑτεραλκέως looks like a Homeric word that could be used with different meanings. It recurs in H. only in 9.103.2, where the Samians εἶδον . . . κατ' ἀρχὰς γινομένην ἑτεραλκέα τὴν μάχην. Though this sentence comes towards the conclusion of the account of the battle, κατ' ἀρχάς shows it refers to the Samians' initial reaction, so 'uncertain' is again the most likely meaning. In Homer, however, ἑτεραλκέα νίκην (*Il.* 7.26 etc.) meant originally 'victory with help from others', and was then taken to mean 'victory to the side that was losing'. The word also appears in Aes. *Pers.* 950–2, where Xerxes complains Ἰάων γὰρ ἀπηύρα, | Ἰάων ναύφαρκτος Ἄρης ἑτεραλκής. The interpretation of the whole stanza is disputed, but the adjective probably means something like 'turning the tide of battle' (Sidgwick) or 'favouring the other side' (E. M. Hall). Other compounds with ἑτερο- naturally imply an inclination etc. to one side or another, as in Hes. *Th.* 544 ἑτεροζήλως 'with partisan bias'.

νὺξ ἐπελθοῦσα διέλυσε: H.'s chronology. H.'s references to nightfall have naturally been used to construct a chronology of events. That this has been difficult, with days seeming to contain more than is likely, may be because H. was concerned less to preserve a chronology than to use nightfall and daybreak as means of articulating his narrative, in the manner of Homer. In book 8, we have the following sequence of temporal indications. The first day sees the first battle and that night ushers in the storm (**12**.1); daybreak (**14**.1) brings relief and a second incident; and the following day (**15**.1) sees the third and major battle, which brings the conflict at Artemisium to an end, as night watch-fires are lit in **19**.2. The sun rises in **23** and there is then a gap for complex events of unspecified chronology, before **54** talks of the day after the capture of the city and **56** closes that day; Themistocles uses the night to reverse the Greek decision. Day dawns (**64**.1) and we have the Persian discussions, concluded by night (**70**.1), when some of the Persians move south (**71**.1), the Isthmus wall is described, Sicinnus' message leads to Persian manoeuvres (**76**.1), and Aristeides arrives (**79**). In the midst of this, at **66**.1, we are told the fleet arrived at Phaleron five days after their sight-seeing at Thermopylae: how precisely the chronology of the army's movements relate to this is not said. At **83**.1 dawn breaks and the battle begins. A very full day finally ends at **107**.1, and there are no further such indications of day and night until 9.8.1: the complexity of events again makes a detailed chronology almost impossible, so H. abandons it. The effect is of a narrative with a clear chronological sequence, but closer inspection suggests the aim may be less historical accuracy than literary structuring. On the other hand, we are already in late September so there are not a lot of days to play with, and even if H. has concertinaed certain events, his account is unlikely to be wildly inaccurate.

Ἀντίδωρος Λήμνιος: Lemnos had been conquered for Darius by Otanes (5.26–7), and by Miltiades for Athens, probably during the Ionian Revolt (6.136.2–140; Lewis, *CAH*² IV 298–9); it returned, however, to Persian control after the failure of the revolt. Antidorus is otherwise unknown. For the motif of desertion, cf. **8, 46**.3, **82**.1.

12–14 A violent storm

This storm is given significance in a number of ways. It occurs at roughly the central point in the Artemisium narrative, and is attributed to the gods, who are said to be trying to even up the balance between the two sides (**13** *fin.*); storms of such severity are indeed unusual at this late stage of the year. Divinely ordained winds generally plague Xerxes' expedition. Faced with the Persian approach, Apollo recommended that the Greeks should 'pray to the winds, as future great allies' (7.178.1). The Athenians, told to pray to 'their son-in-law', interpreted this as Boreas, the North Wind, who had married Orithyia, daughter of Erechtheus: the gods duly sent the storm that destroyed a significant part of the Persian fleet off Mt Pelion (7.188–92), and after the Persian War, they built a temple to Boreas on the river Ilissus (7.189). The fact that the thunder of the current storm also comes from Mt Pelion (**12**.1) links the two divine tempests. The Greek victory is thus divinely sanctioned, not simply won by military skill. Cf. Parker 1996: 154–7; in general on religious matters, Harrison 2000a; Mikalson 2003; Scullion 2006.

After a heightened description of the storm, H. depicts, in roughly equal but very different sections, the fate of the two parts of the Persian force. Though the sailors sailing round Euboea suffer much more than those on land, H.'s account focuses more closely on the reactions of the latter, again recounting their troubles almost in their own words (**12**.2). The fate of the others is known and told, but almost entirely through the narrator: we see little of their reactions as they perish far away and unseen by Persians and readers alike.

12.1 ἦν μὲν τῆς ὥρης μέσον θέρος 'although the season of the year was midsummer'. μέν has its regular subordinating force, with the implication that the subsequent storm (δέ) is therefore in some way uncanny at such a season. ὥρης is a partitive genitive of time, cf. Dem. 21.84 τῆς δ' ὥρας ἐγίγνετ' ὀψέ 'it was late in the year'; **9** δειλίην ὀψίην . . . τῆς ἡμέρης; **144**.5 οὐχ ἑκὰς χρόνου. ὥρη denotes 'any period, fixed by natural laws and revolutions, whether of the year, month or day' (LSJ *s.v.* A). The wind was the 'Hellepontias' (7.188.2), now the *meltemi.*

σκληραὶ βρονταί: the phrase is repeated at the end of the chapter; cf. σκληρὸν δ' ἐβρόντησε Hes. *Th.* 839, fr. 54 (a) 7. These passages describe respectively Zeus' preparations for the destruction of his monstrous opponent Typhoeus, whose defeat inaugurated our orderly world, and the punishment of Apollo; their evocation here thus reinforces the cosmic importance of the storm.

12.2 οἱ . . . ταύτηι: the men at Aphetae, contrasting with those sailing round Euboea in **13**.

ἀπὸ τοῦ Πηλίου: There was a temple of Zeus Akraios on the summit.

12.2 ἐλπίζοντες πάγχυ ἀπολέεσθαι ἐς οἷα κακὰ ἧκον lit. 'expecting to be completely destroyed – into what troubles they had got!', i.e. 'because they had got into such troubles'. οἷος, ὅσος and ὡς in such clauses are equivalent to ὅτι τοιοῦτος etc. Originally these clauses were independent, exclamatory clauses, related paratactically to the rest of the sentence; later they came to depend syntactically on a verb of emotion, as e.g. Xen. *Cyr.* 7.3.14 κατοικτείρων τήν τε γυναῖκα, οἵου ἀνδρὸς στέροιτο, 'pitying the woman for the sort of husband she had lost' (cf. Smyth §2686).

ὁρμημένα: the perfect participle describes a completed action with a permanent result (Smyth §1872d); the torrents surged towards the sea and continued to pour into it.

13 ἡ αὐτή περ ἐοῦσα νύξ 'though it was the same night'; περ is concessive here, it does not emphasise αὐτή (**11**.1n.).

πολλὸν . . . τοσούτωι ὅσωι 'was much more savage, all the more so because'. For the absence of a comparative in the ὅσωι-clause, when the main clause carries the emphasis and the sense of the subordinate clause is essentially 'because', cf. 6.137.4 ἑωυτοὺς δὲ γενέσθαι τοσούτωι ἐκείνων ἄνδρας ἀμείνονας, ὅσωι παρεὸν αὐτοῖσι ἀποκτεῖναι τοὺς Πελασγοὺς . . . οὐκ ἐθελῆσαι, 'they were so much better than those men, because when they could have killed the Pelasgians, they chose not to' (cf. Smyth §2472).

ἄχαρι: though criticised by Longinus (43.1) as 'too undignified and colloquial' a word for such a disaster, is found in H. elsewhere of συμφορά and παθήματα, and is common in the phrase οὐδὲν ἄχαρι πάσχειν 'come to no harm' (e.g. **143**.3); cf. *Od.* 22.392 δόρπου δ' οὐκ ἄν πως ἀχαρίστερον ἄλλο γένοιτο. It is presumably an Ionicism, and Longinus was judging the word by its use in his time.

γὰρ δή: a very common collocation, where δή emphasises the explanatory force of γάρ.

τὰ Κοῖλα τῆς Εὐβοίης: this is said by later sources to be the area between Aulis and Cape Geraestus, below the Euripus channel (Strabo 10.1.2; *suspectus nautis*, Livy 31.47). However, the Persians could not have reached there in the time between their departure in **7**.1 and this storm on the following night. Alternatively, the 'Hollows' may have been near Cyme, where today there is an island called Κοίλη and inlets called Κοιλίαι. From there, news of a disaster there could have reached the Greeks in time to encourage them (**14**.2), whereas it would have taken much longer from Geraestus. But H.'s chronology may not be sufficiently trustworthy to use it as an argument here for the position of the Hollows (cf. **11**.3n.).

φερόμενοι . . . ἐφέροντο: a grimly graphic description of their experience. Only as they are smashed on the rocks does the narrative, in οὐκ εἰδότες, give any insight into their perceptions, and that is merely to show they had no idea what was happening.

ἐποιέετο . . . ὅκως ἂν ἐξισωθείη: this could equally well be an object clause meaning 'every care was taken by the god that the Persian forces were equal to', or a purpose clause 'the god did all this in order that the Persian forces should be equal to'; H. has ὅκως ἄν + opt. in both senses (cf. **7**.1 on ὡς ἄν + opt.).

In 3.108–9, this balance is a principle of the world in general: 'the forethought of the god' ensures in various ways that powerful animals do not dominate the world. This is echoed with a moral tinge in Themistocles' remark in **109**.3 that 'the gods begrudged (ἐφθόνησαν) that one impious and sacrilegious man should be king of Asia and Europe'. This restriction on royal power through either disaster brought on by over-reaching (as in the case of Croesus) or by limitations on their success (as with Darius) is an important aspect of H.'s representation of kings: Immerwahr 1966: 148–88. Cf. too 7.10ε for Artabanus' now clearly prophetic warning to Xerxes that 'the god likes to humble everything that exalts itself, and so even a mighty army can be destroyed by a small one, when the god, in his resentment (φθονήσας), sends panic or thunder and they perish in a way they do not deserve.' For the idea of the gods creating a 'level playing field' in battles, cf. 6.11.3, 109.5 θεῶν τὰ ἴσα νεμόντων; more generally, Immerwahr 1966: 306–26.

14 Each side experiences pleasure, but of different kinds and with different results: the Persians are glad (ἀσμένοισι) just to see the daylight, and are happy to rest and do nothing; the Greeks are encouraged by the arrival of the reinforcements (ἐπέρρωσαν), and successfully attack some Cilician ships. Night again closes this action.

14.1 ἀτρέμας τε εἶχον τὰς νέας: this transitive use of ἀτρέμας ἔχω is unusual; cf. 9.53.4, 54.1; *Il.* 15.318 αἰγίδα . . . ἔχ' ἀτρέμα, and contrast **16**.1 ἀτρέμας εἶχον πρὸς τῶι Ἀρτεμισίωι.

ἀπεχρᾶτο 'it was enough'; the middle is used impersonally only here in Greek.

νέες . . . Ἀττικαί: it is not known what these ships had been doing, but they may simply have been late arrivals. H. has nowhere mentioned the detachment of such a force: in 7.183.1 he seems to imply that the whole Greek fleet left Artemisium and in 192.2 that they all returned.

14.2 φυλάξαντες δὴ τὴν αὐτὴν ὥρην: a kind of resumptive δή (*GP* 225–6), picking up δείλην ὀψίην . . . φυλάξαντες in **9**.1. ὥρα here is close to meaning 'hour' rather than a more general 'time'; for the division of the day into twelve portions, cf. 2.109.3.

Κιλίσσῃσι: possibly a remnant of the 200 sent round Euboea, or some from one of the harbours used in addition to Aphetae, which alone could not have held the whole Persian fleet (cf. Diod. 11.12.5–6).

Though the Cilicians seem to have enjoyed a measure of independence under their kings who bore the name or title *Syennesis* (cf. 1.74.3, 7.98; Aes. *Pers.* 326–8; Xen. *Cyr.* 7.4.2, 8.6.8; *Anab.* 1.2.26), they paid some of the highest sums in tribute, 500 talents of silver (and 360 white horses; 3.90.3); only the Egyptians (700 talents, 3.91.2), Babylonians (1000, 3.92.1) and Indians (360 talents of gold, 3.94.2) paid more. Cilicia was important enough to be a separate satrapy (3.90.3). It was a major naval contributor to the empire, and possessed notable harbours (cf. 6.43.2, 95.1); it provided 100 ships for Xerxes' expedition (7.90). It was rich in agriculture, horses, wood, iron and silver, and manufacturing and trade were also significant. Its warriors wore helmets of a local style and woollen *kithones*, and carried raw-hide shields, two javelins and curved swords (7.91). If correctly identified at Persepolis, they wear rope-like fillets wound round the head and long gowns, and bring rams and other gifts (Schmidt I 87, with Pl. 34; not certain). Their importance makes it odd that Artemisia and Mardonius both list them among the less meritorious elements of the Persian forces (cf. **68**γ with n., **100**.4).

15–18 The second battle

Shame and fear of the King now replace confidence in the Persians, and provoke them to attack at midday, which suggests they sought a final outcome, not a skirmish in the late afternoon in the manner of the Greeks. The tactics on both sides are similar to those in the first battle, the Persians attempting to use numerical superiority to crush the Greeks, but this time, in another presaging of Salamis, the very size and number of their ships is their downfall; not that the Greeks do not suffer severe losses too.

15.1 τρίτηι ἡμέρηι 'on the next day but one'; Greek counts inclusively.

δεινόν τι ποιησάμενοι: cf. **3**.1n.

τὸ ἀπὸ Ξέρξεω 'what Xerxes would do'; cf. 1.159.2 τὸ ἀπὸ σεῦ. The importance of maintaining the King's favour and avoiding his anger recurs in **10**.3, **69**.2, **86**, and **90**.4, and Xerxes is made to highlight fear of their leader as a virtue of Persians as opposed to the free Greek soldiers (7.103.3–4). The Greek traditions of Xerxes' swiftness to anger are fed especially by his treatment of the Hellespont (7.35) and abuse of the corpse of Leonidas (7.238). In his inscriptions, however, he presents a different picture of himself. When he took over one of Darius' epitaphs at Naqsh-i Rustam (DNb (= Brosius no. 103) §3), he arrogated to himself the claim: 'I am not hot-tempered: the things that develop in me during a dispute I hold firmly under control through my mind, I am firmly in control of myself' (XPc). Achaemenid ideology presented the King as calmly wise, unless rightly angered; the Persians' enemies constructed him otherwise, as an oppressive, irascible monarch.

παρακελευσάμενοι 'encouraging each other'; the Greeks respond equally enthusiastically: παρεκελεύοντο, **15**.2. This verb gives a more dramatic picture than the alternative reading παρασκευασάμενοι; cf. 9.102.2 παρακελευσάμενοι ἔργου εἴχοντο προθυμότερον.

τὰς αὐτὰς ταύτας ἡμέρας 'in the course of those very same days'; accusatives in expressions of time show that the whole period is covered by the action. H. in a number of places notes the coincidence of major battles. In 5.108–15, there are two contemporaneous battles at Cypriot Salamis; in 7.166, Gelon and Theron defeat the Carthaginians in Sicily on the same day as the battle of Salamis; and in 9.90.1, 100–101.2, the Persians suffer defeats at Mycale and Plataea on the same day, in each case near a shrine of Demeter (see F&M on 9.102–5 for the details). It may well be that in some of these instances there was an actual coincidence of date, but it may rather be the case that tradition heightened the significance of these battles by these coincidences, which suggest some guiding agency behind the events. See further, Introduction, §5.

15.2 ἦν δὲ πᾶς κτλ. 'the whole struggle for those at sea centred on the Euripus channel, just as it was for those men with Leonidas to guard the pass.' The parallelism between the two battles resides not just in chronology, but also in the form of the conflict.

16.1 μηνοειδὲς ποιήσαντες . . . ἐκυκλεῦντο 'having formed their ships into a crescent, they encircled them.' This seems to be a slightly different tactic from that described in **9–11**. The Persians try to envelop the Greeks, to which the response would normally have been to stay in line abreast. That would not have worked here, so the Greeks attack instead.

παραπλήσιοι . . . ἐγίνοντο 'they fought with equal success', rather than 'of similar fighting strength', because the following clause marks the numerical superiority in the Persian fleet.

16.2 αὐτὸς ὑπ' ἑωυτοῦ ἔπιπτε . . . περιπιπτουσέων περὶ ἀλλήλας 'fell foul of itself . . . fouled each others' oars'; the first use of πίπτω has a more metaphorical sense, the latter a concrete one. There is a further play with words in ἀντεῖχε καὶ οὐκ εἶκε; cf. **1**.1n. The lack of experience amongst the Persian fleet of fighting in such a large group tells here, as the advantage of superior numbers, on which they usually relied, is negated by the geography of the area. This is again a foretaste of what happens at Salamis (**86**, **89**.2).

μὲν δή: δή strengthens μέν: 'though it is true that many Greek ships . . .' (cf. **6**.2n.).

17.1 Αἰγύπτιοι: they provided 200 ships (7.89.2) and 700 talents tribute (3.91.2). Egypt had been brought into the empire by Cambyses in the 520s, an account of which opens book 3. Their navy played a role in the defeat of the Ionian revolt (6.6). They were armed with 'spears for naval warfare and large poleaxes' (7.89.3), which would have helped them in fighting on board ship. They also wore plaited helmets and most had breast-plates, and they carried long swords and shields with thick rims. At Persepolis, they have long fringed gowns (cf. Delegation 19: Schmidt I 88, with Pl. 36; id. III 154, with fig. 50 (Bearer 19)). Despite this prowess, Mardonius is rude about them after Salamis (**100**.4; so Artemisia, **68**γ), though he kept them with him after Xerxes left Greece (9.32).

αὐτοῖσι ἀνδράσι 'crews and all', a 'sociative' dative, where αὐτός is added to the dative to express accompaniment; this is regularly found in military contexts, especially those involving destruction (Smyth §1525; Humbert §§481, 484). Cf. ἀνδράσι τε διηκοσίοισι below.

Ἀθηναῖοι: their triumph was celebrated by Pindar in a dithyramb ('the sons of Athens laid the bright cornerstone of freedom', fr. 77 S-M.), and by Simonides in an epigram set up in the temple of Artemis Proseoea at Artemisium (no. xxiv Page; cf. Plut. *Them.* 8.3).

Κλεινίης ὁ Ἀλκιβιάδεω: this is the Cleinias I, the father of Alcibiades II, who was the grandfather of the famous Alcibiades and himself also kept a private trireme (Thuc. 6.61.6; cf. *LGPN* II *s.v.*(21)). The cost of providing and paying for a trireme was very considerable, and in Athens such private financing of ships was later formalised by the 'liturgy' system. H. preserves the record of another such instance in Philippus of Croton (5.47).

18.1 δρησμὸν δὴ ἐβούλευον: emphatic δή is rare with nouns in prose (*GP* 213–14), so its use here suggests an urgency greater than in **4**.1 δρησμὸν ἐβούλευον. The urgency to retreat despite a perhaps better than expected performance in the battles is to be put down to the damage they had suffered and no doubt a fear that the Persians might do better in the next engagement. In H.'s account, news of Thermopylae has not yet arrived (contrast Diod. 11.13.3; Plut. *Them.* 9.1; this problem upset Plut. *MH* 34).

τῶν νεκρῶν . . . ἐπεκράτεον: to have control over a battle-site and so to be able to pick up one's dead and wreckage was an accepted sign of victory. This is demonstrated in mythical form in 1.82, where the Spartans claim victory in a battle involving 300 Spartans and 300 Argives, because, though two Argives survived but only one Spartan, the Spartan stayed on the battlefield and stripped the enemy corpses.

19–26 After the battle

The action is focused on Greeks and Persians here in almost equal measure, with parallelisms between the two sections. They are both centred on an unusual incident, Themistocles' inscriptions and Xerxes' invitation to the Persians to view the dead at Thermopylae (**22**.1–2, **24**.2). In each case, a message is given in direct speech by H., though in fact they were indirectly relayed to their recipients, by writing and by a herald respectively. These two incidents imply a comparison between Greek and Persian ideology: the appeal to the ultimate unity of the Greek nation in Themistocles' inscriptions contrasts with the royal dismissiveness of Xerxes' remark 'see how Xerxes fights against those men fool enough to hope to overthrow his forces' (**24**.2); problems of Greek unity and Persian arrogance are thus picked up from the previous narrative, and continue H.'s political and psychological analysis. The Artemisium episode closes with Tritantaechmes' explicit contrast of Greek and Persian values, in his surprise that Greeks will compete for nothing more than an olive garland at the Olympic games (**26**.3).

19–20 Themistocles' plans and Euboean forgetfulness

The Euboeans and Themistocles are again prominent in Greek planning, as in **4–5**. Themistocles once again displays the cunning that will lead to the great victory at Salamis. Here, as elsewhere (**57–8, 75**), Themistocles' trickery takes place at night, the time the Greeks associated with cunning (cf. Vidal-Naquet 1981).

19.1 ἀπορραγείη: attempts to detach the Ionians from their current alliance or to create a fifth column in their ranks are repeated themes in H., cf. 6.9.2–4, 13.1 (Lade); 9.98.2–4 (Mycale); this last example is explicitly compared to Themistocles' inscriptions in **22**.

φῦλον: a synonym for γένος, cf. Pl. *Plt.* 260D τοῦ τῶν κηρύκων γένους . . . τὸ κηρυκικὸν φῦλον. It is a *hapax* in H., as are also in this chapter παλάμην and καταθύειν.

τὸ Καρικόν: OP *Karkā*; H. is himself from Caria. The Carians lived in a loose arrangement of towns and hill-top villages, ruled by local dynasts. Caria was poor, so many sought a livelihood abroad through their military skills. They are found in many places, e.g. providing timber for the palace at Susa (DSf (= Brosius no. 45) §4), involved in the coup against and murder of queen Athaliah (Septuagint 4 Kings 11.4, οἱ Χορρί are probably Carians), and writing on the legs of Rameses II at Abu Simbel. They played a significant part in the turbulent history of 6th-century Egypt (H. 2.61.2, 152.4–5, 154.3, 163). Caria was conquered by Croesus (1.28), and by Harpagus for

Cyrus around 547–6 (for this and their customs, 1.171–6). They joined the Ionian Revolt (5.103.2) and, after some reverses, annihilated a Persian army under Daurises (5.117–21). They had always been an important maritime people: in 517 Darius sent the Carian Scylax of Caryanda to explore the Indus river and seek a westward passage to Egypt, prior to his invasion of the Punjab (4.44; Bivar, *CAH*² IV 201–3), and they provided Xerxes with 70 ships (7.93). Homer calls them βαρβαρόφωνοι (*Il.* 2.867; cf. 10.428–9), though in fact their language is probably Indo-European, and related to Hittite and Luvian. It is not yet fully deciphered: cf. Ray 1990; Adiego Lajara 1993; Pope 1999: 192–4; Melchert 2004. They dressed in the Greek manner but carried sickles and daggers (7.93); on the royal tombs they wear a *chlamys* over a *chiton* (Schmidt III fig. 48 (Bearer 30)). Artemisia is their most notable warrior (**68** etc.), and we meet two other notable Carians in book 8, Hermotimus (**104–6**) and Mys (**133–5**). Cf. Strabo 14.2.23–9; Hornblower 1982: 2–24; Ray, *CANE* II 1187–94; H–N 1108–37.

οἷοί τε εἴησαν: the direct form was οἷοί τε ἐσμέν; for the absence of ἄν, cf. *M&T* §§415–16.

19.2 ἐπὶ δὲ τοῖσι κατήκουσι πρήγμασι 'in the present circumstances', as often in H.; κατήκουσι = Att. καθήκουσι.

ὅσα τις ἐθέλοι 'as many as each man wished'; for τις, cf. **109**.4n.

παραίνεέ τε . . . πυρὰ ἀνακαίειν 'he instructed each group of commanders to tell their men to light fires'. The lighting of fires is designed to suggest to the Persians that the Greeks intend to stay where they are that night, but in fact it is to cloak a retreat; for this stratagem, called *pseudopura*, cf. Polyaen. 4.18.2; Frontinus, 1.5.24; 2.5.17.

κομιδῆς δὲ πέρι τὴν ὥρην αὐτῶι μελήσειν 'he would take care of the right moment for their flight'; for the word order κομιδῆς πέρι, cf. **36**.2n.

20 This Euboean neglect of Bacis' oracle is a further example of how failure to heed divine warnings brings its own punishment: the first major episode in H.'s work is Croesus' failure to understand the words of Delphi (1.46–56, 86–92). The Euboeans' mistake and subsequent sufferings contrast with Athens' abandonment of their city in obedience to the 'wooden-wall' oracle and their ultimate success. For the importance of oracles in this book, cf. also **35–9, 77** (possibly spurious), **96, 133–5**; on H.'s Persian War oracles, Crahay 1956: 290–342; Harrison 2000a: 122–57.

20.1 Βάκιδος: H. is our principal source for this seer's oracles, which came to prominence during the Persian Wars. According to schol. on Ar. *Peace* 1071, there were three people of this name, one, the oldest, from Eleon in Boeotia, who was inspired by the Nymphs (cf. Paus. 4.27.4, 10.12.11), one from Attica and one from Caphye in Arcadia; cf. Asheri 1993. The name may be connected with the Lydian *Baki-* 'Bacchus'. Collections of oracles were made early in the historical period, among them those of Bacis: Parke & Wormell 1956: 165–79; Fontenrose 1978: 145–65. Bacis' oracles usually start with 'but when', use animal imagery, offer ritual advice and foretell dreadful events: this one is more straightforward.

οὔτε τι ἐξεκομίσαντο οὐδὲν οὔτε προεσάξαντο ὡς παρεσομένου σφι πολέμου 'they had neither removed anything from their homes nor laid in any stores, as (they would have done) if (they had thought) war was approaching'; i.e. they were completely unprepared. οὐδέν is pleonastic after οὔτε τι (cf. *Lex. s.v.* IV); προεσάξαντο is aorist middle of προ-σάσσω, cognate with σαγή 'baggage', σάγμα 'saddle'. ὡς παρεσομένου σφι πολέμου goes closely with προεσάξαντο, making a single sense-group negatived by οὔτε; ὡς is used with the participle to show that the expectation or otherwise of war belongs to the participants in the action.

20.2 Βάκιδι: a dative 'of citation', a type of locatival dative; cf. Pl. *Rep.* 389E οἷα καὶ Ὁμήρωι Διομήδης λέγει 'the kind of things which, in Homer, Diomedes says' (K–G I 422).

φράζεο often begins oracles; cf. e.g. Ar. *Kn.* 1030 φράζευ, Ἐρεχθεΐδη.

βαρβαρόφωνος: cf. *Il.* 2.867, Κάρων . . . βαρβαροφώνων; also in a Bacis oracle in 9.43.2. The word βάρβαρος becomes frequent in Greek first with H.

βύβλινον: *Cyperus papyrus*, Egyptian papyrus, which got its name from the Phoenician town of Byblos. The reference is to Xerxes' bridge over the Hellespont, which used ropes made of papyrus and esparto grass (7.34–6).

ἀπέχειν 'keep away' is an imperatival infinitive, a feature common in Homer but also found in Attic and Ionic prose (*M&T* §784; Smyth §2013). Indo-European infinitives were originally case forms (accusatives, genitives, ablatives, locatives) of verbal nouns, not related to the rest of the conjugation and without tense or voice; they expressed the root meaning of the verb (cf. Sihler §§551–2). Used on their own, they had the force of a command ordering the realisation of the verb's sense.

πολυμηκάδας 'much-bleating'; presumably a reference to the many different languages spoken in the Persian army; the word is found only here in Greek.

τούτοισι . . . τὰ μέγιστα 'because they paid no attention at all to these words, both in their present troubles and in those they anticipated, it happened that they suffered to the highest degree.' For impersonal παρῆν, normally 'it was possible', meaning 'it happened', cf. 9.70.5 παρῆν τε τοῖσι Ἕλλησι φονεύειν οὕτω ὥστε τριήκοντα μυριάδων; πρὸς τὰ μέγιστα is an adverbial accusative. There are nine dative plurals in a sentence of some twenty words: oracles in this book tend to be accompanied by unusual language, which led Powell to delete them all (cf. **77**nn., **96**.2n.). This is certainly an odd sentence: apart from the numerous datives, προσδοκίμοισι, which means 'expected', is strange in a passage about Euboean forgetfulness.

21 News of Thermopylae causes the Greeks to retreat

The two sentences about the lookouts are parallel in meaning but employ considerable stylistic variation; Artemisium and Thermopylae are again linked. H. will often bring in information at the moment it becomes significant, rather than at the point in the narrative when it actually occurred: cf. on Scyllies in **8**.1.

21.1 Τρηχῖνος: Trachis was the district around Mt Oeta in Thessaly, close to Thermopylae.

ἦν μὲν γὰρ ἐπ' Ἀρτεμισίωι 'that is to say there was at Artemisium'; the anticipatory γάρ introduces the digression on the lookout at Artemisium, and μέν looks forward to ὣς δ' αὔτως ἦν, where the information on the lookout from Trachis is finally given; cf. *GP* 67.

Ἀντικυρεύς: Antecyra was at the mouth of the river Spercheius in the Malian Gulf, just north of Trachis and Thermopylae (cf. 7.198.2); a local man is used as lookout.

κατῆρες ἕτοιμον 'fitted out with oars [and] ready'; κατήρης is a rare word, derived from the root either of ἀρ-αρ-ίσκω 'fit' or of ἐρέτης 'oarsman' (Chantraine 416).

παλήσειε: an extremely rare verb, found in the simple form only here, in an inscription from Egypt (*SB* 9367.10.10 πεπαληκός 'wrecked', of a ship), in the lexicographers (there is also ἐκπαλέω 'dislocate'), and doubtfully in Timoth. 791 fr. 20.48 ἰσόρροπά τε παλευό[i.e.? παλέ[[υ]]ο[ντα, see Hordern 2002: 157). The meaning is deducible from the parallel phrase ἤν τι καταλαμβάνηι νεώτερον τὸν πεζόν at the end of the section.

Ἀβρώνιχος (*LGPN* II *s.v.*(1)) was later an ambassador to Sparta, who was involved in Themistocles' cunning diplomacy to ensure the walls of Athens were rebuilt, despite Spartan suggestions to the contrary (Thuc. 1.91.3).

νεώτερον: νέος often has the sense of 'untoward'; cf. Lat. *novae res* 'revolution'.

οὐκέτι ἐς ἀναβολὰς ἐποιεῦντο = οὐκέτι ἀνεβάλλοντο 'they no longer put off'; cf. Eur. *Heracl.* 270 κλαίων ἄρ' ἅψηι τῶνδε κοὐκ ἐς ἀμβολάς, 'without delay'; ἐς / εἰς in these expressions indicates manner, as in εἰς καιρόν 'opportunely', εἰς δύναμιν (K–G I 471). The Persians now control the mainland, thus isolating the Greeks from the friendly or neutral shore needed for trireme operations (**9**n.).

Κορίνθιοι πρῶτοι: that the Corinthians should be first and the Athenians last may indeed be the result of where they were drawn up, but it also reflects the tension between these two leading Greek nations: cf. **5**, **59**, **61**, **94**.

22 *Themistocles' inscriptions*

This is the only verbatim report of a Greek prose inscription in H. (S. R. West 1985: 285–7; note that H. uses the explicit τάδε not the more approximate τοιάδε or τοιαῦτα), but it is fairly plain that there were no such inscriptions (no trace has ever been found). There is also a blending of genres. Though these words are supposedly inscribed, they take the form of a speech, to which the direct address ἄνδρες Ἴωνες is more appropriate (cf. Xerxes' ἄνδρες σύμμαχοι in **24**.2); formal Greek prose inscriptions do not usually address their readers as an orator his audience, unlike say poetic epitaphs. By contrast, rock-cut Achaemenid inscriptions do include regular personal address to the reader: cf. e.g. DB (= Brosius no. 44) IV §65 'Darius the King says: You who shall hereafter look at this inscription which I have written down and these sculptures, do not destroy (them).'

The use of inscriptions to communicate with the Ionians is a striking conceit, befitting the trickster Themistocles (Leotychidas uses a more conventional herald for a similar appeal before Mycale, 9.98.2–4). For other stories of unconventional methods of communication in H., cf. 1.123–4 Harpagus' letter to Cyrus hidden in a hare and carried by a messenger disguised as a hunter; 5.35 writing on the shaven head of a slave; 7.239 Demaratus' letter to Cleomenes hidden under the wax of a writing-tablet; **128** letters attached to arrows; see also the collection of such stories in Aen. Tact. 31.

The structure of the argument is simple, with ring composition: 'you are acting unjustly in attacking your relations; come over to us; if that is not possible, do nothing; if that is not possible, fight poorly; you are related to us; you are responsible for the war.' It begins with two lapidary sentences, giving the basis of the claim and advice, followed by two conditional clause with εἰ δὲ . . . ὑμεῖς δέ, the second longer and more complex and ending with a clause introduced by μεμνημένοι which repeats the sense of the opening two sentences.

22.1 νέας τὰς ἄριστα πλεούσας: the factors that governed the speed of ships included age; the particular wood used to construct them and how permeable it was; how long they had been in the water, and so how waterlogged the timbers had become; how much bilge had collected and how rough the bottom had become (roughness could reduce speed by up to 20 per cent); and, naturally, how efficient and fit the crew. On 'fast' triremes, cf. Morrison, Coates and Rankov 2000: 276–9.

ἔλεγε: λέγω used of inanimate objects is unusual outside H. He uses it 35×, 9× with γράμματα, but also with e.g. ἀγγελίη, λόγος, χρησμοί, a tripod (5.60), or a statue (2.141.6); cf. *Lex. s.v.* A II; Thuc. 6.54.7 γράμμασι λέγον τάδε, of an inscription.

ἐπὶ τοὺς πατέρας: the Athenians claimed to be the ancestors of the Ionians, and after the founding of the Delian League used that claim to justify their rule over them (cf. 1.147.2, 7.51.2; Solon fr. 4a; Thuc. 1.2.5–6 etc.). Asia Minor was colonised by Greeks from all the main tribes after the fall of the Mycenean kingdoms, but the dialects of the Ionic part of the Asia Minor coastline and of Attica are very close, which points to racial affiliation. Peoples appear to have left Athens for a new start in Ionia perhaps from *ca.* 1050 onwards, but the extent to which Athens was important in the colonisation of Ionia is now disputed: cf. Osborne 1996: 32–7; F&M on 9.106.3. Aristagoras uses a similar argument to persuade the Athenians to support the Ionians in their revolt (5.97.2).

22.2 μάλιστα μὲν πρὸς ἡμῶν γίνεσθε 'preferably, come over to our side', as πρὸς ἑωυτῶν in §3; cf. the use of πρός + genitive to mean 'to someone's advantage', a kind of partitive genitive.

ὑμεῖς δέ: 'apodotic' δέ, that is, δέ used apparently unnecessarily in a main clause after a subordinate clause. This is more frequent in Homer and Herodotus than in Attic prose: 'only in Homer and Herodotus is apodotic δέ really at home' (*GP* 177). H. uses it in conditional sentences more than any other writer, and twice in this sentence. The use seems to be the preservation in syntactic Greek of the intensive force of δέ, which can be seen in such paratactic sentences as 1.112.2 ἐπεὶ τοίνυν οὐ δύναμαί σε πείθειν μὴ ἐκθεῖναι, σὺ δὲ ὧδε ποίησον, 'since I cannot persuade you not to expose it, do *you* therefore do this . . .'; on the rarity of the particular use here, cf. *GP* 180.

ἐκ τοῦ μέσου ἡμῖν ἕζεσθε 'please take a neutral stance'; cf. 3.83.3 ἐκ μέσου κατῆστο, of Otanes not taking part in the contest for the rulership of the Persian empire. ἡμῖν is an ethic dative, 'on our behalf'.

καὶ αὐτοὶ . . . ποιέειν 'and yourselves ask also of the Carians that they do the same as you'.

κατέζευχθε: 2nd pers. pl. perfect passive.

ἀρχῆθεν: i.e. from the time of the Athenians' involvement in the Ionian Revolt; cf. 5.97.

22.3 δοκέειν ἐμοί: an absolute infinitive, which expresses a limitation or qualification of a word or sentence, 'to my way of thinking' (*M&T* §778); cf. (ὡς) εἰκάσαι, 'at a guess' and **20**.2n. on the imperatival infinitive.

ἐπ' ἀμφότερα νοέων 'with a view to two results'; one function of the accusative case is to express the direction of the aim of an action.

λαθόντα τὰ γράμματα βασιλέα 'if the writing went unnoticed by the king'; γράμματα is the subject of the whole ἵνα-clause.

ἐπείτε ἀνενειχθῆι 'whenever the writing was reported'; the omission of ἄν in conditional relative clauses with the subjunctive is rare, and found mostly in poetry and infrequently in H. (cf. 1.216.1 τῆς γὰρ ἐπιθυμήσηι γυναικὸς Μασσαγέτης ἀνήρ, 'whatever woman a Massagetan man desires'; *M&T* §540).

διαβληθῆι 'denounced'; for διαβάλλω used of things rather than people, cf. Dem. 18.28 εἰ . . . προσάγειν τοὺς πρέσβεις ᾤιμην δεῖν, τοῦτό μου διαβάλλει.

ἀπίστους: passive, 'mistrusted'.

23 News of the Greek retreat reaches the Persians

There is a parallelism between this chapter and **21:** a messenger arrives in each; Abronichus' news about Thermopylae led to the Greek retreat, and this messenger announces that retreat to the Persians. Swift ships are dispatched in each case (**22**.1 νέας τὰς ἄριστα πλεούσας ~ **23**.1 νέας ταχέας). On messengers in book 8, cf. **8**n.

23.1 Ἱστιαιεύς: Histiaea (Oreus) is about ten miles west of Artemisium; cf. H-N 656-8. The Histiaeans do not appear on the Serpent Column (**82**.1n.) so, though H. does not say so explicitly, they had presumably medised.

ὑπ' ἀπιστίης: 'incredulity [about reports of present or future fact] is never justified in the tales of Herodotus . . . Correction comes most often in direct observation' (Packman 1991: 405). For ὑπό, cf. **1**.1n.

οὕτω δή often follows a participial clause thus (*Lex. s.v.* δή C 2; cf. *GP* 225, 236–7).

ἡλίωι σκιδναμένωι: poetic; cf. Hom. *Il.* 7.451 ἐπικίδναται ἠώς; Mimnermus, fr. 2.8; Aes. *Pers.* 502; etc.

ἁλής 'all together' is cognate with words expressing association, such as Doric ἁλία 'court', Ἡλιαία, the chief court in Athens, ἡλιαστής, Aeolic ἀολλής 'all together'; the root is probably *_wel-_ 'turn', cf. ϝειλέω, *volvo*, with α-copulative.

23.2 τὸ ἀπὸ τούτου: τό is an adverbial accusative and the phrase means literally '(as far as) after this (was concerned)'. For the use of the article with a prepositional phrase, cf. **10**.1 τὸ ἀπὸ Ξέρξεω, **24**.1 τὰ περὶ τοὺς νεκρούς 'matters concerning the corpses', and phrases like 1.62.3 οἱ ἀμφὶ Πεισίστρατον 'Peisistratus and his men'.

τὴν πόλιν ἔσχον . . . ἐπέδραμον 'they occupied the city of the Histiaeans, and overran all the coastal villages of the Ellopian region, which is the land of Histiaea': the δέ-clause gives a second, closer definition, as in 1.114.5 ὑπὸ τοῦ σοῦ δούλου, βουκόλου δὲ παιδός, 'your slave, the cow-herd's son', **54** Ἀθηναίων τοὺς φυγάδας, ἑωυτῶι δὲ ἑπομένους. The meaning is in fact uncertain, but this sense is preferable to 'they occupied the city of the Histiaeans and of the area known as Ellopia, but overran all the coastal villages', with the μοῖρα being part of the larger γῆ, as in 5.57.1 οἴκεον δὲ τῆς χώρης ταύτης [*sc.* Βοιωτίης], ἀπολαχόντες τὴν Ταναγρικὴν μοῖραν. Ellopia is an old name for the north of Euboea, called after a son of Ion, ancestor of the Ionians (Strabo 10.1.3; H–N 644).

24–5 Persian sightseeing at Thermopylae

Though intended as a morale-booster (**24**.2), in H.'s version this visit to the battlefield becomes a farce, as Xerxes tries unsuccessfully to hide the extent of the Persian losses. There is a story that similarly ridicules Xerxes in **118**. Persian regal arrogance is heard in the herald's words. Such sightseeing breaks are not unparalleled: Xerxes himself was keen to visit Troy (7.43) and see the mouth of the Peneius (7.128), as were the Spartans to see the Persian dead at Marathon (6.120); and when Cambyses invaded Egypt, Greek sightseers followed his army (3.139.1); cf. Thuc. 6.24.3. Tricks with graves are not the sole preserve of Xerxes; cf. 9.85.3, where Greek cities that did not fight at Plataea nonetheless built cenotaphs there to disguise their shame.

24.1 καί: emphatic, 'as many as twenty thousand' (*GP* 320). The rounded numbers here have all the exaggeration of traditions generated by the victors.

φυλλάδα τε ἐπιβαλὼν καὶ γῆν ἐπαμησάμενος: reminiscent of Theog. 428 κεῖσθαι πολλὴν γῆν ἐπαμησάμενον.

24.2 ἄνδρες σύμμαχοι, βασιλεὺς Ξέρξης . . . παραδίδωσι: the tone is that of royal proclamations, cf. **140α**.1n.

τῶι βουλομένωι . . . ἐκλιπόντα: as often, the case shifts into the accusative, the normal case for the subject of an infinitive; cf. **111**.1 σφι . . . λύσοντας.

25.1 οὐδὲν . . . πλοίων σπανιώτερον 'nothing was scarcer than boats'.

οὕτω πολλοί: a rare equivalent of τοσοῦτοι.

πάντες δὲ ἠπιστέατο . . . τοὺς ἑωυτοῦ 'everyone thought (mistakenly; cf. **5**.3n.) that all the corpses lying there were Spartans and Thespians, although they were in fact looking at Helots too. However, Xerxes' actions concerning his own dead did not fool those who went across.' οὐ μὲν οὐδέ is adversative and is sometimes used to contrast two aspects of a person's behaviour or experience, as in **130**.2–3 οὐ προήισαν ἀνωτέρω τὸ πρὸς ἑσπέρης . . . οὐ μὲν οὐδὲ προσεδέκοντο τοὺς Ἕλληνας ἐλεύσεσθαι ἐς τὴν Ἰωνίην; 6.45.1 (*GP* 363). In our case, the subject changes, but it is essentially of the same nature. In other words, the Persians were convinced that the 4,000 Greek dead were all fighting men and did not realise that many of them were the Helots who attended the Spartans; but they did not fall for the trick with the bodies of their own men, because they were lying improbably all in a single place, unlike the enemy.

Θεσπιέας: inhabitants of Thespiae, six miles west of Thebes. They alone willingly stayed with the Spartans at Thermopylae (7.222), and 700 of them were killed. 1,800 were at the battle of Plataea in the following year, though unarmed (9.30.1). *A.P.* 6.344 is a fourth-century inscription in which their participation in Alexander's campaign against the Persians is seen as revenge for their sufferings under Mardonius and Xerxes.

εἵλωτας: the inhabitants of Laconia and Messenia reduced by the Spartans to a kind of serf-class without participation in the political centre; they were assigned to particular estates and paid a fixed quota of the produce. They were distinguished from slaves, and had fewer political rights than the *perioikoi*, who were a kind of half-citizen. Their role in the state is still debated: cf. Luraghi and Alcock 2003. The number of Helots attending a Spartan hoplite presumably varied: τὸν εἵλωτα in 7.229.1 suggests that at Thermopylae each Spartan had but one Helot, though at Plataea each was attended by seven (9.29.1; and cf. **25**.2n.).

25.2 καὶ γὰρ δὴ καὶ γελοῖον ἦν 'and it was indeed ridiculous'. καὶ γάρ means 'in fact', and γάρ is emphasised by δή; the second καί emphasises γελοῖον (*GP* 108, 244). This is the only time H. himself goes so far as to comment that something is γελοῖον (an adjective found again only at 7.209.1), though he is not shy of expressing his opinions generally.

τῶν μὲν . . . οἱ δέ: the Persian dead . . . the Greeks.

τέσσερες χιλιάδες: this is the number on the inscription commemorating the event (7.228.1), but there it refers to the number of those who fought, not those who died. The figures derivable from 7.202.3 and 222 (counting seven helots per Spartiate, cf. §1n.) give 300 Spartans, 2,100 helots (a number of whom will have escaped: cf. 7.229.1) and 700 Thespians = 3,100. Perhaps for this reason Diodorus or his source added a thousand Lacedaemonians to make up the 4,000 (11.4.4–5).

26 Tritantaechmes' 'most noble opinion' on the Olympic games

Tritantaechmes' 'noble opinion' about the Greeks' willingness to compete at Olympia 'not for money but for honour', and his fears for what this shows of their fighting spirit, are dismissed as cowardice by the King, in another display of what, to Greek eyes, would have appeared as unwise arrogance. The difference between Greek and Persian ideology is stark, though the picture is somewhat idealised for the purposes of the episode. While the prizes for Greek games were often of purely symbolic value (cf. Pi. *Ol.* 7.80–7), victory also brought more material rewards, such as dinner in the Prytaneum at public expense, substantial gifts of money etc.; cf. Xenophanes' complaints about the rewards available to athletes but not thinkers in fr. 2.1–11, and generally Young 1984. The Greek leaders have also shown their interest in monetary rewards (**4–5**; cf. **112**), and a large monetary prize will be offered in the battle at Salamis (**93**.2). Tritantaechmes is one of those who act as 'warners', i.e. people with wise opinions who are generally ignored: for Xerxes, his uncle Artabanus in particular plays this role (cf. esp. 7.10–18; **54**.1n.; Bischoff 1932; Lattimore 1939; Pelling 1991). As often, a pithy remark brings the episode to a close.

26.1 αὐτόμολοι . . . ἀπ' Ἀρκαδίης: Arcadia was a poor part of Greece, from which mercenaries at this time regularly came in search of a livelihood (like the Carians, **19**.1n.); cf. Thuc. 3.34.2, 7.57.9, 58.3; Xen. *HG* 7.1.23. Arcadian and Achaean mercenaries made up more than half of Xenophon's Ten Thousand (*Anab.* 6.2.10).

26.2 Ὀλύμπια: held every four years a month after the summer solstice in honour of Zeus, they were pre-eminent among the four main panhellenic games, along with the Pythian at Delphi, the Isthmian and the Nemean. If one presses H.'s chronological indications hard, there is the problem in that the Olympiad is said to be contemporaneous with both the run-up to Thermopylae (at 7.206.2) and with this defection by the Arcadians, but we have seen that oral tradition tends to collapse chronological differences (**15**.1n.).

ἄγουσι καὶ θεωρέοιεν: a striking shift of mood from indicative to optative in indirect discourse. The indicative marks the more important point, the optative adding detail: cf. **140α**.3 οὔτε γὰρ ἂν ὑπερβάλοισθε, οὔτε οἷοί τέ ἐστε ἀντέχειν, **100**.1, **106**.2. In comparable cases where subjunctive and optative appear together thus, the subjunctive can mark the more important point (cf. **6**.2n., **61**.2).

κείμενον: regularly used of prizes from Homer onwards, because the prize was actually put on display; cf. *Il.* 23.273; Soph. *Aj.* 936; Thuc. 2.46.1.

οἱ δὲ εἶπον . . . στέφανον 'they told them of the garland that is given [to the victors] from the olive tree.' This was a wild olive that grew beside the opisthodomus of the temple of Zeus (Paus. 5.15.3). There is an irony in Xerxes' contemptuous dismissal of Tritantaechmes' remark, because Athena's olive seems to lurk behind his defeat: when he decided to attack Greece, a dream of Xerxes crowned with an olive branch that covered the whole earth, but then vanished, was interpreted by the Magi as a sign of world-dominion (7.19); when he burns Athens, Athena's olive on the Acropolis puts out a sudden new shoot (**55**); and Eurybiades and Themistocles receive olive crowns at Sparta for their part in his defeat (**124**.2). In the *Odyssey*, the olive, symbol of Athena and intelligence, marks stages in Odysseus' triumph over adversity (cf. 5.234–6, 476–7, 319–97, 13.122–4, 23.190–1) and in H. too the intelligence of the Athenian Themistocles plays a determining role. For Odyssean aspects of Themistocles, **56-8**n, cf. **92**.2, **125**.1nn; Plut. *MH* 38 says Themistocles was 'named Odysseus because of his cleverness', though where and by whom is not known.

Τριτανταίχμης ὁ Ἀρταβάνου: Tritantaechmes (OP *Ciçantaxma* 'Brave by lineage') is a Median name. The Greek form is influenced by Greek element τριτ- (Schmitt 1967: 121–2), cf. perhaps how Persian 'Masistios', a very tall man, became 'Makistios', perhaps under the influence of the Doric adjective μάκιστος 'tall' (9.20). Tritantaechmes, son of Artaba*n*us, is one of the commanders of the land forces (7.82, 121.3) and significantly, given what he says here, his father had fruitlessly advised Xerxes against the expedition (cf. **54**.1n.). In 1.192.2, Tritantaechmes, son of Artaba*z*us, is satrap of the richest province of Assyria, but his father's name may be a slip by H. or the MSS. In the passage under discussion, some MSS read Τιγράνης, the commander of the Medes and an Achaemenid (7.62.1), who 'surpassed all Persians in looks and size' (9.96.2), for Τριτανταίχμης, but the remark about the Olympics better suits the son of the cautious Artabanus rather than the massive Tigranes.

26.3 παπαῖ: a general exclamation, found in tragedy and Aristophanes, but very rarely in prose. Aeschylus gives it in all cases bar one to easterners (Persians in *Pers.* 1031–2, and the Trojan Cassandra in *Ag.* 1114, 1256); Sophocles gives it mainly to Philoctetes tormented by his wound; Euripides and Aristophanes use it more generally.

Μαρδόνιε: OP *Marduniya*; Balcer 1993: 78–9. He was son of Gobryas (OP *Gaubaruva*, 'Cattle-Possessor'; Elam. *Kambarma*), one of Darius' fellow conspirators and a major figure in his reign. Gobryas married Darius' sister, was entrusted with putting down an Elamite revolt at the start of Darius' reign (DB (= Brosius no. 44) v §71) and is Darius' Spear-Bearer on his tomb (DNc = Brosius no. 112). He receives the largest amount of rations in the Fortification Tablets: cf. Lewis 1997: 353–5. Mardonius himself married one of Darius' daughters, Artazostre (6.43.1; PFa 5 (= Brosius no. 168)), and was put in command of Ionia in the reorganisation of Persian forces there in 494/3. He brought Macedonia and parts of Thrace under Persian control, but lost his fleet off Mt Athos, was wounded and forced to retreat (6.43–5). He was replaced for Darius' campaign against Greece (6.94.2), but according to H. had the most influence over Xerxes before the expedition (7.5.1), and was one of the main commanders of the land forces (7.82, 121.3). After Salamis, he persuaded Xerxes to leave him in Greece to complete the campaign (**100–2**), but died fighting on a white horse at Plataea; his body then disappeared (9.63, 84). Cf. Balcer 1993: 78–9. There is an irony that Mardonius should be the recipient of Tritantaechmes' worry: his failure to reply could be seen as a further sign of the arrogance that eventually leads to his defeat.

27–33 HOSTILITY BETWEEN THESSALY AND PHOCIS

The section comprises two parts, each with two subdivisions. The first concerns the long and ongoing conflict between the Thessalians and Phocians. **27–8** detail the past defeats of the Thessalians and their current attempt to frighten the Phocians into submission with threats of Persian retribution; in **29–30** their arrogant speech is given directly and the Phocians' reply indirectly. In the second, the Persian advance leads to the successful sack of the oracle at Abae (**31–3**), and the disastrous attack on that at Delphi (**34–9**). The Phocians' use of stratagems to defeat a stronger enemy relates the episode thematically to the forthcoming battle of Salamis, and the divine punishment of the Persians at Delphi to the wider theme of divine displeasure at their invasion. On the geography and towns of this area, cf. H–N 399–430; Fossey 1986; McInerney 1999: 40–85, and Gazetteer in 263–332.

27–8 Origins of the Phocian–Thessalian conflict: Phocian stratagems

For the origin of the hostility between Thessalians and Phocians, cf. 7.176.4: these Thessalians came from Thesprotia to colonise Aetolia, to the west of Phocis, and tried to subdue the Phocians who, as here, used cunning measures to keep them out (that the wall mentioned there is ancient, as H. says, is, however, unlikely). Thuc. 1.12.3 dates the migration to the aftermath of the Trojan War, so the hostilities have a long history. (Different traditions are found in Plut. *Mor.* 244A–E and Paus. 10.2). Cf. Keaveney 1995 on this conflict.

The episode also gives in summary form the dilemma the invasion posed to the northern Greeks: whether to submit or keep faith with the other Greeks. The Thessalians were split on the matter: their ruling family, the Aleuadae, sent an embassy to Xerxes offering him support and encouraging him to invade Greece (7.6); but the other Thessalians disapproved. At their request, the Greeks briefly sent a force to guard the pass through Mt Olympus, but it returned after a warning by the Macedonian king, Alexander (for whom, cf. **136**.1n.). They then felt they had no choice but to join the Persians, and became the most helpful of all their allies (7.172–4). H. has Xerxes himself comment on the wisdom of their medising: the diversion of a single river would give control of Thessaly (7.130). Though the Phocians are here loyal to Greece, many later were forced to go over to Mardonius at Thebes, when the Thessalians again seem to have tried to harm their old enemies (9.17–18). Other Phocians continued to harry Mardonius' forces (9.31.5). The conflict is typical of Greek border hostilities which continued over many years, and shows how foreign invasions were used to pursue existing local conflicts. On Phocian–Thessalian relations, cf. McInerney 1999: 173–81.

27.1 Θεσσαλοί: wealthy and powerful Aeolic peoples in the broad plains of northern Greece, who had subjected the local peoples and created an Amphictyony, which also included the Phocians. They had been organised into four tetrads of four cities by Aleuas in the second half of the previous century. Four *tagoi* were charged with organising the military units of their tetrads, which gave the Thessalians considerable fighting power.

Φωκέας: the Phocians were a mixed group of peoples who dealt around Mt Parnassus and Delphi, and had been organised into a federal state with its own army in the sixth century, probably as a result of the pressure of Thessalian influence. Their eponymous hero was Phocus, son of Aeacus.

ἐνέχοντες . . . χόλον 'harbouring a grudge'; χόλος is largely poetic and a more visceral emotion than ἔχθρη.

καὶ τὸ κάρτα 'most especially', adverbial accusative, with καί emphatic.

27.2 σύμμαχοι: perhaps those listed at 7.132.1.

περιέφθησαν: aorist passive of περι + ἕπω 'treat, deal with'.

27.3 κατειλήθησαν ἐς τὸν Παρνησσόν: they will use this refuge again (9.31.5; cf. further **23**.1n.). Mountains are a natural refuge from heavily armed troops: cf. e.g. 6.96, **32**. For the root of the verb, cf. **23**.2n

μάντιν: the *mantis* ('seer, diviner') was a man skilled in divination and an expert in religious matters. They often came from particular families (next note) and moved from city to city: cf. Bremmer 1996. For the importance of seers in military contexts, cf. e.g. 7.221, 9.33–8; Thuc. 3.20.1; Paus. 4.21.7–12; the sepulchral epigram on Cleoboulus ἀμφότερον μάντιν τε ἀγαθὸν καὶ δορὶ μα[χητήν (*SEG* 16 (1959) 193; *ca.* 370); Pritchett 1979: 47–90; Mikalson 1983: 39–49; Jameson 1991; Dillery 2005: 200–9.

Τελλίην τὸν Ἠλεῖον: probably one of the Telliadae, a noted family of seers, amongst whom was also Hegesistratus, Mardonius' Greek *mantis* (9.37.1; cf. Philostr. *Vit. Apol.* 5.25). Elis was also home to another famous family of seers, the Iamidae (cf. 9.33.1; Pi. *Ol.* 6). It was not uncommon for families to provide generations of *manteis*.

γυψώσας: this episode has a faintly ritual or magical quality to it: the Thessalians think it is something uncanny (τέρας, §4). It involves a reversal of normal fighting: hoplites did not fight at night, nor paint their bodies. Smearing with chalk is found in some ritual contexts: the Titans plastered their faces when they destroyed Dionysus (Harpocr. s.v. ἀπομάττων), and early comic performers chalked their faces in a variation on the later mask (Plut.fr. 30.6).

τὸν ἂν μὴ λευκανθίζοντα ἴδωνται 'if they saw anyone who was not whitened'; μή is used because the participle has a generalising force.

27.4 δόξασαι ἄλλο τι εἶναι τέρας 'thinking it a strange and supernatural sight'. For ἄλλος meaning 'strange, bad' cf. Hes. *Op.* 344 εἰ γάρ τοι καὶ χρῆμ' ἐπιχώριον ἄλλο γένηται (with M. L. West's note); Dem. 21.218 ἂν δὲ ἀφῆτε, [δόξετε] ἄλλου τινὸς ἡττῆσθαι 'but if you let him off, you will appear to have given in to something unworthy'; Plut. *Mor.* 187D.

οὕτω: *sc.* ἐφοβήθησαν. There is an ellipsis of the details of the battle, as H. moves straight to the Phocians' taking possession of the bodies on the battlefield after the flight of the Thessalians.

Ἄβας: a town in Phocis with a notable oracle of Apollo, which was consulted by Croesus (1.46.2) and later by Mardonius (**134**.1). Cf. **33**; Paus. 10.35.1–4; H–N 408–9.

ἀνέθεσαν: spoils of war were deposited in temples by individuals, generals or cities, as acknowledgement of the part played by the gods in the victory (cf. Rouse 1902; Pritchett 1979: 240–76, 277–95; Jackson 1991; Lonis 1979: 157–78). Such armour could be costly, with gold and silver decorations, so the dedications could be counted as part of the financial resources of the temple (Thuc. 2.13.4).

27.5 δεκάτη: along with ἀπαρχή and ἀκροθίνια, a technical term for the tithes (i.e. 'tenths') of produce, battle-spoils etc. paid to the gods in gratitude; cf. 5.77.4, **121**n. In fourth-century Athens, a law gave 10 per cent of booty to Athena (Dem. 24.120). The Phocians are careful to make generous gifts to the gods for their unexpected victory: the splendour of the gifts would also be a constant reminder to visitors to these important shrines of the Phocians' victories over more powerful enemies.

περὶ τὸν τρίποδα συνεστεῶτες 'struggling for the tripod'. The use of the genitive is more usual with verbs indicating 'striving for something', the accusative being used with other verbs (Smyth §1693.1b, 3a, c), but there are exceptions to this convention and, since Paus. 10.13.7 tells us that the statues were of Heracles, being restrained by Leto, and Apollo, restrained by Artemis, competing for the Delphic tripod, 'struggling' seems better than 'standing' here. H. not infrequently relates past events to existing monuments and other features (e.g. **39**.2). The struggle between these gods may have reflected that between the Phocians and Thessalians (Asheri).

28 πεζὸν . . . πολιορκέοντας: a plural participle is possible after a collective noun; cf. 7.40.1 στρατὸς παντοίων ἐθνέων ἀναμὶξ οὐ διακεκριμμένοι (Smyth §1044).

ἐσβολῆι: it is about 700 yards wide.

Ὑάμπολιν: not far north of Abae on the Cephisus river (Paus. 10.35.5–7; Fossey 1986: 72–6). It lay on the road to Locris, which was the Thessalian base, according to Plut. *Mor.* 244B. Artemis was its principal deity, and the Elaphebolia festival, which was dedicated to her, celebrated this victory; cf. also Plut. *Mor.* 244B–D.

τάφρον: the Phocians' trick with a ditch is more successful than Xerxes' (**24**.1).

χοῦν δὲ . . . χωρῶι 'having piled up the excavated earth and made it level with the rest of the ground'; for χοῦς, cf. LSJ *s.v.* B.

τὰ σκέλεα: accusative of respect.

29–30 The dispute continued

29.1 τούτων δὴ . . . οἱ Θεσσαλοί 'and so, because the Thessalians were angry with them for both of these reasons'. τούτων is genitive indicating where the anger came from; δή is resumptive (**14**.2n.). The narrative has now come back to the point where the analepsis about the past conflicts began (**27**.1). The language is similar and emphasises the Thessalians' rage at the Phocians' obstinacy: each section uses a slightly unusual expression for that anger: for ἐνέχοντες χόλον see **27**.1n.; ἔγκοτος used as a noun as here seems restricted to H. (LSJ *s.v.* ἔγκοτος II).

ἤδη τι μᾶλλον γνωσιμαχέετε 'now rather accept the fact [though you would not originally have thought so] that . . .' The verb perhaps meant originally 'fight with one's former opinion': cf. γνωσιμαχῆσαι· τὸ μεταβουλεύεσθαι (Bekker, *Anecd.* 228.27; cf. Wilkins on Eur. *Heracl.* 706).

μὴ εἶναι: μή is used with the infinitive in indirect discourse after verbs of agreeing, hoping, expecting, being persuaded, etc. (*M&T* §685; Smyth §§2725–6).

29.2 ἐκεῖνα ἡμῖν ἥνδανε 'we were on the Greek side'. ἐκεῖνα = τὰ τῶν Ἑλλήνων, and looks back to ἐν τοῖσι Ἕλλησι.

πλέον αἰεί κοτε ὑμέων ἐφερόμεθα 'we were always better regarded, carried more weight than you'. The middle of φέρω = 'win for oneself' (cf. LSJ *s.v.* VI 3); ὑμέων is genitive of comparison; and αἰεί is as often strengthened by κοτε.

ἐπ' ἡμῖν . . . ἠνδραποδίσθαι ὑμέας 'it lies in our power [to see that] you are deprived of your land and in addition enslaved'. ἐπί + dative expresses dependence, cf. Xen. *Cyr.* 1.6.8 καθ' ὅσον ἐστὶν ἐπ' ἐμοί 'as far as is in my power'. Tenses of the infinitives outside indirect discourse have no *time* of their own, but mark the *state* of the action, so these perfect passives emphasise the certainty of the events the Thessalians threaten (*M&T* §51; cf. **8**.3n.). πρός is adverbial.

ἡμεῖς μέντοι τὸ πᾶν ἔχοντες: 'in Herodotus, adversative μέντοι predominates over other uses' (*GP* 404). τὸ πᾶν ἔχοντες means 'being in complete control', cf. 7.162.1 οὐδὲν ὑπιέντες ἔχειν τὸ πᾶν ἐθέλετε, Ar. *Birds* 1543 ἤν γ' ἢν σὺ παρ' ἐκείνου παραλάβῃς, πάντ' ἔχεις.

αὐτῶν: i.e. the κακά implied in μνησικακέομεν.

πεντήκοντα τάλαντα: the transfer of such a substantial sum of money would cause a notable shift of resources and power to the Thessalians. Some of the money may have been intended to persuade the Persians not to ravage Phocis, which Thessaly will have hoped to take over undamaged.

τὰ ἐπιόντα: i.e. what the Persians will do unless dissuaded by their allies the Thessalians; cf. for this hostile sense of the verb 7.120.1 τῶν ἐπιόντων κακῶν.

30.1 ἐπαγγέλλοντο: the imperfect of verbs of saying, exhorting etc. is often used where we might expect an aorist, when the point of the command etc. has not been achieved (*M&T* §36; Smyth §1891).

γάρ introduces the explanation of why the Thessalians make the threat they do.

κατ' ἄλλο μὲν οὐδέν 'for no other reason'. κατά + accusative is used to indicate the ground on which something is done; cf. Thuc. 1.60.2 κατὰ φιλίαν τε αὐτοῦ . . . ξυνέσποντο. For the form of expression, cf. 9.109.3 κατ' ἄλλο μὲν οὐδέν, φοβεόμενος δὲ Ἄμηστριν.

ὡς ἐγὼ συμβαλλόμενος εὑρίσκω: it was indeed a brave move by the Phocians to refuse to submit to forces like Xerxes', and therefore hard to explain. Plut. *MH* 35 criticises H.'s cynicism about the Phocians' motives here, but it may not be misplaced. In any case, it redresses to some extent the largely pro-Phocian tone of the narrative of these events so far. H. is not shy of expressing blunt opinions: cf. **3**.2, the Athenian willingness to submit to Spartan command obtained only so long as it suited them; **72, 73**.3 on passivity as the equivalent of medising; 1.62.1; 3.143.2, etc. On H.'s use of the first person, cf. **8**.3n.

30.2 εἰ δὲ . . . τὰ Ἑλλήνων ηὖξον 'if the Thessalians had supported the Greek cause'; the same phrase used of the Phocians occurs in 9.31.5.

παρέχειν . . . εἰ ἄλλως βουλοίατο 'it was possible for them to medise, just as it was for the Thessalians, if they actually wanted to'. For παρέχειν cf. **8**.1n.; for εἰ ἄλλως meaning 'if . . . actually', cf. 7.16γ.1 (of a dream) φανῆναι δὲ . . . ὀφείλει . . . εἴ πέρ γε καὶ ἄλλως ἐθέλει φανῆναι 'it ought to appear to me if it *really* wishes to appear [so it can give a message to us]'; cf. 2.77.3.

ἑκόντες εἶναι: εἶναι is an absolute infinitive (**22**.3n.). This apparently redundant εἶναι is frequent with ἑκών, especially in negative sentences (e.g. **116**.1 οὔτε αὐτὸς ἔφη τῶι Ξέρξηι ἑκὼν εἶναι δουλεύσειν); the infinitive adds the sense 'so far as being willing (etc.) goes' (*M&T* §780; cf. **20**.2n.). Other similar expressions are κατὰ δύναμιν εἶναι 'as far as is possible', τὰ νῦν εἶναι 'for the moment'.

31–3 Thessalian revenge: Persian destruction in Phocis

The Persians' route was probably through the Dhema Pass, which runs between Mt Oeta and Mt Kallidromon in Trachis into Doris, whence they followed the Cephisus river into Phocis. Other routes were possible, and the coastal route was perhaps the most obvious for a large army. However, as H. makes clear, the choice was not Xerxes' but the Thessalians', who wished, by taking the Persians this way, to ensure that as much as possible of Phocis was ravaged. Cf. Kase *et al.* 1991 for the route, with the comments of McInerney 1999: 333–9. Earlier scholars suggested that the army divided, with the cavalry and transports taking the coast road through the recently forced pass of Thermopylae (Hignett 1963: 134–41). For a discussion of the methodology of reconstructing the marches of Xerxes' army, cf. Tuplin 2003. The ravaging of these lands is of a piece with Persian attitudes to those who did not take advantage of proffered opportunities to submit or changed their minds after submitting (cf. **46**.4n., **50**.2, **54**n.).

31 ποδεὼν στεινός: ποδεὼν is literally 'neck of a wineskin', cf. English 'bottleneck'; 30 stades is $3^2/_3$ miles. This ποδέων is where the Asopus flows into the Spercheius river below Mt Oeta (Grundy 1901: 261; Kase *et al.* 1991: 86–9).

εὖρος: accusative of respect.

Δρυοπὶς . . . μητρόπολις: cf. Tyrtaeus, fr. 2.12–15; 1.56.3 and **43** for the movement of the Dorians from Histiaeotis to Pindus, Dryopis and finally the Peloponnese. In myth, the occupation of the Peloponnese was also figured in the 'return of the Heraclidae' (cf. Diod. 4.57–8; Apollod. 2.8). Dryops, 'Oak-man' was the eponymous hero of the area. ἡ χώρη here refers to all of Doris, not just the tongue of land. Cf. Strid 1999.

32.1 κειμένη ἐπ' ἑωυτῆς 'because it lies on its own'; partitive genitive, indicating conditions of existence (Humbert §523).

ἀνηνείκαντο: 3rd person plural aorist middle of ἀναφέρω 'carry goods up'.

32.2 Ὀζόλας Λοκρούς: their epithet was derived in popular etymology from ὄζειν 'smell', either because of their sulphur springs which had been polluted by the bodies of the dead Centaurs (Strabo 9.4.8) or because of their goatskins (Plut. *Mor.* 496F). The Locrians had earlier been driven into three separate regions by the Phocians. For the Locrians' service in the war, cf. **1**.2n. In general, cf. Paus. 10.38; Lerat 1952.

33.1 κατὰ μὲν ἔκαυσαν . . . κατὰ δέ: this separation of the preposition from the verbal element is anachronistically named *tmesis* 'cutting'. Historically, the 'preposition' (better called the 'pre-verb') was not joined with the verbal element, but had an independent existence in the sentence, as is seen regularly in Homer (cf. Horrocks 1981); later it was felt more and more to be connected with the verb and ultimately was united with it. 'Tmesis' is frequent in H., but in a more restricted manner than in Homer; it is used most often with μὲν . . . δέ, οὖν, enclitics, etc. The pattern here, with the verb in the first element only, is Homeric (K–G I 537(g)).

Δρυμὸν πόλιν . . . Χαράδραν κτλ.: for these cities, cf. McInerney 1999: Gazetteer nos. 1–8, 10–15.

θησαυροῖσι: temple sanctuaries, especially panhellenic ones, were regularly places where cities stored valuable items belonging to a god; sometimes special buildings were erected for the purpose (cf. **27**.4n.). They were not just 'banks' for the storing of wealth, but the property in the treasury belonged to the god and constituted an offering to him or her. It could consist of spoils dedicated after special victories, plate, sacrificial implements etc. In times of great crisis, this property could be used by the city for the war effort or other purpose.

χρηστήριον: though sacked and burnt here, it was consulted shortly afterwards by Mardonius (**134**.1). H. saw the statues after this attack (**27**.5), and according to Paus. 10.35.1–3 the Greeks left the ruins as a memorial of Persian impiety. There are still scanty remains of the temple in existence.

πρὸς τοῖσι ὄρεσι 'near the mountains', i.e. before they could get high into the hills; cf. Thuc. 3.78.2 οἱ πρὸς τοῖς Κερκυραίοις, 'those who lived near the Corcyreans'.

ὑπὸ πλήθεος 'in a gang(-rape)'; for this use of ὑπό + genitive, cf. **1**.1n.; the basic meaning is 'by force of numbers'.

34–9 THE PERSIAN ATTACK ON DELPHI

Delphi with its wealth and influence was a regular target for attack in antiquity (Paus. 10.7.1). Here the god saves his shrine from destruction, and Diod. 11.14.4 quotes a Delphian inscription commemorating this event, which was still extant in the 1670s (Merritt 1947: 59–60). The story has been claimed as a 'temple myth', constructed to counter subsequent adverse comment on the role played by Delphi during the Persian Wars, but Delphi's response to the invasion was complex, not unreasonably, given its position and no doubt sound intelligence about the size of Xerxes' forces. If it gave prophecies that implied a Persian victory, such as the first reply given to Athens (7.140) and the ambivalent oracle that allowed the Cretans to avoid becoming involved in the war (7.167), it also gave other more optimistic oracles, such as the 'wooden walls' one (7.141–2; cf. also 148.2–4, 169, 220.3–4); it held out to Sparta the possibility of survival ('either Sparta will be destroyed by the Spartans, or her king will die'; 7.220.3), and gave the Greeks advice on how to gain divine favour (**12–14**n.). Delphi, it appears, played a wisely subtle game, but one should not perhaps be too ready to see anything too suspicious about this. On the workings and position of the Delphic Oracle in Greece, cf. Parke and Wormell 1956; Roux 1976; Price 1985; Sourvinou-Inwood 1991: 192–243.

The relationships between earlier Persian and other eastern rulers and the shrine (cf. **35**.2n.) make it unlikely that the Persians sacked it, and there is in fact no archaeological evidence for major damage. The story, however, fits in with the general Greek denigration of Xerxes and the Persians for impiety: the attack on the most famous shrine in Greece inevitably brings retribution, and H. reminds his reader of Croesus (**35**.2), and so of his disastrous invasion of Persia and Delphi's role in it. There are similar tales in Ctesias: one, that Mardonius was sent by Xerxes to sack the shrine, but died in a hailstorm (*FGH* 688 F 13 (29)); and a second that, after his return to Asia, the eunuch Matacas, on the King's orders, sacked it (ibid. (31)). Plut. *Numa* 9.6 says the temple was burnt by the Medes. In later tradition, the attack by the Gauls in 279 replaced this one as the most famous assault on Delphi in the Greek tradition (cf. Call. *Hy. Del.* 171–95).

After the Persian defeat, Apollo is one of the gods who receives especial thanks (**121–3**n.), but Delphi's influence in political matters was never quite the same again (cf. Parker 1985).

34–5 The Persians divide their forces and march on Delphi

We now follow the exploits of the two halves of the Persian land forces, which headed respectively for Delphi and Athens. H. begins with the march of the major part of the army, which naturally accompanies the King, but then swiftly moves to the other part and its attack on Delphi; we return to Xerxes in **50**. This provides an ABA pattern, and gets round the fact that little of note happened on Xerxes' march: the account of dramatic events at Delphi covers Xerxes' easy march to Athens.

34.1 ἤδη 'from this time onward' (*Lex. s.v.* II 1).

ἐπ' Ἀθήνας . . . ἐς Βοιωτούς: ἐπί means basically 'in the direction of', with also the sense of 'hostilely against', εἰς actually 'into'.

Ὀρχομενίων: Orchomenus was the city of the Graces and Hesiod, and Thebes' main rival for the leadership of Boeotia.

πᾶν τὸ πλῆθος 'the whole population', not the majority as opposed to the aristocracy. In fact, Thespiae, Plataea and some Thebans supported the Greek cause, until the defeat at Thermopylae, when Plataea was isolated (cf. **1**.1n., **66**.2, and 7.132.1; Thuc. 3.52–68).

διατεταγμένοι 'appointed for the purpose'.

Ἀλεξάνδρου: cf. **136**.1n.

ἔσωιζον τῆιδε . . . φρόνοιεν 'they saved them in this way, by their desire to make clear to Xerxes that the Boeotians supported the Persian cause'. τῆιδε looks forward, as almost always, to the participial phrase that follows. These Macedonian agents enabled Alexander both to demonstrate his own loyalty to the Persians and to curry favour with the Boeotians as their saviour.

35.2 βασιλέϊ Ξέρξηι ἀποδέξαιεν τὰ χρήματα: elsewhere in H., βασιλεύς referring to the Great King is used with a personal name in speeches only, so here the expression is to be seen as focalised from the point of view of the soldiers, representing their ideas. In H., the Persian commanders take the initiative in attacking Delphi, but Diod. 11.14.2 attributes an order for the sacking to Xerxes himself; this may well be an instance of the later Greek tradition blackening his name when it could. Presenting Xerxes with booty from Delphi would have brought fine rewards (**85**.3n.).

Delphi had long had connections with eastern rulers: Gyges gave the 'Gygean treasure' for legitimating his rule (1.13–14), and Alyattes rewarded it for a cure (1.25.2); for Croesus, cf. below. Midas, king of Phrygia (**138**.2n.), gave it his throne (1.14.2–3), and Pharaoh Amasis alum towards the rebuilding of the temple (2.180). Darius said that Apollo 'spoke all truth to the Persians' (ML 12.28–9 = Fornara no. 35), and Datis honoured Apollo greatly on Delos, saying that even if Darius had not so instructed him, he had sense enough not to attack the shrine where two gods were born (6.97). The Persians did not destroy shrines unnecessarily. Murray suggests that Delphi was singled out by eastern monarchs, because Apollo would have appeared the main god of the Greeks: 'he was the only god to possess at the great centres of Delphi, Delos and Branchidae a permanent priesthood, temples and oracular shrines on anything like the scale of the great gods of the East' (Murray, *CAH*[2] IV 476).

ἠπίστατο . . . ὅσα λόγου ἦν ἄξια Ξέρξης: there is perhaps an element of exaggeration in this interest ascribed to Xerxes, similar to the suggestion that Darius was a fan of the wrestler Milo (3.137.5; cf. Harrison 2000b: 58–60). On the other hand, he took a good deal from Athens when he captured it, including the bronze statues of the tyrannicides Harmodius and Aristogeiton, which Alexander the Great eventually returned (Arr. *Anab.* 3.16.7–8).

τὰ Κροίσου ἀναθήματα: Croesus was the legendarily wealthy king of Lydia (*ca.* 560–546), who conquered the Greek cities on the Asia Minor coast, but also had cordial relations with them. He made gifts to many Greek shrines (1.92), and sent especially lavish ones to Delphi, because it correctly answered the puzzle that he had set to a number of oracles (1.46–52). Amongst other matters, he consulted Delphi about his planned attack on the rising power of Persia and sought Greek help (1.53–6; cf. 85, 91), but was defeated by Cyrus the Great, according to Greek tradition, after famously misinterpreting the oracle that, if he attacked Persia, he would destroy a great empire (1.71–85; cf. Xen. *Cyr.* 7.2.15–28).

36 A miraculous event at Delphi

36.1 ἀπίκατο . . . κατεστεῶτες, ἐμαντεύοντο: a good illustration of the functions of the different stems of the Greek verb: 'they became sorely afraid [aorist, indicating an instantaneous action], and, being greatly worried [perfect, expressing an action in the past that has continued effect into the time of the main verb], they proceeded to consult the oracle ['inceptive' imperfect, marking the start of an action]'.

κατορύξωσι, ἐκκομίσωσι: subjunctives in an indirect question, because they represent original deliberative subjunctives in the question put to the god; 'are we to bury . . .?'

αὐτὸς ἱκανὸς . . . προκατῆσθαι 'he had always been capable (and so would be this time too) of looking after his own property'. The perfect infinitive (here of προκάτημαι) expresses the certainty of an action (**29**.2n.), here relevant both to the past and to the present case (Humbert §267); cf. Pl. *Prot.* 358C ἀμαθίαν ἄρα τὸ τοιόνδε λέγετε τὸ . . . ἐψεῦσθαι περὶ τῶν πραγμάτων τῶν πολλοῦ ἀξίων; 'do you not call ignorance something like being in error about important things?' The genitive τῶν depends on προ- (Smyth §1384). Gods protect their shrines in various ways: cf. e.g. 3.26.3 (a sandstorm buries the expedition sent to sack the oracle of Zeus Ammon); 6.134–6 (Miltiades is injured trying sacrilegiously to enter the shrine of Demeter); 9.65.2 (no Persian dead are found in the shrine of Demeter at battle of Plataea). *deorum iniurias dis curae* (Tac. *Ann.* 1.73.5).

36.2 σφέων αὐτῶν πέρι: περί is the only 'true' preposition which in prose follows its case (ἕνεκα and χάριν are not strictly prepositions); H. has περί in anastrophe in 25 per cent of cases. Cf. **33**.1n. for prepositions.

πέρην: i.e. across the Gulf of Corinth.

τὸ Κωρύκιον ἄντρον: a large cave on Parnassus, some 500 feet up a steep path, above the plateau on which Delphi stands. It was named after Corycia, a nymph beloved of Apollo, and, like a number of caves, was sacred to the Nymphs and Pan. Cf. Aesch. *Eum.* 22–3 σέβω δὲ νύμφας, ἔνθα Κωρυκὶς πέτρα | κοίλη, φίλορνις, δαιμόνων ἀναστροφή; Paus. 10.6, 32.2–7; Strabo 9.3.1; *BCH* Suppl. 7 (1981), Suppl. 9 (1984). There is a mythical precedent for this flight, during Deucalion's flood (Paus. 10.6.2).

δὲ ὦν 'in short' (*GP* 463).

τοῦ προφήτεω: the priest who ordered and recorded the oracular responses of the Pythia; cf. Price 1985: 141–3.

37–9 The destruction of the Persians

H. injects suspense into this narrative by the threefold repetition of phrases describing the approach of the Persians: **37**.1 ἐπεὶ δὲ ἀγχοῦ τε ἦσαν οἱ βάρβαροι ἐπιόντες; **37**.2 οἱ δὲ βάρβαροι, ἐπειδὴ ἐγίνοντο ἐπειγόμενοι; **37**.3 ἐπεὶ γὰρ δὴ ἦσαν ἐπιόντες οἱ βάρβαροι. They thus constantly approach, but never arrive, before the cataclysmic mixture of thunderbolts, landslides and divine shouts drives them away in confusion. There is a similar technique in the build-up to Salamis (**70**.1n.). These events are focalised first through the Persians (**37**.1 ἀπώρων), and then the focalisation shifts to the Delphians and what they saw (**38** ὥρων) and believe happened (**39**.1 λέγουσι). Finally, the author's voice enters (**39**.2 ἐς ἡμέας), with some physical evidence that would support the truthfulness of the events.

37.1 Ἀκήρατος: otherwise unknown (*LGPN s.v.* IIIB (2)). 'Pure' is a rare name (elsewhere only *IG* 7.1968 from Boeotia, and the author of *A.P.* 7.138), and is suitable for a priest.

πρὸ τοῦ νηοῦ . . . ἱρά 'in front of the temple, weapons, they must have come from inside, and they're the holy ones'; the word order conveys something of the sequence of realisations by the priest on coming upon the weapons. For this focalising of a miraculous event through a character in the narrative, cf. 9.100.1 κηρυκήιον ἐφάνη . . . κείμενον (with F&M *ad loc.*); similarly, the miracles in **84**.2 and **94** are introduced by λέγεται and λέγουσι Ἀθηναῖοι, and that in **65** is told by Dicaeus. H. thus disclaims responsibility for the truth of these events. The weapons would have been lying in front of the east façade of the temple; for this kind of portent, cf. Xen. *HG* 6.4.7; Diod. 15.53.4; Polyaen. 2.3.8; Cic. *Div.* 1.74.

37.2 οἱ δὲ βάρβαροι . . . ἐπιγίνεταί σφι: an anacolouthon (or *non sequitur*), in which the grammatical construction changes in mid-sentence.

ἐγίνοντο ἐπειγόμενοι 'continued to press on'. Cf. the 'periphrastic' construction of εἰμί + present, aorist or perfect participles used in place of a finite part of the verb in the participle to describe a characteristic or situation which persists for some time. γίγνομαι + participle is found thus occasionally in both prose and verse (*M&T* §§45–6; Smyth §1961–2).

Προνηίης Ἀθηναίης: *Pronaia* because her temple stands on the way to Apollo's, about a mile from it (cf. Paus. 10.8.6; *IG* II^2 1126.35; Demangel 1923: 1–41, 1926: 55–107; Bommelaer and Laroche 1991: 47–59). Her intervention is characteristic of her protectiveness: 'more than any other deity Athena is always near her protégés' (Burkert 1985a: 141).

θῶμα . . . φανῆναι 'it is indeed a wonder that weapons should appear of their own accord'; φανῆναι is an explanatory ('epexegetic') infinitive, depending on θῶμα . . . καὶ τοῦτο . . . ἐστί.

δὲ δή: δή strengthens the emphasis regularly placed on the second clause by the use of μὲν . . . δέ (*GP* 257, 259); the automatic movement of the weapons is surprising enough, but nothing compared with what is described in the δέ-clause.

διὰ πάντων φασμάτων lit. 'among all (other) miracles' and so 'beyond, more than'; not a common (or Attic) use of διά, but found in 1.25.2, 6.63.3, 7.83.2; *Il.* 12.104; Pi. *Is.* 3/4.55 ὁ δ' ἔπρεπε διὰ πάντων 'he stood out above all'. The phrase reflects the genitive's original function of indicating the sphere in which an action takes place; compare the local use of διά = 'in the midst of' (LSJ *s.v.* A I 3). This authorial comment creates a pause in the narrative, since the Persians are in the same place at **37**.3 as at **37**.2; the repeated reference to Athena's temple centres the narrative on that significant location.

37.3 γὰρ δή: δή highlights the explanation promised by γάρ (*GP* 243–4).

βοὴ καὶ ἀλαλαγμός: the war-cries befit the armed goddess Athena. Other divine voices will be heard during Xerxes' laying waste of Attica (**65**.1–4), and at the very start of the battle of Salamis (**84**.2).

38 ἴθυ Βοιωτῶν 'straight to Boeotia'; adverbial words used as prepositions are most commonly found with the genitive (Smyth §§1700–2).

ἔλεγον . . . ὡς ὥρων . . .· δύο γὰρ . . . ἕπεσθαι: γάρ in *oratio obliqua* regularly marks the shift from a clause introduced by ὡς etc. to the construction with the infinitive. Greek tends to move fairly quickly into the infinitive construction, in part because it makes clear the extent of the reported speech.

ὡς ἐγὼ πυνθάνομαι: for H.'s use of such local knowledge, cf. Luraghi 2001b.

μέζονας ἢ κατὰ ἀνθρώπων φύσιν ἐόντας 'taller than human stature'. κατά + accusative expresses comparison: cf. phrases like κατὰ νόμον 'in accordance with the law', and Thuc. 2.50.1 χαλεπωτέρως ἢ κατὰ τὴν ἀνθρωπείαν φύσιν 'more than human nature could bear', 7.75.4 μείζω ἢ κατὰ δάκρυα . . . πεπονθότας, 'having suffered troubles too deep for tears'.

39.1 ἐπιχωρίους ἥρωας: Greek heroes were usually mortals whose remarkable exploits, good or bad, had marked them out as superhuman and worthy of reverence and fear after their death. Their worship resulted largely from the eighth- and seventh-century dissemination of the Homeric poems, which caused people to associate local Mycenaean tombs with figures said by Homer to have come from their towns (Coldstream 1976). In nature and cult, they are in many ways the opposite of the Olympians, being 'chthonic' (i.e. living underground), having special rituals that reversed those of the Olympians (nocturnal rites, etc.) and possessing only local influence, but this opposition should not be overemphasised (cf. Scullion 1994). Thus Phylacus and Autonous are local (**39**.1 ἐπιχωρίους) deities, who rise from their tombs to help their worshippers, like Theseus, Heracles and other deities at Marathon (cf. Plut. *Thes.* 35.5; Paus. 1.15.3). In fact, H. seldom mentions such heroic interventions in battles: at Marathon, he tells of a giant warrior (6.117.2–3), but not of Theseus' and other deities' appearances. The Greeks will send a ship to bring the Aeacidae to help them at Salamis, but they are given no explicit role by H. (**64**.2). Cf. in general Brelich 1958; Burkert 1985a: 203–8; Kearns 1989.

Φύλακον 'Guardian', a so-called *redende Name* or 'speaking name', i.e. a name that is appropriate to the character involved; cf. Aceratus, **37**.1n., and e.g. the poet Stesichorus and Hagesichora, leader of a chorus of girls in Alcm. fr. 1. Phylacus reappeared, amidst similar portents, against the Gauls in 279 (cf. Paus. 10.8.7, 23.2). The precise location of his shrine is uncertain, but it may perhaps have been one of the *oikoi* to the north-east of the temple (Bommelaer and Laroche 1991: 46–52). Autonous' shrine is unknown.

τὴν ὁδόν: i.e. the Sacred Way from Daulis to the temple of Apollo.

Κασταλίης: the Delphian spring famous for its inspirational qualities for poets, but also used for purification in temple rites (Eur. *Ion* 94–7, 144–50; Parke 1978).

Ὑαμπείηι κορυφῆι: the right-hand cliff rising sheerly for a thousand feet above the Castalian spring (Str. 9.3.15). Cf. Paus. 10.6.1–4 for the names connected with Delphic sacred geography.

ἐς ἡμέας ἦσαν σόοι: often, by using an imperfect in such phrases, H. makes himself, from the reader's point of view, part of the history he is describing (Rösler 1991: 219).

τούτων . . . ἀπαλλαγὴ γίνεται: a scornful expression; cf. **118**.3 εἰ μὴ τούτων ἀπαλλαγή τις γένηται 'unless we get rid of these men'.

40–82 THE PRELUDE TO SALAMIS

The narrative once again moves alternately between Greeks and Persians, but now with a much greater concentration on the Greek camp. Throughout these sections and the battle narrative (**83–96**) there runs the motif of divine involvement, in Xerxes' sacrifice and the miraculous regrowth of Athena's olive tree (**54–55**); the earthquake, prayers and summoning of the Aeacidae by the Greeks (**64**); the ghostly Eleusinian procession (**65**); oracles (**77, 96**); the arrival of the Aeacidae (**83**.2); the mysterious woman at the start of the battle (**84**.2); and the mysterious boat that approached the Corinthian ship in its (alleged) flight from the battle (**94**.2–3). Expressions and themes recur from the episodes at Artemisium and Delphi: cf. Introduction, §5 ; Immerwahr 1966: 267–87.

40–1 Abandonment of Athens

This episode contrasts with the last, in that Delphi is protected by its presiding deity, but Athens is abandoned by its goddess (**41**.2–3). Each place will ultimately be restored to its position of importance. At Athens, the Persians will be successful only for a time, and the possibility of the regeneration of Athens will be signalled in the regrowth of the olive tree (**55**). Delphi and Apollo will be given rich gifts to mark the victory (**121–3**). Themes recur from the earlier narrative. Like the Euboeans in **4**.2, the Athenians ask that the fleet should pause to let them evacuate their families: the language of **40**.1 recalls **4**.2 ἐδέοντο Εὐρυβιάδεω προσμεῖναι χρόνον ὀλίγον, ἔστ' ἂν αὐτοὶ τέκνα τε καὶ τοὺς οἰκέτας ὑπεκθέωνται. They abandon their homes, like the Phocians (**32**.1) and Delphians (**36**.2), doing so in accordance with an oracle, a motif again found with the Euboeans (**20**) and Delphians (**36**.1): Delphi and the Athenians are saved because they follow the oracles; the Euboeans suffer for not doing so.

40.1 ἐς Σαλαμῖνα . . . πρὸς Σαλαμῖνα: the change in preposition seems to be merely stylistic, as at the end of §2.

πρὸς δὲ καί 'and in addition also . . .' The adverbial use of prepositions has its origins in their earlier independent existence as 'preverbs'; cf. ἐπὶ δέ, σὺν δέ, μετὰ δέ; **33**.1, **36**.2nn.

τὸ ποιητέον ἔσται 'the kind of things they would have to do'. τό = ὅ, i.e. the neuter of ὅς; it is not the definite article. H. has ὅς for τίς in indirect questions 68×, often with the force more of οἷος rather than simply τίς (K–G II 438–9). The future tense with verbal adjectives is rare.

ὡς ἐψευσμένοι γνώμης 'since they were disappointed of their expectations', an ablatival genitive, as often with verbs of separation, loss, deprivation (Smyth §1392). The Athenian disappointment here at not finding the whole of the Peloponnesian forces is reminiscent of the Greeks' contrasting unpleasant surprise at finding Aphetae full of Persian ships (cf. **4**.1 αὐτοῖσι παρὰ δόξαν τὰ πρήγματα . . . ἀπέβαινε). ὡς shows this is the view of the Athenians.

40.2 πανδημεί 'in full force', a compound adverb with its suffix formed on analogy with the locatival suffix in -οι/-ει (found in οἴκοι, ἐκεῖ; Sihler 1995: §259.9); similar forms are ἀθεεί 'without the aid of god', ἀμαχεί 'without fighting'.

ὑποκατημένους 'awaiting'; transitive only here. Such an expectation would have fitted 479 much better than 480, since resistance in Boeotia was most unlikely to be successful at this time, after the loss of Thermopylae.

τῶν μὲν . . . οἱ δὲ ἐπυνθάνοντο 'of the Spartans the Athenians discovered no trace, but they learnt . . .' The Athenians are subject of both clauses, but the pronoun is added to the second to make the contrast between them and the Spartans clearer. This pattern is not infrequent in H.: cf. e.g. 7.6.4 τῶν μὲν ἔλεγε οὐδέν, ὁ δὲ τὰ εὐτυχέστατα . . . ἔλεγε, '[if bad news came,] he said nothing of it, but he did relay the best news'; cf. **60** *init.*

ἐπυνθάνοντο . . . τειχέοντας . . . ἀπιέναι: with verbs of perception, the infinitive and the participle can both be used with very little distinction of meaning (*M&T* §914.1). For the wall, cf. **71**.2n. ἀπιέναι = ἀφιέναι.

41.1 κήρυγμα: there is a major problem here, which was only made more problematic by the discovery at Troezen in 1959 of the so-called 'Themistocles Decree', an inscription relating to the organisation of the evacuation of the city to Troezen and Salamis and to the preparation of forces (cf. ML 23 = Fornara no. 55). There are three main problems: (i) is H.'s account of the proclamation taking place just before Salamis impossible, in that it would have been very difficult to prepare a fleet the size of the Athenians' between June and September, and to announce, organise and begin an evacuation of a city the size of Athens at such short notice? (ii) Is the 'Themistocles Decree', whose lettering dates it most probably to the mid-third century, an edited copy of the fifth-century original or a fabrication? (iii) If genuine, does the Decree refer to June 480 or rather to September 481, as could be suggested by such details as the reference to the decision to send ships to Artemisium, cf. 7.143.3? It seems most likely that the decision to evacuate was taken much earlier than H. says, and that the Decree is a fabrication, because of the numerous problems of anachronistic terminology, questionable strategy and problematic descriptions of decision-making: cf. esp. Lazenby 1993: 102–4; Blözel 2004: 247–54; Cawkwell 2005: 277–80; also Hammond, *CAH*² IV 558–63.

Ἀθηναίων τῆι τις δύναται . . . οἰκέτας 'that the Athenians should save their children and household in whatever way each man could'. Ἀθηναίων is genitive, rather than the expected accusative subject of σώιζειν, through the influence of τις. τις is here used 'distributively', 'each (man) of the Athenians'; cf. 9.17.4 μαθέτω τις 'let each man know'. τῆι 'where' is feminine dative of ὅς, used adverbially (*Lex. s.v.* ὅς B III 6a).

ἐς Τροιζῆνα . . . ἐς Αἴγιναν . . . ἐς Σαλαμῖνα: the decree says [τὰ τέκ]ν[α καὶ τὰς γυναῖκ]ας ε[ἰς] Τροιζῆνα καταθέσθαι . . . τ[οὺς δὲ πρεσβύτας καὶ τὰ] κτήματα εἰς Σαλαμῖνα καταθέ[σ]θ[αι ('they should evacuate their children and wives to Troezen . . . and their old men and possessions to Salamis'; ML 23.8, 9–11 = Fornara no. 55). Troezen treated the refugees generously (Plut. *Them.* 10.3). All three places mentioned here were guarded by the Athenian fleet.

41.2 τῶι χρηστηρίωι: since the Athenian ambassadors had rejected the first oracle given by Delphi, this must refer to lines 8–10 of the second oracle in 7.141.4, 'do not remain, but turn your back and flee', rather than to the opening lines of the first (7.140.2), 'flee to the ends of the earth, leaving your homes and the lofty heights of your circular city'.

ὄφιν: the οἰκουρὸς ὄφις ('guardian snake'), which lived in the temple of Athena Polias (cf. Ar. *Lys.* 758–9). It represented the hero Erechtheus/Erichthonius (the snake is often a symbol of chthonic deities like heroes, cf. Paus. 1.24.7; **39**.1n.), who was the offspring of an attempted rape of Athena by Hephaestus, and became a primordial king of Athens. In his time Athena defeated Poseidon in a competition for the patronage of Athens, and Erechtheus was killed by the disappointed Poseidon whilst defending Athens against the attack by Poseidon's son Eumolpus. His subsequent rebirth as a snake was commemorated at the festivals of the turn of the year in Athens: cf. Powell 1906; Burkert 1966, 1983: 135–61; Parker 1987. That a deity intimately connected with Athena should abandon the city was a clear sign of impending disaster: the 'Decree of Themistocles' records an agreement τὴ[μ] μὲν πό[λιν παρ]ακατ[αθέ]σθαι τῆι Ἀθηνᾶι τῆι Ἀθηνῶμ [μεδεο]ύ[σηι] κ[αὶ τοῖς ἄλλ]οις θεοῖς ἅπασιν φυλάττειν ('entrust the city to Athena, Queen of Athens, and all the other gods to protect', ML 23.4–6 = Fornara 55). Cf. further **41**.3, **53**.1nn.

ὡς ἐόντι 'since they believe it really exists'. ὡς indicates that the Athenians believed in the snake, not that H. did not. In later tradition, this story was rationalised as a trick stage-managed by Themistocles, whereby he caused the priests to explain the disappearance by saying that the goddess had left the city, and so should the Athenians (Plut. *Them.* 10.1). As H. says, however, the Athenians saw no reason to doubt the portent.

ἐπιμήνια: offerings made at each new moon; cf. 6.57.2. Honey-cakes were regularly offered to chthonic deities like Erechtheus; cf. those offered at Trophonius' oracle, where there were also snakes (cf. Ar. *Clouds* 506–8 and schol.; Paus. 9.39.11 with Frazer *ad loc.*; **134**.1n.).

41.3 ὡς καὶ τῆς θεοῦ ἀπολελοιπυίης: that her attendant snake has left the shrine indicates that Athena has gone too (καί). The abandonment of cities by their protecting deities is regularly a sign of imminent disaster; cf. e.g. Aesch. *Sept.* 217–18; Eur. *Tro.* 23–7; Plut. *Ant.* 75.4–5; Bowie 1993: 142–50. The idea is also found in Persian sources. The *Cyrus Cylinder* (*ANET* 315–16; Brosius no. 12; BM 90920) explained Cyrus' destruction of Babylon in terms of the gods' wrath with the activities of the previous king Nabonidus (*Nabū-na'id*): 'the gods who lived in them left their dwelling-places (§9) . . . From . . . the cult places . . . whose sanctuaries had been deserted a long time ago, I returned (their) gods to their (rightful) place' (§§31–2). In Greece, devices such as some form of chain or bonds could be used physically to prevent gods leaving: e.g. Menodotus, *FGH* 541 F 1; Diod. 17.41.7–8, 46.6; Curt. 4.3.21–2; Adrados 1972; cf. also H. 5.85–6.

42–8 Greek forces at Salamis

At the very moment of the dramatic announcement of Athena's abandonment of her city, the narrative moves tantalisingly away to a list of the Greek forces. The catalogue recalls that in **1–2**, but is on a much more impressive scale; indeed, this is the longest catalogue of Greek forces in H. (cf. **1.1–2.1**n.). Though it cannot compete in grandeur, length and ethnographic richness with the spectacular account of the review of Xerxes' troops in 7.59–100, this catalogue gives a sense of the variety of the Greek nation, and suggests a historical depth to that nation that is lacking in the Persian catalogue. The catalogue is arranged by geographical region.

42.1 Πώγωνα 'Beard Harbour'; men who had difficulty growing beards were told 'you'd better go to Troezen' (Suda, *s.v.* Πώγων) because of this harbour.

πλεῦνες νέες . . . πολίων πλεύνων: 54 more ships (378 (**48**) as against 324 (**2**.1, **14**.1)), and nine more states (Hermione, Ambracia, Leucas, Naxos, Cynthos, Seriphos, Siphnos, Melos, Croton), with the loss of the Opuntian Locrians.

42.2 μὲν . . . μέντοι . . . γε 'though he was nauarch . . . he was not, however, of royal stock'. μέντοι is adversative, and γέ emphasises the opposition (*GP* 404–5). The context here suggests that 'nauarch' is being used in the general sense of 'commander of the Greek fleet', rather than technically to refer to the Spartan yearly office of that name. The point of H.'s remark seems to be that one might have expected such an important position to have been held by one of the Spartan kings. Indeed, King Leotychidas took command in the following year (**131**.2, where he is described as 'strategos and nauarch'), but perhaps was not originally given the command of the fleet because the two kings of Sparta could not be out of the city at once (5.75.2), and Leonidas had gone to Thermopylae.

43 The Peloponnesians. Sparta heads the catalogue as the leading state in Greece (**3**.2n.).

Δωρικόν τε καὶ Μακεδνὸν ἔθνος: Macednian is the name H. says the Dorians bore when they lived 'under Ossa and Olympus' (1.56.3; cf. **31**n.). Its basic meaning, if it is Greek, would be 'tall': it is used in *Od.* 7.106 of a tree, and cf. μηκεδανός, μῆκος, μακρός. It may therefore describe the people or indicate that they were highlanders. Its linguistic relationship to Μακεδών looks obvious, but is in fact not certain: cf. Chantraine 659–60; Hammond 1972: 309–10; Hatzopoulos 2003: 215.

Ἐρινεοῦ: one of the three or four original towns of the Dorian tetrapolis in Doris; they are variously named (cf. e.g. Thuc. 1.107.2). For the migration, cf. **31**n. H. chooses the great charter myth of the Dorian occupation of the Peloponnese to start his catalogue and to characterise these peoples.

Δρύοπες: they lived round Mt Oeta, but 'Dryopians' are also found in a number of other parts of the Greek world (**31**n.); for the expulsion, cf. also Diod. 4.37.1–2, and generally Strid 1999.

44 The Athenians. The Plataeans are again closely associated with Athens (**1**.1n.), and the explanation of their absence is allowed to take precedence over the account of Athenian history. This passage runs counter to the idea that H.'s primary audience was the Athenians: they would not have needed to be given the information in §2.

44.1 ἔξω: *sc.* τοῦ Ἰσθμοῦ; 'the mainland beyond the Isthmus', i.e. outside the Peloponnese.

πρὸς πάντας τοὺς ἄλλους lit. 'in comparison to all the others', and so 'surpassing all the others'. For πρός thus in comparisons, cf. Thuc. 3.37.3 οἵ τε φαυλότεροι τῶν ἀνθρώπων πρὸς τοὺς ξυνετωτέρους . . . ἄμεινον οἰκοῦσι τὰς πόλεις; from this comparative use came its use to indicate superiority (Smyth §1695.3c). The Athenians provided 180 out of 378 ships (**1**.1, **14**.1), despite the damage described in **18**. In the newly discovered speech *Against Diondas* 145v, 12–16, Hyperides gives the slightly larger number of 220 ships provided by the Athenians, which may include the 20 ships provided for the Chalcidians (**1**.2); he is making the same point about the importance of the Athenian contribution (I am very grateful to László Horváth, Gyula Mayer, Zoltán Farkas and Tamás Mészáros for letting me see this text before publication).

μοῦνοι is explained by the following clause.

44.2 Πελασγῶν: in this passage, Athenians and Pelasgians are the same race (contrast 6.137–40), and the Athenians are thus glorified by association with the original inhabitants of Greece. This ties in with their oft-repeated claim to be autochthonous, i.e. to have arisen in and never left Attica (cf. Thuc. 1.2.5–6). However, in 1.56–8, H. gives the more traditional view that the Pelasgians were the original non-Hellenic inhabitants of Greece. For this contradiction and its relation to the permeability of the Greek/barbarian opposition in H., cf. Thomas 2000: 118–22; and especially Sourvinou-Inwood 2003a; also Lloyd 1976: 232–4. The Pelasgians are first mentioned in *Il.* 2.840–3 as allies of the Trojans, and the traditions about them are many and complex. H. situates them in all parts: the Peloponnese (e.g. 1.146.1), Attica (1.56.2; cf. 5.64.2, 6.137–40), the north (2.52.3), the islands (2.51.3) and Asia Minor (7.42.1). Thuc. 1.3 gives them much less prominence in early Greek history.

Κραναοί: named after king Cranaus, who is in other traditions successor to Cecrops, first king of Athens (Paus. 1.2.6). The word seems to mean 'rocky', but its etymology is unknown. On the tangled history of the early kings of Athens, cf. Parker 1987. Κραναά was an old name for Athens: Ar. *Ach.* 75, *Lys.* 480; cf. Pi. *Ol.* 7.82, 13.38. H. here weaves various epithets for the Athenians into a historical narrative.

Ἐρεχθέος: see **41**.2n.

Ἴωνος: son, with Achaeus, of Xuthus and Creusa, daughter of Erechtheus; Xuthus was son, with Aeolus and Dorus, of Hellen: Ion, Aeolus and Dorus were the eponymous founders of the three branches of the Greeks. This early tradition is found in Hes. fr. 10a.20–3, and historically 'a controversy about the origins and thus the obligations of the Ionians is fought out through the person of the hero Ion' (Parker 1987: 206, cf. 213 n. 76 for bibliography on Ion). Cf. Eur. *Ion* and **10**.2n.

στρατάρχεω: not an official Athenian term, perhaps used because Ion does not fit easily into the list of early Athenian kings (Parker 1987: 206 with n. 79). He is called 'polemarch' in *Ath. Pol.* 3.2.

45 ἀπὸ Κορίνθου: Leucas was colonised by Corinthians *ca.* 625.

46 The islanders. Though almost all the islands, faced with a fleet the size of Xerxes', had offered earth and water as signs of submission to the Persian king, they had subsequently taken the risky step of abandoning that obligation and fought with the Greeks who opposed the Persians (cf. **46**.4n.).

46.1 Δωριέες ἀπὸ Ἐπιδαύρου: for their split from Epidaurus, cf. 5.83.1 and Paus. 2.29.5.

Οἰνώνη: it gained its later name from the nymph Aegina, raped by Zeus (Paus. 2.29.2); the old name appears e.g. in Pi. *Ne.* 4.46.

46.2 Ἰωνικὸν ἀπὸ Ἀθηνέων: see **10**.2n.

Ἐρετριέες: see **1**.2n.

46.3 Δημοκρίτου: he is the subject of an epigram attributed to Simonides, which praises his exploits at Salamis (*A.P.* 6.2 = XIXa Page).

Νάξιοι δέ εἰσι Ἴωνες ἀπὸ Ἀθηνέων: Naxos was settled *ca.* 1025. The Naxians were given to tactical changes of side: 5.30–4, 6.97.

46.4 γῆν καὶ ὕδωρ: demanding earth and water as signs of submission seems to have been a peculiarly Achaemenid custom. It could be used as a preliminary to detailed discussion of an alliance, and thus took the place of immediate military intervention. The obligations implied by giving earth and water were binding over a long period, and infractions of the alliance justified any action on the part of the King. Interpretation of this demand for earth and water is not easy, but earth and water may have represented symbolically the land of the donor, and in handing them over he was not giving the King his kingdom, but rather swearing an oath of loyalty on it (cf. Kuhrt 1988). Darius had demanded earth and water of the Greek states in 492 (6.48–9), as did Xerxes earlier in 480. He omitted Athens and Sparta, who had thrown Darius' envoys into a pit and a well, as places where earth and water could be got (7.32, 133). Since, however, Athens had earlier given earth and water to Darius' satrap Artaphernes in the hope of an alliance (5.73; *ca.* 507), any subsequent anti-Persian actions could have been counted as grounds for intervention. The only references to this practice are to be found in H. (cf. also 4.127.4, 131–2, 5.17.1–18.1, 6.94.1, 7.131, 163.2, 233.1); no Near Eastern source mentions it.

47.1 ἐντὸς . . . Θεσπρωτῶν 'this side of', so 'to the south and east of'. The suffix -τος has an ablatival function (cf. ἐκτός 'from without'; Palmer 1980: 284), hence its use with the genitive. The Thesprotians lived along the coast of Epirus, in north-west Greece opposite Corfu, extending as far as the Ambracian gulf.

Κροτωνιῆται: situated in southern Italy, on the ball of the 'foot', Croton was settled by Achaeans from the north-east Peloponnese *ca.* 710, and was famous from the mid-sixth century as the home of Pythagoras and his followers, who dominated its politics until expelled towards the end of the century. They have not been mentioned in connection with the fighting before, and do not appear on the Serpent Column (**82**.1n.).

τρὶς πυθιονίκης Φάϋλλος: he was twice victor at Delphi in the pentathlon and once in the foot race; there was a statue of him. He was sufficiently famous to be used later as a type of the fast athlete, as in Ar. *Ach.* 215; *Wasps* 1206; Paus. 10.9.2; *AP Appx.* 297 for his fantastic feats.

48.1 Μήλιοι . . . ἀπὸ Λακεδαίμονος: Melos was resettled *ca.* 900. In Thuc. 5.112.2 the Melians give (in vain) the fact that they have lived on Melos for 700 years as a reason for not submitting to the Athenians.

Σίφνιοι . . . Ἴωνες: Siphnos too was colonised *ca.* 900. It was very wealthy in the sixth century, but was plundered by the Samians *ca.* 525 (3.57–8) and manages but a single ship here. In the fourth century it became, like Seriphos, a byword for insignificance.

ἀριθμός: the figures do not in fact add up, and we are twelve short. Much ingenuity has been expended in trying to make them add up, for instance, by adding δυοκαίδεκα to ἄλλαι πεπληρωμέναι νέες in **46**.1, but the problem has not been satisfactorily resolved. In his more straightforward calculations, H. is usually careful and accurate: cf. Keyser 1986 (esp. 238). Aes. *Pers.* 338–40 gives the number as 310; the discrepancy may come from H.'s failure to take into account losses at Artemisium. Later sources give varying round totals, but textual problems mar their evidence (e.g. Thuc. 1.74.1).

49–50.1 Greek deliberations on where to fight

Eurybiades democratically throws the debate open to all (n.b. τὸν βουλόμενον, §1). Once again, the Peloponnesians express an unwillingness to fight too far from home. Now that northern and central Greece, as well as Attica, are largely in Persian hands, the argument that the Peloponnesians needed to keep the Greeks from those areas happy by fighting to defend their territory begins to have rather less force. The

Peloponnesian want to fight off a friendly shore, in case they have to abandon a naval action after a defeat.

49.1 προθέντος . . . εἰσί 'Eurybiades having suggested that anyone who wished to should give his opinion as to where, amongst the areas that they controlled, he thought it most advantageous to hold the sea-battle.' χωρέων is a partitive genitive depending on ὅκου and stands in the relative rather than in the main clause.

ἀπεῖτο = Att. ἀφεῖτο, pluperfect passive of ἀφίημι.

τῶν δὲ . . . προετίθεε 'he was making his proposal about the rest of their area'.

49.2 συνεξέπιπτον 'were beginning to come out in agreement', a sense possibly deriving from votes falling from an urn (cf. LSJ *s.v.* πίπτω B v 1; **123**.2).

ἐπιλέγοντες 'urging in addition'; the nominative participle is used as if οἱ λέγοντες οἱ πλεῖστοι had stood earlier rather than αἱ γνῶμαι τῶν λεγόντων αἱ πλεῖσται. This is the so-called 'construction according to sense' (κατὰ σύνεσιν or *ad sensum*), where strict grammatical accuracy is sacrificed for clarity.

εἰ νικηθέωσι: εἰ (as opposed to ἐάν) + subjunctive in future conditions is found rarely in Homer; tragedy sometimes uses it but it is very rare in Attic prose (*M&T* §§453–4; Smyth §2327). H. has it 9×, especially in questions; cf. **62**.2 εἰ . . . μὴ ποιήσηις and **108**.4n.

πολιορκήσονται: a future middle used as a passive. Ionic prose uses middle and passive futures without distinction, cf. ἐξοίσονται as a passive in the last clause of this sentence (Smyth §§807–9; K–G I 114).

ἐς τοὺς ἑωυτῶν ἐξοίσονται 'they would (be able to) come ashore (in the lands of) peoples on their own side'. For ἐκφέρομαι thus, cf. LSJ *s.v.* I 4.

50.1 τῶν . . . στρατηγῶν ἐπιλεγομένων ἐληλύθεε 'even while they were deliberating on this, there had arrived an Athenian'. The active of ἐπιλέγω means to say something on a topic, the middle to say something (or have it said) to oneself, and so to consider, deliberate. The pluperfect ἐληλύθεε expresses an action that had reached its fulfilment at the very moment the main action was taking place (*M&T* §52; K–G I 152–3): cf. **114**.1 ἐν δὲ τούτωι τῶι χρόνωι . . . χρηστήριον ἐληλύθεε.

50.2–53 The capture and burning of Athens

We now pick up the narrative of the fate of Athens that paused at **41**, and return to the forces with Xerxes whom we left at **34**. The link to the narrative about the capture of Athens is made by the arrival of an Athenian messenger with the news of the arrival of the Persians in Attica (**8**n.).

There are reminiscences here of the battle at Thermopylae: the Persians expect an easy victory, but are frustrated by a small number of men (7.210.5–12 ~ **51**.2); Xerxes is for a time at a loss (7.213.1 ἀπορέοντος δὲ βασιλέος ~ **52**.2 Ξέρξην . . . ἀπορίηισι ἐνέχεσθαι); they are ultimately successful when a way is found of circumventing the defenders (7.213.1 ~ **53**), who make mistakes (7.218.3 ~ **51**.2). These few men, forced by poverty or duty to stay fatally on the Acropolis, put up a remarkably spirited defence, though superior force and fate (**53**.1) are against them. In Aes. *Pers.* 347–9 the capture of Athens is very much played down: Αγγ. θεοὶ πόλιν σώιζουσι Παλλάδος θεᾶς. | Ατ. ἔστ' ἄρ' Ἀθηνῶν ἔστ' ἀπόρθητος πόλις; | Αγγ. ἀνδρῶν γὰρ ὄντων ἕρκος ἐστὶν ἀσφαλές. For the archaeology of this section, cf. Thompson 1981; Hurwit 1999: 135–6; Mylonas Shear 1999: 119–20.

50.2 Θεσπιέων: cf. **25**.1n.

Πλάταιαν: the Plataeans had evacuated their city in **44**.1. The singular form of the name is found only here in H., beside 22 plural forms.

πυθόμενος Θηβαίων: genitive of the origin of their knowledge. For the hostility between these two neighbours, cf. **1**.1n.

51.1 ἀπὸ δὲ τῆς διαβάσιος κτλ. 'after the crossing of the Hellespont, whence the barbarians had begun their march, they spent a month there in which they crossed into Europe and reached Attica in three more months.' ἔνθεν in H. is always an adverb of place and not time (*Lex. s.v.*; 16×), so here the calculation of the length of the march must be from the Hellespont, and not from the time they left Sardis (7.37.1; roughly in April). In 7.56.1 it is said that the crossing took seven days and nights, but other activities could easily have filled up three more weeks. The three months given for the period between the crossing and arrival in Attica has been thought rather short, but Xerxes met little major opposition on land and the expedition had been four years in the planning (7.20.1).

Καλλιάδεω ἄρχοντος Ἀθηναίοισι: H. uses the specifically Athenian mode of dating, by the name of the 'eponymous' archon who gave his name to the year, to fix the time of the city's destruction; it is used only here in H. ἄρχω is used with the dative in prose only when it means 'be archon of' (Smyth §1537).

51.2 τὸ ἄστυ is the inhabited area of the town as opposed to the Acropolis.

ταμίας τε τοῦ ἱροῦ: there were ten treasurers of the temple of Athena in H.'s time, drawn from the *pentakosiomedimnoi* (*Ath. Pol.* 7.3, 8.1; cf. **33**.1n.). The Decree of Themistocles demanded that [τοὺς δὲ ταμίας καὶ τ]ὰς ἱερέας ἐν τῆι ἀκροπόλε[ι μένειν φυλάττοντας τὰ τῶ]ν θεῶν ('the treasurers and the priestesses are to remain on the Acropolis and guard the gods' property'; ML 23.11–12 = Fornara 55); everyone else was to leave. The temple was the Old Parthenon, for which cf. Hurwit 1999: 132–5.

πένητας . . . ἀσθενείης βίου: this passage suggests that people were expected to pay the costs of evacuation, and those who could not were left behind.

τὴν ἀκρόπολιν: they will have fortified its western end, which had been breached for the construction of the Old Propylon; the rest was defended by the Pelasgic wall and the steep cliffs, where the Propylaea now is, its only unprotected part.

δοκέοντες . . . μαντήιον: i.e. they interpreted differently from Themistocles the phrase in the oracle at 7.141.3 'Far-seeing Zeus grants to Athena that only the wooden wall will remain intact'. They took it literally, because, they argued, the Acropolis had originally been defended by a wooden stockade, and so the oracle must mean that the Acropolis was the place of safety (7.142.1). On the oracle, cf. Blösel 2004: 64–107.

αὐτὸ δὴ τοῦτο εἶναι τὸ κρησφύγετον 'that *this* was the actual place of refuge'. The phrase gives their words in indirect speech. αὐτὸ δὴ τοῦτο is a common collocation

(*GP* 210). The meaning of κρησφύγετον is clear, but not the etymology, except for its connection with φεύγω. Ancient grammarians derived it from Κρής 'Cretan', referring it to caves where the Cretans fled to hide (*EM* 538.1), but nothing more plausible has been suggested.

52.1 καταντίον: i.e. to the north-west, opposite the main entrance.

Ἀρήιον πάγον: this was the meeting place of the Council of the same name, the oldest political institution in Athens. In mythology, this hill was similarly occupied by the Amazons in Theseus' time, though, unlike the Persians, they were driven off by that king (Aesch. *Eum.* 685–90; cf. H. 9.27.4; Isoc. 4.70; Plut. *Thes.* 26–8). This defeat of the Amazons was one of the most popular exploits of Athens' culture hero, and in the fifth century it was celebrated in temple sculptures alongside the defeat of the Persians.

ὅκως . . . ἅψειαν lit. 'whenever having attached flax they set fire to it'; ὅκως is used temporally in Ionic prose (cf. **90**.2, **128**.1; Smyth §2383 A N.3). Some of the arrowheads have been discovered in the excavations.

στυππεῖον: raw flax was often used in association with pitch; cf. Xen. *Cyr.* 7.5.22–3.

καίπερ ἐς τὸ ἔσχατον κακοῦ ἀπιγμένοι, καὶ τοῦ φράγματος προδεδωκότος: καί is redundant, but is used as if another genitive absolute preceded, as in reverse order in 3.127.1 (Darius did not send an army) ἅτε οἰδεόντων ἔτι τῶν πρηγμάτων καὶ νεωστὶ ἔχων τὴν ἀρχήν, 'because affairs were still turbulent and he had only recently taken power'.

52.2 τῶν Πεισιστρατιδέων: Hippias, Peisistratus' eldest son and his successor as tyrant of Athens, had fled the city with his followers when the Spartan king Cleomenes occupied it in 510. Hippias eventually came to Darius' court and was with him at Marathon (6.107); he was now dead. Among those of the Peisistratids and their friends present in Xerxes' entourage would have been Hipparchus, son of Charmus, ostracised in 488/7, the seer Onomacritus (7.6) and Dicaeus (**65**). The Peisistratids were amongst those who had urged Xerxes to attack Greece (7.6.2–5), no doubt in the hope that they would be reinstated as rulers in their homeland. Demaratus, the deposed king of Sparta, is similarly in Xerxes' entourage (**65**.1n.). For the King, such men were useful as negotiators and, because they owed any position they might occupy to him, were likely to be loyal to him. The Persians regularly put cities under the control of local aristocrats, in the hope that the fact they were local would make them acceptable to their subjects (cf. **136**.1n.). On Greek exiles in Persia, cf. Cagnazzi 2001; **75**n.

ὀλοιτρόχους 'stones that roll' < (ϝ)είλέω 'roll' (cf. **23**.1n.); but the ancients derived it from ὀλοός 'destructive' (Σ *Il.* 13.137; cf. Chantraine 794). These stones could have come from the old Mycenaean fortification walls or the West Cyclopean Wall.

ἐπὶ χρόνον συχνὸν ἀπορίῃσι ἐνέχεσθαι: since H. uses χρόνος συχνός to mean anything from a few hours (9.67, 102.3) to a few years (5.94.2), it is hard to know what length of time he envisaged. Battles with the Persians tend to go on 'for a long time':

cf. 6.113.1 (Marathon), 9.62.2, 70.2 (Plataea), 102.3 (Mycale), 119.2; Cyrus had similar problems besieging Babylon: ἀπορίῃσι ἐνείχετο ἅτε χρόνου τε ἐγγινομένου συχνοῦ (1.190.2); cf. F&M on 9.62.2.

53.1 **δή τις** is used when 'the speaker cannot, or does not trouble to, particularize' (*GP* 212). H. does not know precisely how the discovery was made, but since the gods had decreed Athens' destruction, it was inevitable it would come about.

ἔδεε γὰρ κατὰ τὸ θεοπρόπιον: for H.'s use of phrases of this kind, cf. Gould 1989: 73–8.

ἔμπροσθε . . . ἀνόδου 'toward the front of the Acropolis, opposite the gates and the ascent'. The translation is Hurwit's (1999: 136). It is odd that H. calls this end of the Acropolis the 'front': the reference to the shrine of Aglaurus shows us that the east end is meant, but the major entrance had always been at the west. Hurwit resolves the problem by reference to the fact that the 'front' of a Greek temple was regularly the east façade (the cult statue also faced east). H. will be calling the front of the Acropolis that side which faced Athens' civic centre, the Archaic Agora. H.'s knowledge of the Acropolis is not, however, faultless: he is wrong about the location of an inscription on the Acropolis in 5.77.4 (see S. R. West 1985: 283–5).

τῇι δή . . . ἐφύλασσε 'exactly (δή; *GP* 218–19) where no one was on guard'. This motif of the 'unguarded stretch of wall' is not uncommon in tales of the capture of cities; e.g. 1.84.2 (Sardis), 191 (Babylon); Troy had a weak section, built by the mortal Aeacus unlike the rest which was built by gods (Pi. *Ol.* 8.31–46; cf. *Il.* 6.433–4).

ἤλπισε μή: here (and 1.77.4) ἐλπίζω takes the construction of verbs of fearing, in a natural development of its use, especially in poetry, to express unhappy expectations, as in Soph. *Tr.* 111 δύστανον ἐλπίζουσαν αἶσαν. The subject is again the τις of the previous clause.

τὸ ἱρὸν τῆς . . . Ἀγλαύρου: a mid-third-century inscription, which records a decision that it should be placed in the shrine of Aglaurus, has been found at the east end of the Acropolis, suggesting that the shrine was below the great cave there. Cf. Dontas 1983; Lewis *ap.* Burn 1984: 607–8. Aglaurus, daughter of king Cecrops, along with her sisters, was given charge of the casket containing the infant Erichthonius/Erechtheus, born after Hephaestus' attempt on Athena (see **41**.2n.). They were instructed not to look inside it, but did so: when they saw the snaky appearance of the child they threw themselves off the Acropolis (Paus. 1.18.2). So the unexpected sight of the Persians causes some of the defenders similarly to throw themselves off the walls. The reaction is a natural one, but one wonders if some thought of the myth when they realised that they, like the daughters of Cecrops, had made a bad mistake.

53.2 **μέγαρον:** the body of the temple, where the cult image was kept.

τοὺς ἱκέτας: the inside of a temple or sanctuary was sacred and nothing that was polluting, such as sex or death, was permitted in it. Sanctuaries were thus places of refuge for slaves, criminals and others under threat; a temple was ἄσυλος (whence 'asylum'), a place where people and things could not be seized or plundered (συλᾶν), because they were under divine protection. Killing suppliants consequently could have dire consequences: cf. Cleomenes' burning of the Argive suppliants and his subsequent death (6.79–84), or the outcome of the murder of the members of the conspiracy of Cylon in Thuc. 1.126.2–12; cf. Parker 1983: 181–5, and generally on suppliancy, Gould 1973.

ἐπεὶ δέ σφι πάντες κατέστρωντο 'when they had all been laid low by them'; σφί refers to the Persians, and is a dative of the agent, often used with the perfect and pluperfect of passive verbs (Smyth §§1488–94).

ἐνέπρησαν . . . ἀκρόπολιν: The damage done by the Persians was considerable: parts of the Mycenaean walls were completely obliterated, the *Archaios Neos* and Old Parthenon were destroyed, all the stones that had been put in place of the latter being cracked by the heat, along with the temple of Nike and presumably the Great Altar of Athena; the base of the statue of the goddess was ruined and many dedications pulled down and burnt, not least that set up by Callimachus to celebrate Marathon (Hurwit 1999: 136; cf. fig. 105 for this last monument). Later, Xerxes tells Mardonius to offer to restore the Athenian temples as part of his attempt to bring the Athenians over to his side and create a split in the Greek forces (**140**α.2).

The justification for such burning of Greek temples (cf. also **32**.2, **33**) was the burning by the Greeks of Sardis and its temple of the goddess Cybebe (5.102.1, 6.101.3, 7.8β.3, 11.2). This sequence of reciprocal destruction of temples was continued when Alexander the Great burned the palace at Persepolis in revenge for the destruction of the Greek temples by Xerxes (cf. Arr. *Anab.* 3.18.11–12; Strabo 15.3.6). On revenge as a motive in H., cf. de Romilly 1971 and Asheri 1998, esp. 86 on the persistence of the desire for revenge through later centuries. For Persian treatment of foreign religious practices, cf. **54**n.

54–5 A message to Susa, and a miraculous olive shoot

Xerxes' reactions are both celebratory and cautious. He sends a message to Susa to mark the punishment of the city that defied his father, but also orders sacrifice in the Greek manner, to placate the Greek gods and to show that normal local religious activity will continue.

The story of the new shoot from Athena's olive tree is an instructive and ambiguous one. The natural Greek interpretation of it, especially after they had won, was as an omen of the renewal of the city: so it is understood by Dion. Hal. 14.4, and Sophocles alludes to this story in the 'Colonus Ode' of his *Oedipus Coloneus* (694–701): 'there is a thing which I have not heard of in Asia nor as growing in Pelops' great island, a growth that is unconquered, self-renewing, a terror to the spears of the enemy, which flourishes in this land, the grey-leaved olive which nourishes our children.' There would be a parallel in the story of the shady grove that grew up on the tomb of the murdered general of the Ten Thousand, Clearchus: Artaxerxes, who had had him murdered, 'was very remorseful, because he had clearly killed a man beloved of the gods' (Plut. *Art.* 19.5, from Ctesias). That the account of the regrowth is put in the context of the original foundation myth of Athens is also significant.

However, if it was, as H. says, told immediately after the sacrifice, it could equally well have been understood by the Persians and their Athenian allies as a sign of the gods' acceptance of Xerxes' sacrifice, and of a regeneration under *his* rule. The regeneration of a tree would have had a particular resonance for an Achaemenid ruler: Achaemenid kings, like earlier Near Eastern rulers, associated themselves with the fertility of nature, not least in the planting of trees (cf. Xen. *Oec.* 4 *passim*, esp. 20–5; ML 12 (Darius) (= Fornara 35); Strabo 15.3.18; Briant 2002: 232–40). To persuade Xerxes to attack Greece, Mardonius claimed that 'Europe is an extremely attractive country, with all kinds of cultivated trees . . . which a king alone of mortals ought to possess' (7.5.3), and on the march Xerxes rewarded a plane tree for its beauty with gold ornament and an Immortal as guard (7.31). For the olive and Xerxes' expedition, cf. further **26**.2n.

54 Σοῦσα (OP *Çūshā*, Elam. *Shu-sha-an*, OT Shushan, mod. Shush) was formerly, with Anshan, one of the great cities of Elam: it was the capital of Elam as early as the end of the fifth millennium. After its destruction by Ashurbanipal, king of Assyria, in 647/6, it never regained its earlier high importance, but it was a major administrative centre and one of the 'capitals' of the Achaemenid empire, along with Ecbatana, Sardis, Babylon and Persepolis, through which the king regularly progressed, thereby acknowledging the importance of all areas of the empire. Susa was probably used in winter/spring: few of the Persepolis tablets refer to travel there in June to October (Hallock 1969: 41), when lizards and snakes fried if they tried to cross the road (Strabo 15.3.10; in general, cf. Tuplin 1998 (esp. 73 n. 21 on Susa). For the Greeks, it was the main Persian 'capital': Phrynichus' *Capture of Miletus* and Aeschylus' *Persae* are set there. Darius built his palace here, before the one at Persepolis. It had 110 rooms, corridors and courts, and a floor area of 20,675 m^2. Foundation texts describe the construction of the palace and the 16 countries providing construction materials and labour (cf. DSf (= Brosius no. 45), DSz; Dandamayev and Lukonin 1989: 256–9). Cf. Boucharlat 1990; Perrot and Ladiray 1996.

Ἀρταβάνωι: (the first element is *arta-* 'justice'; Balcer 1993: 69–70). He was (half-?) brother of Darius, and as a 'warner' (**26**.2n.) vainly counselled against his invasion of Scythia (4.83) and Xerxes' of Greece (7.10–18, 45–52). He was entrusted with Xerxes' οἶκόν τε . . . καὶ τυραννίδα (7.52.2), though the implication there that he was a 'regent' (ibid. σκῆπτρα . . . ἐπιτρέπω) does not reflect Achaemenid reality: the King was King wherever he went.

δευτέρηι ἡμέρηι 'on the next day', reckoning inclusively. The parallelism of expression with **55**.1 δευτέρηι δὲ ἡμέρηι ἀπὸ τῆς ἐμπρήσιος links these two stories.

Ἀθηναίων τοὺς φυγάδας, ἑωυτῶι δὲ ἑπομένους 'the exiles who, though Athenian, were among his followers'; δέ without a preceding μέν indicates a weak contrast (Smyth §2838). For the exiles, cf. **52**.2n.

τρόπωι τῶι σφετέρωι: Mardonius also uses Greek sacrifices in 9.37.1, but he eventually ignored their warnings (id. 41.4).

εἴτε δὴ . . . τὸ ἱρόν 'he gave this command, either because he had seen a dream, or because he had an attack of conscience because he had burnt the temple'. εἴτε . . .

εἴτε here = ἤ . . . ἤ, as in 1.191.1 εἴτε δὴ ὦν ἄλλος . . . ὑπεθήκατο, εἴτε καὶ αὐτὸς ἔμαθε . . . , ἐποίεε δὴ τοιόνδε, 'whether another suggested it or he learnt for himself, this is what he did' (cf. *Lex. s.v.* εἴτε II 3). For the participle in one clause and indicative in the other, cf. **116**.2 οἱ δὲ ἀλογήσαντες, ἢ ἄλλως σφι θυμὸς ἐγένετο. δὴ ὦν is very common in H. (and Plato) but not elsewhere; here (like καί) it reinforces its εἴτε (*GP* 468–70). Xerxes had been caused great concern by dreams before the expedition (7.10–18), which would justify the first suggestion here.

ἐνθύμιον 'scruple, twinge of conscience'; cf. Parker 1983: 252–4. **Persians and foreign religion**. We have here a case where Greek and Persian perceptions seem to diverge. If for H. ordering a Greek sacrifice is the probable result of a troubled conscience, for Xerxes it would have been normal. Achaemenid kings generally respected the religion of conquered cities, destroying temples only where warnings were ignored: after the Ionian revolt, they spared as they had promised (6.9.3–4) the temples of those Ionians who submitted (6.25.2, Samians), but destroyed those of peoples who did not (6.19.3, 32, 96, 101.3). Their propaganda makes much of this religious tolerance. When Cyrus conquered Babylon, 'there was no interruption (of rites) in Esagila [temple of Marduk] or the (other) temples and no date (for a performance) was missed' (*Nabonidus Chronicle* (= Brosius no. 11), III §§18–19). Jewish sources praise Cyrus for allowing the return of the Jews to Jerusalem and the rebuilding of the Temple (cf. Ezra; and Artaxerxes in Nehemiah 2), and Egyptian ones record Cambyses' reverential treatment of their shrines and the Bull of Apis (Brosius nos. 19–22, 24 with fig. 3; H.'s hostile account in 3.27–9, 37 (Brosius no. 23) is probably a priestly tradition provoked by Cambyses' financial rearrangements of Egyptian temples (Brosius no. 24)). Darius complains of Gadatas' 'ignoring the attitude (νοῦν) of my ancestors towards the god who spoke all truth to the Persians (i.e. Apollo)' (ML 12.26–9 = Fornara 55). The evidence of the Persepolis tablets is the same: 'the economic administration treated the gods equally' (Hallock 1969: 5), and the Fortification Tablets mention offerings to Assyrian and Elamite as well as Iranian gods (e.g. PF 339, 759, 762 (= Brosius nos. 192–4)).

Greek tradition accuses Xerxes of violence against religious institutions: e.g. he murders a priest to steal a statue which Darius had prudently left (1.183.3). Contrast, however, the copious offerings to Athena and the Trojan heroes (7.43.2), the reverence to Athamas (7.197), the cup, crater and sword thrown into the Hellespont (7.54.2–3; H. again questions his motives), and the prayers in the storm off Magnesia to Thetis and the Nereids (7.191.2). Contrast too XPh (= Brosius no. 191) §5: 'Among these countries there was a place where previously demons (OP *daivas*) had been worshipped. Afterwards, by the favour of Ahura Mazda, I destroyed that sanctuary of the demons, and I made proclamation, "The demons had been worshipped!" Where previously the demons were worshipped, there I worshipped Ahura Mazda and Truth (*Arta*) reverently'. Cf. Briant 2002: 550–4.

ἐντεταλμένα: perfect passive participle of ἐντέλλομαι.

55.1 Ἐρεχθέος . . . νηός: for Erechtheus the earth-born, cf. **41**.2n., **53**.1n. It is not certain what this νηός was which H. contrasts with τῶι ἄλλωι ἱρῶι.

ἐν τῶι ἐλαίη τε καὶ θάλασσα: Athena and Poseidon competed to be patrons of Athens in the time of Erechtheus, Athena bringing an olive tree as a gift (Paus. 1.27.2), Poseidon a salt spring and a warhorse (ibid. 26.5). The myth follows the standard pattern of Greek foundation myths: the wilder forces of nature (the sea), are symbolically conquered by more civilised forces (the olive): culture tames nature (cf. Detienne and Vernant 1978: 187–213; Vian 1963). The olive seems to have been outside the Erechtheum in the shrine of Pandrosus, another daughter of Cecrops (cf. **53**.1n.; Philochorus, *FGH* 328 F 67). There is a large cistern under the present Erechtheum, which has been taken as Poseidon's spring; it gave out the sound of the sea when the wind blew, hence H.'s use of θάλασσα. Cf. also Apollod. 3.14.1–2.

μαρτύρια 'as proofs (of their interest in the city)'.

βλαστόν: Thphr. *HP* 2.3.3, Verg. *Geo.* 2.303–13; Pliny, *NH* 17.241 notes exceptional cases of olive trees surviving bad fires.

ὅσον τε 'approximately'. τε in this combination in early writers denotes a habitual or typical action, as Mimn. fr. 2.7–8W μίνυνθα δὲ γίνεται ἥβης καρπός, ὅσον τ' ἐπὶ γῆν κίδναται ἠέλιος ('the fruit of youth lasts a little time, as long as the sun spreads over the earth' (i.e. 'a day')); from this there grew its use without a verb to express 'approximation to a definite standard' (*GP* 524). It is common in H.

56–8 Greek despondency and Mnesiphilus' intervention

The narrative of events in the Greek camp is resumed from **49**. As in **4–5**, Greek despondency provokes desire for flight and for holding the line at the Isthmus. There is a simple pattern: Themistocles persuades Eurybiades to reconvene the council and exchanges words with Adeimantus; makes an impassioned speech; exchanges words with Adeimantus and persuades Eurybiades.

From being the adviser and planner, Themistocles is now advised by his old teacher: inability to listen to a wise adviser causes the downfall of many in H.: when the narrative returns to the Persians, Xerxes will provide another example, by failing to take Artemisia's advice not to fight at Salamis (**67–9**). Mnesiphilus introduces a new argument for not retreating to the Isthmus. So far, such arguments have come from those, like the Euboeans and Athenians, who had an interest in defending their own lands or at least in evacuating their families. Now Mnesiphilus raises the possibility of a chaotic dispersal of the Greeks if they are allowed to retreat south, and the spontaneous flight by some of the Greeks in the previous chapter lends him support: the fragility of the Greek alliance always lurks. The Greeks make the right decision, but as a result not of simple deliberation but of the Athenian threat to abandon the alliance (**62**.2; cf. Pelling 1997a; 2006a: 110–12). Here and in **75**, Themistocles practises his trickery by night, a time regularly associated with cunning in Greek myth and ideology.

The scene is given particular significance by its intertextual relation with the assembly in *Iliad* 2. There, when Agamemnon falsely recounts his dream (*Il.* 2.139–54), there is a noisy and unthinking flight of the Greeks to their ships, as happens here when the message of the capture of Athens' Acropolis is brought (**56**). Then, as the Greeks flee, Odysseus is prompted by Athena and gives impassioned and sententious advice to the individual commanders he stops (155–97), just as Themistocles, encouraged by Mnesiphilus, will advise Eurybiades in private. Once the assembly is reconvened, there is an acrimonious dispute between Odysseus and Thersites (211–77), which is here twice imitated in the exchange between Themistocles and Adeimantus (**59**, **61–2**; and cf. **125** for a closer imitation of this scene, again in the context of rivalry with Themistocles). Odysseus then addresses Agamemnon before the whole assembly, arguing for the continuation of the siege (284–332); and Themistocles similarly makes a speech in the assembly of generals, which is addressed specifically to Eurybiades (**60**). Odysseus saves the Greek expedition, just as Themistocles is about to engineer the Greek victory. Odysseus' words that the Greeks 'like little children or widows weep together, wanting to go home' (288–9) stand as an implied judgement of the runaway Greeks in H. The Iliadic scene which sets in motion the final triumph of the Greeks is thus invoked at the assembly that begins the triumph of the Greeks. Cf. also Blösel 2004: 236–41. For Homer and H., cf. Strasburger 1972; Marincola 2006; Pelling 2006b.

Here, for the first time since events after Thermopylae (7.234–7), direct speech becomes prevalent. It is much used from here until **68** to mark the crucial moment when the decision on where to fight is taken by both sides, and continues to be generally frequent for the next fifty chapters which cover events up to and including the battle. After that, there is a dearth of direct speech until **140–4**. On speeches in H., cf. Hohti 1976; Lang 1984, with exhaustive analyses in 80–149 (47.5 per cent of H.'s speeches are quoted directly (ibid. 143)); Pelling 2006a.

There are also echoes of Marathon (6.109–10), where Miltiades, the architect of the victory, like Themistocles unsuccessful in a discussion of where to fight the Persians, secretly visits and persuades the Polemarch, and offers a similar prospect of glory, in similar language: cf. **60**α n.

56 ὣς σφι κτλ.: ὡς is used four times in as many lines with four different meanings in English: here 'when'; ὡς ἔσχε indirect question; ὥστε . . . οὐδὲ . . . ἔμενον consecutive; ὡς ἀποθευσόμενοι purpose (Macan).

θόρυβον: the panic is a little odd, since the Greeks cannot have expected a virtually undefended Acropolis to survive long, and H. does not say what happened to those who set sail, but it is to be understood as part of the parallelism of this section with *Iliad* 2 (see above).

ἀποθευσόμενοι: for θέω of a sailor, cf. *Od.* 3.287–8 ἐν νηυσὶ γλαφυρῇσι . . . | ἶξε θέων; of a ship, *Il.* 1.483.

νύξ τε . . . καὶ . . . ἐσέβαινον 'when night came . . . then . . . they embarked', a frequent meaning of τε . . . καί in H., cf. **64**.1, **83**.1. There is often asyndeton in these sentences, as though τε both joins this sentence to the last and looks forward to καί.

57.1 Μνησίφιλος: later tradition made him Themistocles' teacher, who handed on Solon's political wisdom to him, but it also tarred him with the brush of Themistocles' amoral politics (Plut. *Them.* 2.4). Though he was once thought fictional, 12 *ostraca* have now been found with his name (cf. Thomsen 1972: 93–4; Brenne 2001: 243–5; *LGPN* *s.v.* II (12)).

57.2 οὔ τοι ἄρα . . . ναυμαχήσεις 'I see: in that case, you can be sure you will have no country left to fight for'. τοι points out to Themistocles what he seems unaware of (*GP* 537), and ἄρα expresses Mnesiphilus' own realisation of it (*GP* 32–3, 40–1, and for the pairing, 555). οὐ . . . οὐδεμιῆς is an emphatic double negative.

οὔτε . . . κατέχειν δυνήσεται . . . ὥστε μὴ οὐ διασκεδασθῆναι 'will not be able to restrain them, so that the force is not scattered'. 'Any infinitive that would take μή, takes μὴ οὐ (with a negative force), if dependent on a negatived verb. Here οὐ is . . . untranslatable' (Smyth §2745; *M&T* §§815–17). Cf. **100**.3n., **119**n.

ἀβουλίῃσι: the plural of abstract nouns can be used in a 'distributive' sense, assigning the quality to a number of people (Smyth §1000 (3)).

ἦν κως δύνῃ '(to see) whether you can'; cf. **6**.1n on εἴ κως.

ἀναγνῶσαι 'induce, persuade', a specifically Ionic use.

58.1 κοινόν τι πρῆγμα συμμεῖξαι 'to share with him a matter of common interest'. For the rare use of the verb with this meaning, cf. LSJ *s.v.* I 4.

58.2 καταλέγει ἐκεῖνά τε . . . καὶ ἄλλα πολλὰ προστιθείς: an anacolouthon; we would expect another present indicative in the καί-clause.

59–63 The Greeks reconsider: debate between Themistocles and Adeimantus

As well as its specific intertexual relationship with *Iliad* 2, this council also recalls the gatherings of gods and men in Homer and Near Eastern poetry (cf. West 1997: 177–81), with which H. shares some motifs. The leader is not totally in control: like Zeus and Agamemnon, Eurybiades must follow prevailing majority opinion, and disputes are conducted in strong language (cf. e.g. *Il.* 4.34–6, where Zeus says Hera would eat the Trojans alive; cf. **61–2**). Getting one's way can involve going behind the backs of others, especially the leader's: Hera and Athena obstruct Zeus' will (e.g. *Il.* 8.350–408), and Themistocles, the human equivalent of Athena's cunning, having twice gone behind the backs of the generals to Eurybiades (**5, 58**), will finally go behind his back in contacting Xerxes (**75**).

59 προθεῖναι τὸν λόγον: this must be the equivalent of λόγον διδόναι 'give the reason', though elsewhere it means 'to open a discussion'.

πολλός 'was passionate'. πολλός basically denotes frequency: cf. 1.98.1 (a question of who should be king) ὁ Δηιόκης ἦν πολλὸς ὑπὸ παντὸς ἀνδρὸς καὶ προβαλλόμενος καὶ αἰνεόμενος, 'Deioces was repeatedly put forward and praised by everyone.' It then comes to denote passion: cf. 7.158.1 Γέλων δὲ πολλὸς ἐνέκειτο λέγων τοιάδε, 9.91.1.

οἷα κάρτα δεόμενος 'as a man does when he is asking a great deal'. οἷα is used (like ἅτε) with a causal participle to give the view of the author (Smyth §2085); contrast the use of ὡς (**7**.2n.).

ῥαπίζονται: whipping was the punishment for breaking Olympic rules, and officials called *rhabdouchoi* were employed for the purpose. Cf. Xen. *HG* 3.2.21 and Thuc. 5.50.4 for this punishment applied to the elderly and distinguished Spartan Lichas.

ἀπολυόμενος 'excusing himself'; cf. Arist. *Rhet.* 1415b37 ἢ διαβάλλειν ἢ ἀπολύεσθαι ἀνάγκη.

δέ γε 'yes, and . . .' is common in retorts, especially in drama (*GP* 153). Adeimantus unwisely trades witticisms with Themistocles, who was noted for his quick repartee: cf. Plut. *Them.* 18.2–5 for examples. Cf. Shapiro 2000 (esp. 105–7) for H.'s use of contradictory *gnomai* in verbal disputes.

60 ἔλεγε . . . λεχθέντων lit. 'he did not now say any of those things said (by him) before', i.e. the things which he had said privately to Eurybiades; οὐκέτι οὐδέν is an emphatic double negative.

οὐκ ἔφερέ οἱ κόσμον 'it was not seemly'; so **142**.2.

ἄλλου λόγου εἴχετο 'he availed himself of another argument'; for ἔχομαι + partitive genitive, cf. LSJ *s.v.* ἔχω C 2.

60 Themistocles' speech. The speech acts as a tactical analysis of the choice facing the Greeks: Artemisia's speech in **68** will consider the same points from a Persian perspective. The speech has a tight rhetorical structure for maximum clarity. It has four main sections: (a) Eurybiades will save Greece, if he does (i) what Themistocles says, not (ii) what his opponents say; (b) the disadvantages of (ii); (c) the advantages of (i); (d) a sententious closure. The middle sections are divided into three points, carefully distinguished, and the parallelism is reinforced by close parallelism of ideas allied to variety of expression, which will be found again, even more strikingly, in the speeches of Thucydides:

πρὸς μὲν τῶι Ἰσθμῶι . . . ἀναπεπταμένωι . . . ἡμῖν . . . ἐλάσσονας
ἢν δὲ τὰ ἐγὼ . . . ἐν στεινῶι . . . πρὸς ἡμέων . . . ὀλίγησι

τοῦτο δὲ ἀπολέεις Σαλαμῖνα
αὖτις δὲ Σαλαμὶς περιγίνεται

ἅμα δὲ . . . ἄξεις . . . κινδυνεύσεις
καὶ μὲν καὶ . . . οὐδὲ ἄξεις . . . προναυμαχήσεις.

The rest of this section gives further advantages, and the final section rounds the speech off again with balance leavened by variation; 'the god' is brought in as a final argument.

60α ἐν σοὶ νῦν . . . Ἑλλάδα: cf. Miltiades to Callimachus before Marathon ἐν σοὶ νῦν, Καλλίμαχε, ἐστὶ ἢ καταδουλῶσαι Ἀθήνας ἢ ἐλευθέρας ποιήσαντα μνημόσυνον λιπέσθαι (6.109.3). For the reader, the success of Miltiades' strategy there supports Themistocles' line of argument here.

ἢν . . . πείθηι . . . μηδὲ . . . ἀναζεύξηις: in parallel clauses like these, when H. uses οὐδέ or μηδέ in the second clause even though the first clause is not negatived, there is always a strong contrast between the two clauses, as in **60**β προναυμαχήσεις . . . οὐδὲ . . . ἄξεις, 6.96.2 οἴχοντο φεύγοντες οὐδὲ ὑπέμειναν (*GP* 190). This turn of phrase is used in Ionic but not Attic prose. ποιέεσθαι is a rare epexegetic infinitive depending on πείθηι; cf. Pl. *Prot.* 338A πείθεσθέ μοι ῥαβδοῦχον . . . ἑλέσθαι; Smyth §1992 N.

βαρυτέρας: Plut. *Them.* 14.3 says the Greek ships were 'lighter and lower', and indeed Phoenician ships seem to have been sturdier to carry more marines (Basch 1980). H.'s 'heavier' is odd therefore. Stein suggested βραδυτέρας.

τοῦτο δέ 'next', an adverbial accusative, used without a preceding τοῦτο μέν; contrast **76**.1.

ἀπολέεις . . . εὐτυχήσωμεν: the distinction in person and number, putting the blame for these significant losses on Eurybiades alone even if the Greeks are successful, is a notable rhetorical move.

ἤν περ καί 'even if in fact'; ancillary περ strengthens words such as εἰ, ἤ (*GP* 487–8).

κινδυνεύσεις τε ἁπάσηι τῆι Ἑλλάδι 'you will put the whole of Greece at risk'; a kind of dative of interest, indicating the object risked.

60β τὰ οἰκότα: here and in §γ Themistocles makes use of the argument from probability (*to eikos*), another example of the influence of sophistic modes of rhetoric in H.'s work, cf. Thomas 2000: 168–212, esp. 168–90.

περιγίνεται 'will be saved'; 'in animated language, the present often refers to the future, to express likelihood, intention' (*M&T* §32).

καὶ μὲν καί 'and furthermore there is also this'; καὶ μέν introduces a new point (*GP* 390).

ὁμοίως . . . Ἰσθμῶι 'if you stay here you will be fighting to defend the Peloponnese just as well as you would be if you fought at the Isthmus'; for τε . . . καί thus, cf. *GP* 515. Themistocles means that a victory at Salamis will have exactly the same effects as one at the Isthmus, and that the narrower confines of Salamis are strategically a better place for the Greek fleet to fight, given its inferiority.

οὐδέ σφεας, εἴ περ εὖ φρονέεις, ἄξεις . . . Πελοπόννησον 'nor will you bring them into the Peloponnese, [and that,] if you are wise, [you will not want to do].' With parenthetic phrases like εἴ περ εὖ φρονεῖς, the thought is compressed and the apodosis omitted: cf. Thuc. 3.44.1 οὐ γὰρ περὶ τῆς ἐκείνων ἀδικίας ἡμῖν ὁ ἀγών, εἰ σωφρονοῦμεν, ἀλλὰ περὶ τῆς ἡμετέρας εὐβουλίας; cf. 1.40.2, 6.11.7. The apodosis is not therefore ἄξεις ἐπὶ τὴν Πελοπόννησον, since Eurybiades hardly needs to be told 'if you are wise, you will not bring the Persians to the Peloponnese'.

60γ δέ γε here has a strong adversative force, with as often 'some tinge of repartee' (*GP* 155); cf. **59**.1n.

Μεγάροισί τε κερδανέομεν περιεοῦσι 'we shall benefit from the survival of Megara', an instrumental dative, though ἐξ or ἀπό is more usual with κερδαίνω (K–G I 435–6).

λόγιον: Themistocles refers here to the oracle quoted at 7.141.4 ὦ θείη Σαλαμίς, ἀπολεῖς δὲ σὺ τέκνα γυναικῶν, which he interpreted as portending success, because otherwise the oracle would have said ὦ σχετλίη Σαλαμίς (7.143.1).

ἐθέλει γίνεσθαι: the subject is an understood repeated οἰκότα, unless something has dropped out of the text. There is a possible parallel in **80**.1 ἴσθι γὰρ ἐξ ἐμέο τάδε [*sc.* ποιεύμενα] τὰ ποιεύμενα ὑπὸ Μήδων. The same idea ends the speech of the

Greek envoys to Gelon in 7.157.3 τῶι δὲ εὖ βουλευθέντι πρήγματι τελευτὴ ὡς τὸ ἐπίπαν χρηστὴ ἐθέλει ἐπιγίνεσθαι.

61 Again, the cunning Themistocles is able to cap a sardonic remark by his main opponent, this time with a serious threat rather than a witty riposte (contrast **59**).

61.1 σιγᾶν τε κελεύων τῶι μή ἐστι πατρίς: *sc.* ἄνδρα as object of κελεύων. The negative is μή because this is a 'generic' relative clause about the class of men without countries (Smyth §2705d). Adeimantus claims Themistocles should not be allowed to vote, because, with Athens in enemy hands, he does not have the same intense interest in the outcome as those whose cities are still at risk. Themistocles will meet a similarly ungenerous remark about state and status in **125**; both remarks ironically look forward to Themistocles' eventual actual loss of his city.

ἐπιψηφίζειν: the context suggests this means 'give the vote to', with a dative of the one consulted, even though this sense is not found again until Lucian (*Timo* 157). The basic meaning 'put to the vote (at the insistence of)' does not fit so well a context in which Themistocles is asking Eurybiades to decide.

παρεχόμενον 'if he could show he had a city', conditional participle.

61.2 ἤ περ is found in epic and Ionic prose only; περ emphasises the difference (*GP* 487; cf. **60**α n.).

ἔωσι: for the contrast with εἴη, cf. **26**.2n.

γάρ introduces the explanation of Themistocles' point about the ships: they will allow the Athenians forcibly to make a home in, and gain land from, any Greek city they choose.

62–3 The seriousness of Themistocles' words is emphasised by the shift back to direct speech after the indirect of the quarrel with Adeimantus. Once again, Themistocles begins with a very forthright address to the leader Eurybiades (σύ), but the closely argued rhetoric of the first speech is replaced by staccato short sentences, crisply articulated: two contrasting short conditional clauses are followed by a blunt statement; and then a long conditional is followed by a threat. The brutal threat to abandon the Greeks and take the vital Athenian ships away means Eurybiades has little choice now.

62.1 ἐπεστραμμένα 'vehement'; perfect passive participle of ἐπιστρέφω.

σὺ εἰ <μὲν> μενέεις καὶ . . . ἔσεαι . . .· εἰ δὲ μή, ἀνατρέψεις τὴν Ἑλλάδα 'if you remain here and, by remaining, are courageous, (well and good,) but if you do not, you will destroy Greece.' In emotional speech, it is not uncommon in contrasting conditional sentences for the apodosis of the first sentence to be omitted, as the speaker or writer hurries on to the important point which is contained in the second, here the destruction of Greece: cf. Pl. *Prot.* 325D καὶ ἐὰν μὲν ἑκὼν πείθηται· εἰ δὲ μή, . . . εὐθύνουσιν ἀπειλαῖς ('and if he agrees willingly, (then all is well) but if not, they call him to account with threats'; also *Il.* 1.135 ἀλλ' εἰ μέν δώσουσι . . . εἰ δέ κε μὴ δώωσι, ἐγὼ δέ κεν αὐτὸς ἕλωμαι; Thuc. 3.3.3; *M&T* §482; Smyth §§ 2346d N.3, 2352a). With εἰ δὲ μή, *sc.* μενέεις. The fuller form can be seen in the calmer remark of Themistocles in **80**.2 ἢν μὲν πείθωνται, ταῦτα δὴ τὰ κάλλιστα· ἢν δὲ αὐτοῖσι μὴ πιστὰ γένηται, ὅμοιον ἡμῖν ἔσται. The broken syntax conveys the almost desperate nature of Themistocles' concern that they follow his course of action.

62.2 Σῖριν τὴν ἐν Ἰταλίηι: i.e. the Siris between Thurii (Sybaris) and Tarentum on the instep of the foot of Italy, not Paeonian Siris north of the Chersonnese (cf. **115**.3). The Athenian claim to this Ionian city seems to rest simply on their avowed leadership of the Ionians: Siris was colonised by Ionians from Colophon (Arist. fr. 584). Themistocles had daughters called Italia and Sybaris (Plut. *Them.* 32.2), which suggests connections with that area: cf. Cimon's diplomatically named son Lacedaemonius (id. *Cimon* 16.1). Such a wholesale emigration was not implausible: the Phocaeans fled to the west to escape Persia in *ca.* 540 (1.163–7; cf. the Scythians in 4.118.2), Bias of Priene proposed a mass Ionian migration to Sardinia (1.170; cf. 5.124.2–126), and the Greeks consider abandoning Ionia and resettling the Ionians after Mycale (9.106.2–3); cf. Demand 1990: esp. 34–44; Braccesi 1995.

λόγια: We know nothing specifically about these oracles, and Themistocles may be making them up to bolster his threat. The Θουριομάντεις of Ar. *Clouds* 332 suggest oracles played an important part in Athens' eventual foundation of Thurii, in 446–3, in which H. seems to have taken part. For the importance of oracles in colonisation, cf. Malkin 1987.

63 ἀπολιπόντων . . . ἐγίνοντο 'if the Athenians were to leave, the rest of the army would not be up to the battle'. The genitive absolute stands for the protasis of the conditional sentence. For the omission of ἄν in such a sentence, cf. Pl. *Rep.* 450D πιστεύοντος μὲν γὰρ ἐμοῦ ἐμοὶ εἰδέναι ἃ λέγω, καλῶς εἶχεν ἡ παραμυθία ('if I trusted that I had any knowledge of what I am talking about, your consolation would be fine'; lit. '(on that supposition) your consolation was fine'; cf. *M&T* §§431–2). The omission of the modal particle ἄν makes the certainty greater.

αἱρέεται: perhaps for dramatic reasons, H. has Eurybiades make the decision himself here; such decisions seem earlier to have been in the hands of the commanders generally.

64–5 Divine manifestations: an earthquake and a miraculous Eleusinian procession

Each side receives one, but where the Greeks take steps to ensure a happy outcome, those on the Persian side seem powerless to act, though they see that the omen is not propitious. The divine plan moves remorselessly on.

64.1 ἔπεσι ἀκροβολισάμενοι lit. 'hurling words at each other like missiles'; a striking metaphor, for which cf. **78**, 9.26.1 ὠθισμὸς λόγων, **81**.1 λόγων ἀμφισβασίη, again of the generals in Salamis. These phrases, always used by H. as narrator, have a comic exaggeration about them, marking a slightly ridiculous element in the Greek disputes. On humour as an aspect of H.'s historiography, cf. Dewald 2006.

σεισμός: the coincidence of an earthquake and sunrise after the decision is taken makes the event particularly significant, and the fact that the quake affects land and sea also suggests a double success, as will happen at sea and on Psyttaleia. Other significant earthquakes are found at 5.85.2, 86.4, 6.98.1.

64.2 εὔξασθαι τοῖσι θεοῖσι: contrast Xerxes' reaction to an eclipse when he marched from Sardis; reassured by the Magi that it portended destruction for Greece, he accepted this interpretation without more ado (7.37.2–3).

Αἰακίδας: descendants of Aeacus, son of Zeus and Aegina, who included his sons Peleus and Telamon, their sons Achilles and Ajax, Neoptolemus etc. They must be physically present at the battle, because heroes had only local influence (**39**.1n.): cf. the stories of the need to possess the bones of Orestes (1.67–8) and Theseus (Plut. *Cimon* 8.5–6); Attic tragedy not infrequently depicts Athens welcoming in foreign heroes, and so ritually taking possession of them. In quite what form the Aeacidae are to be imagined as coming to Salamis is not absolutely clear, but it was most likely as statues, which could represent the presence of the actual divinity. For instance, the Aeginetans loaned the Aeacidae to the Thebans for use against Athens, but they met with little success, and so subsequently exchanged the gods for actual fighting men (5.79–81); the statues of the Tyndaridae accompanied Spartan kings on campaign (5.75.2). Ajax's help was later commemorated at the Aianteia festival, celebrated on Salamis: cf. Deubner 1968: 228; Pritchett 1979: 175–6; Parker 1996: 153–4.

ὡς δέ σφι ἔδοξε, καὶ ἐποίευν 'no sooner had they decided, than they actually began to do it' (note the difference in tenses). καί emphasises the fact, cf. 1.79.2 ὡς δέ οἱ ταῦτα ἔδοξε, καὶ ἐποίεε κατὰ τάχος; cf. also **22**.2n. on the similar use of 'apodotic' δέ.

αὐτόθεν μὲν ἐκ Σαλαμῖνος = ἐξ αὐτῆς Σαλαμῖνος. Telamon and Peleus had had to flee Aegina after murdering their step-brother Phocus (Paus. 2.29.9–10).

65 The scene involving this Eleusinian prodigy at Thria is poignant: two Greeks, exiles from the two leading cities, watch a ghostly festival open to all Greeks, but which their exile excludes them from, and which portends disaster for the empire for which they have left their homeland.

Athena may have left the city, but the gods are still watching over it, as is shown by this ghostly procession from the Eleusinian Mysteries. The rites took place on Boedromion 13–24 (variously in Sept.–Oct.: the Greek calendar does not march with the modern). The most important parts were secret, but other activities took place more publicly. A procession went from Athens to Eleusis, where the rites led to the secret climax in the Telesterion or Anactoron, in which we are told that the Hierophant held up an ear of corn in a blaze of light. Anyone who was not a murderer could take part, but because of the Persian destruction of Athens this ban was extended to non-Greek-speakers (Isoc. *Paneg.* 157; cf. §4).

The structuring myth was that of Demeter and Persephone (Kore), and the initiates won the promise of a blessed afterlife as a result of their participation: 'happy is the earthly man who has seen these things, but he who has not been initiated into them, and who has no share in them, has a very different fate when he dies and goes down to the musty darkness' (*H. Dem.* 480–2). The process of initiation was symbolised as a journey through hardship and darkness leading to light and salvation (Plut. fr. 178; Apuleius, *Met.* 11.23.6–8; and Dionysus' journey to Hades in Ar. *Frogs*). The evocation of a festival offering salvation after hardship, like the earthquake, augurs well for the survival of the Greeks.

We learn later that the Persians had destroyed the Anactoron in their sack of the city, and that Demeter in revenge both ensured that no Persians died on her sacred ground at Plataea (9.65.2), and was prominent in their defeat at Mycale (9.97, 101.1). Cf. *H. Dem.*; Mylonas 1961; F. Graf 1974; Bianchi 1976; Burkert 1983: 248–97; 1987; Carrière 1988: 220–30; Clinton 1992; Sourvinou-Inwood 2003b; for the sources, Farnell 1896–1909: III 343–62.

65.1 Δίκαιος: unknown elsewhere, though the same story features an Ineus in Aristodemus, *FGH* 104 F 1. His name and his father's are rare, but could be significant in this context of a divine portent. It is unusual for H. actually to name his individual sources: cf. 2.28 (a *grammatistes* of Athena), 55 (priestesses of Dodona); 3.55 (Archies of Pitana); 4.76.6 (Tymnes); 6.117 (Epizelus); 9.16 (Thersander); and perhaps Aceratus in **37**.1. He works much more with the 'social memories' of different societies, for which, cf. Gould 1989: 28–32; Luraghi 2001b.

παρὰ Μήδοισι λόγιμος: cf. **5**.2n. on the use of 'Medes'.

ἐκείρετο: not just to destroy Athenian property, but also to feed themselves. Provisioning was obviously a major problem with a force this size and, though formal arrangements were made for Greek cities to feed the army (at great cost to the contributors, 7.32, 118–20), inevitably it had largely to live off the land, especially in hostile territory.

Δημαρήτωι: king of Sparta *ca.* 515–491. He was dethroned on a false charge of illegitimacy by his colleague Cleomenes (6.61–70), whom he had opposed on a number of occasions (5.75, 6.51). He fled to Darius (6.70), and was an accessory to the choice of Xerxes as king (7.3). He accompanied Xerxes to Greece, warning him that Spartan opposition would be implacable (7.101–4, 209, 234–8). He is also said to have cunningly informed Sparta of Xerxes' intention to invade, though H. is unsure how friendly an act this was (7.239). His reward for his services to the King was cities in the Troad (6.70.2). There are many stories about Demaratus in H. which give him a prominent role: their number and complimentary character suggest they may well have come to H. from one or more of his relatives, who were still in Asia Minor in Xenophon's time (*Anab.* 2.1.3, *Hell.* 3.1.6). In book 7, Demaratus gave much advice to Xerxes, but it was not followed, and his advice here that Dicaeus not tell the King is the natural outcome of this: cf. Boedeker 1987: 196, and generally on the picture of Demaratus in H.; Hofstetter 1978: 45–6.

τῶι Θριασίωι πεδίωι: the plain around Eleusis, called after the deme of Thria. The road from Thebes followed by the Persians led to this plain.

τρισμυρίων: this was the conventional estimate of the citizen population of Athens (5.97.2; Ar. *Eccl.* 1132–3; Pl. *Symp.* 175E).

ἀποθωμάζειν . . . ὁτέων κοτε εἴη ἀνθρώπων 'they wondered who on earth caused the cloud'; κοτε emphasises their amazement, as regularly with interrogatives.

τὸν μυστικὸν Ἴακχον: during the procession to Eleusis, which took place on the fourth day of the festival (Boedromion 19 or 20), the cry was Ἴακχ' ὦ Ἴακχε (**65**.4; Ar. *Frogs* 316–17 etc.). Iacchus was a deity who took part in the procession and who, perhaps because of the similarity of name, was associated with Bacchus (F. Graf 1978: 40–78; Burkert 1983: 279). μυστικός, μύστης ('initiate') were derived by the Greeks from μύω, 'to close', especially of the eyes (cf. Chantraine 728): initiation could involve veiling of the eyes and an opening of them to a new status and life.

65.2 ἀδαήμονα 'uninitiated', <*δα- found in δι-δά-σκω, so lit. 'untaught'. It is a poetic word and a *hapax* in H., like σίνος and ἀρίδηλος below: poetic colour suits the mystical subject matter. Cf. the strong poetic colour in **3**.1. Demaratus' ignorance allows H. to tell the episode at length, even though some of his audiences will have known about Eleusis; for such 'secondary' narrators, cf. Introduction, §6.4.

εἰρέσθαί τε αὐτὸν . . . αὐτὸς δὲ εἰπεῖν '(he said that) Demaratus asked . . . and he himself replied'. For the difference in the cases of αὐτόν and αὐτός, cf. Thuc. 4.28.2 [Κλέων] οὐκ ἔφη αὐτός, ἀλλ' ἐκεῖνον στρατηγεῖν 'Cleon said that not he himself, but Nicias was general'; αὐτός refers back to the original speaker.

65.3 κατασκήψηι . . . τράπηται: the subject is the divine cloud. σκήπτω and compounds are regularly used in divine contexts; cf. ἐνεσκήψαν, **39**.2. Dust-clouds had long symbolised the death and confusion of battle (M. L. West 1997: 212–13, 228–9), so the turning of the procession towards Salamis suggests divine sanction for Themistocles' arguments in the Greek council.

65.5 ἢν γάρ τοι ἐς βασιλέα ἀνενειχθῆι: the different ideologies of Greek and Persian are important here again. In H., telling the truth to the king when it is something he might not wish to hear is often represented as dangerous. Asked for his advice by Xerxes, Demaratus once replied: 'King, do you wish me to speak the truth or what will please you?' (7.101.3; cf. also 7.10α, 7.104.1, 105; **69**.1; 9.16, 42.2; Hohti 1974). There is an implied contrast here between the fear of a tyrannical ruler and the ideal of *parrhesia* or *isegoria*, the freedom or equal right to speak, which the Greeks thought characterised their society, and which is praised by H. in 5.78. Cf. further on Artemisia, **69**.1n., for a more nuanced view of the position of those who would advise the King.

ἀποβαλέεις τὴν κεφαλήν: execution by beheading was the standard Persian custom (**90**.3); this particular phrase is found only here.

ἔχ' ἥσυχος: apparently a colloquial expression; cf. Eur. *Hipp.* 1313, *IA* 1133; Ar. *Pl.* 127; cf. Eur. *Or.* 1273 (ἄφοβος ἔχε); Stevens 1976: 34–5.

65.6 ἐκ . . . φωνῆς: ἐκ here is presumably 'after', because 'out of' does not sit easily with 'voice'; cf. **12**.2 ἐκ δὲ τῆς ναυμαχίης ὄμβρος τε λάβρος καὶ ῥεύματα ἰσχυρά.

Δημαρήτου . . . καταπτόμενος 'appealing to Demaratus and others as witnesses . . .' This is a Herodotean usage (here and 6.68.1); the genitive is partitive. As with the account of the salvation of Delphi (**39**.2), H. ends a supernatural episode with evidence to support its truthfulness, without necessarily committing himself to its reality.

66–7 Xerxes consults his leaders

The story of the Persian fleet is picked up from their gruesome sightseeing at Thermopylae (**26**). H. now looks at the question of where to fight from the Persian side, as Xerxes sends Mardonius to seek the views of the allied commanders. As with the Greeks, a figure with the minority view is given a long speech: Artemisia's arguments further corroborate Themistocles' case, but the commander-in-chief decides to fight at Salamis. Divine signs and the wiser human deliberations both point to the advantages of Salamis to the Greeks. After religious miracles, we turn briefly to hard statistics.

66.1 τὸ τρῶμα 'military disaster', cf. 6.132 μετὰ δὲ τὸ ἐν Μαραθῶνι τρῶμα.

Φαλήρωι: the main seaport of Athens as late as 490 (6.116), but gradually replaced from 493/2 by the Piraeus, developed by Themistocles, which had more shelter and more harbours (Thuc. 1.93.3–7).

ὡς μὲν ἐμοὶ δοκέειν: μέν is a weakened form of μήν 'certainly' (cf. Skt. affirmative particle *smā*, μὰ τὸν Δία etc.; Chantraine 695), and was originally an emphatic particle. H. often uses it thus with the first person, when it is not picked up by a δέ (*GP* 359–61; *Lex. s.v.* II 2 d). Its purpose here is to present H.'s opinion in a challenging manner: one might have expected there would have been fewer ships, but H. will have none of it. For δοκέειν as an absolute infinitive, cf. **22**.3n.

οὐκ ἐλάσσονες ἐόντες: despite H.'s confident expression of opinion, there are serious problems. H. says that at Sepias, a promontory near Aphetae (**4**.1n.) there were 1,207 + 120 = 1,327 ships (7.184.1 + 7.185.1). Storms had claimed some 600 (7.190, **13**), but it is unlikely that these numbers could have been made up by the 120 Greek ships mentioned in §2, between the leaving of Artemisium and arrival at Phaleron. H. may be trying here to match Aeschylus' figure of 1207 ships at Salamis (*Pers.* 341–3). The actual numbers are unrecoverable, but H.'s figures are much too high. Figures for the size of later Persian fleets suggest that the number of fighting ships in the navy was not likely to be much more than 300, though some scholars argue for up to 600 (cf. Cawkwell 2005: 260–7). Note that H. says in **13** that there was a near-equality of numbers. As for the land forces, given the lack of opposition they faced, they may not have been substantially reduced in number, though even here H. may be said to make no allowance for the natural reduction in numbers, through illness, garrisons left etc. The figure of 1,207 has been questioned on the ground that it is formed out of two 'typical' numbers, a multiple of twelve and seven (Fehling 1989: 232–4); but see Rubincam 2003 against the notion that H. is overfond of such typical numbers.

ἀριθμόν: accusative of respect.

66.2 **Μηλιέας κτλ.:** for the submission of Malians, Locrians and Boeotians, cf. 7.132.1. It was a Malian who guided the Persians along the secret path to Thermopylae (7.213–15). The Carystians will be punished in **121**. For the Andrians, cf. **108–11**. One Tenian ship will come over to the Greeks before Salamis, bringing confirmation of the Persian blockade (**82**).

πρότερον: in **46**.3–4. They joined the King after the battles at Artemisium.

οὐνόματα: the accusative is unusual with ἐπιμιμνήσκομαι, though it is found with pronouns; cf. the unusual mixture of cases in 6.136.2 τῆς τε μάχης . . . ἐπιμεμνημένοι καὶ τὴν Λήμνου αἵρεσιν.

67.1 ἐκαραδόκεον 'awaited the outcome of'. The word appears to be compounded of καρᾱ- (perhaps = 'completion') and the root of δέχομαι (cf. δωρο-δοκέω 'take bribes'; Chantraine 496). This neutrality did not save Paros from financial penalties (**112**).

67.2 προΐζετο 'he sat on a prominent seat at the front', cf. 4.88.1 Δαρεῖον ἐν προεδρίηι κατήμενον, 7.44, and *prohedria*, the right to front seats at public events (1.54.2, 6.57.2, 9.73.3). **The King in majesty**. Though H.'s economical narrative style says nothing of it, despite the fact that he would have known Mandrocles' painting dedicated in the Heraeum on Samos of Darius ἐν προεδρίηι κατήμενον watching his men cross the Bosporus (4.88), this would have been a scene of great splendour. The audience-scene that once decorated the North Stair of the Persepolis *Apadāna* offers clues, if it represents the reality (cf. Schmidt 1 163–9, with Pls. 119–23, and 132–4, with Pls. 96–9). The King sits on a pleated robe on an ornate straight-backed throne, under an embroidered canopy and with a footstool. His left hand holds a lotus flower, his right a long staff with a globular pommel. Hair and beard are elaborately styled, and he wears a crenellated tiara (*kidaris*), which he alone was allowed to wear upright (Xen. *Anab.* 2.5.23; *Cyr.* 8.3.13; Plut. *Art.* 26.2); bracelets, necklaces and ear-ornaments have left their marks on the reliefs, and Xen. *Cyr.* 1.3.2 speaks of 'eye-liner, facial cosmetics and false hair, in the Median manner' (cf. Ar. *Ach.* 119–21). He wears Persian dress: in Xen. *Cyr.* 8.3.13 Cyrus wore 'a purple tunic shot with white, which none but the king may wear, trousers dyed purple and a purple mantle (*kandys*)'. Xerxes would also have been accompanied by men of the highest noblility, such as the 'Spear-bearer' (*arshtibara*, H. 3.139; **26**.3n.) and 'Bow-bearer' (*vaçabara*). Cf. below and Briant 2002: 216–23; Bittner 1985.

ταξίαρχοι: usually leaders of the ranks of land troops, but cf. 7.99.1 for its use in a naval context.

ἵζοντο ὥς σφι βασιλεὺς ἑκάστωι τιμὴν ἐδεδώκεε 'they sat according to the rank the King had assigned to each amongst them'. σφι is nearly redundant with ἑκάστωι, but can be explained as a generalising ethic dative, 'where they were concerned'. Seating people in an order that displayed their status comparative to others was an important principle in Achaemenid society. Essentially, the 'nearer', in all senses, one was to the King, the higher one's status and potential influence: in 1.134.2, H. sets it down as a general principle of the Persians that 'they honour most those who live nearest them... and least those who live furthest away'. Physical proximity to the King expressed in symbolic terms authority and power. On the monuments, the Crown Prince stands next to the King, and the 'Bow-bearer' and 'Spear-bearer' stand nearby; size also shows the relative importance of the figures. This hierarchisation is noted a number of times in Greek sources and was also maintained in the military camp, where the King's tent was at the centre and his forces were arranged around him, the most trusted closest to him (Xen. *Cyr.* 8.5.8, cf. 1–14, 2.1.25–8). In dining too, there were various hierarchical systems: the king dined alone, with the most honoured diners (*homotrapezoi*, 9.16.2; Xen. *Anab.* 1.8.25, 9.31; also called *syndeipnoi*) in a room close by; the next most honoured dined outside (Heracleides, *ap.* Athen. 145–6A). Xenophon gives Cyrus a strict but shifting *placement* at table, which again indicated where each man stood in his estimation at any particular time (Xen. *Cyr.* 8.4.3–5). Cf. also Xen. *Oec.* 4.8; Briant 2002: 307–12. οἱ περὶ αὐτόν is a regular phrase for close familiars of the king: cf. also Hsch. ἀζῆται· οἱ ἐγγύτατοι τοῦ βασιλέως and Avestan *āzāta-* 'noble'.

Σιδώνιος βασιλεύς: in the review of Xerxes' troops at Doriscus, after he has listed the Persian commanders of the fleet, H. again gives the Sidonian king, Tetramnestus son of Anysus, pride of place as first among the 'most notable', along with the Tyrian Matten (or Mapen; 7.98). H. presumably means these men were the kings, but there is a problem that the known royal names in Sidon at this period appear to be Tabnit and his successor Eshmunazar (Lewis 1997: 355). There is no evidence for Tyrian royal names. The Sidonian king presumably occupied this position of honour because the Sidonians provided the best ships (7.44, 96.1, 99.3), in which Xerxes chose to sail (7.100.2, 128.2). Sidon and Tyre are the main cities of the Phoenicians (**85**.1n.), and the kings of Phoenicia seem to have enjoyed a measure of independence, though they were still subjects of the Persian empire (cf. Xen. *Cyr.* 7.4.2).

68 Artemisia's advice

68.1 Ἀρτεμισίη: daughter of Lygdamis, tyrant of Halicarnassus, and a Cretan mother, she arouses H.'s particular wonder, 'as a woman going to war against Greece' (7.99.1). On the death of her husband, she had assumed control over Halicarnassus, Cos, Nisyros and Calymnos, though she was herself under Persian rule. She brought five of the finest ships, and followed Xerxes voluntarily. Her son (or perhaps nephew) Lygdamis ruled after her, in a turbulent period during which H. was exiled (to which the Halicarnassian property law, ML 32 = Fornara no. 70, may refer; Introduction, pp. 27–8). Cf. Munson 1988.

Women who ruled in their own right are not common in the ancient Near East: women had influence, but usually as queens-consort or princesses. Apart from legendary figures, the best-known ancient female rulers are the queen of Sheba (*Saba'*, southern Arabia; cf. 1 Kings 10:1–13; 2 Chronicles 9:1–12), the Egyptian Pharaoh Hatshepsut (1502–1482 BC) and Semiramis, who was in real life Sammu-ramat, mother of the Neo-Assyrian king Adad-nirari III (810–783). She played an active role in her son's reign, but was never the actual ruler of Assyria. In Greek and Armenian tradition however, she was raised to legendary status (cf. 1.184–7; Diod. 2.4–20 (from Ctesias)), and prompted Arrian's in fact unhistorical remark that 'after Semiramis, it had been accepted in Asia that women should rule men' (*Anab.* 1.23.7). In later Greek historiography, the role played by women behind the throne was transformed into a scheming dominance, in which those other non-men, eunuchs, played an equally ruthless and unscrupulous part; cf. especially Pl. *Legg.* 694C–696A, who marks the greatness of the Persian kings as in inverse proportion to the amount of time that they spent being educated by women in the palace. Wiesehöfer 1996: 79–88 discusses how Greek sources distort the Persian reality. For women in Persia generally, cf. Brosius 1996. For Greece, cf. Mania, who ruled in Aeolis under Pharnabazus (Xen. *HG* 3.1.10–14). Elsewhere, less certainly historical are Tomyris, queen of the Massagetae (H. 1.205–14), and Zarinaea, queen of the Scythians (Ctesias, *FGH* 688 F 7–8). For Caria, Artemisia, sister-wife of Mausolus, and satrap Ada (Arrian above).

68 The speech falls into two parts, each introduced by a statement of her intention to give her opinion (α 1 δίκαιόν ἐστι ἀποδείκνυσθαι ~ β φράσω). The first consists of short clauses and rhetorical questions, with balanced phrases (οὐκ ἔχεις μὲν . . . ἔχεις δέ; ἐμποδὼν δέ τοι οὐδείς . . . οἱ δέ τοι ἀντέστησαν): it is a rhetorical appeal to Xerxes' good sense. The second consists of two coordinated conditionals (ἢν μὲν μὴ ἐπειχθῇς ναυμαχίην ποιεύμενος . . . ἢν δὲ αὐτίκα ἐπειχθῇς ναυμαχῆσαι): the first is elaborately developed grammatically, making its point now by an appeal to logic rather than rhetoric, with a clear progression of ideas (οὐ γὰρ . . . ἀλλὰ . . . οὔτε γὰρ . . . οὔτε . . . οὐδέ); the second crisply expresses her fear. The speech ends again rhetorically with dismissive remarks about the King's warriors in terms of good men having bad servants, which picks up the dismissive comparison of Persian and Greek warriors in terms of women and men at the start of the speech. The forthright nature of her speech is remarkable.

H. has Artemisia make her speech to Mardonius as if she were in fact addressing Xerxes. In Near Eastern or early Greek poetry, messengers will repeat their message to one or more people in the words in which they were given: in *Il.* 2.1–75, Zeus' words are presented three times, by Zeus, Oneiros and Agamemnon. Homer tends to change from third- to second-person pronouns in the repetition, but this device can seem slightly artificial. By having Artemisia address *both* Mardonius (Μαρδόνιε) *and* Xerxes (δέσποτα twice, ὦ βασιλεῦ at the end), and use the second person, H. cleverly superimposes the two recitations of the speech and avoids repetition. For an even more complex example of speech-construction, cf. Alexander's speech in **140**.

The speech reinforces the rightness of Themistocles' arguments: the case that Salamis is salvation for the Greeks is strongly made, and yet the Greek commander initially cannot see it, and the Persian nonetheless decides to fight there.

68α.1 εἰπεῖν μοι imperatival infinitive, cf. **20**.2n.; μοι is an ethic dative = 'please'. Though Xerxes goes amongst his forces, he cannot be addressed directly even by the leading allied monarchs. In general, the King had a group of close advisers drawn from the aristocracy, whom he would consult or entrust with delicate missions; otherwise, access to him was very restricted (H. 1.99, 3.84.2). The advisers were called in OP something like **vith(a)puça* 'prince' or in Aramaic *br byt'* 'son of the (royal) house' (Ezra 7.15; Esther 1.14). The titles were honorific and did not imply a blood-relationship. (cf. Xen. *Anab.* 1.5.15, 1.9.20–8, 6.4; Briant 2002: 307–12).

οὔτε ἐλάχιστα ἀποδεξαμένη 'because I rendered service that was not the least'.

δέσποτα: this address is used in Greek when the speaker is trying to be particularly deferential; at the end, she will use βασιλεῦ, which implies that the addressee is a figure of great power, remote from other beings (Dickey 1996: 90–8). Artemisia begins with a *captatio benevolentiae*, an attempt to secure the goodwill of the addressee through a humble address, marked by hesitation and caution, and ends sententiously with a bold statement of warning tempered by emphasis on Xerxes' grandeur (n.b. σοὶ δὲ ἐόντι ἀρίστωι). Mardonius uses the terms in a similar fashion in **100**, 2, 4.

τὴν δὲ ἐοῦσαν γνώμην . . . ἀποδείκνυσθαι 'reveal my real opinion'. δέ is used after a vocative at the start of a speech to express a contrast with what has preceded, in this case the views of the other commanders: cf. 1.32.1, 115.2 etc. (*GP* 174–5). γνώμην is picked up by τά: cf. 2.51.4 λόγον . . . τὰ . . . δεδήλωται. ἀποδείκνυσθαι puns in Herodotean manner on ἀποδεξαμένη: her display of valour justifies her exposition of her opinion (**1**.1n.).

ἄνδρες γυναικῶν: this remark has an ironic tone, since it is spoken by a woman. The idea of gender reversal is regularly associated with Artemisia's appearances in H.: we have noted H.'s own wonder at her (**68**.1n.); on seeing her prowess in battle, Xerxes comments, 'my men have become women, my women men' (**88**.3); and in **93**.2 the Athenians have put a price on her head, 'because they thought it scandalous that a woman should campaign against Athens'. The jealousy of some of the Persian allies at her popularity with the King no doubt had a gender element too (**69**.1). H.'s and Xerxes' admiration contrasts notably with the attitude of these allies and the Athenians.

68α.2 τί δὲ πάντως δεῖ 'why is it absolutely necessary?'; πάντως with δεῖ, as often in H.

οὐκ ἔχεις μέν: οὐκ, standing thus outside the μέν-clause, negatives both it and the δέ-clause.

ἀπήλλαξαν 'fared'; cf. **39**.1n.

68β.1 ἐπειχθῇς: aorist passive subjunctive of ἐπείγομαι 'be in a hurry'.

68β.2 διασκεδᾷς: the 'Attic' future in -εω, so-called because other dialects used the form in -σω. The Attic future was formed on analogy with the -εω futures of verb-stems ending in ρ, λ, μ, ν (e.g. βαλέω). The origin of the -εω forms is from the future suffix **-ese/o*, which became **-e^{e}/o*, with the loss of intervocalic *-s-* (Sihler §500.3). Thus *διασκεδά-σεις > *διασκεδα-εις > διασκεδᾶις.

πάρα: i.e. πάρεστι.

οὐδὲ αὐτοὺς οἰκός: αὐτούς is picked up and redefined by τοὺς ἐκεῖθεν αὐτῶν ἥκοντας, ἐκεῖθεν being the Peloponnese; the turn of phrase is colloquial.

ἀτρεμιεῖν: the future infinitive after οἰκός is unusual, the aorist (or sometimes present) being the regular tense; it is used on the analogy of the use of the future with verbs like ἐλπίζω (Smyth §1868b).

68γ ὁ ναυτικὸς στρατός κτλ.: almost a quotation of Aesch. *Pers.* 728 ναυτικὸς στρατὸς κακωθεὶς πεζὸν ὤλεσε στρατόν. προσδηλήσεται 'damage in addition'.

πρὸς δέ, ὦ βασιλεῦ, καὶ τόδε ἐς θυμὸν βαλεῦ: an old epic form of expression, e.g. *Il.* 4.39 ἄλλο δέ τοι ἐρέω, σὺ δ' ἐνὶ φρεσὶ βάλλεο σῇισιν (M. L. West 1997: 232–3). This august phrase introduces her coda on Xerxes' excellence.

δοῦλοι: here again Greek and Persian perceptions diverge (cf. **54** ἐνθύμιον n.). In a speech expressing contempt for certain peoples, δοῦλος is clearly pejorative, and reflects the standard Greek view that the peoples of the Persian empire were simply slaves: for Jason, king of Pherae, the Persian King was the only free man in the whole empire (Xen. *HG* 6.1.12). It does not, however, reflect the Persian reality. δοῦλος translates OP *bandaka*, cognate with **banda*- 'bond': cf. Darius' letter to Gadatas, where he addresses him as Γαδάται δούλωι (ML 12.3–4 = Fornara 35). Gadatas' precise status is uncertain, though probably high, if he received a letter from the King. Certainly, on the Bisitun inscription (DB = Brosius no. 44), the high-ranking nobles sent by Darius to suppress the various revolts are regularly *manā bandaka*, 'my *bandaka*.' The word thus indicates at once a bond of loyalty and a subjection to the King, the precise nature of which no doubt depended on the rank of the person in question. It is unlike δοῦλος therefore, which conveys a more scornful tone. Greek preserves the basic idea e.g. in warriors as θεράποντες Ἄρηος, a carpenter as 'slave (δμωιός) of Athena' (M. L. West 1997: 225). For the girdle amongst Iranian peoples as symbolising links between men, cf. the way in which, when Orontes, a traitor to Cyrus the Younger, was condemned to death, at Cyrus' order all those who had tried him 'arose, even his kinsmen, and took him by the girdle to show he was condemned to death' (Xen. *Anab.* 1.6.10). In general, cf. Missiou 1993; Briant 2002: 324–6, 491.

ἐν συμμάχων λόγωι . . . εἶναι 'are counted as your allies'; cf. 3.125.3 ἐν ἀνδραπόδων λόγωι (*Lex. s.v.* 5f).

Αἰγύπτιοι: **17**.1n.

Κύπριοι καὶ Κίλικες: by 525, the Cyprians were under the control of Cambyses, and took part in his campaign against Egypt (3.19.3). They provided 150 ships, and were dressed like Greeks, except that their leaders had *mitrai* ('turbans') and their men *kithones* (7.90). Their history was much tied up with those of the Cilicians (**14**.2n.). They are not depicted at Persepolis nor listed as subject peoples.

Παμφύλιοι: the district to the west of Cilicia, with a heterogeneous population. Little is known of Persian rule here, except that it stopped in 469 (Mellink, *CAH*² IV 225–6). They provided 30 ships, and were armed like Greeks (7.91). They are not depicted at Persepolis nor listed amongst subject peoples.

69–70 Xerxes decides to fight at Salamis

§2 is a remarkable instance of how the opposition between Greeks and barbarians can be deconstructed in H. In theory, the Greek camp operates in a relatively democratic way, with decisions made by the assembled commanders, whilst the Persians are ruled by a monarch. In practice, here at least, Themistocles acts in an autocratic manner in defiance of the other commanders, whilst the King gives the order to follow the majority verdict.

69.1 ὅσοι μὲν . . . οἱ δέ: cf. the contrasting views on the first Greek attack at Artemisium attributed to the Ionians (**10**.2–3); very similar language is used.

συμφορὴν . . . πρὸς βασιλέα lit. 'thought her words a catastrophe, as from one who would suffer some evil at the hands of the King'. This episode shows better than **65**.5 (see n.) the nature of the relationship between the King and those who would advise him. In Achaemenid ideology *Arta* 'truth, justice, right' is set against *Drauga* 'the Lie', as in Darius' epitaph: 'I desire what is Right. I am not a friend of the man who follows the Lie' (DNb (= Brosius 103) §3). *Arta* also has a strong political element, what was 'right' being determined by what helped the King and his dynasty. So here, Xerxes is pleased with Artemisia's expression of opinion because, though it goes against what he wants, she has previously shown herself loyal (σπουδαίην §2), and is now again clearly consulting his interests. Paradoxically, whilst believing that Persian Kings could not be truthfully addressed, Greek writers, not quite understanding the full meaning of *Arta*, interpreted it as a general emphasis in Persian education on just behaviour, especially in truth-telling: H. 1.136.2 'from their fifth to their twentieth year, the Persians teach their sons three things only – horse-riding, archery and telling the truth (ἀληθίζεσθαι)'; cf. Xen. *Anab.* 1.9.3, *Cyr.* 1.2.6; Strabo 15.3.18. This idea runs into trouble in the face of e.g. Darius' casuistical justification of lying in 3.72.2–5. Cf. Briant 2002: 327–30; Wiesehöfer 1996: 79–88.

αὐτῆι, ἅτε . . . τετιμημένης: the usual distinction between ἅτε and ὡς + participle (cf. **7**.2n.) suggests that this reason, as opposed to those here introduced by ὡς, belongs to H. But the distinction is not absolute, and this reason belongs naturally to Artemisia's detractors: stylistic variation has determined the choice. The genitive after the dative pronoun αὐτῆι is Homeric: cf. *Od.* 9.256–7 ἡμῖν δ᾽ αὖτε κατεκλάσθη φίλον ἦτορ | δεισάντων φθόγγον (K–G II 111). This case is different from Ἀρτεμισίηι . . . πεισομένης above, where πεισομένης is genitive dependent on λόγους.

κρίσι 'reply', as in 3.34.5, though elsewhere 'investigation, interrogation'.

69.2 τάδε καταδόξας κτλ. 'being thoroughly convinced, first that his forces had deliberately fought badly off Euboea on the grounds that he was not there – but then he had decided to watch them himself as they fought in the sea-battle.' The construction changes in the δέ-clause from accusative and infinitive depending on καταδόξας to indicative; this has the effect of emphasising the δέ-clause (*GP* 378–9). For the importance of performing well before the King, cf. **85**.3n.

'Of all the Oriental kings, Xerxes is the one who most wants to see and supervise everything for himself' (Immerwahr 1966: 182); cf. 7.43, 44, 56.1, 59.2–3, 100, 128, 212.1; cf. 4.88 for Darius; also Xen. *Anab.* 1.9.14–15, *Cyr.* 8.6.16, *Oec.* 4.6–11; for fear of shaming oneself, cf. H. 6.9.1, 7.107.1, **15**.1, **86**). Achieving recognition by the King often meant catching his eye, since he watched reviews and battles, and inspected lands. Greek sources talk much of the King's 'Eyes' and 'Ears', who would inform him of deeds of all kinds (Aes. *Pers.* 979; H. 1.114.2; Ar. *Ach.* 92; Xen. *Cyr.* 8.2.10–12), but the Achaemenid sources do not mention them (cf. Briant 2002: 343–4). Xerxes' decision to fight may have been influenced by a desire to deal with the Greek navy, so that he could berth his fleet safely somewhere for the winter.

70 If tactically it is not clear why the Persians deploy into their battle-line at this late stage of the day, this movement aids the creation of suspense in the build-up to Salamis. As in the attack on Delphi (**37–9**n.), H. uses the technique of triple narration. (i) The Persians take up position, but we then learn of the Isthmus wall, the Greek deliberations, and Sicinnus' arrival at the Persian camp. (ii) They manoeuvre into position again (**76**), but then we learn of more Greek deliberations, the arrival of Aristeides at the Greek camp, and even further deliberations. (iii) The Greeks prepare for the battle (**83**.1), but a speech of Themistocles intervenes, before the battle actually begins.

οὐκ ἐξέχρησέ σφι ἡ ἡμέρη 'there was not enough of the day left to them'. There has been some telescoping of time in these actions of the Persians: things could not have happened quite so quickly.

70.2 ἀρρώδεον ὅτι: verbs of fearing can be followed by a causal clause introduced by ὅτι; cf. Xen. *Hell.* 3.5.10 ὅτι δὲ πολλῶν ἄρχουσι, μὴ φοβηθῆτε (*M&T* §377).

μέλλοιεν: in indirect discourse, when a cause or reason is attributed to someone else by a narrator or speaker, the mood can be optative (*M&T* §714). For the shift to the indicative πολιορκήσονται, cf. **26**.2n.

ἀπολαμφθέντες = Attic ἀποληφθέντες.

71–3 The Greek wall at the Isthmus

We now briefly see what is happening further south. **73** is a catalogue of shame to be set against the more glorious list in **43–8**, and H. is forthright in his condemnation, which picks up his earlier firmly expressed opinion that the wall was anyway quite useless (7.139). On H.'s opinion on the use of walls as a means of defence, here and elsewhere, cf. Bowie 2006.

71.1 ἐπὶ τὴν Πελοπόννησον 'in the direction of the Peloponnese'; they did not in the end get as far as Megara (9.14).

καίτοι 'and yet' (*GP* 556).

Κλεόμβροτος was the youngest of the triplets, the others being Leonidas and Dorieus, born unexpectedly to the previously infertile first wife of King Anaxandrides (5.41.3). Leonidas succeeded to his father's kingship (7.205.1), and after his death Cleombrotus ruled as regent for Leonidas' son Pleistarchus, but died shortly after leading the army of wall-builders from the Isthmus (9.10). Cleombrotus' son was King Pausanias.

71.2 τὴν Σκειρωνίδα ὁδόν: that part of the road that ran through Eleusis and Megara to the Isthmus. Just after Megara, it becomes a vertiginous path, rough and crumbling, that runs along a ledge six or seven hundred feet above the sea: there is a graphic description of it in Frazer II 546–8. It was thus easy to block. It took its name from the mythical Sciron, who in Megarian tradition was a polemarch who opened the route, but in Athenian tradition was a brigand who asked travellers to wash his feet and, when they obliged, kicked them into the sea. It was also the site of other tragic falls in mythology: cf. Paus. 1.44.6–10.

ἤνετο 'was being brought to completion'. In spring 479, according to 9.7.1, the battlements were being put on (but see F&M *ad loc.* and on 9.8.2 for the uncertainty in H. as to whether it was completed or not). The line of the wall is uncertain: Wiseman 1963 argued from finds that it ran for five miles from Lechaeum to Cenchreae (cf. Diod. 11.16.3), but Gregory 1993: 5 suggests that a line further north and just south of the canal would have been strategically better.

72.1 **Ὀλύμπια δὲ καὶ Κάρνεια παροιχώκεε:** H. refers rather scornfully to the time when, in the month of Carneian Apollo, on learning that Xerxes was at Pieria, the Greeks mustered their armies, but the Spartans refused to let any of their forces march out, apart from the small number with Leonidas, until the end of the Carneia festival on 18 September; the other Peloponnesians used the Olympics as a similar excuse (7.205.3–206; cf. **1**.2n.). The Carneia was a late summer festival dedicated to Apollo, and the most important festival for the Dorian peoples. We are not well informed about it, but it involved *inter alia* ritual imitation of military life; the race of the *Staphylodromoi* 'Grape Runners' to determine the coming fortune of the city; and important musical competitions which drew competitors from all over Greece. It was connected by the Dorians with the capture of Troy and the Dorian Migration. Cf. Burkert 1985a: 234–6; for the importance of performing all rituals correctly amongst the Spartans, cf. 9.7.1 where the Spartans had not done what the Athenians expected because 'they considered it of the greatest importance to arrange all the affairs of the god' (see F&M *ad loc.*), and generally Parker 1988.

παροιχώκεε: i.e. they had no festivals to use as an excuse for not helping the other Greeks. This recalls how, on previous occasions when the Carneia was being celebrated, the Spartans had first of all refused to come immediately to Marathon (6.106), and had then sent Leonidas to Thermopylae with only a token force, intending to send the rest after the festival (7.206); the Olympic games were also used as an excuse in the latter case. H. is even more explicit in his condemnation of these peoples in **73**.3.

73.1 **αὐτόχθονα:** claims of autochthony, i.e. being born of the earth where they lived, were used to justify a race's right to inhabit its lands; cf. Thuc. 1.2.5–6 for Athens. Such claims could be reinforced by tracing one's lineage back to an animal connected with the earth, such as a snake: cf. **55**.1n. On the Arcadians, cf. 1.146.1, 2.171.3.

Κυνούριοι: possibly the inhabitants of a strip of land on the Argolic Gulf south of Argos, but see Gomme, Andrewes and Dover on Thuc. 5.67.2, p. 108–9 for the problems of locating Orneae and Cynuria.

ἐκ μὲν . . . ἐκ μέντοι 'though they never left the Peloponnese, nevertheless they did leave their own original land'. They settled on the north coast, after being driven out by the Dorians: cf. 1.145, 7.94; Paus. 5.1.1–2; Strabo 8.7.1.

73.2 **Δωριέες . . . Δρύοπες:** cf. **31**n., **43**n.

Αἰτωλοί: cf. Paus. 5.3.5–7, where the Aetolians are given Elis as a reward for the help they gave the Dorians in their migration into the Peloponnese.

Λήμνιοι: they were the descendants of the Argonauts, who had stayed on Lemnos and married local women, before being driven out by the Pelasgians. They then returned to their original home, where they took over the land of the Paroreatae in Triphylia in the west of the Peloponnese (4.145–8).

Ἀσίνη: in southern Messenia; cf. Paus. 4.14.3, 34.9–12.

73.3 **Ἴωνες . . . καὶ [οἱ] περίοικοι:** a vexed passage, which has not been satisfactorily explained. Pausanias, at 2.25.6, derives the Orneatae from Orneus, son of Erechtheus, which would give them an Ionian origin, but he then gives an Argive origin in 3.2.2. The reference to them as περίοικοι is often explained by the suggestion that the Argives had reduced them to a status like that of the περίοικοι in Laconia.

ὑπό τε Ἀργείων ἀρχόμενοι καὶ τοῦ χρόνου 'as a result of being ruled by the Argives and by the passage of time'. ὑπό governs τοῦ χρόνου, but in a different sense: ὑπὸ Ἀργείων is a genitive of the agent dependent on ἀρχόμενοι; ὑπὸ τοῦ χρόνου is instrumental. This is stranger than the zeugma in **106**.4: Πανιώνιον μέν νυν οὕτω περιῆλθε ἥ τε τίσις καὶ Ἑρμότιμος.

κατέατο = ἐκαθῆντο, from καθίημι.

ἐμήδιζον: on medising generally, cf. Gillis 1979: 39–81.

74–5 Greek dissatisfaction and Themistocles' message to Xerxes

This section is structured in a manner similar to **56–64**. Panic leads to discussion of tactics and the majority is against remaining at Salamis. Themistocles takes the initiative and, with the aid of a confidant, makes another secret approach, this time to the Persians. Since the arguments among the Greeks were the same (**74**.2 περὶ τῶν αὐτῶν), H. says nothing more of them, and direct speech is used for the crucial moment, Sicinnus' message to the Persians (**75**.2–3).

74.1 περὶ τοῦ παντὸς θέοντες lit. 'running (the race) that involved everything', i.e. 'fighting for their lives'. The metaphor of the 'race' for someone's life is first found in *Il.* 22.161 περὶ ψυχῆς θέον Ἕκτορος ἱπποδάμοιο, and is common in tragedy (Eur. *Alc.* 489, *Or.* 878 etc.). The text is uncertain. The MSS have περὶ τοῦ παντὸς δρόμου θέοντες, but δρόμου seems otiose, and it seems best to delete it with Lobeck as a gloss on παντός. This may be supported by the fact that elsewhere H. does not use δρόμος in this expression: cf. 7.57.1, **102**.3 (though note ἀγῶνας here), **140α**.4, 9.37.2; contrast Ar. *Wasps* 376–7 τὸν περὶ ψυχῆς δρόμον δραμεῖν.

τῆισι νηυσὶ . . . ἐλλάμψεσθαι 'they did not expect that they would distinguish themselves with their navy'. ἐλλάμψεσθαι is the future middle infinitive of ἐλλάμπομαι. There is an element of desperation here, since a naval defeat would mean the Persians could circumvent the blocked road with their fleet.

ὅμως ταῦτα πυνθανόμενοι 'in spite of learning of these preparations'; ὅμως renders the concessive force of the participle explicit (Smyth §2082).

οὐκ οὕτω . . . ὡς περὶ τῆι Πελοποννήσωι: again, worry about their homeland dominates the Peloponnesians' thinking. For the expression, contrast the Persians in Susa in **99**.2 οὐκ οὕτω δὲ περὶ τῶν νεῶν ἀχθόμενοι . . . ὡς περὶ αὐτῶι Ξέρξηι δειμαίνοντες.

74.2 ἕως 'for a time', contrasting with τέλος δέ; ἕως thus as an adverb = τέως is Homeric.

θῶμα ποιεύμενοι = θωμάζοντες.

ἐξερράγη: the subject, 'their discontent', has to be supplied from the context.

οἱ μὲν . . . Ἀθηναῖοι δέ: these nominatives are used as if ἔλεγον not ἐλέγετο had preceded.

μηδὲ . . . μάχεσθαι 'they should certainly not stay and fight'; μή is used as a negative in indirect discourse in emphatic statements, especially with reference to the future (Smyth §§2723–7; *M&T* §685).

75 This story of Themistocles' treating with the enemy commander may seem almost fanciful, but it is already found in Aes. *Pers.* 353–73, where the message, sent at nightfall (364–5) not at night (μέσαι νύκτες, **76**.1), is more deceptive, and actually causes the Persian fleet to move. In Aeschylus the message says nothing of Greek discord, the unity of the Greeks being a major theme of the tragedy. At *Pers.* 355 Themistocles is just ἀνὴρ . . . Ἕλλην ἐξ Ἀθηναίων στρατοῦ, but Aeschylus does not name individual Greeks. Given the odds stacked against the Greeks and the likelihood that Xerxes would have imagined (if he did not know) that the Greeks would have disagreed about the wisdom of opposing him, such a message would not have come as a great surprise to the Persians. Here, they could have thought, was a man who wished to become a 'benefactor' of the King (**85**.3n.) by betraying his compatriots, an act which, in the circumstances, must have seemed to the Persians eminently sensible for anyone who wished to survive the inevitable Greek defeat and enslavement. For the question of how Themistocles could have plausibly contacted Xerxes again after tricking him in this way, cf. **110**.2–3n.

75.1 ἑσσοῦτο τῆι γνώμηι 'he was losing the argument'. The imperfect shows the matter is still open; contrast the perfect tense in **130**.3 κατὰ μέν νυν τὴν θάλασσαν ἑσσωμένοι ἦσαν τῶι θυμῶι, 'as far as fighting at sea was concerned, their confidence had gone'.

Σίκιννος: here he is just Themistocles' messenger, but in Aeschylus he is talked of as an '*alastor* or evil *daimon*' (*Pers.* 354). His fame and name were no doubt the reason that later tradition attributed the satyric *sikinnis* dance to him (Clem. Alex. *Paed.* 1.7.55.2).

παιδαγωγός: the slave who took boys to school and generally supervised their conduct and education. Another *paidagogos* will supervise the evacuation of Xerxes' children after the battle (**104**).

Θεσπιέα: Thespiae needed new citizens, having lost 700 at Thermopylae (cf. **25**.1n.).

75.2 διαδράντας 'once they start to run away'; the aorist participle can describe an action which coincides with the time of the main verb, and marks its beginning and development (Smyth §1872c).

75.3 καὶ τοὺς μή: μή is used with participles describing a class or group, οὐ when specific people are meant (Smyth §2734).

76 Manoeuvres of the Persian ships

It is here that the problems of understanding H.'s account of the preliminaries and of the battle begin. His account in summary is as follows. The Persian fleet, after its sightseeing at Thermopylae (**24**), came down the Euripus channel to Phaleron (**66**); H. says the whole fleet, except the Parians, went there (**67**.1 πάντες). Having decided to fight in the narrows, Xerxes ordered his fleet to put to sea towards Salamis, arrayed in order, but the late hour meant they simply prepared to fight the next day (**70**.1); why they did this and whether they returned to their bases is not clear. It is also perhaps likely that events took place over more days than H. allows. Sicinnus then took his message (**75**), and in the present chapter the Persians decide to act immediately. They do three things, articulated by τοῦτο μὲν . . . τοῦτο δὲ . . . τοῦτο δέ: (i) they land 'many of the Persians' on the island of Psyttaleia; (ii) they advance their west wing towards Salamis κυκλούμενοι, i.e. 'in an encircling motion' (cf. **10**.1), so that 'the Greeks should not be able to flee but be hemmed in on Salamis'; (iii) the ships stationed off Ceos and Cynosura put to sea, and 'held all the strait as far as Munychia'. The problems with all this are discussed below. For bibliography on Salamis generally, cf. **83–96**n.

The chapter interweaves the two manoeuvres in an ABBA pattern: Psyttaleia; movement of ships; reasons for moving ships; reasons for Psyttaleia. The strategies are carefully worked out, but neither will succeed.

76.1 Ψυττάλειαν: this island is important for any reconstruction, but its identification is disputed. It is described as 'between Salamis and the mainland' and where 'men and wrecks would be most likely washed ashore, because it stood in the πόρος of the battle'. The meaning of πόρος is not clear: it could mean the heart of the battle, or where battle and especially the wreckage would drift. There are two possible identifications of Psyttaleia, Lipsokoutali or Ayios Yeoryios (see map 3).

In favour of Lipsokoutali are the following points. (a) The Persians occupied Psyttaleia 'in silence, so the Greeks would not notice' (§3); this would be difficult on Ayios Yeoryios, given its proximity to the Greeks. (b) Strabo 9.1.14 lists the islands Psyttaleia and Atalante immediately before Peiraeus, suggesting that Ayios Yeoryios is one of the 'Enchantress' islands he has mentioned before. (c) A scholion to Aes. *Pers.* 447 says Psyttaleia is 5 stades from Salamis, exactly the distance from Lipsokoutali to Cynosura (Cape Varvari) on the promontory of Salamis. (d) Michael Akominatos, metropolitan at Athens *ca.* 1175–1204, describes seeing from Hymettus 'islands that still have their ancient names, Psyttaleia, Salamis, Aegina' (*Letter* 9 II 13–14) and only Lipsokoutali is visible from Hymettus. (e) There are remains of ancient monuments on Lipsokoutali and Cape Varvari, at the narrowest point, which could be the Greek trophies. (f) The name *Lipsokoutali* could be derived as follows: *Psyttaleia* > **Le Psouttali* > *Lipsokoutali*, since the article was regularly added to or falsely detached from Greek names in Frankish times, cf. *La Crémonie* < *Lakédémonie* (cf. Burn 1984: 473). Cf. Wallace 1969 for a full discussion.

ἀνῆγον: the verb is first used in a transitive and then in an intransitive sense. The former group are probably the Phoenicians, who are later said to be on 'the wing towards Eleusis and the west' (**85**.1).

κυκλούμενοι: as for how far up the eastern side of Salamis the Persian fleet should be imagined as stretching, cf. **83–96**n. 'Encircling' is one of the motifs in H.'s account of a number of battles which link them together in significant ways: cf. Introduction, §5.

τὴν Κέον τε καὶ τὴν Κυνόσουραν: the location of these two places is a further problem. They are usually taken to refer to places within the Bay of Salamis: Ceos, which is otherwise unknown, could be either the small island, just south of Cape Varvari, now called Talantonisi, or Zea, a harbour on the Peiraeus peninsula; and Cynosura ('Dog's Tail'), the long tongue of land on the east side of Salamis, now Cape Varvari. Asheri 1993: 68–9, however, taking this passage with the opening two lines of the oracle in **77**.1, points out that there is no ancient evidence for these identifications, and identifies Ceos as the well-known Cycladic island of that name lying off Sunium, and Cynosura as the promontory with that name which points south from Marathon. Thus the reference would be to ships not inside the Bay of Salamis but ranged along the east coast of Attica, waiting to move in, because Phaleron could not have held the whole fleet. He argues further that an oracle originally referring to Marathon has been transferred to Salamis. Actions (ii) and (iii) above (**76**n.) would then be sequential: the main fleet entered the channel, then these ships blocked the exits. However, the uncertainties over the authenticity of **77** (see nn.), and the fact that H. says that all the Persian ships were at Phaleron make this problematic. On either reading, the ships at Ceos and Cynosura are a surprise after the 'all' of **68**.1.

76.2 **τῶν ἐπ' Ἀρτεμισίωι ἀγωνισμάτων** 'their successes at Artemisium'; on ἀγώνισμα, cf. Johnson 1994: 232–4.

ἐς τὴν νησῖδα . . . τῶνδε εἵνεκα, ὡς κτλ. 'they put some of the Persians on the islet called Psyttaleia for these reasons, so that, since when the sea battle took place it was there especially that the bodies and wreckage would be carried – because the island lay in the way of the forthcoming sea-battle, they would be able to save their own men and destroy the enemy.' However one analyses this sentence, the grammar is awkward. One is faced with the choice, either of having ἵνα repeat the final conjunction ὡς, which is perhaps defensible as a colloquialism, or having ὡς qualify ἐξοισομένων, thus giving the Persians' view, in which case the gap between ὡς and its participle is uncomfortably large. The former is preferred in the text. Aes. *Pers.* 450–3 gives a similar motivation for the occupation of this island. Persian soldiers are chosen as crack troops (400, according to Paus. 1.36.2); Aes. *Pers.* 441–2 describes them as 'the most brave in spirit and noted for their nobility, among the most trusted by the King'.

76.3 **οὐδὲν ἀποκοιμηθέντες παραρτέοντο** 'they made their preparations, having no sleep that night'; οὐδέν goes with the participle. Cf. Aes. *Pers.* 382 καὶ πάννυχοι δὴ διάπλοον καθίστασαν | ναῶν ἄνακτες πάντα ναυτικὸν λεών.

[77 H. on prophecy]

This chapter was rightly excised by Krueger. The case against it rests on the following grounds. (i) The introduction of a confession of faith in oracles is very abrupt. (ii) The chapter comes awkwardly between the two sentences **76**.3 οἱ μὲν δή . . . and **78**.1 τῶν δὲ ἐν Σαλαμῖνι . . . , which contrast much more naturally with each other than would sentences about Persian manoeuvres and the desire not to disbelieve oracles; furthermore, the contrast between the silence of the Persians and the noisy debate of the Greeks is also lost. (iii) 'The expression of the first sentence . . . is peculiar . . . that of the last, delirious' (Powell). (iv) There are unusual expressions in the oracle, some of which seem to be caused by the reuse of only partially understood epicisms, though it is true that abnormal expressions in the oracle need not necessarily affect the question of the authenticity of the whole chapter. (iii) is the strongest single objection and joined with the other three constitutes a major case against the authenticity of the chapter.

The chapter is defended by Asheri 1993 who, following earlier suggestions, argues that the oracle was originally concerned with Marathon, and later reapplied to Salamis. It would thus describe the ships blockading Marathon Bay from Cynosura (cf. **76**.1n.) to Artemis' shrine at Brauron to the south of the Bay: the 'bridge' is metaphorical, and the expression 'bronze will clash with bronze, and Ares will stain the sea with blood' refers to the hoplite battle at Marathon and subsequent fight in the sea (cf. 6.112–15). In the reapplication, πέρσαντες was substituted for an original πορθῆσαι (depending on ἐλπίδι), so that it could now refer to Xerxes' recent actual capture of the city. Oracles were indeed moved from one event to another, but this oracle seems no more especially suited to Marathon than Salamis, and blood in the sea suits Salamis better. Furthermore, the strange Greek of the prose parts of the chapter remains unexplained on this hypothesis. Cf. also 9.43 for another passage with an oracle of Bacis, where again there are grammatical oddities.

77.1 οὐ βουλόμενος . . . καταβάλλειν: καταβάλλω is unusual with non-personal objects: the nearest parallel is Democr. fr. 125 ἡμέας καταβάλλεις, where the human body's senses are speaking; the title οἱ καταβάλλοντες (*sc.* λόγοι) 'Knock-down Arguments' ascribed to one of Protagoras' works would be another, though the title may not be original. Asheri argues that H. is not claiming belief in all oracles indiscriminately, but only in those that are clear and shown to be true by events (1993: 72–6), but even if this were a good example of a clear oracle, the argument would be more persuasive if τοὺς ἐναργέως λέγοντας were written. This is also the only place where H. explicitly emphasises the importance of clarity in oracles (Harrison 2000a: 130–2).

ἐς τοιάδε πρήγματα ἐσβλέψας: since oracles in H. are usually introduced in some way, one expects τοιάδε to look forward, as it does in 192 of its 199 occurrences. Asheri, however, argues that the πρήγματα are the events just described which prove the oracle correct, and compares Aes. *Pers.* 800–2 εἴ τι πιστεῦσαι θεῶν | χρὴ θεσφάτοισιν, ἐς τὰ νῦν πεπραγμένα | βλέψαντα . . . This is not, however, an exact parallel and leaves the oracle with no introduction.

ἀλλ' ὅταν is a regular start to an oracle (**20**.1n.).

Ἀρτέμιδος χρυσαόρου . . . Κυνόσουραν: on the traditional view of Ceos and Cynosura (**76**.1n.), the headland will be either on Salamis, where there was a temple of Artemis and the trophy was set up (Paus. 1.36.1), or perhaps on the shore near Munychia, where there was a temple of Artemis Munychia (Paus. 1.1.4); Ceos and Brauron also had shrines of Artemis. Asheri justifies taking the 'headland' of Artemis to refer to Ceos off Sunium by reference to the two shrines to Artemis there, and to the fact that we know nothing of such shrines on the other Ceos, posited in the bay of Salamis.

χρυσαόρου: an epithet found elsewhere of Apollo, Demeter, Orpheus, Perseus and Zeus, but not of Artemis, who is furthermore shown but once with a sword in art, on the Louvre Tityos vase (cf. Richardson 1974 on *H. Dem.* 4).

γεφυρώσωσι: apparently 'join by a bridge', though this sense is not found elsewhere; it would describe the manoeuvre in **76**.1. For the verb in epic, cf. *Il.* 15.357 (Apollo fills the Achaean trench to make a causeway) γεφύρωσεν δὲ κέλευθον, and 21.245 (of the tree Achilles uses to get out of a river) γεφύρωσεν δέ μιν αὐτὸν | εἴσω πᾶσ' ἐριποῦσ'; Kirk on *Il.* 5.87–8.

λιπαράς was a cliché for Athens. In *Ach.* 639–40 Aristophanes chides the Athenians for the ease with which they succumbed to flattery: εἰ δέ τις ὑποθωπεύσας λιπαρὰς καλέσειεν Ἀθήνας, | ηὕρετο πᾶν ἂν διὰ τὰς λιπαράς 'if anyone, in an attempt to curry favour, called Athens "shining", he got all he wanted because of this "shining"'; cf. Pi. *Is.* 2.20, *Ne.* 4.18–19; Eur. *Tro.* 803 etc. The adjective literally describes things that are shiny with oil or fat, and so splendid-looking.

σβέσσει: this future with -σσ- is found elsewhere only in [Theoc.] 23.26, probably a much later poem which itself is textually very difficult.

Κόρον, Ὕβριος υἱόν: personifications tend to have varied genealogies; cf. Pi. *Ol.* 13.10 Ὕβριν, Κόρου μάτερα and Theog. 153 (= Solon, fr. 6.3) τίκτει τοι Κόρος Ὕβριν.

δοκεῦντ' ἀνὰ πάντα πιθέσθαι: 'meaningless' (Powell), and it is certainly odd; it appears to mean 'expecting everything to obey him'. Again, Homeric phraseology and word-positioning appear to be imitated, cf. the line-end *Od.* 17.21 σημάντορι πάντα πιθέσθαι 'to obey one's leader in everything'. Given the oddities in the oracle, there seems little point in trying to emend.

77.2 ἐς τοιαῦτα κτλ.: again, the Greek is strange, for three reasons. The shift from ἐς τοιαῦτα to the dative λέγοντι is harsh, and ἀντιλογία and ἀντιλέγω are not used elsewhere with the preposition ἐς (πρός is used); ἀντιλογίας λέγω = ἀντιλέγω is found only here. Stein's deletion of ἐς, as if intruded by dittography from ἐς τοιάδε in §1, helps but not very much.

οὔτε παρ' ἄλλων ἐνδέκομαι 'nor do I accept them from anyone else'; the phrase is used with more clarity in **142**.1 μήτε λόγους ἐνδέκεσθαι παρὰ τοῦ βαρβάρου 'nor to consent to the suggestions of the King', from which it may have been imitated.

78–82 Aristeides and Themistocles

The story of the Greek council is picked up from **74**. There is a mildly comic irony about the violence of the debate, when we know that they are already surrounded. As often in H., direct speech is used for the crucial news, conveyed in the private discussion between Themistocles and Aristeides (**79–80**), while Aristeides' speech to the council is in indirect speech; the focus remains on the main characters and their relationships. This private discussion balances that between Themistocles and Mnesiphilus (**57**), which began this section from the destruction of Athens. Themistocles listens to advice again, and the reconciliation of the two great Athenian rivals before the battle is a further good sign.

78 ὠθισμός: for other striking metaphors for the violence of the Greek debates, cf. **64**.1n.

ὥσπερ . . . εἶναι 'they expected them to be in the place where they saw them drawn up during the day'. ὥσπερ = ὡς (*Lex. s.v.* ὥσπερ 2); for the infinitive with δοκέω of things that are not the case, cf. **110**.1n.

79.1 Ἀριστείδης was one of the major Athenian politicians of the period (cf. *LGPN* II *s.v.*(32)). He was a friend of the reformer Cleisthenes, and was said by some to have been a *strategos* at Marathon. Rivalry with Themistocles resulted in his ostracism in 483/2 (*Ath. Pol.* 22.7; 123 *ostraka* with his name have been found; Lang 1990: 35–40; Brenne 2001: 114–17). At Salamis he commanded the hoplites on Psyttaleia (**95**), and was sole commander of the Athenian army at Plataea (9.28.6). He subsequently helped Themistocles ensure the rebuilding of the Athenian walls, and influenced the allies' preference for Athenian leadership over Spartan. He organised the tribute levels of the Delian League, with a fair assessment of contributions, and was generally known as 'the Just'. Plut. *Arist.* 7.5–6 has the famous story about his ostracism, in which an illiterate man, not recognising Aristeides, asked him to write 'Aristeides' on a potsherd, and when asked why he wished to ostracise Aristeides said he was tired of hearing him called 'the Just'. Aristeides was often contrasted as the just and aristocratic man with the scheming and democratic Themistocles; Thucydides, however, defends him (1.138), There is also the witty remark of Callaeschrus, based on the fact that Aristeides' deme was Alopecae ('Fox Deme'), that he was μᾶλλον τῶι τρόπωι Ἀλωπεκῆθεν ἢ τῶι δήμωι 'a fox more by character than by deme'. He died in the early 460s. See Plutarch's *Life*.

ἐξωστρακισμένος: ostracism was introduced by Cleisthenes in 508/7 (*Ath. Pol.* 22), to make it possible for the Athenians to expel for ten years any politician they thought too powerful or disruptive. The first recorded ostracism, however, was not till 487 (cf. ML 21 = Fornara 41). If a motion for an ostracism was put, the Athenians voted by tribes in the Agora, inscribing the name of the man they wished to expel on potsherds (*ostraka*). The rules are not entirely clear, but anyone ostracised was exiled for ten years but kept his property and citizen rights, either (i) because 6,000 votes were cast and he had a majority, or (ii) because he had 6,000 votes against him. Similar institutions existed in Argos and Syracuse where, since olive leaves (*petala*) were used, it was called *petalismos* (Diod. 11.85–8, Hsch. *s.v.*).

In 480, there was a general recall of the Athenians who had been ostracised, including Aristeides. The 'Decree of Themistocles' (ML 23.45–7 = Fornara no. 55; **41**.1n.) says τοὺς μὲν μεθεστηκότας τὰ [δέκα] ἔτη ἀπίεναι εἰς Σαλαμῖνα καὶ μένειν αὐτοὺς ἐ[κεῖ ἕως ἄν τι τῶι δήμ]ωι δόξηι περὶ αὐτῶν ('those banished for ten years are to go to over Salamis and wait until the people comes to some decision about them'). This recall took place either sometime before July (*Ath. Pol.* 22.8) or slightly later (Plut. *Aristeid.* 8.1). Cf. Thomsen 1972; Lang 1990; Brenne 2001; Siewert 2002; Forsdyke 2005.

79.2 στὰς ἐπὶ τὸ συνέδριον 'standing at (the entrance to) the meeting' (ἐξεκαλέετο shows he was not in the meeting).

79.3 στασιάζειν . . . ἐργάσεται lit. 'it is right that we have been competing with each other both in the past and especially now, about the question of which of us will do more good to his country.' Expressions with ἄλλος τε . . . καί place the emphasis on the words that follow καί. On περὶ τοῦ ὁκότερος κτλ. and the article's ability to make words or phrases substantival, cf. Smyth §1153.

79.4 ἴσον ἐστί . . . Πελοποννησίοισι 'it is all the same whether the Peloponnesians say a lot or a little about sailing away from here'; the dative Πελοποννησίοισι depends on ἴσον.

80 Themistocles' speech echoes the phraseology of Aristeides': αὐτὸς αὐτόπτης γενόμενος ≈ ἐγὼ γὰρ αὐτόπτης . . . γενόμενος; αὐτός σφι ἄγγειλον and ἀλλά σφι σήμηνον αὐτὸς παρελθών ≈ ἀλλ' ἐσελθών σφι ταῦτα σήμηνον; περιεχόμεθα πανταχόθεν ≈ περιεχόμεθα . . . κύκλωι. It also contains a certain amount of repetition and word-play: χρηστὰ . . . ἤγγειλας . . . χρηστὰ ἀπαγγέλλων . . . ἄγγειλον; γενέσθαι, αὐτὸς αὐτόπτης γενόμενος; ἐδέομην . . . ἔδεε; οὐκ ἑκόντες . . . κατίστασθαι . . . ἀέκοντας παραστήσασθαι. There is something similar in his speech in **109**.2–3. It is a shrewd move on his part to get the 'just' Aristeides, who has not before been party to the quarrel over tactics, to convey to the Greeks the news that marks the triumph of Themistocles' strategy. Themistocles displays no false modesty.

80.1 τὰ γὰρ . . . ἥκεις: understand τούτων with αὐτόπτης.

ἐξ ἐμέο τὰ ποιεύμενα ὑπὸ Μήδων: understand another ποιεύμενα with ἐξ ἐμέο 'at my insistence' (K–G II 564).

παραστήσασθαι is transitive; *sc.* ἐς μάχην.

80.2 οὐ πείσω, ὡς οὐ ποιεύντων lit. 'in the circumstances of (their belief that) the barbarians are not doing this, I shall not persuade them', i.e. 'I shall not persuade them that the barbarians are doing this'. ὡς οὐ ποιεύντων is a genitive absolute describing the belief of the Greeks, as is shown by the use of ὡς (cf. **7**.2n.). ὡς does not introduce an indirect statement depending on πείσω, for if it did, there would be no οὐ with the participle. For this construction, cf. Soph. *Aj.* 281 ὡς ὧδ' ἐχόντων τῶνδε ἐπίστασθαί σε χρή lit. 'believing this to be so, you must understand (it is so)' = 'you must understand this is so'; *M&T* §917; Smyth §2122.

ἢν μὲν πείθωνται . . . εἴπερ περιεχόμεθα: in these two conditional clauses, the subjunctive πείθωνται expresses uncertainty over whether the Greeks will be persuaded; the indicative περιεχόμεθα by contrast states the plain fact that if they are indeed (περ) completely surrounded, there will be no longer any question of running away.

81 ἔλεγε . . . φάμενος 'there is no real tautology, for the participle denotes the full account of which the main verb introduces an excerpt' (Dunbar on Ar. *Birds* 472); such apparent tautologies are not uncommon in H.; cf. 1.118.2 ἔφη λέγων and Stein *ad loc.*

παραρτέεσθαι . . . ὡς ἀλεξησομένους 'he advised them to make preparations in order to defend themselves'.

82.1 ἀπιστεόντων δὲ τούτων: that the Greeks will not believe Aristeides justifies Themistocles' unwillingness to try to persuade them himself (**80**.2).

αὐτομολέουσα: if Panaetius had been part of the Persian fleet assigned to Ceos and Cynosura (cf. **76**.1n.), he could quite easily have escaped to the Greek fleet.

ἀνὴρ Παναίτιος: nothing else is known of him or his father (*LGPN* I *s.v.*(13). If ἀνὴρ Παναίτιος is correct, ἀνήρ serves 'to introduce a person not previously mentioned, – being more respectful than τις' (Jebb on *Ajax* 45); cf. *Il.* 11.92 ἄνδρα βιήνορα, Soph. *Ajax* 817 etc.: it is a poetic expression.

ἐνεγράφησαν . . . ἐς τὸν τρίποδα: after their victory, the Greeks catalogued on a monument dedicated to Apollo at Delphi the names of the races who had fought the Persians: το[ίδε τὸν] | πόλεμον [ἐ]- | πολ[έ]μεον· | Λακεδ[αιμόνιοι] | Ἀθηναῖο[ι] | Κορίνθιοι κτλ. (ML 27 *Coils* 1–2 = Fornara 59). This consisted of a golden tripod resting on a column made of three intertwined serpents, on whose coils the names were carved. The column is still extant in Istanbul. The Tenians do indeed figure in the list of participating Greek cities on the Serpent Column, and appear to have been added after the first inscription of names since they (like the Siphnians) are on a coil that has four rather than the usual three names (ML 27 *Coil* 7). Strictly speaking, therefore, the inscription is not on the actual tripod as H. says, but on the coils of the three serpents that supported it. 'Tripod' may be shorthand for the whole monument, but H. is again inaccurate in 9.81.1, where he says the serpent had three heads, despite the fact that he must have seen the Column at Delphi; cf. S. R. West 1985: 280–1. The Tenians are again recorded on the base of the statue of Zeus at Olympia, which celebrated the victory at Plataea (Paus. 5.23.1–2). Cf. **66**.2 for their medising after Thermopylae and Artemisium.

κατελοῦσι: dative plural of the aorist active participle of καταιρέω (Att. καθ-).

τῆι πρότερον . . . τῆι Λημνίηι: cf. **11**.3.

83–96 THE BATTLE OF SALAMIS

83–4 The battle begins

The narrative of the battle can be analysed into three segments, the two armies receiving roughly equal treatment.

83–84 Greek preparations and views on how the fighting started.
85–90 The fighting from the Persian side.
91–96 The fighting from the Greek side.

'It is characteristic of H. that the sections preceding and following the action are always more important than the battle itself' (Immerwahr 1966: 69; cf. 238–305 on H.'s battles). Thus H. gives a perhaps surprisingly small amount of detail about the battle beyond general statements and accounts of a small number of incidents, which are not the most vital in terms of the outcome. H. himself admits to a certain amount of ignorance in **87**.1: 'as for the rest of the Persians and Greeks, I cannot say exactly how they fought.'

Nor are the movements, positions and alignments of the two fleets now firmly reconstructable, as the disagreements amongst historians show (there is a similar problem with other battles, such as Mycale: cf. F&M on 9.102–5). The Greek fleet was based on the eastern side of Salamis, though precisely which harbour(s) it used is uncertain. The Persians, having occupied the harbours on the Attic coast, came up the channel, 'in three lines', according to Aes. *Pers.* 366–7. The numbers of ships were probably 2–3:1 in the Persians' favour.

How far up the channel the Persians penetrated is uncertain. Some (e.g. Asheri) put them all the way up the coast opposite Salamis, which would be supported by **85**.1 'the Phoenicians held the wing off Eleusis and to the west' (though since Eleusis is situated to the north of the bay, this makes 'west' problematic). Such a deployment would also have enabled the Persians to prevent the Greeks from escaping round the back of Salamis. On the other hand, since Themistocles was keen to engage them in the narrows, it is more likely that the Athenians attacked them in the narrows by Ayios Yeoryios, using the *diekplous* (**9**n.) to break through their lines. The narrowness of the channel (about 1,300 yards) would have allowed only 80 triremes to row abreast, thus reducing the Persians' numerical superiority (cf. Morrison, Coates and Rankov 2000: 59–60).

Diod. 11.17.1–18.2 and Plut. *Them.* 12.5 (from Ephorus) speak of an Egyptian squadron which was sent round the western end of the island, to block the Greeks' exit; but the absence of any mention in H. suggests this is further rationalising on the part of Diodorus and Plutarch. (cf. **41**.2n.). Aes. *Pers.* 366–8 τάξαι . . . ἄλλας . . . κύκλωι νῆσον Αἴαντος πέριξ need not refer to these Egyptians.

H. concentrates on certain episodes rather than giving an account of the whole battle. This may in part be the result of the fact that the tactics of trireme battles, involving ramming and boarding, meant that individual triremes were involved in only one or two incidents per battle; it may also reflect Homeric practice of concentrating on individual *monomachiae*. It also, however, allows H. to comment implicitly on the nature of historiography (see below).

For accounts of the battle, cf. Hignett 1963: 193–239; Immerwahr 1966: 267–82; Hammond, *CAH*² IV 569–91; Burn 1984: 450–75; Lazenby 1993: 151–97; Balcer 1995: 257–72 (a Persian perspective); Green 1996: 167–98; de Jong 1999: 262–71; Morrison Coates and Rankov 2000: 55–61, 152–6; Strauss 2004: 151–253. The principal ancient sources are, from the fifth century, Aes. *Pers.*; Timotheus, *Persians*; Choerilus, *Persika* (Bernabé 1996: 191–208); and later Plut. *Them.* 10–17; Diod. 11.14–19; see also Asheri 282–5. For H. and Aeschylus, cf. Pelling 1997b.

83–4 We have here the repetition of the motif of a messenger bringing news and so moving the action on, once the trustworthiness of his news is established (**83**.1 ~ **76**.1). The arrival of the ship bearing the Aeacidae at the very moment that the Greeks begin to embark is an excellent omen for the coming battle. Themistocles' speech is in a long tradition of pre-battle orations that goes back at least to the *Iliad*, but H., having already used a number of important speeches, does not let another one get in the way of the description of the start of the battle.

83.1 τὰ λεγόμενα . . . ῥήματα: for the pleonasm, cf. 1.109.1 ἔφραζε . . . τὸν πάντα Ἀστυάγεος ῥηθέντα λόγον. On the interpretation of the first two sentences, cf. Graham 1996.

ἠώς τε διέφαινε: in H., this is little more than a temporal marker, but in Aes. 384–407 the daybreak is much more symbolically charged. All is light, sound and rapid movement: the sun rises, the Greeks cry out, a trumpet sounds, the Greek fleet sets forth and a great and glorious patriotic cry goes up. H.'s build-up is much more low-key, with a string of simple sentences, until the dramatic moment in **84**.2.

In the Attic calendar, the battle coincides with the date of procession to Eleusis during the Mysteries, Boedromion 19 or 20, which corresponded to 23 or 24 September in 480.

καὶ οἳ . . . ποιησάμενοι, προηγόρευε εὖ ἔχοντα μὲν . . . Θεμιστοκλέης 'they gathered the marines together, and out of all of them Themistocles foretold good fortune'; the plural participle seems to be hanging, but H. writes as if a number of speakers were about to be listed and their performances judged (note the position of μέν after εὖ ἔχοντα not προηγόρευε), but does not consider them worth mentioning (cf. K–G I 288–9 for the use of the participle thus). It is indeed likely that each contingent was addressed by its own leaders. εὖ ἔχοντα is often taken to mean 'well', but there is no parallel for such an adverbial use in H., and προαγορεύω does not just mean 'speak', but 'announce' or 'foretell', so εὖ ἔχοντα will be its object.

τὰ δὲ ἔπεα . . . ἐγγίνεται 'his words were all about the contrast between the many better and worse aspects that are found in man's nature and constitution.' ἀντιτιθέμενα ('contrasting') agrees with ἔπεα and governs <τά> κρέσσω. δή with universalising relatives like ὅστις, ὅσος, makes the relative comprehensive (*GP* 221–2).

83.2 ἡ ἀπ᾽ Αἰγίνης τριήρης: **64**.2.

84.1 Ἀμεινίης δὲ Παλληνεύς: Ameinias (*LGPN* II *s.v.*(32)) is made brother of Aeschylus by Diod. 11.27.2, Ael. *VH* 5.19, and *Vita Aesch.* 4, but Aeschylus was from Eleusis not Pallene. In Plut. *Them.* 14.3, Ameinias is from the deme of Deceleia.

ἐξαναχθείς 'having moved forward'; middle voice.

ἐμβάλλει: ramming is referred to a number of times in this battle (**86**, **87**.2–4, **90**.1–2, **91**, **92**; cf. Aes. *Pers.* 408–11, 418–19), whereas reference to capture is less common (**85**.2, **90**.2, both by members of the Persian fleet). Salamis may, however, have been unusual in the prevalence of ramming (Cawkwell 2005: 223–5). For the ram (ἔμβολος), cf. Morrison, Coates and Rankov 2000: 168–9, 221–2.

συμπλεκείσης . . . οὐ δυναμένων: the first participle refers to the ship Ameinias struck, the second to both ships embroiled in the same tangle.

84.2 Ἀθηναῖοι: similarly, in Aes. *Pers.* 409–11 a 'Greek ship' starts the battle, hitting a Phoenician one. If the Athenians were indeed stationed opposite the Phoenicians, as H. says (**85**.1), this ship would have been Athenian. The competing versions here are the result either of a desire of different peoples to claim the credit for initiating the great victory, or of the difficulty of knowing what exactly happened along an extended battle-line.

δαιμόνιοι: the adjective, from δαίμων and so meaning 'amazing', can have a variety of tones, depending on the context. Here it is indignant, perhaps 'Gentlemen, you amaze me!' as in 4.126, 7.48; cf. Dickey 1996: 141–2, 280. Divinities have a tendency sometimes to address mortals somewhat harshly: cf. e.g. Hes. *Th.* 26, where the Muses speak to Hesiod, ποιμένες ἄγραυλοι, κάκ' ἐλέγχεα, γαστέρες οἶον, imitated by Epimenides, fr. 1, spoken by Truth or Justice or perhaps both, Κρῆτες ἀεὶ ψευσταί, κακὰ θηρία, γαστέρες ἀργαί.

μέχρι κόσου ἔτι πρύμνην ἀνακρούεσθε: the rhetorical question 'how long . . .' referring to something unsatisfactory has a long pedigree in Near Eastern and Greek poetry; cf. e.g. Ps. 13.1 'How long wilt thou forget me, O Lord?'; Callin. fr. 1.1–2 μέχρις τέο κατάκεισθε . . . , | ὦ νέοι;, in an elegy performed at a symposium, and punning on κατακεῖσθαι 'lie idle (at table)/be inactive (in battle)' (M. L. West 1997: 257–8). πρύμνην ἀνακρούεσθαι is 'to row astern a little . . . they do this so as not to appear to be obviously retreating' (schol. Thuc. 1.50.5).

85–90 The battle viewed from the Persian perspective

This section can be analysed as follows (italics point to repeated features):

A **85** disposition of the fleets; how *the Ionians* fought for the Persians. *Xerxes* rewards his best fighters.

B **86** *comparison* of fighting and fortunes of Greeks and Persians.

C **87–8** *Xerxes* observes Artemisia's exploit.

B **89** *comparison* of casualties of Greeks and Persians.

A **90** backfiring of Phoenician accusations against *the Ionians*, when *Xerxes* sees a fine exploit by them.

These episodes enable H. not only to describe the battle, but also to do two further things: (i) analyse and reflect on relationships in the Persian forces, and (ii) speculate on the nature of historical recording and judgement. (i) The fact of Xerxes' observation of the battle is stressed throughout, and the importance of noting the names of those who perform well so they can be rewarded frames the episode: in **85**, Samians are rewarded by Xerxes, Theomestor becomes a tyrant, and Phylacus 'was recorded (ἀνεγράφη) as a benefactor' (§3); and in **90**.4n. 'scribes recorded (ἀνέγραφον), with father's name and city, the names of trierarchs who had performed some notable deed'. However, the down-side of this royal observation is that chaos is caused in the Persian fleet by their very enthusiasm to impress Xerxes by their exploits (**86, 89**.2): there is an absence of a coherent strategy.

(ii) The episodes in **87** and **90**, linked by the involvement each time of three ships, illustrate the problems of a system that involves rewards based on observed actions. In the first, Artemisia gains greater credit with the King, despite the fact that she 'commits a crime' (**88**.1), because no one realises she has attacked a friendly ship. In the second, the accusation by the Phoenicians against the Ionians is not looked into, because Xerxes happens to see a striking exploit by an Ionian ship and settles the matter in their favour; a friend at court of the Ionians, Ariaramnes, also helps. This has relevance for the historian too: error and chance determine the interpretation of events. Just as Xerxes makes mistakes which are duly recorded in writing, so the historian, who relies on such reports or even his own judgement, can similarly produce an inaccurate record. H. states explicitly that it is not known exactly why Artemisia attacked her own ship (**87**.3), so judgement of her actions is made problematic, for King and historian alike. Cf. further Christ 1994.

85.1 κατὰ μὲν δὴ Ἀθηναίους ἐτετάχατο Φοίνικες . . . κατὰ δὲ Λακεδαιμονίους Ἴωνες: κατά = 'opposite'. The Athenians were on the Greek left, the Spartans on the right, the position of honour, as befitted their overall command: cf. 6.111.1. The reference to Phoenicians and Ionians is picked up at the end of this section (**90**). ἐτετάχατο is 3rd person plural, pluperfect passive of τάσσω (< **tag-*, as in ταγοῦχος 'office-holder').

Φοίνικες: from the end of second millennium they were a great trading nation. There is evidence for their activities from Morocco to Nineveh, and it is one of their voyages which starts off H.'s own work; Homer describes them as 'famed for their ships, cunning fellows, bringing countless baubles in their black ship' (*Od.* 15.415–16). They were part of the Babylonian and Assyrian empires, and came under Persian rule sometime before 525 (3.19.2–3). Darius conquered the islands 'through possession of the Phoenician fleet' (Thuc. 1.16), and they provided Xerxes with 300 ships (7.89.1). Tyre and Sidon were their main cities, and they founded others such as Cadiz, Marseilles and Carthage (*qarṭ ḥadasht* 'New Town'). Their version of the Semitic alphabet led to the alphabets for e.g. Aramaic, Hebrew, Greek and Latin, and thus gave the world much more accessible systems of writing than e.g. the cuneiforms of Akkadian, Elamite and Old Persian. In the gathering of the army in **67**.2, their kings hold pride of place. Their importance in the Achaemenid empire may also be reflected in the fact that Phrynichus made Phoenician women the chorus of his *Phoenissae* (*TrGF* 3 F 8 = Aes. *Pers. Hypoth.* 1–6). The Phoenician soldiers were dressed in Greek helmets, with linen corselets, rimless shields and javelins (7.89.1). Cf. Moscati 1999.

τὸ πρὸς Ἐλευσῖνός τε καὶ ἑσπέρης κέρας: for the difficulty, cf. **83–96**n.

μέντοι is essentially temporal here: 'now, a few of them' (*GP* 406). For the ἐντολαί, cf. **22**.

85.2 ἔχω: the capture of an enemy ship would have been the kind of thing whose memory would have been preserved by the successful captain and his family, so H. could have heard these stories when in Asia Minor. For H.'s periodic refusal to give information he possesses, cf. 7.224.1 (the names of the 300 at Thermopylae); Lateiner 1989: 74–5.

Θεομήστορός τε . . . καὶ Φυλάκου: Theomestor's time for enjoyment of the tyranny of Samos (§3) was short, since Samos returned to the Greeks in 479, after a secret embassy was sent, unbeknown to him (9.90.1, 99.1, 103.2, 106.2–4). His name is unique and grand. Cf. 6.25 for a similar gift of Samos to Aeacus by Darius, for services rendered. Phylacus is otherwise unknown. He shares a name with one of the heroes at Delphi who punished the Persians for their attack (**39**.1): cf. Introduction, §5 for H.'s use of names to link episodes.

85.3 εὐεργέτης: 'amongst the Persians good deeds are highly valued and bring greatness' (3.154.1). **Reward for good deeds** to the royal house was crucial to the functioning of the Achaemenid empire (Gould 1991). Cf. DB (= Brosius no. 44) IV §63 'the man who supported my (royal) house, him I treated well'; also I §8; DNb (= Brosius no. 103) §§4, 6; Xen. *Anab.* 1.9.11–13, 20–8, a eulogy of Cyrus the Younger after his death; Darius' letter to Gadatas, 'for this, there will be laid up the greatest gratitude (*charis*) in the King's house' (ML 12.15–17 = Fornara 35); and Xerxes' to Pausanias (Thuc. 1.129.3, next note). The Persepolis *Apadāna* had an immense relief depicting peoples of the empire bringing the King gifts characteristic of their countries. The King's favour was shown by gifts of cities and territory, positions of power (3.160.2, 9.107.3), distinctive clothes (especially a Median robe (3.84.1)), ceremonial privileges (no one else could help the King onto his horse if Tiribazus, *hyparchos* of western Armenia, were present (Xen. *Anab.* 4.4.4)), or honorific titles (the Egyptian Udjahorresnet boasted 'the King caused me to be beside him as a companion administrator of the palace' (Brosius no. 20 §1)). Amongst Greeks, gifts entailed an obligation to reciprocate; in Persia the King was at the centre, dictating the relationship (exaggeratedly shown by the tale of Pythius the Lydian, 7.27–9, 38–9; cf. the parody of royal reward and punishment in **118**.3–4). When the King travelled it was necessary to bring gifts, but the manner of giving was as important as the gift itself: a handful of water could bring great rewards (Plut. *Art.* 4.3, 12.3–4, 14.1; Aelian, *VH* 1.31.3). Royal gifts had to be accepted or there could be appalling consequences (Plut. *Art.* 14.5–16), but on his birthday, at the *tukta* ('perfect, complete'), the King had to grant any Persian noble's request (9.110.2, though the obligation was probably not as strong as H. makes it; cf. Plut. *Art.* 26.3). Cf. Wiesehöfer 1980; Briant 2002: 302–23.

ἀνεγράφη: the physical recording of important events such as battles is attested across ancient Near Eastern societies. Scribes record Xerxes' conversations with his troops (7.100.1–2; cf. **90**.4), and Xerxes wrote to Pausanias 'your good deed is recorded (ἀνάγραπτος) in our house' (Thuc. 1.129.3; cf. last note and the passages collected in *FGH* 696). For how these records might be used, cf. Esther 6:1–2 (written *ca.* 150–100): '[Ahasuerus, i.e. Xerxes] commanded to bring the book of records of the chronicles; and they were read before the king. And it was found written, that Mordecai had told of Bigthana and Teresh, two of the king's chamberlains, the keepers of the door, who sought to lay hand on the king Ahasuerus'; Mordecai is then suitably rewarded. In Assyrian art, we see men with clay tablets and scrolls recording details of battles (perhaps as war artists as well as scribes), loot and, more grimly, the number of enemy killed by individual soldiers, who bring the heads as evidence (Reade 1988: 47–9, e.g. BM WA 118882).

ὀροσάγγαι: possibly from Old Persian **varu- sanha-* 'widely famed' (Schmitt 1967: 131). It is used by Sophocles in plays on Trojan subjects (frs. 183 (*Marriage of Helen*), 634

(*Troilus*)), supposedly in the sense σωματοφύλακες; Nymphis, *FGH* 432 F 6, however, translated it as ξένοι βασίλειοι.

Περσιστί: in a small number of cases, H. discusses Persian words. In 6.98.3, he translates the names of Darius, Xerxes and Artaxerxes, but inaccurately; in **98**.2, he records the name of the Persian messenger service; in 9.110.2, he translates the name τυκτά, of a feast, as 'perfect'; cf. Schmitt 1967. For H.'s interest in foreign languages, cf. Harrison 1998.

86 σὺν κόσμωι . . . οὔτε τεταγμένων: Aes. *Pers.* 399–400 also stresses the order of the Greeks: τὸ δεξιὸν μὲν πρῶτον εὐτάκτως κέρας | ἡγεῖτο κόσμωι; his Persians begin in an orderly way (374–83), but ultimately there is again confusion (412–23). When the battle turns against them, Persian disorder recurs at Plataea (9.59.2, 65.1), but their Greek allies also suffer from it (9.67–9). The contrast of Greek order with barbarian disorder has a literary counterpart in the Greeks and Trojans at their first battle in *Il.* 3.1–9, where an almost moral distinction is implied between Greek silence and Trojan uproar. Here, however, though H. regrets their lack of organisation, he is keen to avoid any charge of cowardice against them.

ἔμελλε . . . ἀπέβη 'it was likely that some such fate would befall them as actually did'.

καίτοι ἦσάν γε [καὶ ἐγένοντο]: although εἰμί and γίνομαι need not mean quite the same thing – γίνομαι can mean 'prove to be' (*Lex. s.v.* III 2) – having them both here does not yield good sense. καίτοι qualifies what the author has just said.

μακρῶι ἀμείνονες αὐτοὶ ἑωυτῶν ἢ πρὸς Εὐβοίηι: lit. 'they were better by far than themselves, than they had been off Euboea' (i.e. at Artemisium). The reflexives ἑαυτοῦ etc. are added to comparative statements when a subject is both compared to itself and said to show a quality in a greater than normal degree; sometimes the particular quality or aspect is added with ἤ: cf. 2.25.5 ὁ δὲ Νεῖλος . . . τοῦτον τὸν χρόνον οἰκότως αὐτὸς ἑωυτοῦ ῥέει πολλῶι ὑποδεέστερος ἢ τοῦ θέρεος (K–G II 313–14); **137**.3 διπλάσιος . . . αὐτὸς ἑωυτοῦ. H. repeatedly stresses how well the Persians fought in various battles: cf. 9.62.2–3, 102.2–4.

θεήσασθαι: **69**.2.n.

87–8 Artemisia's cunning

87.1 οὐκ ἔχω εἰπεῖν ἀτρεκέως is used again in 6.14.1 of the battle of Lade; cf. **8**.2n.

87.2 καὶ ἣ οὐκ ἔχουσα . . . ἔδοξέ οἱ: an anacolouthon, leaving ἣ οὐκ ἔχουσα hanging; cf. 7.177 ἅπαντα γὰρ προσκεψάμενοι . . . ταύτηι σφι ἔδοξε δέκεσθαι. Here the parenthesis eases the shift in construction.

ἡ δὲ αὐτῆς: *sc.* νηῦς.

πρὸς τῶν πολεμίων μάλιστα 'very near the enemy'; the genitive is ablatival, used to mark the point *from which* the distance is measured, cf. **120** ἵδρυται πρὸς τοῦ Ἑλλησπόντου μᾶλλον 'is situated nearer the Hellespont', and expressions like εἴχοντο δὲ τούτων 'positioned next to these' (6.8 etc.).

φέρουσα intransitive with the passive sense 'rapidly borne along' is very rare; cf. Aeschin. 3.82 καὶ εἰς τοῦτο φέρων περιέστησε τὰ πράγματα. It is an extension of the intransitive uses of the verb to mean 'lead' (of roads etc.), 'conduce to', 'portend' (*Lex. s.v* II 1–3).

Καλυνδέων: Artemisia attacks a ship of her own contingent, captained by Damasithymus who was amongst the most notable commanders in Xerxes' navy (7.98). Damasithymus is here from Caly*nd*a, a noted city on the borders of Caria and Lycia (H–N 1119); in 7.99.2, the island of Caly*dn*a is one of Artemisia's possessions. There could be confusion of names here, but Damasithymus' grand position and the expression 'a friendly ship' (and not 'one of her own ships') suggest that he was not a mere subject of another ruler.

87.3 εἰ μὲν . . . ἐόντων, οὐ μέντοι ἔχω γε εἰπεῖν 'whether . . . really, I cannot say'. Emphatic μέντοι usually comes early in its sentence and is rare outside dialogue (*GP* 400–1), so perhaps here its dramatic later appearance makes its clause almost an answer to the direct question behind the εἰ-clause: 'Did they have a quarrel before?' 'Well, I really don't know.' Cf. Aeschin. 1.98 ὅτι ταῦτ' ἀληθῆ λέγω, ἐνταῦθα μέντοι . . . τοὺς μάρτυρας παρέξομαι (the only other example quoted by *GP* that is not in a dialogue).

87.4 τε γάρ without a subsequent καί or τε is rare and often disputed (cf. *GP* 536; Mastronarde on Eur. *Phoen.* 1313). Here the complexity of the sentence explains the absence: the second piece of good fortune is finally introduced by τοῦτο δέ in **88**.1.

τριήραρχος: as we learn when he realises his mistake in **93**.1, this was the Ameinias of **84**.1.

αὐτοῖσι: i.e. the Greeks.

88.1 τοῦτο μὲν . . . διαφυγεῖν τε καὶ μὴ ἀπολέσθαι 'on the one hand, it so happened to her advantage that she escaped and was not killed'; διαφυγεῖν and ἀπολέσθαι are added as infinitives explanatory of τοιοῦτο. This episode is linked to its counterpart by the repetition συνήνεικε ὦν οὕτω ὥστε Ἰώνων τε τοὺς στρατηγοὺς μὴ ἀπολέσθαι (**90**.1).

88.2 καὶ δή is common in Ionic but not Attic prose and is used freely by H. Here it draws attention to a notable feature of the story (cf. *GP* 248), the noting of Artemisia's impressive performance, which is also highlighted by the use of direct speech.

καὶ τοὺς φάναι 'and they said, "Yes, it is"'. φημί is regularly used thus (LSJ *s.v.* III); contrast the opposite in 6.61.4 λέγεται . . . τὴν . . . κελεῦσαι οἱ δέξαι, τὴν δὲ οὐ φάναι 'it is said that she asked her to show [the child] to her, but the woman refused.'

ἐπίσημον: this was a bow or stern ornament used to identify a ship. It could be either some sort of figurehead or painted decoration (3.37.2 gods, 3.59.3 boars) or a flag or other removable decoration (Morrison and Williams 1968: 120, 133–4): cf. **92**.2.

88.3 καὶ τὸ . . . γενέσθαι 'and the fact that no one from the Calyndian ship survived to accuse her'; the 'articular' infinitive (infinitive with the article) here governs a complex clause. Though they did not know it, in making the infinitive into a noun by adding the article, the Greeks were in fact returning it to its original substantival use; cf. **20**.2.

οἱ μὲν ἄνδρες γεγόνασί μοι γυναῖκες: the seriousness of this comment may be judged by H.'s remark that 'the greatest reproach amongst the Persians is to be called worse than a woman' (9.107.1; cf. 20). Such a remark caused Artaÿntes, one of the defeated generals at Mycale, to attempt to kill his detractor Masistes (ibid.). In Aeschylus, much is made of the effeminate side of the Persians, in a stereotyping that has its roots in Homer's Trojans (especially Paris) and continued to be a feature of Greek construction (and Western construction generally) of the Easterner. Though this central panel of the description from the Persian side involves gender reversal, H. does not exploit this stereotype of effeminacy, but barely hints at it.

89–90 Persian casualties and the Phoenicians' fatal attempt to blame the Ionians

89.1 ἀπὸ μὲν ἔθανε . . . ἀπὸ δὲ ἄλλοι: cf. **33**.1n.

Ἀριαβίγνης was brother to Xerxes and commander of the Ionians and Carians (7.97; Balcer 1993: 110).

ὀλίγοι δὲ . . . Ἑλλήνων 'some of the Greeks too died, but only a few'; ὀλίγοι contrasts with πολλοί earlier.

ἅτε γὰρ νέειν . . . διένεον 'since they knew how to swim, those whose ships were destroyed, the ones not killed in the hand-to-hand fighting, swam to Salamis'. The order of clauses has something conversational about it. ἐν χειρῶν νόμωι = ἐν χερσὶ; cf. 9.48.2 ἐς χειρῶν νόμον ἀπικέσθαι (LSJ *s.v.* I 1e). This sentence and the next are neatly structured: νέειν ἐπιστάμενοι – διεφθείροντο – διεφθάρησαν – νέειν οὐκ ἐπιστάμενοι. On the ideological importance of swimming, cf. **8**.1n.

90.1 διέβαλλον . . . ὡς προδόντων 'they began to slander the Ionians, (claiming) that it was the Ionians' fault that their ships had been destroyed, because (in their eyes) the Ionians had turned traitor.' The genitive προδόντων after the accusatives Ἴωνας and ἐκείνους can be explained by the fact that, in indirect discourse, a participle with ὡς can appear in the genitive in place of whatever case is strictly demanded by the grammar (*M&T* §§916–17; cf. **80**.2n.)

90.2 Σαμοθρηικίη: the Samothracians, from the island off the Thracian coast, were not strictly Ionians, but they would have been *Yaunā* to Xerxes (**10**.2n).

κατεδύετο 'began to sink, became water-logged', with which contrast the subsequent aorists κατέδυσε, καταδυσάσης; the Samothracian ship was actually sunk.

ἅτε δὴ ἐόντες ἀκοντισταί 'it was just because they were javelin-throwers'; δή provides a slight emphasis (*GP* 218, 221).

90.3 οἷα ὑπερλυπεόμενος 'because he was very angry'; οἷα + participle is causal.

90.4 ὅκως . . . ἴδοι: cf. **52**.1n.

κατήμενος: cf. Aes. *Pers.* 466–7 ἕδραν γὰρ εἶχε παντὸς εὐαγῆ στρατοῦ, | ὑψηλὸν ὄχθον.

πατρόθεν 'with his father's name'. So Darius lists the names of his fellow conspirators on DB in the form 'Gobryas by name, the son of Mardonius, a Persian' (=

Brosius no. 44, IV §68). Though Greek name-lists regularly include the patronymic, specifying its inclusion can be a mark of honour: cf. *Il.* 10.68 πατρόθεν ἐκ γενεῆς ὀνομάζων ἄνδρα ἕκαστον; H. 6.14.3 ἐν στήλῃ ἀναγραφῆναι πατρόθεν (of brave sailors).

οἱ γραμματισταί: cf. **85**.3n.

πρὸς δέ τι καὶ προσεβάλετο 'in addition, Ariaramnes, a friend of the Ionians, contributed somewhat to the demise of the Phoenicians by his presence.' For προσβάλλω + genitive, cf. Eur. *Med.* 284 συμβάλλεται δὲ πολλὰ τοῦδε δείματος, 'many things contribute to this fear', and perhaps (though the reading of the verb is disputed) Thuc. 3.36.2 προσξυνεβάλετο οὐκ ἐλάχιστον τῆς ὁρμῆς αἱ Πελοποννησίων νῆες.

Ἀριαράμνης: OP *Ariyāramna* 'Having the Aryans at peace'. It is uncertain which Ariaramnes we are to imagine here, but since he appears not to be in the battle, it is more likely he was the Ariaramnes who was satrap of Cappadocia and led an exploratory expedition to Scythia before Darius' campaign there (Ctesias, *FGH* 688 F 13 (20); Balcer 1993: 64–5), than the one whose death is recorded at Salamis by Plut. *Them.* 14.3 (cf. *Mor.* 173B–C, 488C–F; Balcer 1993: 136).

91–96 The battle from the Greek side

The previous section was based around Xerxes' perceptions of the battle and his recording of them. In this section, the technique is different, but matters of history and power are again important. Of these two episodes, involving competing claims by, respectively, Athenians and Aeginetans and Athenians and Corinthians, the first is, as far as the battle is concerned, of little consequence, and the second is false. Their significance, however, is that the first looks back to events a decade ago, and the second looks forward to the situation between Athens and Corinth in H.'s own time: together they represent a wide chronological span of mutual suspicion. The perspective on events therefore is not so much that of the characters in them as of the historian and his readers. Just as Xerxes could not easily tell the truth of events before his eyes, so historian and reader must with difficulty decide between Athenian and Aeginetan, and Athenian and Corinthian versions of events they did not witness. History is politicised: Athens charges Aegina with medism and the Corinthians with desertion, though both charges are rejected. Both Xerxes and the Athenians wish to control the record of the fighting, but Xerxes' recording and rewarding, for all its uncertainties, contrasts with the Athenian use of false testimony against their allies. Even with a great battle like Salamis, the truth is hard to find.

These speculations are encouraged by the structural similarities between the two sections looking at the battle from the Persian then Greek sides. Generalising accounts of notable deeds (**91, 93, 95**) are again interwoven with longer episodes (**92, 94**). The episodes both involve encounters of ships, and there is another three-ship incident. Artemisia's attack on an allied ship is now viewed from the Greek side (**93**). Similar themes recur also: conflict between allies (**92**), mirrors Artemisia's attack on a friendly ship (**87–8**), and slander of allies (**94**), mirrors the Phoenician accusations against the

Ionians (**90**); questions of loyalty to the cause are again important. Persian and Greek ideologies are examined through these juxtapositions.

91 οἱ μὲν δὴ . . . ἐτράποντο: nameless men turn to their task, in a chilling ellipsis of the Phoenicians' execution, which echoes the killing of the Euboeans' animals in **19**.2 ἐτρέποντο πρὸς τὰ πρόβατα.

92.1 ἐνθαῦτα συνεκύρεον νέες: there are five ships mentioned: (1) Themistocles' which, while pursuing (2) an anonymous ship, meets (3) that of his ally Polycritus the Aeginetan, which has just attacked (4) a Sidonian ship, which itself in an earlier incident (7.179, 181) had attacked (5) an Aeginetan ship on guard off Sciathos, on which was the Aeginetan marine, Pytheas. It was in this last incident that Pytheas had so distinguished himself that the Persians bound his wounds, took him to their camp and eventually put him on the Sidonian ship, whence his countryman Polycritus rescued him. Persian admiration of their enemy Pytheas may contrast with the mutual hostilities of the Greeks.

Πολυκρίτου τοῦ Κριοῦ: Polycritus appears only in this episode. Crius was a noted wrestler, whose name 'Ram' inevitably made him the butt of jokes: cf. 6.50, 73.2; Simon. fr. 507.1; Ar. *Clouds* 1355–6, with scholia. For his history, cf. **92**.2n.

τὸν δὴ περιάγουσα ἅμα τοῖσι Πέρσῃσι 'carrying whom, as well as its Persian crew'.

92.2 βώσας . . . ὀνειδίζων 'he shouted at Themistocles and taunted him, making mocking reference to the Aeginetans' medising'. The history behind this goes back to the Aeginetans' giving of earth and water to Darius in 491. The Athenians feared the Aeginetans had done this in order to get Darius' forces to attack Athens, and so persuaded the Spartan king Cleomenes to go to Aegina to arrest those responsible; Crius and other leading Aeginetans were taken as hostages to Athens (cf. 6.49–50, 73). Polycritus thus shows the Athenian Themistocles what Aeginetan 'medising' means now, by smashing into a Persian ship.

ἐπεκερτόμησε . . . ὀνειδίζων: for the collocation of these verbs, cf. *Il.* 2.255–6 ἧσαι ὀνειδίζων, ὅτι οἱ μάλα πολλὰ διδοῦσιν | ἥρωες Δαναοί· σὺ δὲ κερτομέων ἀγορεύεις, where Odysseus upbraids Thersites, in an episode which is again evoked in a context with Themistocles in **125** (*q.v.*). ἐπικερτομέω is confined to epic in early Greek (cf. Clarke 2001). On H. and Homer, cf. Pelling 2006b.

ὑπὸ . . . στρατόν 'under the protection of the land army'; so in 9.96.2.

93.1 ἤκουσαν . . . ἄριστα Αἰγινῆται: cf. Pi. *Is.* 5.48–50 (for Phylacides of Aegina) 'now Salamis, city of Ajax, could claim that in war it was saved by her sailors in Zeus' destructive rain, in the hailstorm of gore that slew countless men.'

ἐπὶ δὲ Ἀθηναῖοι 'and after them, the Athenians'.

Εὐμένης . . . Ἀναγυράσιος: from the deme of Anagyrus on the south coast of Attica, named after the stinking bean trefoil (*anagyrus*), and famous for its bad-tempered *daimon* (schol. Ar. *Lys.* 67); cf. Frazer on Paus. 1.31.1. Eumenes does not appear elsewhere (*LGPN* II *s.v.*(5)).

εἰ μέν νυν ἔμαθε ὅτι . . . πλέοι 'if he had known that Artemisia was sailing'. Normally, an imperfect indicative of direct discourse is retained in indirect discourse after past tenses (there being no separate imperfect optative), but the present optative is sometimes used when, as here, it is clear that the optative is standing for an imperfect (*M&T* §673).

93.2 **παρεκεκέλευστο** 'an order had gone out (*sc.* to take her alive)'.

μύριαι δραχμαί = one and two-thirds talents. Pay for a soldier or craftsman in the fifth century was about one drachma a day, so this represents some twenty-seven years' wages for such a man in full-time employment – or just over half a bribe to Adeimantus (**5**.2; cf. **4**.2n.).

ὃς ἄν: supply τῶι ἀνδρί as antecedent.

δεινὸν γάρ τι ἐποιοῦντο γυναῖκα κτλ.: cf. **68**α.1n.

94 A false tale of Corinthian desertion

This is a good example of H.'s technique of giving considerable space to a story along with good reasons for not believing it: cf. **118**n. This fits his declarations that 'I am obliged to say what is said, but I am absolutely not obliged to believe it' (7.152.3), and 'the less credible story must also be recounted, because it is current' (3.9.2). Here the tale is manifestly false for the time it refers to, but contains a truth about the future, which H.'s readers will appreciate. After 460, relations between Athens and Corinth deteriorated (Thuc. 1.103.4, 105.1), and this story would have particular resonance after the involvement of Adeimantus' son Aristeas or Aristeus in fighting against the Athenians at Potidaea in 432, and his summary execution by the Athenians, when he was captured with Spartan and other ambassadors on their way to Persia to seek help (cf. H. 7.137.3; Thuc. 1.60–5, 2.67; Carrière 1988: 236–41).

Plutarch accused Herodotus in passages such as this of acting 'like painters, who use shadow to highlight the bright parts of their work; so he strengthens his criticisms by means of denials and deepens suspicions by ambiguity' (*MH* 28). He also spends a good deal of time refuting this story (*MH* 39), which, he points out, conflicts with e.g. the inscription the Athenians allowed the Corinthians to set up on Salamis ('Stranger, we once dwelt in the well-watered city of Corinth: now Ajax's island Salamis holds us'; cf. ML 24), with the Corinthians' position immediately after the Athenians on the Serpent Column (ML 27 *Coil* 2 = Fornara no. 59; **82**.1n.); and with Adeimantus' epitaph ('this is the tomb of that Adeimantus, through whose counsels Greece crowned herself with the garland of freedom'; Plut. *MH* 39 = *A.P.* 7.347). The Corinthians also distinguished themselves at Mycale (9.105).

94.1 **τὰ ἱστία ἀειράμενον:** in battle, sails were taken down or even left ashore (Thuc. 7.24.2, 8.28.1; Xen. *HG* 2.1.29). To raise sail was therefore a sign of flight: cf. the Samians at Lade, who 'raising their sails, deserted their place in the line' (6.14.2).

τὴν στρατηγίδα: *sc.* νέα.

94.2 **ὡς δὲ ἄρα φεύγοντας γίνεσθαι:** in indirect discourse, when the main verb is in the infinitive, the verb in a temporal or relative clauses is sometimes put into the infinitive by assimilation (*M&T* §755).

τῆς Σαλαμινίης: *sc.* γῆς; 'topographical genitive' indicating their position.

<τὸ> ἱρὸν Ἀθηναίης Σκιράδος: this shrine is of uncertain location; Strabo 9.1.9 says that *Sciras* was the old name for Salamis.

τὸν οὔτε πέμψαντα . . . Κορινθίοισι 'which no one appeared to have sent, and which came upon the Corinthians when they knew nothing of what was happening in the battle'. τόν standing outside the first οὔτε-clause suggests that there will be two such negative relative clauses of which it is object. However, the construction shifts, and the repeated οὔτε has two different functions: the first governs the infinitive φανῆναι, the second the participle εἰδόσι. This divine boat recalls the appearance of the mysterious woman at the start of the battle (**84**.2).

τῶν ἀπὸ τῆς στρατίης 'the situation in the army'. This is an example of the 'attraction of the preposition'. One expects ἐν τῆι στρατίηι, but the use of ἀπό combines the two notions of 'the state of affairs *in* the army' and 'news *from* the army'; cf. 5.34.1 ἐσηνείκαντο τὰ ἀπὸ τῶν ἀγρῶν ἐς τὸ τεῖχος = 'they brought the things that had been in the field out of them and inside the wall'; Aes. *Ag.* 521 κῆρυξ Ἀχαιῶν χαῖρε τῶν ἀπὸ στρατου; cf. Fraenkel *ad loc.*; K–G I 546.

τῆιδε δὲ συμβάλλονται . . . τὸ πρῆγμα 'this is how they reckon that the event was divinely inspired'. τῆιδε looks forward, as always in H., except 2.104.2: cf. 3.68.3 ὑπώπτευσε τὸν μάγον ὡς οὐκ εἴη . . . Σμέρδις . . . τῆιδε συμβαλλόμενος, ὅτι τε οὐκ ἐξεφοίτα ἐκ τῆς ἀκροπόλιος, 'he suspected that the Mede was not Smerdis, on this reckoning, that he did not leave the acropolis.' The point is that these Corinthians, being absent from the battle because they had run away, could not otherwise have known the facts about it which were given by the figures in the boat, and so the fact that they *did* turn back to the battle shows that this supernatural event must be true.

94.3 καὶ δή 'even now'. The combination's basic function is to show that an event is actually taking place at a particular moment; it is often equivalent to a dramatic ἤδη (*GP* 252).

ὅσον αὐτοὶ ἠρῶντο 'just as they prayed they would'; the verb is ἀράομαι, which is generally poetic outside H.

λεγόντων . . . λέγειν 'when they said this – you see [anticipatory γάρ; **5**.1n.] Adeimantus did not believe them – they said the following.' The construction changes: it starts with a genitive absolute participle describing the divine figures, but then makes them the subject of the main verb λέγειν (for a similar instance, cf. **90**.1n.; Smyth §2073; *M&T* §850); the point of this construction is to emphasise the idea in the genitive absolute. λεγόντων and λέγειν are in the present tense, because verbs of saying can stand in the present when their effects start in the past and continue into the present: cf. ὅπερ λέγω 'as I said' (Smyth §1885a).

ὡς αὐτοὶ . . . ἢν μὴ νικῶντες φαίνωνται 'they were ready to be taken for hostages and slain, if the Greeks were not victorious for all to see' (Godley). For νικῶντες φαίνωνται, cf. **110**.1n. A similar offer to act as hostages until they were proved correct was made by the secret Samian embassy to the Greeks before Mycale (9.90.3).

94.4 ἐπ' ἐξεργασμένοισι 'when it was all over'; locatival dative of time.

95–6 The end of the battle

Aeschylus too puts this exploit on Psyttaleia after the defeat of the Persian ships, but makes it a very much grander affair (447–64), perhaps to give to the hoplites an exploit to match that of the fleet: both arms of the Greek forces thus have credit in the victory. There is a different version again in Plut. *Arist.* 9.1–2, with material from later sources. Cf. Fornara 1966 for the suggestion that the emphasis or otherwise given to this episode reflected political rivalry between the aristocratic and democratic elements, representing hoplites and sailors; also Harrison 2000b: 97–102.

95 ὀλίγωι τι πρότερον: 79.2.

96.1 διελέλυτο 'finally over'; the pluperfect is sometimes used in temporal clauses, where the aorist is usual, to mark an act as 'doubly past' (*M&T* §59).

96.2 An oracle is used as a closural device to a battle or other event, as after Lade and the capture of Miletus (6.19.2); cf. also **20**. However, the language of this section is awkward (see below) and the chapter's authenticity has been questioned by Powell (**20**.2n.).

Κωλιάδα: this was the site of an important shrine of Aphrodite, but its precise location is uncertain. Paus. 1.1.5 puts it about two and a half miles from Phaleron, perhaps at modern Cape Cosmas; Strabo 9.1.21 near Anaphlystus. Its priestess was important enough to have a seat in the theatre (*IG* II² 5119), though its rites gave the shrine a slightly risqué reputation: Ar. *Clouds* 52, *Lys.* 1–3.

ὥστε ἀποπλῆσαι . . . τοὺς Ἕλληνας: taking the text as printed, this would mean 'so that it fulfilled the prophecy, not only all the prophesying about the sea-battle by Bacis and Musaeus, but also what was said many years before these events about the wrecks that were brought ashore here, in an oracle by Lysistratus, an Athenian oracle-monger, which all the Greeks had forgotten.' As in **77**, a passage involving an oracle is couched in very awkward Greek. It is as if its author initially meant τὸν χρησμόν to refer only to the prophecy of Lysistratus, but then brought in Bacis and Musaeus, thus making what starts out as a single oracle cover two different oracles given at two different times by different people. That Bacis and Musaeus are both said to be the authors of the first oracle is also awkward. The subject of ἀποπλῆσαι will be the west wind, though this makes for a further awkwardness, in that the wind's bringing of the wrecks strictly fulfils only Lysistratus' oracle, not Bacis' and Musaeus' more general one(s). ἀποπλῆσαι has been emended by editors to a passive, in the light of Lorenzo Valla's translation *ut impletum sit*, but this does not solve all the difficulties. As with **77**, the strangeness of the Greek points to later interpolation. The simplest deletion is τὸν χρησμὸν . . . ἐξενειχθέντα, but the two datival clauses with two different grammatical functions in ἐν χρησμῶι . . . χρησμολογῶι are not pleasing.

Μουσαίωι 'the Man of the Muses', a significantly named famous mythical poet and seer, who is mentioned in the same breath as Orpheus, Homer and Hesiod (cf. e.g. Ar. *Frogs* 1031–5; Pl. *Rep.* 364E). He is especially connected with Eleusis, where he was said to be the father of Eumolpus, the ancestor of the main priestly family at Eleusis. His oracles were collected around 500. He is also closely associated with Orphic religion, and poems of an Orphic nature are ascribed to him. For the ancient evidence, cf. Kern 1922.

Λυσιστράτωι . . . χρησμολόγωι: Lysistratus is not otherwise known (*LGPN* II *s.v.*(1)). χρησμολόγοι were professional seers who provided and interpreted oracles, not so much from major centres like Delphi, but from seers such as Bacis (**20**.1n.), Musaeus, Epimenides etc. Their oracles had been written down early on and were then referred to later events. χρησμολόγοι offered guidance in various activities, but by the end of the fifth century their stock seems to have fallen, as the *polis* took control of religious affairs, and such 'unofficial' religious types were mistrusted: cf. e.g. Ar. *Kn.* 960–1099, 1229–48; *Peace* 1043–1126; *Birds* 959–91; Thuc. 2.8.2, 5.26.3, 8.1.1; Burkert 1962.

φρύξουσι 'will roast, parch (barley)'. Barley was a staple food, and when parched was easier to husk (cf. Ar. *Clouds* 1358). Solon is said to have made brides take a roasting pan (φρύγετρον) to their wedding, as a symbol of their role in providing food for the household (Pollux 1.246).

97–125 THE AFTERMATH

97 Xerxes' reactions to the defeat

After the broad canvas of the battle narrative, we move to the King's private discussions. The section interweaves the Persian reactions to defeat with a description of their messenger-system and the revenge of Hermotimus. The deliberations are divided into two sections (**97, 101–3**). Xerxes first plans a diversionary move to disguise his intention to withdraw not just from his own men, presumably to avoid panic, but also from the Greeks, so that they do not conceive the plan of destroying the bridges by which his army had marched into Greece. Then, in a wonderful scene of highly rhetoricised court intrigue, he holds discussions with Mardonius and Artemisia: the former seeks to atone for encouraging an expedition that has gone spectacularly wrong; the latter thinks coldly in terms of the preservation of the King's and her own interests. This debate mirrors the ones before the battles.

97 Greek sources make Xerxes' flight undignifiedly precipitate: in Aes. *Pers.* 465–71, 480–514 it is even more so than here. It is probable, however, that some days passed before he left. Furthermore, it is possible, but no more, that there was a revolt in Babylon by one Shamash-erība in 479, and that Xerxes left to deal with this because of Babylon's crucial position at the heart of the empire (Briant 1992); the exact chronology is uncertain, however, and the dating has been challenged (cf. Kuhrt 1997: 302–4; Tuplin 1997: 395–403). If there was such a threat, then it was wise for the King not to be absent on an expedition at the edge of his empire. Greek tradition preserves a version of events which puts the King in the worse light.

97.1 ἔμαθε 'understood', not 'learnt', since Xerxes is watching. Cf. 7.209.2, where it is reported to Xerxes that the Spartans at Thermopylae are practising athletics and combing their hair; Xerxes summons the Spartan king Demaratus, ἐθέλων μαθεῖν τὸ ποιεύμενον πρὸς τῶν Λακεδαιμονίων.

κινδυνεύσηι: still dependent on δείσας μή.

δρησμόν: it is now the Persians' turn to think of flight; earlier this word was applied to the Greeks (**4**.1, **18, 56, 74**.2).

ἐπίδηλος 'transparent (in what he intended)'.

χῶμα . . . διαχοῦν: 'cognate' accusative, where noun and verb are from the same root, as **109**.2 εὕρημα εὑρήκαμεν; cf. also **113**.1n. Xerxes seeks to construct a mole across the channel between Salamis and the mainland, which is a mile across at its shortest point and four fathoms (24 feet) deep. This is a much disputed passage, and it is indeed hard to see the point of such a mole. The massive nature of the undertaking makes it very unlikely that he would have constructed such a mole purely as a blind, unless one thinks that he had no such serious intention and merely gave the order to avoid rumours and speculation on how he would react the defeat. Later sources (Ctesias, *FGH* 688 F 13 (30); Strabo 9.1.13) say it was started before the battle, but this could be a rationalisation, made after his flight caused the idea of building a mole seem pointless. Even for Persian engineers (cf. Introduction, pp. 4–5) this would have been an enormous task. The Samians built a remarkable mole, 400 yards long and in a harbour up to 120 feet deep (3.60.3), but Xerxes' mole would have been a much bigger project.

γαύλους: a round-shaped merchant vessel, particularly associated with Phoenicia (cf. 3.136–7; Epicharm. fr. 54K). *Gaulos* was the Greek name of the island of Gozo near Malta.

ὡς ναυμαχίην ἄλλην ποιησόμενος: for all their losses in the battle, the Persians clearly had enough ships to make fighting a further battle eminently feasible; that is how the Greeks saw it (**96**.1).

97.2 πολεμήσειν: though with verbs like παρασκευάζω the infinitive is regularly present or aorist, the future is also used on analogy with verbs such as μέλλειν, ἐν νῶι ἔχειν. ἐκ παντὸς νόου 'in real earnest' here may therefore have influenced the use of the future.

98–9 The Persian messenger system

This passage neatly combines ethnographic description with narration: even as Xerxes' messenger is travelling to Susa, the system he is using is described; and after the description, the messenger duly arrives. The Hittites (*ca.* 1700–1200) had developed roads, and the Assyrians a postal service. Roads (about 8,000 miles in all) and messenger service enabled close political, economic and military control of the vast Achaemenid empire. H. says the horses ran for a day, which seems to be supported by the fact that the majority of Persepolis tablets concerning rations deal with single days (Hallock 1969: 6; Miller 1997: 114–17). The post-stations were situated about twenty miles apart: some 20 stations have been identified on the Persepolis tablets in the 375 miles between Persepolis and Susa. Rations were issued for single days, suggesting the *katagogai* ('inns') and *kataluseis* ('caravanserais', H. 5.52.1) were one day's journey apart; these were decorated and some had gardens attached (cf. **138**.2n.). Travel was extensive: the Persepolis travel-tablets (PF 1285–1579, 2049–57; PFa 12–23) speak of travellers from Susa and Persepolis to Egypt, Bactria, Babylonia, and Hindush. There were 'express messengers' (Elam. *pirradazish*, PF 1285 (= Brosius no. 185)), who travelled alone or with up to three companions; 'elite guides' (Elam. *barrishdama lakkukra*, PF 1317–18 (= Brosius no. 186–7)), who accompanied important foreigners and single women; caravan leaders (Elam. *karabattish*, PF 1341 (= Brosius no. 188)); and guards and guard-stations (PF 1250 *da'ubattish*, 1272 *dattabara* 'law-officers'; H. 1.23.3, 5.35.3, 7.239.3). Locals were impressed by these roads: the Thracians reverently left Xerxes' road unploughed and unsown (7.115.3), and the Greeks attributed their foundation to mythical figures (Diod. 2.13.5, 22.3–4). The Greeks had nothing comparable, relying on *hemerodromoi*, 'day-runners' as messengers (e.g. 6.105.1). Cf. also Xen. *Cyr.* 8.6.17–18; Ctesias, *FGH* 688 F 33; Hallock 1969: 6, 42; D. F. Graf 1994; Briant 2002: 357–87.

The description is also reminiscent of Aeschylus' account of Clytaemnestra's beacons that announced the fall of Troy: cf. *Ag.* 282–3 φρυκτὸς δὲ φρυκτὸν δεῦρ' ἀπ' ἀγγάρου πυρὸς | ἔπεμπεν ('beacon sent forth beacon by means of the courier-fire'); 312–13 τοιοίδε τοί μοι λαμπαδηφόρων νόμοι, | ἄλλος παρ' ἄλλου διαδοχαῖς πληρούμενοι ('such was the manner of my torch-bearers, each fulfilling his duty as substitute for the last'). A chain of beacons reminiscent of a torch-race announced the fall of Troy, and now a chain of messengers, also like a torch-race, take the news of another eastern defeat in the reverse direction. H. repeats Aeschylus' ironic move of talking of a victory over the East in terms of one of the glories of the eastern empires. This Aeschylean intertext associates Salamis with the last great Greek victory over the East. The Greeks at Salamis, it is hinted, have achieved something on a par with the mythical heroes at Troy. This is also how Simonides represents the battle of Plataea in the recently discovered fragments of his poem on that subject: having praised the Greeks at Troy, he asks the Muse to help him sing of the Spartans who gained glory at Plataea (cf. *IEG*², pp. 118–22, esp. fr. 11). Other, Iliadic, intertexts scattered through the book carry the same message (cf. **56–8**n., **92**.2nn.).

98.1 ταῦτά τε ἅμα . . . καὶ . . . συμφορήν: ἅμα + τε . . . καί = 'at the same time as'; cf. 4.150.3 ἅμα τε ἔλεγε ταῦτα καὶ ἐδείκνυε ἐς τὸν Βάττον. There are here ironic verbal echoes of the last messenger sent to announce the triumph at Thermopylae; cf. **54** Ξέρξης ἀπέπεμψε ἐς Σοῦσα ἄγγελον ἱππέα, Ἀρταβάνωι ἀγγελέοντα τὴν παρεοῦσάν σφι εὐπρηξίην.

τούτων δὲ . . . θνητὸν ἐόν 'than these messengers there is nothing faster that is mortal'.

ὁσέων ἂν ἡμερέων . . . διεστᾶσι 'however many days the whole journey requires, that number of horses and riders are stationed at intervals'; ἡμερέων is a genitive of the measure of time (Smyth §1325).

οὔτε νιφετὸς κτλ.: this is reminiscent of Homer's description of the Elysian Plain οὐ νιφετός, οὔτ' ἂρ χειμὼν πολὺς οὔτε ποτ' ὄμβρος (*Od.* 4.566), and οὔτε . . . οὐκ . . . οὐ is a largely poetic collocation (K–G II 289). The evocation of this famous passage contributes to the almost superhuman nature of this service; this and the poetic tinge ironically contrast with the disastrous news that is being carried. H.'s words were placed on the 1914 façade of the New York General Post Office, and became the US Postal System's unofficial motto.

μὴ οὐ κατανύσαι: the double negative with the infinitive, as regularly after a negatived verb of prevention (*M&T* §807; Smyth §2742).

τὴν ταχίστην 'as quickly as possible'; adverbial accusative.

98.2 κατ' ἄλλον <καὶ ἄλλον>: the MSS all have simply κατ' ἄλλον, but this cannot mean the required 'from one to another'; cf. ἄλλος παρ' ἄλλου διαδοχαῖς πληρούμενοι in the Aeschylus passage quoted above. Valla's translation has *in alium atque alium*, hence the supplement <καὶ ἄλλον>, which could easily have been lost through haplography after the similar κατ' ἄλλον. ἄλλος καὶ ἄλλος is not found elsewhere in H., but this is no reason to reject it, since it is not common generally: cf. Xen. *Cyr.* 4.1.15 ἄλλην καὶ ἄλλην πειρασόμεθα διώκειν; Euclid, 1.7 οὐ σταθμήσονται πρὸς ἄλλωι καὶ ἄλλωι σημείωι 'cannot be constructed from one point and another' (cf. LSJ *s.v.* ἄλλος II 3). κατά would have its distributive sense (cf. e.g. Aeschin. 3.182 δέκα δραχμαὶ κατ' ἄνδρα 'ten drachmas for each man'; Smyth §1690.2c), but it is hard to find convincing parallels.

παραδιδόμενα: *sc.* as subject τὰ ἐντεταλμένα, for which cf. **54**n.

λαμπαδηφορίη: on torch-races, cf. Jüthner, *RE* 12.569–77.

Ἡφαίστωι: we know of only one torch-race in honour of Hephaestus, the Hephaesteia in Athens (*IG* I³ 82.30–2; Ar. *Frogs* 131, 1087–98 and schol.), but the god may be specified as a further reminiscence of Clytaemnestra's beacon speech, which begins with his name (*Ag.* 281).

ἀγγαρήιον: the etymology of this word is uncertain. It may be borrowed from Akkadian *egirtu* 'letter' *via* Aramaic: cf. Mancini 1994. It and its cognates came in later Greek and Latin to be used of public or private duties and of servile activity: cf. LSJ *s.vv.* ἄγγαρα and following words, and in *Suppl.*; Chantraine 8 *s.v.* ἄγγαρος. Interestingly, Ἀνγάριος appears as a Greek personal name as early as the seventh or even eighth century (*Corinth* 15(3).1).

99.1 ἡ μὲν δὴ πρώτη ἐς Σοῦσα ἀγγελίη: the road from Sardis to Susa (described by H. in 5.52–4), which Xerxes' messengers will have used for most of their journey, was about 1,550 miles long, involving 111 stages (5.53).

ὡς ἔχοι Ἀθήνας: optative in indirect discourse in historic sequence, depending on ἀγγελίη.

οὕτω δή τι: 'the δή has a certain sense of irony ... as though Herodotos were thinking of the groundlessness of their rejoicing' (Shuckburgh); cf. *GP* 208–9 (viii) and (xii).

ὥς = ὥστε (*Lex.* B IX).

μυρσίνηι . . . θυμιήματα: the same materials were used when Xerxes prayed to the Sun at the Hellespont (7.54.1); cf. Alexander's welcome into Babylon as conqueror (QC 5.1.20).

99.2 κιθῶνας . . . κατερρήξαντο: Aeschylus makes this a frequent reaction of the Persians to bad news: *Pers.* 199 πέπλους ῥήγνυσιν; cf. 125, 468, 537, 832–6, 1030, 1060; H. 3.66.1; Ctesias, *FGH* 688 F 41. The *kithon* was the regular dress of the Persian noble; it had sleeves and was richly embroidered (7.61.1, confirmed by many representations in art).

οἰμωγῆι . . . ἀπλέτωι: the same expression recurs at the death of Masistius, respected most after the King and Mardonius (9.24, with 6.58.3–59 for other expressions of Persian grief). This brief proleptic passage is the only description H. gives of the emotive reactions in Persia, which are so graphically portrayed by Aeschylus. The Greeks attributed excessive grief to easterners, but H. is very much more restrained here than the tragedian.

ἐν αἰτίηι τιθέντες 'laying the blame on', only here for ἐν αἰτίηι ἔχοντες; cf. 3.3.2 ἐν ἀτιμίηι ἔχει . . . ἐν τιμῆι τίθεται. Mardonius had encouraged Xerxes to undertake the expedition (7.5–6.1, 9), and this clause justifies the steps he is about to take to preserve his reputation.

περὶ τῶν νεῶν . . . περὶ αὐτῶι Ξέρξηι: Macan tries to distinguish between the cases as follows, 'it was not grief arising about the ships (that had been lost), but fear centred on the King's person (lest he should never return)'. However, **74**.1 οὐκ οὕτω περὶ σφίσι αὐτοῖσι δειμαίνοντες ὡς περὶ τῆι Πελοποννήσωι, 'less afraid for themselves than for the Peloponnese', suggests there is no difference. Their concern for the king reflects the absolutely central place he held in Persian society: cf. **85**.3n., **118**.3–4.

100 Mardonius advises Xerxes with an eye to the future

Once again, H. presents the Persian command as a place where tactical thinking is dominated by the King's likely reaction (cf. **65**.5n., **69**.1n.): Mardonius is represented as thinking about saving his own skin and his personal reputation, rather than about the best course of action for all. When he speaks to Xerxes, however, it is as one who has thought about all the options open to the King (e.g. ἄλλην ἔχω καὶ ἐκ τῶνδε βουλήν, §3). It is a masterly piece of court rhetoric. It combines almost hectoring instructions (μήτε λυπέο . . . μήτε συμφορὴν . . . ποιεῦ . . . μὴ δὲ δυσθύμει . . . μὴ ποιήσηις . . . ἐμοὶ πείθεο) with repeated deference to the King's likely wishes: εἰ μέν νυν δοκέει . . . εἰ δὲ καὶ δοκέει . . . εἰ δ᾽ ἄρα τοι βεβούλευται . . . εἴ τοι δέδοκται; the perfects suggest that of course the King has already made a decision on the matter. It makes light of the losses (§2); stresses the Greeks' ultimate powerlessness (§2–3); and shifts the blame onto the allies (§4). It ends with a remark that is at once self-deprecating (ἐμὲ . . . χρή) and vengeful (δεδουλωμένην). The headstrong nature of Mardonius, seen here in his offer to reduce Greece with only a portion of the army, will become all the more apparent in book 9, cf. esp. 9.41–2, 48–9.1, 58–9, with F&M *ad locc.* and their Introduction 9–11. The apparent cleverness of Mardonius' calculations will be somewhat dented by Artemisia's even more cynical analysis in **102**.

100.1 δώσει . . . εἴη: for the difference in moods, cf. **26**.2n., **106**.2. Mardonius thinks he will certainly pay the penalty for having persuaded Xerxes to attack Greece, but that there may be a possibility of redeeming himself by great deeds.

ἢ κατεργάσασθαι . . . ἢ . . . τελευτῆσαι: both infinitives depend on ἀνακινδυνεῦσαι 'to take a gamble on'.

ὑπὲρ μεγάλων αἰωρηθέντα 'playing for high stakes'. The stake is rule over Greece, which he must have expected Xerxes would give him, once he had conquered it.

100.2 δέσποτα: cf. **68**α.1n.

οὐ γὰρ ξύλων . . . ἵππων 'wooden planks are not what our most important conflict is all about, but men and horses'; though ξύλον can be used poetically of a ship, here the tone is scornful. For the idea, cf. Aesch. *Pers.* 348–9 Ατ. ἔτ' ἄρ' Ἀθηνῶν ἔστ' ἀπόρθητος πόλις; | Αγ. ἀνδρῶν γὰρ ὄντων ἕρκος ἐστὶν ἀσφαλές; Soph. *OT* 56–7 ὡς οὐδέν ἐστιν οὔτε πύργος οὔτε ναῦς | ἔρημος ἀνδρῶν μὴ ξυνοικούντων ἔσω; Thuc. 7.77 ἄνδρες γὰρ πόλις, καὶ οὐ τείχη οὐδὲ νῆες ἀνδρῶν κεναί; Alcaeus, 112.10.

σοὶ δὲ οὔτε τις . . . ἠπείρου τῆσδε 'neither will any of these (Greeks), who think that victory (τὸ πᾶν) has been achieved (κατεργάσθαι, pf. pass. inf.) by themselves, attempt to oppose you by leaving either their ships or the mainland here.'

ἠντιώθησαν: i.e. at Thermopylae.

100.3 εἰ δὲ καί 'but if on the other hand'; καί reinforces the disjunction between the two conditional clauses (*GP* 305).

οὐδεμία ἔκδυσις μὴ οὐ . . . εἶναι δούλους 'there is no way the Greeks can escape paying for their actions now and in the past, and becoming your slaves'. μὴ οὐ is the regular negative after negatived verbs of preventing (**57**.2n.), and is also found when a positive expression (as here ἔκδυσις) is negatived by οὐ or α-privative (*M&T* §817; Smyth §2746).

εἰ δὲ ἄρα τοι βεβούλευται 'but if, as may be the case (ἄρα), you have decided'. Mardonius cunningly leaves to the end the option he wants Xerxes to choose.

100.4 οὐδὲν γὰρ ἐν Πέρσῃσι . . . πρηγμάτων 'no damage at all to your affairs has come at the hands of the Persians'. ἐν Πέρσῃσι acts almost as a dative of the agent with the perfect δεδήληται; cf. Thuc. 7.8.2, where Nicias sends a letter so that his opinion will be μηδὲν ἐν τῶι ἀγγέλωι ἀφανισθεῖσαν, 'in no way distorted by the messenger'; Soph. *Aj.* 519 ἐν σοὶ πᾶσ' ἔγωγε σώιζομαι. Mardonius means the actual Persians here, who were the central body of the army.

ὅκου 'in what respect'.

Φοίνικες κτλ.: **85**.1n.

οὐδὲν . . . τὸ πάθος 'this misfortune has nothing to do with the Persians'.

100.5 ἤδη ὦν 'so then'. The combination is often used by H. to introduce a point that follows logically from what precedes; here it introduces Mardonius' conclusion.

τριήκοντα μυριάδας: that the number of 300,000 is too high is generally agreed, but what the actual number was is hard to estimate. Logistically, 60–70,000 is most likely: Burn 1984: 511.

101–3 Xerxes asks Artemisia for a second opinion

For Artemisia's benefit, Xerxes strips the defensive rhetoric from Mardonius' speech, and pares it down to the two options. This paraphrasing is another variation on the epic habit of repeating speeches verbatim: cf. **68**n.

101.1 ὡς ἐκ κακῶν 'as far as was possible given his misfortunes'; cf. Thuc. 7.42.2 ὡς ἐκ κακῶν ῥώμη τις ἐγεγένητο. ὡς with prepositional phrases conveys a sense of comparison: cf. Thuc. 6.20.2 ἐπὶ γὰρ πόλεις . . . μέλλομεν ἰέναι μεγάλας . . . τό τε πλῆθος, ὡς ἐν μιᾶι νήσωι, πολλάς 'we are about to go against cities that are large and, as to their number, given that it is (only) a single island, many' (cf. K–G II 494).

βουλευσάμενος ἔφη ἀποκρινέεσθαι 'he would tell him after consultation'. βουλεύω and cognate words are used seven times in this paragraph and twice more at the start of the next. This emphasis on consultation rather deflates Mardonius' fourfold presumption that the King has made up his mind (**100**n.).

τοῖσι ἐπικλήτοισι 'councillors', members of the King's inner group of close advisers (cf. **67**.2n.).

101.2 μεταστησάμενος τοὺς ἄλλους: that the King removes his councillors and his bodyguard conveys the highest distinction on Artemisia, who last time could address him only through an intermediary (**68**).

δορυφόρους: the royal bodyguard, who may be the soldiers depicted on glazed polychrome bricks from the palace of Darius at Susa, wearing richly decorated Persian costume, carrying bows and quivers and holding spears with the rounded end balanced on their advanced right foot (a motif found at Susa since the second millennium; Amiet 1988: fig. 81; Curtis 2000: fig. 47; BM WA 132525).

ἔλεξε Ξέρξης: this summary of Mardonius' speech using similar language is a variant of Homer's wholesale repetition of speeches when they are relayed to a third party. On the ways in which H. conveys speeches within speeches, cf. **68**n., **140**n.

βουλομένοισι . . . ἀπόδεξις 'an opportunity to accomplish something would find them willing'; the emphasis is on the participle. On ἀπόδεξις in H., cf. Bakker 2002: 25.

101.4 ἐπιτύχω: a deliberative subjunctive retained in the indirect question; cf. **36**.1n. That the indirect-question construction had its origin in paratactic sentences can be seen here: lit. 'advise: following which course of action am I to succeed in having planned well?'

102 In her speech, Artemisia is the consummate courtier: she flatters the King, and shows her prime concern is his interests: his safety and that of his dynasty or 'house' must be assured (§2), and all achievements in the empire are his. She also protects herself: it is clearly safest to recommend the King's retreat, since (i) if disaster followed a recommendation to stay, Artemisia would be in Mardonius' current position, and (ii) any disaster that befalls Mardonius will be nothing to do with the King. The clear logical thinking of her earlier speech is again evident (cf. **68**n.). She even meets the objection that the expedition will not have achieved its aim, by emphasising that Athens has been sacked. Xerxes obviously intended to achieve more, but her implication is presumably that it was Athens that sacked Sardis, and he has had his revenge. Perhaps there is also the hint that though Darius had asked to be constantly reminded of that city at dinner (5.105.2), he had not, unlike his son, been able to burn it.

102.1 χαλεπὸν μὲν . . . εἴπασαν 'on the one hand, it is difficult to hit on the best advice in what one says when someone consults you'; μέν is picked up by μέντοι.

Artemisia begins with a deferential remark, which contrasts with Mardonius' imperatives.

102.2 σὸν τὸ ἔργον: there is something of a flattering exaggeration in this idea that all achievements belong to the King. On the Bisitun inscription, Darius, describing the suppression of the many revolts, uses repeatedly a formulaic phrase of the type: '(There was) a Persian, Hydarnes by name, my subject (*bandaka*; **68**γ n.), him I made their [i.e. the army's] chief. I said to them: "Go forth, defeat that Median army that does not call itself mine!" . . . By the favour of Ahura Mazda my army defeated that rebellious army utterly' (DB (= Brosius no. 44) II 25 etc.). Though he sums up with 'This is what I did' (e.g. ibid. IV 51), he clearly gives credit to his commanders.

σέο τε . . . περὶ οἶκον τὸν σόν 'if you and the power of your house survive'; *sc.* περιεόντων with πρηγμάτων, and for πρήγματα 'power', cf. *Lex. s.v.* 4. τῶν πρηγμάτων περὶ οἶκον τὸν σόν has been queried, but it is fairly close to periphrastic expressions such as 1.174.4 τὰ περὶ τοὺς ὀφθαλμούς = τοὺς ὀφθαλμούς, **24**.1 τὰ περὶ τοὺς νεκρούς.

As important as the King's safety is that of the royal house (OP *viθ*, Akkad. *bītu*, Aramaic *bīt* (whence names like 'Bethlehem'); οἶκος 'household, (royal) family' is used in Greek in very similar ways). This importance can be seen in inscriptions: cf. the examples quoted in **85**.3nn.; DPh (= Brosius no. 134) §2 'may Ahura Mazda protect me and my royal house'; and H. 6.9.3 νῦν τις ὑμέων εὖ ποιήσας φανήτω τὸν βασιλέος οἶκον.

102.3 οὐδέ τι . . . ἀπολέσαντες 'even if the Greeks do win, it will be no sort of victory, since they will (only) have killed one of your slaves'; τι goes with νικῶσι.

πυρώσας τὰς Ἀθήνας: this phrase picks up Xerxes' own first expression of intent πυρώσω τὰς Ἀθήνας (7.8β.2), and these are the only two instances of this largely tragic verb in H. (Chiasson 1982: 158).

103 ἥσθη τε: picked up, not by a καί, but by ἐπαινέσας δέ.

Ἔφεσον: here began the road to Sardis which then joined the Royal Road to Susa. It is a further distinction, after her private interview with the King, for Artemisia to be given the task of escorting home the royal children.

νόθοι: 'the Persians each have several legitimate wives (κουριδίας γυναῖκας), but they also possess very many more concubines (παλλακαί)' (1.135; cf. Deinon *FGH* 690 F 27; Plut. *Mor.* 140B). These 'bastards' will have been the children of women of the highest status among the latter. The difference between the two classes of women seems to be that wives, but not concubines, were formally married, and 'bastards' could not succeed to the throne if there were children of wives alive (3.2.2; Darius II in 424 was an exception, and he earned the epithet *nothos*). Though such *pallakai* had very high status (Greeks never call them *hetairai*), the distinction was important. When Cambyses demanded a daughter of Amasis in marriage, 'Amasis, troubled by and afraid of Persian power, could neither give nor deny his daughter [to Cambyses], because he knew well that Cambyses intended to have her not as his wife (γυνή) but as his concubine (παλλακή)' (3.1.2; cf. Xen. *Cyr.* 4.3.1, *Ages.* 3.3; Ctesias, *FGH* 688 F 13 (10)). In other words, *pallakai* could be women of high status but foreign birth.

Polygamy was practised by rulers to ensure sufficient sons from whom to choose a suitable successor, to fill key posts in the empire, and to be able to form alliances with and reward other important families at home and abroad. Large numbers of children were encouraged: 'if you shall not conceal this record [of Darius' deeds] . . . may your offspring be numerous!' (DB (= Brosius no. 44) IV 60; cf. H. 1.136.1 (rewards from the King for the largest families)). Persian nobles also possessed many *pallakai* of lower status. Cf. in general Sancisi-Weerdenburg 1983; Brosius 1996: 31–4, 89–90, 94–5, 191–2; Briant 2002: 277–86.

104–6 The revenge of the eunuch Hermotimus

Now that Xerxes has decided on his next moves, the narrative pauses for a vignette about a leading eunuch in his entourage. The story is an apparently simple one of revenge for mistreatment, fitting the pattern so often found in H. of punishment for crimes. It has a folk-tale symmetry, as the punishment repeats the crime: the good man prospers by his talents and triumphs over his enemy; the bad loses his prosperity and, in the mutual castration of father and sons, his house and lineage.

However, Hornblower (2003) argues that this tale does not record a true episode involving historical individuals, but that it is a 'signifier' for the catastrophe which befell Chios in 494 BC when, as a reprisal for the Ionian Revolt, the Persians castrated the Chian boys and deported the girls. The first part of the story stands allegorically for the Greek colonisation and subjugation of the indigenous inhabitants of the eastern Aegean, such as the Carians, and their expression of their identity by the creation of the Panionium: it is important both that the name *Panionios* is unique and a kind of *Festname* (a name derived from festivals and cult centres), and that like Ion, founder of the Ionians, Panionius has four sons. The second part stands for the Persian reprisals for the revolt, as Hermotimus has taken on the status of a Persian through his time at Sardis; Panionius and his family are utterly destroyed, as happened to the Chians in 494. The punishment takes place at Atarneus, a place associated in H. with pollution and death: cf. esp. 1.160, and also 6.4, 28. The positioning of the story at the moment of Xerxes' defeat indicates that this defeat is itself revenge for the Persian atrocities on Chios. For the folk-tale pattern, Hornblower adduces the story of Joseph in Genesis 37–45. This is an attractive reading, though it is perhaps a little awkward that the context is the preservation of the Persian King's children. Cf. also Griffiths 2001 (esp. 172); Braund 1998: 164–70 (esp. 166–7).

104 Πηδασέα: (Carian *p-a-d-s-'s*), from Pedasus, not far from Halicarnassus in Caria.

φερόμενον δὲ οὐ τὰ δεύτερα lit. 'who did not gain second prize amongst the eunuchs', i.e. was the most trusted. This is an athletic metaphor; cf. *Il.* 23.537–8 ἀλλ' ἄγε δή οἱ δῶμεν ἀέθλιον . . . | δεύτερ'.

εὐνούχων: literally 'guardians (ἔχω) of the royal bed (εὐνή)' (cf. e.g. 3.130.4). The term covers a wide range of different people from menial servants to trusted advisers of kings. Pictures of beardless adult males on Assyrian and Achaemenid reliefs may be eunuchs. In Greek sources, they are an important feature of ancient Near Eastern courts, and appear regularly in H., but there is a growing consensus that the Greeks may have exaggerated the number of actual castrati among 'eunuchs' in the Achaemenid court, and that the term was in fact an honorific court title. It is an odd fact that most of the important Achaemenid eunuchs have Iranian names, which has suggested to some that they were not castrati. There are references to them in Hittite and Urartian sources, and Assyrian sources make a distinction between *sha ziqni* ('the bearded') and *sha rēshi* (lit. 'chief'), but the translation of the latter as 'eunuchs' is problematic (Kuhrt 1995: 529–31); there are similar problems with OT *sarish*, translated 'eunuch' or 'court official'. Apparently 'inappropriate' titles for high officials are not uncommon: 'Nabu-zer-iddina, chief baker' heads a list of important Babylonian palace functionaries, but was also chief of the armed forces (2 Kings 25.8–21; *ANET* 307–8; Kuhrt 1995: 605–7); cf. the Persian *arshtibara* 'Spear-Bearer' and *vaçabara* 'Bow-Bearer', two of the most honorific posts (cf. **67**.2n.), and also the British royal family's 'Gentlemen of the Bedchamber'.

In Greek literature, eunuchs are said to have been acquired in various ways, such as tribute (500 Babylonian boys sent yearly to the king (3.92.1)), war booty, or from slave traders like Panionius (**105**.1). Castration seems to have been by crushing or removal (total or partial) of the genitals. Greek tradition paints two contrasting pictures of eunuchs. In Xen. *Cyr.* 7.5.58–65, Cyrus makes use of them in Persia because, having no families, their loyalty could be assured by appropriate treatment (cf. also **105**.2). By contrast, in writers such as Ctesias, Quintus Curtius and Plutarch, they tend to be scheming and untrustworthy, sexually ambiguous and often in league with equally deceitful princesses and queens (for a critique of this idea, cf. Wiesehöfer 1996: 79–88; Brosius 1996: 105–22, on women). Cf. in general Briant 2002: 268–77; Llewellyn-Jones 2002.

[οἱ δὲ Πηδασέες . . . Ἑρμότιμος ἦν]: this passage is excised by most editors because it seems to be an awkward (though not exact) paraphrase of 1.175, perhaps brought in here as an explanation of Πηδασέα by a scribe who remembered the earlier passage. H. could have put the passage in twice, but there are also verbal oddities: ἀμφικτυόνες, here 'dwellers-around', is not used elsewhere in prose except of the Delphic Amphictyons; ἀμφί + gen. in a local sense is very unusual (only Eur. *Hipp.* 1132 τὸν ἀμφὶ Λίμνας τρόχον and perhaps Theoc. 25.9 νέμονται ἐπ' ὄχθαις ἀμφ' Ἑλισοῦντος; K–G I 489); ἐντός is used in expressions of time (LSJ *s.v.* I.3), but has little meaning here with χρόνου.

πώγωνα: the abnormal change in the nature of the priestess portends a change for the worse in the natural world. This is a real medical condition, called the Achard-Thiers syndrome. Such women have inevitably been a source of fascination: cf. Ribera's painting of Magdalena Ventura in the Tavera Hospital, Toledo and Sánchez Cotán's of Brígida del Río, 'la barbuda de Peñaranda', in the Prado.

105.1 ἤδη emphasises the superlative μεγίστη; cf. Hermotimus' words at the dénouement of the story ὦ πάντων ἀνδρῶν ἤδη μάλιστα ἀπ' ἔργων ἀνοσιωτάτων τὸν βίον κτησάμενε (**106**.3).

ἀνοσιωτάτων: it is a mark of H.'s cultural broad-mindedness that he does not in general pass adverse judgement on the many foreign customs he records. Two further exceptions are his extreme distaste for Babylonian ritual prostitution of women at 1.199.1 ('most shameful') and disapproval of circumcision at 2.37.2 ('they put cleanliness before appearance'); passages like 1.203.2, 3.101.1, 4.180.5, on public sex indulged in 'like animals', need not be critical. H. is aware that different customs fit different races: cf. esp. 3.38 (given a choice men will always choose their own *nomoi*, as was shown when Darius suggested, to their horror, that Greeks and Indians exchange burial customs). Cf. Redfield 1980. For H.'s use of anticipatory expressions of this kind to engage the reader's interest, cf. Munson 1993.

εἴδεος ἐπαμμένους lit. 'who had reached (perfect middle of ἐφάπτω) beauty'.

ἐς Σάρδις τε καὶ Ἔφεσον: Sardis (Lydian *Sfarda*; OP *Sparda*; Dusinberre 2003) and Ephesus were important markets on the Royal Road (5.54), with temples served by eunuch priests, of Cybele at Sardis (cf. 5.102.1; Juv. 8.176), and of Artemis at Ephesus (Strabo 14.1.23).

χρημάτων μεγάλων: even in more recent times, the survival rate for castration was not high, thus increasing the value of those who did survive.

105.2 πίστιος εἵνεκα τῆς πάσης 'because of their complete trustworthiness'. πάσης in this position is emphatic; for the idea that eunuchs were especially trustworthy, cf. **104**n.

τοῦτον brings us back to Hermotimus.

καὶ οὐ γὰρ . . . Ἑρμότιμος 'and then – you see Hermotimus' fate was not all bad – '; καί joins the sentence ἀπικνέεται κτλ. to the last, and γάρ introduces a parenthetic comment (cf. **5**.1n.). The story is told in an apparently artless, almost conversational manner.

106.1 ὅρμα 'was preparing to lead'; inceptive imperfect.

κατὰ δή τι: cf. **53**.1n.

Ἀταρνεύς: a city near the coast opposite Lesbos. It was given to the Chians as a reward for handing over the Lydian Pactyes after his revolt against Cyrus (1.153–61; esp. 160.3–5).

106.2 οἱ ὑπισχεύμενος . . . ποιήσει 'promising him all the things he would do in return for this (good fortune)', lit. 'promising how many things'; the shift to the future indicative from the optative ἔχοι emphasises the certainty of this act (**26**.2n.).

ἢν . . . οἰκέῃ ἐκείνῃ 'if he would live there', i.e. in Atarneus.

106.3 ὡς δὲ ἄρα: ἄρα draws the reader's attention to the fact.

τί σε ἐγὼ . . . ὅτι κτλ. 'what harm did I do to you, myself or any of my family, to you or any of yours, in respect of which . . .?'; ὅτι is adverbial accusative and picks up τί. The awkward syntax represents Hermotimus' highly emotional state.

τὸ μηδὲν εἶναι 'a nothing'. Expressions of this kind are negatived by μή when they describe an abstract idea, but by οὐ when they indicate a fact (as in Thuc. 3.95.2 τὴν οὐ περιτείχισιν, 'the fact that there had been no blockade'; cf. Smyth §2736). Contrast Mardonius' scornful remark about the Spartans in 9.58.2 οὐδένες ἅρα ἐόντες ἐν οὐδαμοῖσι ἐοῦσι Ἕλλησι. Creon's despairing ἄγετέ μ' ἐκποδών, τὸν οὐκ ὄντα μᾶλλον ἢ μηδένα (Soph. *Ant.* 1324–5) exploits the difference: he is not just an abstract 'no-one', but is as if he were not alive; cf. also *Aj.* 1231 οὐδὲν ὢν τοῦ μηδὲν ἀντέστης ὕπερ, with Jebb *ad loc.*

μέμψασθαι is the MSS' reading. Powell supported Madvig's and Cobet's μέμψεσθαι (despite the great rarity and uncertainty of ὥστε + future infinitive outside indirect discourse (*M&T* §591)), on the grounds that 'the future on which logically the consecutive depends ("and I will punish you") is suppressed; the futurity must therefore be expressed in the consecutive clause itself.' But the futurity is supplied by τὴν ἐσομένην δίκην.

106.4 αὐτοῦ: *sc.* τὰ αἰδοῖα from the previous sentence. The mutual castration of father and sons marks the obliteration of Panionius' house and lineage.

περιῆλθε ἥ τε τίσις καὶ Ἑρμότιμος: a zeugma, almost grimly comic.

107 Xerxes leaves for Persia

H. quickly describes what was no doubt a major logistical task, but which has no particular significance. Matters presumably proceeded rather more slowly than he suggests.

107.1 ποιέειν . . . ὅμοια 'to make his actions match his words in what he attempted', a variation of ποιέειν . . . πειρᾶσθαι 'to try to make'.

ταύτην μὲν τὴν ἡμέρην: apparently the day of the battle, though much is crammed into it by H.'s narrative.

ἐς τοσοῦτον ἐγίνετο 'matters went so far'; impersonal, contrast **126**.1 ταῦτα μέν νυν ἐς τοσοῦτον ἐγένετο.

ὡς τάχεος εἶχε ἕκαστος 'as fast as each could'; τάχεος is partitive genitive, cf. 6.116 ὡς ποδῶν εἶχον; **111**.2 θεῶν χρηστῶν ἥκοιεν εὖ is similar (K–G I 382–3).

διαφυλαξούσας . . . βασιλέϊ 'to make sure the bridges were safe for the king to cross'; the attribution of this act to the ships rather than the Persians, and the dative of advantage + epexegetic infinitive are both unusual.

107.2 Ζωστῆρος: a promontory in Attica, south of Phaleron, so named because Leto loosened her girdle (ζωστήρ) there in preparation for the birth of Apollo and Artemis on Delos; cf. Pausanias 1.31.1.

ἔδοξάν τε νέας εἶναι: the flight is thus presented as not just hasty but panicky too. Cf. the even more ludicrous episode that is said to have occurred on Xerxes' retreat in **118**. H. is, however, also happy to make gentle fun of Greek timidity at sea: cf. **132**.3.

108 Eurybiades opposes Themistocles' plan to pursue the Persian fleet

After Xerxes' deliberations, we now have another Greek council, and familiar motifs recur from the debates before Salamis. Themistocles' tactical skill is again displayed in his encouragement to the Greeks to do exactly what Xerxes most feared (**97**.1). He proposes a course of action, but is again opposed by the Peloponnesians, this time successfully. He instigates another clandestine meeting, between Sicinnus and the Persians (cf. **75**), but this time not in order to see his tactics followed, but with a view to his own future career, in case he should fall out with Athens. H. thus merely hints at events beyond the end of his history, which readers will fill in for themselves.

108.1 Ἄνδρον: one has to pass Andros, 80 miles east of Salamis, to get to the Hellespont by ship; cf. **111**.1n. for the reason for stopping here.

108.2 διὰ νήσων τραπομένους: i.e. they should let the Persians return along the coast, whilst they themselves took the quicker route across the Aegean, moving from island to island. This is a similar strategy to the one adopted by Miltiades after the victory at Marathon, and as in that case the account is hostile to the general involved (6.132–6). In each case, the intention was to punish those islands that had not helped Greece and could be useful to the Persians as a base for future naval attacks on the Greek mainland.

πλέειν ἰθέως ἐπὶ τὸν Ἑλλήσποντον: it is a little surprising that Themistocles should have suggested such a plan; the sailing season was nearly over, and Attica was in the hands of the Persians.

Eurybiades' speech. Eurybiades is finally given a more prominent role than heretofore: we finally hear his views at some length. His speech is, however, given only indirectly. This allows an important tactical moment to be marked by speech, but not in such a way that it has the prominence of the earlier, even more crucial debates, whose importance direct speech characterised.

Eurybiades' oration is structured through a simple parallelism, but also employs some diversity; its relative clarity and plainness suit a Spartan. After a pair of conditional sentences, two groups of three clauses follow, each dependent on a dative participle (ἄγοντι μὲν . . . ἐπιχειρέοντι δέ):

> οὔτε τι προχωρέειν οἷόν τε ἔσται τῶν πρηγμάτων
> οὔτε τις κομιδὴ τὸ ὀπίσω φανήσεται
> λιμῶι τέ οἱ ἡ στρατιὴ διαφθερέεται.
>
> πάντα τὰ κατὰ τὴν Εὐρώπην οἷά τε ἔσται προσχωρῆσαι κτλ.
> ἤτοι ἁλισκομένων γε ἢ πρὸ τούτου ὁμολογεόντων
> τροφήν τε ἕξειν σφέας τὸν ἐπέτειον . . . καρπόν.

The first group are simple sentences, co-ordinated by οὔτε τι . . . οὔτε τις . . . τε. The second, at times echoing the first, convey the more graphic and worrying picture through a slightly more elaborate grammatical structure. A coda with the logical deduction from these arguments ends the speech.

108.3 ὡς ἄγοντι μὲν . . . ἐπιχειρέοντι δέ: these two groups of clauses represent the likely thoughts of Xerxes, as is shown by ὡς; the participles are conditional ones.

οὔτε τι . . . πρηγμάτων: the subject is τι . . . τῶν πρηγμάτων.

ἐπιχειρέοντι δέ 'if however he were to be active and take control of affairs, all of Europe would be likely to go over to him, by city and by nation, as they were either actually captured or came to an agreement before that; he would also have the annual crops the Greeks produced, year after year.' ἁλισκομένων and ὁμολογεόντων are genitive absolutes describing how the submissions would come about; αἰεί reinforces ἐπέτειον.

108.4 ἀλλὰ . . . γάρ 'but [whatever the force of these speculations, they did not matter] because he did not think the Persian would remain . . .' ἀλλὰ γάρ is a combination with a variety of meanings (cf. *GP* 98–108); here both should probably be taken with δοκέειν; cf. **5**.1n. for 'anticipatory' γάρ.

ἐατέον ὦν εἶναι: *sc.* τὸν Ξέρξην.

ἐς ὃ ἔλθηι: the subjunctive without ἄν in temporal clauses is a feature of H. and poetry (in Attic only with μέχρι (οὗ); Smyth §2402). The omission of ἄν is an archaism, going back to the time before ἄν/κε were used to distinguish the prospective use of the subjunctive (expressing the speaker's expectation of what would happen) from the voluntative (expressing what the speaker wanted to happen); cf. Palmer 1962: 149.

109 Themistocles changes his advice

109.1 ἐκπεφευγότων περιημέκτεον 'were angry because the barbarians had escaped'. When transitive, περιημεκτέω takes a dative, so ἐκπεφευγότων is a genitive absolute with a causal sense (K–G II 54), and περιημέκτεον is used absolutely, as in 1.114.4 μᾶλλόν τι περιημέκτεε.

ὁρμέατο is an unaugmented pluperfect middle: 'they had conceived the desire to sail (and still held it)'.

καὶ ἐπὶ σφέων αὐτῶν βαλόμενοι 'even attacking on their own'; ἐπί + the genitive of personal pronouns expresses dependence. The stage is here set for the subsequent increasing separation of Athenians and Peloponnesians.

βουλοίατο is optative because it records the view of the Athenians, a verb of saying being implied in περιημέκτεον.

109.2–4 *Themistocles' speech.* This is a highly rhetorical utterance, that relies more on emotion than logic. It has five parts, in an ABCBA pattern with the gods at the centre: (i) a generalisation, based on claimed personal experience, that defeated men *fight* better a second time; (ii) a deduction from that experience about *their own* best moves after their success; (iii) a reminder that that success belongs to the *gods*; (iv) encouragement to look after *their own* lives and property; (v) and the prospect of *action* in the spring: Ἰωνίης, the last word, is the rallying-cry. The encouragement to action in the spring is rhetorically clever: it will please those who want a pause now, as well as those who feel they should follow up their advantage, and, furthermore, leaves open the possibility of a change of mind in spring if that proves more sensible. Its opening is remarkable for rhetorical effects: πολλοῖσι παρεγενόμην ~ πολλῶι πλέω . . . γενέσθαι; four words beginning with ἀν(α)-; εὕρημα . . . εὑρήκαμεν; §3 contains six pairs of words or phrases. Similar features appear in his speech to Aristeides in **80**. The word-play characterises Themistocles as a master of sophistic rhetoric.

πολλοῖσι . . . ἀκήκοα 'I have been present on many occasions, and have heard of many more, when it happens that men, who have been driven into dire straits because they have been defeated, make up for and retrieve their earlier inadequate performance.' Since it correlates with πολλῶι πλέω, πολλοῖσι is grammatically neuter; ἀναμάχεσθαι and ἀναλαμβάνειν explain τοιάδε: lit. '. . . such things happen, (namely) that men . . .'

ἐς ἀναγκαίην ἀπειληθέντας: the verb is ἀπειλέω (LSJ *s.v.*A) 'be driven into', not ἀπειλέω 'threaten'; cf. 1.24.4, 9.34.2.

εὕρημα . . . Ἑλλάδα: this sentence is hard to explain. A possible explanation (if the text is sound) is that εὕρημα εὑρήκαμεν acts as a verbal phrase with ἡμέας . . . Ἑλλάδα as its object. εὕρημα εὑρίσκω is a cognate-accusative expression meaning 'I have a stroke of luck', so the sentence would mean something like 'we have had a stroke of luck as far as we ourselves and Greece are concerned.' For this combination of verb + an accusative of the idea which is contained in the verb + object, cf. Aeschin. 3.181 Μιλτιάδης δέ, ὁ τὴν ἐν Μαραθῶνι μάχην τοὺς βαρβάρους νικήσας; Dem. 19.293 Κτησιφῶντα γραφὴν ἱερῶν χρημάτων ἐδίωκε; Pl. *Apol.* 39c τιμωρίαν . . . πολὺ χαλεπωτέραν . . . ἢ οἵαν ἐμὲ ἀπεκτόνατε (cf. Madvig 1853: §26b). However, one would naturally expect here a participle meaning e.g. 'having saved'.

νέφος τοσοῦτον: though νέφος can be used neutrally in the metaphorical sense (*Il.* 4.274 νέφος . . . πεζῶν), it is also regularly used of unpleasant or dangerous things, e.g. Soph. *OT* 1313–14 σκότου (of blindness), Eur. *Med.* 107 οἰμωγῆς; cf. LSJ *s.v.*2. Powell notes that τοσοῦτον ἀνωσάμενοι νέφος ἀνδρῶν would end a hexameter, and the poetic tone suits the moralising nature of this passage (cf. also on ἀτάσθαλον and ὃς . . . ὃς below).

109.3 ἐφθόνησαν: that envy is a key aspect of the gods is stated early in H.: τὸ θεῖον πᾶν . . . φθονερόν τε καὶ ταραχῶδες (1.32.1, cf. 3.40.2, 7.10ε, 7.46.4; and also Aes. *Pers.* 361–2 οὐ ξυνεὶς δόλον | Ἕλληνος ἀνδρὸς οὐδὲ τὸν θεῶν φθόνον). However, this should not be overemphasised: φθόνος and cognate words are more often applied in H. to men than gods (Lateiner 1989: 196–7). For the idea that the gods keep competing powers in the world in balance, cf. **13** ἐποιέετό τε πᾶν ὑπὸ τοῦ θεοῦ, ὅκως ἂν ἐξισωθείη τῶι Ἑλληνικῶι τὸ Περσικὸν; and, applied to the natural world, 3.108–9 where H. gives examples of how divine *pronoia* has seen to it that 'timid and tasty animals have many young, so that they are not eaten up and disappear from the earth, but savage and terrible creatures have few.'

ἀτάσθαλον is usually poetic, but is found 6× in H., once in the description of Xerxes' words to the Hellespont as βάρβαρά τε καὶ ἀτάσθαλα (7.35.2).

ὃς . . . ὃς: 'the anaphora of the relative with asyndeton is rare and solemn' (Powell); this fits the religious nature of this part of the speech. The flogging of the sea is in 7.35.

109.4 ἀλλ' εὖ γὰρ κτλ.: Themistocles' coda varies its syntax for rhetorical effect. It looks as though εὖ . . . ἔχει . . . ἡμῖν 'for the present time of year it is as well for us to . . .' will introduce two infinitive clauses contrasted by νῦν μέν and ἅμα δέ; but after the first infinitive ἐπιμεληθῆναι the καί τις clause introduces an exhortatory tone with its jussive subjunctives, and another jussive then replaces the infinitive expected in the ἅμα δέ clause. This allows Themistocles to end with the rousing καταπλέωμεν ἐπὶ . . . Ἰωνίης.

τις . . . ἀναπλασάσθω: τις is used in a collective sense, 'let each man' (Smyth §1267). For rhetorical purposes, H. forgets that Athens is still in Persian hands.

ἀνακῶς ἐχέτω 'let him pay attention to'; ἀνακῶς, almost always found with ἔχειν, may possibly be connected with *κοϝέω (cf. ἀ-κούω, *caveo*) 'hear, understand' (Chantraine 83–4).

παντελῶς: an exaggeration, but this is rhetoric, not a description of the actual circumstances.

109.5 ταῦτα ἔλεγε . . . ἐγένετο: this story has been understood as meant further to blacken Themistocles' name, but Fornara 1971: 71–2 notes that he lies in the Greek cause. Furthermore, it has a dramatic purpose: the anecdote would 'to his audience have appeared to be the ultimate example of Themistocles' capacity to look after himself'. The ἄρα in ἢν ἄρα τί μιν καταλαμβάνηι . . . πάθος is masterly: in a conditional protasis it has the sense 'if, after all' (*GP* 37–8), so H. ironically allows Themistocles to entertain for a moment the idea that his relationship with Athens may deteriorate, as his readers know full well it did. H. again relies on the readers' ability thus to supplement his account with their own knowledge of the future in his portrait of Pausanias in book 9 (Fornara 1971: 62–6).

ἀποθήκην ποιήσεσθαι: an unparalleled expression, meaning 'to lay in a store (of gratitude) for himself'. If this story of the second message were true (on which question cf. **110**n.), Themistocles could have been acting quite cynically in his own interest, but equally he could have been playing a subtle diplomatic game, working hard for Greece whilst keeping channels open to the Persians. This could have enabled him, after a Greek defeat, not only to justify himself to the Persians (as H. suggests), but more particularly to influence Persian treatment of the defeated peoples.

ἐς τὸν Πέρσην: to King Artaxerxes according to Thuc. 1.135.2–8, in a letter dateable to 465/4; cf **110**n. The date of his ostracism is not certain: cf. Siewert 2002: Index *s.v.* 'Themistokles'; **4**.2n.

τά περ ὦν καὶ ἐγένετο 'which indeed actually (καί) happened'; περ ὦν stresses the reality of what was only supposed in the preceding conditional (*GP* 421).

110 Themistocles contacts Xerxes again

The question of how, after his first deceptive message (**75**), Themistocles could contact Xerxes again has been the subject of much debate: cf. Marr 1995 for a full discussion of the sources and problems, and suggestions as to how this story came about; also Lazenby 1993: 167–70, 199–202. It has been argued that Sicinnus' original message is cleverly worded, so that the nearest it came to major misinformation was the claim that the Greeks would not fight (**75**.3). It does encourage Xerxes to fight to prevent the Greeks escaping, but he has already decided to do that and the Persian ships are on the move (**69**.2–**70**.1); it is anyway up to Xerxes and the Persians to frame a suitable battle plan. Xerxes might well have been willing to treat with anyone, especially one as important as Themistocles, who might wish to change sides: compare the double game that Alexander played (**136**.1n.). Even so, the particular circumstances of this supposed second message make it somewhat unlikely.

Thuc.1.137.3–4 quotes a letter which he says Themistocles wrote to King Artaxerxes I seeking sanctuary, after he had left Athens: 'The letter says, "I Themistocles have come to you, as one who of all the Greeks did the most harm to your house, when I had to defend myself against your father who was attacking me. However, I did much more good to him at the time of his retreat, when I was safe and he was in great danger. A favour is owed to me in return (he cites both the forewarning message sent by him from Salamis to Xerxes to withdraw from Greece, and the subsequent Greek failure to destroy the bridges at that time, which he falsely claimed in his letter had been due to him), and now I am here able to do you great benefits, but pursued by the Greeks because of my friendship with you"' (§4). The parenthesis is Thucydides' paraphrase of part of the letter not quoted in full; the translation of it is Marr's (cf. 1995: 62–4). This letter would support the idea of a second message, but may itself be a later creation. The varying traditions about the second message may have grown up later in the century when Themistocles' actions and intentions became the subject of dispute.

If the story is a later fiction, Artaxerxes was anyway later sufficiently persuaded by Themistocles to offer him not just sanctuary but also great wealth (**4**.2n.): Themistocles may have made much of the fact (true or false, **108**.2n.) that he has persuaded the Greeks not to go to the Hellespont, and/or Artaxerxes may have seen a propaganda value in having a Greek as famous as Themistocles in his control. The Persians had treated remarkably generously other individuals who had done them (often great) disservice. Cyrus kept his attacker Croesus honourably at court (1.88.1), and H. says Darius would have pardoned Histiaeus despite his involvement in the Ionian Revolt, had he not been murdered before he had the chance (6.30). When Miltiades' son Metiochus was captured by the Persians, he was given property and a wife, though his father was responsible for the execution of Darius' envoys (cf. 6.41; and especially 3.15.2–3 on Persian humane treatment generally of the sons of rebellious kings; also **140**α.1, β.4 for Xerxes' offer to forgive the Athenians their 'misdeeds' if they will join him).

110.1 διέβαλλε 'was being deceitful', 'putting them off the scent' (Shuckburgh); cf. 5.107 Ἱστιαῖος μὲν δὴ λέγων ταῦτα διέβαλλε, Δαρεῖος δὲ ἐπείθετο.

δεδογμένος . . . ἐφάνη 'since he had seemed to be clever before, and now it was obvious that he actually was clever and full of wise advice'. As a rough rule, φαίνομαι is used with a participle to express what is plainly the case, but with an infinitive to express what may or may not be true (*M&T* §914.5; Smyth §2143); δοκέω is constructed only with the infinitive because it involves appearance.

110.2 τοῖσι . . . φράσαι 'whom he trusted, even though they might face every form of torture, to keep silent about the things he ordered them to tell the king'. The danger involved in Themistocles' approach to the King is clear here: if caught by the

Greeks, these men, because they were slaves, could well be tortured for information. In Ctesias, *FGH* 688 F 13 (30), Themistocles and Aristeides are together responsible for encouraging the flight of the king.

ἀναβὰς παρὰ Ξέρξην: this time, Sicinnus sees Xerxes himself rather than just his commanders. The economy of H.'s narrative can be seen here. That Sicinnus should be able to go straight to the King is, given the way in which access to him was restricted (**68**α.1n.), somewhat unlikely, and there is no mention of interpreters; no reply is given. Similar is the direct access of the herald to the King in **114**.1 and that of the fisherman to the tyrant Polycrates in 3.42.

110.3 Θεμιστοκλέης . . . Θεμιστοκλέης: the repetition not only helps to fix the name in Xerxes' mind, but in the second case makes Sicinnus' words echo Themistocles' original command: 'Tell him Themistocles the Athenian, wishing to help you . . .' Something of Themistocles' pride comes across, and Sicinnus' grand recital of Themistocles' name, his father's name and his qualities not only contrasts with his anonymous ἔπεμψέ με στρατηγὸς ὁ Ἀθηναίων in **75**.2, but also paints Themistocles as a man worthy to be a potential 'Benefactor' to the King (**85**.3n.).

111–12 Greek money-collecting

The tenor of the narrative is again unflattering to Themistocles, but again enough is said to make plain the fact that he and the Greeks sought money from those who had sided with the Persians or at least had not helped the Greeks. The witty remarks of the Andrians do not disguise or excuse their pro-Persian stance, and the unwillingness to contribute could be construed as an unfriendly act towards the Greek war effort that receives a condign response. The strategy seems to be to bring the islands of the Cyclades back into the Greek fold in order to make it difficult for the Persians to use them as a base: Miltiades attempted something similar after Marathon (6.132–3). This money-collecting expedition is characterised as private profit-making, but in reality may rather have been an attempt to generate funds to cover the very considerable costs of naval campaigning. Such money-gathering is a standard feature of Greek campaigns in the fifth and fourth centuries; cf. also 9.114–21.

111.1 ἀπέδοξε μήτ' ἐπιδιώκειν 'had decided that they would not pursue'; μή is regularly used pleonastically with the infinitive to reinforce the negative aspect of verbs such as those of denying, restraining, deciding against, etc. (*M&T* §815).

λύσοντας: the accusative, despite the use of dative σφι earlier, is the result of the influence of the infinitive, the subject of which is normally in the accusative; cf. **24**.2n.

τὴν Ἄνδρον: the Andrians were part of the Persian fleet at Salamis (**66**.2).

περικατέατο: cf. **73**.3n.

111.2 Ἀναγκαίην: for H.'s use of the idea of the compulsion of necessity in its religious and political forms, cf. Munson 2001b.

ὡς ἥκοιεν . . . δοτέα εἶναι: . . . ὡς . . . ἦσαν: the construction of the indirect discourse changes twice (**26**.2n.).

κατὰ λόγον ἦσαν ἄρα 'the Athenians were indeed, from what he said, very reasonably great and fortunate'. The imperfect and ἄρα together suggest with a certain irony that the Andrians had not, or at least pretend they had not, fully appreciated just how fortunate the Athenians were (*M&T* §39).

θεῶν . . . ἥκοιεν εὖ 'were well supplied with useful gods'. With ἥκω and intransitive ἔχω, adverbs of manner like εὖ are used with the genitive; cf. 5.62.3 χρημάτων εὖ ἥκοντες (Smyth §1441; **107**.1n.).

111.3 εἶναι . . . ἐκλείπειν . . . φιλοχωρέειν . . . δώσειν have been attracted into the infinitive in the subordinate clauses of an accusative and infinitive construction (**94**.2n.).

γεωπείνας ἐς τὰ μέγιστα ἀνήκοντας lit. 'short of land, reaching it to the highest degree', i.e. 'as short of land as one could be'. There is no exact parallel; 5.49.3 ἐς τὰ μέγιστα ἀνήκετε ἀρετῆς πέρι 'you have reached the highest pitch of valour' is nearest.

Πενίην τε καὶ Ἀμηχανίην: the Andrians are humorously made to cap the remark of Themistocles, replacing his Πειθώ and Ἀναγκαίη with the similar-sounding personified abstractions. This is the third time that Themistocles has been the recipient of a smart remark: there is a crescendo in his replies, from a riposte (**59**), to a threat (**61**), to a siege; cf. also **125**. A similar paradoxical remark was made, in similar circumstances, by the Thessalians in 7.172.3 οὐδαμὰ γὰρ ἀδυνασιῆς ἀνάγκη κρέσσων ἔφυ ('necessity was never stronger than inability').

ἐπηβόλους 'in possession of'.

112.1 πλεονεκτέων: πλεονεξία is a characteristic which Thucydides particularly associates with the Athenians (1.77.3–4). The shift in the portrayal of Themistocles from saviour at Salamis to extortioner has been seen as Herodotus' reflection of the way in which the Athenians went from being the saviours of Greece against the Persians to an oppressive imperial power; cf. e.g. Fornara 1971: 66–73; Evans 1991: 75–81.

διὰ . . . χρεώμενος 'using the same messengers' (cf. **110**.2–3); cf. 1.99.1 δι' ἀγγέλων δὲ πάντα χρᾶσθαι for the meaning 'deal with through messengers'. The presence of χρεώμενος, deleted by some editors, is supported by the survival of the final sigma in the papyrus.

112.2 Καρυστίων: for their medising, cf. **66**.2; for Paros, 6.133.1, and **67**.1, where they took neither side.

πολιορκέοιτο διότι ἐμήδισε: the moods differ because aorist indicatives without ἄν in subordinate clauses in indirect speech are not normally changed to the optative (though in fact in such causal clauses with ὅτι and ὡς the change does happen: *M&T* §693).

εἰ δὲ δή 'but whether in fact'.

112.3 καίτοι . . . γε 'on the other hand, for the Carystians at any rate . . .'; καίτοι is adversative, γε stresses the word it follows (*GP* 564).

τούτου εἵνεκα 'as a result of this', i.e. their payment of the money.

λάθρηι: remarks were made at the time about Themistocles' increase in wealth (Aelian, *VH* 10.17), and the lyric poet Timocreon attacked him for the way he used his money (which did not include helping Timocreon; Plut. *Them.* 21).

113 Mardonius selects his army

Two chapters concerning Mardonius (**113–14**) precede two longer sections with different versions of Xerxes' retreat (**115–17** and **118–20**). The chapters on Mardonius are in ill-omened juxtaposition: his selection of forces is followed by Xerxes' unintentionally prophetic remark to the Spartans that 'Mardonius will make suitable amends' for Leonidas' death (§2).

113.1 ἐξήλαυνον . . . τὴν αὐτὴν ὁδόν: a 'cognate' accusative; cf. **97**.1n., except that here the accusative is not from the same root as the verb, but has a similar meaning to it (Smyth §1567). The road is presumably the main one through Eleusis to Thebes, but it is possible that another, via Deceleia to Tanagra, was also used, the route taken by Mardonius (9.15). For routes into Attica, cf. Ober 1985: 101–29.

ἔδοξε . . . ἀνωρίη εἶναι τοῦ ἔτεος: ἔδοξε is used here in two different ways in the two clauses, (i) impersonally, 'it seemed good to Mardonius', and (ii) with ἀνωρίη as subject 'it seemed not the right time of year'. ἀνωρίη is found only here, but cf. the adjective ἄνωρος, LSJ *Suppl. s.v.*; for the genitive, cf. Antiphon, 2.1.4 ἀωρὶ τῶν νυκτῶν 'late at night'; **12**.1n.

113.2 ἀθανάτους: so called, according to H., because there were always exactly 10,000 of them; when one died, he was replaced by another (7.83.1). They were the elite of the land forces and crucial to the King's power and security (cf. Xen. *Cyr.* 7.5.66–8, 8.5.3). They may have incorporated the select group of one thousand, distinguished by golden pomegranates on the ends of their spears, who formed the King's bodyguard (7.41.2; Heracleides, *FGH* 689 F 1; Diod. 17.59.3; Arr. *Anab.* 3.11.5; cf. **101**.2n. for their possible appearance). Persepolis reliefs suggest that Persians, Medes and Elamites served in this unit (cf. Young, *CAH*² IV 91 n. 72). On campaign, they travelled in style: 'they had wagons in which were their concubines and a large and elaborate retinue; and their food was carried, separately from the other soldiers, by camels and yoke-animals' (7.83.2; cf. Introduction, §4). They fought under Hydarnes at Thermopylae and were used in the encirclement of the Greeks via the path shown by Ephialtes (7.211, 215, 218). Cf. Briant 2002: 261–2.

113.2 Ὑδάρνεος: (OP *Vidarna*) a Persian and *strategos* of the coastal dwellers of Asia Minor, who had tried in vain to persuade Spartan ambassadors to come over to the King's side (7.135; cf. Balcer 1993: 125–6). He may have been son of the Hydarnes who was one of Darius' seven conspirators (DB (= Brosius no. 44) IV §68; H. 3.70.2; Lewis 1977: 84 n. 14), and was put in charge of suppressing the revolt of Media in 522–521 (DB (= Brosius no. 44) II §24–5); he was later made hereditary satrap of Armenia.

λείψεσθαι βασιλέος lit. 'to be left behind away from the King': the verb is middle in form but passive in sense (cf. **49**.2n); the genitive is ablatival.

τὴν ἵππον τὴν χιλίην: there were two such elite cavalry troops (7.40.2, 41.1).

Μήδους: here to be distinguished from the Persians. They were armed like Persians, with the *tiara*, tunics with metal fish-scale armour, trousers, wicker shields, long bows and a quiver, short spears and a short sword (7.62.1; cf. 61.1). On Achaemenid reliefs, where they often alternate with Persians, they characteristically wear a domed felt hat with a tassel or a *bashlyk* (a three-knobbed headdress with muffler flaps), ear ornaments, belted coat with a Median sword hanging in an elaborately decorated scabbard at the right side (Schmidt I Pl. 120), long trousers and strapped shoes.

Σάκας: OP *Sakā* 'Scythians' covers a great swathe of peoples along the northern borders of the empire, from Sogdia (OP *Sugda*) to the Thracians (*Skudra*) west of the Black Sea. There were three branches: south of Kazakhstan, the *Haumavargā* ('who drink *hauma*', an intoxicating ritual drink of crushed fly-agaric mushrooms (Skt. *sóma*)); east of the Caspian Sea, the *Tigraxaudā* ('Pointed-hat Scythians'); and north of the Black Sea, the *Paradraiyā* ('Scythians across the sea'; cf. 4.1–144). In 7.64.2, H. says Xerxes' Sacae were 'Amyrgians', i.e. the *Hauma*-drinkers, who, as he says, had trousers, daggers and battle-axes: see the reliefs on the *Apadāna* (Delegation 17; Schmidt I Pl. 43; III Pl. 103D) and royal tombs (Bearer 14; Schmidt III fig. 43). However, he also gives them pointed hats, something they (unlike many Scythians) do not have on the monuments. The hats are probably H.'s mistake, but the *Haumavargā* may well have been the ones who accompanied Xerxes: they take precedence over the *Tigraxaudā* in the Achaemenid inscriptions and appear to have been important guardians of the north-east frontier. For the problems, cf. Schmidt III 111–16.

The nomadic Scythians moved into the Near East in the seventh century, troubling the Assyrians and the Medes (cf. 1.103.3–106). As mounted bowmen, feared for their repeated cavalry attacks and retreats, they were amongst the most important warriors in the army, serving permanently in many parts of the empire: statuettes of Sakai wearing *bashlyks* (previous note) and long narrow trousers have been found from Egypt to Central Asia. They improved the technology of bows and arrows in war, had distinguished themselves at Marathon (6.113.1), and would do so again at Plataea (9.71.1). They served also as marines alongside the Persians and Medes on Persian ships (7.96.1, corroborated by a Babylonian document (*VS* 20.49)). Their commander was Hystaspes, son of Darius and Atossa (7.64.2). On the Scythians, cf. Sulimirski and Taylor *CAH*² III pt.2 547–90; S. R. West, 2002.

Βακτρίους: OP *Bāxtrish*, the inhabitants of one of the most important central Asian kingdoms, roughly northern Afghanistan. It was conquered by Cyrus sometime in the 540s (cf. 1.153.4), and Darius lists Bactrians as his subjects (e.g. DPe (= Brosius no. 133) §2; cf. H. 3.92.2). Their importance is shown by the fact that Bardiya, Cyrus' elder brother, was made satrap of Bactria, as a consolation for not getting the kingship; Aes. *Pers.* 732–3 cites Susa and Bactria as emblematic of the Persian empire as a whole. Bactria was a producer of high-quality art from the third millennium onwards. It conducted trade with Mesopotamia (notably in lapis lazuli), and its oases were highly fertile agriculturally, thanks to impressive irrigation works. Though part of the empire, archaeology suggests that their material culture was unaffected by Achaemenid domination (Lyonnet 1990). They were Iranian-speakers, and armed with Median helmets, reed bows and short spears (7.64.1, 86.1). On the monuments they wear belted coats and trousers, hairnets, elaborate ear pendants and Median swords; their gift is a Bactrian camel (*Apadāna* Delegation 15; Schmidt I 88 with Pl. 41, III Pl. 102F; royal tombs, Bearer 6; ibid. III 148 with fig. 41).

Ἰνδούς: OP *Hinduyā*, from *Hindush*, modern Sind (all from Indo-Iranian *sindhu* 'a frontier', with *s* > *h*, as regularly in OP). These were people from the Indus valley, which Darius had conquered (4.44; they appear regularly on the inscriptions). In Babylonia they formed part of military colonies which, in return for land, paid taxes and provided a certain number of warriors (Dandamayev and Lukonin 1989: 147, 232). In fifth-century Babylon, there were *indumāja*, 'chiefs of the Indians', with Babylonian and Iranian names (ibid. 311). Their tribute was 360 talents of gold dust, and H. calls them the most populous nation known to the Greeks (3.94.2). They wore cotton armour, and had cane bows and arrows tipped with iron; some were on horseback, some in chariots, drawn by horses or wild asses (7.65, 86.1). On the *Apadāna*, their leader has a long skirt with a cape over it, his followers short skirts and bare upper body; they bring a donkey, axes and, possibly, gold dust (Delegation 18; Schmidt I 89 with Pl. 44; III 152 with Pl. 103G). Cf. Vogelsang 1990.

καὶ τὸν πεζὸν καὶ τὴν ἵππον: i.e. both the foot-soldiers and the cavalry of all the races mentioned.

113.3 τοῖσι εἴδεα . . . πεποιημένον 'choosing those who had notable personal appearance and any whom he knew to have performed valiant deeds'. The construction shifts from the relative τοῖσι (with which *sc.* τούτους depending on διαλέγων) to εἰ τέοισι 'if by any'; τέοισι is dative of the agent (**53**.2n.). τε should strictly follow τοῖσι therefore, but follows εἴδεα as if there was to be another, parallel noun clause. εἴδεα is a 'distributive' plural, used, as often with abstracts, to refer to single things held by a number of people (Smyth §1004).

Beauty and size were a major aspect of power and authority in Achaemenid society. H., after describing Xerxes' spectacular forces, comments 'of all the tens of thousands of men there no one, for beauty and stature, was worthier than Xerxes to hold that command' (7.187.2), and Tigranes, 'the best-looking (κάλλεϊ) and tallest man in Persia' (9.96.2) commanded the army left by Xerxes to hold Ionia. In Xen. *Cyr.* 4.5.57, Cyrus the Younger similarly chooses men for their looks (cf. *Cyr.* 7.4.14), and Xenophon says Cyrus adopted and recommended the Median mode of dress because 'if anyone had a physical defect the dress would help to conceal it, and it made them very tall and handsome' (*Cyr.* 8.1.40). Cf. also *Cyr.* 2.2.28–31; Pl. *Alc.* 121D; and the Ethiopians, who chose their king by size (H. 3.20.2). To select fighting men for their beauty was an oddity among the Greeks: cf. the *lochos* of handsome youths put together by the *paiderastes* Episthenes (Xen. *Anab.* 7.4.8) and perhaps the Theban Sacred Band.

στρεπτοφόρους τε καὶ ψελιοφόρους: these torques and armlets were characteristic wear of aristocratic Persians (9.80.2, Xen. *Anab.* 1.8.29, *Oec.* 4.23; etc.), and were given as marks of honour at the Persian court (Xen. *Anab.* 1.2.27). In the Oxus treasure, there are superb examples, with the ends decorated with winged griffins and other animal heads, and with inlaid glass and coloured stones (BM 124017; Curtis 2000: fig. 69; cf. Bittner 1987: 247–9).

ἐπὶ δέ 'and in addition'; the adverbial use of the preposition (cf. **40**.1n.).

πλῆθος μὲν οὐκ ἐλάσσονες: appears to contradict πλεῖστον ἔθνος Πέρσας. Most editors delete more or less of the sentence.

ῥώμηι δὲ ἥσσονες: it is a constant theme in Greek tradition (and perhaps also Persian) that the Medes were much more luxurious-living and self-indulgent than the Persians, who came from poorer lands and were consequently hardier; cf. e.g. 1.125–6, 9.122; Xen. *Cyr.* 4.1.13–14, 8.8.15.

114 Xerxes' ill-omened reply to a Spartan embassy

On this episode, cf. Asheri 1998: 65–75.

114.1 ἐξ ἐκείνου: ἐκ + genitive of the agent = ὑπό is a feature of Ionic prose (and especially H.) and tragedy, more than of Attic prose (K–G I 460).

114.2 ὦ βασιλεῦ Μήδων: this expression is used twice elsewhere in H.: 1.206.1, where queen Tomyris chides Cyrus for the his expansionist desires, and 7.136.2 where Spartan spies refuse to perform *proskynesis* before Xerxes. These suggest it is not a deferential form of address; cf. also **5**.2n.

Λακεδαιμόνιοί τέ σε καὶ Ἡρακλεῖδαι: a grand formula, perhaps with a religio-legal tone fitting the formal claim made here. The Heracleidae are possibly the two kings, descended from the hero, but equally the two words could essentially mean 'Spartans'.

ὁ δὲ γελάσας: 'the only two men who laugh more than once in Herodotus are the mad King Cambyses and the insatiate King Xerxes (six times and four, respectively)' (Lateiner 1977: 178); for Xerxes, cf. also 7.103.1, 105, 209.1. Laughter, especially scornful, not infrequently points to coming disaster in H.

τοιγάρ 'right, in that case'; τοιγάρ marks a strong logical connection. This is apparently the only instance of this combination in prose; it is found in drama (usually iambics) and in Homer, where it is used in replies to requests (*GP* 565–6).

ὅδε δίκας δώσει: Xerxes is talking ironically, and the meaning is best captured by the English word 'requite', which has a double meaning. Xerxes means that Mardonius will 'requite the Spartans as they deserve', i.e. 'repay' them by inflicting another defeat like Thermopylae on them. In the event, the words turn out to have the other meaning, 'make amends': Mardonius is killed at Plataea, 'and so atonement was made (δίκη . . . ἐπετελέετο) by Mardonius to the Spartans for the death of Leonidas, according to the oracle' (9.64.1). δίκας διδόναι is used in five of its 17 uses of Mardonius (also 7.5.2; **100**.1; 9.58.4, 64.1; Lateiner 1980): he is a man marked out for punishment.

The words are a κληδών, a chance utterance that turns out to be prophetic in a way not intended by the speaker. This is shown by the use of δέκεσθαι (§1) and δεξάμενος (**115**.1), a technical verb for 'recognising' an oracular remark, cf. 1.63.1 δέκεσθαι τὸ χρησθέν, 9.91.2 δέκομαι τὸν οἰωνόν. For other such unintentionally prophetic remarks, cf. the story of Perdiccas in **137**.4–5 (n.b. δεκόμεθα . . . τὰ διδοῖς, §5); 7.57, 9.16.

115–17 The sufferings of Xerxes' retreating army

The two versions of Xerxes' retreat are constructed out of similar elements. The first describes the physical *hardships* of having too little and then too much food; in between, there are the loss of the *royal* chariot to the Paeonians, and the cruel *punishment* of a king's disobedient sons. The second tells of the *hardships* of the storm; the *royal* gifts to Abydos; and Xerxes' alleged cruel *punishment* of the helmsman. H. emphasises the hardships on the retreat, but it is notable that Xerxes still has time to arrange for the care of his sick soldiers and to reward Abdera in a suitably regal manner; and Artabazus, his escort with 60,000 men, has not lost so many men that he cannot immediately begin campaigning again on leaving the King (**126**.1). This later chapter is in effect an implicit commentary on Greek traditions on the supposed Persian losses on the retreat. As with the Athenian allegations against Corinth (**94**), H. records a second, more extreme story, but rejects it.

Aeschylus' version of the retreat (*Pers.* 480–514) is notably more graphic and terrifying: through a 'poeticised cartography' (E. M. Hall), each place mentioned marks ever greater suffering. The climax is the attempted crossing of the frozen Strymon, when the sun, in the play the enemy of the Persians, rises and melts the ice, thus punishing the men who yoked the Hellespont. The motif of the chariot is also used in a more symbolically powerful manner: the shift from riding in a fine chariot to loss of that chariot is an important visual motif of Xerxes' disaster (176–200, 607–9, 1000–1). The historian is more restrained in his picture of the retreat.

115.1 ἐν . . . ἡμέρῃσι: the context makes it fairly clear that H. means 45 days from leaving Thessaly, not Athens as some have argued. That Xerxes took so long contradicts the claim that he was in headlong flight, and indeed he was travelling through lands that were still nominally loyal to him and where he had garrisons (7.106–7, 113.1).

ἀπάγων . . . οὐδὲν μέρος, ὡς εἰπεῖν 'bringing back not a fraction of his army, so to speak'. ὡς εἰπεῖν is an absolute infinitive modifying a general statement; cf. **22**.3n.; Smyth §2012b. This is an obvious exaggeration (as ὡς εἰπεῖν rather implies), but Greek tradition made much of the contrast between Xerxes' march into and out of Greece.

115.2 τῶν δενδρέων τὸν φλοιόν: the inhabitants of the Bruttian town of Petelia also ate bark, when besieged by Himilco (Livy, 23.30.3). Though no doubt resorted to only in desperation, the cambium layer between the wood and outer bark does in fact contain nourishment (Yardley 2003).

ἡμέρων 'cultivated'.

115.3 ἵνα 'wherever.'

115.4 τὸ ἱρὸν ἅρμα: this chariot, drawn by eight white horses, and with its charioteer following behind on foot holding the reins because no mortal was allowed to ascend it, preceded Xerxes' chariot when the expedition left Sardis and when they crossed the Hellespont (7.40.4, 55.3). Xenophon too puts this chariot in Cyrus' great procession after his ascent to the throne: it is followed by a chariot of the Sun and a third chariot decked in purple (*Cyr.* 8.3.12). For an idea of its appearance, cf. the gold model, resembling the chariots that appear on royal seals, in the Oxus treasure (BM 123908 = Curtis 2000: fig. 70; cf. fig. 64; Curtis and Tallis 2005: cat. 399 = BM 89132).

Διός: the name of the Greeks' main god is used for Ahura Mazda (OP **ahura* 'Lord' + **mazdhā* 'wise'; Gk. Ὡρομάσδης), the main deity of Zoroastrianism. On the complex question of H.'s use of names for foreign gods and their relation to Greek gods, cf. Thomas 2000: 274–82; Harrison 2002: 208–22; Scullion 2006: 198–204. Zeus is also identified with Ahura Mazda on fourth-century votive inscriptions found on the terrace at Persepolis (Dandamayev and Lukonin 1989: 270). Zoroastrianism is one of the world's longest-surviving religions, with adherents still especially among the Parsees, descendants of the Persians who fled to India from the Muslims in the seventh to eighth centuries AD (cf. Boyce 2001). It was founded by Zoroaster (Avestan *Zarathushtra*), who lived at some uncertain time between 1000 and 600, and to whom are ascribed the still-extant *Gāthās* (verse hymns) of the *Avesta.* Put very simply, in Zoroastrian theology, Ahura Mazda, personifying light, life and truth (*Arta*), is opposed by Anra Mainyu (Areimanius), personifying darkness, death and the Lie (*Drauga*): cf. Darius' words quoted in **69**.1n. Darius appears to have made Ahura Mazda the supreme deity of his pantheon, perhaps as a unifying feature of his empire: the god is not mentioned in Persian documents prior to Darius. On DB, Darius mentions Ahura Mazda 69 times, giving him credit for his accession and victories, in imitation of Babylonian kings who justified their reign by claiming to have been chosen by their main god, Marduk. Ahura Mazda is represented as a bearded and crowned male figure holding a ring (an ancient Mesopotamian symbol of kingship), and sitting in a disc which has the wings, tail and legs of a bird (cf. Brosius no. 44, with figs. 5a, b): this figure has taken over the iconography of the chief Assyrian god and protector of kings, Ashur (cf. Root 1979: 169–76, 210–15).

νεμομένας: *sc.* τὰς ἵππους; they are male horses in 7.40.4, 55.3.

116.1 Βισαλτέων βασιλεύς: a king Mosses is known from coinage from the period *ca.* 500–480 (Head 1911: 199–200).

οὔτε αὐτὸς ἔφη . . . τοῖσί τε παισί: οὔτε . . . τε is an idiom used frequently in H., when some sort of negative is implied in the second clause, as here in ἀπηγόρευε 'he forbade'; cf. Pl. *Prot.* 360D οὔτ' ἐπινεῦσαι ἠθέλησεν ἐσίγα τε, 'he didn't want to agree and he said nothing' (*GP* 508).

116.2 οἱ δὲ . . . πόλεμον: for the combination of a participle in one of two coordinated clauses and an indicative in the other, cf. **54**n. ἄλλως emphasises the second of two alternatives: 'or else'.

117.1 ἐντεταμένας: Aesch. *Pers.* 798–800 implies that they were still intact.

117.2 οὐδένα τε κόσμον: adverbial accusative.

ὕδατα μεταβάλλοντες: Hippocrates' *Airs, Waters and Places* discusses different kinds of water and their effects on health (7–9); significant changes of water (or season or air) lead to physical changes in the body. For Hippocrates, the equable climate of Asia rendered its inhabitants less robust and warlike than the Greeks, whose land and seasons are changeable: 'endurance of body and mind are not possible where there are not violent changes' (§19; cf. 16, 23–4). For H.'s interest in and engagement with contemporary medical theories, cf. Thomas 2000: 28–74.

118–20 A false tale about Xerxes' retreat refuted

This is a further example of H. giving a more colourful version of an event which is rejected as untrue alongside a duller but true version (cf. **94**). The striking nature of the fictitious version suggests that perhaps, though it is factually untrue, it still conveys a kind of truth about autocracy: cf. Flory 1987: 49–79, and 56–62 on this story and those in 1.75 (Thales) and 3.9 (leather water pipes). The whimsical behaviour of the tyrant here is stereotypical: H. alludes colourfully to the stereotype and then firmly rejects it, leaving the reader to resolve the paradox.

118.1 ὁδοιπορίῃσι 'by land-marches'.

118.2 **Στρυμονίην:** a north-north-east wind of notable force; cf. Aesch. *Ag.* 192–8; Arist. *Vent.* 973b17.

χειμαίνεσθαι is passive; *sc.* Xerxes.

γεμούσης . . . κομιζομένων 'because the ship was full, since a large number of the Persians who were being transported along with Xerxes were on its deck'; ὥστε is used by H. to give a causal sense to a participle (*GP* 527).

τὸν βασιλέα: a relatively rare use of the article for the King of Persia; in H. it is absent 10× more often than it is present (*Lex. s.v.* 4). OP essentially lacked the article (Kent 1953: 85), so the Greek use of βασιλεύς without it may have been influenced by this.

118.3 **τις:** cf. **109**.4n.

118.4 προσκυνέοντας 'performing *proskynesis*', i.e. showing deference, but not, as is often thought, by prostrating themselves on the ground. In Achaemenid art, men are depicted showing deference to the King by raising the right hand with the palm facing the mouth (perhaps touching the lips, if the Greek word, based on κυνέω 'kiss', is accurate), whilst inclining the upper body slightly: see the Mede on the North Stair of the *Apadāna* at Persepolis (Root 1979: Pl. xvii; E. M. Hall 1997: fig 3). This was probably a very old gesture of deference: the cuneiform ideogram for 'give homage, pray' combines the ideas of 'hand' and 'mouth'. The Greeks, however, seem to have interpreted *proskynesis* as involving prostration on the ground, cf. 7.136.1 προσκυνέειν βασιλέα προσπίπτοντας; Aes. *Pers.* 588–9 οὐδ' ἐς γᾶν προπίτνοντες ἄρξονται. This may be because there were times when easterners (as many still do) did prostrate themselves, but this was usually only in extreme circumstances, such as defeat or gratitude: 'all the people of Babylon . . . knelt before him, kissed his feet, rejoiced at his kingship' (*Cyrus Cylinder* (= Brosius no. 12) §18); cf. Xen. *Cyr.* 7.5.32), and in a custom inherited from the Assyrians, vassal kings kissed the feet of Persian rulers (Root 1979: 266). Unlike Egyptian or Mesopotamian art, however, Achaemenid art does not show people prostrating themselves before the king: even the rebels on the Bisitun relief are standing, and the defeated usurper Gaumata is being trampled, not prostrating himself. The Greeks, who used the kissing gesture only to gods, saw *proskynesis* to mortals as further evidence for the Persians' servile nature: the greatest proof of Greek liberty after the Persian Wars is that 'you do not perform *proskynesis* to any man as master but to the gods' (Xen. *Anab.* 3.2.13; cf. Isoc. 4.151). Thus a perfectly normal gesture in one culture was given heavy symbolic meaning by the other: the appropriateness of doing obeisance to Alexander was hotly debated (Arr. *Anab.* 4.10.5–12). Cf. Bickerman 1963; Neil on Ar. *Kn.* 156; Briant 2002: 221–2.

δωρήσασθαι . . . ἀποταμεῖν: the tale ends with a parodic vignette of the way in which the King is the fount of reward and punishment.

119 οὗτος 'this is the . . .' οὗτος refers back to the story in the previous chapter, picking up ἄλλος ὅδε λόγος from its beginning.

οὔτε ἄλλως . . . πάθος 'especially as regards what happened to the Persians'. The construction of τὸ πάθος is difficult; it is probably better to take it as a nominative rather than as an accusative of respect depending on πίστος, but both are hard to parallel. One might, however, expect something like Powell's <κατὰ> τό.

εἰ γὰρ δὴ ταῦτα . . . ἐς τὴν θάλασσαν 'for if these things had been said by the helmsman to Xerxes, amongst ten thousand opinions I do not have one that would oppose the idea that the king would have done something like this: namely, to have made those on the deck go into the ship's interior, since they were Persians and the foremost of them, and that he would have thrown into the sea a number of the rowers, who were Phoenicians, equal to that of the Persians.' The grammar is complex. The sentence starts with an accusative and infinitive construction depending on μίαν [γνώμην] οὐκ ἔχω ἀντίξοον. μὴ οὐ is used with ποιῆσαι, as regularly in such expressions: cf. **57**.2n. καταβιβάσαι is an infinitive that explains ποιῆσαι. At τῶν δὲ ἐρετέων, however, the construction changes from the accusative + infinitive of the μέν-clause depending on the whole phrase μίαν . . . ἀντίξοον, to a δέ-clause depending on γνώμην alone, introduced by ὅκως = ὡς or ὅτι (as often in H. but not Attic): 'I have no opinion . . . that he would not have thrown'.

The shift in the construction of the indirect discourse here is not unparalleled, but it is awkwardly done, and the unusual nature of this syntax has led some editors to delete all of **119–20**, or all but the opening οὗτος . . . πιστός. On the other hand, the critical attitude and mode of argument are characteristic of H.: for H.'s modes of proof and their links with contemporary science and philosophy, cf. Thomas 2000a: 168–248.

120 καὶ τόδε μαρτύριον: having argued from what was likely in **119**, H. now provides more concrete evidence that the story in **118** cannot be true. There are three parts to the proof: (i) there is firm evidence that Xerxes went to Abdera, in the gifts he gave that city; (ii) he was still travelling by land when he came to Abdera; (iii) Abdera is further on towards the Hellespont than Eion. Therefore (iv) the story that he threw the Persians overboard after sailing from Eion cannot be true, because he would already have passed Eion on foot by the time he got to Abdera.

Ἄβδηρα (H–N 872–5) was probably a Persian naval base (6.46–7). During Xerxes' advance, it suffered considerably from the need to entertain the Persian troops, Megacreon ironically remarking that his countrymen should give thanks for the gods' kindness in making Xerxes happy with but one meal a day (7.118–20). For the honouring thus of whole communities by the King, cf. Xerxes and Acanthus (7.116), and the Ariaspians, nicknamed 'Benefactors' for their help to Cyrus (Arr. *Anab.* 3.27.4); generally, cf. **85**.3n.

ἀκινάκηι: a short sword or dagger, made of gold or iron plated with gold, and worn stuck into a sash by Persians on monuments (cf. 7.54.2, 9.80.2) and by Medes hanging by the right side (a fine example in Schmidt I Pl. 120, cf. ibid. 165–6; Miller 1997: 46–8). The handle and scabbard could be richly decorated, with floral, hunting and animal motifs (cf. BM 123923 = Curtis 2000: fig. 67). It was a valuable gift, all the more so when given by the King: cf. 7.54.2 (Xerxes to the Hellespont); Xen. *Anab.* 1.2.27, 8.29; Plut. *Art.* 15.2; Aelian, *VH* 1.22. On monuments, wearing it where others do not seems to have been a mark of especial status (Schmidt III 112). The King's *akinakes* was credited with the power of controlling the weather: cf. Ctesias, *FGH* 688 F 45b (9); Polyaen. 7.11.12; also H. 4.62.2. Cf. Bittner 1985: 199–207.

τιήρηι χρυσοπάστωι: this was a loose felt cap (not a turban) worn by nobility and warriors (7.61.1; cf. **67**.2n.). If the sword was a regular gift, a royal tiara was a special one. For χρυσόπαστος, cf. Aes. *Ag.* 776 τὰ χρυσόπαστα ἔδεθλα.

ἐλύσατο τὴν ζώνην: such was Xerxes' haste to return that he had not had time to change his clothes; cf. 5.106.6, where Histiaeus promises Darius not to remove his cloak until he reaches his goal.

Apart from the incident of amorous intrigue in 9.108–113, Xerxes' active role in the *Histories* is now over.

ἵδρυται πρὸς τοῦ Ἑλλησπόντου μᾶλλον 'is situated nearer the Hellespont than'; Greek uses a genitive of the place from which the distance is measured (**87**.2n.).

ὅθεν δή 'whence he is supposed'; δή expresses H.'s doubt.

121–3 Greek honours to gods and men

After a false tale involving the comparative status of Persians and Phoenicians, we have actual instances amongst the Greeks where questions of honour cause difficulties: (i) Apollo (or at least his priests at Delphi) claims not to have been given quite enough offerings (**122**); (ii) Greek attempts to award the *aristeia* to the most important warrior founder on self-importance (**123**); and (iii) honours to Themistocles at Sparta cause trouble in Athens (**124–5**). Competition for symbolic or concrete marks of honour (*philotimia*) was endemic in aristocratic Greek society, and contrasts with the Olympic ideal commented on by Tritantaechmes in **26**. Furthermore, the bickering and lack of generosity among the Greeks contrasts with the Persian nobles' (albeit fictional) willingness to sacrifice themselves for their King. Greek disunity extends even to the award of prizes.

121.1 ἐξελεῖν . . . ἐξεῖλον: the pun links this episode with that concerning Andros in **111–12**; for this use of words with different senses, cf. **1**.1n.

Κάρυστον . . . δηιώσαντες: despite their payment of moneys in **112**.2–3.

ἀκροθίνια 'the first fruits, finest part', literally 'the top of the heap', derived from ἄκρος and θίς. For the custom, cf. **27**.5n. For the dedication of whole ships, cf. also Thuc. 2.84.4, 92.5, but more usually the prows were cut off and dedicated (H. 3.59.3; cf. Xen. *Hell.* 2.3.8, 6.2.36). For the Persian spoils from Salamis, cf. Miller 1997: 33–4, and 29–62 on spoils from the Persian Wars generally.

ἐς Ἰσθμὸν ἀναθεῖναι: at the temple of Poseidon in the Isthmian games enclosure (cf. **123**.2; Paus. 2.1.7); ἀναθεῖναι is epexegetic infinitive after ἐξεῖλον.

ἐπὶ Σούνιον: to the temples of Athena and Poseidon, presumably.

τῶι Αἴαντι: the battle was commemorated at the Aianteia and Mounychia festivals; Parker 1996: 153–4.

αὐτοῦ ἐς Σαλαμῖνα = ἐς αὐτὴν Σαλαμῖνα; cf. **64**.2 αὐτόθεν ἐκ Σαλαμῖνος; *Il* 2.237 αὐτοῦ ἐνὶ Τροίηι; H. 9.11.1 αὐτοῦ τῆιδε. For αὐτοῦ of motion towards, cf. H. 2.178.1 αὐτοῦ ναυτιλλομένοισι.

121.2 ἀνδριάς: H. does not say of which god. Paus. 10.14.5 mentions a large statue of Apollo at Delphi, a dedication from the spoils of Salamis and Artemisium, but he does not mention the ship's prow. The Greeks who swore to oppose the Persians also swore to give Apollo a tithe of the property of those who medised (7.132.2), and a tithe of the immense booty captured after Plataea was also given to him (9.81), including the famous Serpent Column (**82**.1n.). There was a painting representing Salamis holding a ship's figurehead alongside Greece at Olympia (Paus. 5.11.5), and a huge statue of Zeus commemorated Plataea (9.81.1).

δυώδεκα πηχέων = of about eighteen feet, a genitive of measure (Smyth §1325). The Greek cubit was about $18^1/_2$ inches (47 cm), the 'royal' about 21 inches (53 cm) (cf. 1.178.3).

Ἀλέξανδρος: for the statue, cf. [Dem.] 12.21 and for the episode that led to its creation, Dem. 23.200. The dedication would help to delete the memory of Alexander's flirtation with the Persian cause (**34**; **136**.1n.).

122 τὰ ἀριστήια: i.e. their prize for their performance in the battle (**93**.1). Quite why Apollo should have demanded this is not easy to explain. Perhaps the Aeginetans dedicated it themselves and this story was later told at Delphi to explain why the Aeginetans made a special dedication, as well as being associated with the communal one (Asheri).

ἀστέρας χρυσέους possibly represent, like Lysander's two stars representing the Dioscuri dedicated after the final defeat of Athens at Aegospotami (Cic. *de div.* 1.75), the Dioscuri and Apollo Delphinios (cf. Hornblower 2004: 225), or Aeacus, Peleus and Telamon (Asheri; cf. **64**.2).

ἐπὶ τῆς γωνίης 'in the corner (of the opisthodomus)'. The silver crater, holding 600 amphorae and used at the Theophania festival, was given by Croesus (**35**.2n.). The positioning of the prize next to Croesus' crater is perhaps significant: objects marking Delphi's significant involvements in the East are juxtaposed.

123.1 ἀνὰ πόλεμον τοῦτον: this phrase and the unusually solemn procedure suggest that this was not just the prize for the battle of Salamis, but for the war as a whole (cf. Hamel 1998: 191–3).

123.2 ἔφερον . . . ἐπὶ . . . τῶι βωμῶι 'cast their votes on the altar'. Since it is not clear exactly how this vote operated – whether there was one vote or two, how the votes were cast, whether urns were used, etc. – , it is perhaps unwise to alter the text, despite the fact that elsewhere the phrase used is ἀπὸ τοῦ βωμοῦ φέρειν, cf. e.g. Dem. 18.134 καὶ ταῦτα ἀπὸ τοῦ βωμοῦ φέρουσα τὴν ψῆφον ἔπραξαν, id. 43.14; Plut. *Them.* 17.1 ἐπει γὰρ ἀναχωρήσαντες εἰς τὸν Ἰσθμὸν ἀπὸ τοῦ βωμοῦ τὴν ψῆφον ἔφερον οἱ στρατηγοί; id. *Peric.* 32.2. Cf. Pliny, *NH* 34.53 for a vote that reaches a similar impasse.

ἐμουνοῦντο lit. 'were left on their own', and so presumably 'were left with but a single vote', but this is hard to parallel.

δευτερείοισι here means 'second votes', not, as is usual, 'second prize'.

124–5 Themistocles honoured in Sparta; an ungracious reaction

For a discussion of these honours in their Spartan context, cf. Jordan 1988.

124.1 οὐ βουλομένων . . . φθόνωι 'although the Greeks did not want to resolve this matter because of their mutual jealousy'.

124.2 μεγάλως δὲ ἐτίμησαν: the Spartan treatment of Themistocles here may have been caused by their desire now to pursue a naval campaign, so that by harrying Mardonius' communications and fomenting revolt in Asia Minor they could get Mardonius out of Greece without having to fight him on land. For a naval campaign, Athens was essential, and the appointment of a king, Leotychidas, in place of Eurybiades, as commander of the naval arm also suggests naval action was seriously envisaged (**131**.2). Themistocles, however, played no part in the campaign of 479: the reasons and events are hazy, but Athenian displeasure either at his honouring by Sparta or more likely at his proposed policy, may have led them not to elect him a general for the following year, or, it would seem, ever again (Diod. 11.27 gives a more cynical account). Aristeides (**79**.1n.) and Xanthippus (**131**.3n.) were elected.

ἀριστήια μέν νυν . . . στέφανον ἐλαίης 'they gave the prize for excellence (in battle) to Eurybiades (in the form of) a crown of olive; (the prize) for wisdom and ingenuity they gave to Themistocles, and he too received a crown of olive.' When Plutarch used this passage, he wrote (*Them.* 17.1) Εὐρυβιάδηι μὲν ἀνδρείας, ἐκείνωι δὲ σοφίας ἀριστεῖον ἔδοσαν θαλλοῦ στέφανον, which led Cobet to add in our passage <ἀνδρηίης> after Εὐρυβιάδηι to balance σοφίης καὶ δεξιότητος. However, ἀριστήια regularly refers to the prize for valour in war and so contains the idea of 'valour'; the genitives then depend on the idea of 'prize' in ἀριστήια.

σοφίης δὲ καὶ δεξιότητος: after the final Greek victory, Themistocles built a small temple to Artemis Aristoboule ('Of the best counsel') in his deme of Melite, with a statue of himself inside (Plut. *Them.* 22.1–2). It was desecrated after his disgrace but renovated in the fourth century (Threpsiades and Vanderpool 1964). Cf. Plut. *Them.*

15.2 on Simonides' description of Salamis in *The Battle of Salamis:* 'that noble and famous victory . . . was won by the common bravery and enthusiasm of the men who fought in the sea-battle and by the intelligence and astuteness (γνώμηι καὶ δεινότητι) of Themistocles.'

ὄχωι . . . καλλιστεύοντι: ὄχος is a poetic word for a grand vehicle.

124.3 αἰνέσαντες . . . προέπεμψαν: strictly, the participle refers to the Spartans generally, the main verb to the youths, but since the latter are included in the former, the construction makes no distinction between them. For this procession, one might compare Plut. *Lyc.* 26.3, where successful candidates for the *gerousia* toured the sanctuaries of the city accompanied by young men and women.

ἱππέες: this elite corps of men under 30 performed a number of functions on behalf of the Spartan state, mainly militarily, as the royal bodyguard, but also politically as diplomats and administrators; cf. Jordan 1988: 560–5. According to Xen. *Rep. Lac.* 4.3 they were chosen each year by three *hippagretai*, selection being a mark of high honour; cf. H. 1.67.5.

μοῦνον δή: asyndeton and δή emphasise the exclusivity of this mark of honour for Themistocles. The Athenian envoy at the negotiations at Sparta in 432 will remind the Spartans of this honour, to prove the magnitude of the Athenian contribution to the defeat of the Persians in providing so great a general (Thuc. 1.74.1).

125.1 Τιμόδημος Ἀφιδναῖος: he is otherwise unknown (*LGPN* II *s.v.*(16)). Aphidna is a deme of the tribe Acantis, situated north-east of Deceleia. Timodemus is replaced by an anonymous inhabitant of Seriphos (an island noted for its insignificance) in Pl. *Rep.* 329E6–330A.

ἄλλως δὲ . . . ἀνδρῶν 'but not otherwise one of the prominent men in the state'; ἄλλως strengthens the opposition with the previous clause. ἐπιφανής is used generally here, cf. Thuc. 2. 43. 3 ἀνδρῶν γὰρ ἐπιφανῶν πᾶσα γῆ τάφος.

καταμαργέων: a very strong word to describe Timotheus' rabid manner; this compound is found only here, and μαργάω is rare and poetic.

ἐνείκεε: this passage is reminiscent in context and language of Thersites' outburst against Agamemnon (*Il.* 2.211–77); νεικέω, an epic verb found in earlier prose only here and in 9.55.2, appears there thrice (221, 224, 243). Both Timodemus and Thersites are described as hostile to their opponents (cf. ἔχθιστος, ibid. 220); both are from the less distinguished parts of society; Thersites complains that Agamemnon gets prizes through the efforts of others (ibid. 225–40), as does Timodemus about Themistocles (διὰ τὰς Ἀθήνας ἔχοι τὰ γέρεα . . . ἀλλ' οὐ δι' ἑωυτόν); each man is worsted by a figure of great cleverness, Odysseus and Themistocles. For another episode involving Themistocles which recalls Thersites, cf. **92**.2 and n.

ὡς . . . ἔχοι: there are no satisfactory parallels for either νεικέω or προφέρω + ὡς thus, but both verbs naturally imply a verb of saying that could introduce this indirect quotation of Timodemus. προφέροις also occurs in Odysseus' speech to Thersites (ibid. 251).

125.2 οὕτω ἔχει τοι 'quite right', ironically. In strong statements of this kind, τοι can comment unfavourably on the previous speaker's words; cf. καίτοι **86**n. (*GP* 542).

οὔτ᾽ ἂν ἐγὼ ἐὼν Βελβινίτης . . . Ἀθηναῖος 'if I had come from Belbina, I would not have been so honoured by the Spartans; but neither would you, even though you are an Athenian'; i.e. birth *and* valour are both necessary to achieve the kind of honour paid to Themistocles by the Spartans. Belbina, a tiny island off Sunium (H–N 622), stands here for a completely unimportant place. Timodemus has no better luck in his attempt to score off Themistocles than did Adeimantus in **59** and **61**.2, or the Andrians in **111**. Apart from a passing reference by H. in 9.98.4, Themistocles now disappears from view.

126–9 ARTABAZUS ATTACKS OLYNTHUS AND POTIDAEA

126–8 Potidaea revolts

The King is in Sardis, having (allegedly) lost most of his army; Mardonius is in winter quarters in Thessaly, awaiting his disaster in book 9. We now see the fate of the army that had escorted Xerxes: the Greek tradition wishes to make the destruction of the Persians as complete as possible. As off Magnesia (7.188–92), around Euboea (**12**) and at Salamis, disaster comes to the Persians from the sea, and their watery grave balances the death of the Olynthians in the marsh (**127**). Their deaths are associated with an act of sacrilege (**129**.3), as is the case with those who attempted to sack Delphi (**38–9**) and those who burnt the shrine of Demeter at Eleusis (9.65.2).

126.1 Ἀρτάβαζος, a cousin of Darius, was commander of the Parthians and Chorasmians (7.66.2), and held in high esteem by Xerxes (9.41.1); he was still active, fighting the Athenians in Egypt, in the 460s (Diod. 11.75; cf. Balcer 1993: 84–5). He may have been son of the Pharnaces (OP *Farnaka*; Elam. *Parnaka*) who was the most important official in the treasury at Persepolis under Darius (cf. Lewis 1997: 359; Brosius nos. 140–3). Artabazus urged caution on Mardonius in the lead-up to Plataea (9.41.2–4), but in his annoyance at Mardonius' scornful rejection of his advice, he and his 40,000 men abandoned the Persian lines at the start of the battle and made their way home (9.66). Xerxes later made him satrap of Dascylium (on the south coast of the Sea of Marmara), in order to promote the intrigues with Pausanias (Thuc. 1.129.1), and his descendants followed him in the satrapy (cf. Lewis 1977: 52; Gomme, Dover and Andrewes on Thuc. 8.6.1). The references to Artabazus in H. are notable for their favourable nature, which has led to the idea that he was an important source for H. on the Persian empire. Cf. also **26**n. on Tritantaechmes.

στρατοῦ τοῦ Μαρδόνιος ἐξελέξατο 'the forces, which Mardonius had chosen'; τοῦ is for τόν through attraction of the relative into the case of its antecedent στρατοῦ. That Artabazus immediately thinks of campaigning after leaving the King rather contradicts the idea that the Persians had lost most of their men in the hardships described in **115** and **117**.

126.2 Παλλήνην: the western peninsula of Chalcidice.

Μαρδονίου τε χειμερίζοντος . . . καὶ οὐδέν κω κατεπείγοντος 'since Mardonius was in winter quarters and was not yet pressing him'; Artabanus seizes an opportunity for some activity on his own behalf, now he no longer has the King to look after. If the text is sound, καὶ . . . κατεπείγοντος is added as if the clause had begun Μαρδονίου χειμερίζοντος τε, in a kind of anacolouthon: cf. 9.55.1 ὡς δὲ ἀπίκετο ὁ κῆρυξ . . . ὥρα τέ σφεας κατὰ χώρην τεταγμένους καὶ ἐς νείκεα ἀπιγμένους αὐτῶν τοὺς πρώτους, where τε would more naturally come after σφεας (cf. *GP* 518–20).

οὐκ ἐδικαίου . . . μὴ οὐκ ἐξανδραποδίσασθαι 'he did not think it right, since he had come upon the Potidaeans in a state of revolt, not to reduce them to slavery'; for μὴ οὐ, **57**.1n. Cf. 7.122–3.1 for the help given to the Persians on their way through Greece by Potidaea and Olynthus.

126.3 παρεξεληλάκεε: pluperf of παρεξελαύνω. For the tense, cf. **50**.1n.

ὣς δὲ καί 'and likewise also'.

127.1 Ποτείδαιαν: on Pallene, a city founded by Corinth; H–N 838–9.

ἀπίστασθαι 'that they were contemplating revolt'; the present tense describes something as going on, so can be used to express an intention or attempt ('conative' present, *M&T* §25).

Βοττιαῖοι: they were expelled from their land between the Haliacmon and Axius rivers into the Chersonnese some time after the Temenid dynasty came to power *ca.* 640, probably by Alexander, son of Perdiccas; cf. Thuc. 2.99–100 and **137–44**. Cf. Flensted-Jensen 1995.

λίμνην: possibly the Βολύκη λίμνη, to the east of the city.

Κριτοβούλωι: not otherwise known, but no doubt a Greek who could be expected to be loyal to the Persian King.

128.1 Τιμόξεινος: known only for this exploit (cf. also Polyaen. 7.33.1).

ὅντινα μὲν τρόπον ἀρχὴν . . . οὐ γὰρ ὦν λέγεται 'I cannot say in what manner [he arranged the betrayal] at first, for the very reason that nothing is told.' The two accusatives τρόπον and ἀρχήν are adverbial, 'οὖν adds to γάρ the idea of importance or essentiality' (*GP* 446), and μέν is picked up by μέντοι. For the admission of the limitations of oral tradition in οὐ γὰρ ὦν λέγεται, cf. 1.49; 7.60.1; **133**.

τοξεύματος . . . πτερώσαντες: not entirely clear, but it seems that they wrapped the letter round the arrow near the butt-end, where there were notches (γλυφίδας) either to give the fingers a better grip or for fitting feathers into; they then put the feathers of the arrow over the letter to hide it. Aen. Tact. 31.25–7 quotes the story with περί instead of παρά, but that may be an attempt to clarify what he thought happened. For such means of communication, cf. Plut. *Cimon* 12.3; Polyaen. 2.29.1; Caes. *BG* 5.48.5–10; for other cunning modes of communication, cf. **22**n.

128.2 συμμαχίη 'allies'; abstract for concrete.

128.3 καταπλέξαι 'to implicate him'; for the sense, cf. perhaps καταδέω 'convict' in 2.174.2 ὅσοι δέ μιν κατέδησαν φῶρα εἶναι, 4.68.3.

μὴ νομιζοίατο εἶναι Σικιωναῖοι . . . προδόται: a striking instance of how Greek states could forgive crimes when to do so was in the greater interests of the state. The defence that one's crimes were to the benefit of the city was frequently mounted in the Athenian courts.

129 A remarkable flood-tide destroys the Persians

129.1 παρῆισαν: i.e. the Persians were on the north side of Potidaea, which completely blocks the isthmus, and, wishing to attack its south side but having no ships, tried to go round it through the shallows (τέναγος), aided by the very low tide. Cf. Aristeus' similar operations in Thuc. 1.63–4.

129.2 ὡς δὲ τὰς δύο . . . τὰς διελθόντας χρῆν εἶναι ἔσω ἐν τῆι Παλλήνηι 'when they had covered two parts of the journey and there were three left, having crossed which must have brought them into Pallene'; the imperfect χρῆν is used for something that was a possibility but did not in fact happen (*M&T* §§415–19; Smyth §1776).

πλημυρίς: though the Mediterranean is generally free of tides, there are places where shore and currents conjoin to produce them; cf. e.g. 7.198.1.

ὅση οὐδαμά κω . . . πολλάκις γινομένη lit. 'of such a size as never yet occurred, according to the locals, though a flood-tide often happens'; γινομένη is nominative since it refers to the same sort of flood-tide as ὅση.

νέειν . . . οὐκ ἐπιστάμενοι: cf. **8**n.

129.3 Ποσειδέωνος: the eponymous god of the city. The name 'Potidaea' reflects the spelling of the god's name with a *-t-*, found in the dialect of Corinth whence Potidaea was founded. On the complex variety of spellings of the god's name, cf. Chantraine 930–1.

οἵ περ καί 'these were exactly (περ) the men . . .'

130–44 THE FOLLOWING SPRING

130–2 The fleets reassemble; mutual reluctance to advance

Spring of 479 opens the new campaigning season. The mutual fear that was a factor at Artemisium now resurfaces. Tactically, this caution made sense, since neither side wanted to risk a battle where they might be severely mauled, but there is something mildly wry about the well-travelled H.'s remarks on the Greek mainlanders' limited knowledge of the eastern Aegean (**132**.3). The Ionian ambassadors' plot against Strattis of Chios and its betrayal balances the story of Artabazus' failed intrigue with Timoxenus at Potidaea (**128**). Again, cunning is as much an instrument of policy as military force. The fleets will remain frozen in their mutual fear until 9.90, whilst the fate of the Persian land army is recounted in the bulk of book 9.

130.1 Περσέων . . . ἐπεβάτευον 'the majority of the *epibatai* were Persians and Medes', i.e. the most trusted peoples fought and kept discipline on deck.

130.2 Μαρδόντης τε ὁ Βαγαίου: Mardontes was commander of the 'tribes that came from the Red Sea and from the islands where the King installs those called the Exiles' (7.80), and may well be the *Mardunda* of the Persepolis Fortification Tablets who was deputy satrap of Susa in 499–4 (PF 1352.8–9; Balcer 1993: 157). He died in a brave rearguard action conducted by small bands of Persians after the rout at Mycale (9.102.4). His father may have been the Bagaeus son of Artontes who was entrusted with Darius' letters which cunningly encompassed the death of the satrap Oroetes (3.127–8). One *Bakeya* appears on PF 823 (= Brosius no. 161) in connection with the 'princess' (Elam. *dukshish*) Ishtin, most likely his wife and daughter of Darius. Lewis 1997: 355–6 suggests we see here the reward which Bagaeus got from Darius, and which his family continued to enjoy under Xerxes.

Ἀρταΰντης Ἀρταχαίεω: OP **Artavanta*, 'Pursuing justice' (Schmitt 1967: 129). He survived Mycale (9.102.4), but nearly murdered Masistes, Xerxes' brother, because of Masistes' insulting analysis of his generalship there (9.107). Here and in 7.63, the MSS have Ἀρταχαίου, which most editors change to Ἀρταχαίεω, making his father the huge, stentoran-voiced Artachaees son of Artaeus who supervised the construction of the Athos canal (7.22.2; cf. 7.117 for his obituary). MSS and papyrus offer very varied versions of the Persian names in this section.

ἀδελφιδέος αὐτοῦ Ἀρταΰντεω προσελομένου Ἰθαμίτρης 'Ithamitres, Artaÿntes' nephew, Artaÿntes himself doing the choosing'; αὐτοῦ goes with προσελομένου in an unusual order which makes Krüger's transposition Ἀρταΰντεω αὐτοῦ attractive. All that is known of Ithamitres is that he too escaped at Mycale (9.102.4): note, however, that his presence here is due to an emendation (see *apparatus criticus*).

130.3 οὐ μὲν οὐδὲ προσεδέκοντο 'not that they expected . . .' (*GP* 363; **25**.1n.).

κατὰ μέν νυν . . . τῶι θυμῶι 'as far as (prospects on) the sea were concerned, in their hearts they had little confidence'.

131.1 δέκα καὶ ἑκατόν: a surprisingly small number. Quite why there were so few ships is hard to say. We don't know how many of these were Athenian, but it is clear that they had not sent as many as they could: the Persians had at least 300 (**130**.2). Perhaps there was less confidence in Athens about the naval strategy, so they were loath to commit too many ships at once?

131.2 Λευτυχίδης (*LGPN* IIIA *s.v.* Λατυχίδας (2)) has already appeared in 6.65–73, 85–6 where he became king in place of Demaratus (for whom, cf. **65**.1n.), but his pedigree is given here at the important point where he takes command of the Greek forces. A similar technique is used with Leonidas, who appears in book 5, but has his pedigree given only shortly before Thermopylae (7.204), and Alexander, who first appears in 5.19–21, but is given his ancestry only in **135–9**, when he becomes important in Greco-Persian relations. The first actual king in this genealogical list is Theopompus; the seven men who follow him were a younger branch of Theopompus' descendants, which branch did not gain the throne until the deposition of Demaratus. For the parallel pedigree of Demaratus, cf. Paus. 3.7, and on such genealogies in H., Mitchell 1956. About most of these names little or nothing is known. Euryphon (usually Eurypon) is the eponymous founder of the Eurypontid royal house, to which Leotychidas belonged.

τῆς ἑτέρης οἰκίης: the first royal house was the Agids, descended from Agis; both royal houses traced their lineage back to Heracles (7.204). On Spartan king-lists, cf. Cartledge 2002b: 293–8.

131.3 δυῶν: almost all editors have accepted Paulmier's ἑπτά, to bring H. into line with the list in Paus. 3.7.5–6. Gilula 2003: 79–80, however, points out that the fact that Leotychidas' father and grandfather were not kings means this list is a genealogy and not a king-list, and that altering H.'s text to fit a list composed many centuries afterwards is methodologically unsound.

Ξάνθιππος: father of Pericles. He married Cleisthenes of Sicyon's daughter Agariste, who when pregnant with Pericles dreamt of giving birth to a lion (6.131.2; cf. *LGPN* II *s.v.*(7)). He had successfully prosecuted Miltiades for his conduct of the campaign on Paros in 490–489 (6.136.1), and was himself ostracised in 484 (*Ath. Pol.* 22.6; 23 *ostraca* bearing his name have been found: Brenne 2001: 310–12; Siewert 2002: 71). He presumably returned from exile in the general amnesty (**79**.1n.). After Mycale, unlike the majority of the Greek fleet, he refused to withdraw from the campaign, and conquered Sestos at the head of the Athenian ships (9.114–20).

132.2 Ἡρόδοτος: an interesting coincidence of name. He is otherwise unknown, but Hornblower 2003: 56 suggests that his father's name points to the priestly clan of northern Ionia, the Basilidae, and that this Herodotus may be the source of the story of Strattis. Pape 1911: *s.v.* lists 20 men with H.'s name.

σφίσι γενόμενοι 'making a compact with each other', so 'conspiring together'. As is often the case, σφίσι is a direct reflexive = ἑαυτοῖς, and so here equivalent to ἀλλήλοις; cf. **9** λόγον σφίσι αὐτοῖσι ἐδίδοσαν, 7.145.1 διδόντων σφίσι λόγον καὶ πίστιν.

Στράττι: tyrant of Chios, possibly from as long ago as Darius' expedition to Scythia in 512 (4.138.2), though perhaps with a gap during the Ionian Revolt; cf. *LGPN* I *s.v.* (1).

132.3 οὔτε . . . εἶναι: the construction changes abruptly from a causal participle to an independent clause; the negative οὔτε is picked up by τε with a positive sentence (cf. LSJ *s.v.* οὔτε II 4; **116**.1n.). The passage gives us an interesting insight into the average mainland Greek's geographical knowledge of the eastern Mediterranean. Few in the navy would have had cause to sail so far from home.

τὴν δὲ Σάμον . . . ἴσον ἀπέχειν 'and they thought as a matter of conjecture that Samos was as far away as the Pillars of Heracles'; δόξηι shows the speculative nature of their ideas. The Pillars of Heracles were the Straits of Gibraltar; what exactly these 'Pillars' were was much speculated upon in antiquity (cf. Strabo 3.5.5).

τὸ πρὸς ἑσπέρης . . . Σάμου 'the part to the west beyond Samos'.

χρηιζόντων τῶν Χίων 'though the Chians asked them'; concessive.

δέος . . . σφεων 'fear maintained the distance between them.' It was not until July in the following year that Leotychidas was persuaded to move to Samos, encouraged by Samian patriots (9.90–2).

133–9 Two ambassadors of Mardonius: Mys and Alexander

Mardonius, in preparation for his campaign, sends ambassadors both to gods and to men. He first consults a similar selection of oracles to Croesus (in 1.46), and in a similar way: a written record is again taken, and one oracle seems to be crucial (**133–6**). Mardonius will also concern himself with Greek forms of divination at Plataea, before abandoning them when the sacrifices do not recommend battle (9.37.1,

38.2. 43, 45.2). Thus, Croesus at the start of the *Histories* is eventually undone through misunderstanding an oracle, and Mardonius, the last major Persian actor, suffers defeat and dies after ignoring divine indications.

He then sends Alexander of Macedon to Athens to persuade them to change sides. This episode is in two parts: (i) Alexander's earlier history and the history of his family (**136–9**), and (ii) his embassy to Athens and discussions there (**140–4**).

133–5 Mardonius sends Mys to consult oracles; a remarkable response at the Ptoum

133 χρηστήρια: for foreign kings and Greek oracles, cf. **34–9**n., and for Persians and foreign religions **54**n. Mardonius used Greek seers, the Elean Hegesistratus and the Leucadian Hippomachus (9.37.1, 38.2), as did Cyrus the Younger, who had Silanus, an Ambraciot (Xen. *Anab.* 1.7.18); the Athenian Onomacritus brought Xerxes many oracles which helped persuade him to make his expedition (7.6.3–5).

Εὐρωπέα . . . Μῦς: Mys is only known for this exploit. That he was a Carian is suggested by his recognition of that language; his name is a not uncommon Greek one, but Carians used Greek and Carian names. His city is probably Euromus, for whose inhabitants the adjective Εὐρωπεύς appears to be a variant for Εὐρωμεύς (Carian *u-r-o-m-'s*); it is found on two first-century coins and a third-century inscription from Laodicea, as well as in H. and Paus. 9.23.5; cf. Steph. Byz. *s.vv.* Εὔρωμος, Εὐρωπός; Robert 1950.

ἐντειλάμενος . . . ἀποπειρήσασθαι lit. 'ordering him to go everywhere in order to make oracular consultations [at those oracles] of which it was possible for them to make trial'; the antecedent of τῶν is a partitive genitive χρηστηρίων implied in πανταχῇ . . . χρησόμενον. The absence of Delphi from the list is consistent with events in **36–9**.

134.1 Λεβάδειαν: a Boeotian town to the west of Lake Copais, famed for the oracle of Trophonius: cf. Fossey 1988: 343–9; Schachter 1981–94: III 66–89; H–N 445–6. At this, after elaborate ritual preparations, one descended into a chamber and entered a narrow chasm feet-first, only to be whisked in violently and to come out later head-first and in a state of some shock. Priests then interpreted the things one had experienced below. There is a first-hand account in Paus. 9.39.5–14. Consultation could sometimes be such an experience that one did not smile again, hence the popular saying of the grim-faced, 'he's been to the oracle of Trophonius' (Apostolius, 6.17 etc.). It was the subject of mockery in comedy: cf. Ar. *Clouds* 506–8; Cratinus fr. 239. Pausanias 9.37.5–7 attributes a story of great trickery to Trophonius (it is attributed to an anonymous Egyptian thief in H. 2.121), which results in his being swallowed by the earth, like Amphiaraus (see below).

φαίνεται . . . Τροφώνιον: on the usual interpretation, both here and at the shrine of Amphiaraus, Mys employs another to do the consultation for him; i.e. grammatically φαίνεται governs the participles ἀπικόμενος and πείσας. Asheri, however, argues that this implies that the oracle was open only to locals, which we know is not true, and takes φαίνεται with καταβῆναι; the local would then have been hired as a guide.

But Mys seems equally loath to do the consultation himself at Amphiaraus' shrine, though as a foreigner he could have done so, and Pausanias' detailed account does not mention the use of guides.

Ἄβας: cf. **27**.4n., **33**.

Ἰσμηνίωι Ἀπόλλωνι: the oracle stood on the Ismenian Hill by one of the city gates, near the river Ismenus. The god's statue was of cedar-wood, and the priest each year was a youth of noble family, the Daphnephorus (Paus. 9.10.2–4). Cf. Schachter 1981–94: I 77–85.

ἔστι δὲ . . . χρηστηριάζεσθαι 'it is possible, as at Olympia, to seek oracles from the sacrifices there.' The reference is to the use as oracles of the behaviour of fires during sacrifice: cf. Pi. *Ol.* 8.1–3 'Olympia, where the men of prophecy seek the will of Zeus by inspecting the offerings in the fire' (Ὀλυμπία . . . ἵνα μάντιες ἄνδρες ἐμπύροις τεκμαιρόμενοι παραπειρῶνται Διός). This was also the custom in Thebes: cf. Soph. *OT* 21 ἐπ' Ἰσμηνοῦ τε μαντείαι σποδῶι; *Ant.* 1005–11; Eur. *Phoen.* 1255–8 with Mastronarde and the scholia *ad loc.*

κατεκοίμησε 'he caused him to lie down'. 'Incubation', sleeping in a holy place, was a regular means of consulting an oracle or seeking healing from the gods (Deubner 1900; Halliday 1913: 128–34). There is a long account of incubation in the shrine of Asclepius in Ar. *Pl.* 653–763; cf. Eur. *IT* 1259–67.

Ἀμφιάρεως: Amphiaraus was a famous seer, like Trophonius (see above), swallowed up by the earth during the failed expedition of the Seven against Thebes: cf. *Thebaid*, fr. 9D; Paus. 1.34.2–5. Consultants of his oracle sacrificed a ram and slept on its fleece; Amphiaraus himself had begun to prophesy in his sleep when still alive (Paus. 2.13.7). Plutarch supplies the dream given to Mys' consultant: he was killed by a stone thrown by an attendant of the god, which corresponds to the manner of Mardonius' own death in Plutarch (*Arist.* 19.1–2), but not in H. 9.64.2. The shrine described by Pausanias is at Oropus in the border region between Attica and Boeotia; if H. means this shrine, then ἐς Θήβας should be interpreted loosely as 'into Theban territory'. Cf. Schachter 1981–94: I 19–26.

134.2 οὐδενὶ ἔξεστι: it was sometimes the case that particular peoples were barred from particular rites or that people could not participate in certain rituals in cities not their own (cf. Bowie 1995: 467–8). An aetiological myth often gave the reason for the unusual prohibition. Cf. 1.143–5, 171.5–6, 2.47.1, 5.72.3, 6.81.

διὰ χρηστηρίων ποιεύμενος 'communicating with them through oracles'; cf. **112**.1n.

ὁκότερα . . . τούτων 'to choose one of these two options'. Neuter pronouns are often used in the plural for a singular idea; cf. Xen. *Symp.* 2.19 ἐχειρονόμουν δέ· ταῦτα γὰρ ἠπιστάμην, 'I waved my arms, because I knew how to do this' (Smyth §1003).

ἅτε μάντι 'as a *mantis*' (for which, cf. **27**.3n.); ἅτε is so used adverbially in Pindar and H., and sometimes in tragedy (*GP* 526).

τοῦ ἑτέρου ἀπεχομένους 'giving up the other alternative'.

135.1 ἄρα is regularly used to introduce a surprising fact in indirect speech, sometimes also as a disclaimer of responsibility for its truth (*GP* 38).

Πτώιου Ἀπόλλωνος: this shrine was under the summit of Mt Ptoum (Strabo 9.2.34; Paus. 9.23.5–6; Schachter 1981–94: 1 52–73).

καλέεται: indicative, because this is a parenthesis by H. himself, and not part of the indirect discourse.

135.2 παρελθεῖν . . . ἕπεσθαι δέ: παρελθεῖν is attracted into the infinitive though in the subordinate clause (**94**.2n.); δέ is apodotic (**22**.2n.).

ἀπὸ τοῦ κοινοῦ 'from the state'.

ἀπογραψομένους: oracles were recorded by priests, e.g. on lead tablets at Dodona, but also by those doing the consultation, as in 7.142.1, where the Athenians write down the more propitious second oracle about the Persian invasion.

However, against the common notion that oracles were regularly written down at this time, cf. Dillery 2005: 215–18, 225–6, who notes that out of more than 100 cases, H. says an oracle was written down only three times (here, 1.47–8 (Croesus), 7.142.1), and that in each case the recording has an importance in its context, as most obviously in the cases of Croesus and Mys.

ἔμελλε: *sc.* ὁ θεός.

πρόμαντιν: a regular word, like προφητής (**36**.2n.), for the oracular mouthpiece of a god; cf. 1.182.2 the priestess of Apollo at Patara, 6.66.2 the Pythia at Delphi, etc.

135.3 οὐδὲ ἔχειν ὅ τι . . . πρήγματι 'and did not know what to make of the matter before them'. χρήσωνται is a deliberative subjunctive, which is often found in relative clauses with οὐκ ἔχω, when something stands between the speaker and the fulfilment of their desire. ὅ τι is an interrogative acting as a relative, lit. 'they did not have in respect of which to treat . . .' (cf. the direct 'in what way are we to treat . . .?'). Cf. *M&T* §572; Smyth §2546–7.

τὴν ἐφέροντο δέλτον 'the tablet they were carrying'; for τὴν δέλτον τὴν ἐφέροντο.

Καρίηι . . . γλώσσηι: that an oracle high on a mountain in Boeotia should reply in the native language of an enquirer suggests that the message was of considerable importance. However, H. tantalisingly closes down the narrative without revealing what was in fact said, though he gives his surmise as to what was said in **136**.3. Whatever it was, Mardonius made the mistake of ignoring it. For Greek oracles using foreign languages, cf. the story that attributes to Delphi a pun on the Libyan *battus* 'king' in 4.155. On the Carian language, cf. **19**.1n.

136 Mardonius sends Alexander to Athens

136.1 ἐπιλεξάμενος ὅτι δὴ λέγοντα ἦν 'having read what it was that the various oracles said'. δή is emphatic; for periphrastic λέγοντα ἦν, cf. **37**.2n.

Literacy. Darius says of his Bisitun inscription, 'it was written down and read (aloud) before me' (DB (= Brosius no. 44) IV §70), and in Akkadian, the term translated as 'read' has the primary meaning 'call out'. No doubt Mardonius too had the oracles read to him: as a Persian noble, he was most likely illiterate and ignorant of foreign languages (though there is a Persian noble who speaks Greek in 9.16.2, Leotychidas relies on barbarian ignorance of Ionic Greek when he shouts to the Ionians in the Persian army before Mycale, 9.98.4). Xenophon seems to exclude learning to read and write from his account of Persian aristocratic education: 'the boys spend their time learning justice . . . just as our boys learn their letters' (*Cyr.* 1.2.6). Specially trained scribes were needed to cope with the cuneiform writing systems of Akkadian, Elamite and Old Persian; Aramaic, the administrative *lingua franca* of the empire, was easier, but nobles would scarcely have troubled to spend time acquiring literacy, a craft of servants.

Ἀλέξανδρον: Alexander I, son of Amyntas and king of Macedonia *ca.* 494–452. Known as *Philhellen*, he was very keen to be thought Greek (5.22) and invited Greek poets to his court. He was skilled at being (or presenting himself as being) a friend to both sides in the Persian Wars. According to what was probably a piece of propaganda for Greek consumption, when *ca.* 511 his father gave Darius' messengers earth and water and the Persians behaved lasciviously towards the Macedonian women, Alexander had them killed by disguising smooth-chinned armed men as women. He escaped punishment by giving his sister to the Persian general Bubares (5.17–21). In 7.173.3, he pointed out to the Greeks the folly of opposing the King, as he will again here (**140**), which could be interpreted as kindness to the Greeks or loyalty to the King; and in 9.44–5, his striking night-time visit to the Greek lines could, in the event of a Greek victory, be balanced against his troops' support for Mardonius. Cf. also **34**.1n. He later extended his kingdom as far as the Strymon (Thuc. 2.99), taking control of a rich mine from which he minted the first Macedonian coinage (5.17.2; cf. Hammond 1979: 104–15). His skilful handling of his relationships with the Achaemenids laid the foundations of the great Macedonian monarchy of the future. Cf. Hammond 1979: 98–104, 1989: 43–8; Scaife 1989; Badian 1994.

Βουβάρης directed the work on the canal through the peninsula of Athos (7.22.2); see previous note for the marriage.

Ἀμύντης ὁ ἐν τῆι Ἀσίηι: the lengthy parenthesis allows H. to recall the earlier story and add a further fact about the honour shown by Persian Kings to this family; cf. Balcer 1993: 83.

Ἀλάβανδα: the name is a problem, since there was a city in Caria with this name near Tralles (7.195; H–N 1110–11), but none recorded for Phrygia. Badian 1994: 115–16 suggests it was a relatively unimportant town which was given to the younger Amyntas as a consolation prize, after the loss of Macedonia from Persian control meant that they would not be able to install him as a satrap-king on Alexander's death. That the son of an Achaemenid should have a Macedonian name might come from a desire to make their future ruler acceptable to the Macedonians.

πρόξεινος: acting like consuls today, these were local citizens who were officially appointed by other states to represent the interests of their citizens in the city where the *proxenos* resided; in return, the *proxenoi* were granted privileges and honours by the appointing state. Alexander may have become a *proxenos* as a result of his father's relationship of *xenia* with the tyrants. Cf. Walbank 1978, esp. 63–7 on Alexander, the first recorded Athenian *proxenos*; Geschnitzer, *RE* Supp. 13 (1973) 629–730.

εὐεργέτης: cf. **140β**.2 n.

136.2 πολλὸν ἄρα: ἄρα conveys Mardonius' interested reaction to the revelation of this fact about the Athenians. Cf. Pl. *Symp.* 198C καὶ ἐνενόησα τότε ἄρα καταγέλαστος ὤν, 'and – now I see it – I realised I was foolish then . . .'; cf. **111**.2, **135**.2.

τά τε . . . ἐπίστατο 'and he knew that the sufferings at sea that had befallen the Persians the Athenians especially had caused'.

136.3 τά περ ἂν καὶ ἦν 'which would indeed have been the case'; for καί **109**.5n.

οὕτω τε ἐλογίζετο . . . Ἑλληνικῶν 'as a result, he considered that his position would be superior to that of the Greeks'.

τάχα δ' ἂν . . . προλέγοι, συμβουλεύοντα 'perhaps the oracles also foretold this to him, when they counselled him'. H. sometimes uses an optative to express a tentative conjecture about the past: cf. 1.70.3 τάχα δὲ ἂν καὶ οἱ ἀποδόμενοι λέγοιεν ἀπικόμενοι 'perhaps those who sold it would have said on their return', 5.59, 7.180, 184.3, 214.3, 9.71.3, which is unusual, given that the optative naturally looks to the future. Homer provides parallels, e.g. *Il.* 4.223 ἔνθ' οὐκ ἂν βρίζοντα ἴδοις Ἀγαμέμνονα 'then you would not have seen Agamemnon dozing', where ἴδοις refers to Homer's audience, not someone in the past battle. It seems that these Homeric optatives express potentiality without any limitations of time, except those that arise from the context. H.'s usage is a development of these (cf. *M&T* §§442–3; this is not certainly found in Attic).

τοῖσι: i.e. the oracles.

137–9 Alexander's ancestry; how Perdiccas created the Macedonian monarchy

For such legendary stories of how men ascended to kingship in unlikely ways, cf. Gyges' seeing Candaules' wife naked (1.8–14), Cyrus elected 'king' by his playmates (1.114), Psammetichus using his helmet for a libation (2.147.4, 151), and the accession of Darius, when his horse was the first to whinny after the sun rose (3.84–7). In the manner of many folk-tales about origins, this story concentrates on the earliest and most recent characters, Perdiccas and Alexander; cf. Thomas 2001. The traditions and problems surrounding the early Macedonian history and kingship are examined by Hammond 1972: 430–41 (esp. 433–5 on this passage), 1979: 3–14, 1989: 16–19, 37–48; cf. Rosen 1978; Zahrnt 1984; Sourvinou-Inwood 2002; and the full bibliography in Asheri 346–7. On the various problems of topography, see most recently Hatzopoulos 2003, who concludes that the brothers' route as here described was 'from Bravas (or Daskion) to Polyphyton, fording the Haliacmon near Polymelos and over Mt Bermion through the Kastania pass and Leukopetra to the Gardens of Midas at or near Beroea' (212).

137.1 ἕβδομος: i.e. counting himself. Greek regularly counts both ends of a series, even if it may seem odd to count a man amongst his own ancestors; cf. 1.13.2 (of

Croesus) τὸν πέμπτον ἀπόγονον Γύγεω, 91.1; **15**.1n. Thuc. 2.99–100 agrees with the number and descent here.

ἐξ Ἄργεος: most likely not the Peloponnesian Argos (*pace* Thuc. 2.99.3, 5.80.2), but Argos in Orestis near the source of the Haliacmon in southern Macedonia (cf. Appian, *Syr.* 63; Strabo 7, fr. 11). The claimed relationship with the more famous Argos could have been an attempt to lend prestige to Temenid rule; cf. Kelly 1976: 38–50.

Τημένου: a Heraclid, who took Argos for the Heraclids and became the founder of the line of Argive kings (Paus. 2.18.7; 38.1; Theopompus, *FGH* 115 F 393; Ephorus, *FGH* 70 F 115).

ἐς τὴν ἄνω Μακεδονίην . . . ἐς Λεβαίην πόλιν: 'Upper Macedonia' was in the Pierian mountains, north of Mt Olympus; cf. Zahrnt 1984: 346–7. Lebaea is harder to place, but probably south of Mt Bermion on the Haliacmon (Hatzopoulos 2003: 207–13). The Macedonian capital was eventually at Aegae, near Vergina.

137.2 ἐπὶ μισθῶι 'for hire'; ἐπί + dative is used of circumstances and conditions, and so of prices.

βασιλέϊ: called Cisseus in Paus. 9.40.8 and Eur. *Archelaus* (cf. Hyginus, *fab.* 219).

νεώτατος: it is a common folk-tale and mythical motif for the youngest of a group to be the most significant: cf. 4.5 and 9–10 for two versions of the origins of the Scythian dynasty involving the youngest son. Zeus is the youngest of the Olympians when he overthrows his father Cronus, and Marduk, the great king of the Babylonian gods, is the last-born of Ea. Cf. Thompson 1955–8: VI (Index) *s.v.* 'Youngest'.

τὰ λεπτά: i.e. sheep and goats. This detail is significant: the goat was a symbol of the Macedonian kings and appeared on Macedonian coinage (Hammond 1979: 104–15); it also refers to the capital Aegae and appears in the charter oracles for Temenid rule (Diod. 7.16; Justin 7.1.7–12).

ἀσθενέες χρήμασι: a dative of manner indicating in respect of what they were poor; this dative is found largely with intransitive adjectives (Smyth §1516).

137.3 ὅκως: 52.1n.

τοῦ παιδὸς τοῦ θητός, Περδίκκεω 'the servant-boy, Perdiccas'.

διπλήσιος . . . αὐτὸς ἑωυτοῦ 'it became twice its own size'. The doubling is an omen of Perdiccas' future kingship; compare perhaps the Spartan kings' double portion at banquets (6.57.1; cf. 7.103.1). For αὐτὸς ἑωυτοῦ, cf. **86**n.

εἶπε: *sc.* ἡ γυνή.

ἐσῆλθε 'occurred to'; impersonal.

137.4 θεοβλαβής: i.e. the gods made him say something that had an outcome very different from what he intended; cf. 1.127.2 where Astyages, forgetting he had served Harpagus' son to him at dinner, made him commander against Cyrus, ὥστε θεοβλαβὴς ἐών. Cf. **114**.2 for a similarly unintentionally prophetic remark about Mardonius by Xerxes.

137.5 περιγράφει τῆι μαχαίρηι . . . ἀρυσάμενος τοῦ ἡλίου 'drew round the sun with a knife onto the floor of the house, and when he had done this, scraping up the sun into his lap . . .'; ἡλίου is partitive genitive. By scraping the sun into his lap, Perdiccas thus symbolically takes possession of the house and land of the king, and so of the Macedonian kingship. That it is the sun, and not the earth, that is important is suggested not just by H.'s explicit statement, but also by the fact that the sun appears as a symbol of Macedonian kingship on coins, shields and the *larnakes* discovered at Vergina (Tripodi 1986). Cf. also Deinon, *FGH* 690 F 10 where Cyrus dreamt that the sun visited him and he tried three times to touch it, unsuccessfully; the three attempts were interpreted by the Magi as each portending ten years of kingship. For the knife and kingship, cf. perhaps the symbolic power of the Persian King's *akinakes* to control the weather (**120**n.). For the motif in folk-tale, cf. Thompson 1955–8: R.9.1; for earth as a symbol of ownership of land, cf. e.g. Pi. *Py.* 4.28–56.

138.1 οἷόν τι . . . διδόμενα: the repetition ὁ παῖς . . . κείνων ὁ νεώτατος is a little awkward; Stein deleted ὁ παῖς, making the king the subject of the first clause. σὺν νόωι is 'with serious intent', 'with something in mind'.

ποταμὸς . . . τῶι θύουσι: the river is most likely the Haliacmon (cf. §2n.), though the omission of its name contributes to the fairy-tale atmosphere (Asheri). Sacrifice to rivers is regular; 'each city worships its river or spring' (Burkert 1985a: 174); Asheri suggests that horses may have been sacrificed at the river, as by the Persians at the Strymon (7.113.2).

σωτῆρι 'as their saviour', in apposition to τῶι; for such comparisons without ὡς, cf. K–G II 495–6.

138.2 ὥστε τοὺς ἱππέας μὴ οἵους τε γενέσθαι διαβῆναι: there is the same motif in the story of the destruction of the Egyptian charioteers in the Red Sea, when the Israelites left Egypt to settle in Israel (Exodus 14).

ἐς ἄλλην γῆν τῆς Μακεδονίης: the area between Mt Bermion and the Haliacmon. 'The rest of Macedonia' (§3) will be the lands beyond.

κήπων: i.e. a **'paradise'**, the spacious and lavishly provided parks of Near Eastern monarchs and aristocrats. 'The canal crashes from above into the gardens; fragrance pervades the walkways; streams of water as numerous as the stars of heaven flow in the pleasure garden': so Ashurnasirpal II, ninth-century king of Assyria, described his gardens, listing 41 varieties of tree collected from his empire (Grayson 1976: 174; cf. *ANET* 558–60). The Persians called the gardens *paradayadā*, cognate with Avestan *pairi-daēza*, 'surrounded by a wall', whence 'paradise' (Elam. *partetash*). They were a mixture of pleasure-gardens (Esther 1.5; Diod. 2.13.1–4) and country park: 'there were splendid wild animals, some in enclosed parks, others in open spaces, while a river, full of all sorts of fish, surrounded the palace; and there were plenty of birds too, for those who were skilful in fowling' (Xen. *HG* 4.1.15–16, the satrap's paradise at Dascylium; cf. *Anab.* 1.2.7–9, 1.4.10, 2.4.14). PFa 33 (= Brosius no. 110; cf. also PFa 1) lists 4,981 seedlings of olives, apples, quinces, mulberries, pears, dates and other, unknown, trees, to be planted at four paradises. The gardens required complex irrigation systems, such as aqueducts (cf. also the cows at Susa who downed tools when they had put the requisite number of jars of water on their paradise (Ctesias, *FGH* 688 F 34)). These paradises expressed two important aspects of Achaemenid royal ideology: the king as hunter is an old Near Eastern motif of royal protection for his people, and Achaemenid kings linked themselves with natural fertility (**54–5**n.). There are echoes of these gardens, in e.g. Alcinous' garden in *Od.* 7.112–32. Cf. Briant 2002: 200–3, 232–40); Tuplin 1996: 80–131.

Μίδεω: many Greek traditions are attached to this man. Midas captured the Silen, who spoke philosophically with him (see below §3n.); Midas returned him to Dionysus and was rewarded with the touch of gold. Greek tradition made him the founder of the Phrygian kingdom (Arr. *Anab.* 2.3.1–6). Mita, king of the Muski, appears in Assyrian sources first in 718, as a conspirator against the Assyrian king Sargon II, with whom he was later reconciled. Greek sources add little: he was the first barbarian king to give gifts to Delphi (**35**n.), and he committed suicide when the Cimmerians invaded and ravaged his prosperous kingdom and massive citadel (Strabo, 1.3.21). A skeleton, which may be his, of a short man in his early sixties has been found at his capital, 'Midas City' (now Yazılıkaya, between Eskishehir and Afyon). It was laid on purple and brown textiles, inside a log coffin. There was furniture for a funerary banquet and 150 bronze vessels, the most comprehensive Iron Age drinking set ever found, and remains of a feast of spicy lamb and lentil stew, fermented grape-wine, barley beer and honey mead. His name appears on Phrygian inscriptions at his capital: *midai* | *lavag<e>taei* | *vanaktei* 'to Midas, leader of the people and lord' (cf. Gk. λαϝαγέτας, ϝάναξ; Brixhe and Lejeune 1984: nos M-01a, d, T-02d, G-137). Cf. Hawkins, *RdA* VIII 271–3; Sams, *CANE* II 1147–59; Mellink, *CAH*² III pt 2 622–43; Voigt and Henrickson 2000.

Γορδίεω: he gave his name to Gordium (mod. Yassıhüyük) for which see Mellink, *CAH*² IV 228–31; the town was later famous for its knot cut by Alexander the Great.

αὐτόματα: plants etc. growing of their own accord is a traditional feature of golden ages and places of a magical fertility; cf. e.g. Hsd. *Op.* 117–18 καρπὸν δ' ἔφερε ζείδωρος ἄρουρα | αὐτομάτη.

ἑξήκοντα φύλλα 'sixty petals', a remarkable number, until the breeding of modern varietes.

138.3 Σιληνός: a kind of satyr. Though best known for their licentious behaviour, satyrs were also connected with more than human wisdom: cf. Pl. *Symp.* 215A, 216D; Arist. fr. 44; Verg. *Ecl.* 6; Seaford 1984: 7. In later versions, Midas mixed wine into the Silen's spring to gain his wisdom, and the Silen gave him the message that it was best for a man never to have been born, and second best to die as soon as possible. This story is found in Greek art from the second quarter of the sixth century; the first reference in Greek literature is Tyrtaeus, fr. 12.6. Cf. Miller, *LIMC* VIII 1 846–51.

139 Ἀμύντεω: he appears as a tentative foil to his son in the massacre of misbehaving Persian guests in 5.17–21. For such honorific genealogies, cf. 7.204 (Leonidas), **131** (Leotychidas), 9.64 (Pausanias). Apart from Amyntas, the kings are merely names. Aeropus (cf. **137**.1) and Argaeus are names borne by kings after this Alexander. On this list and the different lists in later writers, cf. Momigliano 1975; Hammond 1979: 3–14, 31–9.

140–4 Debate at Athens

After the folk-tales, *paradeisoi* and Silens, we now return to very serious politics and the question of Athens' future allegiance. The section consists of four speeches, with a brief narrative passage (**141**). The speeches stand alone, with only the briefest of introductory statements, lending the passage a lapidary quality which underlines the crucial nature of the decision facing the Athenians. The nearest parallel is the equally significant constitutional debate between Otanes, Megabyxus and Darius, after the overthrow of the usurper Smerdis (3.80–2). The speeches are arranged in a simple pattern: two speeches addressed to the Athenians by Alexander and by the Spartans precede two by the Athenians addressed to Alexander and to the Spartans. There are 47 such groups of four speeches in H.; cf. Lang 1984: 24–31, 106–13.

The Athenians' great defence of their commitment to *to hellenikon* makes a stirring ending to the book. The Alexandrian editor who chose to end his papyrus-roll at this point knew what he was doing (cf. **1**.1n.).

140 Alexander's speech

This is the longest and technically most interesting of the speeches. It contains a number of notable narratological features. First, there is the 'nesting' of the speeches. H. will often, in the speech of an envoy, give in direct speech the words of the one who sent him (e.g. 1.69, Croesus' words relayed by messengers), but Alexander goes one stage further: he encompasses two other speeches, quoting Mardonius who in turn quotes Xerxes. The order of *voices* is Alexander, Mardonius, Xerxes, but the first two merely introduce the next speaker, so the order of *speakers* imitates the original chronological one, Xerxes, Mardonius, Alexander. This nesting technique is reminiscent of, but again more complex than, Artemisia's speech in **68**, spoken to Mardonius but addressed to the King. Remarkably for economic documents, a small number of Persepolis tablets also use nesting of speeches: 'Tell Harrenā the cattle-chief, Parnaka spoke as follows: "Darius the king ordered me saying: '100 sheep from my estate (are) to be issued to Irtashduna [Gk. Artystone] the princess'"' (Fort. 6764; cf. PF 1792, 1806). A scribe with frustrated literary ambition?

H. characterises the three speakers by means of stylistic variation. Xerxes is crisp: he starts with a first-person statement; gives a command to Mardonius, one to the Athenians, another to Mardonius; and ends in the first person. Mardonius begins almost grudgingly, with a veiled threat and a forceful 'I tell you this'. In a curt question he immediately accuses the Athenians of madness, before explaining that charge with a sevenfold use of the second person plural: the onus is on the Athenians to see the point. §4 starts and ends with equally curt imperatives, provides little in the way of argument, and finishes with an implication that the Athenians might try tricks. It is the impatient speech of one forced to defend a course of action of which he does not approve, in relation to peoples for whom he seems to have little but contempt. He seems more comfortable speaking obsequiously to his sovereign (cf. **100**.2–5) than tactfully persuading his enemies into an alliance. It is a brilliant characterisation of the haughty nobleman, and the *hybris* points (for Greeks at least) to his ultimate complete failure.

As a skilled operator and clearly realising the diplomatic deficit in Mardonius' speech, Alexander is very much more emollient. He immediately reminds the Athenians that the previous words were Mardonius'. He softens Mardonius' hammer-blows with much more emotionally and syntactically nuanced sentences (n.b. λεήνας, **142**.4). β.3 makes use of the genitive participle to sum the situation up with remarkable economy. Where Mardonius could only say the alliance was 'for the best' (κάλλιστα) and to be accepted because the King wanted it (α.4), Alexander cleverly stresses the *value* to the Athenians of the alliance. He ends by noting that it is to them alone that the King is making his request, and by emphasising that the request is that the King should be *their* friend: a lesser rhetorician might have put that the other way round.

140α.1 ἐγεγόνεε μὲν δὴ ὧδε 'so that was how Alexander had come about'. The contrast in tense with ὧδε ἐγένετο in **139** has point: the pluperfect views the matter from the standpoint of the time of which H. is speaking, the aorist states the simple fact of his origin.

Μαρδόνιος τάδε λέγει: this recalls the formulation 'X the King says', which is peculiar to Persian inscriptions (cf. H. 5.24.1; 7.150.2); Mardonius seems almost to be arrogating royal authority to his words.

140α.2 τοῦτο μὲν . . . τοῦτο δέ = μὲν . . . δέ, as **76**.1.

αὐτόνομοι: this word and *autonomia* almost always (cf. 1.96.1) refers to the position of a weaker state allowed or attempting to exercise some freedom under the rule of a stronger. It appears to be a word that grew up under the Athenian empire to express the aspirations of the Athenian allies to restrict Athenian power, and so would be an anachronism here, giving the passage a relevance to events later in the century. H. would mean that the Athenians were to be 'autonomous' but that they would have in effect to capitulate to the Persians: one might compare the privileges given the Ionians by Mardonius' 'democracies' in 6.43.3, which remained firmly under Persian control. Cf. Bickerman 1958; Ostwald 1982: esp. 15–16. The Persian empire did allow certain peoples a measure of autonomy, so long as their loyalty to the King was not in doubt and was suitably expressed when required, or because more control was not practically possible. This was true in the case of the Phoenicians (cf. **67**.2n., **85**.1n.), and of certain more remote pastoral and nomadic tribes.

ἱρά . . . ἀνόρθωσον: cf. **54** ἐνθύμιον n.

ἤν δὴ βούλωνταί γε 'if indeed (δή) they really (γέ) wish': 'γέ denotes that the speaker . . . is not concerned with what might or might not be true apart from the qualification laid down in the subordinate clause' (*GP* 141–2). Xerxes is portrayed as willing to do almost anything to get the Athenians to agree to his offer of an alliance.

τούτων δὲ ἀπιγμένων 'now that this message [from the king] has arrived'. Mardonius here begins to speak in his own voice, taking the part of one who must do his master's bidding.

ἤν μὴ . . . αἴτιον γένηται 'unless your view of things is the reason (why I cannot do what the King orders)'. αἴτιον is the MSS reading; some editors have felt the lack of a negative expression representing the thought in the bracket, and so accept Valckenaer's ἀντίον 'an obstacle'. τὸ ὑμέτερον is like τὰ ὑμέτερα in **75**.2–3, 'your affairs', and almost = ὑμεῖς, cf. 3.155.4 ἢν μὴ τῶν σῶν δεήσηι 'if there is no failing on your part'; for the singular, cf. 4.127.1 οὕτω τὸ ἐμὸν ἔχει.

140α.3 νῦν τί μαίνεσθε . . . ἀνταειρόμενοι 'given all this, why are you madly raising war against the King?'; νῦν is sometimes used at the start of a question that grows out of the previous remarks (K–G II 117).

οὔτε οἷοί τέ ἐστε ἀντέχειν τὸν πάντα χρόνον: the justice of this analysis, repeated by Alexander in β.2, is acknowledged by the Greeks when they discuss future policy after the final victory at Mycale (9.106.2). For the shift in mood from optative to indicative, cf. **26**.2n.

τοῦ περ . . . φρονέετε 'which you cannot (possibly) hope for, if you have any sense'; cf. **60**β n.

ἄλλη . . . παραπλησίη: *sc.* δύναμις. Kelly 2003 argues that rumours of the size of the Persian forces were an important part of a psychological propaganda campaign designed to overawe the Greeks.

140α.4 μὴ ὦν βούλεσθε: the present imperative in prohibitions often calls for abstention from an action already begun (Smyth §1841a).

παρισούμενοι 'by trying to make yourselves equal'.

θέειν . . . περὶ ὑμέων αὐτῶν: cf. **74**.1n.

βασιλέος ταύτηι ὁρμημένου 'now that the King has made this *démarche*', almost 'gone down this road'.

ἔστε ἐλεύθεροι . . . συνθέμενοι: the asyndeton contributes to a rousing end to the speech (cf. Denniston 1952: 112–14). The Athenians will provide their own definition of 'free' in **143**.1 ἐλευθερίης γλιχόμενοι ἀμυνεύμεθα οὕτως ὅκως ἂν καὶ δυνώμεθα.

ἄνευ τε δόλου καὶ ἀπάτης: phrases of this sort regularly appear in actual treaty texts in Thucydides, as 4.118.1 ἀδόλως καὶ ἀδεῶς, 5.18.3, 47.1 ἀδόλους καὶ ἀβλαβεῖς, and also in speeches in H. (1.69.2, 9.7α.1). τε is sometimes placed after a word that governs two conjoined words, rather than after the first of the two; cf. Pl. *Prt.* 316D τοὺς ἀμφί τε Ὀρφέα καὶ Μουσαῖον (*GP* 518). From here, Alexander becomes the speaker.

140β.2 περὶ μὲν εὐνοίης . . . οὐδὲν λέξω: it is notable that H. does not have Alexander give the details of his benefaction to Athens, which might have increased the power of his arguments. However, Badian 1994: 122–7 suggests that it was Alexander who had suggested that the Athenians turn to the King for support and ensured the success of the appeal, when in 508/7 they were in a very vulnerable position after the expulsion of Cleomenes and Isagoras. If he is right, for Alexander to mention such an event at a time like this would have been very unfortunate.

ἐνορῶ γὰρ ὑμῖν οὐκ οἵοισί τε ἐσομένοισι 'I see that you will not be able', an unparalleled use of ἐνορᾶν with the dative of the object instead of the accusative (as τοῦτο in the next clause), probably on analogy with the synonymous σύνοιδα + dative (Stein).

καὶ γάρ '(but I don't see this) because . . .'; the particles explain why it is that he *has* come with this message.

δύναμις . . . καὶ χεὶρ ὑπερμήκης: for this conjunction, cf. 4.155.4 τέωι δυνάμι, κοίηι χειρί;, said in response to an apparently impossible demand. 'Long-armed' may be metaphorical, as here or in Ov. *Her.* 17.166 *an nescis longas regibus esse manus?*, but Plut. *Art.* 1 claims that Xerxes' successor, Artaxerxes μακρόχειρ, had a right hand longer than his left. Cf. Pollux 2.150.1.

140β.3 ἦν ὦν . . . τὴν γῆν κεκτημένων 'if therefore you do not immediately agree, when the Persians are offering you generous terms on which they are willing to agree, I fear for you, because most of all the allies [μάλιστα . . . τῶν συμμάχων πάντων together; genitive of comparison] you live in the path [of Mardonius' invasion] and must alone always be threatened with destruction, since you possess a land that is marked out as [lit. 'and'] a battle-ground'. It is not strictly true that Athens lay in the path of any march made by Mardonius to the Peloponnese: Alexander is using mild rhetorical exaggeration to make his point. Mardonius does, however, sack Athens when this offer is refused (9.1). μεταίχμιον is the space between two armies (6.77.1; Sol. 37.9). Mardonius was in fact to discover the disadvantages of fighting in Attica (9.13).

140β.4 ἀλλὰ πείθεσθε: ἀλλά marks 'a transition from arguments for action to a statement of the action required' (*GP* 14). Alexander ends with a reminder of the important fact that they need not fear reprisals for their mauling of the Persian fleet, if they agree to the Persian offer. For Persian leniency to those who have previously damaged their interests but have the potential to benefit them in future, cf. **110**.2–3n.

141–2 The Spartan ambassadors' speech

141.1 τῶν λογίων: perhaps these are the oracles which Cleomenes took from the Acropolis containing dire warnings about the Athenian threat to Sparta and which the Peisistratids had left behind when they fled eventually to Persia (5.90.2; cf. **52**.2n.).

ἔδεισαν . . . Ἀθηναῖοι: the threat was a real one; Athens had earlier threatened to abandon the alliance if the Spartans did not fight at Salamis (**62**.2). This shows again how fragile was the notion that because one belonged to the Greek race one's allegiance naturally lay with the Greeks.

141.2 σφεων . . . τὴν κατάστασιν 'the appearance of both of them' (before the Athenians), i.e. of Alexander and the Spartan messengers. κατάστασις is used in this sense only in H. (also 3.46.1, 9.9.1).

ἐπίτηδες ὦν ἐποίευν 'so they did this on purpose'; ἐποίευν is used absolutely, as in 7.168.3.

ἐνδεικνύμενοι 'attempting to make clear'; the present participle can describe an attempted action (Smyth §1872a.3).

142 The speech of the Spartans. After Alexander's rhetorical fireworks, the Spartans are given a rather lower-key speech (cf. that of Eurybiades in **108**.2–4). They take a high moral line at beginning and end, but in the middle strike the warmer note of an offer to look after Athenian families for the duration of the war: concern for their families had earlier especially motivated Athenian policy-making (**60**β). Their final remark about the untrustworthiness of barbarians picks up Mardonius' last remark (**140**α.4).

142.1 διαδεξάμενοι 'taking up'; τὸν λόγον 'the argument' is understood from ἔλεγον.

ἡμέας δέ 'us too have the Spartans sent'; ἡμέας is emphatic, and δέ contrasts them with Alexander (for δέ at the start of a speech in H., cf. *GP* 172).

μήτε . . . κατὰ τὴν Ἑλλάδα 'nor do anything radical, harmful to Greece'; for νέος in this sense, cf. **21**.1n.

142.2 οὔτι γε ἄλλοισι . . . ὑμῖν δὲ δή 'certainly not for any other Greeks, and especially not for you of all people'. γε emphasises οὔτι; the piling up of negatives is striking, emphasising a certain desperation on the part of the Spartans. For adversative δὲ δή, cf. *GP* 259.

ἠγείρατε γὰρ . . . πᾶσαν τὴν Ἑλλάδα 'you started this war, when we wanted nothing of it; it was about your sphere of influence at first that the conflict began, but now it has spread to the whole of Greece.' This is a problematic but intriguing passage. The MSS all have περὶ τῆς ὑμετέρης ἀρχῆς 'about your empire', but against this it is objected that it introduces an apparent anachronism, since it does not make a lot of sense to talk about the 'Athenian empire' in 480. ἀρχή would have to refer rather generally to the idea of the Athenian leadership of the Ionians (cf. **22**.1n.), and to the initial conflicts in the Ionian Revolt which the Athenians had supported. This would be one of a number of passages in H. which in their context look anachronistic, but which together give his work a relevance to the events of his own time, when the Athenian empire has replaced the Persian as the problematic and in many eyes oppressive power block in the Mediterranean.

Some editors have adopted emendations such as Schaefer's adverbial accusative ἀρχήν 'in the beginning', or Wesseling's ἀρχῆθεν 'from the beginning', comparing Themistocles' remark to the Ionians that 'ἀρχῆθεν hostility between Greek and barbarian was caused by you' (**22**.2); with ὑμετέρης then *sc.* γῆς (cf. e.g. **3**.2 περὶ τῆς ἐκείνου of the King's empire). νῦν δέ in the following clause would then contrast with ἀρχήν.

On the other hand, one could argue that the sense 'at the start' is already prominently present in the first and last words of the first part of the sentence, ἠγείρατε 'you started' and ἐγένετο 'began'. If we keep ἀρχῆς, the sentence would then have a doubly balanced structure: '*you* started the war; *we* wanted nothing to do with it: it was *your sphere* that was initially involved; now *all of Greece* is affected by the consequences.' The Spartans are made to speak in a way that it is better to regard not as anachronistic, so much as proleptic: they speak as their descendants later in the century were to speak. The reference to 'freeing many peoples' in the next sentence also fits the later Athenians as well, if not better, than those of 480. The paradosis is also defended by Gilula 2003: 85–7.

ἠγείρατε γὰρ τόνδε τὸν πόλεμον: by their support for the Ionian Revolt, 'the start (ἀρχή) of the troubles between the Greeks and the barbarians' (5.97).

142.3 ἄλλως τε . . . ἀνασχετόν: a problematic sentence. ἄλλως τε is 'and besides'; cf. e.g. Soph. *OT* 1114 ἄλλως τε τοὺς ἄγοντας ὥσπερ οἰκέτας | ἔγνωκ' ἐμαυτοῦ. As the text is transmitted, τούτων ἁπάντων appears to have no construction. No satisfactory solution has been found. What is printed in the text presumes that καί was lost after the -θαι of γενέσθαι, which would be an easy mistake for a scribe to make. It might be argued that this reading risks creating confusion with the common use of ἄλλως τε . . . καί 'especially', but this expression tends not to start a sentence, so a Greek would not necessarily have looked for a καὶ that went with ἄλλως τε here. (For ἄλλως τε 'especially' followed by a καί which is not connected with it, cf. K–G II 250–1).

μέντοι marks a shift in the Spartans' speech from criticism to sympathy. The particle, regularly adversative in H. (**29**.2n.), has the implication 'but leaving what we have just said aside (though we mean it)', i.e. it allows the criticism to stand, even as the speech moves on to less controversial matters.

καρπῶν ἐστερήθητε διξῶν ἤδη 'you have already lost two harvests'. The Spartans must be speaking with an eye to the future, because so far the Athenians have lost only the harvest of the current year, 480, as a result of their abandoning of Attica (cf. **50**). For rhetorical purposes, to make the Athenian situation look as bad as possible, the Spartans presume that the harvest of 479 will also be lost. It is not entirely unreasonable for the Spartans to imagine that this second harvest will also be lost in the continuing conflict, if Mardonius were to reoccupy Attica, as Alexander suggests he would (**140β**.3). Themistocles has advised the Athenians to go to their homes and sow their autumn crops (σπόρου ἀνακῶς ἐχέτω, **109**.4), and those who did return and sow their crops must have abandoned them again at the approach of Mardonius, because when he takes Athens for the second time, he finds it empty: most of the Athenians are on Salamis or in the fleet (9.3, 13; H. does not go into details about who returned from Salamis, which remained the seat of the Athenian council, 9.5). As it happens, Mardonius does not ravage the countryside, in the hope that the Athenians will come over to him (9.13.1), but the Spartans could not know that, or perhaps they suppress the possibility to make their case stronger.

ἐστερήθητε . . . οἰκοφθόρησθε: the aorist describes a single act of deprivation, the perfect an event with continuing import ('you have lost your homes').

142.4 τὰ . . . οἰκετέων ἐχόμενα 'those of your household who are unfit for war'. The participle of ἔχομαι is regularly used thus in H. to mean 'be of the nature of' (*Lex.* C 2): cf. 3.25.4 τὰ εἶχον σιτίων ἐχόμενα 'what they had in the way of food'.

ἔστ' ἂν ὁ πόλεμος ὅδε συνεστήκηι 'as long as this war continues'; for this sense of the perfect, cf. 1.74.2 τῆς μάχης συνεστεώσηις, 7.225.1 τοῦτο δὲ συνεστήκεε μέχρι οὗ οἱ σὺν Ἐπιάλτηι παρεγένοντο 'this (battle) continued . . .' (LSJ *s.v.* συνίστημι B II 1).

λεήνας τὸν Μαρδονίου λόγον 'smoothing out [the harshness of] Mardonius' words'. 'Smooth' in connection with words regularly implies deceit; Solon 34.3 καί με κωτίλλοντα λείως τραχὺν ἐπιφανεῖν νόον ('[they thought] that, though I flattered them smoothly, I would reveal my harsh intention').

142.5 τύραννος: the Spartans use a pejorative word; the only time Alexander's kingship is specifically mentioned, he is called βασιλεύς (9.44.1)

ὑμῖν δέ γε: for the 'tinge of repartee', cf. **59**n.; 'he has to behave like this, but you don't'.

143 The Athenian reply to Alexander

The longest speech comes last, divided in two by an authorial intervention at **144**.1: however dramatic the rhetoric of the speeches, the unadorned quality of this part of the narrative is thus maintained, as it is again at the end, when the Spartans are said simply to leave. The speech has an ABC CBA pattern, the first triad addressed to Alexander, the second to be conveyed to Mardonius: (A) advice to Alexander on his recent behaviour; (B) we will defend ourselves (ἀμυνεύμεθα); (C) you will never persuade us to make a treaty (ὁμολογῆσαι) with the barbarian; (C) we will never make a treaty (ὁμολογήσειν) with Xerxes; (B) we will defend ourselves (ἀμυνόμενοι); (A) advice to Alexander on his future behaviour. The phrase 'proxenos and friend', placed at the end, reminds Alexander of his obligations.

143.1 This reply was given by Aristeides according to Plut. *Arist.* 10.3–6. By giving it to the Athenians, H. is able to keep the focus on their behaviour as a nation.

ἀμυνεύμεθα: future.

καί emphasises δυνώμεθα, 'as much as ever we are able'.

μήτε σὺ ἡμέας πειρῶ . . . οὔτε ἡμεῖς πεισόμεθα: the negatives differ because one introduces a command, the other a statement; the shift emphasises the second clause. The slight anacoluthon in the thought allows the parallelism of the clauses to stress the contrast between Alexander's behaviour and that of the Athenians.

143.2 ἔστ' ἂν ὁ ἥλιος: such oaths on apparently unchanging natural phenomena are not uncommon. Compare e.g. the oath of the Phocaeans that they would not return to their country until a lump of iron, which they had dropped into the sea, rose to the surface again (1.165.3).

μήκοτε ὁμολογήσειν: for emphatic μή in indirect discourse, cf. **74**.2n.

ἀλλὰ θεοῖσί τε . . . καὶ τοῖσι ἥρωσι: πίσυνοι governs θεοῖσι συμμάχοισι and ἥρωσι; μιν is governed by ἀμυνόμενοι.

ὄπιν: in Homer, this word means the 'anger' or 'vengeance' of the gods, but in H. and later it means the reverence owed by men to the gods.

143.3 τοῦ λοιποῦ: *sc.* χρόνου.

144 The Athenian reply to the Spartans; the importance of 'Hellenism'

This speech attempts to characterise the Athenians as selflessly devoted to the ideal of Greek freedom and contains fine sentiments. On the other hand, there are also other tones. To begin a speech 'That the Spartans should be afraid . . .' borders on the provocative, and to refer to that fear as 'shameful' increases the provocation. The Athenians seem rather annoyed that the Spartans should think they would ally with Xerxes, but it was a not unreasonable fear. The subsequent high-flown defence of

Attica as a place to live sits a little oddly with Attica's known poverty of soil (Thuc. 1.5), and with Themistocles' earlier threat to abandon his homeland if he does not get his way (**62**.2). It sits least well with the Athenians' later declared intention to join the Persians, when they think (wrongly, as it happens) that the Spartans have let them down by not sending the army they promised (9.11). Their more noble account of the things preventing them allying with Xerxes is made up of two sentences with repetition and variation, the repetition emphasising Athenian loyalty to things Greek, and the exact centre of the speech contains its main message in an ἔστ᾽ ἄν clause, as did the speech to the Spartans (**143**.2). They at last acknowledge Spartan concerns for their well-being, but in a way that is tinged with a curious self-righteousness in the face of the difficulties they know they will face (**144**.4n.). Panhellenism thus marches with touches of self-importance and self-absorption.

144.1 τὸ μὲν δεῖσαι Λακεδαιμονίους 'that the Spartans should be afraid'; 'articular' infinitive, with the subject as usual in the accusative (**88**.2n.). μέν is picked up by ἀτάρ, here marking a strong contrast between the clauses (*GP* 54).

ἀτὰρ αἰσχρῶς γε . . . καταδουλῶσαι τὴν Ἑλλάδα 'but it is really to your shame that you appear to be afraid, despite the fact that you know well the Athenian spirit, (which believes) that there is not so much gold anywhere in the world nor a land so greatly superior in attractiveness and fertility, on acceptance of which we would be willing to medise and enslave Greece.' The construction is equivalent to οὔτε χρυσός ἐστι τοσοῦτος, οὔτε χώρη οὕτω ὑπερφέρουσα, ὥστε . . ., but the potential relative clause τὰ ἡμεῖς κτλ. replaces the ὥστε-clause which τοσοῦτος and οὕτω might lead one to expect. οἴκατε governs ἀρρωδῆσαι, which is qualified by αἰσχρῶς; ἐξεπιστάμενοι is concessive; ὅτι introduces the description of the φρόνημα, as in the Greek 'I know you, who you are' construction. καταδουλῶσαι meets the Spartan accusation in **142**.3 (n.b. δουλοσύνης).

144.2 πολλά τε γὰρ καὶ μεγάλα . . . μηδ᾽ ἢν ἐθέλωμεν 'there are many great and powerful considerations preventing us from doing this, even if we wanted to.' ταῦτα is the object of μὴ ποιέειν; μηδέ is used with ἐθέλωμεν because of the preceding μή (regular after a verb of hindering), but like that μή is omitted in translation.

πρῶτα μὲν . . . αὖτις δέ introduce the two categories of considerations, one involving their duty to the gods, the other their duty to the Greeks. Athens rather grandly (indeed grandiosely) shows how aware it is of the importance of its relationships to gods and men. The fears about Athenian conduct expressed by the Spartans are, it is suggested, deeply misguided, given the broad moral vision of the Athenians.

τὸ Ἑλληνικόν, ἐὸν ὅμαιμόν τε καὶ ὁμόγλωσσον 'Greekness, which shares one blood and one language'. It was their victory in the Persian Wars which helped crystallise a notion of 'Greeks' as against 'non-Greeks' or *barbaroi*: current scholarship debates whether this followed soon after or rather later than the victory. There is a strong 'pan-hellenic' aspect to the *Iliad*, and there existed Hellenus, whose descendants gave their names to the Dorians, Ionians and Aeolians, but there does not seem to have been so strong a sense of 'Greekness' as there was after the defeat of

Persia: Thuc. 1.3.3 notes that Homer has no single term for 'Greeks' as opposed to others.

H. here defines 'Greekness' in terms of four things: shared genetics, language, religion and customs. Though there were similarities in these areas across the Greeks, there were also differences. It is now generally thought that the Greeks came into Greece in a single wave, rather than at separate intervals, but membership of ethnic groups such as 'Dorians' or 'Ionians' could be more important than membership of the 'Greek' race. Their dialects, though descended from a common language, 'proto-Greek' (cf. Palmer 1980: 3–26), developed in some cases such differences that not all Greeks were in fact mutually comprehensible, and the separate dialects might reasonably be thought of as different languages (cf. Morpurgo Davies 1987; for useful discussions of the dialects, cf. Chadwick 1956; Risch 1981; for language and ethnicity in the fifth century, cf. J. M. Hall 1995). They shared certain religious festivals, such as the great penteteric games at Olympia, Delphi, the Isthmus and Nemea, and cult sites such as the oracles at Delphi and Dodona, but otherwise their religious activity was of a remarkable variety. So it was with their customs. It was now, however, possible to override such differences for rhetorical purposes. Given the effect that the Persian Wars had on Greek notions of ethnicity, one must allow for the possibility that the 'definition' of hellenicity here is focalised more from H.'s own time than from the view in 480.

On Greek constructions of their identity at this time, cf. Diller 1962; E. M. Hall 1989; Cartledge 2002a; J. M. Hall 1997, 2002 (esp. 172–205).

144.3 ὑμέων μέντοι ἀγάμεθα τὴν προνοίην: μέντοι introduces the transition from high-minded refutation of Spartan insinuations to a (rather brief) final acknowledgement of the fact that the Spartans had offered to help the Athenians in their plight. This mirrors the Spartans' similar use of μέντοι in **142**.3 (see n.) to move from their insinuations to the offer of help, and the subsequent words pick up Spartan expressions (οἰκοφθορημένων, ἐπιθρέψαι, οἰκέτας), but there is an element of ingratitude and even sanctimoniousness in the 'tit-for-tat' manner in which the Athenians do this.

ἔχουσαν 'pertaining, relating to', as often (*Lex. s.v.* B 3 b).

144.4 καὶ ὑμῖν μὲν ἡ χάρις ἐκπεπλήρωται, ἡμεῖς μέντοι: ὑμῖν is dative of the agent, as regularly with the perfect passive. μὲν . . . μέντοι makes for a much stronger contrast than μὲν . . . δέ: there is thus again just a hint of dismissiveness in this sentence.

λιπαρήσομεν οὕτω ὅκως ἂν ἔχωμεν 'we will get by in whatever way we can'; ὅκως introduces an indefinite relative clause.

ὡς οὕτω ἐχόντων 'since things are as they are'; cf. **80**.2n.

144.5 οὐχ ἑκὰς χρόνου lit. 'not far-off in time', a partitive genitive, with which cf. ὀψὲ τῆς ἡμέρας 'late in the day', **12**.1n.

ἐπειδὰν τάχιστα: *sc.* παρέσται before this.

ἡμέας 'you and us'. In 9.6, the Athenians complain that the Spartans 'ignored the Persian invasion of Attica and did not meet them in Boeotia', and repeat the charge in 9.7β.1 'you promised to meet us in Boeotia, but let us down and ignored the invasion of Attica'; those passages pick up this one. Wesseling's ὑμέας is not necessary, since both armies are to meet there, and it makes for a better ending to the speech if the Athenians rouse both themselves and their principal allies to further efforts against the Persians.

οἱ μέν: the Spartans. The δέ-clause will describe Mardonius' move south from Thessaly, towards Athens.

BIBLIOGRAPHY

Adiego Lajara, I.-J. 1993: *Studia carica: investigaciones sobre la escritura y lengua Carias*, Barcelona.

Adrados, F. R. 1972: 'Los coros de la "Paz" y los "Dictiulcos" y sus precedentes rituales', in *Studi classici in onore di Q. Cataudella*, Catania: 173–85.

Alberti, G. B. 1983: 'I papiri e l' "archetipo" di Erodoto', *Prometheus* 9: 193–6.

Alty, J. 1982: 'Dorians and Ionians', *JHS* 102: 1–14.

Amiet, P. 1988: *Suse: 6,000 ans d'histoire*, Paris.

Armayor, O. K. 1978: 'Did Herodotus ever go to the Black Sea?', *HSCP* 82: 45–62.

Armayor, O. K. 1980: 'Sesostris and Herodotus' autopsy of Thrace, Colchis, inland Asia Minor, and the Levant', *HSCP* 84: 51–74.

Asheri, D. 1988: *Erodoto, le Storie, libro I*, Rome.

Asheri, D. 1993: 'Erodoto e Bacide: considerazioni sulla fede di Erodoto negli oracoli (Hdt. VIII 77)', in M. Sordi (ed.), *La profezia nel mondo antico*, Milan: 63–76.

Asheri, D. 1998: 'Platea vendetta delle Termopili: alle origini di un motivo teologico erodoteo', in M. Sordi (ed.), *Responsabilità, perdono e vendetta nel mondo antico*, Milan: 65–86.

Badian, E. 1994: 'Herodotus on Alexander I of Macedon', in S. Hornblower (ed.), *Greek Historiography*, Oxford: 107–30.

Bakker, E. J. 2002: 'The making of history: Herodotus' *historiês apodexis*', in Bakker, de Jong and van Wees 2002: 3–32.

Bakker, E. J., de Jong, I. J. F. and van Wees, H. 2002: *Brill's companion to Herodotus*, Leiden, Boston and Cologne.

Bakker, M. P. de 2007: 'Speech and authority in Herodotus' *Histories*', Diss. Amsterdam.

Balcer, J. M. 1993: *A prosopographical study of the ancient Persians royal and noble c. 550–450 BC*, Lewiston, Queenston and Lampeter.

Balcer, J. M. 1995: *The Persian conquest of the Greeks 545–450 BC*, Konstanz.

Bandiera, A. 1997: 'Per un bilancio della tradizione papiracea delle Storie di Erodoto', *Akten des 21. Internationalen Papyrologenkongresses Berlin, 1995*, Stuttgart and Leipzig.

Baragwanath, E. 2005: 'Studies in motivation and narrative technique in Herodotus', Diss. Oxford.

Barth, H. 1968: 'Zur Bewertung und Auswahl des Stoffes durch Herodot (die Begriffe θῶμα, θωμάζω, θωμάσιος und θωμαστός)', *Klio* 50: 93–110.

Basch, L. 1980: 'M. le Professeur Lloyd et les trières: quelques remarques', *JHS* 100: 198–9.

Bernabé, A. 1996: *Poetae epici Graeci*, I, Stuttgart and Leipzig.

Bianchi, U. 1976: *The Greek mysteries*, Leiden.

Bichler, R. and Rollinger, R. 2000: *Herodot*, Hildesheim.

Bickerman, E. J. 1958: 'Autonomia: sur un passage de Thucydide (I, 144, 2)', *RIDA* 5: 313–44.

Bickerman, E. J. 1963: 'A propos d'un passage de Charès de Mytilène', *PP* 18: 241–55.

Binder, G. 1964: *Die Aussetzung des Königskindes Kyros und Romulus*, Meisenheim am Glan.

Bischoff, H. 1932: 'Der Warner bei Herodot', Diss. Marburg.

Bittner, S. 1987: *Tracht und Bewaffnung des persischen Heeres zur Zeit der Achaimeniden*, 2nd edn., Munich.

Blösel, W. 2001: 'The Herodotean picture of Themistocles: a mirror of fifth-century Athens', in Luraghi 2001a: 179–97.

Blösel, W. 2004: *Themistokles bei Herodot: Spiegel Athens im fünften Jahrhundert: Studien zur Geschichte und historiographischen Konstruktion des griechischen Freiheitskampfes 480 v. Chr.*, Stuttgart.

Boedeker, D. 1987: 'The two faces of Demaratus', *Arethusa* 20: 185–201.

Boedeker, D. 1988: 'Protesilaos and the end of Herodotus' *Histories*', *ClAnt.* 7: 30–48.

Bommelaer, J.-F. and Laroche, D. 1991: *Guide de Delphes: le site*, Athens and Paris.

Boucharlat, R. 1990: 'Suse et la Susiane à l'époque achéménide: données archéologiques', *AchHist.* 4: 149–75.

Bowen, A. J. 1988: 'The place that beached a thousand ships', *CQ* 49: 345–64.

Bowen, A. J. 1992: *Plutarch, The Malice of Herodotus*, Warminster.

Bowie, A. M. 1993: *Aristophanes: myth, ritual and comedy*, Cambridge.

Bowie, A. M. 1995: 'Greek sacrifice: forms and functions', in A. Powell (ed.), *The Greek world*, London: 463–82.

Bowie, A. M. 2004: 'The narratological role of social and religious rituals in Herodotus' *Histories*', in D. Yatromanolakis and P. Roilos (eds.), *Greek ritual poetics*, Harvard: 261–78.

Bowie, A. M. 2006: 'Herodotus on survival: city or countryside?', in I. Sluiter and R. Rosen (eds.) *City, countryside, and the spatial organization of value in classical antiquity*, Leiden: 119–37.

Boyce, M., 2001: *Zoroastrians: their religious beliefs and practices*, London.

Braccesi, L. 1995: 'Troia, Atene, Siri', *Hesperìa* 5: 61–73.

Brandenstein, W. and Mayrhofer, M. 1964: *Handbuch des Altpersischen*, Wiesbaden.

Braund, D. 1998: 'Herodotus on the problematics of reciprocity', in C. Gill, N. Postlethwaite and R. Seaford (eds.), *Reciprocity in ancient Greece*, Oxford: 159–80.

Brelich, A. 1958: *Gli eroi greci: un problema storico-religioso*, Rome.

Bremmer, J. N. 1996: 'The status and symbolic capital of the seer', in R. Hägg (ed.), *The role of religion in the early Greek polis*, Stockholm: 97–109.

Brenne, S. 2001: *Ostrakismos und Prominenz in Athen: attische Bürger des 5. Jhs. v. Chr. auf den Ostraka*, Vienna.

Briant, P. 1990: 'Hérodote et la société perse', in G. Nenci and O. Reverdin (eds.), *Hérodote et les peuples non grecs*, Vandoeuvres and Geneva: 69–104.

Briant, P. 1992: 'La Date des revoltes babyloniennes contre Xerxès', *StIr* 21: 7–20.

Briant, P. 1997: 'Chronique', *Topoi* Supplément 1 (= *BHAch* 1): 1–127.

Briant, P. 2001: *Bulletin d'histoire achéménide*, II, Paris.

Briant, P. 2002: *From Cyrus to Alexander: a history of the Persian empire*, tr. P. T. Daniels, Winona Lake.

Brinkman, J. A. 1989: 'The Akkadian words for "Ionia" and "Ionian"', in R. F. Sutton (ed.), *Daidalikon: studies in memory of Raymond V. Schoder, S.J.*, Wauconda: 53–71.
Brixhe, C. and Lejeune, M. 1984: *Corpus des inscriptions paléo-phrygiennes*, 1, *Texte*, Paris.
Brock, R. 2003: 'Authorial voice and narrative management in Herodotus', in Derow and Parker 2003: 1–16.
Brosius, M. 1996: *Women in ancient Persia, 559–331* BC, Oxford.
Brown, S. C. 1988: 'The *Mēdikos logos* of Herodotus and the evolution of the Median state', *AchHist* 3: 71–86.
Burkert, W. 1962: '*Goes.* Zum griechischen "Schamanismus"', *RM* 105: 36–55.
Burkert, W. 1966: 'Kekropidensage und Arrhephoria: vom Initiationsritus zum Panathenäenfest', *Hermes* 94: 1–25.
Burkert, W. 1983: *Homo necans: the anthropology of ancient Greek sacrificial ritual and myth*, tr. P. Bing, Berkeley, Los Angeles and London.
Burkert, W. 1985a: *Greek religion: archaic and classical*, tr. J. Raffan, Oxford.
Burkert, W. 1985b: 'Herodot über die Namen der Götter: Polytheismus als historisches Problem', *MH* 42: 121–32.
Burkert, W. 1987: *Ancient mystery cults*, Cambridge, MA and London.
Burkert, W. 2005: *Babylon, Memphis, Persepolis: eastern contexts of Greek culture*, Cambridge, MA.
Burn, A. R. 1984: *Persia and the Greeks: the defence of the West, c.546–478* BC, 2nd edn. with a postscript by D. M. Lewis, London.
Buxton, R. 1992: 'Imaginary Greek mountains', *JHS* 102: 1–15.
Cagnazzi, S. 1975: 'Tavola dei 28 logoi di Erodoto', *Hermes* 103: 385–423.
Cagnazzi, S. 2001: *Gli esìli in Persia*, Bari.
Carrière, J.-C. 1988: 'Oracles et prodiges de Salamine: Hérodote et Athènes', *DHA* 14: 219–75.
Carter, E. and Stolper, M. W. 1984: *Elam: surveys of political history and archaeology*, Berkeley.
Cartledge, P. A. 1990: 'Herodotus and "the Other": a meditation on empire', *EMC* 34: 27–40.
Cartledge, P. A. 2002a: *The Greeks: a portrait of self and others*, 2nd edn., Oxford.
Cartledge, P. A. 2002b: *Sparta and Lakonia: a regional history 1300 to 362* BC, 2nd edn., London, Boston and Henley.
Cartledge, P. A. and Greenwood, E. 2002: 'Herodotus as critic: truth, fiction, polarity', in Bakker, de Jong and van Wees 2002: 351–71.
Cartledge, P. A. and Harvey, F. D. (eds.) 1985: *Crux: essays in Greek history presented to G. E. M. de Ste. Croix on his 75th birthday*, London.
Casson, L. 1971: *Ships and seamanship in the ancient world*, Princeton.
Cawkwell, G. 2005: *The Greek wars: the failure of Persia*, Oxford.
Chadwick, J. 1956: 'The Greek dialects and Greek prehistory', *G&R* 3: 38–50; repr. in G. S. Kirk (ed.), *The language and background of Homer*, Cambridge 1964: 106–18.
Chambers, M., Cockle, W. E. H., Shelton, J. C. and Turner, E. G. 1981: *The Oxyrhynchus Papyri*, 48, London.

Chiasson, C. C. 1982: 'Tragic diction in Herodotus: some possibilities', *Phoenix* 36: 156–61.

Christ, M. R., 1994: 'Herodotean kings and historical inquiry', *ClassAnt* 13: 167–202.

Clarke, M., 2001: '"Heart-cutting talk": Homeric κερτομέω and related words', *CQ* 51: 329–38.

Clinton, K., 1992: *Myth and cult: the iconography of the Eleusinian Mysteries*, Stockholm.

Coates, J. F., Platis, S. K. and Shaw, J. T. 1990: *The trireme trials 1988: report on the Anglo-Hellenic sea trials of* Olympias, Oxford.

Coldstream, J. N. 1976: 'Hero-cults in the age of Homer', *JHS* 96: 8–17

Connor, W. R. 1988: '"Sacred" and "secular": ἱερὰ καὶ ὅσια and the classical Athenian concept of the state', *Anc. Soc.* 19: 161–88.

Cook, J. M. 1983: *The Persian empire*, London.

Cooper, G. L. 2002: *Greek syntax: early Greek poetic and Herodotean syntax* (after K. W. Krüger), III–IV, Ann Arbor.

Crahay, R. 1956: *La Littérature oraculaire chez Hérodote*, Paris.

Curtis, J. 2000: *Ancient Persia*, 2nd edn., London.

Curtis, J. and Tallis, N. (eds.) 2005: *Forgotten empire: the world of Ancient Persia*, London.

Dandamayev, M. A. 1985: 'Herodotus' information on Persia and the latest discoveries of cuneiform texts', *SStor* 7: 92–100.

Dandamayev, M. A. & Lukonin, G. 1989: *The culture and social institutions of ancient Iran* (Eng. edn. by P. L. Kohl; tr. D. J. Dadson), Cambridge.

Demand, N. H. 1990: *Urban relocation in archaic and classical Greece*, Bristol.

Demangel, R. 1923: *Le Sanctuaire d'Athéna Pronaia* (*FdD* II 5e fasc. 1e fasc.), Paris.

Demangel, R. 1926: *Le Sanctuaire d'Athéna Pronaia* (*FdD* II 5e fasc. 3e fasc.), Paris.

Denniston, J. D. 1952: *Greek prose style*, Oxford.

Derow, P. S. and Parker, R. C. T. (eds.) 2003: *Herodotus and his world: essays from a conference in memory of George Forrest*, Oxford.

Detienne, M. and Vernant, J.-P. 1978: *Cunning intelligence in Greek culture and society* (tr. J. Lloyd), Hassocks and New Jersey.

Deubner, L. 1900: *De incubatione capita quattuor*, Leipzig.

Deubner, L. 1968: *Attische Feste*, 2nd edn., Berlin.

Dewald, C. 2006: 'Humour and danger in Herodotus', in Dewald and Marincola 2006: 145–64.

Dewald, C. and Kitzinger, R. 2006: 'Herodotus, Sophocles and the woman who wanted her brother saved', in Dewald and Marincola 2006: 122–9.

Dewald, C. and Marincola, J. 2006: *The Cambridge companion to Herodotus*, Cambridge.

Dickey, E. 1996: *Forms of address: from Herodotus to Lucian*, Oxford.

Diller, H. 1962: 'Die Hellenen-Barbaren-Antithese im Zeitalter der Perserkrieg', in *Grecs et barbares, Entretiens Hardt* VIII, Vandoeuvres and Geneva: 39–68.

Dillery, J. 1996: 'Reconfiguring the past: Thyrea, Thermopylae and narrative patterns in Herodotus', *AJP* 117: 217–54.

Dillery, J. 2005: 'Chresmologues and *manteis*: independent diviners and the problem of authority', in S. I. Johnson and P. T. Struck, *Mantikē: studies in ancient divination*, Leiden and Boston: 167–231.

Dontas, G. S. 1983: 'The true Aglaurion', *Hesperia* 52: 48–63.

Drews, R. 1973: The *Greek accounts of Eastern history*, Cambridge, MA.

Dunbar, N. 1995: *Aristophanes: Birds*, Oxford.

Dusinberre, E. R. M. 2003: *Aspects of empire in Achaemenid Sardis*, Cambridge.

Ehrhardt, C. 1988: *RAC* 14 *s.v.* 'Herodot', Stuttgart: 849–61.

Eliade, M. 1965: *The myth of the eternal return or, cosmos and history* (tr. W. R. Trask), corr. edn., Princeton.

Evans, J. A. S. 1991: *Herodotus, explorer of the past*, Princeton.

Farnell, L. R. 1896–1909: *Cults of the Greek states*, I–V, Oxford.

Fehling, D. 1989: *Herodotus and his 'sources': citation, invention and narrative art*, tr. J. G. Howie, Leeds.

Flensted-Jensen, P. 1995: 'The Bottiaians and their *Poleis*', in M. H. Hansen and K. Raaflaub (eds.), *Studies in the ancient Greek polis*, Stuttgart: 103–32.

Flory, S. G. 1987: *The archaic smile of Herodotus*, Detroit.

Flower, M. 2006: 'Herodotus and Persia', in Dewald and Marincola 2006: 274–89.

Fontenrose, J. 1978: *The Delphic Oracle: its responses and operations, with a catalogue of responses*, Berkeley, Los Angeles and London.

Fornara, C. W. 1966: 'The hoplite achievement at Psyttaleia', *JHS* 86: 51–4.

Fornara, C. W. 1971: *Herodotus: an interpretative essay*, Oxford.

Forsdyke, S. 2005: *Exile, ostracism, and exclusion: the politics of expulsion in ancient Greece*, Princeton.

Forsdyke, S. 2006: 'Herodotus, political history and political thought', in Dewald and Marincola 2006: 224–41.

Fossey, J. M. 1986: *The ancient topography of eastern Phokis*, Amsterdam.

Fossey, J. M. 1988: *Topography and population of ancient Boeotia*, I, Chicago.

Fowler, R. L. 2003: 'Herodotos and Athens', in Derow and Parker 2003: 305–18.

Frazer, J. G., 1913: *Pausanias' Description of Greece*, I–VI, London.

Fried, L. S. 2004: *The priest and the king: temple–palace relations in the Persian empire*, Winona Lake.

Frost, F. J. 1968: 'Scyllias: diving in antiquity', *G&R* 15: 180–5.

Georges, P. B. 2000: 'Persian Ionia under Darius: the Revolt reconsidered', *Historia* 49: 1–39.

Gibson, C. A. 2004: 'Learning Greek history in the ancient classroom: the evidence of the treatises on progymnasmata', *CPh* 99: 103–29.

Gillis, D. 1979: *Collaboration with the Persians*, Wiesbaden.

Gilmore, J. 1885: *The fragments of the Persika of Ctesias*, London and New York.

Gilula, D. 2003: 'Who was actually buried in the first of the three Spartan tombs (Hdt. 9.85.1)? Textual and historical problems', in Derow and Parker 2003: 73–87.

Gould, J. 1973: '*Hiketeia*', *JHS* 93: 74–103.

Gould, J. 1989: *Herodotus*, London.

Gould, J. 1991: *Give and take in Herodotus* (The Fifteenth J. L. Myers Memorial Lecture), Oxford.
Graf, D. F. 1994: 'The Persian royal road system', *AH* 8: 167–89.
Graf, F. 1974: *Eleusis und die orphische Dichtung Athens in vorhellenistischer Zeit*, Berlin.
Graham, A. J. 1996: 'Themistocles' speech before Salamis: the interpretation of Herodotus 8.83.1', *CQ* 46: 321–6.
Grayson, A. K. 1975: *Assyrian and Babylonian chronicles*, New York.
Grayson, A. K. 1976: *Assyrian royal inscriptions*, II, Wiesbaden.
Grayson, A. K. 1996: *Assyrian rulers of the early first millennium* BC, II, *858–745* BC, Toronto, Buffalo and London.
Green, P. 1996: *The year of Salamis: 480–479* BC, London.
Gregory, T. E. 1993: *Isthmia*, V, *The Hexamilion and the Fortress*, Princeton.
Grenfell, B. P. and Hunt, A. S. 1919: *The Oxyrhynchus Papyri*, 13, London.
Griffiths, A. 2001: 'Kissing cousins: some curious cases of adjacent material in Herodotus', in Luraghi 2001a: 161–78.
Griffiths, A. 2006: 'Stories and story-telling in the *Histories*', in Dewald and Marincola 2006: 130–44.
Grosso, F. 1958: 'Gli Eretriesi deportati in Persia', *RIFC* 36: 350–75.
Grundy, G. B., 1901: *The Great Persian War and its preliminaries: a study of the evidence, literary and topographical*, London.
Hall, E. M. 1989: *Inventing the barbarian: Greek self-definition through tragedy*, Oxford.
Hall, E. M. 1994: 'Drowning by nomes: the Greeks, swimming, and Timotheus' *Persians*', in Khan 1994: 44–89.
Hall, E. M. 1997: *Aeschylus: Persians*, Warminster.
Hall, J. M. 1995: 'The role of language in Greek ethnicities', *PCPS* 41: 83–100.
Hall, J. M. 1997: *Ethnic identity in Greek antiquity*, Cambridge and New York.
Hall, J. M. 2002: *Hellenicity: between ethnicity and culture*, Chicago.
Halliday, W. R. 1913: *Greek divination: a study of its methods and principles*, London.
Hallock, R. T. 1969: *Persepolis Fortification Tablets*, Chicago.
Hallock, R. T. 1978: 'Selected Fortification Texts', *Cah. D. A. F. I.* 8: 109–36.
Hallock, R. T. 1985: 'The evidence of the Persepolis Tablets', in I. Gershevitch (ed.). *The Cambridge History of Iran*, II, Cambridge: 588–609.
Hamel, D. 1998: *Athenian generals: military authority in the classical period*, Leiden, Bonn and Cologne.
Hammond, N. G. L., 1972: *A history of Macedonia*, I, Oxford.
Hammond, N. G. L. 1982: 'The narrative of Herodotus VII and the Decree of Themistocles at Troezen', *JHS* 102: 75–93.
Hammond, N. G. L. 1989: *The Macedonian state origins, institutions and history*, Oxford.
Hammond, N. G. L. and Griffith, G. T. 1979: *A history of Macedonia*, II, Oxford.
Hanson, V. D. (ed.) 1991: *Hoplites: the classical Greek battle experience*, London.
Harrison, T. 1998: 'Herodotus' conception of foreign languages', *Histos* 2 (www.dur.ac.uk/Classics/histos/1998/harrison.html).
Harrison, T. 2000a: *Divinity and history: the religion of Herodotus*, Oxford.

Harrison, T. 2000b: *The emptiness of Asia: Aeschylus' Persians and the history of the fifth century*, London.

Harrison, T. 2002a: 'The Persian invasions', in Bakker, de Jong and van Wees 2002: 551–78.

Harrison, T. (ed.) 2002b: *Greeks and Barbarians*, Edinburgh.

Hartog, F. 1988: *The mirror of Herodotus: the representation of the Other in the writing of history*, tr. J. Lloyd, Berkeley.

Harvey, F. D. 1985: '*Dona ferentes*: some aspects of bribery in Greek politics', in Cartledge and Harvey 1985: 76–117.

Hatzopoulos, M. 2003: 'Herodotus (8.137–8), the manumissions from Leukopetra, and the topography of the middle Haliakmon valley', in Derow and Parker 2003: 203–18

Head, B. V., 1911: *Historia nummorum: a manual of Greek mathematics*, Oxford.

Hemmerdinger, B. 1981: *Les Manuscrits d' Hérodote et la critique verbale*, Genoa.

Hignett, C. 1963: *Xerxes' invasion of Greece*, Oxford.

Hofstetter, J. 1978: *Die Griechen in Persien: prosopographie der Griechen im persischen Reich vor Alexander*, Berlin.

Hohti, P. 1974: 'Freedom of speech in speech sections in the *Histories* of Herodotus', *Arctos* 8: 19–27.

Hohti, P. 1976: *The interrelation of speech and action in the Histories of Herodotus*, Helsinki and Helsingfors.

Hordern, J. H. 2002: *The fragments of Timotheus of Miletus*, Oxford.

Hornblower, S. 1982: *Mausolus*, Oxford.

Hornblower, S. 1983: *The Greek World 479–323 BC*, London.

Hornblower, S. 2003: 'Panionios of Chios and Hermotimos of Pedasa', in Derow and Parker 2003: 37–57.

Hornblower, S. 2004: *Thucydides and Pindar: historical narrative and the world of epinikian poetry*, Oxford.

Horrocks, G. C. 1981: *Space and time in Homer: prepositional and adverbial particles in the Greek epic*, New York.

Hurwit, J. M. 1999: *The Athenian Acropolis: history, mythology, and archaeology from the Neolithic era to the present*, Cambridge.

Immerwahr, H. R. 1966: *Form and thought in Herodotus*, Atlanta.

Isager, S. 1998: 'The pride of Halikarnassos', *ZPE* 123: 1–23.

Jackson, A. H. 1991: 'Hoplites and the gods: the dedication of captured arms and armor', in Hanson 1991: 228–49.

Jacoby, F. 1913: 'Herodotos', *RE* Suppl. 2: 205–520.

Jameson, M. H. 1991: 'Sacrifice before battle', in Hanson 1991: 197–228.

Janko, R. 1992: *The Iliad: a commentary, books 13–16*, Cambridge.

Johnson, W. A. 1994: 'Oral performance and the composition of Herodotus' *Histories*', *GRBS* 35: 229–54.

Jones, T. B. and Snyder, J. W. 1961: *Sumerian economic texts from the third Ur dynasty*, Minneapolis.

Jong, I. D. F. de 1997: '*Gar* introducing embedded narratives', in A. Rijksbaron (ed.), *New approaches to Greek particles*, Amsterdam, 175–85.

Jong, I. D. F. de 1999: 'Aspects narratologiques des *Histoires* d'Hérodote', *Lalies* 19: 217–75.

Jong, I. D. F. de 2001: 'The anachronical structure of Herodotus' *Histories*', in S. J. Harrison (ed.), *Texts, ideas, and the classics: scholarship, theory and classical literature*, Oxford: 93–116.

Jong, I. D. F. de 2002: 'Narrative unity and units', in Bakker, de Jong and van Wees 2002: 245–66.

Jordan, B. 1988: 'The honors for Themistocles after Salamis', *AJP* 109: 547–71.

Kase, E. W., Szemler, G. J., Wilkie, N. C. and Wallace, P. W. 1991: *The great Isthmus corridor route: explorations of the Phokis–Doris expedition*, I, Dubuque.

Kearns, E. 1989: *The heroes of Attica*, London.

Keaveney, A. 1995: 'The medisers of Thessaly', *Eranos* 93: 30–8.

Kelly, T. 1976: *A history of Argos to 500 BC*, Minneapolis.

Kelly, T. 2003: 'Persian propaganda – a neglected factor in Xerxes' invasion of Greece and Herodotus', *Iranica Antiqua* 38: 173–219.

Kent, R. G. 1953: *Old Persian: grammar, texts, lexicon*, 2nd edn., New Haven.

Kern, O. 1922: *Orphicorum Fragmenta*, Berlin.

Keyser, P. 1986: 'Errors of calculation in Herodotus', *CJ* 81: 230–42.

Khan, H. A. (ed.) 1994: *The birth of European identity: the Europe–Asia contrast in Greek thought 490–322 BC*, Nottingham.

Krentz, P. 1991: 'The *salpinx* in Greek battle', in Hanson 1991: 110–20.

Kuhrt, A. 1987: 'Usurpation, conquest and ceremonial: from Babylon to Persia', in D. Cannadine and S. R. F. Price (eds.), *Rituals of royalty: power and ceremonial in traditional societies*, Cambridge, 20–55.

Kuhrt, A. 1988: 'Earth and water', *AchHist* 3: 87–99.

Kuhrt, A. 1995: *The ancient Near East: c. 3000–330 BC*, II, *From c. 1200 to 330 BC*, London.

Kuhrt, A. 1997: 'Some thoughts on P. Briant, *Histoire de l'empire perse*', *BHAch* 1: 299–304.

Kuhrt, A. 2007: *The Persian Empire: a corpus of sources from the Achaemenid Period*, London.

Labarbe, J. 1957: *La Loi navale de Thémistocle*, Paris.

Lachenaud, G. 1978: *Mythologies, religion et philosophie de l'histoire dans Hérodote*, Paris.

Lang, M. L. 1984: *Herodotean narrative and discourse*, Cambridge, MA.

Lang, M. L. 1990: *The Athenian Agora*, 25, *Ostraka*, Princeton.

Lateiner, D. 1977: 'No laughing matter: a literary tactic in Herodotus', *TAPA* 107: 173–82.

Lateiner, D. 1980: 'A note on δίκας διδόναι in Herodotus', *CQ* 30: 30–2.

Lateiner, D. 1989: *The historical method of Herodotus*, Toronto.

Lattimore, R. 1939: 'The wise adviser in Herodotus', *CPh* 34: 24–35.

Lazenby, J. F. 1987: 'The diekplous', *G&R* 34: 169–77.

Lazenby, J. F. 1993: *The defence of Greece 490–479 BC*, Warminster.

Lecoq, P. 1997: *Les Inscriptions de la Perse achéménide: traduit du vieux perse, de l'élamite, du babylonien et de l'araméen, présenté et annoté par Pierre Lecoq*, Paris.

Legrand, P.-E. 1955: *Hérodote: introduction*, Paris.
Lenardon, R. J. 1978: *The saga of Themistocles*, London.
Lerat, L. 1952: *Les Locriens de l'ouest*, Paris.
Leumann, M. 1950: *Homerische Wörter*, Basle.
Lewis, D. M., 1977: *Sparta and Persia*, Leiden.
Lewis, D. M. 1985: 'Persians in Herodotus', in M. H. Jameson (ed.), *The Greek historians: literature and history. Papers presented to A. E. Raubitschek*, Saratoga: 101–17.
Lewis, D. M. 1997: *Selected papers in Greek and Near Eastern history*, ed. P. J. Rhodes, Cambridge.
Lightfoot, J. L. 2003: *Lucian: On the Syrian Goddess*, Oxford.
Lillo, A. 1991: 'Ionic κώς, ὅκως, ὅπως, Thessalian κις: a phonetic problem of analyzable compounds', *Glotta* 69: 1–13.
Llewellyn-Jones, L. 2002: 'Eunuchs and royal harem in Achaemenid Persia', in S. Tougher (ed.), *Eunuchs in antiquity and beyond*, London and Swansea: 19–49.
Lloyd, A. B. 1976: *Herodotus Book II: commentary 1–98*, Leiden.
Lloyd-Jones, H. 1999: 'The pride of Halicarnassus', *ZPE* 124: 1–14.
Lonis, R. 1979: *Guerre et religion en Grèce à l'époque classique: recherches sur les rites, les dieux, l'idéologie de la victoire*, Paris.
Loraux, N. 1981: *Les Enfants d'Athéna: idées athéniennes sur la citoyenneté et la division des sexes*, Paris.
Luckenbill, D. D. 1926–7: *Ancient records of Assyria and Babylon*, I–II, Chicago.
Luraghi, N. 2001a: *The Historian's craft in the age of Herodotus*, Oxford.
Luraghi, N. 2001b: 'Local knowledge in Herodotus' *Histories*', in Luraghi 2001a, 138–60.
Luraghi, N. 2006: 'Meta-*historie*: method and genre in the *Histories*', in Dewald and Marincola 2006: 76–91.
Luraghi, N. and Alcock, S. E. (eds.) 2003: *Helots and their masters in Laconia and Messenia: histories, ideologies, structures*, Cambridge, MA and London.
Lyonnet, B. 1990: 'Les Rapports entre l'Asie centrale et l'empire Achéménide d'après les données de l'archéologie', *AchHist* 4: 77–92.
Madvig, J. N. 1853: *Syntax of the Greek language, especially of the Attic dialect* (tr. H. Brown, ed. T. K. Arnold), London.
Malkin, I. 1987: *Religion and colonization in ancient Greece*, Leiden.
Mancini, M. 1994: 'Etimologia e semantica del gr. ἄγγαρος', *Glotta* 73: 210–22.
Marincola, J. 1997: *Authority and tradition in ancient historiography*, Cambridge.
Marincola, J. 2006: 'Herodotus and the poetry of the past', in Dewald and Marincola 2006: 13–28.
Marr, J. 1995: 'Themistocles and the supposed second message to Xerxes: the anatomy of a legend', *AClass* 38: 57–69.
Masaracchia, A. 1977: *Erodoto: le Storie, libro VIII, la battaglia di Salamina*, Milan.
McInerney, J. 1999: *The folds of Parnassus: land and ethnicity in ancient Phocis*, Austin.
McNeal, R. A. 1983: 'On editing Herodotus', *AC* 52: 110–29.
Meiggs, R. 1972: *The Athenian empire*, Oxford.

Melchert, H. C. 2004: 'Carian', in R. D. Woodard (ed.), *The Cambridge encyclopedia of the world's ancient languages*, Cambridge: 609–13.
Merkelbach, R. and Stauber, J. 1998: *Steinepigramme aus dem griechischen Osten*, 1, Stuttgart and Leipzig.
Merritt, B. D. 1947: 'The Persians at Delphi', *Hesperia* 16: 58–62.
Mertens, P. and Strauss, J. A. 1992: 'Les papyrus d'Hérodote', *ASNP* Ser. 3, 22: 969–78.
Mikalson, J. D. 1983: *Athenian popular religion*, Chapel Hill and London.
Mikalson, J. D. 2003: *Herodotus and religion in the Persian Wars*, Chapel Hill and London.
Miller, M. C. 1997: *Athens and Persia in the fifth century BC: a study in cultural receptivity*, Cambridge.
Missiou, A. 1993: 'Δοῦλος τοῦ βασιλέως: the politics of translation', *CQ* 43: 377–91.
Mitchell, B. M. 1975: 'Herodotus and Samos', *JHS* 95: 113–22.
Mitchell, F. 1956: 'Herodotus' use of genealogical chronology', *Phoenix* 10: 48–69.
Moles, J. 1996: 'Herodotus warns the Athenians', *Papers of the Leeds International Latin Seminar* 9: 259–84.
Moles, J., 2002: 'Herodotus and Athens', in Bakker, de Jong and van Wees 2002: 33–52.
Momigliano, A. 1975: 'La leggenda di Carano, re di Macedonia', in *Quinto contributo alla storia degli studi classici e del mondo antico,* 1, Rome: 425–33.
Momigliano, A. 1979: 'Persian empire and Greek freedom', in A. Ryan (ed.), *The idea of freedom: essays in honour of Isaiah Berlin*, Oxford: 139–51.
Morpurgo Davies, A., 1987: 'The Greek notion of dialect', *Verbum* 10: 7–28.
Morrison, J. S. 1991: 'The Greek ships at Salamis and the *diekplous*', *JHS* 111: 196–200.
Morrison, J. S., Coates, J. and Rankov, N. B. 2000: *The Athenian trireme: the history and reconstruction of an ancient Greek warship*, Cambridge.
Morrison, J. S. and Williams, R. T. 1968: *Greek oared ships, 900–322 BC*, Cambridge.
Moscati, S. 1999: *The Phoenicians*, New York.
Munson, R. V. 1988: 'Artemisia in Herodotus', *ClAnt* 7: 91–106.
Munson, R. V. 1993: 'Herodotus' use of prospective sentences and the story of Rhampsinitus and the Thief in the *Histories*', *AJP* 114: 27–44.
Munson, R. V. 2001a: *Telling wonders: ethnographic and political discourse in the work of Herodotus*, Ann Arbor.
Munson, R. V. 2001b: '*Ananke* in Herodotus', *JHS* 121: 30–50.
Murray, O. 1972: 'Herodotus and Hellenistic culture', *CQ* 22: 200–13.
Murray, O. 1987: 'Herodotus and oral history', *AH* 2: 93–115.
Mylonas, G. E. 1961: *Eleusis and the Eleusinian mysteries*, Princeton.
Mylonas Shear, I. 1999: 'The western approach to the Athenian Acropolis', *JHS* 109: 86–127.
Nachtergael, G. 1977: '*Les Galates en Grèce et les Sotéria de Delphes*', *Acad. Roy. Belg., M. cl. Lettres*, 2nd ser. lxiii/1, Brussels: 15–205.
Nock, A. D. 1972: *Essays on religion and the ancient world*, selected and edited by Z. Stewart, Oxford.

Ober, J. 1985: *Fortress Attica: defense of the Athenian land frontier 404–322 BC*, Leiden.

Osborne, R. G. 1996: *Greece in the making, 1200–479 BC*, London and New York.

Ostwald, M. 1982: *Autonomia: its genesis and early history*, New York.

Ostwald, M. 1991: 'Herodotus and Athens', *ICS* 16: 137–48

Paap, A. H. R. 1948: *De Herodoti reliquiis in papyris et membranis Aegyptiis servatis*, Leiden.

Packman, Z. M. 1991: 'The incredible and the incredulous: the vocabulary of disbelief in Herodotus, Thucydides, and Xenophon', *Hermes* 119: 399–414.

Palmer, L. R., 1962: 'The language of Homer', in A. J. B. Wace and F. H. Stubbings, *A companion to Homer*, London: 75–178.

Palmer, L. R. 1980: *The Greek language*, London.

Pape, W. 1911: *Wörterbuch der griechischen Eigennamen*, Braunschweig.

Parke, H. W. and Wormell, D. E. W. 1956: *The Delphic oracle*, 1, *the history*, Oxford.

Parke, H. W. 1978: 'Castalia', *BCH* 102: 199–219.

Parker, R. C. T. 1983: *Miasma: pollution and purification in early Greek religion*, Oxford.

Parker, R. C. T. 1985: 'Greek states and Greek oracles', in Cartledge and Harvey 1985: 298–326.

Parker, R. C. T. 1987: 'Myths of early Athens', in J. N. Bremmer (ed.), *Interpretations of Greek mythology*, Beckenham: 187–214.

Parker, R. C. T 1988: 'Spartan religion', in A. Powell (ed.), *Classical Sparta: techniques behind her success*, London: 142–72.

Parker, R. C. T. 1996: *Athenian religion: a history*, Oxford.

Pasquali, G. 1952: *Storia della tradizione e critica del testo*, 2nd edn., Florence.

Pearson, L. 1960: *The lost histories of Alexander the Great*, New York.

Pelling, C. B. R. 1991: 'Thucydides' Archidamus and Herodotus' Artabanus', in M. A. Flower and M. Toher (eds.), *Georgica: Greek studies in honour of George Cawkwell*, London, 120–42.

Pelling, C. B. R. 1997a: 'East is east and west is west – or are they? National stereotypes in Herodotus', *Histos* 1 (http://www.dur.ac.uk/Classics/histos/1997/index.html).

Pelling, C. B. R. 1997b: 'Aeschylus' *Persae* and history', in id. (ed.) *Greek tragedy and the historian*, Oxford, 1–19.

Pelling, C. B. R. 2002: 'Speech and action: Herodotus' debate on the constitutions', *PCPS* 48: 123–58.

Pelling, C. B. R. 2006a: 'Speech and narrative in Herodotus', in Dewald and Marincola 2006: 103–21.

Pelling, C. B. R. 2006b: 'Homer and Herodotus', in M. J. Clarke, B. G. F. Currie and R. O. A. M. Lyne (eds.), *Epic interactions: perspectives on Homer, Virgil and the epic tradition presented to Jasper Griffin by former pupils*, Oxford: 75–104.

Pernot, L. 1995: '"Le Plus Panégyrique des historiens"', *Ktèma* 20: 125–36

Perrot, J. and Ladiray, D. 1996: 'Susa – city of splendour', in J. G. Westenholz (ed.), *Royal cities of the biblical world*, Jerusalem: 234–83.

Pfeiffer, R. 1968: *History of classical scholarship from the beginnings to the end of the Hellenistic age*, Oxford.

Podlecki, A. J. 1975: *The life of Themistocles: a critical survey of the literary and architectural evidence*, Montreal and London.

Pohlenz, M. 1937: *Herodot: der erste Geschichtsschreiber des Abendlandes*, Leipzig and Berlin.

Pope, M. 1999: *The story of decipherment: from Egyptian hieroglyphs to Maya script*, rev. edn., London.

Posener, G. 1936: *La Première Domination perse en Égypte*, Cairo.

Powell, B. 1906: *Erichthonius and the three daughters of Cecrops*, Ithaca.

Powell, J. E. 1937: 'Puns in Herodotus', *CR* 51: 103–5

Price, S. R. F 1985: 'Delphi and divination', in P. E. Easterling and J. V. Muir (eds.), *Greek religion and society*: Cambridge: 128–54.

Pritchett, W. K. 1974: *The Greek state at war*, II, Berkeley, Los Angeles and London.

Pritchett, W. K. 1979: *The Greek state at war*, III: *Religion*, Berkeley, Los Angeles and London.

Pritchett, W. K. 1993: *The liar school of Herodotos*, Amsterdam.

Raaflaub, K. 1987: 'Herodotus, political thought, and the meaning of history', *Arethusa* 20: 221–48.

Ray, J. D. 1990: 'An outline of Carian grammar', *Kadmos* 29: 54–83.

Reade, J. 1988: *Assyrian sculpture*, 2nd edn., London.

Redfield, J. 1980: 'Herodotus the tourist', *CPh* 85: 97–118.

Rhodes, P. J. 2003: 'Herodotean chronology revisited', in Derow and Parker 2003: 58–72.

Richardson, N. J. 1974: *The Homeric Hymn to Demeter*, Oxford.

Riemann, K.-A. 1967: 'Das herodoteische Geschichtswerk in der Antike', diss. Munich.

Risch, R., 1981: 'Die Gliederung der griechischen Dialekte in neuer Sicht', in A. Etter and M. Looser (eds.), *Kleine Schriften*, New York and Berlin, 269–89 (= *MH* 12 (1955) 61–76).

Robert, L. 1950: 'Le Carien Mys et l'oracle du Ptōon (Hérodote, VIII, 135)', *Hellenica* 8: 23–38.

Rollinger, R. 2000: see Bichler and Rollinger 2000.

Romilly, J. de, 1971: 'La Vengeance comme explication historique dans l'oeuvre d'Hérodote', *REG* 84: 314–37.

Rood, T. 1998: *Thucydides: narrative and explanation*, Oxford.

Root, M. C. 1979: *The king and kingship in Achaemenid art: essays on the creation of an iconography of empire*, Leiden.

Rosén, H. 1962: *Eine Laut- und Formenlehre der herodotischen Sprache*, Heidelberg.

Rosen, K. 1978: 'Die Gründung der makedonischen Herrschaft', *Chiron* 8: 1–27.

Rösler, W. 1991: 'Die "Selbsthistorisierung" des Autors: zur Stellung Herodots zwischen Mündlichkeit und Schriftlichkeit', *Philologus* 135: 215–20.

Rouse, W. H. D. 1902: *Greek votive offerings: an essay in the history of Greek religion*, Cambridge.

Roux, G. 1976: *Delphes: son oracle et ses dieux*, Paris.

Rubincam, C. 2003: 'Numbers in Greek poetry and historiography: quantifying Fehling', *CQ* 53: 448–63.

Russell, D. A. 1973: *Plutarch*, London.
Sacks, K. S. 1976: 'Herodotus and the dating of the battle of Thermopylae', *CQ* 26: 232–48.
Saerens, C. 1990: 'Papyrus d'Hérodote et tradition manuscrite', *Studia Varia Bruxellensia* 2: 177–92.
Saïd, S. 2002: 'Herodotus and tragedy', in Bakker, de Jong and van Wees 2002: 117–41.
Sancisi-Weerdenburg, H. 1980: *Yaunā en Persai: Grieken en Perzen in een ander perspectief*, Groningen.
Sancisi-Weerdenburg, H. 1983: 'Exit Atossa: images of women in Greek historiography on Persia', in A. Cameron and A. Kuhrt, *Images of women in antiquity*, rev. edn., London: 20–33.
Sancisi-Weerdenburg, H. 1989: 'Gifts in the Persian empire', in P. Briant and C. Herrenschmidt (eds.), *Le Tribut dans l'empire perse*, Paris: 129–46.
Sancisi-Weerdenburg, H. 1994: 'The orality of Herodotus' *Medikos Logos* or: the Median empire revisited', *AchHist* 8: 39–55.
Sancisi-Weerdenburg, H. 2002: 'The personality of Xerxes, king of kings', in Bakker, de Jong and van Wees 2002: 579–90.
Sansone, D. 1985: 'The date of Herodotus' publication', *ICS* 10: 1–9.
Scaife, R. 1989: 'Alexander I in the Histories of Herodotus', *Hermes* 117: 129–37.
Schachter, A. 1981–94: *Cults of Boeotia*, I–IV, London.
Schmitt, R. 1967: 'Medisches und persisches Sprachgut bei Herodot', *ZDMG* 117: 119–45.
Schmitt, R. 1971: '"Méconnaissance" altiranischen Sprachgutes im Griechischen', *Glotta* 49: 95–110.
Schmitt, R. 1982: 'Achaemenid throne-names', *AION* 42: 83–95.
Scullion, J. S. 1994: 'Olympian and chthonian', *ClAnt* 13: 75–119.
Scullion, J. S. 2006: 'Herodotus and Greek religion', in Dewald and Marincola 2006: 192–208.
Seaford, R. A. S. 1984: *Euripides: Cyclops*, Oxford.
Shahbazi, A. S. 1985: *Old Persian inscriptions from the Persepolis Platform* (*Corp. Inscr. Iranicarum* I.I.I), London.
Shapiro, S. O. 2000: 'Proverbial wisdom in Herodotus', *TAPA* 130: 89–118.
Siewert, P. (ed.) 2002: *Ostrakos-Testimonien*, I, *Die Zeugnisse antiker Autoren, der Inschriften und Ostraka über das athenische Scherbengericht aus vorhellenistische Zeit (487–322 v. Chr.)*, Stuttgart.
Sihler, A. L. 1995: *New comparative grammar of Greek and Latin*, New York and Oxford.
Smyth, H. W. 1894: *The sounds and inflections of the Greek dialects: Ionic* (Oxford).
Sourvinou-Inwood, C. 1991: *'Reading' Greek culture: texts and images, rituals and myths*, Oxford.
Sourvinou-Inwood, C. 2002: 'Greek perceptions of ethnicity and the ethnicity of the Macedonians', in L. M. Castelnuovo (ed.), *Identità e prassi storica nel Mediterraneo greco*, Milan: 173–203.

Sourvinou-Inwood, C. 2003a: 'Herodotos (and others) on Pelasgians: some perceptions of ethnicity', in Derow and Parker 2003: 103–44.

Sourvinou-Inwood, C. 2003b: 'Festivals and mysteries: aspects of the Eleusinian cult', in M. Cosmopoulos (ed.), *Greek mysteries: the archaeology and ritual of ancient Greek secret cults*, London and New York 2003: 25–49.

Stadter, P. 1992: 'Herodotus and the Athenian *Arche*', *ASNP* 3rd ser. 22: 781–809.

Stevens, P. T. 1976: *Colloquial expressions in Euripides, Hermes Einzelschriften* 38.

Stevenson, R. B. 1997: *Persica: Greek writing about Persia in the fourth century* BC, Edinburgh.

Stolper, M. W. 1987: 'Bēlshunu the Satrap', in *Language, literature and history* (Fest. E. Reiner), New Haven and London: 389–402.

Stolper, M. W. 2005: 'Achaemenid languages and inscriptions', in Curtis and Tallis 2005: 18–24.

Strasburger, H. 1955: 'Herodot und das perikleische Athen', *Historia* 4: 1–25.

Strasburger, H. 1972: *Homer und die Geschichtsschreibung*, Heidelberg.

Strauss, B. 2004: *Salamis: the greatest battle of the ancient world, 480* BC, London.

Strid, O., 1999: *Die Dryoper: eine Untersuchung der Überlieferung*, Uppsala.

Stüber, K. 1996: *Zur dialektalen Einheit des Ostionischen*, Innsbruck.

Szemerényi, O. 1975: 'Iranica v', *AcIr* 5: 313–94.

Talbert, R. J. A. 1989: 'The role of the Helots in the class struggle at Sparta', *Historia* 38: 22–40.

Thomas, R. 2000: *Herodotus in context: ethnography, science and the art of persuasion*, Cambridge.

Thomas, R. 2001: 'Herodotus' *Histories* and the floating gap', in Luraghi 2001a, 198–210.

Thompson, D. B. 1956: 'The Persian spoils in Athens', in S. S. Weinberg, *The Aegean and the Near East (Studies H. Goldman)*, New York: 281–91.

Thompson, H. 1981: 'Athens faces adversity', *Hesperia* 50: 343–55.

Thompson, S. 1955–8: *Motif-index of folk literature: a classification of narrative elements in folktales, etc.*, I–VI, Copenhagen.

Thomsen, R., 1972: *The origin of ostracism: a synthesis*, Copenhagen.

Threpsiades, J. and Vanderpool, E. 1964: 'Themistokles' sanctuary of Artemis Aristoboule', *Arch. Delt.* 19: 26–36.

Tomlinson, R. A. 1976: *Greek sanctuaries*, London.

Tougher, S. 2002: *Eunuchs in antiquity and beyond*, London.

Tozzi, P. 1978: *La rivolta ionica*, Pisa.

Tripodi, B. 1986: 'L'"emblema" della casa reale macedone', *Ancient Macedonia* 4: 653–60.

Tuplin, C. J. 1985: 'Imperial tyranny: some reflections on a classical Greek political metaphor', in Cartledge and Harvey 1985: 348–75.

Tuplin, C. J. 1994: 'Persians as Medes', *AchHist* 8: 235–56.

Tuplin, C. J. 1996: *Achaemenid Studies*, Stuttgart.

Tuplin, C. J. 1997: 'Achaemenid arithmetic: numerical problems in Persian history', *BHAch* 1: 365–421.

Tuplin, C. J. 1998: 'The seasonal migration of Achaemenid kings: a report on old and new evidence', *AchHist* 11: 63–114.

Tuplin, C. J. 2003: 'Xerxes' march from Doriscus to Therme', *Historia* 52: 385–409.

Untersteiner, M. 1949: *La lingua di Erodoto*, Bari.

Vansina, J. 1973: *Oral tradition*, Harmondsworth.

Vian, F. 1963: *Les Origines de Thèbes: Cadmos et les Spartes*, Paris.

Vidal-Naquet, P. 1981: 'The Black Hunter and the origin of the Athenian *ephebeia*', in R. L. Gordon (ed.), *Myth, religion and society: structuralist essays by M. Detienne, L. Gernet, J.-P. Vernant and P. Vidal-Naquet*, Cambridge and Paris 1981: 147–62.

Vogelsang, W. 1990: 'The Achaemenids in India', *AH* 4: 93–110.

Voigt, M. M. and Henrickson, R. C. 2000: 'Formation of the Phrygian state: the early Iron Age at Gordion, *Anatolian Studies* 50: 37–54

Walbank, M. B. 1978: *Athenian proxenies of the fifth century* BC, Toronto and Sarasota.

Wallace, P. W. 1969: 'Psyttaleia and the trophies of the battle of Salamis', *AJA* 73: 293–303.

Wallinga, H. T. 1993: *Ships and sea-power before the great Persian War: the ancestry of the ancient trireme*, Leiden, New York and Cologne.

Weber, U. and Wiesehöfer, J. 1996: *Das Reich der Achaimeniden: eine Bibliographie*, Berlin.

Weidner, E. F. 1931/2: 'Die älteste Nachricht über das persische Königshaus. Kyros I. ein Zeitgenosse Ashshurbanipals', *Archiv für Orientforschung* 7: 1–14.

West, M. L. 1997: *The east face of Helicon*, Oxford.

West, S. 1999: 'Sophocles' *Antigone* and Herodotus Book Three', in J. Griffin (ed.), *Sophocles revisited: essays presented to Sir Hugh Lloyd-Jones*: Oxford: 109–36.

West, S. R. 1985: 'Herodotus' epigraphical interests', *CQ* 35: 278–305.

West, S. R. 2002: 'Scythia', in Bakker, de Jong and van Wees 2002: 437–56.

Whitehead, I. 1987: 'The periplous', *G&R* 34: 178–85.

Wiesehöfer, J. 1996: *Ancient Persia from 550* BC *to 650* AD, London and New York.

Wiesehöfer, J. 1980: 'Die "Freunde" und "Wohltäter" des Grosskönigs", *Studia Iranica* 11: 7–21

Wiseman, J. R. 1963: 'A trans-Isthmian fortification wall: notes on hellenistic military operations in the Corinthia', *Hermes* 32: 248–75.

Wood, H. 1972: *The Histories of Herodotus: an analysis of the formal structure*, The Hague and Paris.

Yardley, J. C. 2003: 'Bark and leaf-eating in Petelia (Livy 23.30.3)', *AHB* 17: 158.

Young, D. C. 1984: *The Olympic myth of Greek amateur athletics*, Chicago.

Young, T. C. 1980: '480/79 BC – a Persian perspective', *Iranica Antiqua* 15: 213–39.

Zahrnt, M. 1984: 'Die Entwicklung des makedonischen Reiches bis zu den Perserkriegen', *Chiron* 14: 325–68.

INDEX

1. GREEK

2. GENERAL

Lightning Source UK Ltd.
Milton Keynes UK
UKHW022232060122
396753UK00008B/65

9 780521 575713